MW00813688

THE POWER OF A TALE

THE POWER
OF A TALE

Stories from the Israel Folktale Archives

Edited by Haya Bar-Itzhak
and Idit Pintel-Ginsberg

WAYNE STATE UNIVERSITY PRESS
DETROIT

Library of Congress Control Number: 2019950420
ISBN 978-0-8143-4208-4 (hardcover); ISBN 978-0-8143-4209-1 (ebook)

Published with support from the fund for the Raphael Patai Series in Jewish Folklore and Anthropology.

In memory of Prof. Dov Noy, the founder of the IFA,
and to the storytellers and transcribers of the IFA.

CONTENTS

The Road on the Holiday of Shavuot (IFA 23011)   **383**
    Narrated by Aharon David Rabinovitch (Belarus);
       transcribed by Itzhak Ganuz
    Commentary by Itzhak Ganuz

THE STORYTELLERS

The following photographs represent only those storytellers whose photos are archived at the IFA and thus do not include images for each storyteller in this volume.

 Hamza Abu Zidan

 Mina Abu-Rokan

 Reuven Adi

 Muhamed Arsan Madjis Abu Zeid

 Moshe Attias

 Yiftah Avrahami

 Abner Azulay

 Yossi Bar Sheshet

 Avraham Barazani

 Zalman Ben Amos [Kastrol]

 Yeshua Ben David

 David Cohen

 Heftsiba Dadon

 Nissim Damti

 Rivka Daniel

 Esther Elfassy

 Esther Elizra

 Leah Gad

 Sima Goldenberg

 Yosef Goldman

 David Itsicovitc

 Kahana Sh.Z

 Zevulun Kort

 Mordechai Hillel Kroshnitz

 Berta Lieber

 Tamar Lugasi

 Haya Mazouz

 Haya Nahumzon

 Dov Noy

 Eliezer Papo

 Levana Sasson

 Ya'acov Shaham

 Hinda Sheinfarber

 Shimon Toder

Zipora Zabari

Illustrations

ACKNOWLEDGMENTS

We take pleasure in thanking all who assisted with the publication of this book, which celebrates the Jubilee of the Israeli Folktale Archives named in honor of Dov Noy. We are especially indebted to Professor Dan Ben-Amos, the editor of the Raphael Patai series, for his initiative to publish the English version of this volume, and to the anonymous reviewers for their encouragement and excellent suggestions for improving the manuscript. Our deepest thanks to Kathryn Wildfong, former editor-in-chief, who has made our association with Wayne State University Press a particularly happy one; to Mindy Brown, copyeditor; Kristin Harpster, editorial, design, and production manager, and Kristina Stonehill, promotions manager, for their dedicated work.

A special thanks to Mr. William Gross, who provided us with photos of objects from his family's extensive collection of Judaica.

Finally, we extend our deepest thanks to the scholars who contributed to this volume. Without them this project would not have materialized.

Introduction

The Israel Folktale Archives and the Preservation of the Cultural Heritage in Israel

Haya Bar-Itzhak

The Israel Folktale Archives (IFA), renamed in honor of its founder, Professor Dov Noy, in 2001, was established in Haifa in 1955 in conjunction with the municipality's Museum of Ethnology and Folklore. Its goal was to record, collect, and document the folktales told by members of the various ethnic communities living in Israel. The IFA has been affiliated with the University of Haifa since 1983. Its academic director from that year until 1992 was Professor Aliza Shenhar. It has been my privilege to serve in this position since 1992 until 2014. Since 2014 Professor Dina Stein serves in this position. In addition, the IFA has been blessed with three brilliant and dedicated scholars who have filled the vital role of scientific coordinator of the archive: Edna Hechal (1955–2003), Dr. Idit Pintel-Ginsberg (2003–14), and Dr. Haya Milo since 2014. The policy of the IFA is set by the IFA scientific board, which includes folklore scholars from all Israeli universities.

The 1950s marked a period of mass immigration to Israel, which gained its independence in 1948. The diverse communities that arrived in the country from east and west brought with them many traditions and stories. A major factor in the establishment of the IFA and the definition of its policies was the fear that these immigrants' varied cultures would wither and disappear as a result of their encounter with Israeli culture. Thus the work of collecting and documenting this cultural diversity was a rescue operation of the sort prominent in folklore studies in those days. It is important to remember, too, that this effort was an attempt to resist the dominant ideological and political goals of the State of Israel at the time, which aimed not only to gather in the exiles but also to mix them in the melting pot of a new society: one that would reject Diaspora traditions and forge a uniform and hegemonic Israeli culture. By recording, documenting, and thereby perpetuating the traditions of the various immigrant groups, the IFA challenged this attitude.[1]

Today the IFA contains more than twenty-four thousand folk narratives collected from narrators of various ethnic groups, making it the largest collection of Jewish folk narratives ever. Amassed over a period of more than fifty years, it is the largest reservoir of the Jewish imagination in the world, with no rival anywhere. The archive's holdings also include folk narratives of the non-Jewish groups living in Israel: Muslim and Christian Arabs, Bedouins, Druze, and Circassians.

By founding the IFA, Dov Noy established a vital national and international institution for the preservation and study of folk narratives. But the inspiration for its establishment and work, as well as for the various projects it has conducted over the years, can be traced back to the earliest days of Jewish folklore studies in Eastern Europe, where it all began. The great Yiddish writer Isaac Leib Peretz (1852–1915) brought Jewish folklore to the forefront in Warsaw when he began collecting Yiddish folk songs in 1890. The historians Saul Ginsburg (1866–1940) and Pesach Marek (1862–1920) also began collecting Yiddish folk songs; they published the anthology *Di Yidishe Folkslider in Rusland* (*Yiddish Folk Songs in Russia*) in 1901. In 1908 Ignatz Bernstein (1836–1909) published the expanded edition of his collection of Yiddish proverbs and sayings. In 1912 Y. L. Cahan (1881–1937) published a collection of Yiddish folksongs with melodies.

But the apex of fieldwork in folklore studies before World War I was the expedition led by S. An-Ski (pseudonym of Shlomo Zainwil Rapoport, 1863–1920). Around 1888 An-Ski left the insular Jewish community in his hometown of Vitebsk and made the town of Yekaterinoslav his base; later, captivated by the spirit of Russian populism—the *Narodnichestvo*—An-Ski lived among coalminers and began studying Russian folklore. Subsequently, during his years as a political exile in Paris, he became familiar with European and especially French folklore. The Russian populism that had molded his worldview and his close acquaintance with Russian and European folklore eventually shaped his approach to Jewish folklore, which he saw as a means for uncovering the modern Jewish experience and as the symbolic language of Jewish history. The radical change in the direction of his life seems to have occurred in 1900, following the death of Piotr Labrov (1823–1900)—the *Narodnik* theoretician who had employed An-Ski as his secretary—and after the pogroms that took place in Russia in 1905 and 1906. The catalyst for his new focus on Jewish folklore was his encounter with the work of I. L. Peretz, which taught An-Ski that modernism and European sensibilities could be expressed in Yiddish and be based on Jewish folklore.

The culmination of An-Ski's folklore work was the ethnographic expedition he led, which set out on July 1, 1912. For An-Ski this was the sacred mission of his life, a project about Jewish life on a national scale. The expedition passed through some seventy shtetls (archetypal East European Jewish places of residence) in Volhynia and Podolia, recording stories, songs, and proverbs, and documenting and collecting items of material culture. Additionally, the expedition's findings led to the compilation of an exhaustive questionnaire about the Jewish life cycle; edited by the Russian-Jewish ethnologist Lev Sternberg (1861–1927), the survey encompassed 2,087 questions, divided into five categories that ranged from conception to death. The expedition's work placed folklore and ethnography squarely at the center of the intellectual discourse of Jewish studies and set fieldwork at the heart of folklore studies.[2]

Another institution that helped place fieldwork at the center of the discipline was YIVO (the *Yiddisher Visenshaftlekher Institut*) and its ethnographic commission. YIVO, founded in 1925, accorded folklore an important status. The main goal of the ethnographic commission, which was established on October 27, 1925, was to organize the collection of Jewish folklore materials "wherever the Yiddish language lives."[3] The priority assigned to fieldwork stemmed both from the dominant approach in folklore studies at the time—which was that a large and well-cataloged archive was a precondition for research—and from the fear that, under the pressure of modernization, these materials were liable to disappear, so that whatever could be salvaged must be salvaged without delay. The ethnographic commission set up a network of volunteer collectors (*zamlers*) throughout Poland and elsewhere, based in Yiddish cultural institutions and especially schools. Notices of the establishment of this network were published at meetings, in periodicals, and in the YIVO *Bulletin*. The following ad appeared in *Yugnt Veker* (November 1925), the organ of the Bundist youth published in Warsaw: "The [YIVO] ethnographic commission hereby issues a fervent enthusiastic call to all lovers and friends of Jewish folk creation, especially teachers in Jewish schools and young people everywhere: help us collect the treasures of Jewish folk creation! In the cities and the towns, wherever the Yiddish language is alive! . . . Don't let them be lost."

Each month the commission published questionnaires about specific folklore topics on which the collectors were to focus. But they were given full freedom to collect other items. A hallmark of the commission's work was the personal relationship it developed with the *zamlers*. It corresponded with them on a regular basis and paid attention to their requests, thereby spurring their motivation. The *zamlers'* names were published in the YIVO *Bulletin*; some of their harvested materials eventually appeared in its publications. The collection of folklore materials is often viewed as YIVO's most notable achievement, accomplished over the span of a very few years.

The establishment of the IFA and its methods were inspired by the YIVO project. But, since its establishment, IFA has focused on research beyond simply recording and collecting. The main research projects, after collecting stories, were indexing and publication:

1. Indexing the tales according to the narrator's country of origin;
2. Indexing the tales according to the name of the narrator and the collector;
3. Indexing the tales according to the Aarne-Thompson tale-type index and Jewish oikotypes;
4. Indexing the tales according to the characters that appear in them;
5. Publication of annual collections of folktales, accompanied by scholarly notes.[4]

Over the years the IFA has evolved substantially, and developments in research methods have also spurred changes in IFA policy:

1. There has been a transition from manual transcription to audiotaping and, more recently, to video recording.
2. Questionnaires (one relating to the narrator and one to each story) have been developed to document the storytelling event and its cultural context.
3. Several large fieldwork projects have been conducted.

In particular, ethnographic expeditions set out to work in two towns in the northern part of Israel which were populated overwhelmingly by new immigrants: Beit-She'an and Shlomi (1977–1979 and 1980–1982, respectively). I will describe these two projects in turn.

THE BEIT SHE'AN PROJECT

The Beit She'an project had several goals:[5]

1. Collecting folk narratives from local residents, to be archived at the IFA;
2. Making the citizens of Beit-She'an, young and old alike, more aware of the importance of their ethnic communities' cultural heritage, thus motivating them to preserve it and incorporate it into the educational and cultural life of the town;
3. Involving university students in fieldwork to give them a taste of collecting folktales and applying the theoretical concepts learned in the classroom.

Modus Operandi

The project proceeded along two main tracks:

1. Over the course of a year, we ran a regional study group that focused on the culture of ethnic communities in Israel. Each session involved a guest lecturer and folklore presentations by residents of Beit She'an and the environs who represented one of the major ethnic groups there, including Jews from Kurdistan, Morocco, Yemen, and Iran.
2. All through the year there, meetings with local educators and high-school pupils were held to encourage them to record the stories of their relatives and acquaintances. During the year we got to know most of the storytellers, took down their addresses, and developed a trusting relationship with them. Approximately eighty folktales were transcribed during this year.

The long-term intensive work created mutual familiarity and trust among the residents and the researchers. This facilitated the success of the fieldwork, which involved students and faculty from the University of Haifa, Hebrew University, and Oranim College. The collectors lived in Beit She'an while doing the fieldwork. Each storyteller was notified a week prior to the arrival of the collectors. A recording center was set up at an advertised location so that narrators whose addresses we had not obtained could go there if they wished. In the hopes of locating additional storytellers, we also visited senior citizens' clubs and recorded stories there.

Every collector was given a tape recorder so that all the stories could be recorded. Recordings were made in the morning. In the afternoon we met to report on the materials collected, exchange impressions, and get new addresses. Afternoons were also devoted to making recordings. In the evening we had review meetings, and transcribers filled in the narrator questionnaires and typed up some of the recordings. We also held two storytelling events with the participation of local residents.

Our methods for raising awareness of the importance of folklore materials and ethnic culture, and for enlisting the assistance of teachers and high-school pupils, are reminiscent of the approach pioneered by the YIVO ethnographic commission. On the other hand, sending university faculty and students into the field for a protracted period more closely resembles the method of the An-Ski expedition, which worked in specific places and dispatched researchers there to collect folklore materials.

Lessons from Our Fieldwork in Beit She'an

Several important methodological findings were gleaned from our time in Beit She'an:

1. The storytellers' responses to our fieldwork show the importance of doing preparatory groundwork before an expedition arrives in the field. Our informants were open to us because our yearlong presence made them more aware of the project. They talked freely, treated us as their welcome guests, and referred us to other storytellers they knew.
2. Local guides are essential for finding addresses. The familiar faces of the guides, most of them high-school pupils, also made storytellers feel more relaxed and confident.
3. Collectors who contemplate spending only a limited amount of time in a place must understand in advance that most of the stories they record will not be recounted during ritual events. The opportunity to record stories told during ritual events requires an invitation to such ceremonies and a much longer visit.

Results of the Project

We collected approximately three hundred stories in Beit She'an. Some of these were published in various issues of the IFA series "A Tale for Each Month" (1979), edited by Dov Noy, and others in *Folktales from Beit-She'an*, which was edited by Aliza Shenhar and me.

Different ethnic groups were found to prefer different genres. Immigrants from Iran, Kurdistan, and Iraq recounted mainly fairy tales and novellas, whereas the bulk of stories told by Jews from Morocco were sacred legends.

We discovered local saints of Moroccan Jews about whom we had not been aware previously, such as Rabbi Yihye Lahlu and Rabbi Yosef Etah. Stories of the miracles they performed and their sacred gravesites were living folklore for the elders of the community.

We found folktales that are told chiefly to children. The narrator Sultana Simhi told us a story titled "Shangol, Mangol, and Abetabetangol," which she and her children said had been told to the children of their family for as long as they could remember. Another woman, Freha Dadya, told us "Open the Door, Children!"; it too was a tale for children.

We could see the changes that emerged in stories our narrators had brought from their countries of origin as a result of their encounter with Israeli culture. This was manifested with regard to geography (place names) as well as in the choice of images and metaphors. For example, one narrator compared the speed at which King Solomon flew through the air to that of a

Skyhawk military jet. Changes in lifestyle also affected the mode of storytelling. One evening, the audience listening to Shlomo Ezra of Beit She'an asked him to abridge his story
because they had to get up early the next morning to go to work.

THE SHLOMI PROJECT

The project in Shlomi[6] was influenced by our experience in Beit-She'an, chiefly with regard to
our setting up a recording center, meeting with local teachers, and running local meetings about
folklore. Nevertheless this project was very different from its predecessor. Above all this project
was conceived in part as a way to turn the town into a research workshop for the University of
Haifa, involving the collection of folksongs (directed by Professor Joseph Chetrit) and material
culture (directed by Professor Yedida Stillman) as well as folk narratives. There were several
differences from the Beit-She'an project:

1. At that time (the 1980s) the population of Shlomi consisted almost exclusively of Moroccan immigrants, so the project focused on them.
2. In Shlomi, unlike in Beit She'an, we preferred to record stories in their original language,
   the Jewish dialect of Moroccan Arabic. This meant that we had to employ collectors
   fluent in that dialect. The emphasis on language strongly recalls the work of the YIVO
   ethnographic commission, which was affiliated with the institute's philological section
   and emphasized the spoken vernacular—Yiddish. Recording stories in the original language produced tales marked by a linguistic richness not found in what we had collected
   from Moroccan Jews in the past.
3. The collection work was done with scholarly awareness of both text and context, which
   encompasses the narrator's artistry as a performer and the storytelling event, relations
   between the audience and the narrator, and the time and place of telling.

This approach produced a different type of documentation. We designed narrator and story questionnaires that, when synthesized, made it possible to study each narrator's genre repertoire,
the storytelling event as a motive for changing the genre, ethnic definitions of genres, and so on.
The composition of special questionnaires harks back to the work of the An-Ski expedition, whose
crowning achievement was its life-cycle questionnaire.

The research in Shlomi was summed up in two books: *Folktales from Shlomi*, published in
Hebrew by the University of Haifa, and *Jewish Moroccan Narratives from Israel*, published
in English by Wayne State University Press. Here there is a basic difference from the work of
YIVO, reflecting changes in orientation and research. The YIVO ethnographic commission made
a clear distinction between the collector and the scholar; the ultimate fate of the vast amounts of
material gathered was left to the decision of some scholar in the future. This also solved the problem of the commission members themselves, most of whom were self-taught folklorists. The IFA

expeditions were directed by qualified scholars at a time when the emphasis was on context, performance, and the storytelling event. The products of our going out to the people were not limited to anthologies of stories but also included academic scholarship, found both in the anthologies themselves and in many articles based on the two projects.

Recent years have seen a number of changes at the IFA. Thanks to a research grant I received from the Israel Academy of Sciences and Humanities to fund a computerized comparative study of the IFA's holdings, all the stories have been digitized and will be made available online. The stories were subjected to poetic and thematic analysis on the basis of keywords. This will eventually produce a computerized database to provide scholars with information on almost every topic, including places mentioned in the tales, characters, customs and beliefs, genres, and more.

Collections of stories from the IFA have been published in Israel and elsewhere, accompanied by a weighty scholarly apparatus. In addition to those mentioned above, three volumes of stories from the IFA, with extensive annotations by Dan Ben-Amos, were published by the Jewish Publication Society over these past years. The present collection of IFA stories was published in Hebrew in 2009 to mark the institution's fiftieth anniversary. Its stories are accompanied by commentaries by folklorists and their students from Israel and abroad.

The IFA's influence on culture in Israel and abroad extends beyond the ivory tower. Some of the three hundred to five hundred people who visit the archives every year are not academics. The Israeli educational system makes extensive use of its holdings; and some stories have been included in school readers. Many adaptations of IFA stories have been published for children, with some of them proving extremely popular. Stories from the IFA collection have been used as the basis for plays for children, performances by professional storytellers, and the works of several authors.[7] It seems likely that at least some of this work will return to us as part of the new cycle of folk culture in Israel and abroad.

If I may hark back to the romanticism of the nineteenth century, we see that, in addition to IFA's scholarly contribution, stories that came from the people returned to them in various ways, fueling a dynamic renewal of culture in general and of folk culture in particular.

THE STORIES AND THE STORYTELLERS

This collection, which marks the fiftieth anniversary of the Israel Folktale Archives, was initially planned to include fifty-one stories from its holdings. Some contributors referred to more than one version of a story or to more than one story and asked that they, too, be included. As a result the final volume contains fifty-three stories.

The authors of the articles chose the stories from the more than 24,000 in the archives. The criterion for selection was that the tales had not previously appeared in an IFA publication. The editors also wanted to represent as many ethnic groups as possible among those with stories in the IFA.[8]

The stories here come from twenty-six different ethnic communities, according to the standard IFA classification. There are twenty-two Jewish communities: Afghanistan (2 stories), Belarus (2),

Bulgaria (1), Ethiopia (1), Georgia (1), Germany (1), Greece (1), India (1), Iran (2), Iraq (3), Iraqi Kurdistan (1), Israel (2),[9] Israel, Ashkenazi (3), Israel, Sephardi (2), Lithuania (1), Morocco (7), Poland (6), Romania (2), Tunisia (2), Yemen (2), and Yugoslavia, Sephardi (1). There are also four non-Jewish groups: Bedouin (2), Druze (2), Muslim Arab (4), and Christian Arab (1).

The stories were told by nineteen women (two by the same person) and thirty three men. The storytellers came from all walks of life and from different ethnic backgrounds. Some had a university degree; others had no formal education at all. They worked in many diverse fields and were of different ages. Some were long-settled in Israel, while others were recent arrivals. They all shared one conspicuous quality—their talent as storytellers. These tales were not created in a vacuum. The folk narrative is anchored in tradition, but it is modified and renewed by each narrator as he or she tells it to different audiences and in different performance contexts.

The stories are presented here in the order of their entry into the IFA, as indicated by their serial numbers. Those selected were collected from the 1950s until very recently.

The Language

In the IFA's early years, most of the stories were transcribed in Hebrew. One reason for this was that the collectors had insufficient command of the storytellers' native languages. When the latter's knowledge of Hebrew was limited and incidental, the story may be told in broken and ungrammatical Hebrew. When they did know Hebrew well, the register employed is a direct outgrowth of their education, individual style, and the prevailing spirit of the time. The stories collected in the 1950s and 1960s are often told in an elevated and even flowery style, as was thought proper for literature in those days. When the use of spoken Hebrew became legitimate, stories began to be recounted in it—just as we find in folk narratives from many places, expressing what is essentially an oral culture.

At the IFA the rule is to transcribe (record or videotape) stories without modification or editing. This is what we did for the stories published here. From time to time, when necessary, we added clarifying notes.

Since the 1980s (see my earlier comments on the Shlomi project), we have insisted that stories be transcribed in the original language, if the narrator wishes.

The Collectors

Its team of collectors is very important for the IFA. A look at those whose work is included here yields an interesting picture. Some of the stories (chiefly those dating to the early years of the IFA) were written down by volunteers who felt a special attraction to folktales; they labored with great dedication, moved by their love of and appreciation for the field. Nevertheless, their transcription was not always accurate. Collectors often allowed themselves to modify the story as they set it down, to the extent that some stories are actually the joint product of the narrator and the transcriber. The transcriber's influence on the text has been addressed here; some of the commentaries deal with this matter specifically.

Many of the tales were collected by undergraduates and graduate students at Israeli universities, usually as an ethnographic assignment for courses or seminars or as part of their thesis work. These stories, as well as those collected by university scholars doing ethnographic research and then deposited with the IFA,[10] were transcribed precisely as told, in keeping with the principles of ethnographic collection of folklore; in many cases they are accompanied by contextual details.

THEMES, GENRES, AND COMMENTARIES

The stories in this collection deal with many and varied themes: destruction and redemption; the Diaspora and the Land of Israel; the Holy Temple and synagogues; relations between Jews and non-Jews—blood libels, martyrdom, pogroms, miraculous deliverances, and more; saints and rabbis; historical events, such as the Chmielnicki uprising of 1648–49 and the rescue of the Jews of Irbil from a pogrom in 1941; festivals—Hanukkah, Passover, Shavuot, and Lag ba'Omer; the lifecycle—birth and circumcision, growing up, marriage, old age and death; relations between the sexes; fundamental values of the narrating society, such as respect for parents and hospitality; wisdom and folly; ritual objects; pilgrimages to sacred shrines; stones; demons; dragons and witches; immigration to and absorption in Israel; the building of the land, including the symbolism of the flying camel emblem of the Levant Fair and the construction of the Polgat factory; and a tale about the power of a tale.

With regard to genre the stories fall into many categories: mythical tales, historical legends, sacred legends, demon legends, realistic legends, *märchen* of various sorts, novellas, jokes and anecdotes, and personal narratives. Some stories can be assigned to more than one genre—a topic addressed in some of the chapters here.

The authors who contributed chapters are senior scholars of folk literature who teach at universities in Israel and abroad and their students (some of them recently minted PhDs, others still pursuing a graduate degree).

The contributors employed diverse approaches to analyze and interpret the stories. The methods applied include the classic comparative approach, which looks at tale types, oikotypes, and motifs; formalism, which considers narrative roles and narrative functions; structuralism, which aims to uncover the story's deep structure and its binary contrasts; the psychological approach, which analyzes the tales using psychological theories ranging from Freud to Lacan; and Marxist theories, which see the folktale as an expression of the class struggle.

The articles are evidence of the lively research being conducted today on folk literature. The field is not stagnating. The younger generation of folklorists continues to expand and innovate, building on their teachers' work.

The stories and commentaries here are a sort of plum pudding offered for the delectation of readers and scholars, as appropriate for the IFA jubilee volume.

NOTES

1. For survey of the first years of the IFA, see Noy 1967, 142–54; Noy 1961, 99–110; Pintel-Ginsberg and Hechal 2005, 225–32.
2. On An-Ski and the ethnographic expedition, see Noy 1982, 94–107; Bar-Itzhak 2010, 28–33.
3. On the study of Yiddish folklore, see Gottesman 2003, 111–70.
4. On the IFA publication series and other IFA publications, see Noy 1980, 200–218. See also the list of IFA publications at the end of this volume.
5. For a survey of the Beit She'an Project, see Bar-Itzhak 1979a, 142–43; Bar-Itzhak 1979b, 149–57.
6. On the Shlomi project, see Bar-Itzhak and Shenhar 1993a.
7. See, for example, Pinhas Sade, *The Book of the Jewish Imagination* (Jerusalem: Schocken, 1983).
8. The unequal representation of the different ethnic groups in the archives must be taken into account. Obviously those with a particularly large number of stories receive more generous attention in this collection.
9. These are stories that have no link to the teller's country of origin and are a clear expression of Israeli folktales.
10. It is interesting to note that some stories in this category were transcribed as told by family members—parents and grandparents.

BIBLIOGRAPHY

Bar-Itzhak, Haya. 1979a. "A Survey of the Beit She'an Project." *Yeda Am* 19 (45–46): 142–43. [Hebrew]

———. 1979b. "Beit She'an Project 1977–1978." In *A Tale for Each Month 1978*, ed. Dov Noy, 199–257. Jerusalem: Center for Folktale Research. [Hebrew]

———. 2010. *Pioneers of Jewish Ethnography and Folkloristics in Eastern Europe.* Ljubljana: Studia Mythologica Slavica–Suplementa, Scientific Research Center of the Academy of Science and Arts.

Bar-Itzhak, Haya, and Aliza Shenhar. 1993a. *Jewish Moroccan Folk Narratives from Israel.* Detroit: Wayne State University Press.

———. 1993b. "Processes of Change in Israeli Society as Reflected in Folklore Research: The Beit She'an Model." *Jewish Folklore and Ethnology Review* 11 (1–2): 2–11.

Gottesman, Itzik Nakhman. 2003. *Defining the Yiddish Nation: The Jewish Folklorists of Poland.* Detroit: Wayne State University Press.

Noy, Dov. 1961. "The First Thousand Folktales in the Israel Folktale Archives." *Fabula* 4: 99–110.

———. 1967. "Recording Folklore from Storytellers in Israel: A Ten-Year Project." *Bitfutsot Ha'gola* 8 (39): 142–54. [Hebrew]

———. 1980. "The Folktales Publication Series in Israel." *Shevet Va'Am* 9: 200–218. [Hebrew]

———. 1982. "An-Ski in Jewish Folkloristics." *Jerusalem Studies in Jewish Folklore* 2: 94–107. [Hebrew]

Pintel-Ginsberg, Idit, and Edna Hechal. 2005. "Narrating Stars—The Jubilee of the Israel Folktale Archives (IFA)." *Yeda Am* 30–31: 225–32. [Hebrew]

Shenhar, Aliza, and Haya Bar-Itzhak. 1981. *Folk Narratives from Beit-She'an.* Haifa: University of Haifa. [Hebrew]

———. 1982. *Folk Narratives from Shlomi.* Haifa: University of Haifa. [Hebrew]

THE BRIDE AND THE DEMON

IFA 335

NARRATED BY HAYA NAHUMZON (LITHUANIA)

In a small, remote village in Lithuania, not far from the town of Kovno, lived a poor and meager Jewish family that barely made a living. The father was a poor shoemaker who repaired shoes and boots for farmers from the surrounding villages. Each day, with his tools on his back, he wandered among the villages and the gentile farmers' dwellings. And so he passed from village to village, from gentile to gentile, from farmer to farmer, and repaired their shoes. This was his livelihood; the wage for his labor was meager, just bread and water. With great sorrow and effort, he earned his daily bread. But nevertheless the man was happy and satisfied, for why someone should complain to the Lord? If it was destined from heaven that at the cost of his life he should earn his bread, why should he complain to the dweller above?

His consolation—a glimpse of hope and light—was the Shabbat and his only daughter, Feigele. On Fridays he arrived home early to amuse and cheer his wife, and most of all, his only daughter, Feigele, for she was his comfort in life and his hope for entertainment. In his hands he would bear her, and she was an unfailing source of comfort and delight.

Feigele was kind and gentle, the epitome of perfection and beauty. She was his sole solace, for he loved her so, and his soul was tied to hers.

So his life passed in peace and tranquility until Feigele grew up and reached puberty, and it was her time to marry. Many were talking about her; matchmakers from all around did not stop knocking on their door, for her name, beauty, and kindness reached far.

But the man would keep his beloved daughter as an apple of his eye. He chose a fitting groom—a good and nice young man from a respectable and rich family—so that nothing would be lacking for his only daughter. Everything went well, and at the right and proper time, the terms were signed, and Feigele was a bride. Now, she was closely watched by her mother, aunts, and grandmothers, and the good women neighbors guarded her and kept an eye on her: "Feigele, eat that"; "Feigele, the day is almost over and you didn't taste a thing yet"; "Feigele don't be alone, it is firmly forbidden to leave a bride alone, without company, for the wise men said: *Three should not be left alone: the sick, the pregnant woman, and a bride, for God forbid, the devil could denounce you*." And Grandma added to that; she attached a special talisman over Feigele's heart to protect her from the evil eye.

They surrounded her from all over, and Feigele had no break. Her wish was to get out of the circle that surrounded her, to be by herself a bit, and to go to the nearby forest close to her village without any company. The day arrived; she escaped from the vigilant eyes of the ones surrounding her and reached the forest. She filled her lungs with the pure forest air and wandered deep into the woods, unaware of the time and the approach of nightfall.

When she finally regained her senses and wanted to return home, a demon suddenly appeared, disguised as the *paritz* (gentile landlord) who lived in his mansion not far from her village. The *paritz*-demon approached Feigele, bowed politely and graciously to her, and offered to accompany her home. Feigele accepted his offer and walked with him a short while, until she realized that this was not the way to her village. For the *paritz*-demon was directing her on a different path, a way she had not gone before. Her heart was beating hard; fear grabbed her, for her heart told her she had fallen into a trap. So she said to the *paritz*: "This is not the way to the village."

The *paritz* did not listen to her and tried to grab her hand to lead her forward. Feigele realized that a lot of trouble was about to befall her. She gathered the rest of her strength: In one hand she held the talisman that her grandmother had given her, and with her other hand she gave the *paritz* a strong push; and from her mouth came a roar: "The Lord is my strength and my fortress, who should I fear."

The demon in the *paritz* disguise disappeared at once, and Feigele ran with the rest of her strength back to her village, without looking back, and so she escaped a great disaster.

Transcribed by Moshe Vigiser

COMMENTARY TO
"THE BRIDE AND THE DEMON"

IFA 335

IDIT PINTEL-GINSBERG

This tale is a Jewish demon legend. At the center of the plot stands the maturation of a young Jewish girl—her transition from childhood, through puberty, and then to marriage. At the same time there exists the tension within the Jewish community, which derives from its coexistence with a non-Jewish population. In this tale coexistence is a geographic and economic inevitability, but it is also a physical and moral threat to the Jewish society. The plot focuses

LITHUANIAN JEWESS.

on the fate of one girl, but, in a hidden stratum, it insinuates the dangers threatening the whole community's existence.

This Jewish legend does not belong to any international tale type, but the plot development is close to that of international type AT 888* (The Princess Flees to the Forest to Escape Marriage), while the tale's ending is close to the international type AT 817* (Devil Leaves at Mention of God's Name). In this tale there are several motifs that resemble international ones: T 311.1 (Flight of Maiden to Escape Marriage); D 815.1 (Magic Object Received from Mother); D 1470.1 (Magic Wishing Object Causes Wishes to Be Fulfilled); L 162 (Lowly Heroine Marries Prince); G 303.16.8 (Devil Leaves at Mention of God's Name, which is also a tale type, as mentioned above).

This tale was told by Haya Nahumzon, who lived in Herzliya, Israel. She was born in 1911, in Srednik,[1] a shtetl near Kovno, Lithuania. Nahumzon mentioned that the heroine of the tale also lived there. Nahumzon's family, along with six hundred other Jews living in the area, were murdered by the local Lithuanians. She immigrated to Israel on her own in 1934. She lived first in Kibbutz Givat Brenner and later on in Herzliya, where she met and married Moshe Vigiser, one of the first highly motivated tale collectors of IFA. Nahumzon told Vigiser her stories, which were connected to the folkways and traditions of her homeland and town of birth.

This tale describes a small, remote village and its daily realities. Four plot parts can be identified. In the first, the exposition, we have a seemingly pastoral description of a poor Jewish family's life over the years. The father is a shoemaker, a low trade position among Jews. All week long he resides in non-Jewish neighborhoods and returns home just for the Shabbat—the sacred time. He considers his existence God's decree, and he does not consider himself responsible for the fact that he is leaving the domain of Jewish society. In the description of the father's return for Shabbat, his special relationship with his daughter is revealed. Although it is mildly implied, there is an incestuous tension. The narrator describes his relationship with his wife using almost the same words as those describing his relationship with his daughter: "he arrived home early to amuse and cheer his wife, and most of all, his only daughter." Further on, his ties with his daughter are described more extensively: "she was an unfailing source of comfort and delight. . . . She was his sole solace, for he loved her so, and his soul was tied to hers." The word "delight," or *oneg* in Hebrew, has an evident erotic connotation, especially within the Shabbat context, wherein the sexual union of a married couple on Friday night is considered a *mitzvah* known as "Shabbat delight" (*Oneg Shabbat*). The tale's exposition deploys the relationships of a person who lives contrary to the human and Jewish social norms: He acts within a non-Jewish space during secular time and creates an incestuous tension during sacred time. Although the family members live within the confines of the Jewish village, they are disconnected from it, physically and normatively.

The second part of the plot takes place within the larger family and the Jewish village, when the young girl reaches the age of marriage. The time span described here is much shorter than in the exposition, extending from the girl's adolescence to the period of her wedding preparations. Here the characters' actions represent the norms and values of the Jewish society. They intend to resolve the family's existential situation: to eliminate the Oedipal tension by marrying off the daughter and thereby to return the family to Jewish society. The father has difficulties separating from his daughter—"The man would keep his beloved daughter as his own eyesight"—but finally he agrees; he chooses for her the ultimate groom, one physically, morally, and financially superior. After the father separates from his daughter, he is replaced by a group of women belonging to the Jewish society in the village, made up of female members of the extended family—the aunts, the grandmothers, and also the women living in the annex space (the good neighbors). They physically surround the girl: They protect her, feed her, and create a space around her that is secluded from men and the known Jewish world. They explain their actions as complying with a rabbinical order whose function is to protect the girl from Satan's allegations. The rabbinical tradition the tale refers to is from the Babylonian Talmud (Tractate Berachot 54b):

Rab Judah said: Three persons require guarding, namely, a sick person, a bridegroom, and a bride. In a Baraitha it was taught: A sick person, a midwife, a bridegroom and a bride. Some add: a mourner, and some add too: scholars at night-time.

Rashi comments here that the guarding is against demons.

Those in danger are a sick person and the couple about to be wed, and to this list are added, from an earlier source, a pregnant woman and rabbinical scholars. This tradition is based on a folk belief that demons seek to hurt people whenever the opportunity arises. When someone is sick and weak, he is an easy target for demonic abuses, and thus he must be closely guarded from them. When a person is in a joyful situation, he is also vulnerable, because the demons are jealous of him (Noy 1971). Thus there is fear that demons will hurt the couple about to get married. This issue is mentioned in the Book of Tobit, from the first centuries CE, which describes how Asmodeus the Demon kills Sara Bat Reuel's intended grooms even before their nuptial nights. The folk belief that demons attack especially during these moments reflects the tremendous anxiety and fears such events produced (Yassif 1999; Bilu 1982). In the present tale this belief may express the society's anxiety over preserving its ways and sacred norms (Bar-Itzhak 1982). Here this way of life is assured by the realization of the marriage and the assurance that the family structure will carry on. Its nonfulfillment is concretized as a demonic and destructive aspect that threatens the proper existence of this society. Of the list of people left vulnerable when left alone, in addition to the sick person, our tale emphasizes female characters: the pregnant woman and the bride. The explanation given for the guard in the tale is that these situations stimulate Satan's indictments. This assertion is an adaptation taken from various rabbinical sources: The Mishnah states that women die during childbirth because they do not strictly adhere to their three divine commandments or *mitzvot* (Mishnah Shabbat 2.6)—*nidah* (menstrual purity), *challah* (extraction of a portion of dough), and *nerot* (lighting Shabbat candles). The Midrash adds on to the Mishnah ruling and explains it: In times of danger, Satan denounces the wrongdoing of people (Midrash Tanhuma Vayigash 1).

Our tale connects the guarding of the bride and the danger of satanic denunciation. The women watch over the girl through active physical care. They smother her and feed her. Magic protection is offered to her as well, in the form of a talisman against the evil eye which her grandmother places over her heart. The tale does not elaborate on the nature of this talisman, but amulets against the evil eye were common in Jewish communities; they were fashioned from jewels, silver or other metals, written parchment, colored beads, and took various forms (Schrire 1966; Shachar 1981).

It is interesting to compare the women guarding over the bride to the traditional watch of men over a newborn on the night before the circumcision (*Wachnacht*)—a common medieval custom. The men on this watch are active within the sacred domain: they pray and read biblical verses of a protective nature (Trachtenberg 1977 [1939], 46, 106, 157), while the female guardians act within the natural domain, performing a physical and magical watch.[2]

In the third part of the plot, which lasts less than a day, the young girl succeeds in breaking through the women's protective ring and escapes to the forest, which serves as her asylum. In various IFA folktales originating from Poland, the motivation behind the bride's escape to the forest is apparent. In these tales the young girls seek refuge from their distress in the forest, as, for example, in the tale IFA 18142, "The Bride Who Escaped from Her Groom," where the young girl wishes to avoid the matchmaking she resents ("And she ran away through the window in her wedding dress. She escaped to the forest and feared the wild beasts"); and in the tale IFA 20347, "The Good Daughter" ("And here, at the end of the wedding, after all the guests left, nobody knew about her great sorrow. . . . One day the rumor spread that she disappeared from home and vanished. Some said they saw her lying down between the thick trees"). In the tale IFA 20357, "The King's Wrath," the young girl is taken to the forest by the Prophet Elijah, so she can reunite with her destined fiancé, whom the king expelled.

In our tale the forest is opposed to the village, which represents the cultural domain. The escape to the forest is an exit to the natural domain—the boundless, dangerous realm dominated by demonic forces. These domains symbolize not only the real hazards awaiting a young girl walking alone but also her soul's inner world: her desires, her curiosity, her will to rebel and demand independence. Walking during the day within the boundless domain leads to the most dangerous time—the night—in which the demonic forces rule. The time spent in the forest is in a way the liminal stage of a rite of passage (Turner 1969). The young girl detaches herself from her childhood, her parents' home, and the women's circle. This stage—figuratively represented by the forest—also represents the dangers awaiting her while disconnecting from her previous groups of belonging: the threats of the non-Jewish world, represented here through the gracious gentile[3] who appears in a demonic form, a demon disguised by the face of a known gentile. The gentile/demon leads her through an unknown path, hinting at what may happen to her. The possible scenarios, from romantic to violent, are not described but rather left to the audience's imagination. According to the folk belief— which has a basis in the Jewish tradition originating from rabbinical sources—a demon can present itself as a human being, male or female, and can marry a person and then kill him or her after the relationship (Alexander 1991, 1995; Dan 1968; Yassif 1999; Zfatman 1987). Does the gentile/demon want to seduce the girl, convincing her to go with him into the non-Jewish/demonic world and live with him in adultery? Does he intend to rape her? Kill her? In any case, the path takes her away from her family and community, and brings her closer to a physical and moral ruin.

The fourth and last part of the tale is about salvation and return. It takes place first in the forest and ends in the Jewish village, over the course of only a few hours. Feigele holds the talisman given to her by her grandmother, firmly pushes away the man/demon, and recites a verse. This verse—"The Lord is my strength and my fortress, whom should I fear"—combines two different biblical citations, one from Jeremiah 16:19 ("O Lord, my strength, and my fortress, and my refuge in the day of affliction") and the second from Psalms 27:1 ("The Lord is my light and my salvation; whom shall I fear? The Lord is the strength of my life; of whom shall I be afraid?").

It may be that the recurrence of the word "strength" in the two verses—in Hebrew, *maozi* and *maoz*—created a connection between them and their merging into one in the tale. This fusing of the two verses is unknown in the written traditions, but it may point here to an oral women's tradition.

The struggle of the young woman transpires simultaneously in three dimensions: the physical-tangible, the symbolic, and the psychic. In the physical-tangible dimension, the young woman pushes firmly against a violent man and succeeds in chasing him away with her shouts. In the symbolic dimension, the girl struggles with an unnatural being—a demon—by means of a symbolic system (Bilu and Witztum 1994), by waving an object and pronouncing magical words. The mix of action and recitation is a magic ritual whose function is to channel meaning. The words perform metaphoric mirroring, while the use of the symbolic object is a performative act (Harari 1998; Tambiah 1973; Tambiah 1985). The words express metaphorically the overcoming of fears and the strength of belief in a savior and shield who will overpower the threatening dangers. The object/amulet has symbolic magical power against the evil eye. When the young girl holds it in her hands, she somehow wields a defensive weapon and repels the threat to her. In a Jewish context, loudly reciting sacred words is an empowering activation of the holy domain, and it creates a separation between the girl and the profane world (that is, the demonic domain). The demon is scared away from the holy domain and vanishes (Trachtenberg 1977 [1939]). In the psychic dimension, the girl struggles with her own fears and impulses; she becomes aware of the destructive dimension inside her and succeeds in overcoming it.

The return of Feigele to the Jewish village, to her home and her groom, is a symbolic return to Jewish norms. This is the third stage in a rite of passage: unification with the new attending group. She gives up the previous group—her childhood, and her relations with her father, who is connected to the non-Jewish world—and accepts herself as an adult woman and bride in the Jewish society.

The positive ending of the tale in fact represents the reacceptance of conventional societal norms. In this case, it is the return of the girl to Jewish society and her entrance into the world of married wives—the traditional role reserved for her in the society that tells the story. This tale is also a reinforcement of the folk custom in which women guard the bride, and proves its validity and effectiveness.

Notes

1. Srednik is the Yiddish name for the village Seredzius, in Lithuania, situated at latitude 55° 05′N and longitude 23° 25′E.
2. On the different types of rituals according to gender, see Rubin 1995.
3. In the tale he is called "the *paritz*," which sounds similar to the Hebrew word *pritzut*, or lust—an association that may not be accidental.

Bibliography

Aarne, Antti, and Stith Thompson. 1961. *The Types of the Folktale: A Classification and Bibliography*. FF Communications no. 184. Helsinki: Suomalainen Tiedeakatemia.

Alexander, Tamar. 1991. "Theme and Genre: Relationships between Man and She-Demon in Jewish Folklore." *Jewish Folklore and Ethnology Review* 14, nos. 1–2: 56–61.

———. 1995. "Design of the Demon Story Genre: Marriages between a Man and a Demon." In *A View into the Lives of Women in Jewish Societies*, ed. Yael Atzmon, 291–307. Jerusalem: Zalman Shazar Center for Jewish History. [Hebrew]

Bar-Itzhak, Haya. 1982. "Modes of Characterization in the Sacred Legend of Oriental Jews." In *Studies in the Literature of Oriental Jews*, ed. Haya Bar-Itzhak and Aliza Shenhar, 1–21. Haifa: University of Haifa. [Hebrew]

Bilu, Yoram. 1982. "Demonic Explanations of Disease among Moroccan Jews in Israel." *Jerusalem Studies in Jewish Folklore* 2: 108–23. [Hebrew]

Bilu, Yoram, and Eliezer Witztum. 1994. "Ben Zoma Glimpsed and Was Damaged: On Mystical Beliefs and Practices among Psychiatric Outpatients." *Alpa'im* 9: 21–43. [Hebrew]

Dan, Yosef. 1968. *The Esoteric Theology of Ashkenazi Hasidism.* Jerusalem: Bialik Institute. [Hebrew]

Harari, Yuval. 1998. "How to Do Things with Words: Philosophical Theory and Magical Deeds." *Jerusalem Studies in Jewish Folklore* 19–20: 365–92. [Hebrew]

Noy, Dov. 1971. "Folklore." *Encyclopaedia Judaica*, vol. 6: 1375–84; 1396–1405.

Rubin, Nissan. 1995. *The Beginning of Life: Rites of Birth, Circumcision, and Redemption of the First-Born in the Talmud and Midrash.* Tel Aviv: Hakibbutz Hameuchad. [Hebrew]

Schrire, T. 1966. *Hebrew Amulets.* London: Routledge and Kegan Paul.

Shachar, Isaiah. 1981 [1971]. "Amulets." In *The Jewish Tradition in Art*, 237–318. Jerusalem: Israel Museum.

Tambiah, Stanley J. 1973. "Form and Meaning of Magical Acts: A Point of View." In *Modes of Thought: Essays on Thinking in Western and Non-Western Societies*, ed. R. Horton and R. Finnegan,199–229. London: Faber.

———. 1985. "The Magical Power of Words." In *Culture, Thought and Social Action*, 17–59. Cambridge, MA: Harvard University Press.

Trachtenberg, Joshua. 1977 [1939]. *Jewish Magic and Superstition.* New York: Atheneum.

Turner, Victor. 1969. *The Ritual Process.* London: Routledge and Kegan Paul.

Van Gennep, Arnold. 1975 [1960]. *The Rites of Passage.* Chicago: University of Chicago Press.

Yassif, Eli. 1999. *The Hebrew Folktale: History, Genre, Meaning.* Bloomington: Indiana University Press.

Zfatman, Sara. 1987. *The Marriage of a Mortal Man and a She-Demon: The Transformations of a Motif in the Folk-Narrative of Ashkenazi Jewry in the Sixteenth–Nineteenth Centuries.* Jerusalem: Academon. [Hebrew]

Stone Restrains Redemption

IFA 489

Narrated by Aharon Nini (Iraq)

One of the Western Wall stones was once used for idolatry. And as long as it remains in the wall, the Redemption will not arrive. No one knows which one it is, and where exactly it is located.

Once, a young man arrived in Jerusalem. He spoke three languages—the Holy language, Hindu, and Arabic. He introduced himself as David from the tribe of Reuben, and claimed that he held a "Name," and with its help he will remove the stone that prevents the Redemption.

When, with the Sages of Jerusalem, he arrived at the Western Wall, they all suddenly fell asleep, and when they awoke, they did not find the messenger. The Sages of Jerusalem raised their voices and cried, for they knew that the time had not yet arrived, and the Redemption would be delayed.

Transcribed by Dov Noy

THE OLD SYNAGOGUE IN PRAGUE

IFA 502

NARRATED AND TRANSCRIBED BY DOV NOY (POLAND)

The old synagogue in the city of Prague, capital of Czechoslovakia, was built from stones of the Temple. When Titus the Wicked, may his name and memory be blotted out, destroyed the Temple and the People of Israel went into exile, they carried with them stones from the Temple. And in all the routes they took, they carried them and cared for them with holy love and heartaches, fulfilling the verse (Psalm 102:15), "for your slaves wanted its stones and its aches desired."

When they arrived in the city of Prague and built the synagogue there, they placed stones from the holy Temple in its walls.

STONE IN THE TEMPLE ORIGINATED FROM SINAI

IFA 553

NARRATED BY A LONGTIME JERUSALEM RESIDENT (ISRAEL, SEPHARDI)

All the stones of the Temple in Jerusalem were from Jerusalem and its hills. Only one stone came from overseas. But it was not a stone from a regular place, for it was from the holy Mount Sinai. It was placed in the Western Wall of the Temple.

And this is why the Western Wall was not destroyed and it is the sole remnant, because of the stone from the holy mountain, where the Torah of truth was given.

(Transcribed by Dov Noy)

Commentary to "Stone Restrains Redemption," "The Old Synagogue in Prague," and "Stone in the Temple Originated from Sinai"

IFA 489, 502, 553

Idit Pintel-Ginsberg

These three tales were all recorded by Dov Noy in 1958.[1] The tale "Stone Restrains Redemption" (IFA 489) was told by Aharon Nini and originated from Iraq. The tale "The Old Synagogue in Prague" (IFA 502) was told by Noy and originated in Poland. The tale "Stone in the Temple Originated from Sinai" (IFA 553) was told by a long-time resident of Jerusalem.

These three tales are all religious legends involving two intertwining topics: the sacred space of the People of Israel, and the mythical-historical rhythmus of destruction-exile-redemption, which is interpreted in Jewish culture as the People of Israel's existential cycle. Each tale emphasizes only one stage in this cycle, but in the plots' background stands the entire continuum.

These two main topics are discussed through an object—the stone—and its appearance in three contexts:

- A stone from Mount Sinai is inlayed in the Western Wall, explaining why this particular wall is the only remnant since the Second Temple's destruction (IFA 553).
- The stones from the destroyed Temple were brought to Prague and used to build the synagogue there (IFA 502).
- A stone used for idolatry is embedded in the Western Wall and delays the Redemption (IFA 489).

The stone (or stones') properties—the physical ones and the ones attributed to it in the Jewish cultural context—are at the core of each tale's plot. On the one hand, its firmness, hardness, permanence, and changelessness are transferred to a symbolic sphere and express the Jewish worldview: the eternity of Israel, the firmness of the bonds between God and his people, the hardness of the principle of reward and punishment. On the other hand, in the cultural context, the stone was used as building material for the Temple Mount and the Temple. The Shtiah stone—the floor stone of the Holy of Holiest—was considered the axis mundi, the center of the universe and the direct connection between this world and the celestial one.

The stone, in the Jewish cultural context, is central to the issues of impurity and purity. One of its aspects—which is not expressed in the tales discussed here—is its purity and its ability to prevent impurity; in particular, to avert impurity caused by touching the dead (Levine 1989–91; Magen 1988; Magen 1994). Another aspect, which stands in the background of one of the tales, is the belief that stones can be impure (Pintel-Ginsberg 2000).

The tale "Stone in the Temple Originated from Sinai" (IFA 553) joins a series of Jewish sources that deal with the question of why the Western Wall survived destruction. Noy points to two trends among the answers offered: the historical-rational trend, which aims to find the reason in historical-cultural military terminology and to tie it to the conquest and destruction itself; and the ethical-imaginary trend, which is not interested in the historical or pseudo-historical truth—for it is constrained by time limitation—but prefers the eternal truth that lies beyond the specific event (Noy 1966, 46). Based on Noy's distinctions, it is possible to ascribe tale IFA 553 to the ethical-imaginary trend. Yet, by acuminating these distinctions, one could ascribe this tale to another trend, which we will call "cultural-symbolic."

The stone from Mount Sinai, thanks to which the Western Wall was saved, points to the continuity of holiness and the divine providence that derived from the first holy space, Mount Sinai (where Israel became a people and where the people had a direct and ultimate encounter with God). The holiness of the space and its founding status are symbolized in the stone from Mount Sinai. Although this stone did not stop the total destruction of the holiest parts of the Temple Mount and the Temple itself, it saved the Western Wall from ruin. The stone's protective nature symbolizes the providence principle and the eternity of Israel. The redemption in this tale is the very existential and cultural continuity of the Jewish people, the evidence of the holy space in the past and its minimalistic embodiment in the Western Wall.

The tale "The Old Synagogue in Prague" (IFA 502) has many written sources, as Noy has shown.[2] Its closest variant appears in Micha Yosef Bin Gorion's *Mimekor Yisrael* (1966), tale 158.

"Of the Temple stones"—The old synagogue in Prague was built from the Temple's stones. When Israel went to Exile, they took with them stones from the Temple because of their love for the Holy and for their sorrow and distress, to follow the verse words: (Psalms 102:15) "For thy servants take pleasure in her stones." And when they came to Prague, they built there a synagogue and put there also stones from the Temple.[3]

The stones of the destroyed Temple symbolize the continuity of the physical and spiritual existence of the people. Although the real holy center was destroyed, and the people in exile lost its space, its spiritual existence remained. The stones of the Temple carried within them the holiness attached to the holy space and conveyed this holiness to the Diaspora as well.[4]

The people in exile thus realistically and metaphysically are carrying the stone of an edifice. Although the transit of a holy object, the stone, from the Land of Israel to Prague is itself something of an exile, it enables the establishment of a symbolic substitute (Bar-Itzhak 2001). The old Prague synagogue becomes the sacred space in which the people return to become holy, through alternative rituals crystallized after Israel's destruction (in 70 AD). This enables—even if only temporarily—an unmediated bond between the exiled people and its world of beliefs, its spiritual existence and its cultural heritage.

The people's unwillingness to be cut off from the Temple's stones is described in this tale as an act of great love toward the sacred space and as an act of constant yearning. But the concealed narrative expresses the tremendous strengths of a people who believed in rebuilding and restoring life after destruction and devastation.

This tale, which was still told after the Holocaust, also carries the message of the return to and founding of the State of Israel. The powers of rehabilitation and healing are seen as characteristic of the People of Israel's self-image. However, it is reasonable to assume that this tale was told even before World War II, and it thus can be seen as having an additional message: the glorification of the Diaspora and Jewish diasporic life. As Haya Bar-Itzhak has pointed out: "The spatial connection between Poland and the Land of Israel occurs . . . through the medium of stones from the Holy Temple that are incorporated into the walls of the local synagogue. . . . The Land of Israel remains the sanctified space for which the Jews yearn; it radiates a measure of sanctity on the landscapes and synagogues of their present abode" (Bar-Itzhak 2001, 40).[5]

The tale "Stone Restrains Redemption" (IFA 489) attributes the delay to the fact that one of the Western Wall's stones had been used for idolatry, and to the failure to extricate the offending stone. This contradicts entirely the theme of "Stone in the Temple Originated from Sinai" (IFA 553), which, as we have seen, ascribes the wall's survival to a stone that originated from a holy source. Noy pointed out the polarization of various concepts regarding the Western Wall in folktales. He maintained that the remains not only represented comfort in the future and in the promise of a return to a glorious past, but also served as an eternal proof of a dreadful failure, a testimony to the void and the absence. Thus the tales developed an ambivalent attitude toward the wall, including attributing impurity to it (Noy 1966, 54).

In this tale, ancient written traditions reverberate. The first part of the tale is very close to the testimony of the sixteenth-century rabbi Rafael Tarbot, and there is a consensus among scholars that the messenger in the tale refers to David Hareuveni (Cassuto 1963, 343; Eshkoli 1993, 94):

And he claimed he has been dispatched by Reuven tribe's king in Jerusalem, to remove a stone from the Western Wall of our Glorious Temple. Created by Yerovam Ben Nabbat, by means of sorcery, this stone, as long as it is a part of the Wall, prevents Israel from returning from exile. And this lad prided himself that he removed it, in front of the Gaon, our mighty glorious Nagid, the great priest, Rabbi Itzhak Solal.[6]

An additional sixteenth-century source is the book of visions by Rabbi Haim Vital. In Haim Vital's dream description, he was the one who extracted the stone from the wall.[7] Noy introduced an additional source from the seventeenth century, which told of a young man "who arrived in Safed, dispatched by King Chananel of the Reuben Tribe, in order to remove from the Western Wall a stone used for idolatry" (Noy 1966, 55). And indeed the young man succeeded in doing so by pronouncing the Holy Name of God. The stone was lost after it was removed from the wall.

The last part of our tale, where the explanation for the missed Redemption is given, reminds us of the tale of Rabbi Itzhak Luria (the Ari), who wanted to lead his pupils to Jerusalem on Shabbat eve. The Ari explains that his pupils' hesitation delayed the Redemption and caused the return to exile.[8] Although our tale is based partially on ancient sources, it seems that the story-teller created a complete narrative whose message diverged from the earlier tales. At the center of the plot stands the missed opportunity for removing an idolatrous stone from the Western Wall, and thereby also the missed opportunity for Redemption, which is in total contrast to the written sources where the hero succeeds.

The act of removing a stone used for idolatry relates to the motif of stones' inherent impurity in Jewish culture. The concept derives from two different views: One is the functional view, according to which a stone should be removed if it was originally intended to be used for idolatry (Mishnah Avoda Zara 3:7). The second is the physical view, termed "the leprosy plague" in the Bible (Leviticus 14:33–55), whereby a house's stone wall, if covered with colored spots, is considered to be infected. The only way to make the house safe for human use is by removing the stone from the wall. The person assigned this task is a priest, who extracts it and takes it to an impure site outside the encampment's boundaries. The theme of a plagued stone and its treatment was further developed in the Midrash (Leviticus Raba, 17:7), where it imparted the necessity of destruction and exile, and the hope for redemption. The plagued stone's end symbolized the fate of Israel's people. The stone's leprosy stood for Israel's sins, its extraction from the wall symbolized the exile, and the extractor was God. Replacing it with a pure stone represented the redemption of a people that had cleansed itself of its sins. Placing the stone back in the house symbolized the return to Zion, the return of the Jewish people to its sacred space (Pintel-Ginsberg 2000, 191–92). In our tale the plot's structure reminds one of the stone's handling stages as described in the Bible, but there are some important differences. In the biblical ritual the active character, the priest, is in the sacred space; in the Midrash's symbolic reading, this character is God, the ultimate sacred entity. In our tale the main characters are the historical David from the Reuben tribe (who may be, as mentioned earlier, David Hareuveni) and the collective character of the Jerusalem sages. This is the sole IFA tale where the name of David from the Reuben tribe is mentioned (as opposed to Elijah the prophet, the ultimate savior in Jewish folk literature, who is present in more than six hundred IFA folktales).

David from the Reuben tribe does not seek to extract the stone through a realistic action, as would the biblical priest, but instead uses a magic ritual centered on pronouncing God's Holy Name. His failure is not a consequence of his lacking mystical/magical abilities but instead is caused by the Jerusalem sages' sleep. It is not clear whether their falling asleep was caused by a heavenly power or their lack of faith. It is possible that the storyteller is conveying his belief in a magical reality that is centered on bringing redemption by pronouncing holy names in front of an audience. The criticism in this case centers on the people, who do not believe in an imminent salvation. And indeed, when the sages wake up, they find that the envoy has disappeared and taken with him the chance for an imminent Redemption.

The storyteller chooses to describe the character of the savior through ambiguous expressions that put his integrity in question: "a young man," "[h]e introduced himself as David from the tribe of Reuben, and claimed that he held a Name." The doubt raised is a partial criticism and even condemnation of the "Redemption-hastening" acts. The claims of this savior character are in total opposition to the belief that Redemption will come not by magically forcing it but by the ethical readiness of the people. Therefore the stone of idolatry implanted in the Western Wall symbolizes the reality in which the People of Israel live, in impurity, and this is the real reason Redemption is not yet possible. This message is totally different from the written sources, as mentioned by Noy: "These tales promise: now, when the obstacle is removed, that Redemption will be possible" (Noy 1966, 55).

Notes

1. IFA 489 was published in the newspaper *Omer*, December 15, 1961. IFA 502 was printed in a publication for new immigrants (see Noy, ed. 1959, 38) and annotated (ibid., 49–50); this version was adapted into easy Hebrew. IFA 553 was translated into German and published in 1976 by Heda Jason (Jason 1976, 37; 291).
2. Noy, ed., 1959, 49–50, note 15.
3. Micha Yosef Bin Gorion in *Mimekor Yisrael*, page 127, pointed at this tale's sources: *Sipurim Nehmadim* (Zhitomir, 1903), tale 7, and *Der Born Judas*, vol. 5 (Leipzig, 1924), tale 194, 305.
4. For other traditions on holy stones used to build synagogues in the Diaspora, see Noy 1959, 49–50, note 15.
5. See also Bar-Itzhak 2001, 154, and note 45 on page 175.
6. From manuscript 111 in *Floteon*, folio 44, quoted in Moshe Idel's introduction to Eshkoli 1993, xxxvii; Cassuto 1963, 353; Noy 1966, 55; Vilnay 1954, 104. Historically, however, David Hareuveni may not have practiced magical or Kabbalistic rites (Benmelech 2011, 48). David Hareuveni was born in 1490 and died in 1535. He sought to hasten Redemption through political and military means. His activities throughout the Mediterranean basin created a messianic tumult, particularly among the Converso.
7. See Moshe Idel's note in his introduction to Eshkoli 1993, xxxvii–xxxviii.
8. This tale is mentioned in the "Shlomel letter" included in the book *Shivhey Haari* (Praises of the Ari), printed in the eighteenth century (Dresznitz 2006, 16–17, 56–57; see Kefir, ed., 1981, 17–76). This tale, with alterations, was also published in Micha Bin Gorion's *Mimekor Yisrael*, 288, tale no. 479, where it is titled "The Missed Moment." It has been retold orally to the present day. The Israel Folktale Archives (IFA), named in honor of Dov Noy, situated

in the University of Haifa, Israel, has two versions of the tale: IFA 13542, narrated and recorded by Boaz Hadad, from Jerba, Tunisia, and IFA 16159, recorded by Orna Padida and narrated by Shimon Shebabo, from the Sephardic Jerusalem community.

BIBLIOGRAPHY

Bar-Itzhak, Haya. 2001. *Jewish Poland: Legends of Origin.* Detroit: Wayne State University Press.

Benmelech, Moti. 2011. "History, Politics and Messianism: David Ha Reuveni's Origin and Mission." *AJS Review* 35, no. 1 (April 2011): 35–60.

Bin Gorion, Micha Yosef. 1966. *Mimekor Yisrael.* Tel Aviv: Dvir. [Hebrew]

Cassuto, Moses. 1963. "Who Was David Hareuveni?" *Tarbitz* 32: 339–59. [Hebrew]

Dresznitz, Solomon Shlomel Ben Hayim. 2006. *Tales in Praise of the Ari.* Jerusalem: Chileha Leoraita Institute.

Eliade, Mircea. 1965. *Le Sacre et le profane.* Paris: Gallimard.

Eshkoli, Aharon Z. 1993. *The Story of David Hareuveni.* Jerusalem: Mosad Bialik. [Hebrew]

Harari, Yuval. 1998. "How to Do Things with Words: Philosophical Theory and Magical Deeds." *Jerusalem Studies in Jewish Folklore* 19–20 (1997–98): 365–92. [Hebrew]

Jason, Heda. 1976. *Märchen aus Israel.* Dusserldorf: Eugen Diederichs Verlag.

Kefir, Elkanah, ed. 1981. *The Complete Book of Shivhey Haari.* Tel Aviv: N.p. [Hebrew]

Kunin, Seth. 1994. "Judaism." In *Sacred Place,* ed. Jean Holm and John Bowker, 115–33. London: Continuum.

Kushelevsky, Rella. 2014. "Sites of Collective Memory in Narratives of the Prague Ghetto." In *Framing Jewish Culture: Boundaries and Representations,* ed. Simon Bronner. Jewish Culture Studies Series, vol. 4. Oxford: Littman Library of Jewish Civilization.

Levine, Baruch Abraham. 1989–91. "The Impure Dead and the Cult of the Dead: Polarization and Opposition in Israelite Religion." *Bitzaron* 10: 80–89. [Hebrew]

Magen, Yitzhak. 1988. *The Stone Vessel Industry in Jerusalem in the Days of the Second Temple.* Tel Aviv: Society for the Protection of Nature in Israel. [Hebrew]

———. 1994. "Jerusalem as a Center of the Stone Vessel Industry during the Second Temple Period." In *Ancient Jerusalem Revealed,* ed. Hillel Geva, 244–56. Jerusalem: Israel Exploration Society. [Hebrew]

Moshe, David. 1963. "Who Was David ha-Reuveni?" *Tarbiz* 32: 339–59. [Hebrew]

Noy, Dov. 1962. "The Western Wall in Our Folktales." *Mahanayim* 71: 46–48. [Hebrew]

———. 1966. "Folktales about the Western Wall." *Mahanayim* 107: 44–45. [Hebrew]

———. ed. 1959. *The Diaspora and the Land of Israel.* Jerusalem: Sha'ar. [Hebrew]

Pedaya, Haviva. 1997. "Metamorphoses in the Holy of Holies: From the Margin to the Center." *Jewish Studies* 37: 53–110. [Hebrew]

Pintel-Ginsberg, Idit. 2000. "The Phenomenology of a Cultural Symbol in Judaism: The Stone as a Case Study in Rabbinic and Midrashic Literature." PhD diss. Haifa: University of Haifa. [Hebrew]

Schwarzbaum, Haim. 1994. *Roots and Landscapes,* ed. Eli Yassif. Beer Sheva: Ben-Gurion University Press.

Vilnay, Ze'ev. 1954. *The Legends of Eretz Israel (Jerusalem, Judea, Dead Sea and Samaria).* Jerusalem: Kiriat Sefer. [Hebrew]

THE HANUKKAH MIRACLE:
HANNAH AND HER SEVEN SONS

IFA 1724

NARRATED BY DR. S. Z. KAHANA (ISRAEL, ASHKENAZI)

It was the first night of Hanukkah. All the family members and some of Father's students were at home. Father lit the candles, and we sang "*Maoz Tzur Yeshuati*" loudly. Afterward, we sat at the table by the oil lamp and studied the laws of Hanukkah. Father peered through his glasses at the Talmud while we listened intently for something to happen outside. It was a rainy night, a storm wind was blowing, and rain came crashing down from time to time, shaking the doors and windows. Dark clouds covered the sky and sowed fear everywhere. And then Father suddenly sat up and pricked up his ears, listening carefully: Someone was walking down the lane with a cane; a strange walk, that of an old man dipping his feet in rain puddles.

We heard nothing. We told Father that he was imagining it. But he insisted he could hear it and was surprised that anyone was out on a night like this. Suddenly, Father went pale and cried out: "He's standing and banging with his stick on the paving stones of the lane." He said he could hear a loud knocking and also the murmuring of words of prayer. Who was it? He wanted to go outside and see. He put on fine silk garments, took his stick, and was about to open the door on his way out, but we held him back because it was dangerous.

The next evening, the same thing happened again, and this time father said that he could hear two knocks of the stick, and the day after, three. Father was very upset and begged us to let him go outside to see what the old man was doing. He was very insistent and opened the door, and we followed him.

Outside it was pitch black, and the darkness was almost palpable. We moved in the direction from which Father said the sound of the knocking had come; it was coming from the corner of the alleyway. When we approached the spot, we found the elderly R. Isaac of the Nachmanides Synagogue. R. Isaac was known as a long-time Kabbalist, as one who was familiar with the secret mysteries, one of the great Kabbalists of Jerusalem. We were astonished to see him outside on such a rainy and stormy night, and we asked him why. R. Isaac lifted his head and looked at us with his dark eyes and answered with a question: "Did you see the light?"

"We didn't see anything," we responded.

"Look well and see," was his answer. We listened to him and looked carefully, but we saw nothing. However, it seemed to Father that he could see a jet of light bursting forth from the depths of the earth, and he expressed his amazement.

R. Isaac looked intently into my late father's face as if to see if he really could see something, and after he was convinced that he indeed could, he turned his face only toward him and whispered: "It is good that you have come, very good. I am glad. I was very concerned and now I am relieved." And he continued: "The world thinks that Hanukkah came to the world because of the miracle of the cruse of oil that burned for eight days. And that is indeed the case. But what is the value of this miracle, that we should celebrate it? And why did it burn for eight days, and from where did it take the light? On the external, manifest level, the holiday celebrates the candles that burned; however, on the inner, mystical level, the holiday really celebrates the 'light' that attached itself to the candles to keep them blazing for eight days. The light," continued the old man, "has always emanated from here, from this crooked lane. It emanates from inside, from within the earth."

R. Isaac said these things quietly and calmly, but his words could be heard despite the storm. We looked at him with wonderment at hearing his words, and Father asked him what he was trying to say. "Very simple," answered R. Isaac, and as he spoke, he lifted up one of the stones paving the lane and said: "Here, deep down, in a cave inside a cave, lie Hannah and her seven sons, eight sparks of light. The sages tell us of the courage of the mother and the sons: Without them, there could not have been a victory. They provided the strength and valor to rise up, and from them came the light for the eight days of Hanukkah. From them, from these eight, came the light, from Hannah and her seven sons. These eight gave the light for the eight days, one for each day, and the light of Hanukkah is their light. Each day of Hanukkah is one of the eight martyrs who sanctified God's name, the mother together with her sons, and the light increases from one day to the next."

When R. Isaac saw that Father was listening to him attentively and could see from his expression that he was grateful to him, he continued and revealed even more: "In fact, Hannah's real name was Miriam, Miriam daughter of Tanhum, but she is called Hannah because of Hanukkah, whose name and letters teach us that the light of Hanukkah comes from her and her sons."

"But what does that have to do with this place?" we asked.

"It is connected, and quite strongly. It is a tradition of many generations that in this place, in this lane, are buried Hannah and her seven sons." And he continued to bolster his words with the story itself. "This place had an attendant who came every year to bang on the stones and lift up one paving stone to draw out the light. That old attendant died and was taken to heaven, and he gave me his stick, and I continue to carry out his vocation." The old man sighed and said. "Now, I too am getting old, and I have no one to pass it on to after me, and you are the rabbi of Old Jerusalem and of this lane, and you are also a priest from the tribe of Levi, the third tribe. For the three knocks that you heard, and because you heard my steps and saw the light—all these signs testify that you are the man, and you will receive the stick from me."

Immediately the two men, the old R. Isaac and Father, began to speak in whispers. Of what they spoke I was not privileged to hear. To this day I do not know if Father accepted the vocation or if he refused. We never heard anything more about it and never spoke of it again.

Transcribed by Haim Dov Armon

Commentary to "The Hanukkah Miracle: Hannah and Her Seven Sons"

IFA 1724

Rella Kushelevsky

ocal legend in Jerusalem has it that Hannah and her seven sons are buried in the Jewish Quarter of the city, near the Hurva Synagogue of R. Judah the Hasid. The narrow, twisting lane, with its steps, extends from Jaffa Gate to Jews' Street and crosses Habad Lane, also known as "Or ha-Hayim." In the past the name of the lane was "Hannah and Her Sons." It is under those steps, as the elders of Jerusalem tell it, that Hannah and her seven sons are buried. That is why all those who ascend the steps become so easily fatigued (Vilnay 1977, 119; Weiss 1986, 215). This etiological tradition is apparently very late, and unlike the case for another tradition of Eretz Israel, which situates their tombs near Safed, we have no testimonies to it that predate the twentieth century.[1] One who contributed to its preservation was Shmuel Zanvil Kahana, the son of Shlomo David Kahana, the rabbi of the Old City who lived in the courtyard of Or ha-Hayim, located on the same lane.[2] In a story called "Hannah's Rock" or "Hannah and Her Seven Sons Lane," Shmuel Zanvil Kahana related this folk tradition in his own way (Kahana 1954; Kahana 1977). The story appears in two separate compilations with certain variations, and it is preserved in the Dov Noy Israel Folkltale Archive (IFA) in Haifa University.[3] However, it is not the story per se that interests us here but rather its function in marking a much broader popular and national phenomenon, which functions as the contextual frame of the story. From this perspective, the story coalesces with S. Z. Kahana's activities as director-general of the Ministry of Religious Affairs in the 1950s, as the person who established the Association for the Preservation of the Holy Places, under the auspices of the ministry, and as the director in charge of the Mt. Zion sites.[4]

It was Hanukkah time, relates Kahana, the eve of the fall of the Old City of Jerusalem to the Jordanians in Israel's War of Independence. While all the inhabitants of the city were firmly settled in their homes due to the darkness and the pouring rain, the family members of the rabbi of the Old City, Shlomo David Kahana, could hear steps and the banging of a walking stick approaching their home, which then moved away, in the direction of the end of the lane. When this was repeated on the two following nights of Hanukkah as well, the rabbi and his son hurried out into the street to see who was walking there. They arrived at the corner of the lane, where they were surprised to encounter the well-known elderly Kabbalist R. Isaac of the Nachmanides Synagogue. In their presence, he knocked with his stick on one of the lane's paving stones, lifted it up, and told the rabbi about the cave underneath, where Hannah and her sons were buried. From this cave their light emerges, the light of Hanukkah—which is hinted at in the name "Hannah"—from which all the Hanukkah lamps draw light. With these words R. Isaac the Kabbalist passed on his stick, which had a silver knob, to the rabbi of the Old City, the father of the story's narrator, instructing him to knock on the paving stone each year, to draw out the light of Hannah and her seven sons from within their tomb to bring its light to all the Hanukkah lamps in the world.[5]

In Kahana's story the folk tradition of the tomb of Hannah and her sons is turned into an esoteric family tradition deposited with his father, the city's rabbi, so that it would be passed on afterward to his son after him, as a symbol of leadership. The two are tasked from this time forward with enabling the light to flow from within the tomb and to be spread throughout the Jewish world by means of the Hanukkah candles. As the staff of God was passed down from one generation to the next among the nation's chosen, so too was the staff of the elderly Kabbalist passed down to the rabbi of the Old City, and afterward to his son.[6] Just as Moses struck the rock to cause the water to flow from it, so must they strike the stone to cause the light to flow.[7] The succession ceremony involving the passing down of this tradition included a test of leadership as well: He who sees the light emanating from the stone is worthy of receiving it.[8]

The tradition of the tomb, which is now a family tradition that expresses an awareness of leadership, is intertwined with the national narrative. The event we are told about occurred on the eve of the fall of the Old City, which is why the elderly rabbi is unable to carry out his mission. But the existence of the State of Israel in the background of the story guarantees that it will be carried out again one day, by his son.[9] From the perspective of the narrator, the events of the past anticipate the present.

A broader context of the story is the phenomenon of the "sacred geography" in Israel.[10] Yoram Bilu (2005) refers to the sanctification of the expanse in popular religion and in the sacred ritual, as well as in Israel's civil religion, by means of state rituals. The graves of the national and local righteous, official monuments, cemeteries, and national museums are all sites of ritual that become "sites of memory."[11] The phenomenon becomes established by means of governmental bodies, in response to popular and national initiatives, and also as a catalyst. We will focus on two of these ritual types: the rituals of saints—or as Elhanan Reiner terms it (Reiner 1988), the "ritual of the holy places"—and the rituals of the state.

A ritual of a holy place is "a defined ritual: going to a certain site at a regular time or in honor of known events, praying, the making of vows and giving of charity in honor of the holy place [lighting candles], the use of magical formulations" (Reiner 1989, 228). The expectation is of immediate, visible results, and the purpose of the ritual is to exploit the magical potential embodied in the holy place.[12] In Israel millions of people visit the tombs of righteous rabbis in Meron, Netivot, Tiberias, and many other places, where mass celebrations are held. The roots of the phenomenon, as it is currently expressed mainly among Jews originally from North Africa, lie in the traditional veneration of saintly rabbis in Morocco, as we know from the work of Issachar Ben-Ami (Ben-Ami 1984; Bilu 2005, 75–82).

In addition to these holy rituals, and also combined with them, are the rituals of the state. In the state's formative years following its establishment, the emblems of Israeli sovereignty took shape by means of Memorial Day and Independence Day ceremonies. The emblems of the state were invested with their meaning in the context of Jewish heritage in accordance with a secular-Zionist narrative. As Bilu explains (2005), the Aliya (immigration, but literally "ascent") to Israel has replaced the *aliya* (ascent by pilgrimage) to the Holy Temple in Jerusalem, and the *aliya al hakarka* (settling the land) has replaced the *aliya la-Torah* (being called up to the Torah). The "sites of memory" were determined by means of official monuments, military cemeteries, and national museums. The annual, chronological succession of Holocaust Remembrance Day, followed by the commemoration of Israel's war dead on Memorial Day and then Independence Day celebrations, as well as the overall typographical system of Yad Vashem and the military cemetery, with its special section for the country's luminaries, embody an ethos of "from Holocaust to rebirth," "They died that we may live," and "glory and heroism." In the context of Hanukkah, which lies at the center of the story we are discussing, we can see an emphasis on the victory of the Maccabees—like the few against the many in the Zionist ethos—as opposed to the motif of the miracle of the cruse of oil.

The contextual framework of the combined rituals of the saints and of the state comes up in Kahana's story. The sanctification of God's name, or martyrdom, of Hannah and her seven sons during a period of terrible persecution and oppressive decrees is presented here as something that propelled the victory of the Maccabees in their war against the many. And this is what the elderly Kabbalist explains to the rabbi:

> The world is in a state of error. They believe that we celebrate Hanukkah because of the miracle of the cruse of oil that burned for eight days. But that is not all: Hanukkah comes to thank Hannah and her seven sons, who sanctified the heavens and died so as not to transgress the Torah; one Hannah and seven sons—they are eight and they constitute the source of the miracle and the light. If not for their *courage*, the spirit of the *courage* of Matityahu and his sons could not have been awakened. If not for their devotion, there would not have been a miracle of Hanukkah. (current volume, "The Hanukkah Miracle: Hannah and her Seven Sons"; emphasis added)

The Zionist-secular ethos of "glory and heroism" is modified in the story based on the religious-Zionist ethos. It is the spiritual courage that sustains the physical heroism.

The narrative time—encompassing the fall of the Old City in 1948 and its liberation in 1967—places the narrator and his father in key roles in the historical progression that includes within it the years 1948–67.[13] The walking stick with the silver knob they possess is intended to advance the process of redemption; the establishment of the State of Israel is one stage in this process, representing the "dawn of the redemption" and continuing from the Six-Day War until the coming of the Messiah. As long as the Old City of Jerusalem is held by the Arabs, the stick remains hidden in Mt. Zion, but with the liberation of the city, the narrator returns to the Old City to bang on the rock of Hannah. In the eschatological, analogical narrative, the staff was hidden in the ark of the Temple, and when the time comes, it will be passed on to the Messiah. Mt. Zion plays a central role in this narrative as an alternative to the historical sites which, until 1967, were not part of the State of Israel. The symbolism of the tomb of Hannah and her sons is thus shifted, or rewritten, to Mt. Zion. In Kahana's reworking of the story after the Six-Day War, an epilogue is indeed added about the return of Kahana, as the son of the rabbi, to the "original" site of the tomb of Hannah and her sons in the Old City of Jerusalem.

This is then a new story of initiation, which melds into the religious-Zionist narrative to whose constitution Kahana was partner as the director in charge of the holy places. In the context of his position as director-general of the Ministry of Religious Affairs and the founder of the Association for the Preservation of the Holy Places, Kahana sought to "judaize the Galilee" by means of renovating the tombs of saintly rabbis in the north and, as an expression of the right of the Jewish people to the Land of Israel, to turn Mt. Zion into a spiritual center for the Jewish people and an alternative to other holy sites that remained outside Israel's 1948 borders. In addition to David's Tomb, further "sites of memory" were established on Mt. Zion, such as the Chamber of the Holocaust, the Temple Mount Lookout, and the site where the Hasmonean torch is lit on Hanukkah (Bilu 1997–98, 72; Bilu 2005, 278–79). This last site is of particular significance in the context of the story under discussion here, which, as we've noted, connects the heroism of Hannah and her seven sons with that of the Maccabees. The story appears not only to mark the phenomenon of the pilgrimage to the holy places in its popular modes in Israel but also to express Kahana's role in its framing within the religious-Zionist narrative in the 1950s.

NOTES

1. I have discussed this subject in another article: Rella Kushelevsky, "Re-Reading 'The Mother and Her Sons' in Light of the Heterotopia of Their Tomb," *Jerusalem Studies in Jewish Folklore* 24–25 (2006–7): 123–24.
2. This legend apparently continues to live among the locals to this day. One resident told Nehama Cohen, the daughter of S. Z. Kahana, of his family's custom of visiting Hannah Lane on Hanukkah, at the site where Hannah is thought to be buried. I am grateful to Nehama Cohen for sharing this with ne.
3. The story's IFA number is 1724, where it is catalogued under the heading "Hannah and Her Seven Sons." I am thankful to Nehama Cohen for relating the versions of the story to me and to Idit Pintel-Ginsberg, who directed me to the IFA 1724 version, as well as the IFA 14426 version, which preserves the tradition of their tomb as being located in Safed.
4. In this context, see his book (Kahana 1954). In his books on Mt. Zion, Kahana refers to himself as "the director."
5. A reprint of the story, in 1977, under the heading "Hannah's Rock," describes the return of the story's narrator to the Old City of Jerusalem, after the Six-Day War, to rekindle Hanukkah lights with the light of Hannah and her seven sons.

6. The tradition of the staff held by the first generations and by the kings can be found in a number of sources. In this context, see my article, Rella Kushelevsky, "'Aaron's Rod'—An Exploration of One Criterion for Establishing a Thematic Series," *Jerusalem Studies in Jewish Folklore* 13–14 (1991–92): 210–11, and the list of sources therein.

7. In "Hannah's Rock" the father is instructed to strike one of the stones at the place where Or ha-Hayim Street and Habad Lane intersect.

8. This is also how it appears in "Hannah and Her Seven Sons Lane" and in IFA 1724.

9. This position of the implied narrator can be seen in a later version of the story, "Hannah's Rock," where the narrator indeed returns to the Old City after its liberation in the Six-Day War in order to strike the stone.

10. The following discussion is based on Yoram Bilu (1997–98), and the last chapter of his most recent book (2005), 236–80.

11. "Sites of memory" are, according to Pierre Nora, as quoted by Yoram Bilu (2005), 65: "[s]ites that connect to a mythic past and a transcendental reality, and abound with symbolic meanings of spirituality and holiness." See Pierre Nora 1989.

12. Reiner refers to a pilmagrage known as "Ziyarah," which was common in the Middle Ages in the east (Reiner, 1988, 228).

13. The self-image of the figure of the chosen leader was also constructed by means of the narrator's identity as a priest. The staff of Aharon the priest is also the staff of Moses, the staff of God, and the stick of the elderly Kabbalist, which was passed on to the father of the narrator to mediate between the light of Hannah and her seven sons and the light of the People of Israel. The version in "Hannah and Her Seven Sons Lane" indeed notes that Kahana was of the priestly tribe and also rabbi of the Old City, facts that qualify him for the role.

BIBLIOGRAPHY

Ben-Ami, Issachar. 1984. *Saint Veneration among the Jews in Morocco*. Jerusalem: Magnes. [Hebrew]

Bilu, Yoram. 1997–98. "The Sanctification of Space in Israel: Civil Religion and Folk Judaism." *Jerusalem Studies of Jewish Folklore* 19–20: 65–84. [Hebrew]

———. 2005. *The Saints' Impresarios: Dreamers, Healers, and Holy Men in Israel's Urban Periphery*. Haifa: Haifa University Press. [Hebrew]

Kahana, Shmuel Zanvil. 1954. *The Lamp of the Mountain: Legends of Mt. Zion*. Jerusalem: Mossad Har Zion. [Hebrew]

———. 1977. "Hannah's Rock." In *Legends for Hebrew Holidays and Festivals*, ed. Rachel Inbar. Jerusalem: Brit Ivrit Olamit. [Hebrew]

Kushelevsky, Rella. 1991–92. "'Aaron's Rod'—An Exploration of One Criterion for Establishing a Thematic Series." *Jerusalem Studies in Jewish Folklore* 13–14 (1991–92): 210–11.

———. 2006–7. "Re-Reading 'The Mother and Her Sons' in Light of the Heterotopia of Their Tomb." *Jerusalem Studies in Jewish Folklore* 24–25: 123–24.

Nora, Pierre. 1989. "Between Memory and History: Les Lieux de Memoire." *Representations* 26: 7–24.

Reiner, Elhanan. 1988. *Pilgrims and Pilgrimage to Eretz Yisrael, 1099–1517*. PhD diss., Hebrew University, Jerusalem.

Vilnay, Ze'ev. 1977. *Legends from the Land of Israel*. Jerusalem: Kiryat Sefer. [Hebrew]

Weiss, Shraga. 1986. *Holy Sites in the Land of Israel*. Jerusalem: Reuven Mas. [Hebrew]

The Girl and the Cossack

IFA 1935

NARRATED AND TRANSCRIBED FROM MEMORY
BY DAVID COHEN (POLAND)

Long ago, when Chmielnicki the bone-crusher ran wild with his Cossacks across the steppes of Ukraine, devastating Jewish communities by flame and sword, a troop of Cossacks reached this remote and isolated town. Worn out by pillage and murder, they decided to rest in the town, and swore they would not harm the Jews; the latter welcomed them into their homes and even fed them and their horses.

One of the Cossacks was smitten with the rabbi's daughter, a ravishing beauty who was already betrothed. This Cossack would not let the innocent girl alone. When he saw that sweet talk would not win her heart, he threatened that he and his companions would set fire to the town and slaughter its Jews—starting with her father, the rabbi.

At this point, the Cossacks' manner was not what it had been before, and rumors began circulating among the Jews that the Cossacks had evil designs against them. These rumors were spread by the Cossack whose mad love for the rabbi's daughter blazed fiercely inside him.

This pure virgin saw that disaster would befall the town because of her. She remembered what Judith had done to Holofernes and decided to emulate her.

So one summer's evening, when the Cossack would not leave her alone—first courting her with sweet words, then threatening her—she gave him a radiant smile and told him, "Wait for me at midnight, on the hill overlooking the town, and I will come to you."

And so it came to pass at midnight. The rabbi's daughter climbed to the top of the hill, where the Cossack stood burning with lust, his arms open wide to embrace her. Reaching inside her dress, she pulled out a sharp dagger and plunged it into the Cossack's heart. Then she walked quietly down to the river and plunged into its watery depths.

The next morning, when the Jews of the town discovered the Cossack's body, they hid his death from his comrades and buried him on the hilltop. Several days later, when the River Styr spat out the body of the rabbi's daughter, they buried her in the Jewish cemetery.

Ever since, the place has been called "Cossack Hill."

COMMENTARY TO
"THE GIRL AND THE COSSACK"

IFA 1935

HAYA BAR-ITZHAK

The tale was transcribed in the early years of the IFA by David Cohen, apparently from memory. Cohen was born in Slobodka, in the Novogrudok district of what is now Belarus, in 1894. In his youth he left home and wandered across Ukraine, supporting himself as a homilist and storyteller. According to his account, deposited in the IFA, he frequently moved his audience to tears. Later he joined the Slonim Hasidim and lived among them for several years. He then attended the Volozhin yeshiva before moving to Vienna, where he published sketches, novellas, and legends in a Yiddish newspaper. In 1924 he immigrated to Mandatory Palestine, where he

worked as a teacher, journalist, and counselor for the Working Youth (Ha'Noar Ha'Oved) movement.

Our story is a legend set in Volhynia, in an unnamed town—though we are told that it lies on the banks of the River Styr, in which the heroine drowns herself. Also mentioned is Cossack Hill, whose name is attributed by this etiological legend to a Cossack who tried to seduce a Jewish girl but ended up being killed by her and buried there. The story is a historical legend from the period of the Chmielnicki pogroms (1648–49). It begins with a reference to Bogdan Chmielnicki, known as "the bone-crusher"; in this way the storyteller draws an analogy to one of the ultimate oppressors in Jewish history—the Roman emperor Hadrian. The pogroms were part of the Cossack uprising led by Chmielnicki against their Polish overlords. At first the Cossacks routed the Polish forces and overran many cities and towns in Ukraine, Podolia, and Volhynia. They got as far as Zamość and Lublin, and raided Pinsk and Gomel in the north. Hundreds of Jewish communities were wiped out during the course of the rebellion waged by Cossacks, Tatars, and Ukrainian peasants and townsfolk. It is estimated by some scholars that roughly half of Polish Jewry was killed. In their chronicles, the Jews of Poland referred to these pogroms as the destruction of the Third Temple; the mourning and gloom that descended on the survivors provided fertile ground for the rise of Sabbateanism.

Polish Jews recounted many legends about the Chmielnicki pogroms, especially in the districts mentioned earlier. According to S. An-Ski:

Nearly three hundred years have passed since those terrible days, and legends that have never been written down or published are still alive throughout Podolia and Volhynia. Not only do they live eternally; they are also fresh and impressed on every aspect of the Jews' daily life. There is not a single place there where Jewish blood has not been spilled. There is no old building dating back to that era or martyr's grave that is not saturated with legends or without accounts of the events of that past. To this very day, the small, half-dry river near Polonnoye is known as the *Rezinka* (Russian for slaughter), because "that is where Krivonos rinsed the blood off his sword after slaughtering all the residents of Polonnoye; for many years after the river's waters flowed red with blood." In every cemetery there are tombstones that tell of the martyrdom of the spiritual heroes of yesteryear. In every town there are memorial tombstones, stone wells, and synagogues. The Jews dance around a few stones on *Simhat Torah* and during weddings. On *Tisha B'Av*, children visit cemeteries holding wooden swords, which they shatter on the martyrs' tombstones and then stick into the ground. In short, the legend struck roots in its lifetime and has lived on without interruption throughout the generations for decades and centuries (An-Ski 1920, 12)[1]

The fact that David Cohen told this story in the 1950s supports An-Ski's concluding comment. It also indicates the vitality of the legends about the Chmielnicki pogroms even after the Jews had left those districts and the State of Israel was born.

At the heart of the story is the confrontation between the Cossack, who lusts for the rabbi's daughter and wants to possess her at any price, and the beautiful girl, who is already betrothed. This assigns our story to the genre of Jewish Polish legends about women in times of persecutions, many of which are set during the Chmielnicki pogroms. In this category the heroines are young virgins assaulted by ruffians who threaten not only their chastity but also the lives of their families and of all the Jews living in the area. The most famous stories of this type are two that appeared in *Yeven metzulah* (*Abyss of Despair*), the chronicle of the Chmielnicki pogroms compiled soon after the events by Nathan Note Hannover (Hannover 1968 [1653], 38). The first tells of a girl who is captured by a Cossack but then takes advantage of the man's belief that she has supernatural powers and tricks him into shooting her.[2] The second story tells of a girl who deceives a Cossack by agreeing to marry him in the church on the other side of the river. On the way there, she jumps into the water and drowns. The two stories view the girls' deaths as exemplifying martyrdom, even though one of them committed suicide. These and other legends about the Chmielnicki pogroms were passed down among Polish Jews; some of them were collected in H. J. Gurland's *Annals of the Persecutions of Israel* (Gurland, 1972 [1887], 33–37), including "The Cossack and the Damsel," "The Bride and the Groom," and "The Hetman and the Damsel."

While the girl in our story, who drowns herself in the River Styr, dies in a way that resembles the fates of the young women in the second story from *Yeven metzulah*, her heroic act is closest to that in "The Hetman and the Damsel":

THE HETMAN AND THE DAMSEL

While the Cossacks were pillaging the houses of Teverov, several rogues happened upon the house of a rich Jewish magnate of that town. When they opened the door, they bumped into a lovely damsel who was trying to escape. The Cossacks captured her alive. After killing her parents before her eyes and helping themselves to their property, it was time to rape her. But one of the lot interfered and would not let them satisfy their lust—for, he said, this damsel ought to be their chief's mistress.

So they brought the unfortunate girl to the hetman, whose tent was pitched opposite the cemetery of the Jews of Teverov. When evening came the hetman ordered everyone out of the tent. His servants complied at once, leaving the hetman alone with the girl. He tried to seduce her, telling her about all his wealth and property and promising her a life of comfort and ease if she gave herself to him and became his mistress. But the damsel stopped up her ears and hardened her heart and paid no attention to the words of her base seducer.

The hetman, furious at being rebuffed, jumped on her. But the damsel, working up her courage, drew his saber from its sheath on the tyrant's thigh and struggled with him for almost half an hour. When she could hold out no longer, she seized hold of two candles that were burning on the table and set fire to the walls of the tent. In a flash the whole tent and everything in it were ablaze. The damsel jumped through the flames and burning walls of the tent and ran into the old cemetery, where she hid among the tombs.

The Cossacks were astonished and disheartened when they discovered the scorched corpse of their hetman. Believing that the damsel had been burned to a cinder, they did not search for her body.

On the third day the Cossacks left the town. The Jews began to come out from their hiding places and bury their dead. When they reached the cemetery, they found the girl fluttering between life and death there among the graves. There was not a place on her body without a sore; all bruises and welts and festering sores. They labored in vain to heal her; the girl fainted away; after she had spoken a few words, telling them, with trembling lips, what had happened to her, she gave up her soul and died.

The Jews buried her in that grave. To this day, the people of Teverov still tell about and sorrow over this holy martyr.

Gurland 1972 (1887), 33–34

This story, like ours, involves physical valor and prowess. The heroine resists the Cossack commander, warding him off with his own sword; when at length her strength fails her, she sets fire to the tent. Because this is a legend—that is, the narrating society considered it to be a true story ("to this day, the people of Teverov still tell about and sorrow over this holy martyr")—the heroine must survive long enough to give an account of what happened.

In addition to the religious confrontation, all the tales about young women during the Chmielnicki pogroms feature a sexually charged encounter between the heroine and a Cossack. The pogroms bring into contact people who would not have met in the normal course of events, when Jewish girls were cloistered in their homes and not exposed to the lustful eyes of non-Jews. In such unsettled times, however, the girls in these stories find themselves having to deal with murderers and rapists. But they are not depicted as helpless—quite the contrary. Despite their youth and inexperience, despite the trauma they have experienced, and despite the unprecedented nature of the encounter and conflict, each of them, in her own way, takes her destiny into her own hands and overcomes her assailant. All of these stories end with the heroine's death, interpreted as the sanctification of God's name and accounted as martyrdom.

An analysis of Jewish legends about women in times of persecution in East European tales, including those from other periods,[3] reveals several paradigms:

(1) *The heroine kills the oppressor.* Sometimes she manages to retain her innocence, but in other instances she must surrender her innocence before she can overcome him. This sort of heroine is associated with archetypal figures of ancient Jewish literature, notably Judith. Our story falls into this category, and even includes explicit mention of Judith and Holofernes, whom the heroine remembers when planning her deed.

(2) *The heroine chooses to die rather than surrender her innocence.* Most of the legends mentioned earlier fall into this category. In most of them the young women employ the age-old weapon of the weak—deception. Sometimes the woman tricks the villain into killing her; sometimes she deceives her assailant and kills herself; and sometimes she prays to God, who takes her soul. Our story also involves elements of this pattern, inasmuch as the girl deceives the Cossack to get him to come to their midnight assignation. In addition, she commits suicide by drowning herself in the River Styr.

(3) *The heroine surrenders her innocence, but only to help her people.* Despite her deviant behavior, she is not depicted in a negative light. In the folk narratives of Polish Jews, for example, we find the beloved of King Casimir the Great, Esterke, who is associated with positive role models of ancient Jewish literature, notably the biblical Queen Esther (Bar-Itzhak 2001, 113–32). While our heroine preserves her chastity, her act is also understood as intended to protect the entire community, because the Cossack has threatened to harm her fellow Jews if she refuses to yield to him. This legend and other legends set in times of persecution assign women characteristics they do not possess at other times. These stories construct women who are not only heroic but also deviating from traditional gender behavior. Events compel them to take a stand in the public sphere. Although the legends do uncover the peril that threatens women in the public space, they also reveal the women's strength, ability, and resourcefulness to guard what is most sacred to the narrating society.

Although we may assume that these stories were originally told by women, the written texts we have today were set down by men. In other words these legends about women in times of persecution received the stamp of approval of male patriarchal Jewish society. Patriarchal Jewish culture accepted cultural heroines who crossed gender boundaries in times of persecution. This phenomenon is not unique to Jewish culture and can be found in other conservative patriarchal societies as well. In times of persecution, when the social order is disrupted by some external agency, the comprehensive code of values and norms is blurred, and the society is forced, whether or not it wants to, to establish a new order. In this new order some values may have to be sacrificed to preserve those that are most important, placing them in the category of those for which one should die rather than transgress. Because Jewish men cannot uphold the social order or protect their women during times of persecution, the creation of cultural heroines who cross the boundaries of their gender behavior serves this objective.

In times of persecution these women were set up as revered heroines whose resistance to oppressors, decisions to die to defend their chastity, and willingness to do everything they could to protect their community turned them into admired cultural heroines worthy of emulation. This ensured that women would stand vigil over society's most cherished values in periods when the men could not do so. But it also allowed the female voice to be heard in ways that were not countenanced during more peaceful times in the history of Polish Jewry.

NOTES

1. An-Ski bases his writing on the findings of the ethnographic expedition he headed, which toured these districts between 1912 and 1914 to gather folklore materials (Bar-Itzhak 1999, 363–69; 2010, 27–33).
2. This story served as the inspiration for ballads by Shaul Tchernichovsky and Ya'akov Cahan, and for Shalom Ash's novel *Kiddush Ha-Shem* (Ash 1926, 218–24).
3. Other East European Jewish legends about women in times of persecution deal with women who save synagogues or who are involved in blood libels. Those heroines are mature women, however, rather than unmarried girls (Bar-Itzhak 2001, 150–54).

BIBLIOGRAPHY

An-Ski, S. 1920. "Folk Legends about the Pogroms of 1648–49." *Ha'olam* 27 (5): 12–14. [Hebrew]

Ash, Shalom. 1926. *Kiddush Ha-Shem*. Tel Aviv: Dvir. English translation by Rufus Learsi. Philadelphia: Jewish Publication Society.

Bar-Itzhak, Haya. 1999. "The Essay 'Jewish Ethnopoetics' by S. An-Ski." *Chuliyot* 5: 363–69. [Hebrew]

———. 2001. *Jewish Poland: Legends of Origin*. Detroit: Wayne State University Press.

———. 2010. *Pioneers of Jewish Ethnography and Folkloristics in Eastern Europe*. Ljubljana: Scientific Research Center of the Academy of Science and Arts.

Gurland, H. J. 1972 [1887]. *Annals of the Persecutions of Israel*. Jerusalem: Kedem. [Hebrew]

Hannover, Nathan Note. 1968 [1653]. *Yeven Metzulah (Abyss of Despair)*. Ed. Yisrael Halperin. Tel Aviv: Ha'Kibbutz Ha'Meuhad. [Hebrew]

DEATH AS A GODFATHER

IFA 1937

NARRATED BY SIMCHA BRACHA (BULGARIA)

Many year ago, in a faraway land, lived a happy couple, but one thing clouded their happiness: They didn't have any children. After many years passed, the woman gave birth to a son. Then there was no limit to their happiness, and the father decided to seek the most honest man in the world in order to name his son after him.

So he went on his way, walking day and night, and along the way he encountered an old man and greeted him. The old man asked him, "What are you looking for?" The man replied, "I am looking for an honest man, so I can name my son after him." The old man said, "I am willing to come and give you my name." "Who are you?" asked the man. "I am God," replied the old man. "No," answered the man. "You are not honest. One year you give happiness, one year you give sorrow, one year health, another sickness. There is no justice with you," he said, and left.

The man went on and met a man holding keys in his hand. He greeted the man, who asked, "What are you looking for?" The man replied, "I am looking for an honest man who will give me his name for my son." The man with the keys replied, "I will come with you if you are willing to accept me." "Who are you?" asked the man. "I am the guard of the Garden of Eden and Gehenna," the guard replied. "No, I do not agree," said the man. "You are not righteous. You let whoever you like enter the Garden of Eden, and you send whoever you don't like to Gehenna."

The man continued on his way until he met an old woman who was bent down and leaning on her cane. He greeted her with a heartfelt hello and told her what he was seeking. "I am willing to come and give your son my name," said the old woman. "Who are you?" the man asked. "I am Death," the woman answered. The man looked at her and thought for a minute, and said, "Yes, you are righteous and just. When the time comes, you are considerate with the righteous, the sick, or the healthy. When the time comes to die, you end life in an instant."

The man brought the old woman to his house. He had a great celebration, and Death gave the boy her name. When the guests left, Death said to him, "You have given me great honor. Therefore I will tell you a secret with which you can earn a lot of money. But remember, the secret must remain only between us—when you see a sick man, you can heal him if you see me standing at the head of his bed, for you can be sure he will recover. But if you see me at the foot of his bed, you will know that he will die. People will pay you for your ability to foresee their fate." Before long, the man became very wealthy. When someone was sick, they would invite him into their home in order to learn their fate.

Thus many years passed, and the man and Death remained dear friends. Once in a while they visited each other. One day Death told him, "Come with me, and I'll show you the Chamber of

Life. I've never revealed this secret to anyone." They went into a very large room where they saw thousands of oil candles, some with long wicks, others with shorter ones. The man asked, "Why aren't they even?" Death answered, "If a person's wick is longer, his life will be longer. And if it is shorter, his life will be shorter."

While they were in the Chamber of Life, they saw a candle with a long wick and a bright flame surrounding it. "Whose candle is this?" the man asked. "It is your son's," the old woman answered. The man was very happy to hear this. Then he saw a candle that was flickering and looked like it was about to go out. "And whose candle is this?" he asked. "Yours," Death answered. The man fell to his knees and begged her, "Please, take some of the oil of my son and add it to my candle." "No," Death answered. "Do you remember when we first met? You told me you were looking for an honest man. You know that when it is time for someone to die, I kill him."

The man went back to his home very sad, but at least he knew that he had found an honest person. And there he awaited his own death.

Transcribed by Rachel Heller

COMMENTARY TO
"DEATH AS A GODFATHER"

IFA 1937

HOWARD SCHWARTZ

IFA 1937, "Death as a Godfather," is a Bulgarian folktale recounted by Simcha Bracha and transcribed by Rachel Heller. At the center of the story is a father who has decided to name his newborn son after an honest man, and who has set out on a quest to find such a man. As such it can be classified primarily as a quest tale. Quest tales make up a good percentage of folktales, and perhaps half of all fairy tales are quests. This story is not a fairy tale, but it has supernatural elements (the encounters with God and Death), and the quest itself has many parallels among IFA stories. One close parallel is IFA 7830, collected by Zevulon Kort from Ben-Zion Asherov of Afghanistan. This is a tale about a Jew who sets out on a quest to find justice. Underlying both of these stories is a likely echo of the famous Greek legend recounting how Diogenes walked through the marketplace of Athens with a lantern, searching for an honest man. This seems to demonstrate the influence of Greek tradition on Jewish folklore.

"Death as a Godfather" is somewhat rare in that it includes an encounter with God in the form of an old man. Most Jewish tales have meetings with various messengers of God, above all with Elijah, instead of direct encounters with God. God generally remains in heaven. In stories about ascents on high of rabbis and other holy figures, such as the Baal Shem Tov, God is inevitably described as seated on His throne of glory. Even stranger is the fact that the man in the story rejects God, saying, "You are not honest. One year you give happiness, one year you give sorrow, one year health, another sickness. There is no justice with you." With this rejection, the purpose of the story becomes apparent: to raise a complaint about the general unfairness of life in this world, and to lodge this complaint directly against God. The underlying bitterness of this accusation makes it clear that this is an outspoken folktale that has cast aside the general awe in which God, the Creator, is held in Jewish tradition. As such it goes far beyond the kind of theology found in most rabbinic texts, although it does echo the famous story in the Babylonian Talmud (Bava Mezia 59b) of the rabbis who insisted that God stay out of their discussions. The coda to that story has Elijah encounter God and asking Him how He felt about it. God is said to have replied, "My children have overruled Me! My children have overruled Me!"

Continuing in his quest, the father then meets a man who identifies himself as the guard of Gan Eden and Gehenna. The father also rejects the guard on the grounds that "you let whoever you like enter the Garden of Eden, and you send whoever you don't like to Gehenna," implying that these are arbitrary decisions that are entirely up to the guard. This follows the general theme of the overall unfairness of life that dominates in the story. Yet it differs from the general tradition about such guards.

The notion of a guard outside Gan Eden derives, of course, from Genesis 3:24, where God "stationed east of the Garden of Eden the cherubim and the fiery ever-turning sword, to guard the way to the tree of life." There is a separate tradition, found in the Zohar and in many folktales, of a guardian of Gehenna. This figure is identified in the Zohar as Samriel, and his decisions are anything but arbitrary—he can admit to Gehenna only those whose names appear in the giant book he consults whenever anyone arrives at the gates of Gehenna (Zohar 1:62b).[1] It is true that Ecclesiastes Rabbah 7:23 identifies Gan Eden and Gehenna as being side-by-side: "What is the distance between Gan Eden and Gehenna? A handbreadth." This makes the notion of a single guardian for them both feasible. Further, Adam is described in *The Testament of Abraham* as sitting on a golden throne outside the gates to Paradise and to Gehenna, where he observed the many who entered the broad gate of Gehenna and the narrow gate of Paradise.

The third figure whom the father meets on his quest is Death. Here there is a serious textual problem—Death is first identified as an old woman, "bent down and leaning on her cane," and later in the story as an old man. The traditional identification of Death is as a man, so the initial identification of Death as a woman is quite unusual. The father acknowledges that death is "righteous and just," as well as impartial: "When the time comes to die, you end life in an instant."

The father brings the old woman to his house, and there is a celebration in which Death gives the child her/his name. Just how long the father's quest has taken is not mentioned in the story, but if he follows tradition, this is the *brit* ceremony that takes place on the eighth day after the boy's birth. And Death is given the honored role of the godfather, who holds the baby during the circumcision. However, the role of the godfather is generally given to a man, and, in any case, the notion of Death as a godfather is very strange.

As a reward for the honor the man has given her (or him), Death reveals a secret about how to cure those who are sick: If he sees Death at the head of the bed, the sick person will live; if Death is standing at the foot of the bed, the sick person will die. This secret makes it possible for the poor man to become wealthy. Note that the story veers away here from the original quest—to find an honest man—and fuses a separate theme: that of an agreement with Death (or another supernatural figure).

This kind of agreement is a familiar one in Jewish folklore. An early version of this tale is found in the Babylonian Talmud (Me'ilah 17b), concerning the demon Ben Temalion, who agrees to assist Rabbi Simeon Bar Yohai by entering the body of the emperor's daughter in order to save the Jews. Another variant is IFA 3523, told by David Hadad. Here it is Ashmodai, the king of demons, who makes the agreement with a man the demon king saves from suicide. Another variant, wherein the agreement is made with the Angel of Death, is found in *Yiddishe Folkmayses*, edited by Y. L. Cahan (1931).

Then IFA 1937 takes yet a new direction and fuses an episode about "wicks of life"—those born with long wicks have long lives and those with shorter ones, short lives. This returns, of course, to the original and primary theme of the story, that life is essentially unfair. Note that this episode is a variant of IFA 7830, where a man arrives at a cottage filled with oil candles and is told by a mysterious keeper-of-the-candles that a person's life lasts as long as his candle continues to burn, but ends when the candle burns out. (Another variant is IFA 8335, collected by Moshe Rabi and told by Hannah Hadad, regarding a cave containing bottles of oil: The oil in each bottle represents the lifespan. Individuals live until their oil is exhausted.) This clearly demonstrates that these two stories are close variants, in that both consist of a quest episode (to find justice in IFA 7830 and to find an honest man in IFA 1937), followed by an episode about candles or wicks that indicate how long a person will live. In both stories, as well, the man discovers that his own candle is about to burn out. In IFA 7830 the man who sought justice tries to steal oil from the candle next to his. The primary theme in that story concerns the nature of justice and the man's failure to live up to his own ideals. In IFA 1937 the man who stood up to God now trembles before Death on learning that his own time has nearly come to an end, and he is even willing to take some of his son's light (life) to extend his own. Here, in the last-minute failure of the protagonists to live up to their ideals, the two stories are perfectly parallel. And in a return to the primary theme of honesty, Death reminds him that he had been searching for an honest person and that he had found one. Thus the conclusion of the story reinforces the theme that no one escapes death.

From a typological perspective the quest portion of IFA 1937 belongs to AT 461A ("The Journey to the Deity for Advice or Repayment"). The encounters with God, the guard of Gan Eden and Gehenna, and Death belong to AT 751A ("A Man Invites God to His House"). The arrangement Death makes with the man belongs to AT 332 ("Godfather Death"), AT 1164D ("The Demon and the Man Join Forces"), and AT 1862B ("The Sham Physician and the Devil in Partnership"). The episode about the wicks belongs to AT 934E ("The Magic Ball of Thread"), and AT 1187 ("Meleager—Permission to Live as Long as Candle Lasts"). Thus IFA 1937 is clearly an amalgam of several tale types.

Note

1. See also Sofer (1994), *Sippurei Ya'akov* 7, and Shenhar-Alroy (1986), *Sippurim Mi-she-kevar*, no. 27.

Bibliography

Aarne, Antti, and Stith Thompson. 1961. *The Types of the Folktale: A Classification and Bibliography*. FF Communications no. 184. Helsinki: Suomalainen Tiedeakatemia.

Cahan, Yehuda Leib. 1931. *Yidishe Folkmayses*. Vilna: Yidishe Folklor Bibliotek. [Yiddish]

Shenhar-Alroy, Aliza. 1986. *Sippurim Mi-she-kevar: Children's Folktales*. Haifa: University of Haifa. [Hebrew]

Sofer, Ya'acov. 1994. *Sippurei Ya'akov* (*Tales of Ya'acov*). Edition annotated by Gedalia Negael. Jerusalem: Carmel. [Hebrew]

THE DANCE OF THE ARI (RABBI ISAAC LURIA)

IFA 3590

NARRATED BY ISRAEL BER SCHNEERSOHN (ISRAEL, ASHKENAZI)

Four leaders—four pillars—lived in Safed in the time of the Ari, and the four constituted the spiritual leadership of the city: Rabbi Joseph Caro, author of the *Beit Yosef* and the *Shulhan Arukh*; the Ari, Rabbi Isaac Luria Ashkenazi; Rabbi Meir Alsheich, the brilliant preacher; and Rabbi Elazar Azkary, author of *Sefer Haredim*.

Rabbi Joseph Caro was the city rabbi. The Ari, whose daughter married Rabbi Joseph Caro's son, was Safed's spiritual guide and the leader of its Kabbalists. Rabbi Moses Alsheich captured hearts with his passionate sermons. But Rabbi Elazar Azkary maintained a low profile and served as the Ari's beadle. Elazar Azkary's life was shrouded in mystery. The man was unassuming and lived by the principle, "Walk humbly with your God."

It was the Ari's custom that every Lag ba'Omer he would go up with his students, his "cubs," and prostrate himself at the grave of Rabbi Simeon Bar Yohai in Meron. Normally an ascetic much given to solitary meditation, he excelled in rejoicing and gladdening hearts on Lag ba'Omer.

One Lag ba'Omer, the Ari went up with his "cubs" to Meron, as was his wont, and they danced together in ecstatic devotion.

On the edge of the circle of dancers, carried as though on a wave of mighty song, an elderly man was dancing by himself. The man, who had a long, white beard and was elegantly dressed, wore white clothes with a Sephardic hat. He danced with growing enthusiasm, his eyes closed, radiating glory and mystery with all his being. From time to time, the mysterious old man would join the circle of his people dancing, and then went back to his own solo dance.

Suddenly, the Ari approached him, grasped his hand, and the two of them began a breathtaking *mitzvah tantz*.

The two whirled together for a long time, and a great blue-gold light joined the candles' flames. The rapturous dance of the Ari and the marvelous old man continued for a long time.

Suddenly, the Ari grabbed Rabbi Elazar Azkary by the hand and pulled him into their circle. Now the trio danced a furious dance, the likes of which had never been seen at Bar Yohai's grave in Meron.

They trio danced for many hours. The Ari's disciples and all those at the memorial celebration gazed at them in wonder.

When they finally stopped dancing, the Ari's students came up to him, and some of them made bold to ask:

—Forgive us, master, for our question. We do not know this old man you danced with; he must certainly be a great man, and great was his merit to dance with you. But it is not worthy of our master and teacher to dance together with Rabbi Azkary, the town beadle. Even if he is a God-fearing Torah scholar, it is not worthy for our rabbi, the rabbi of all Israel, to dance with him alone.

The Ari heard them out, and a smile crept to his lips. Then he answered: "If the holy *tanna* Rabbi Simeon Bar Yohai danced alone with me, as unworthy as I am, wouldn't it be a great honor for me to dance with him?"

The students understood that the handsome old gentleman was Rabbi Simeon Bar Yohai in the flesh and asked no more questions.

Thus was revealed the greatness of Rabbi Elazar Azkary, author of *Sefer Haredim*, which was founded and built upon the verse, "All of my bones will say [Lord who is like you]." And when this secret was made known, Rabbi Elazar Azkary coined the motto, "The day has come when we said, it is time to act for the Lord" (from the preface to *Sefer Haredim*).

So it was thanks to the Ari's dance on Lag ba'Omer, at Bar Yohai's grave in Meron, that the great secret of Rabbi Elazar Azkary, who was also called by his book's name, *The Haredim*, was also revealed.

Transcribed by Yeshayahu Ashani

Commentary to
"The Dance of the Ari
(Rabbi Isaac Luria)"

IFA 3590

Eli Yassif

The storyteller, Israel Ber Schneersohn, originally from Safed, the mystical city in the upper Galilee, tells his story to people in his own community. His first goal as storyteller is to establish the credibility of his narrative. For this he utilizes the available means of both his chosen narrative genre— the legend—and the local knowledge of place and time: The path from Safed to the holy site in Meron and the yearly festival/ritual of Lag ba'Omer (the thirty-third day of harvest) are elements well known to every member of the Safed community as part of their everyday lives. The historical background of the golden age of Safed in the sixteenth century—the names of the great rabbis of that time, quotations from the book authored by one of the central figures in the story (Rabbi Elazar Azkary)—is also meant to deepen the linkage of the narrative to the place as well as its "authenticity."

However, most of the narrative details appearing in the tale could not have taken place in historical reality. The sacred ritual at Meron on Lag ba'Omer, starting with a parade of songs and dances from Safed all the way to Meron, is a present-day ceremony, and was not observed, as far as we know, at the time the story describes—that of Luria's sixteenth-century Safed.[1] It is true that the four rabbis mentioned in the story—Rabbi Joseph Caro, Rabbi Isaac Luria Ashkenazi (the Ari), Rabbi Moshe Alsheich, and Rabbi Elazar Azkary—lived in Safed during that time, but the relationships among them were far from ideal. In reality there was a strong rivalry among them, as well as tensions between the study of legal Jewish law and mystical visions, among the various synagogues, and among the different Jewish communities.[2]

Elazar Azkary also was not in fact a synagogue's beadle but one of the eminent students of Rabbi Luria and the author of an important moral book (*Sefer Haredim*). There is also no evidence that Luria incorporated dance into his ritualistic observance of the holiday.[3]

Such incongruities between story and historical reality are not important in themselves, as it is already well established that folk narratives do not "reflect" reality, but are essential means for interpreting its tensions and aspirations.

From this perspective we can conclude that the function of most narrative elements presented here is to paint the sixteenth-century reality of Luria's time with the colors of the Hasidic movement (which was founded only in the second half of the eighteenth century): its customs, beliefs, and goals. This happens on almost all narrative levels: In this story Luria plays the role of the Hasidic *rebbe* (the *admor*, or leader of the Hasidic community); Alsheich is the preacher; and Azkary is the beadle. These narrative functions are well known from the Hasidic stories and the nineteenth-century structure of the East European *shtetl*. We can also interpret in the same way the widespread narrative motif of the "hidden holy *zaddik*"[4] (righteous person), derived from Hasidic narratives, which is an integral part of this story as well.

Rabbi Elazar Azkary was chosen from among Luria's disciples because he was known as an ascetic figure who preached extreme moral conduct in everyday life, as evidenced by his book, which was well known in Hasidic circles. Thus he was naturally closer to Hasidic ideals than were the other persons of the golden period of Safed. Following these narrative elements, Azkary is described at the beginning of our story not as one of the favored and learned disciples of Luria—which he really was—but as a naïve beadle, despised by the other disciples, whose holiness was revealed to the public only by Luria, the group's leader, and its supernatural mentor, Rabbi Simeon Bar Yochai.

The story corresponds fully with Hasidic literature and its system of beliefs. Another narrative element—the ritualistic—also follows this path, as revealed through the central function of ritual dance in Hasidic ideology. The ecstatic ritual dance, led by the *admor*, sweeps everyone up in its heat and passion; dance is one of the basic rituals of every mystical movement,[5] and it became one of the central components of the Hasidic movement as well.

The Hasidic movement's adoption of sixteenth-century Lurianic mystical concepts did not begin with this story, but it can be observed since the beginning of the movement in the late eighteenth century. The Lurianic hagiography, *Praises of the Ari*, is mentioned as the basis and inspiration for the first (and most fundamental) Hasidic text to be published in book form, *Praises of the Baal Shem Tov* (1814). One of the central Hasidic collections of stories, *Sefer Sippurei Kedoshim* (*Book of Tales about the Righteous*, 1866), begins with a story about Luria, and the same applies to other collections of Hasidic tales.

However, while embracing Lurianic Safed at the beginning of the Hasidic movement was one of the means Hasidism used to achieve legitimation, this cannot be the reason behind the creation and telling of a story like "The Dance of the Ari" in the second half of the 19th century. By 1961, when this tale was recorded, the Hasidic movement was not only established and legitimate but also the most popular and authoritative movement within contemporary Orthodox Jewish communities. This is yet another proof of the importance of the data attached to each story recorded in the IFA. At that time, just over ten years after the founding of the State of Israel, the struggle over state rituals—the nation's cultural identity—had become an urgent issue. The ceremonies commemorating Independence and the memorials of recent events (the Holocaust and the struggle for the State), including Holocaust Remembrance Day, and the half-ritual, half-military pilgrimages to Masada Rock and the Tel-Hai site in Upper Galilee, took shape as essential public rituals defining Israeli identity. These were "new" or "invented" state rituals. Yet the older traditional and religious rituals continued to struggle for their place in the new Israeli reality. The ritual ceremony of Lag ba'Omer in the small Upper Galilee village of Meron was one of the most prominent of these. Thus a folktale connecting the golden age of the past and the contemporary Hasidic reality could function as a means to strengthen and establish this Upper Galilee ritual and make it a significant element in the shaping of a new Israeli identity.[6]

This story has also an important local implication. As I have stated elsewhere,[7] sixteenth-century Safed legends cannot be defined, as they had been in the past, as only saint's legends (concentrating on Luria). These legends are, and function as, local legends. They are connected, spatially and mentally, to Safed and its environs, and their function is to enhance the connection of the community to their habitat. I suggest interpreting the story of "The Dance of the Ari" in a similar way. While on the surface it belongs to the cycle of Luria's hagiography, its deeper meaning should be seen in a different light.

The story's meaning is deeply anchored in the locale in which it was told, encompassing the storyteller; the recorder and publisher; the ceremony of Lag ba'Omer, when the narrated events occurred; and the road from Safed to Meron. To this should be added the great Safed personalities depicted in the tale and the mythical-Kabbalistic figure of Rabbi Simeon Bar Yohai, whose burial place is "precisely" there. As an outcome of this it appears that the story should be understood first and foremost as a local legend, and therein lies its primary meaning and function.

We shall refer here again to the information attached to the story, as it was recorded in the IFA records. The late 1950s and early 1960s witnessed a great struggle for the identity of Safed, the holy city. Israeli artists—painters, sculptors, and architects—discovered the beauty of Safed: its colorful alleys, its mysticism and mystery, the spectacular views of the Upper Galilee seen from every corner of the old city. A colony of artists was established there, and Safed became, step by step, the artistic capital of Israel. These developments were far from welcomed or accepted by the ultra-Orthodox community of the old city. The liberal, open, and even promiscuous lifestyles of the artists, and the secular hordes of guests who came to visit the galleries mainly on Shabbat and holidays, were, in the eyes of the Orthodox, grave desecrations of the sacred city.

"The Dance of the Ari" was recounted by R. Israel Ber Schneersohn, a member of the sacred Lubavitch family that founded Chabad, the largest sector of the Hasidic movement. He is also described in the recorded data as one of the leaders of the local Hasidic movement. The main narrative technique used in the tale is the clear anachronistic establishment of Luria's persona and milieu as those of a Hasidic rabbi. The central claim of the story is that the contemporary Hasidic movement represents the legitimate continuation of the golden age of Luria's Safed and his group of mystics. It is thus the contemporary Hasidic community of Safed, the legitimate heirs to the golden age Safed—rather than the secular/artistic community that has tried to change the city's traditional/religious essence—that must provide the city its moral character. In this way the anachronistic shaping of the story is not only a narrative device but a central tool in the struggle for the identity and character of the holy site and its place in Israeli society in the formative years before the 1967 war.

Yeshayahu Ashani, who recorded this story, is not an anonymous figure. He is known as one of the foremost writers of Safed, whose book, *In the Alleys of Safed* (Safed, 1962), was one of the main vehicles for carrying the Safed myth to the larger Israeli public. Ashani can be considered neither a professional author nor an ethnographer; he is what I have termed in the past a "folk-writer"—a person belonging to the community, and attentive to its traditions, who is rewriting them in his own language and style. The following passage is an example:

> On the edge of the circle of dancers, carried as though on a wave of mighty song, an elderly man was dancing by himself. The man, who had a long, white beard and was elegantly dressed, wore white clothes with a Sephardic hat. He danced with growing enthusiasm, his eyes closed, radiating glory and mystery with all his being. . . . The two whirled together for a long time, and a great blue-gold light joined the candles' flames.

Such elevated style, full of pathos and a neo-spiritual atmosphere, as well as the detailed description of the mens' attire and movement, can be found neither in folk narratives nor in Hasidic stories. However, even a brief comparison of this narrative style to that in Ashani's *In the Alleys of Safed* reveals their origin. The "learned" note Ashani adds to the story, about the association of this story to Azkary's influential *Sefer Haredim* (Book of the Pious)—"written after in-depth reading of R. Elazar Azkary's *Sefer Haredim*"—is meant to emphasize his similarly "learned" status: He is not a regular, naïve collector of stories but an enlightened author who is basing his observations on philosophical books. To these half-collectors, half-authors of folk tales we owe much of the folk narratives available to us.[8]

Thus we can read this story on three different levels. The first one is that of its sources, the oldest of which is the model of *Praises of the Ari* from sixteenth-century Safed, in conjunction with the widespread motif of "the hidden *zaddik*" of Hasidic literature. The second level was created, as I have outlined, by the Hasidic community and its representative/narrator R. Israel Schneersohn. From here the ancient Safed legends merged with recent Hasidic stories and were connected to the local ritual of the celebration in Meron. This formation of the tale creates a new and meaningful narrative, which takes part in the struggle over the cultural identity of the young State of Israel. The third level concerns the "folk-writer" Yeshayahu Ashani. Like many other folk-writers, Ashani collected the story from its storyteller but did not consider himself obliged to reproduce its plain language and style or the thin descriptions of events and realistic details. He rewrites the tale so it will fulfill his artistic aspirations and those of his future readers, in the new cultural community of the young state.

NOTES

1. For a summary of this topic, see Benayahu 1962, 9–40.
2. In this matter, out of the rich scholarship see Rozen 1980, 73–101; Hacker 1984, 63–117; Horowitz 1987, 273–84.
3. It may even be the opposite, that dancing during the festival was considered morally unruly, and was specifically forbidden; see Benayahu 1962, 27–28.
4. See Klapholz 1977; Nigal 2008.
5. See, for example, Elstein 1998; Idel 1995.
6. Shokeid and Deshen 1999, 98–113; Azaryahu 1995.
7. Yassif 2005.
8. Rosenberg 1991, Eli Yassif: Introduction, 7–72.

BIBLIOGRAPHY

Azaryahu, Maoz. 1995. *State Cults: Celebrating Independence and Commemorating the Fallen in Israel, 1948–1956.* Sde Boker: Ben-Gurion Research Center. [Hebrew]

Benayahu, Meir. 1962. "The *Hanhagot* of Safed Kabbalists in Meron." In *The Book of Safed—Research and Sources*, ed. Itzhak Ben-Zvi and Meir Benayahu, 9–40. Jerusalem: Ben-Zvi Institute. [Hebrew]

Elstein, Yoav. 1998. *Ecstasy and the Hasidic Tale.* Ramat Gan: Bar Ilan University Press. [Hebrew]

Hacker, Joseph. 1984. "Disaster Does Not Come to the World but for Ignorants: Jezeeya Tax Payment by the Rabbis in Sixteenth-Century Eretz Israel." *Shalem* 4: 63–117. [Hebrew]

Horowitz, Carmi. 1987. "Notes on the Attitude of Moshe Ben Yosef Mitrani (Mabit) toward the Safed Hasidim." *Shalem* 5: 273–84. [Hebrew]

Idel, Moshe. 1995. *Hasidism: Between Ecstasy and Magic.* SUNY Series in Judaica: Hermeneutics, Mysticism, and Religion. Albany: State University of New York Press.

Klapholz, Israel Jacob. 1977. *The Thirty-Six Hidden Saints: A Collection of Stories from Tzadikim Nistarim Gathered from Reliable Sources and Arranged According to Topics.* 2 vols. Tel Aviv: Peer Hasefer. [Hebrew]

Nigal, Gedalyah. 2008. *The Hasidic Tale.* Oxford: Littman Library of Jewish Civilization.

Pachter, Mordechai. 1981. "The Life and Personality of R. Eleazer Azikri as Reflected in His Mystical Diary and in *Sefer Haredim*." *Shalem* 3: 127–47. [Hebrew]

Rosenberg, Yehudah Yudl. 1991. *The Golem of Prague and Other Wondrous Deeds.* Collected and Introduced by Eli Yassif. Jerusalem: Mossad Bialik. [Hebrew]

Rozen, Minna. 1980. "The Situation of the Musta'rabs in the Inter-Community Relationships in Eretz Israel from the End of the Fifteenth Century to the End of the Seventeenth Century." *Cathedra* 17: 73–101. [Hebrew]

Shivhey Ha'Besht. 1992. ed. Avraham Rubinstein. Jerusalem: Reuven Mass. [Hebrew]

Shokeid, Moshe, and Shlomo Deshen. 1999. *The Generation of Transition: Change and Continuity in the World of the Jews of North Africa.* Jerusalem: Ben Zvi Institute. [Hebrew]

Yassif, Eli. 2005. "In the Fields and Deserts: On Space and Meaning in Safed Legends." *Cathedra* 116: 67–102. [Hebrew]

THE MISERLY *MOHEL* AND THE DEMONS

IFA 5151

NARRATED AND TRANSCRIBED BY ZEVULUN KORT (AFGHANISTAN)

There was once a wealthy man with substantial assets who was very miserly and unwilling to give away any of his fortune. Poor people who approached him left empty-handed. They got to know him and used to bypass his house. To avoid having to give charity, he did not visit the synagogue on weekdays but prayed alone. Only one *mitzvah** was dear to his heart: He was a *mohel*,† and whenever he was called out, even to villages a long distance away, he put down his work and went to perform the circumcision, free of charge—not for the sake of reward.

Once, a man came to the *mohel* and invited him to his village to circumcise his baby son. The *mohel* put down his work, closed his store, and set out with the man. They walked and walked, and the next day reached a high mountain and a village with several grand houses. They entered a beautiful building, where the *mohel* remained while the father of the baby went to fetch something from the market. The *mohel* wandered around the rooms. He looked at all the beautiful furniture; everything was magnificent, everything was beautiful. While walking from room to room, he came upon the mother of the baby.

When the mother saw him, she said:

> Please come here. I have something to tell you before my husband returns. You should know that he is not a human being but is one of the demons. I, like you, am human. When I was young, they kidnapped me and brought me here. Now, I am lost. If you wish to leave and not remain here like me, accept neither food nor drink, nor any of their gifts, because as soon as you derive pleasure from anything of theirs, you will be unable to leave.

The *mohel* was very frightened at having fallen into the demons' lair. He thanked the woman, left her room, and went to the guest room to wait for the baby's father to return. Everyone arrived, including many guests. Tables were set, and they sat down to eat. They invited the *mohel* to join them, but he pleaded tiredness and a lack of appetite and refused to eat, in spite of their entreating.

The following day everyone went to the synagogue with the baby. The *mohel* performed the circumcision, and everyone was invited to the festive religious meal at the baby's father's house. They sat around well-laid tables and invited the *mohel* to participate in the meal. He said that he was fasting that day, so they postponed the party until the evening.

---

* A *mitzvah* is a commandment in Jewish law
† A *mohel* is a Jewish man trained to circumcise newborn baby boys.

In the evening they sat at the lavishly laid tables once again and invited the *mohel* to join them. The *mohel* complained that he did not feel well and was unable to eat a thing. Once again he managed to slip away and excused himself from participating in the meal. Everyone else sat and ate, and when the meal was finished, the host invited the *mohel* to his room. The *mohel* was very frightened, convinced that he was about to be killed. In fear and trembling, he accompanied his host into a chamber. Inside the room were objects of silver and gold, and many expensive jewels. The host told the *mohel* to choose whatever keepsake he wanted, as payment for his work, but the *mohel* said: "I lack nothing."

The host took him to another room, where there were precious stones, pearls, and diamonds. When invited to choose from the riches, the *mohel* replied: "I lack nothing. I have everything I need."

The host took him to one last chamber, where bunches of keys were hanging on the walls. The *mohel* stared in wonder. "Why are you astonished?" asked the host. "I have shown you so many expensive things that did not impress you at all, and yet simple bunches of keys leave you astounded!"

The *mohel* replied: "Those keys are identical to my own keys."

The host said to him:

Come. Now I will tell you the secret. I am chief of the demons. Some demons are appointed to watch over misers. When misers spend no money and give no charity, the demons take their keys and keep them here, with us, and the misers cannot use their money. You are one of those misers. That is why your keys are here, with me, and you cannot use your money. Since you performed a *mitzvah*, by coming here to circumcise my son, and refused to accept a reward, I'm telling you these secrets, and because you tasted nothing in my house, you can return to live with your own kind. If you had tasted even something small, or if you had had something to drink, you would have remained with us. And now, I am returning your keys to you and sending you home, on the condition that you will change your ways and will give alms to the poor and to anyone who asks, whether poor or rich. If you do as I tell you, you will live a good life.

The host took him back to his wife and children. The *mohel* became generous and gave charity to everyone in the town. Everyone liked him and respected him, and he has lived a good and happy life ever since.

THE CAT DEMON

IFA 8902

NARRATED BY HEFTSIBA DADON (MOROCCO)

There was once a midwife who went to attend to a pregnant woman. The woman gave birth to a son. The road was dark, so to light her way home, the midwife held a candle. Suddenly, the candle went out. She lost her way, and prayed to God: "How will I find my way home? I have such a long way to go."

All of a sudden she noticed a cat, which was talking by her side. It said: "What is wrong?"

"I have lost my way," she said.

The cat said: "All right, follow me. I know the way," and she gave the midwife a match with which to relight the candle. They walked and walked, and on reaching the midwife's house, she bade the cat goodbye and gave it a blessing: "May it be God's will that I shall rescue you, just as you have rescued me."

One evening, about a year later, there was a knock at the door. A man entered and said: "A woman is about to give birth"—and the midwife went with him. He took her a long, long way, and there, in the house, a young woman was lying in bed.

Later, she gave birth to a son. As the midwife was sitting with her, the young woman said: "Do you know who I am? I am a demon. A year ago, I was a cat, and you gave me a blessing. If they invite you to eat with them, refuse, because if you eat anything, you too will turn into a demon. Say that you are fasting for seven days. After that they will show you a chamber full of gold, silver, and pearls. Say no. And when they ask you what you want, say: 'Only a small rug.' If you sit on it at home, you will grow rich. None of the other things there are real and will turn into stones when you get home." The relatives came, and indeed everything that the woman predicted was said. When they asked the midwife what she would like, she asked for the rug, which they gave her. Later, as she was preparing to leave, the newborn baby was crying and crying, and they asked: "What can we do for him?"

A woman relative stood up, and said: "He is crying. Another woman has just borne a son. The babies are the same age." (It was said that whenever a baby demon was born, a human was born at the same time). "The human baby is quiet and is not crying. Go and switch them."

The midwife saw the woman switching the babies when the human mother's back was turned, and she said: "Bring me the baby, and I will dress him." When the others weren't looking, the midwife stuck a pin into the sole of the baby's foot, and he began to cry and cry. Everyone said: "What! Is this one crying too? Take him away and bring our baby back." And they did.

When the baby demon was returned, the midwife fed him sugar water. He calmed down, and they took the midwife back home.

Early the next morning, she ran swiftly to the house of the human mother and found the baby screaming and crying. She said: "Bring me the child."

She took him and removed the pin from his foot, and the child calmed down.

She then told the mother the whole story, and said to her: "From now on, never turn your back on a baby."

She gave her a blessing and went directly to the great rabbi of the time, Rabbi Joshua ben Nun, and told him the story from beginning to end.

He said: "This is not the first I have heard about demons abducting children or adults. I will finish this once and for all."

What did he do? He imposed a ban and excommunicated them. Since then the demons have been living in the underworld; we never see them and they frighten us no more.

(Transcribed by Deborah Dadon-Wilk)

COMMENTARY TO "THE MISERLY MOHEL AND THE DEMONS" AND "THE CAT DEMON"

IFA 5151 IFA 8902

EDNA HECHAL

The two tales "The Miserly *Mohel* and the Demons" and "The Cat Demon" were classified as Oikotype AT 476*-*A. Following a reexamination of all the versions of these tales that are registered in the IFA, we believe that a distinction should be made between the versions of "The Miserly *Mohel*," which indeed belong to the aforementioned oikotype, and the versions of "The Cat Demon," which are closer to the international type AT 476* ("In the Frog's House: Midwife to the Demons").

AT 476* ("In the Frog's House: Midwife to the Demons") tells of a woman who pledges her friendship to a frog and succeeds in releasing the souls kept prisoner in his home. She assists the frog's wife with household chores; she empties the garbage and takes it home, where the refuse turns into gold.

The sixteen versions of this type, which are registered in IFA, originate in Morocco, Syria, Israel (Sephardi), Yemen, Turkish Kurdistan, Iraqi Kurdistan, Iraq, and Bukhara. More than a third (six) of the versions are from the cultural area of Kurdistan and Iraq. Two of the versions have been published.[1] Eleven of the versions were told by women, and indeed, the tale is unmistakably a woman's tale: The two main characters are women, in the clearly feminine roles of midwife and mother.

Unlike the tale of "The Miserly *Mohel* and the Demons," in which the storytellers specifically mention that the mother is both Jewish and human, there is no such emphasis in "The Cat Demon." The mother is a demon, sometimes in animal form (a cat or a lizard), although references to Jewish family and society can be found in most of the tales.

Most of the midwife tales demonstrate a clear intention to personalize the story, and to find links to the storyteller's family history: the source of the family's economic wealth,[2] a gold leaf that is passed down from generation to generation but which becomes lost in the last generation, and so forth.[3]

Our tale has several unique characteristics: In most of the tales, the midwife is rewarded with garlic or onion skin, which turns into gold on her arrival home. In our version, however, the situation is reversed: The mother/cat demon warns the midwife against eating any food or accepting any treasures that are offered to her, and instructs her to request a small rug: "If you sit on it at home, you will grow rich. None of the other things there are real and will turn into stones when you get home."

The second part of our story includes a child-switching episode: The demon baby cries and is exchanged with a human baby when its mother's back is turned. The midwife sticks a pin in the human baby's foot, and he screams. The demons switch the babies back. The midwife calms the demon baby, and once at home, she hurries to the human baby's family, pulls the pin out of his foot, and says to the baby's mother: "From now on, never turn your back on a baby." This is the source of the custom that prohibits mothers and newborn babies from being left alone, without protection against the demons.

The final part takes the tale from the personal to the etiological realm, in which the midwife recounts the events to the great rabbi, Joshua ben Nun,[4] who imposes a ban on the demons and excommunicates them from the human world: "Since then the demons have been living in the underworld."

Twelve versions of oikotype AT 476*-*A are registered in the IFA ("Miser Circumciser" [*Mohel*]). A miser is strictly adherent to the commandment in Jewish law (*mitzvah*) of ritual circumcision, and to this end he is willing to travel to remote locations. He is called to circumcise the newborn son of a demon father and a human mother. The mother warns the *mohel* not to eat any of the food offered him; if he does so, he will be forced, like her, to remain in the land of the demons.[5] In return for the *mitzvah*, the demon father, who has confiscated the keys to the miser's treasure, returns them to their rightful owner. Once the keys are released from the demons, the *mohel* is no longer forced to be excessively mean, and he becomes generous and well liked in society.

The twelve versions of this tale in the IFA originate in Greece, Yugoslavia, Israel (Sephardi), Persia, Afghanistan, Bukhara, Czechoslovakia, Romania (2), Poland (2), and Russia. Half of the versions are from Eastern Europe, and four of the versions have been published.[6]

Nine of the twelve versions in IFA were told by men. And indeed the story is a man's tale, with a male protagonist, the miserly *mohel*, and the change he undergoes. The tale appears repeatedly in many Jewish anthologies.[7]

Our tale was written from memory by the collector Zevulun Kort (born 1916, Herat, Afghanistan; died 1995, Tel Aviv). Between 1957 and 1990 he collected 524 folktales, most of them from narrators who emigrated from Afghanistan. The tales are registered in IFA. He also published a selection of stories in two books: *The Princess Who Became a Flower Bouquet* (Tel Aviv, 1974) and *Folktales from the Jews of Afghanistan* (Tel-Aviv, 1983). This tale is similar to the version printed in *Mimekor Yisrael*. The story belongs to the legend genre (see note 5). Due to his strict adherence to the *mitzvah* of ritual circumcision, the *mohel* is able to regain the keys to his treasure from the demons. His transformation from miserliness to generosity changes his social status in the community: "Everyone liked him and respected him, and he has lived a good and happy life ever since."

NOTES

1. IFA 279: Noy 1963, no. 12; IFA 4564: Bahrav 1964, no. 48 = Noy 1976 (*Animal Tales*), no. 39.
2. See IFA 16468 (Iraqi Kurdistan).
3. See IFA 14732 (Israel, Sephardi); 4564 (Turkish Kurdistan); 279, 16468, 16477, and 20412 (Iraqi Kurdistan); 11339 (Iraq); and 8140 and 18928 (Bukhara).
4. The name of the rabbi, Joshua ben Nun, is puzzling. We found no reference to the scriptural figure in connection with demons. The banishing of demons, limiting their temporal and spatial activities among humans, is associated with Rabbi Hanina ben Dosa. See Babylonian Talmud, Tractate Pesahim 112b.
5. It is noteworthy that the demons live a Jewish lifestyle. According to Haya Bar-Itzhak, the demonic legend is a subgenre of the sacred legend (Bar-Itzhak 1982).
6. IFA 9182: Noy 1972, no. 7; IFA 9246: Rabbi 1976, no. 28; IFA 10097: Attias 1976, no. 10; IFA 12044: Varenbod 1976, 76–77.
7. See Bin Gorion 1969, story 651 and its reference list.

BIBLIOGRAPHY

Aarne, Antti, and Stith Thompson. 1961. *The Types of the Folktale: A Classification and Bibliography*. FF Communications no. 184. Helsinki: Suomalainen Tiedeakatemia.
Attias, Moshe. 1976. *The Golden Feather: Twenty Folktales Narrated by Greek Jews*. Haifa: Haifa Municipality, Ethnological Museum and Folklore Archives. [Hebrew]
Bahrav, Zalman. 1964. *Sixty Folktales Collected from Narrators in Ashkelon*. Haifa: Haifa Municipality, Ethnological Museum and Folklore Archives. [Hebrew]
Bar-Itzhak, Haya. 1982. "Modes of Characterization in the Sacred Legend of Oriental Jews." In *Studies in the Literature of Oriental Jews*, ed. Haya Bar-Itzhak and Aliza Shenhar, 1–21. Haifa: University of Haifa. [Hebrew]
Bin Gorion, Micha Yosef. 1969. *Mimekor Yisrael*. Tel Aviv: Dvir. [Hebrew]
Noy, Dov. 1963. *Folktales of Israel*. Chicago: University of Chicago Press.
———. 1972. *A Tale for Each Month, 1971*. Haifa: Haifa Municipality, Ethnological Museum and Folklore Archives. [Hebrew]
———. 1976. *The Jewish Animal Tale of Oral Tradition*. Haifa: Haifa Municipality, Ethnological Museum and Folklore Archives, Israel Folktale Archives. [Hebrew]
———. 1980. "Is There a Jewish Folk Religion?" In *Studies in Jewish Folklore: Proceedings of a Regional Conference of the Association for Jewish Studies held at the Spertus College of Judaica*, ed. Dov Noy and Frank Talmage, 273–85. Cambridge, MA: Association for Jewish Studies.
Rabbi, Moshe. 1976. *Our Fathers Told*. 3 vols. Jerusalem: Bakal. [Hebrew]
Varenbod, Nehemia. 1976. *Nehemia Ba'al Guf: The Tale of a Coachman*. Tel Aviv: Aleph. [Hebrew]

THE STORY ABOUT DOBUSH

IFA 5167

NARRATED AND TRANSCRIBED FROM MEMORY BY SHIMON TODER (POLAND)

In the times of the Besht there was a robber in the Carpathians, in Ukraine, who kept the entire region in fear. He was known as Dobush. There were many legends about Dobush's life, about his childhood, and about his meeting with the Besht and the good relations between the two. Here is one story, as I registered it in 1930. I heard it during one of the conversations in the library that stood near the Jewish center in Stanislav.* The library was headed by Reuven Fahn, a writer and researcher of the Karaites and the period of Jewish Enlightenment. It was a place where well-educated people used to discuss various literary and cultural issues. In most cases the poet Nathan Stockhamer was among the participants. The name of the person who told this story was not stored in my memory. Yet I do remember that the story was told in connection to the publication of Reuven Fahn's book *The History of Karaites*, which in addition to the principles of the Karaite faith also addressed the life of Karaites in Galich at that time. Thus from one issue to another we came to this story.

Dobush's father died, and his mother became a widow while still in her third month of pregnancy. She was left without any help and without bread at home. The only person who used to bring her some food was a Jew, the owner of the inn. She was a hardworking woman and was ashamed to live on the alms. So she used to do various jobs in the field to sustain herself, and when she returned home, she worked in her household.

In one of the last months of her pregnancy, she went to the forest to pick up some brushwood to warm her house and to prepare some porridge. When she bent to pick up the brushwood, the birth pangs began. The child was born before she could return home. The mother was all alone in the forest, as nobody was nearby. So she took her gardening scissors, cut the umbilical cord, wrapped the baby in one of her skirts, and prepared to go home.

While busy with swaddling the baby and preparing to return home, she heard the sounds of horses stomping and dogs barking. The mother realized that hunters had entered the forest. She became frightened that they would harass her. She put the baby in the sack that she had brought for the brushwood, tied it to her waist, and ran as fast as she could.

Running home quickly, she didn't notice that the baby had dropped out of the sack and had been left behind in the forest, wrapped in his mother's skirt. Only upon her return did she realize

---

* Now Ivano-Frankivsk.—L.F.

the misfortune that had occurred. She started to wail and to tear her hair. The neighbors came to sympathize with her sorrow, but nobody was brave enough to go to the forest to search for the lost baby. All of them knew how dangerous it was to be in the way of the landlord and his servants during hunting time.

The landlord spent three days and three nights in the forest, enjoying his time with his servants. And all this time the mother remained by the window of her hut, which was the closest to the forest. She wanted to see the hunters when they returned.

And at that very moment that the mother mourned over her child, who had died so dreadfully as a result of the noble's entertainments, the baby was lying on the fallen leaves. A she-dog that had lost her puppies was standing nearby, guarding him from the wild animals. The she-dog pulled at the bundle, which she had found in her path, and found the baby's face. She stood above it and fed the baby with her milk.

Three days later the hunters returned home. The mother ran out of her hut and into the forest. She wanted at least to find the remnants of her child in order to bury them. The mother walked along the lanes feeling deep sorrow in her heart, with tears running down her face. She peered into every bush on her way, trying to find the traces of her baby, who had been torn to pieces. Instantly she noticed an animal standing motionless. The mother ran forward, crying, as she thought the animal was licking the last bone of her baby. When she came close, she saw a dog near a bundle that was wrapped in a skirt whose color she immediately recognized. She picked up a branch from the ground and intended to throw it to the dog. But then she became afraid that it might hit the body of her dead baby. The mother ran toward the dog, grabbed it by the fur, and threw it aside. Then she bowed over the baby, saw him alive, with the drops of milk on his lips, and fainted from such great joy.

The dog, which at first was frightened of the person who had appeared so suddenly, returned to try to help the woman. It ran from her to the baby and back, whining, until the woman regained consciousness.

When the mother recovered, she hurried to the baby and unfolded the bundle. The baby burst into tears. The mother examined the child, made sure that he was whole and unharmed, and couldn't believe her own eyes. She sat up on her knees to embrace the baby with her one arm and the she-dog with the other. She didn't know what to do first: praise the miraculous rescue of the child or express her gratitude to the she-dog, which was standing nearby, for saving his life.

The mother got up, pressed the baby to her breasts, and hurried home. The dog followed them. On her way home the mother was soundlessly praying to God, thanking him for sending a good guard for her baby.

The rumor of the great miracle spread quickly. And the neighbors and relatives came to witness it. The Jewish owner of the inn was among them. On seeing that the hairy baby resembled a bear, he gave him the nickname "Dobush," which means "little bear."

When Dobush grew up and became what he became, everybody recounted how he had been miraculously saved in childhood. And he hated the nobles and was fond of animals.

COMMENTARY TO
"THE STORY ABOUT DOBUSH"

IFA 5167

LARISA FIALKOVA

This story was transcribed by Shimon Toder (1903–73) from memory, and he supplied a short introduction. Toder was a collector of Jewish folk proverbs and stories; twenty-nine of his stories are registered in IFA.

This story is a historical legend, as it recounts the story of a true-life protagonist (Jason 1975, 58), focusing on the birth and magical rescue of Oleksa Dobush. Dobush was born in 1700, in Pechinizhin, in the Pokuttya region of the Carpathian Mountains, to a poor Hutsul family. His father's name was Vasyl; his mother's name is unknown. In the Ukrainian tradition his second name is known variously as Dovbush, Dobosh, or Dovboshchuk.

The name "Dobush" is sometimes attributed to his father's alleged service as a military drummer (*dobosh*), but this attribution is not confirmed by historical sources. From 1738 until his tragic death in 1745, Dobush was a famous leader of the *opryshoks* (or *oprishki, opryszki*). *Opryshoks* were social brigands or "noble robbers"; they represented an anti-feudal and national liberation movement active in the Carpathian Mountains, mostly in the Hutsul region, Pokuttya and Bukovyna (Bukowina, Bucovina), from the sixteenth to the early nineteenth century. There is no general agreement among scholars about the term *opryshoks*. It is variously explained as deriving from the Russian words *ryskat* (scour, hunt after, prowl), *oprichnik* (private person), or *oprochnik* (separated, asunder); the Romanian word *opresk* (forbid); or the Latin word *opressor* (in the sense of violator, disturber, destroyer of the rich—primarily the *shliakhta* or *szlachta*, i.e., Polish nobles).

The Carpathian Mountains form a border area. The location of the Carpathians between Poland, Moldova, and Hungary enabled the *opryshoks* to escape to another country when the highland caves at home were not safe enough for them. While this mountain region harbored *opryshoks*, the Poles called it "the region of robbers." The nobles were afraid to come near it. In 1745 Polish nobles called on the people to kill Dobush, promising anyone who succeeded exemption from feudal duties. This idea appealed to a peasant named Stepan Dzvinchuk, but apparently Dobush became aware of this fact, and he attacked Dzvinchuk's house. Dobush was mortally wounded by Dzvinchuk on August 23, 1745, in Kosmach, and he tried to escape to the forest. On August 24, Dzvinchuk called on the people to search for Dobush; he was soon found, still alive, by a group that included two priests and an arendar. Dzvinchuk asked Dobush why he had attacked, but he neither responded nor repented. The same day Dobush died from his wounds. His corpse was cut into twelve pieces and displayed at various venues to frighten the peasants. This information was recounted in a letter written by Ian Kolandovskii, the mayor of the city of Iabluniv, on August 26, 1745 (Hrabovets'kyi 1994, 114–19, 266–68).

Dov Noy was the first scholar to note the existence of the Dobush character in Jewish Hasidic legends, where this robber is either named or anonymous. In Jewish sources the central episodes of Dobush's biography are connected not to his attacks on the nobles but rather to his meetings with a holy Hasid in the Carpathian Mountains. In most cases this holy man was the Baal Shem Tov himself, although other great Hasidic rabbis occasionally can be found in his stead. In the cases when Dobush is presented as an anonymous robber, he is recognized only through the context of his meeting with the holy Hasid (Noy 1960). Dobush is familiar both in Hasidic Jewish folk literature as well as in multilingual Jewish fiction and poetry based on folk sources, including a Sh. Y. Agnon story, a Shimshon Meltzer ballad, and the poetry of Meir Bossak and Naftali Gross, among other sources. Yet these representations are rather meager when compared to the image of Dobush in Ukrainian culture, be it in folklore (legends, epic and lyric songs), fiction and drama, or plastic arts and tapestries. In Ukrainian culture he is perceived as a noble-robber resembling Robin Hood, with the diffusion of his reputation as a bandit and a hero. As Dobush divided among the poor the property stolen from the rich, Ukrainians tend to perceive him more as the defender of and fighter for social justice rather than as a criminal. Although there are also Ukrainian legends recounting the meeting of the Baal Shem Tov with Dobush, this aspect is marginal in such tales. Similarly, the tale of Dobush is marginal within the Jewish stories about the Baal Shem Tov.

The relationship between Dobush and the Jews, however, does play a part in Ukrainian folklore about him. Perceiving wealthy Jews as allies of the Polish feudal lords, Dobush attacked them along with the rich in general (Hnatiuk 1910, 111–13, 115–20). But he did not plunder poor Jews; his dislike for Jews was more social than religious or ethnic, and was relatively moderate overall. Instead of harming a poor Jew, for example, he might instead give him some money for Shabbat (Hnatiuk 1910, 111; Vincenz 1936, 241).

The current story differs from the typical Jewish legends about Dobush in that there is no holy Hasid at all. Its Jewish character appears only at the beginning and very end of the tale, which is typical for "Judaized" universal stories (Shenhar 1987, 10). It is connected with the incidental but important figure of the Jewish innkeeper. It was he who helped the hero's widowed mother. It can be assumed that this supportive behavior of a Jew toward Dobush's mother influenced Dobush's relatively tolerant attitude toward Jews. An interesting historical fact mentioned in Kolandovskii's letter is that a Jewish innkeeper was staying with Dobush up to his last moment, and he gave him water to drink. According to the legend, the Jewish innkeeper gave the hero his nickname. It is also significant that the Hebrew word for bear is *dov* (singular; *dubim*, plural). Clearly, the name "Dobush" (as it sounds and is written in Jewish texts) resembles the Hebrew *dov/dubim* (bear/bears). This ending of the tale makes the legend into a *midrash*, a literary form typified by the interpretation of a name according to the logic of Hebrew and Jewish traditions. The use of the names of animals for humans is common in *midrash* (e.g., Zvi–deer, Ze'ev–wolf, Zipora–bird, etc.). The *midrash* can be found in Jewish traditions from the Old Testament to the present. According to Bar-Itzhak, midrashic naming is accomplished by various linguistic means: puns, alliterations, etiological legends, and so on (Bar-Itzhak 2001). In our case the historical legend seems also to be an etiological one. A foreign name becomes understandable through the new meaning it acquires in the Hebrew language. Another important aspect of this legend is that a hirsute, excessively hairy appearance is a universal sign of the Other, be it in the world of uncivilized nature or extramundane phenomena (Belova 2005, 51–52).

Finally, the miraculous rescue of a future hero by a she-dog recalls the myth of Romulus and Remus and the she-wolf. This motif is widespread in many cultures and constitutes an important part of Lord Raglan's scheme of a mythical hero's biography (Fialkova 2011, 13).

As Shimon Toder wrote, this is a story he drew on from memory; it was not collected during actual fieldwork. No information about the performance (gestures, facial expressions, intonation, pauses) is provided.

BIBLIOGRAPHY

Bar-Itzhak, Haya. 2001. "The Geography of Jewish Imagination: Po-Lin among Trees with Leaves from Gemara." In *Jewish Poland: Legends of Origin*, 24–44. Detroit: Wayne State University Press.

Belova, Olga. 2005. *Etnokul'turnye stereotipy v slavianskoi narodnoi traditsii (Ethnocultural Stereotypes in the Slavic Folk Tradition)*. Moscow: Indrik. [Russian]

Fialkova, Larisa. 2011. "Oleksa Dovbush: An Alternative Biography of the Ukrainian Hero Based on Jewish Sources." *Fabula* 52 (1/2): 92–108.

Hnatiuk, Volodymyr. 1910. "Narodni opovidannia pro opryshkiv" ("Folk Tales about Opry-shoks"). In *Entohrafichnyi zbirnyk* (Ethnographic collection), 26. L'viv: Naukove tovarystvo imeni T.G. Shevchenka. [Ukrainian]

Hrabovets'kyi, Volodymyr. 1994. *Oleksa Dovbush*. Lviv: Svit. [Ukrainian]

Jason, Heda. 1975. *Ethnopoetics: A Multilingual Terminology*. Jerusalem: Israel Ethnographic Society.

Noy, Dov. 1960. "The Legends about the Besht in the Carpathians." *Mahanayim* (Shavuot): 66–73. [Hebrew]

Shenhar, Aliza. 1987. "The 'Judaization' of Universal Folktales." In *Jewish and Israeli Folklore*, 1–5. New Delhi: South Asian Publishers.

Vincenz, Stanislaw. 1936. *Na Wysokiej Połoninie: Obrazy, Dumy i Gawędy z Wierchowiny Hucul-skiej* (On the High Uplands), part 1. Warsaw. [Polish]

Rabbi Ephrayim Elnekave and the Lion

IFA 6432

Narrated by Abner Azoulay (Morocco)

Rabbi Ephrayim Elnekave, a great man in every sense of the word, was the head rabbi in the city of Tlemcen, in Algiers. It was not his custom to stay at home studying within the confines of his home, but instead he would venture out among the community members and teach Halakha [Jewish law]. Sometimes he left his home and traveled to distant villages, to instruct the people in the ways of Jewish law and provide them with knowledge of the Torah.

Once he traveled far away from his village of Tlemcen, and when he wanted to return home, he was forced to journey with a large company—a caravan procession—to reach his distant village. The people in the caravan procession were Arabs, peddlers, and merchants. They walked for days through the desert. Friday arrived, and Rabbi Elnekave told the head of the caravan that he could not continue on with them without desecrating the Shabbat. The headman then explained to the rabbi that they could not stop in the desert because it was a dangerous place—full of animals and robbers—and he was responsible for the entire procession. The rabbi told the caravan leader that he needn't wait for him, and that everyone should continue on their way, as he took full responsibility for protecting his soul on his own. The rabbi would not travel on with them; he would not desecrate the Shabbat. The members of the procession continued on their way, shaking their heads at the Jewish rabbi who refused to join them—who knew what his end would be?

Rabbi Ephrayim stood next to a tree, drew a circle around him, put down his bundle, and began to prepare for Shabbat. As the sun began to sink, Rabbi Ephrayim stood within the circle and began to pray aloud, "*L'cha dodi, l'krat kala,*" and afterward, he recited the evening prayer. Suddenly, the roar of a lion shattered the silence. Rabbi Ephrayim saw the lion approach the circle. Rabbi Ephrayim continued to pray, and after finishing, he blessed the wine and took out two loaves of bread, sliced one of them, and began eating the first Shabbat meal. The lion sat outside the circle, looking on in silence. Rabbi Ephrayim finished eating the evening meal, sang the Shabbat *zmirot*, put his bundle under his head, and went to sleep. The next day, he awoke, prayed, and ate the second and third meal of Shabbat, while the lion crouched outside the circle. As the end of the Shabbat approached, after Rabbi Ephrayim had finished the *Havdalah* service, he saw a long snake coming toward him. The lion leapt to Rabbi Ephrayim's feet, as if to say: "Get up on my back!"

Rabbi Ephrayim climbed onto the lion's back and stretched out upon his neck, holding the snake which, in his hand, had been transformed into a bridle. The lion ran, sure-footed as an arrow shot from the bow. Early the next morning—on Sunday—the lion brought Rabbi Ephrayim to the marketplace in the city of Tlemcen and placed him on his feet, among the members of the caravan procession.

When they saw the rabbi descending from the back of the lion, they knew they were in the presence of a true *zaddik* [holy man]. They went and asked his forgiveness. The rabbi, of course, forgave them, and returned to his home.

[The storyteller explains that the depiction of Rabbi Ephrayim on the back of a lion is very common in North Africa.]

Transcribed by Moshe Rabbi

COMMENTARY TO
"RABBI EPHRAYIM ELNEKAVE AND THE LION"

IFA 6432

AVIDOV LIPSKER

The Israel Folktale Archives at Haifa University contains ten documented versions of the folktale about the miraculous deeds of the tale's hero, who subjugates a lion, rides on his back, and becomes a *zaddik*.[1] The discussion here relates to three of these versions: two are Jewish versions, which attribute the deed to two wondrous figures. The first version, which appears in this narrative— "Rabbi Ephrayim Elnekave and the Lion" (IFA 6432)—was recorded by Moshe Rabbi and narrated by Avner Azoulay. Azoulay was born in 1912 in the city of Sefrou, in Morocco, where he taught Hebrew language and literature, and was active in both the Jewish community and the Zionist movement. After years of activist work, promoting the *aliya* of thousands of Sefrou Jews to Israel, Azoulay himself immigrated to Israel in 1956. More than forty of his stories have been recorded in the IFA, all of them by Moshe Rabbi.

The second version, "Ariel" (IFA 12043), was recorded by Tamar Alexander and narrated by Leon Margi, from Tangier. The third version—"The Founding of the Village of Ein al-Asad" (IFA 21858)—is Druze and was recorded in Hebrew by Yusuf Badran.

In each of these versions, the wandering hero finds himself on a dangerous journey, during which he wins the protection of a lion on whose back he rides until the last station of the journey. In this folk narrative, this act is clearly the central narrative function and serves as the plot's climax. It is a function that includes permanent pictorial, emblematic components; that is, a function with a unified motif-based composition—one referred to in thematology as *motifeme*.[2] In the three IFA versions, this *motifeme* receives a unique design that is based on a special direction or trend in the telling of traditional folktale narratives that have already been recorded.

I first became interested in these versions as the result of a research project on the narrative tradition of Ashkenazi Jews—specifically the hagiography about Rabbi Shmuel the Hasid and Rabbi Yehuda the Hasid (Lipsker 1996). These stories can be found in Hebrew versions in the medieval Brill Manuscript, appearing in full in the anthology *Hasidut Ashkenaz in the History of Jewish Thought* compiled by Joseph Dan. Dan presents an important review discussing the link between this series of stories and the tradition of the Kalonymus family of Italy and its Babylonian roots.[3] This series of stories from the Brill Manuscript contains a special version of the tale, about Rabbi Shmuel the Hasid, who creates a lion and then forces him to carry wheat to be ground before Passover. This version also became part of the storytelling tradition of the Old Yiddish–language narrative; it appears in a Yiddish manuscript from the sixteenth century and in the early printing of the *Mayse Bukh* (Basel, 1602), the best-known collection of stories written in Old Yiddish.[4]

In two articles dedicated to these stories, I suggested that we add the Ashkenazi link established by the research of Reuven (Robert) Bonfil, who discovered the early Babylonian roots of this narrative tradition and its movement to Italy in the tenth century. Bonfil showed that the fabula of the lion devouring the ass, and the subjugation of the lion by the story's hero, present dramatic power exchanges, which the hero displays by riding on the back of the lion.[5] In the Ashkenazi tradition the *motifeme* of riding on the back of a lion is often missing; several of its variants discuss only the discovery of an important rabbi and the magical deeds he enacts (as in the third version in the partial list that follows); but in most versions the *motifeme* of the subjugation of the lion and the hero's riding on its back is the main part of the story. The Ashkenazi tradition includes the following tales:

1. "The Story of Aaron of Baghdad," *Megillat Ahima'atz*, 1054.
2. "Rabbi Todros of Rome, Creator of a Lion," *Raze Rabah*, thirteenth century.
3. "Rabbi Yehuda the Hasid, Exiled from Mainz Because of His 'Teivat HaShemot,'" *R. Shlomo Luria's Responsa* (1570), no. 29.
4. "Rabbi Shmuel the Hasid Saves a Lion from a Panther," *Mayse Bukh* (Basel, 1602), tale no. 160.
5. "Rabbi Shmuel the Hasid Creates a Lion Using Names," *Mayse Bukh* (Basel, 1602), tale no. 162.

The story version that appears in Old Yiddish (no. 162 in the *Mayse Bukh* anthology) tells the tale of Rabbi Shmuel the Hasid, who was preparing wheat for Passover. Suddenly, it began to rain. In an attempt to complete the *mitzvah*, he created a huge lion by uttering holy names. The rabbi then strapped the wheat onto the beast's back and jumped on himself, then brought the wheat to its destination. In return for this deed and the magical use of holy names, he was punished with exile.

In the tales I've listed, beginning with the *Megilat Ahima'atz* (*The Scroll of Ahima'atz*), an exemplary figure is banished and exiled, despite the fact that he acts to fulfill a *mitzvah*. However, this action is perceived as a magical or supernatural transgression, one that requires punishment. This specific and fascinating *motifeme*—making use of holy names—disappears from the later folktale versions, despite its hidden dramatic potential: the taming of a wild beast through magic. Remnants of this tale, however, are clearly seen—together with the unique addition of the lion and the snake—in the version regarding Rabbi Ephrayim Elnekave, one of the better-known versions of the "Ariel" stories.[6] In this version the snake threatens the hero, who has wandered in exile far from his home, but as part of the miracle, the snake becomes a bridle in his hand, with which the hero then subjugates the lion. This addition brings to mind the symbol of the chimera—a lion with the tail of a snake—the mythological beast from the bestiary of Mediterranean Basin mythology; its form is known to us from the Roman statue of the beast, cast in bronze, that was excavated from an archaeological dig in Florence. (It is today one of the most important exhibits at the National Archaeological Museum of Florence.) The breaking down of this symbolic emblem—the "disconnection" of the tail from the body of the lion—is a sort of neutering of its mythic, supernatural quality. The Rabbi Ephrayim Elnekave version of the tale isolates this part of the symbol—the snake—as a separate foundation that threatens the holy man and is afterward used as a bridle, with which he controls the lion. This part symbolizes the version's movement away from its magical tradition, and its movement toward the religious *telos* of piety and the fulfillment of *mitzvot*. This *telos* is hinted at in the well-known rhetorical configuration of "a snake wrapped around his heel," an expression of how one continues to pray even when threatened by danger, and which is hidden within the motif of the subjugation of the lion.

This *telos* endorses the tradition of the folktale narrative versions in using the lion to carry or grind the wheat (as in the story about Rabbi Aharon from Baghdad from the *Megilat Ahima'atz*) and in fulfilling the *mitzvah* of keeping the Shabbat, which does not require external aid but rather is simply a break from daily activity. This break in response to a holy day (Shabbat), which stops the convoy's chain of events and progression of movement, requires no action (such as the grinding and transport of grain) but encourages, rather, inaction. In this way the horizon line of the religious *telos* is completely blurred—as this is a line of active intervention that comes from outside. Nevertheless, the hero in the folk narrative is required to do something—he must commune with himself over the simple Halakhic ritual of blessing the wine and the bread. Therefore he must only be determined and stand his ground to fulfill a *mitzvah*, and to realize the promise made by his forefathers. Making the circle brings to mind, of course, Choni the Circle-Drawer. Although the theoretical appeal is missing, the swearing of an oath and the fulfilling of an ultimatum by God which, in the well-known story about Choni, brings down rain. It is not any kind of act of protest regarding the certainty of God—it is rather simply a type of circle of protection into which the hero enters by the strength of his own faith. The Jewish tradition in both of the folktales in the IFA focuses on the folk ethos of fulfilling *mitzvot*, of the unwavering belief in fulfilling the *mitzvot* that protect all believers, especially when faced with the dangers of the desert borderlands that lie between home and the unknown cities to which travelers journey. Exile, once again, is not a punishment, as it was in the earlier series with which the *Megillat Ahima'atz* begins or in the geography of the Ashkenazi Hasids; setting out on a journey is in itself an act of choice and an encounter that tests one's faith and one's belief in fulfilling *mitzvot*.

From this point of view, the Jewish story tradition intersects with the story from the Islamic space—a complete intersection of meeting and sharing with the same cultural, religious, and spiritual spaces. In the story told by the Druze from the village Ein al-Asad, the important leader (Sheikh Abed Alkedad Algilani, descendant of Al-Hassan II ben Ali ben Avi Talb) comes from Baghdad to the Land of Israel by way of Lebanon, and, like his Jewish counterparts, he is exposed to the hostility of strangers on the borderlands he must cross during his journey. As mentioned earlier, the heroes in the Jewish versions are escorted by non-Jews and do not receive support when they ask to stop to honor the Shabbat. Likewise, the Arab traveler is singled out as a "stranger/ foreigner," dressed in a cape that does not reflect the local style of dress, and the village children and monks at Ein al-Asad throw stones at him.

It is possible that the Druze version—whose narrative space resides with the monastery that maintains the Christian tradition in the Galilee—served to bring back to life the motif of the devouring of the ass by the lion. This motif, as I mentioned in an earlier article (Lipsker 1996, fn 1), is of Syrian origin, from the fifth century, and was the core of the Eusebius Sophronius Hieronymus (c. 342–420) legend that appears in the *Legenda aurea*. This legendary version is the source of the motif of the lion devouring the ass and its subjugation by the holy man, only after which it evolved into the ancient series that passed from Babylonia into Italy and then appeared in *Megillat Ahima'atz*.[7] However, despite the rejuvenation of the pictorial motif of the lion devouring the ass, the Druze folktale does not have the same magical foundation of swearing an oath through magic that appears in the ancient Jewish versions.

Thus it seems that the Druze folk tradition, similar to the Jewish tradition, preferred the folk narrative version, which relates a simple and innocent *telos* of piety and the fulfilling of daily *mitzvot* by the faithful over the more ancient tradition that examines the relationship between supernatural powers and daily tradition.

NOTES

To Yoav Elstein, thematologist of Israeli folk literature and the chief editor of the *Encyclopedia of the Jewish Story*.

1. This is a Jewish oikotype: AT **776C-B (IFA): A man refuses to travel on the Sabbath Eve, but catches up with the caravan procession on Saturday night, as he rides up on a lion's back.
2. The concept of *motifeme* indicates a unit at the functional level, which organizes motifs under the umbrella of a single literary function. The term was coined by Alan Dundes, who referred to Vladimir Propp's concept of function. For further details on the subject, see Elstein and Lipsker 2004–5, 38–39.
3. On the historical links that connect the Kalonymus family in Italy with the founding fathers of Hasidut Ashkenaz and the significance of the *Megillat Ahima'atz* (*The Scroll of Ahima'atz*) in relation to this dynasty, see Dan 1989–90, 109–36.
4. Stories in praise of Rabbi Shmuel the Hasid and his son Rabbi Yehuda the Hasid were printed from the Hebrew anthology that includes forty stories (26 are stories in praise of Rabbi Shmuel the Hasid and Rabbi Yehuda the Hasid), some in Hebrew and others in German, in Brüll 1889, 20–54. The manuscript is from Innsbruck, Ashkenaz (1596), and it is indicated as Jerusalem 803182 (the tales about Rabbi Shmuel and Rabbi Yehuda the Hasid, 108b–112a); it appears in its complete form in Dan 1989–90, 194–208. A comparison with Yiddish

manuscripts is provided by Meitlis 1961, 35–41. Meitlis edited a collection of stories made up of several published by Brill (20 stories), from a Frankfurt manuscript (8 stories), from a Yagga manuscript (5 stories), and from an Innsbruck manuscript (26 stories), among the same stories from the *Mayse Bukh* (Basel, 1602; 27 stories that appear in the section between the notes 158–83).

5. See also his pioneering article on the history of Hasidut Ashkenaz in the Middle Ages. Y. N. Simhony was the first to record the narrative versions of the exiled *zaddik* in the hagiographic tradition of the Ashkenazi Hasid. Simhony restored all the links, although he ignored one version—that of the Raza Rabba. Simhony was the first to link the legendary foundation with the person of Rabbi Aharon, in the historical transference of the secrets of Babylonia to Italy and Ashkenaz. See his article: Simhony 1986–87, 52. See, in particular, the study that established this question of the historical basis of the legend, in Bonfil, 1988–89, 99–135. In this series, they also discuss Eli Yassif 1984, 41–56, as well as his article "Studies in the Narrative Art of 'Megilat-Ahima'atz'" (Yassif 1984, 2, 18–24); and the chapter "The Historical Legend" (Yassif 1994, 325)

6. See Thompson B557.10 ("Person Carried by Tiger"; Thompson 1955, 454). We also make a connection to the story "Androcles and the Lion" which appears in Indian anthologies from the eighteenth century. In later Jewish literature, the story "Ariel" is also especially well known, as is the "Story of the Flea and the Lion," which appear together in the Bin Gorion anthology, *Mimekor Yisrael* (Bin Gorion 1965–66, 177–78). The folk motif was documented by Abraham Stahl (1970, 167–69). Stahl relates stories that present riders of lions, as narrated in Jerba and collected by Rabbi Shoshan Cohen, in *The Wonders of the Zaddikim* (1934–35), as well as in David Idan, *In Praise of the Zaddikim* (Jerba, 1918–19).

7. Ryan and Ripperger 1969, 591–89. See an additional version in Loomis 1948 (the chapter "The Folklore of Christian Legend," 58–59). For yet another version, see Bollandus 1684–1940, col. 1, 389.

BIBLIOGRAPHY

Aarne, Antti, and Stith Thompson. 1961. *The Types of the Folktale: A Classification and Bibliography*. FF Communications no. 184. Helsinki: Suomalainen Tiedeakatemia.

Bin Gorion, Micha Yosef. 1965–66. *Mimekor Yisrael*. Tel Aviv: Dvir. [Hebrew]

Bollandus, Joannes. 1684–1940. *Acta Sanctorium*, vol. 1, Antwerp. Vol II. Parisiis: V. Palme.

Bonfil, Reuven (Robert). 1988–89. "Myth, Rhetoric, History? A Study of *Megillat Ahima'atz*." In *Culture and Society in the History of the Jews of the Middle Ages*, ed. R. Bonfil, M. Ben-Sasson, and Y. Heker, 99–135. Jerusalem: Zalman Shazar Center, Israeli Historical Society. [Hebrew]

———. 2009. *History and Folklore in a Medieval Jewish Chronicle: The Family Chronicle of Ahima'atz ben Paltiel*. Boston: Brill.

Brüll, N. 1889. *Jahrbücher für Jüdische Geschichte und Literatur* IX, 20–54. Frankfurt.

Dan, Joseph. 1989–90. "Hasidut Ashkenaz through the Generations." In *Hasidut Ashkenaz in the History of Jewish Thought I*, unit 3. Tel Aviv: Open University. [Hebrew]

Elstein, Yoav, and Lipsker, Avidov. 2004–5. "Foundations in the Thematology of Israeli Literature." In *Sippur Okev Sippur: The Encyclopedia of the Jewish Story I*, ed. Yoav Elstein, Avidov Lipsker, and Rella Kushelevsky. Ramat Gan: Bar Ilan University. [Hebrew]

Lipsker, Avidov. 1996. "The Zaddik's Exile—The Exile of Rabbi Yehuda the Chasid from Speyer to Mainz." Presented at the Rabbi Yehuda the Hasid of Regensburg Conference, Regensberg, Germany.

———. 2008. "Transgression and a Slumberous Magic in the S. Y. Agnon Story, 'There Were Two Scholars in Our City.'" *Alpayim* 32 (April): 132–48. [Hebrew]

Loomis, Charles Grant. 1948. *White Magic*. Cambridge, MA: Medieval Academy of America.

Megillat-Ahima'atz. 1953–54. Ed. Benjamin Klar. Jerusalem: Mossad Rav Kook and Tarshish.

Meitlis, Jacob. 1961. *De shevachim fun Rebbe Shmuel en Rebbe Yehuda Hasid*. London: Kedem. [Yiddish]

Ryan, W. Granger, and Ripperger, Helmut. 1969. *The Golden Legend*, vol. 2. Translated and adapted from the Latin. Salem, NH: Ayer Company.

Simhony, Ya'acov Naftali. 1986–67. "Hasidut Ashkenaz in the Middle Ages." In *Religion and Society in the Context of Hasidei Ashkenaz*, ed. Even (Israel) Marcus. Jerusalem: Zalman Shazar Center. [Hebrew].

Stahl, Abraham. 1970. *Tales of Ethnic Groups*. Jerusalem: Ministry of Culture and Education. [Hebrew].

Thompson, Stith. 1955. *Motif-Index of Folk-Literature*. Vol. 1. Copenhagen: Rosenkilde and Bagger.

Yassif, Eli. 1984. "Folktales in the *Megillat-Ahima'atz* and Their Movement in the Oral Tradition of the Middle Ages." In *Yad L'Hayman—Research Collection in Memory of A. M. Haberman*, ed. Tzvi Malachi, 41–56. Tel Aviv: Berman Institute. [Hebrew]

———. 1994. "Studies in the Narrative Art of *Megillat-Ahima'atz*." *Jerusalem Studies in Hebrew Literature* 4: 18–24. [Hebrew]

———. 1999. *The Hebrew Folktale: History, Genre, Meaning*. Bloomington: Indiana University Press.

THE PRINCESS IN THE WOODEN BODY

IFA 6859

NARRATED BY ESTHER ELIZRA (MOROCCO)

In a big city, there once lived a king. The king had a beautiful queen. He had no sons, but he had one daughter. The daughter looked like her mother and surpassed her beauty. The mother died, and the daughter remained with the father. She lived with her father, and he cared for her very well. He said: "If my daughter didn't look like her mother, I would go out of my mind. I will never forget my wife."

The girl grew up, and her father said to her: "Listen to what I have to say to you. Only you will I wed."

The daughter said: "A father does not marry his daughter."

He told her: "You have no choice. This is the way it will be."

The daughter was vexed and wept, and tried to think what was best to do. One day, she went to a woman and said: "My mother is dead, and you are like my second mother." She told her what her father had said, and she began to weep.

The woman said: "I cannot advise you on this matter. But ask your father for an evening gown, made all of the finest pearls and gems."

The daughter went to him and said: "I ask you to give me an evening gown. If you can do this, I will marry you."

He answered: "Yes. I will give you more than this."

The next day, the finest pearls and gems were brought to the daughter. Many women sat and sewed her gown. When she put it on, the gown was more brilliant than the light.

She went once again to her father and said: "I ask now for a day gown with a sun."

He said: "I will give you all you ask, and then you will wed me."

He went to the best jewelers, and they made a gown that was more beautiful than the first.

The daughter took up the gowns and went to the woman: "Look, I have asked my father for everything. What must I do now?"

The woman replied: "You must help yourself. Go to the carpenters and tell them to make you a costume from wood. Everything must be made from wood; only leave holes for your eyes. It will take several weeks to prepare. Ask your father for more time to prepare for the wedding."

The daughter went to the carpenters and asked them to prepare the clothing. They were frightened: "Why do you want this clothing?"

She began to weep and said: "My mother is dead, and my father wants to wed me. Make me the clothing, and I will pay you whatever you ask."

It took two weeks to make the clothing.

At home, she said to her father: "Wait one more month until the wedding."

He agreed.

Once the wooden clothing was finished, she put it on, took the two gowns, jumped onto a horse, and left home, riding from one town to another, so that the people would let her leave the lands of her father. She left the city and wandered from place to place. She finally arrived at the sea and wanted to throw herself into the waves. But suddenly, from afar, she saw a new, big ship. She called out to the people on the ship and asked: "Where are you from?"

They answered: "We are the first to travel on this ship."

She said: "May I travel with you?"

They said: "Where are you from? What is your name? What is the name of your father?"

She said: "I have no name. I have only a wooden body. Neither father nor mother have I. I was born from wood."

They agreed to take her onto the ship. When the ship sailed, she went to the galley to help, to cook and clean.

"How can a wooden body clean and help us so much?" The people on the ship were frightened, but they loved her greatly for the beauty of her eyes.

The ship sailed on. They reached land, and the ship was welcomed. An officer went aboard and led the people off the ship, until no one was left.

He saw her and asked: "Where is this from?"

They answered: "This is a wooden body that we found in the sea and brought aboard the ship."

The officer saw that she was a hard worker.

The ship's owner made the officer an offer: "Take a gift for yourself from the ship; take anything you like."

The ship's owner agreed to give the wooden body to the officer.

A year passed, and they reached the officer's country. He held a party at his home and invited the king. When the guests arrived, they all looked at the wooden body. The table was laid, the house arranged, everything was done by the wooden body. The guests, together with the king, entered the house and said: "Where is this person from?"

The officer answered: "It is not a person; it is a wooden body."

They asked: "Where was the body born?"

The officer replied: "The body was born of wood, not from a woman's body." Everyone was amazed to see a wooden body working and cleaning.

After the party the officer offered to give the king a gift. The king wanted no gift; he wanted only her, the wooden body. And nobody realized she was a young woman; they all thought she was only a wooden body.

The officer said: "I also received it as a gift, and now I give it to you."

She went with the king, her suitcase in hand. The king and the wooden body traveled for seven days to the land of the king, back from his visit to the officer's country.

The king said to his wife: "We have received a good gift. It knows well how to work." The queen took her and gave her a room in which to sleep and food to eat.

Meanwhile, the king, the daughter's father, had fallen ill from seeking out his daughter but never finding her.

The king who had received the wooden body as a gift held a banquet in his country. Everyone made merry there and feasted. The king came out with his wife and children and invited the wooden body to come with them, but the body said: "I am not allowed out because everyone will gaze upon me. When you return, I will go in; and when you leave, I will leave."

They went through the town, and the body stayed home and cleaned. The daughter thought: "I grow weary of this life. I have not even tried on the gowns that I took away from my home." She went and bathed and put on the evening gown and, alone, left the house of the king. She went to the place where the banquet was being held. The people were frightened when she entered among them, but they only had eyes for her. The king's son saw her, took her hand in his, and they began to dance. He asked her: "What would you like to drink?"

She replied: "I do not drink, but I will have a glass of arak."

He went off to search for it in the town, and she returned home, took off her gown, and put on the wooden body once more. The prince returned and searched for her in vain. At the end of the ball, he went home and fell ill. He would neither eat nor drink. His father asked him: "What has happened to you, why do you not get up?"

The son replied: "I will get up, but I ask that the ball continue for three days, today and tomorrow."

The father agreed: "Yes, I will do as you bid. I know you did not find the maiden, but have no fear."

The son said: "It was my mistake; I did not ask her who her father is or where she is from."

The father said: "Perhaps she will come again today?"

Another ball was held that same evening. She stayed at home and did as she had the day before; she put on her day gown and went to the ball. When she entered the room, the prince took her hand in his, and they began to dance. He asked her: "First of all, what is your name?"

She replied: "I have no name. I cannot tell you."

"What is the name of your father, your mother?"

She replied: "I do not know them."

She had to leave early to change her clothes. Her shoe fell off, and while the prince bent down to look for it, she disappeared. At home once again, she put on her wooden body. The prince said: "We will search the town and find her."

They searched, but did not find her.

Then he said: "We have one more night, the last night of the ball, and if I don't find the maiden . . ."

The king and his family left for the ball, but the prince remained at home. The prince said: "This night, I will keep watch over the wooden body. Maybe the maiden comes out of the body."

He pretended to be ill and promised to come in one hour. After they had gone, the prince got up, washed himself, dressed, and said to the body:

"Come and close the door after me; I am going to the ball."

While she was closing the door, he quickly hid under her bed.

When she had finished her work, she came into the room to dress and put on her gown; he saw everything, came out of hiding from under the bed, and caught her.

"So! This is what you do every night? You say you are a wooden body?"

"I will tell you everything." She told him her life's story and about her gowns: "This is how I was until now; now you have caught me."

He replied: "And you, what do you want? Marry me."

She said: "If you are destined for me, I have no reason to flee."

She dressed, and they went to the ball together. The prince said to the king: "Look, this is the wooden body."

The parents were very happy, because she was very beautiful. The king made them a wedding, and they lived happily enough.

One day, the maiden said to the prince: "Three years have passed, and I would like to write a letter to my father."

He agreed. The daughter wrote to her father: "I did everything out of respect for you. I left the city of my birth; I have seen much trouble in my life. Now, I have married a great prince. If you would like to visit me, come. If not, then I will visit you."

The king had been ill for three years, thinking grievous thoughts about his wife and daughter, both beautiful and both utterly lost to him. One day, the king received a letter. He opened the letter and read it: "My daughter is alive. My life is one of sorrow. I have been destroyed by my thoughts of her." And then he died. But before he died, he wrote: "No man killed me. I died of longing for my daughter and my wife."

The letter he wrote remained together with the letter from his daughter. The viziers read the daughter's letter and wrote to her, telling of the king's death, saying she could come. She then came with her husband to the city of her father. The prince became king, and she, queen. They took the king's treasures and lived a long life.

Transcribed by Billy Kimhi

COMMENTARY TO
"THE PRINCESS IN THE WOODEN BODY"

IFA 6859

HAYA MILO

The story "The Princess in the Wooden Body" (IFA 6859) was recorded in Ma'alot by Billy Kimhi and narrated by Esther Elizra. Elizra was born in the Tafilat district in Morocco in 1937; she made *aliya* to Israel with her family in 1962, after many detours and hardships. Her stories were told to her by her parents and neighbors.

This story has two IFA versions: one from Tunisia ("The Father Who Wanted to Wed His Daughter"; IFA 1035) and another from Bukhara ("The Maiden and the Wooden Clothing"; IFA 9294).

All three stories belong to tale type AT 510B ("A Dress from Gold, Silver, and Stars"), a subtype of the "Cinderella" (AT 510) tale type.

According to the Aarne-Thompson classification index, this fairy tale is comprised of four parts. At the center of the first part is the demand of the father—usually a king—to wed his own daughter. In the second part the maiden escapes from her father with the help of magical gowns or a sort of wooden body or costume that serves to hide her. Over the course of her travels, the maiden becomes a servant in the palace of a prince who humiliates her or treats her unkindly. In the third part, the real identity of the princess is exposed by a forgotten shoe or some other identifying sign, like a ring concealed in a loaf of bread or a cake baked by the maiden. The tale concludes with the marriage of the maiden and the prince.

Two of the Jewish versions also among the IFA tales—"The Princess and the Wooden Body" (IFA 6859), from Morocco, and "The Father Who Wanted to Wed His Daughter" (IFA 1035), from Tunis—clearly satisfy the criteria of the AT 510B subtype, while the third story, from Bukhara (IFA 9294), is a conglomeration of two different tale types: The first part is based on the Jewish oikotype "There's No Escaping Fate," while the story's continuation reflects AT 510B.

THE FAIRY TALE'S OEDIPAL FOUNDATION

It is customary to perceive tales of the "Cinderella" type as a story of the feminine adolescence and maturation process, which traces the feminine lifecycle from childhood until adulthood. In the fairy tale the period of childhood is symbolized by separation from the mother; the daughter's maturity is symbolized by her marrying the prince or by pregnancy and childbirth, a characteristic addition of Jewish tales of this type (Bar-Itzhak 1993).

The assumption that Oedipal foundations are at the base of the Cinderella story has been clearly noted by Bettelheim (Bettelheim 1976, 194). Bettelheim perceives in the fairy tale the symbolic expression of the young girl's desire to inherit her mother's place and marry her father. As a result of the feelings of guilt associated with these fantasies, she feels worthy of punishment, hence her escape or humiliation. Therefore the daughter's adolescence and maturation process is one in which she overcomes Oedipal impulses, transferring her feelings of desire for her father onto the other male figure (the prince). Moreover, in the real lives of various cultures, even in modern times, the usual process of adolescence and maturation may well go awry: The daughter is not the one, in her childish longings, who wishes to marry her father; it is rather the father who asks to engage in intimate relations with his daughter. Therefore the fairy tale—which places at its center the breaking of a social taboo but distances any evidence of it through the use of symbolic language—can serve as a platform for describing those experiences that cannot be spoken of in an overt and detailed manner. One of the most common of these unspeakable experiences and well-kept secrets, found among most cultures, is the experience of incest or rape. In this commentary I will show that many similar thematic lines exist between the personal stories—recorded on Internet blogs—of young women who are victims of incest and the story before us.

The blogs to which I compare the tale "The Princess in the Wooden Body" appear on an Israeli website dedicated to the support of sexually abused victims. The name of the site is "*Macom*" (the Hebrew word for "place"). The site's goals are to provide information, encourage and facilitate discourse concerning incest, and enable communication among those affected by it. The many personal blogs on the site allow the victims to tell their own stories and share their experiences, coping methods, feelings, thoughts, and so forth. All the bloggers I reference here are native Israeli, Hebrew-speaking women who live in Israel. Although they remain anonymous and appear on the site only with nicknames (a central characteristic of virtual communication, which enables them to express themselves freely), they all share common past experiences, having been victims of incest as young girls or teenagers. The bloggers state that they use the blogs as part of their recovery process and to provide testimony for the traumatic events they experienced. The site is open to the public.[1]

A comparison of the tale and these personal stories reveals "The Princess in the Wooden Body" as a story in which the young woman's normative process of adolescence and maturity is disrupted in a violent way. The result is a split feminine existence: The young woman's adolescent body becomes the exclusive property of the man, and the disassociation from her independence forces a form of partial existence on her, one that is hollow and limited—where she exists as a "wooden body." The young woman's recovery from the miserable existence that has been forced on her is a process that ends with her leaving the "wooden body" in which she has lived. She learns to reconnect with life from a place of strength expressed, among other ways, in her ability to face her father.

BREAKING THE TABOO: A FATHER'S REQUEST TO MARRY HIS DAUGHTER

In this story, the teller skips the characteristic introduction to the genre and begins immediately with the plot: "In a big city, there once lived a king." The father, who is left a widower, misses his wife greatly, and so, turning to his daughter, he expresses a clear and unequivocal demand: "Only you will I wed." On the realistic level, we perceive the father's desire to marry his daughter, and his desire (unrepressed) to have sexual relations with her.[2] The shocked daughter reminds her father in her childish way that "a father does not marry his daughter." But the brief discussion concludes with the father's decisive statement: "You have no choice. This is the way it will be." The storyteller does not associate the father's demand with any of the explanations we find in the other Jewish versions: not with the oath sworn by the mother (the former queen) that whoever should find her gold bracelets, her widowed husband will wed (IFA 1035), nor even with the fact that the father didn't know that the beautiful girl he met was his daughter (IFA 9294). The realistic explanation in the text, which is well known to us "from life," accordingly lends the father's demand a realistic validity. A father who desires his own daughter doesn't require reasons or explanations. No explanation can stand up against the breaking of such a basic and deep taboo, one of the three sins against "preservation of life" punishable by death or excommunication.

HELP FROM A WOMAN

In her crisis, the maiden seeks help: "One day, she went to a woman" and told her about her predicament. We learn that the girl turns to a woman for help, but the teller doesn't tell us anything about the "woman," except that she is of the female sex. Is she a neighbor? A family member? We do not know. Haya Bar-Itzhak finds in the "Smeda Rmeda" stories that, in a family, "loyalty only exists among women related by blood; in contrast, the absence of blood relations engenders conflict and loathing" (Bar-Itzhak 1993, 343). In this story we see that the opposition between the women, against the backdrop of the absence of blood relations, is not expressed; although it would seem that they are not family members. The "woman," as a woman, is an ally, and as such does not refuse to help the girl. She tries to help to the extent that she is able. But we see that there is little she can do to help, and she doubts her own abilities. The advice the woman offers the girl does not cancel out the evilness of the deed itself but only brings about a brief delay.

She cannot save the girl—certainly not by openly opposing the father, the king. The woman thus turns to feminine wiles for help: the only power available to the weak. The things she tells the girl to ask of her father seem impossible: "ask your father for an evening gown, made all of the finest pearls and gems." These tasks, however, which the father accomplishes with ease, empha-size the helplessness of the girl before a man who wields such power in his world. The gowns, whose function is to emphasize and make more prominent the heroine's femininity and sensuality, serve the father's purpose—which is to see his daughter as a spouse, a wife, in every sense of the word. After the first two tasks have been completed, the girl goes back to the woman. The third time, in accordance with the poetic rules of folktales, the woman prefaces her words with the sen-tence: "You must help yourself." On the overt level of the story, the advice relates to the making of the wooden clothing or body: "tell them to make you a costume from wood. Everything must be made from wood; only leave holes for your eyes."[3] The wooden body stands in opposition to, and in contradiction with, the gowns mentioned previously, and its purpose is to take away the girl's femininity and hide her from the surrounding environment, since the heroine's sexual maturity and her developing femininity prove to be obstacles. On the covert level, however, the assertion "You must help yourself" may be understood as a piece of advice for life: The young woman's initiation is being guided by the advice of an older woman. The woman tells the girl that she needs to take her fate into her own hands. Therefore, as soon as the wooden clothing is ready, "she put it on, took the two gowns, jumped onto a horse, and left home, riding from one town to another."

THE TRANSFORMATION FROM "DAUGHTER" TO "WOODEN BODY"

In the international tale type, the maiden receives supernatural assistance and escapes with the help of magical clothing, some of which are made of wood (motif D 1473.1: "Magic Wand Fur-nishes Clothes" [Thompson 1933, 215]; motif D 1050.1: "Clothes Produced by Magic" [Thomp-son 1933, 107]). The fantastic mode in which the story is told is one of the conditions that define the genre and the possibility to perceive fairy tales as a symbolic expression of deep and repressed feelings that are, from the point of social taboos, among other things, part of this mode. The presence of supernatural forces and wondrous guiding principles is interpreted, for the most part, according to the psychodynamic approach, as expressions of unconscious humanity, as symbols that represent the collective aspect of a human's soul (Raufman 2003). The supernatural mode of the tale "The Princess in the Wooden Body" is expressed particularly in the character of the magical transformation the girl undergoes—the way in which she disappears and escapes—every time she puts on the wooden body: She transforms from a whole person, with a body and soul, to a "wooden body" without life, which no one would be interested in; and, in the words of the teller, from a "daughter" to a "wooden body." The central theme of of the heroine's transforma-tion and her ongoing existence as a "wooden body" encourages us to treat it as the tale's central characteristic.

MENTAL ESCAPISM: EXISTING IN THE BODY ALONE

Escape, either physical or mental, is one possible strategy of women threatened with incest. On the plot level, the story fulfills the option of physical escape despite the fact that this option is often difficult to realize in real life. On a symbolic level, mental escape is often the only remaining choice open to incest victims. Mental escape of a certain type can be accomplished by disconnecting the body from the mind. Existing "in body only" means existing separately from ourselves: becoming a "wooden body."

The act of separating the body from the mind appears repeatedly in many of the personal stories of rape victims on the Macom site. (In what follows, I refer to the victims using the writers' pseudonyms.) In one example, Ricky writes in her poem, "Death": "Now in the bed lay only a body with no soul."[4] Mirit's poem includes these lines: "The body remembers / and the soul is wounded, / the body remembers, / frozen . . . contaminated, / the body remembers but the soul retreats, / the body remembers, / and the heart breaks"[5]

The central poetic characteristic in the tale—the reference to the heroine as a "wooden body"— also appears in many of these modern-day personal stories, where the young women refer to themselves as a "doll" or a "wooden doll." (See as well the young girl in IFA 1035, "Wooden Doll.") The wooden doll or wooden body are both objects, both lifeless. Mirit writes on Macom:

> I am a doll that stopped breathing
> Started dreaming
> Wandering
> To escape from the body
> From herself
> I am the doll. . . .[6]

During her wanderings, the girl of our tale wants to put an end to her life. How can this desire to end her life be explained? Is it only her fear of her father, or is it her realization of the difficulties of her solitary existence? The teller does not explain but briefly mentions that she "wanted to throw herself into the waves." A comparison with the personal blog stories is helpful here as well. A central theme in these stories of young women who experience sexual assault is the desire to die and disappear. Poems and stories about the act of suicide—an act that will release the writer from her unbearable and unceasing internal pain—appear in most of their writings.[7] The girl boards the passing ship, and it takes her away. But when she is asked, "Where are you from? What is your name? What is the name of your father?" she answers with a statement that echoes repeatedly throughout the text, one that defines her identity and the meaning of her existence: "I have no name. I have only a wooden body. Neither father nor mother have I. I was born from wood." With these words she transforms herself from a girl into only a wooden body. It is a body that exists independent of and disconnected from the mind and the soul: a lifeless, wooden body.

Furthermore, her denial of the existence of her mother in the words, "I was born from wood," is another theme the maiden in the story shares with women who experience incest. Victims writing on the Macom site often blame their mothers, who witnessed the abuse but remained silent. By their silence the mothers became accomplices to the crimes perpetrated against their daughters.[8]

The heroine's existence inside the wooden body revolves around her assigned housework, which she carries out to the amazement of the others: "The table was laid, the house arranged, everything was done by the wooden body." Because she is "only a body," she is perceived as an object that can be given away: The officer who offers to give his guest, the king, a gift, gives him the "wooden body" with the words: "I also received it as a gift, and now I give it to you." Great sorrow and pain can be heard in the teller's voice when she says: "And nobody realized she was a young woman; they all thought she was only a wooden body."

THE TALE'S CONCLUSION: THE RECOVERY PROCESS

In accordance with the tale type, the real identity of the young woman is revealed to the prince when he hides under her bed on the night of the third day of the ball. The prince discovers that the "body" he knows so well is the same beautiful girl he fell in love with at the ball, and they are married.[9]

The story ends with the father being punished, which is a deviation from the international version but along the same lines as the characteristic addition to the Jewish oikotype of the "Cinderella" type, which concludes with the punishment of the villain (Bar-Itzhak 1993, 331). The girl says: "Three years have passed, and I would like to write a letter to my father." Moreover, the number 3 functions in the story as a formulaic numeral; numbering the time in years indicates that the time since her escape is long enough, and she is now mentally capable of meeting face to face with her father, the aggressor. A similar theme may also be found among the present-day personal stories on Macom, which position the direct conflict opposite the father-aggressor as a necessary phase in the woman's recovery process.[10]

The meeting between the daughter and her father in our story is not realized. Ironically, the father's excitement on receiving the letter written by his daughter serves to increase his sorrow, and he collapses and dies. However the poetic justice does not end there, with the daughter indirectly punishing her father and avenging herself. Before he dies, the father clearly writes: "No man killed me. I died of longing for my daughter and my wife." It would seem that a certain justice is expressed in the secret wish of the female storyteller for the father-aggressor to admit his guilt, only after which he is punished.

From the story's conclusion we can see the message at the base of the Jewish version, according to which "women can only be saved and redeemed when a male figure steps in. This being so, the woman must take the initiative and act so as to merit deliverance at the hands of a man" (Bar Itzhak 1993, 116). Her activity is not directed toward the man, and she doesn't manipulate him to engage in any task. An opposite example is that of Smeda Rmeda (IFA 16446), who asks her father for the right thing—the nuts. The "wooden body" heroine asks her father for the wrong things, because in the end she cannot save herself but only postpone her sentence. She shows activity and initiative to ensure her physical and mental survival; she is determined to exist in body only to preserve her mind and soul. The mind-body unity between the "daughter" and the "body" is not the result of activity and initiative directed toward the man but rather the outcome of initiative and activity directed inward, toward the heroine's inner self.

The final recovery of the heroine derives from her ability to shed the "wooden body," to return and reconnect to herself, and to confront her father. However, it is important to remember that she is able to accomplish these acts only after she is married; she is no longer the possession of the all-encompassing, all-knowing father but has found the protection of another male figure. The father's death is within the realms of a secret wish fulfillment—the aggressor will receive his just punishment, while the heroine will be able to return to the bosom of society without taking on herself the burden of guilt and shame. The viziers who read the father's letter and "wrote to her, telling of the king's death, saying she could come," provide her, from their elevated position, with the personal and social approval for which she has yearned.

A similar theme may also be found in the modern-day personal stories on the Macom site, which describe the recovery process whereby the female victim must confront the aggressor and reconnect with the surrounding environment from a place of strength rather than weakness.[11]

The difficult and cruel reality is that full and complete recovery from abuse is often impossible, but the folktale, because of its very nature, gives the woman the possibility to realize her hidden wishes and achieve a full recovery. And indeed: "She then came with her husband to the city of her father. The prince became king, and she, queen. They took the king's treasure and lived a long life."[12]

NOTES

1. Macom, which has published these stories, is dedicated to the treatment of sexual assault victims: http://www.macom.org.il/rooms/rooms.php. My commentary here does not deal with Internet blogs in themselves and does not pretend to explore or provide an explanation for this medium. This subject requires a separate study. In my discussion I use the blogs as a preliminary source of information regarding incest victims' feelings, attitudes, thoughts, etc. For further reading, see Milo and Raufman 2014.

2. Incest occurs more commonly than we would like to believe. According to data from the Israel Council for the Treatment of Sexual Abuse, the number of referrals to assistance centers for victims of sexual assault in 2016 was 47,901. The numbers shows an increase of 15% compared to the previous year, and of 34% increase compared to 2011. 90% of the victims were females. Among them, 60% were minors, under the age 18. The most common type of injury was rape or attempted rape (58%). One out of three—(27%) was victim of incest. For further information about the numbers of victims of sexual abuse in Israel, see the Knesset report (in Hebrew): https://www.knesset.gov.il/mmm/data/pdf/m03643.pdf

3. Except for the fact that it is made of wood, the clothing resembles the traditional costume worn by religious Muslim women, which covers them from head to toe, leaving only a small opening for the eyes. We can assume that the description of the clothing stems from the cultural reality of the story told within the Muslim context.

4. http://www.macom.org.il/rooms/ricky3.php 02.91 (28.12.17)

5. http://www.macom.org.il/rooms/mirit14.php 5.2.2004 (28.12.17)

6. http://www.macom.org.il/rooms/mirit12.php 2.04 (28.12.17)

7. For example, see www.macom.org.il/suzzan8.php: "The blue water becomes stormy, it rages and roils; she jumps into the sea's wet embrace, and is swept away . . ." (July 1992). In the tale, the sea provides not only the end but also the opportunity for salvation. According to its archetypal meaning, as related by Annis Pratt (Pratt 1981), the sea is perceived as a fundamentally feminine space, part of the "green" world that is connected to nature and freedom. It is apparently not a coincidence, then, that the young woman finds an opportunity for her salvation in the sea.

8. From a letter that appears on the Macom site, written by a young girl, Suzzan, to her mother. The writer concludes her letter to her mother, who didn't prevent her father from abusing Suzzan for many years, with these words: "I am disgusted by you, I miss you, I hate you and I love you . . . but I have to say goodbye. Goodbye, Mother." http://www.macom .org.il/rooms/suzzan2.php. Accessed December 28, 2017.

9. It is important to mention that the motif of the shoe that falls from the girl's foot exists in the story, but it does not fulfill any function in terms of proving the identity of the heroine.

10. From the preface to a letter written by a young woman to her father, which appears on http://www.macom.org.il/rooms/ricky4.php: "After 12 years of silence, in July 2003, I decided to meet with my father. This is the letter that I wrote a few lonely hours before the meeting. When I meet my father, I want to be very direct . . . very decisive and very honest. I want to leave the meeting with the feeling that I have come full circle and experienced closure in my life; after confronting him, I want to simply move on with my life."

11. From a January 10, 2006, post to the Forum for Victims of Sexual Abuse on the Macom site: "I often feel tucked away inside myself, as if I live inside a bubble, disconnected from the world around me. . . . Recovery means being in the opposite situation, a situation where the aggressor is weaker than us, and we are in the stronger position. I've always had these kinds of fantasies. In my dreams, I see myself screaming at her without mercy. Standing up for myself. But sometimes reality deals us a blow from inside, a strong blow. Whenever I think I've recovered, it suddenly turns out that I still have a long way to go, and that I still haven't gotten out of this bubble."

12. The story's happy ending reminds us of the liberating power of stories that are told in public, and the strength of stories in the recovery process—a theme that many of the Macom writers mention. For example, here is the first page from the blog of Meofefet, a young girl who was the victim of sexual abuse: "Some days, everything is fine, other days, everything is bad. There are some days when I am still 11 years old, sitting scrunched up on the brown leather couch, scared, without any will of my own, wanting nothing; an object, a doll, while there are other days when I remember that I am 15 years old and that I haven't sat that way for years, I have a will and desires; I am a human being and need to be related to as such. All of these days are in search of a story. Throughout all of these days, I look to see where my own story will appear, and somewhere, in the back of my head, this small voice tells me that this story is mine, and so I must be the one to tell it. The first version of The Room was written as a memorial, in memory of a tormented soul/mind and a polluted body, a monument of survival, for the rebirth of the phoenix which, even if it dies sometimes, is always reborn and rises up from out of the ashes. Here I am, exposed once again. Without inhibitions and without shame. Here is my story." http://www.macom.org.il/rooms/meofefet1.php

BIBLIOGRAPHY

Aarne, Antti, and Stith Thompson. 1961. *The Types of the Folktale: A Classification and Bibliography*. FF Communications no. 184. Helsinki: Suomalainen Tiedeakatemia.

Bar-Itzhak, Haya. 1993. "'Smeda Rmeda Who Destroys Her Luck with Her Own Hands': A Jewish Moroccan Cinderella Tale in an Israeli Context." *Journal of Folklore Research* 30 (2/3): 93–125.

Bettelheim, Bruno. 1976. *The Uses of Enchantment: The Meaning and Importance of Fairy Tales*. New York: Knopf.

Milo, Haya, and Ravit Raufman. 2014. "'The Princess in the Wooden Body': Israeli Oral Versions of 'The Maiden in the Chest' (ATU 510B*) in Light of Incest Victims' Blogs," *Journal of American Folklore* 127, no. 503 (Winter): 50–71.

Pratt, Annis. 1981. *Archetypal Patterns in Women's Fiction*. Bloomington: Indiana University Press.

Raufman, Ravit. 2003. "Examining Folktales as a Feminine Genre by Means of the Affinity between Dream Narratives and Folktales." PhD diss. Haifa: Haifa University. [Hebrew]

Thompson, Stith. 1933. *Motif-Index of Folk-Literature*. Vol. 2. Indiana University Studies vol. XX, study no. 100. Bloomington: Indiana University Studies.

THE KING WHO TRUSTED HIS KINGDOM TO HIS DAUGHTERS

IFA 7202

NARRATED BY SIMA GOLDENBERG (ROMANIA)

The king ruled his kingdom with a hard hand. The people groaned under the heavy burden of taxes and [realized that] the king didn't care how hard they worked and how much they suffered. Only a few people in the kingdom, tax collectors and clerks, were satisfied. They lived in rich palaces while the poor lived in meager, shabby tents and shacks.

The king and queen had three daughters but no sons to inherit the throne when the time should come.

The princesses grew up to become beautiful, well-educated young women, as becomes a royal family. However, the king and queen were worried: What would become of their dear daughters when they would reach the marriageable age?

One day, the king developed a plan. He thought, "I'd like my daughters to find suitable husbands who would lead the country after I die, each according to his talents. One of my sons-in-law should become commander of the army, another should manage the finances, and the best of the three should inherit the kingship from me when I'm too old to rule." Then the king called on his three daughters—the oldest, the middle, and the youngest—and told them, "My dear daughters, you have grown up and developed well, as befits princesses. Now it is time to think about your future. I have decided to test you: I will give each of you a precious stone, a gem worth a lot of money. Each of you shall do with the stone as she likes. This way I'll see how well you are suited for your future."

The oldest daughter said, "My father, my lord, I'll take my gemstone to the jeweler and ask him to place it in a jeweled setting, tied to a gold chain. I'll hang the chain around my neck, and that way I can keep my eye on it all the time."

The second daughter said, "I shall order the builders to build a high tower. I'll place a golden scepter on its top, and put the gemstone at the top of the scepter. This way the gem will lighten the darkness of night, and its luminance shall be visible far into the distance. This way, your capital city will be known far and wide."

The third daughter didn't know what to do with her gem. She asked her father to give her more time to think about it until she made up her mind. But the king was not willing to wait. Instead, he immediately gave the first gem to his older daughter and told her, "My daughter, I shall not stop you from doing as you wish. Go to the jeweler and ask him to make you a fabulous, masterpiece jewel in which to place your stone; just make sure you always guard it from danger."

The king then turned to fulfill his middle daughter's request and ordered the builders to construct a high tower. They put the second daughter's gem in the scepter and placed it on top of the tower. The gem lightened the darkness of night for long distances, thus enhancing the grandeur of the kingdom.

The youngest daughter also received her gemstone, but she didn't tell the king what she would do with it. The king thought, I shall let my youngest daughter ponder over it, and we shall see what happens.

The youngest princess started walking around the capital city, visiting remote neighborhoods where poor people and beggars lived. One day she entered a shack. Immediately she smelled the dense, putrid air of this poor dwelling. She sneezed, and her eyes opened wide in the dark room. She saw a young mother lying on her deathbed with seven naked, small children crawling around her and crying for food. Soon the mother would die, and the children would be orphaned, alone, and helpless. The princess felt sorry for them. She went to the market, sold the gem for a lot of money, and bought medicine, food, and clothing for the poor family. She returned to them and started to take care of them all, until the happy mother recovered to see her sated and well-dressed children. Nothing remained of the money the princess had received for the gem; she had saved nothing for herself. The princess returned to her father's palace empty-handed. The king was angry at his spendthrift daughter and banished her.

The girl walked around the country looking for shelter. She went from one town to another and from one village to the next, working hard for her basic sustenance. Her royal dress became worn out, her slippers fell apart, and her gentle feet that had always been well taken care of by her maids now turned rough from walking and from the hard work she had to do for a living.

One day the princess sat down to rest under a tree on a mountain slope. She was tired and wearing a ragged dress. As she sat there, she saw a dwarf pushing and rolling large stones from the top of the mountain, then walking down and collecting the stones to make a fence around a piece of land. Though she was very tired, the princess couldn't stand seeing the poor little man toil alone, so she joined him and helped him accomplish his difficult task.

The dwarf thanked the girl for her kindness and said, "Thank you, maiden, for your kindness and for the help you extended to me. This is a sign that God gave you the gift of compassion. Now, because you care about people's suffering, I shall give you a precious gift." As he spoke, he took a chain off his neck and placed it in her hand. The chain was connected to a tiny wooden caddy, inlaid with golden ornaments.

"This caddy can do many things," said the dwarf. "When you are in trouble and weep about your bad luck, open the cover of the caddy and allow a tear to enter it. This tear shall then turn into a precious diamond. Sell the diamond, and with the money you receive, you will be able to support yourself and many more poor and miserable people."

The young princess accepted the special necklace and hung it around her neck. She bid farewell to the man and went on her way. As she passed by an orchard, she saw a land-owner ruthlessly tyrannizing his workers. While they were digging canals, the owner was beating them with a whip, and the workers moaned in pain. The young princess felt sorry for the suffering workers, and tears started to suffocate her throat. Then she remembered the little caddy that hung over her heart. She opened its cover and let a warm tear fall in. Immediately the tear turned into a diamond, shimmering in a myriad of colors. The compassionate daughter went to the market and sold the diamond for a great deal of money. She gave most of the money to the poor orchard workers and kept the rest for herself.

This scene was repeated over and over as the tender-hearted princess helped many unfortunate people, until her name became famous and glorious all over her father's country.

One day the older princess went to swim in the sea, with the gem-jewel fastened around her neck. Suddenly there was a storm, and the princess quickly took off the jewel and clenched it in her hand. But alas, a huge wave engulfed her. The older princess was forced to let go of the jewel, which sank to the bottom of the sea.

At the same time, a huge eagle flying in the sky spotted an eye glittering on the top of a tower. The eagle thought it was the eye of a rival eagle, whose other eye he had already plucked out, and now it wanted to pluck out this eye, too. It stuck its beak right into the scepter and swallowed the gem, the king's gift to his second daughter. She, too, went back to her father's palace, empty-handed and despondent. Thus, two of the three gems the king had bequeathed to his daughters were now lost.

A neighboring king sensed that the father of the three princesses had become old and weak. He knew that this king had no sons to continue to rule the country after him, and wickedly decided to steal the kingdom from its old king. The neighboring king declared war against the father of the three princesses and appointed his son, the crown prince, to command his army.

The king realized that his country was in danger of invasion and declared a general draft. But the people would not fight for the ruthless king and his cruel clerks. Young men hid in caves and behind rocks and refused to fight the king's enemy. The youngest princess knew that the people respected her for her kindness, charity, and support of the needy. What did she do? She appealed to them persuasively. She told them that their homeland was in danger and had to be saved from the cruel invader who wanted to enslave them. She promised to treat the people with benevolence and compassion ever after.

The princess's request was graciously accepted by the young men. They gathered in army camps to prepare for battle, and the knights trained with their special weapons. Then they all marched together to face the enemy; none remained at home.

The enemy king and his son saw the courageous battalions and regiments facing them; immediately, they gave up their plan of invading the old king's country.

Meanwhile the glory of the merciful princess, adored by all, reached the ears of the young prince. He wanted to marry her. The crown prince sent messengers to ask the old king for permission to marry his youngest, but wisest, daughter. The king approved the match, and the two neighboring kings then made a peace treaty and married off their children.

The benevolent princess became the wife of the neighboring prince. When the time came they became king and queen, and ruled the two countries, now united into one, in the paths of humbleness and grace. And the king's two older daughters remained old maids for the rest of their lives.

Transcribed by Zalman Baharav

COMMENTARY TO "THE KING WHO TRUSTED HIS KINGDOM TO HIS DAUGHTERS"

IFA 7202

YAEL ZILBERMAN

The narrator of this tale is Sima Golden-berg, who was born in Eastern Roma-nia in 1914 (in Tulcea, in Dobrogea County) to parents of Romanian and Turkish origin. Sima worked as a seamstress and ran her own firm. She was an ardent Zionist and always dreamed of moving to Israel/Palestine. Her dream came true in 1964. Sima settled in the city of Ashkelon and continued to work in her profession. Her deep conviction of the righteousness of the Zionist cause helped her acclimate quickly in Israel. Sima often integrated fables in her speech and stories.

The feminist interpretation of folktales has been undergoing significant changes over recent decades. While the tales merited sharp criticism in the 1960s due to the stereotypical passivity and submission of their heroines, they were reevaluated in later decades and viewed, instead, as providing a complex expression of positive characteristics, such as courage, wisdom, and survivability.[1] Researchers such as Kay F. Stone and Troborg Lundell add that, while folk narrative offers a variety of heroine behaviors and attributes, passive heroines tend to be chosen by editors of popular tales collections, Walt Disney Studios scriptwriters and producers,[2] and at times folklorists—who choose to focus on the acquiescence of their female protagonists.[3]

By the 1980s feminist criticism concentrated on the dynamic relations weaved between tales and their interpretation by the narrator (who is most often female) and her audience, thereby stressing the storytelling process in its various contexts.[4] This trend is part of a rich feminist, non-essentialist critique that does not endorse a tale as a whole but rather sees it as made up of "sites" representing clashing historical and social frames. According to this critique, tales reflect social norms in a conflictive manner and enable expression of both the normative and the subversive (Baccilega 1993).

One of the contemporary trends in feminist critique of tales is reference to their gender aspects in the context of their social class and financial situation. For example, Elisabeth Panttaja offers a refreshing and exciting class-based analysis of the Cinderella tale. Panttaja contends that the tendency of feminist and neo-Marxist criticism to adopt a gender-related psychological interpretation created a focus on the personal and sexual aspects of the tale and its gender aspects in complete isolation from its political contexts.[5] In truth, despite the leaning of the tale toward the universal, it is no less anchored in real-life cultural and sociopolitical contexts. In most cases this context is feudal, monarchic, and patriarchal.

The figures in the tale belong to two diagonally opposed classes: aristocracy (kings, queens, princes, and princesses) and commoners, including craftsmen and women (lumberjacks, millers, tailors/seamstresses), or shepherds, hunters, and warriors. According to Lutz Röhrich, this polarity, beyond a narrative ploy enhancing tension, expresses not the dominance of higher classes but rather the subversion of accepted social structures by the lower classes. This is expressed in the frequency of motifs, such as the poor man who finds a treasure, the commoner who becomes king, and so forth. Thus the tales give vent to the sentiments of the people and to their hearts' desires (Röhrich 1986).

In contrast to Röhrich, Jack Zipes claims that the Grimm brothers' collection expresses capitalist and bourgeois values that befit feudal societies. According to Zipes, though some of the low-class figures are transformed into elites, this only serves to strengthen and not subvert bourgeois values and power relations such as obedience and patience. Moreover, such examples of social mobility prove that individuals can compete for higher status in the social hierarchy only by accumulating property and gaining power. While rulers may change in the tales, the patriarchal structure and the master-servant power relationship is always preserved (Zipes 1982, 58–59). Panttaja points at the duality expressed in fairy tales, between their wish to preserve past experience, including conflictive moral stands between the people and the rulers, and their goal of creating a new reality.[6]

This duality is clearly present in the tale at hand (IFA 7202), a Romanian Jewish tale type that is partly categorized as a secondary AT 923B ("Princess in Charge of Her Fate"). Usually this tale type consists of the following parts or moves:

1. A king asks his three daughters to tell him who controls their fates. The two older daughters reply that it is their father, the king, but the youngest daughter answers that it is only herself. Following this she marries a poor or crippled man and lives with him in frugality. In some variants of this type, she is expelled from the palace or kingdom for her brazen answer.

2. Using her wisdom and skills, the youngest princess makes a poor man rich and eventually turns him into a king, or she cures his illness. In some variants she herself becomes rich and marries a prince.

3. The old king, who visits the new king, recognizes his daughter and admits that she is indeed responsible for her fate. In some variants he loses his kingdom and

wanders around until he reaches his daughter's dwelling (Aarne and Thompson 1961).

The present variant, "The King Who Trusted His Kingdom to His Daughters," only partially conforms to this general pattern. The youngest princess is expelled, cures a sick woman, and helps many people; yet she does not turn a poor man into king but rather becomes rich and marries a prince. In the end her father, who is threatened with the loss of his kingdom, does not actually lose it, and at any rate he never admits that his youngest daughter was correct about her fate (or anything else). This tale also partially correlates to the Jewish oikotype formulated by Heda Jason, which combines type AT 923 ("Love like Salt") and the secondary types AT 923A ("Love like Wind in Striking Sun") and 923 B.[7] The present tale does not start with the king's question to his three daughters and the younger daughter's defiant answer, but with a test that he devises for them. Having no sons, the king wants his daughters to choose suitable husbands to rule the country after his death. He gives each of them a valuable gemstone to test their ability to make good decisions—that is, to choose appropriate husbands.

Unlike her older sisters, the youngest princess recognizes that she does not know how to use her gemstone, so she departs on a quest. On her way she meets the poor people of the kingdom and sells the gemstone to help them. She then returns to the palace empty-handed and is expelled for her alleged wastefulness. A dwarf whom she helps gives her a magical caddy that can turn tears into diamonds. Using the caddy, she is able to make a living and help many people. Meanwhile, a neighboring king decides to take over the old king's country. At first the people refuse to fight for their country because of the cruelty of the king and his clerks, but with the persuasion of the princess they finally agree. Upon seeing the masses ready for battle, the rival king and his son change their mind about the war, and instead the prince marries the princess, whereas her older sisters remain unmarried.

Unlike in equivalent variants, which may open with the wife's or daughter's statement of her superiority (e.g., "only the woman/wife creates the home," "all is in the hands of the woman/ wife and by the woman," "luck depends on the woman/wife"), and thus anticipate gender strife,[8] in this variant the main conflict is class strife between the rich and the poor, or oppressors and oppressed, whereas the gender and generational conflicts are secondary. In its other variants, too, the woman/wife proves her superiority through helping the poor and making them rich, at times richer than the king. But she does so only within the home sphere, thereby fulfilling the "good wife" function through executing household chores such as lighting the fire, doing the laundry, sewing, cooking, and looking after the children. By contrast the heroine in this tale acts in the public sphere from the start. The class conflict, stressed already at the beginning, derives from the injustice existing in the kingdom, where the king and his tax collectors and rich clerks all live in luxury while the poor live in shabby tents and shacks. It is also emphasized that the king rules iron-handedly and imposes heavy taxes regardless of the people's poor livelihood. Poverty is described in greater detail than is usual for descriptions in folktales: the darkness and airlessness in the poverty-stricken home; the young, dying mother and her seven naked, starving children; the crushing labor of the dwarf pushing large stones; and the orchard-owner harassing his workers. All these exemplify the misery and suffering of the lower classes.

The main value expressed by this tale is that of preferring the good of the people over one's own good. The choices of the older sisters, to decorate themselves or the capital city with the gemstone they receive, are shown to be unjust and even unprofitable, as both lose their stones whether in the sea or to an eagle. Only the younger princess, who sells the stone for medicine, food, and clothing for the poor, never loses her gemstone—or rather, its worth. Moreover, thanks to the help she extends to the poor, she receives respect and gratitude from them. This, in turn, enables her to convince them to fight—while the king is unable to force them—and finally she marries a prince. On the political plane, if the gemstone test was meant to determine who is entitled to lead the people, then this is a "socialist fable" about the suffering of the masses and commitment of the leadership to alleviate their suffering, thereby strengthening the regime as well. In this regard—unlike other variants of this tale type which make the woman responsible for her individual fate—this story stresses the responsibility of the entire society and especially those who have power to support the ordinary poor people.[9]

Notwithstanding all this, the tale also expresses monarchical and patriarchal voices and sentiments. First, as mentioned earlier, the king never acknowledges his past misdeeds or the fact that his youngest daughter was correct in her assessments, and he wasn't. Unlike the case in a similar Jewish-Moroccan variant (IFA 5066), here the king is never ashamed and silent. The fact that the daughter helps her father out of trouble yet never merits his recognition and apology weakens the message about her righteousness, wisdom, and victory. Second, unlike some of the other variants, this tale ends not with intermarriage of classes but with a prince marrying a princess. This means that, despite the tale's solidarity with the poor and their misery, and though the princess herself lives in poverty during her quest—searching for food, wearing a simple dress and worn-out shoes—eventually she marries back into her original class, and thus the monarchic order is preserved. Moreover, the marriage becomes part of a peace treaty between two rival kings who unite, thereby strengthening the monarchic institution. Third, no less problematic, is the fact that the princess uses her power to persuade the people to fight for the kingdom against their inclinations—behavior that is certainly incongruent with the tale's socialist-Marxist message.[10]

Thus the same heroine who helps the people and identifies with them also prevents them from protesting against the injustice of the system. She takes advantage of their sympathy/admiration (or their dependence on her money) to manipulate them to act according to her will and presents the rival king as a ruthless enemy who would otherwise enslave them, although this is exactly the conduct of her father, their present king. In Marxist terms she creates a false consciousness, presenting the ruling ideology as working for the good of the people, though it does exactly the opposite. Fourth and last, side by side with her proactive, independent behavior throughout the tale is the emphasis placed on her traditionally feminine features at the very end of the tale. In the course of the tale she is depicted as demonstrating initiative, resourcefulness, a strong sense of justice and social awareness, and even physical strength (to help the dwarf push stones uphill), but in the end she is described as a woman of extraordinary beauty and charming grace, as well as a merciful and gentle nature—qualities that make her a suitable match for her prince.

It seems that this variant, despite its explicitly subversive and socialist messages, is simultaneously also more traditional and feudal than others.[11] This may be related to the historical and political context in which this tale was transmitted to Sima, namely that of the communist regime that ruled Romania as of the late 1940s (until she left for Israel in 1964). It is likely that this variant has gone through a process of oicotypification (creation of a local tale type) to the atmosphere of mid-twentieth-century Romanian communism by criticizing social inequality yet never depicting the abolishment of inequality, all within an ostensibly egalitarian system. In other words, despite all the energy invested in hard work, mutual help, and war prevention, the system remains the same. It may well be that this variant was mandated to accommodate an environment that did not allow for freedom of thought, speech, and criticism: Despite the existence of a magical caddy—which transforms tears into diamonds that are used by the heroine on behalf of the poor and downtrodden—still the means of production remain forever in the hands of the kingdom. The king and queen may lead the people on the "paths of humbleness and grace" but not on the paths of social equality.

Notes

1. Marilyn Jurich contends that viewing the fairy-tale heroine as a passive figure is a superficial reading, because even as a victim her morality and intellect often make her stronger than her victimizer(s). Thus even seemingly obedient heroines can fight and effectively undermine their oppressor(s) (Jurich 1986).
2. For a thorough social critique of the Disney industry, see Dorfman and Matterlart 1975.
3. Lundell shows that the type and motif indices are systematically biased in labeling similar actions differently according to the gender of the protagonist. Princes are characterized as active even when they do very little, and princesses are habitually presented as passive, dependent, and weak no matter what they do. See Stone 1975; Lundell 1983.
4. This direction of research is well exemplified in the essay collection of Lalita Handoo and Ruth B. Bottigheimer (1999).
5. Panttaja claims that the conflict between Cinderella and her dead mother on the one hand, and her step-mother and sisters on the other, represents the class conflict between aristocracy and bourgeoisie. The tale reserves the happy ending for the aristocracy-born bride, not for her ambitious lower-class rivals. Moreover, presenting the sisters as incompatible for the higher class through the glass-slipper test and as morally and physically inferior strengthens negative perceptions of lower classes. See Panttaja 1993.
6. See Panttaja 1993. The debate about the conformist/subversive nature of the fairy tale is part of a much broader and more fundamental discussion about the revolutionary potential of folklore materials, mainly from a Marxist point of view. See, for example, the argument between Limon and Zipes: Limon 1983; Limon 1984; Zipes 1982; Zipes 1984.
7. IFA has forty-four variants of this type. The present tale matches them only partially with regard to the following elements: I C b—the princess's banishment; II c—financial success

and marriage to a prince; II e—activation of a magical object. For further discussions of this type, see Jason 1965, 116.

8. Five of the six IFA variants of the secondary type AT 923B include a gender conflict: 5066, 6188, 6312, 6501, and 8229. Considering IFA 637, this remains unclear, as it exists only as a tale synopsis.

9. Mutual help and support of the poor are of great importance in folk literature in general and in Jewish lore in particular. Dov Noy's annotated collection of Romanian Jewish folktales exemplifies this principle. Often the message behind the poor people's plea for financial help from the rich is that they deserve this assistance and are entitled to it, whether because they work for it as the employees of the rich or due to communal responsibility as instructed in the Torah. See Noy 1967.

10. It is worthwhile to stress the distinction between intra- and extratextual Marxist critique; i.e., between the narrator's socialist awareness as expressed in her narrative and my reliance on Western, neo-Marxist research tools, which is what I attempt here. I thank Prof. Galit Hasan-Rokem of the Hebrew University for her enlightening remarks concerning this distinction.

11. In another Romanian Jewish variant of AT 923, "The King and His Three Daughters" (IFA 5956), the princess who is sent to do household chores in another palace finally marries a prince.

BIBLIOGRAPHY

Aarne, Antti, and Stith Thompson. 1961. *The Types of the Folktale: A Classification and Bibliography*. FF Communications no. 184. Helsinki: Suomalainen Tiedeakatemia.

Alexander, Tamar, and Dov Noy. 1989. *The Treasure of Our Fathers: Judeo-Spanish Tales*. Jerusalem: Missgav Yerushalaim. [Hebrew]

Baccilega, Cristina. 1993. "An Introduction to the Innocent Persecuted Heroine Fairy Tale." *Western Folklore* 52 (1): 1–12.

Dorfman, Ariel, and Armand Matterlart. 1975. *How to Read Donald Duck: Imperialist Ideology in the Disney Comic*. New York: International General Press.

Handoo, Lalita, and Ruth B. Bottigheimer, eds. 1999. *Folklore and Gender*. India: Zooni Publications.

Jason, Heda. 1965. "Types of Jewish-Oriental Oral Tales." *Fabula* 7: 115–224.

Jurich, Marilyn. 1986. "She Shall Overcome: Overtures to the Trickster Heroine." *Women's Studies International Forum* 9 (3): 273–78.

Limon, Jose. 1983. "Western Marxism and Folklore: A Critical Introduction." *Journal of American Folklore* 96 (379): 34–52.

———. 1984. "Western Marxism and Folklore: A Critical Reintroduction." *Journal of American Folklore* 97 (385): 337–44.

Lundell, Troborg. 1983. "Folklore Heroines and Type and Motif Indexes." *Folklore* 94: 240–46.

Noy, Dov. 1967. *Folktales from the Jews of Romania*. Together, the Tribes of Israel series, ed. Baruch Rand. Jerusalem: Ministry of Education. [Hebrew]

———. 1970. *Jewish Folktales from Tunis*. Jerusalem: Jewish Agency, Haifa Municipality, and Israel Folktale Archives. [Hebrew]

Panttaja, Elisabeth. 1993. "Going Up in the World: Class in 'Cinderella.'" *Western Folklore* 52 (1): 85–104.

Röhrich, Lutz. 1986. "Introduction." In *Fairy Tales and Society: Illusion, Allusion, and Paradigm*, ed. Ruth B. Bottigheimer, 1–9. Philadelphia: University of Pennsylvania Press.

Stone, Kay F. 1975. "Things Walt Disney Never Told Us." *Journal of American Folklore* 88 (347): 42–50.

Yeshiva, Miriam. 1963. *Seven Folktales*. Haifa: Haifa Municipality, Ethnological Museum and Israel Folktale Archives (IFA). [Hebrew]

Zipes, Jack. 1982. "Who's Afraid of the Brothers Grimm? Socialization and Politicization through Fairy Tale." In *Fairy Tales and the Art of Subversion: The Classical Genre for Children and the Process of Civilization*, 45–70. New York: Wildman Press.

———. 1984. "Folklore Research and Western Marxism: A Critical Reply." *Journal of American Folklore* 97 (385): 329–37.

THE SIX SISTERS FROM THE MOUNTAINS

IFA 7370

NARRATED BY YAFFA COHEN (IRAQ)

Once there were six sisters. They lived in the mountains with their mother and father. One day, as he was leaving for work, the father said: "My daughter, bring me some food"—to which the daughter readily agreed. In the morning her mother told her: "Go. Bring this food to Daddy." Once again, the daughter agreed. She took the food and went along, until she reached a place full of mud. She wanted very much to stop and play with the mud. She put down the food and started playing, forgetting all about her father. She played and played, until she fell fast asleep. When she awoke, it was already evening. She said: "Oh, my goodness. I didn't bring Daddy his food . . ."

When she arrived back home, her father asked: "My daughter, why didn't you bring me my food?" She answered: "There was mud on the path, and I couldn't get through." Then he said: "Tomorrow you won't come, but your younger sister will." When dawn broke, the younger sister took food and set out to bring it to her father. She reached a hill full of flowers, and she also forgot about the food, playing with the flowers and saying: "Why do I need to bring Daddy this food? I'll take these flowers and the food and bring them to Grandmother, who will kiss me." Afterward she went to her grandmother and told her: "I have brought you food and flowers." The same thing happened to the next three sisters: All three failed to bring the food. But on the sixth day, the mother told the youngest sister to bring the father his food. After walking halfway, she reached a high mountain. She climbed up until she reached the middle of the mountain, where she found a very shiny box. Using her hands, she dug and dug until she uncovered a small golden box full of gold. She marked the place, covered it with sand, and went directly to her father, completely forgetting the food.

She went to her father and said: "Come on, what are you working for?" He asked her: "Why do you ask? You have never before asked me such a question." So she answered: "I have a reason. Come home, and I'll tell you why." They went home, and she told him: "Bring a sack, and let's go." He asked her: "Where are we going?" To which she replied: "Somewhere." They walked to the mountain, climbed up the hill to where the box was hidden, dug, and found the golden box. They put it in the sack and went down the hill.

When they reached home, they told the mother and sisters what had happened. They all slept through the night. In the morning, the father woke up, took some gold, and went to the big city. He asked his daughters what presents they would like; each sister asked for something else. The youngest asked for two little kittens; the eldest asked for a necklace; the second sister asked for shoes; and so on, each sister asking for a present of her own. The father bought everything they asked for and began his homeward journey. On his way he encountered a pool with rocks. One of the kittens stopped there to drink water. He left the kitten where it was and continued on his way. When he reached home, the sisters saw him and ran toward him, asking him whether he had brought what they asked for, and he said yes. He gave each girl her present; only the youngest daughter didn't get what she wanted—she had asked for two kittens, but received only one. She said: "I asked for only two small things, and you brought only one." The father said: "I left one kitten near the pool. I stopped to drink there and forgot the second kitten. I will go and bring it now."

He went away, and when he reached the pool, he saw an eagle with the kitten in its mouth. The eagle asked: "Who owns this kitten?" The father answered: "I do. Give it to me. It's for my daughter." The eagle said: "If you give me your daughter, I'll give you the kitten." The father said that he couldn't possibly give his own daughter to an eagle, to which the eagle replied: "Whether you give her to me or not, I'll take her, and if not, I'll destroy the entire city." The father went back home sadly, and asked his oldest daughter if she wanted to marry the eagle, and she said no. Then he said: "If you don't marry him, he will destroy our city." The oldest daughter realized she had to go with the eagle.

The eagle took her to his house and gave her a man's heart, urging her to eat it straightaway. He said: "If you refuse to eat it, I'll kill you." Then he went out to work, and she threw the heart onto the rubbish heap. When the eagle came back, he turned to his wife and asked: "Did you eat the heart?" She replied: "Of course I did." But the heart said: "I'm here on the rubbish heap." The eagle took the heart and killed the girl. There were twelve chambers in the eagle's house, and he put her into the last one. Then he went to her father and told him: "Your daughter is dead. I want the second one. If you refuse me, I will destroy the whole city." The second daughter went to the eagle's house, and the same thing happened to her. And so on and so forth, with the third, the fourth, and the fifth daughter, until only the youngest daughter remained.

When the eagle came to take her, she followed him with no fear. She said nothing. When he went out to work, he gave her the heart and said: "By the time I return, you must eat the heart, or else I will kill you." The youngest daughter had two little kittens. She cut the heart into small pieces and fed them to the kittens. The eagle came home and asked: "Did you eat the heart?" And she said: "I did." The eagle said: "Should I call it?" And she answered: "Call it, I don't mind." The eagle called: "My heart, my heart, where are you?" The heart answered: "In the stomach." The eagle was pleased, and said: "Now you are my wife." And he gave her all the keys to the house, telling her: "You may enter all the chambers, except the last one."

After the eagle left, she opened the first chamber, which was full of silver. She opened the second chamber, which was full of gold. She touched the gold with her little finger, and her finger turned to gold. She was frightened and wrapped her finger in a handkerchief. When the eagle came home, he asked: "What happened to your little finger?" To which she replied "I hurt it with a knife." So the eagle asked the knife: "Knife, knife, why did you hurt my wife?" The knife began cursing: "I didn't hurt her finger." The eagle asked: "So who did?" The wife said: "It was the broom." The eagle asked: "Broom, broom, why did you hurt my wife?" But the broom said: "I didn't hurt her." Finally the eagle said: "I'm opening the room." Then he saw the gold. He took it and put his wife into the gold to her throat.

The day after, he went to work again. She entered the twelfth chamber and saw all her sisters hanging in the air. She thought to herself: "He'll probably do the same thing to me. I had better run away from here." And that's exactly what she did. The eagle came back but didn't find his wife. He started hitting himself and crying: "Where is my wife?" Finally he opened all the rooms until he reached the last one, where she had forgotten her keys. When the eagle saw them, he knew she had been there. He understood that she had run away because she was afraid. She went back to her mother and father, who were now old. They hugged her and kissed her, and the eagle stayed alone, all by himself.

Transcribed by Ya'acov Avitsuk

COMMENTARY TO
"THE SIX SISTERS FROM THE MOUNTAINS"

IFA 7370

RAVIT RAUFMAN

This tale was recorded in the IFA in 1966.[1] It was transcribed by Ya'acov Avitsuk, who heard the story from Yaffa Cohen, a new immigrant who had arrived in Israel from Iraq in 1951.

Typologically this tale can be identified as a conglomerate: The first part of the tale belongs to tale type AT 425 ("Beauty and the Beast" or "The Search for the Lost Husband"), while the second part of the tale belongs to tale type AT 311 ("Bluebeard" or "Three Sisters Rescued from the Power of an Ogre"). This tale type includes six plot stages: (1) The forbidden chamber—The ogre takes the sisters away against their will, housing them in his castle and forbidding them entrance into one room, which they enter despite his decree; (2) the ogre kills the sisters for their

act of disobedience; (3) their youngest sister rescues them; (4) the sister deceives the ogre by carrying a bag; (5) the sister disguises herself as a bird; and (6) the sister punishes the murderer.

The IFA has four tales in which the salient motives characterizing tale type AT 311 can be identified—tale numbers 6216, 6283, 7325, and 7370 (the present tale)—and which present the greatest similarity to the international type.

An interesting characteristic of the Jewish-Iraqi version (7370) is the way in which the tale type combines aspects of tale type AT 425, which appears in the first part of the story. The connection between the two story parts is rather vague, and each one could stand on its own as a separate story. In the first part of the story, the father who goes to work asks his daughters to bring him food. One after another the girls fail to accomplish this task for different reasons; the youngest one finds a chest full of gold, yet she too fails to bring the father his food. Later on the father goes to town, and each daughter requests a gift. The eagle, which steals the youngest daughter's gift, warns the father that if he refuses to give up one of his daughters, the whole city will be destroyed. As a result the girls are given up, one by one, to the eagle. Another interesting feature of this Jewish-Iraqi version of the tale which is missing from the international type is the heart-eating motif (Q478.1 "The Eaten Heart"; Thompson 1957, 238). The claim here is that these two aspects, which appear together in this version, are associated with each other, and that in understanding the act of eating the heart as a concrete expression of the idiomatic expression "eat her heart out," it is possible to understand how the Jewish oikotype, which appears as a conglomerate, was created.

The idiomatic expression "eat her heart out" appears in many languages. Among others, it appears variously in Hebrew, English, and Arabic—the prevalent languages spoken among the Iraqi people and Iraqi Jews. However, in all languages the phrase expresses the same thing: regret and jealousy. As a concrete act, this motif can be found in romantic novels in the father–daughter context or in bride–mother-in-law relationship. These relationships are characterized by jealousy, guilt, and regret, as when an unfaithful wife is unknowingly forced to eat her lover's heart. The way this idiomatic expression functions in the tale to represent feelings of guilt and regret helps us understand the connection between the two parts of the story: The daughters who failed to respect their father in the first part of the tale are forced to eat a heart in the second.

The relationships between concrete and symbolic layers of the conscious mind, and between verbal expressions and somatic symptoms, were studied by Sigmund Freud during the early stages of the development of psychoanalytic theory. In *Studies on Hysteria*, Josef Breuer and Freud described the creation of somatic symptoms as a symbolization of verbal expressions (Breuer and Freud 1955 [1893–95]). In an essay that attempts to trace the development of Freud's ideas, Yoav Yigael relates the case description of Cacilie. Here Freud describes the way in which, during one of her acute attacks of facial neuralgia, Cacilie remembered a period when she had been extremely angry with and bitter toward her husband after he insulted her. Suddenly, while speaking, she put her hand on her cheek and cried out loudly with great pain, saying: "It was like a slap in the face." The somatic pain had become indicative of a specific kind of psychic suffering. This is how the creation of symbolic conversion is explained: by thoughts simultaneously accompanied by both physical pain and a given somatic pain. The latter becomes representative of the former in what Freud calls the "associative reverberation of the psychic life" (Yigael 2001, 179–80). Another example appears when Cacilie tells Freud that, when she was fifteen years old, she was resting in bed under the strict supervision of her grandmother. The sharp pain between her eyes she felt then is explained in analysis as actually being associated with her grandmother's "penetrating" stare, and the thought that her grandmother suspected her of something. In this case the unpleasant feeling of being "under the scrutinizing eye" of someone, with suspicion directed against her, is converted into somatic pain. Yigael mentions that Freud's use of the "symbolic" is different from and almost antithetical to its accepted use, and to his own later employment of the concept. For example, when we relate to a flag as a symbol, the effect is of a high concentration in one object (the extent of which cannot be accurately assessed) of values, standpoints, and emotions. In Freud's later works, the somatic symptom becomes a representative symbol that implies or stands for an abstract idea or repressed conflict. Conversely, while working on *Studies on Hysteria*, and in the context of the affiliation between verbal expression and somatic "expression," Freud saw the symptom as a precise translation of an idiom into a specific sensation (Yigael 2001, 180). Freud even adds that this is not a matter of an overdeveloped imagination; on the contrary, the hysteric relates literally to the linguistic expression. After a number of actual insulting remarks, the feeling of "a stab in the heart" or "a slap in the face" is the reliving of a sensation to which the linguistic expression owes its origin. It appears that Freud is trying to say that these are the simplest and most primitive verbal expressions, which are connected to sensation in a way that has no more freedom than the connection between sanctions and the body's various organs. The hysteric is "right" in preserving the original meaning of words and indicates the outstanding strength of their innervations (Yigael 2001, 180).

As a magical genre the wonder tale—characterized by old, archaic ways of thinking—gives, in the story's Jewish-Iraqi version, a concrete expression of feelings that carry deep meaning. We must remember that, in many cases, the wonder tale's way of describing feelings, emotions, and thoughts is by describing concrete actions. Thus choosing a concrete action to describe feelings of guilt and regret is quite natural in the realm of the wonder tale. The daughters, who failed to respect their father's will, are punished by the eagle and are forced to do something that testifies to their feelings of guilt and regret.

The significance of the eagle in Jewish culture helps explain the affinity between this bird and the character of the father; the eagle, with its qualities of authority and mercy, can feel pity, but it can also punish and execute revenge. The Bible contains numerous descriptions testifying to the bird's mercy, such as: "As an eagle stirreth up her nest, fluttereth over her young, spreadeth abroad her wings, taketh them, beareth them on her wings" (Deuteronomy 32:11). In some cases the eagle appears as an image of God: *"Ye have seen what I did unto the Egyptians, and how I bare you on eagles' wings, and brought you unto myself"* (Exodus 19:4). However, as a big, strong bird, the eagle often appears as an image of the enemies of Israel: *"The Lord shall bring a nation against thee from far, from the end of the earth, as swift as the eagle flieth; a nation whose tongue thou shalt not understand"* (Deuteronomy 28:49). Another example appears in the following prophecy: *"And say, Thus saith the Lord GOD; A great eagle with wings, longwinged, full of feathers, which had divers colors, came unto Lebanon, and took the highest branch of the cedar"* (Ezekiel 17:3).

The eagle, which simultaneously encompasses the qualities of mercy and authority, is a fitting symbol for the character of the father, as reflected in the Jewish-Iraqi version of the tale. As usual in wonder tales, the story reveals nothing about the father's feelings. He expects his daughters to bring him food, and the youngest one is the only one to try to accomplish her mission. His special efforts to bring her the kittens testify to his feelings for her. The fact that he gives his older daughters to the eagle before he gives the youngest one also might reflect his emotional priorities. All his other feelings and emotions, with all the complexity and depth one might expect from a father being betrayed by his own daughters, are revealed in the wonder tale in only a subtle, indirect way, by using the concretization of an idiomatic expression.

The youngest daughter, who acts most faithfully of all the sisters, is not punished. From a psychological point of view, we might find Oedipal mechanisms at play here, since the youngest daughter doesn't stay at the eagle's house but instead comes back home to her beloved father. However, this explanation does not sufficiently elucidate the way this version differs from other versions of tale type AT 311 around the world. The question here is how to understand the special addition of the heart-eating motif, whose origin is not necessarily in the Jewish tradition but whose integration into tale type AT 311 is exclusive to the Jewish-Iraqi version. It seems we must search for the answer in a broader view of the processes of adaptation of international folktales into Jewish culture. Examining these processes reveals that sometimes the major course of adaptation is not necessarily achieved through clear, overt Jewish characteristics but rather through a narrative structure that doesn't have any overt Jewish characteristics; instead, it is merely characteristic of the Jewish versions (Yassif 1992). It is thus possible to understand the passivity of the women in the Jewish versions of tale type AT 425, which unveils the complexity of the status of women in the Jewish family. We must remember that the wonder tale is a genre that deals the most with relationships inside the family, and many of the changes in the Jewish versions reflect cultural and familial values. Within this context it is clear how the heart-eating motif in the Jewish-Iraqi version serves to concretize concepts such as guilt and regret, which are associated with familial relationships and the dictate to respect the father. Thus the wonder tale avoids direct instruction, preferring instead to instruct in a more symbolic, indirect manner. By exposing the meaning of idiomatic expressions hidden in the concrete plot, one can understand the fate of the youngest daughter, who regrets the behavior of her older sisters toward their father.

NOTE

1. This tale is also discussed in my article dealing with realizations of idiomatic expressions; see Raufman 2012.

BIBLIOGRAPHY

Aarne, Antti, and Stith Thompson. 1961. *The Types of the Folktale: A Classification and Bibliography*. FF Communications no. 184. Helsinki: Suomalainen Tiedeakatemia.

Breuer, Josef, and Sigmund Freud. 1955 [1893–95]. *Studies on Hysteria*. S. E. II. London: Hogarth Press.

Raufman, Ravit. 2012. "Realizations of Idiomatic Expressions in Israeli Oral Wonder Tales: A New Interpretative Method." *Fabula* 53 (1/2): 20–45.

Thompson, Stith. 1957. *Motif-Index of Folk-Literature*. Vol. 5. Bloomington: Indiana University Press.

Yassif, Eli. 1992. "Reevaluating the Ways in Which International Folktales Adjusted to the Jewish Folklore of Recent Generations." *Jerusalem Studies in Jewish Folklore* 13–14: 275–302. [Hebrew]

Yigael, Yoav. 2001. "Dual Identification and the 'Weight of Responsibility.'" *Psychoanalysis and Contemporary Thought* 24 (2): 175–202.

THE WISE SHEIKH AND THE MENORAH

IFA 8271

NARRATED BY LEAH GAD (AFGHANISTAN)

Once upon a time there was a very learned Muslim sheikh. He was also very good-hearted. People from all over would come to him to receive cures.

The sheikh would receive the patient, talk to him, and then go into another room and shut himself away. Then he would come out and say: "This patient has a chance to live; give him this or that remedy." Or he would say: "There is no chance, it is not worthwhile to waste efforts on him."

Everything the sheikh said proved to be true.

In the same town lived also a Jewish *hakham*; he was very pious, learned, and good-hearted. His name was famous all over the country. The *hakham* heard of the deeds of the gentile sheikh. He wondered and said to himself, "How is it possible that a gentile would be so successful—would know so many secrets and reveal mysteries?"

The *hakham* wanted to meet the sheikh and talk to him, but he was too shy. He wondered why he, who had been studying the Torah and the laws of Israel in sanctity and purity, still did not know these secrets, while the non-Jew knew more than he and surpassed him in wisdom. The *hakham* sent the head of the community to speak to the sheikh and arrange an interview with him.

The head of the community went to the sheikh and spoke to him; he told him that the *hakham* wanted to meet him and asked to set a time for a meeting.

The sheikh said he had also heard of the Jewish *hakham*, and he wanted very much to meet with him and hear what he had to say. He asked the leader to tell the *hakham* to come and meet him as soon as possible. The leader delivered the message, and the *hakham* went to see him.

The sheikh received him cordially and honored him greatly. They sat and talked about this and that. The sheikh would ask, and the *hakham* would answer. The sheikh wondered at the erudition of the *hakham*. When the conversation ended, the *hakham* rose and wanted to leave; the sheikh said: "I greatly enjoyed your visit. I would like you to come every two or three days so we can converse."

They parted warmly, and the *hakham* went home. Two days later the sheikh realized that the *hakham* had not come to visit, so he sent one of his servants with a horse for the *hakham* to ride. The servant mounted the *hakham* on the horse, and he came to visit the sheikh. The sheikh greeted him and embraced him, and they kissed.

Said the sheikh: "Since we parted I could not rest, my soul has been bound to you."

Again he offered the *hakham* refreshments, and they sat and talked. The sheikh asked, and the *hakham* answered, and both were content. And so things went: Every few days the *hakham* would visit, they would talk as old friends, and both were pleased. During one of the visits, the sheikh asked the *hakham* something, and the *hakham* replied instantly but added another matter of which the sheikh had not known nor heard. Now the *hakham* questioned the sheikh, and the sheikh did not know the answer. The sheikh bowed his head before the *hakham* and said: "Please explain it to me."

The *hakham* said: "I studied this and it cost me a fortune. How can I explain it to you for free?"

The sheikh said: "I will pay whatever you request."

The *hakham* said: "No way do I trade my knowledge for money or even for gold, because I do not lack money or gold, thank God. I would like to ask you to exchange wisdom for wisdom."

The sheikh said: "Is there any wisdom that I have and you don't? You are so full of knowledge."

The *hakham* said to him: "There is one thing. When you pray for the sick, you know if they are going to live or die. If you explain this to me, I will also teach you."

The sheikh said: "This is difficult. I cannot reveal this to anyone, as my father had made me swear not to disclose this to anyone, as had his father before him. This has come down to us as a legacy from the former generations."

The *hakham* said: "I have also been sworn not to teach anyone. But as I am learning something in exchange, it is permitted to do so, and so it is for you."

The sheikh said to him: "I wish it would be permitted. But I fear you will not be able to fulfill what I will tell you, as one has to prepare oneself intensively."

The *hakham* said: "I am ready for anything."

The sheikh said to him: "If so, go home now and prepare yourself. Fast from this evening on for two days; do not eat anything. After you finish fasting be careful not to eat meat or fish, and do not drink wine. Then immerse yourself and put on clean clothes. On the days you fast, you should also immerse yourself in the morning and in the evening, and then you will be ready."

The *hakham* took it upon himself to do everything the sheikh said. He went home, immersed himself, began to fast, and prayed with great devotion. For two days he fasted and did not eat a thing. Morning and evening he would wash himself, put on clean clothes, and pray with great intention.

On the morning of the third day, the *hakham* got up, immersed himself, put on clean clothes, and went to the house of the sheikh while still fasting.

As he entered the sheikh's house, the sheikh rose and said to him: "I can see from your appearance that you have done as I asked."

The *hakham* was feeble and pale; he had not touched any food for three days.

The sheikh was worried for the *hakham*'s health and said to him: "Come, I will show you now."

The sheikh showed him into a room. He opened the door with a key, of which he was the sole owner. As they proceeded into the room, he locked the door behind them so no one could enter. They reached a beautiful garden, in the center of which was a pool filled with clean water. The whole garden was well nourished and bright. There were two chairs by the pool, and on them two sets of clothes. The sheikh said: "We will immerse ourselves here before we enter the holy place."

They immersed themselves, put on the clothing, and strolled around the garden. At the extremity of the garden was a small building made of marble stones; the doors were gilt and painted with wonderful pictures.

The sheikh said to the *hakham*: "Here we are. I will open the door, and we will enter. And you should do precisely as I do."

The sheikh opened the door, and they entered. The *hakham* saw a beautiful, bright room; in front of him was a curtain made of precious material embroidered with golden threads. The sheikh kneeled and bowed seven times. Reluctantly the *hakham* did the same. He regretted doing so, as he thought to himself that there might be some idol there. So he closed his eyes and envisioned the synagogue and the ark. After that the sheikh told him: "Approach the curtain and draw it back; there you shall find what you are seeking. But be extremely cautious."

The *hakham* approached, raised the curtain, and what did he see? A menorah plaque, and above it inscribed: "I have set the Lord always before me"—a plaque that is to be found in all the synagogues of the Jews.

As the *hakham* saw this, he was relieved that he did not bow in vain. He kissed the menorah, stepped back, closed the door, and pulled down the curtain. And they both left.

The *hakham* said to the sheikh: "I have not seen anything unusual except for that which is found in all our synagogues, and you said I would find what I sought and I would learn."

The sheikh said to him: "This is it! The letters you saw written above are the Name of God. When someone asks me to pray for him, I enter and look: If the letters shine and glow, the sick person will heal. If the letters do not shine, he will die."

The *hakham* taught the sheikh what he wanted to learn and returned home.

The *hakham* cried and tormented himself and said: "How is it that the non-Jews venerate our sacred things, and at the same time we disrespect them and do not revere their sanctity?"

Transcribed by Zevulun Kort

Commentary to
"The Wise Sheikh and the Menorah"

IFA 8271

Esther Juhasz

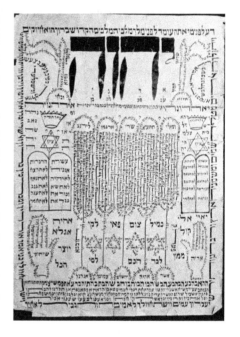

The following discussion will read a folktale through the perspective of the material object that plays a major role in it. The object that stands at the center of the story presented here is the Shiviti-Menorah plaque.

The Shiviti-Menorah is a devotional plaque or image, densely inscribed with biblical verses and texts, that is commonly found in Jewish places of worship and dwellings; it is also frequently seen as a page in the *siddur* (prayer book). Customarily it contains two core components: a depiction of the seven-branched Temple menorah inscribed with the words of Psalm 67, and the verse "I have set the Lord always before me" (Psalm 16:8), with God's name enlarged and emphasized. It is a religious folk image that is intended to invoke piety; it functions as a mnemonic aid and a protective amulet. Traditionally it is referred to either as "Shiviti" or "menorah."[1]

The Shiviti-Menorah plaque and its religious significance are the focal points of the story "The Wise Sheikh and the Menorah," which is told among Sephardi and Oriental Jewish communities. This story revolves around the significance of true faith, which is embodied in this prevalent votive plaque and revealed only through an inter-religious discourse.[2]

The version of the tale I will examine here is that recounted by Zevulun Kort, who heard it first in his childhood in Afghanistan and again in Tel Aviv, as told by his elder sister, Leah Gad, in 1962. I will compare this rendition to other versions.

It seems that all versions of the tale recounted in the last generations are based on the written versions of the story first published in the compilation by Itzhak Farhi, *Matok Midvash*, based on oral accounts, and copied by Rabbi Yosef Shabetay Farhi in his book *Oseh Pele*. The story has various titles: "The Good Sheikh," "The Story of the Ishmaeli *Hakham*," "The Good Sheikh and the Menorah," and "Rabbi Galante of Blessed Memory and the Shcikh." The titles emphasize the exemplary figure of the Muslim sheikh, whose function is to set an example of piety and faith for the Jews and thereby to induce them into repentance. Only in our tale version does the title mention the "menorah," the miraculous intermediary object that bestows on the sheikh supernatural predictive powers regarding the prognosis of sick people.[3]

The story is a moral tale revolving around several themes, including the lack of faith and piety among Jews, as exposed in the inter-religious discourse between Jews and Muslims and between the Jewish rabbi and the Muslim sheikh. There is no overt debate between the two religions, and the moral of the story is an inner criticism of the Jews' lack of faith, which is contrasted powerfully with the pious behavior of the Muslim sheikh.

The story underscores also the status and function of religious objects as manifestations of religious values. The Shiviti-Menorah plaque is a sacred object believed to embody the divine presence; it serves as a mediating object of faith that is also believed to possess magical protective and predictive powers. The story reproves the Jews for failing to see the fundamental truths of their faith that are symbolically embodied in this plaque, particularly those centered around the sacred name of God, which is accentuated visually in the plaque. Looking at the divine name and meditating on it is thought to imbue the believer with the encompassing presence of God, as it is recommended in the verse: "I have set the Lord always before me" (Psalm 16:8).[4] But concurrently this meditative gaze should also be a reflective look at man's deeds, inducing him to mend his ways. Paradoxically, in our story the only person who can trigger this reflectivity is an outsider, the sheikh, who belongs to another religion but recognizes the force of the Jewish faith more than the Jews do themselves.[5]

I will start with an analysis of the material evidence regarding the object that stands as the central symbol in this story: its form, structure, description, location, and function.

The descriptions in several tales vary:

IFA 8271: "A menorah plaque, and on it is inscribed, 'I have set the Lord always in before me . . . [as] in all the synagogues of the Jews.'"

IFA 4283: A shining copper *tasa* (plaque) is inscribed in relief with the words, "I have set the Lord always before me."

IFA 8818: As they open "the last door and [go] through it," they see a large *parokhet* (torah ark curtain), and on it large letters, and above them *menorot* (lamps), and above them a Hebrew inscription: "I have set the Lord always before me."

Matok Midvash and *Oseh Pele*: "[And] he saw inside the *heikhal* [Sephardi: the Torah ark in the synagogue] a beautiful, wonderful plaque inscribed with the form of the menorah in a marvelous painting, and written above it, 'I have set the Lord always in before me,' and the letters of the Name of the Lord, *Shem HaVaya*, are very large."

In one version the material mentioned is copper, and the plaque is called *tasa*, which is one of terms Sephardi Jews use for the Torah breastplate. In another it is a textile *parokhet*—the curtain hung in front of the ark. Other versions do not mention either the material or how the inscriptions are made. All versions, except one, cite the Shiviti verse, which is inscribed on the plaque, and the presence of the menorah on the tablet. When the texts refer to the presence of a menorah or *menorot*, they do not specify whether it is the seven-branched Temple lamp, but the *Oseh Pele* version says that the form of the menorah is inscribed and not painted or sketched. This alludes to the menorah form inscribed with the words of Psalm 67, as is typical of Shiviti-Menorah plaques. The story attests also to the already established identification between the two core elements that comprise the Shiviti-Menorah plaque, the juxtaposition of which is actually its essence. These two core components, which display no overt connections between them, were combined in late seventeenth and early eighteenth centuries into one plaque, and have become inseparable, interchangeable, and identified with one another.[6] The typical structure of the Shiviti-Menorah plaques in which the Shiviti verse is set above the menorah is repeatedly described, as well as the common practice of enlarging the letters of the Name of God in the Shiviti verse to become a central focus of the plaque.

Thus it is quite evident that all versions refer to the typical Shiviti-Menorah plaque as "in all the synagogues of the Jews," a religious image with which the Sephardi Jews are well acquainted. The material details that emerge in the various versions of the story are a testimony to the ubiquitous presence of the Shiviti-Menorah plaque. This acquaintance with the Shiviti-Menorah as a customary synagogue object—known to the narrators as well as to their audience—is an important component of the rabbi's reaction when he sees the plaque unveiled before him at the climax of the story: He notes that he has not seen anything new or unknown to him.

In the story the Shiviti-Menorah emerges as a customary object, with a widely accepted presence, which exemplifies and symbolically signifies true faith and piety. Nevertheless it should be noted that, although the Shiviti-Menorah touches on key issues at the very heart of Jewish belief, it is not an object prescribed by religious precepts. It is a noncanonical object designed not to fulfill a commandment but as an aid to devotion. It is the product of folk religion—a creation that expresses religious devotion. It embodies a religious recommendation to be followed by the believers and the devout in fulfilling the commandments.

The positioning of the Shiviti-Menorah in our story—within the *heikhal* hidden behind doors and veils—is both unusual and significant. It diverges from the prevailing custom in Sephardi and Oriental synagogues, where numerous Shiviti-Menorahs are usually hung on all the walls of the synagogues, sometimes flanking the *heikhal* or above it, or on the *bimah*.[7]

IFA 8271: "At the extremity of the garden was a small building made of marble stones; the doors were gilt and painted with wonderful pictures. . . . [Inside] the *hakham* saw a beautiful, bright room; in front of him was a curtain made of precious material embroidered with golden threads. . . . The *hakham* approached, [and] raised the curtain."

IFA 4283: In the fourth room are a *heikhal* and a *parokhet*.

Matok Midvash and *Oseh Pele*: One building is beautifully constructed, its doors made of pure silver, beautifully painted with various paintings the likes of which cannot be found even in the palaces of kings. "And he opened the door, and he saw a marvelous building, and opposite the entrance a small *heikhal*, on top of which a *parokhet* wonderfully embroidered with precious stones and gemstones. . . . The doors of the *heikhal* are gold and gemstones . . . [and] inside the *heikhal* is a plaque."

As mentioned earlier, *heikhal* is the term used by Sephardi and Oriental Jews for the Torah ark in the synagogue. But the word also means "temple," and the use of this term along with the descriptions of the sumptuous ark might allude also to the Temple.

The Shiviti-Menorah in this story is situated inside the Torah ark, in the actual place of the Torah scroll, which is the most sacred and significant ritual object in the synagogue. Thus this devotional object—which does not have a prescribed place in the synagogue nor a defined function in the ritual—replaces the Torah scroll. It is thus raised to a central place physically and spiritually by virtue of its location. The elevated status allocated to the Shiviti-Menorah is also evident through the extreme reverence the sheikh shows toward it, similar to that expressed toward the Torah scroll. The remote location of the ark in which the Shiviti-Menorah is hidden and the numerous dividing and protective doors, screens, veils, and wrappings that shield it, are similar to those shielding the Torah scroll. In addition the purification and ablutions required to see it unveiled resemble the purification required of a Torah scribe (*sofer stam*) when he is preparing to write the Torah scroll and especially the sacred, ineffable Name.

This positioning of the Shiviti-Menorah as an equivalent to the Torah scroll, and the reverence shown toward it, signal an emanation of the sacredness of the Torah scroll onto the Shiviti-Menorah. This equivalence seems to indicate also that the Shiviti-Menorah is conceived as representing the Divine presence in a manner somewhat similar to the way the Torah scroll does so. The reverence for the plaque that bears the Name of God, graphically highlighted, is comparable to the veneration of the Torah scroll, which contains the sacred names of God both materially and symbolically. According to some traditional mystic interpretations, the entire text of the Torah is believed to be composed of the Holy Names of God through various combinations of letters, or even: "The entire Torah is like an explication of and a commentary on the [Ineffable] Name of God."[8] In the Shiviti-Menorah the divine presence is represented by the ineffable Name of God the Tetragrammaton contained in the Shiviti verse. The Shiviti verse calls the believer to be constantly aware of the divine presence and to attempt to visualize it.

Functionally, in this story, the divine presence revealed in the Shiviti-Menorah represents the bearer of divine knowledge who knows the fates of men. This knowledge and protective power can be transmitted, through the intermediary of the Shiviti-Menorah, to humans, but not to all of them—only the few worthy of it. Those worthy of receiving the knowledge and power are those who respect and venerate it and perform all the required preparations—in this case the Muslim sheikh. The sheikh serves as an intermediary who passes on information regarding the prognosis of ill people.

The presence of light is understood to be a good omen of life. This way of revealing fates by means of flickering lights is known from the *Urim Vetumim* on the breastplate (*hoshen*) of the high priest,[9] but it alludes also to the magical power attributed to the light of the menorah in the Shiviti-Menorah. These powers of the menorah are summarized in an abbreviated formula written on some Shiviti-Menorah plaques: "Whoever looks at the menorah [and] daily reflects upon it, it is accounted as though he himself had lit the menorah, and he is assured a place in the world to come. Whoever recites Psalm 67 from a text whose words are set out in the form of a menorah, no evil shall befall him, and he shall succeed in his endeavors"[10] This means that the power of the menorah is put into effect for a person through symbolic devotional actions the individual performs, and thus he is protected in this world and will be redeemed.

In the story the power of the menorah is not protective, but it is revelatory; it serves as a means to commune with supernal worlds that are open only to the initiated. The sheikh, after a process of purification, is let into the sacred. He prays with intention (*kavanah*), proper devotion, and bows, and only then is he considered worthy of receiving the hidden knowledge passed through the flickering lights. In this story, extraordinarily, the worthy person is a non-Jew, the Muslim sheikh.

That it is a non-Jew who venerates the Holy Name more than the Jews—and who performs acts of profound devotion that make him worthy of receiving the hidden knowledge—is the focal point of this story. This means that the Jews need an external mentor to guide them in their own religious framework.

The story reproves the Jews for disrespecting the Name of God when they mention it in vain or in false oaths. There might be also an implied criticism of the Jews' disrespect toward an object bearing the Holy Name. When people see the Shiviti-Menorah in the synagogues, they are so accustomed to it that they do not pay attention to its presence. As a consequence they do not properly respect its sacredness, and they need an external indicator to do so, to remind them about how to relate to God and his name. The Jews, and even the wise devout rabbi, did not acknowledge the sacredness and the force embodied in the Shiviti-Menorah until they saw its power manifested only to those who treated it with utmost respect and veneration.

In IFA 8818 the rabbi says:

If an Arab non-Jew can believe and be helped by these words, "I have set the Lord always before me," how could we—the Jews who have this verse in all our synagogues—how is it that we do not bow a great bow as we enter the synagogue? Before every entrance we should make two ablutions, and we should fast. We should purify ourselves in order to be worthy of entering this holy place. If an Arab can believe in this verse and benefit from the power of this holy verse, we Jews all the more so.

Apart from the moral of the story, there seems to be implied in it the belief in the "power of images"[11] to empower people in their faith and "enlighten" them. These images are also believed to transform people through their "right" gaze. The Jews see these Shiviti-Menorahs around them all the time, but do not actually see them anymore. They fail to look at the images as one should. But after a person from outside the community has freshened their eyes and spirit to look at this image as if one has been prepared to witness the divine presence, their vision can be transformed, and they can be restored to the right path.

NOTES

1. This plaque's creators and users refer to it either as "shiviti" (mainly among Ashkenazim) or "menorah" (among Sephardim and Oriental Jews). For methodological reasons I refer to it according to its two core components: "Shiviti–Menorah."
2. The present discussion is based in part on my PhD dissertation, "The 'Shiviti-Menorah': A Representation of the Sacred—Between Spirit and Matter" (Hebrew University of Jerusalem, 2004). For a reference to this story, see pp. 332–34.
3. I am indebted to Prof. Dov Noy for introducing me to this story and to Edna Hechal, emeritus scientific coordinator of IFA, for providing me with the versions of this story. On the different versions of the story, see Farber-Ginat and Noy 1970, 89–90. The first printed version: Itzhak Farhi, *Matok Midvash* (Jerusalem, 1842); the second: Yosef Shabetay Farhi, *Oseh Pele* (Livorno, 1869). On the contribution of *Oseh Pele* to Jewish folk literature, see Yassif 1982. Other versions in IFA include: IFA 8818, narrated by Itzhak Bitton (Israel, Sephardi) and transcribed by Tamar Alexander, 1972; IFA 4283, narrated by Rabbi Hanun (Jerusalem) and transcribed by Reuven Nana, 1962. A reference to this story also appears, facing the Menorah page, in the prayerbook *Siddur Sefer Beit El* (Livorno, 1878).
4. Another translation of the verse is, "I am ever mindful of the Lord's presence."
5. This moral, which seeks to return young Jews to faith and religion, is a principal objective of the *Oseh Pele* compilation (see Yassif 1982, note 2).
6. On the implicit connections between the menorah inscribed in the words of Psalm 67 and the Shiviti verse, see Juhasz 2004, chapter 3.
7. In Ashkenazi synagogues there is usually one Shiviti plaque on the lectern in front of the *hazan*.
8. Joseph Gikatilla, *Sha'arei Orah*, quoted in Scholem 1974, 171. On this Kabbalistic concept, see ibid., 170–71.
9. The flickering light of the *hoshen* served to discover sinners (Tanhuma, Genesis, Vayeshev, Achan's Sin). See Bialik and Ravnitzky 1952, 80.
10. *Beit Oved, Prayerbook for the Days of the Week According to the Sephardi Rite* (Livorno, 1948). For the English translation, see Juhasz 1999, 150.
11. This phrase is the title of David Freedberg's (1989) pioneering book on the subject.

BIBLIOGRAPHY

Bialik, Haim Nahman, and Y. H. Ravnitzky, eds. 1952. *The Book of Legends*. Tel Aviv: Dvir. [Hebrew]

Farber Ginat, Asi, and Dov Noy. 1971. *A Tale for Each Month 1970*, 89–90. Haifa: Haifa Municipality. [Hebrew]

Farhi, Itzhak. 1842. *Matok Midvash*. Jerusalem. [Hebrew]

Farhi, Yosef Shabetay. 1869. *Oseh Pele*. Livorno. [Hebrew]

Freedberg, David. 1989. *The Power of Images: Studies in the History and Theory of Response*. Chicago: University of Chicago Press.

Juhasz, Esther. 1999. "The Amuletic Menorah." In *In the Light of the Menorah: Story of a Symbol*, ed. Yael Israeli, trans. David Louvish, 147–51. Jerusalem: Israel Museum.

———. 2004. "The 'Shiviti-Menorah': A Representation of the Sacred—Between Spirit and Matter." PhD diss. Jerusalem: Hebrew University. [Hebrew]

Scholem, Gershom. 1974. "The Torah as the Mystical Name of God." In *Kabbalah*, 170–71. New York: Meridian.

Sefer Beit El. 1878. Livorno: Avraham Hamoy.

Yassif, Eli. 1982. "The Influence of 'Oseh Pele' on Jewish Folk Literature." *Jerusalem Studies in Jewish Folklore* 3: 47–66. [Hebrew]

THE RICH MISER

IFA 9400

NARRATED BY AVRAHAM BARAZANI (IRAQ)

There has never been a miser like Kassem El Tandoori, and there will never be such stinginess as his. To this day the people of Iraq, young and old, call extraordinary misers "Kassem." Here is the story the people of Iraq tell about him.

Once, in honor of his son's wedding, and at the family's request, he bought a new pair of shoes, but soon the soles were torn due to his excessive walking. Kassem asked the shoemaker to fix the soles by adding extra soles to the original ones with the help of some nails. But soon enough he needed to repair his shoes once again, and the shoemaker added more soles on top of the others, and also glued some leather pieces to the heels. Of course, the shoes became very heavy. His family's requests to replace them with a new pair were rejected, despite the words of scorn and derision that came to his ear about the shape of his shoes and his stinginess. Then, one Friday, Kassem went to the bathhouse. He sat on the bench at the entrance, took off his clothes, put his shoes under the bench, and went to bathe. Five minutes later the district governor, holding in his hands new shoes, also came to the bathhouse, and he put his clothes and shoes next to Kassem's clothes.

Kassem finished bathing before the governor. Next to his seat and clothes, he found new shoes. He was sure that his son had found the opportunity to get rid of his old shoes and replace them with new shoes. Kassem wore them and went about his business. Five minutes passed, and the governor came out of the water. He looked for his new shoes, but they had disappeared. The shoes were stolen, and no one saw the thief. Suddenly they saw Kassem's shoes under the bench. No doubt the rich miser Kassem is also a thief! Kassem was asked to appear before the judge, who accused him of stealing the governor's shoes. The proof was Kassem's worn shoes, which were returned to him. Kassem's claims were denied by the judge, and he was fined a large sum for the offense. He had no choice but to pay the fine. Then he took his old shoes and headed to the Tigris River. He threw his shoes into the river and thought he got rid of them.

A short time later a few fishermen came to the river. They cast their net into the river, and as they lifted it, the net was very heavy. The fishermen thought there was a shark or a whale in the net. To their surprise, they found Kassem's old shoes instead.

They recognized Kassem's shoes right away, and thought that they were stolen from him. So they decided to return them immediately. When they arrived at Kassem's house, they found the door locked and the window open. So they threw the shoes through the window. Kassem had stored wine bottles on shelves in front of the window, to sell them in the future at a higher price. Unfortunately for him, the bottles of wine broke. Kassem came home, and the large amount of wine that he had bought and hoped to sell on the black market was floating on the floor. Why? Because of his shoes!

Kassem decided to bury the shoes in a hidden place to get rid of them. At night he took his spade and started digging a hole in the wall of a house. The guards saw him and thought he was a thief making his way into the house, so they dragged him to court, and he was fined a large sum of money.

This time he decided to bury them in the road. He dug a hole in the road and put the shoes inside. It turned out that this place was a sewage extension, and the shoes interrupted the flow of sewage. The local residents had no choice but to dig up the sewage line to find out what happened. In doing so, they reached the place where Kassem had buried his shoes. Immediately they recognized them, because who does not know Kassem's shoes?!

Again Kassem was led to court, where he was accused of causing trouble for the people of the neighborhood. His arguments did not help him, and he was fined. Now he decided to wear his shoes again as before. He washed them and put them on the roof to dry. A cat passed on the roof, put one of the shoes in its mouth, and jumped to the parallel roof edge. As the cat jumped, the shoe, due to its weight, fell out her mouth and directly onto the head of a boy who was passing by.

Because of the heavy weight of the shoe, the child died from the blow on the spot. Of course, Kassem was tried for causing the child's death as well as for his irresponsible behavior. This time Kassem was fined an amount bigger than ever. He turned to the judge and said: "Your Honor, please save me from my shoes and the trouble they caused me. I am ready to pay any amount that you ask for this favor." He told the judge about all the events that had happened to him and the huge amounts of money he had paid. The judge laughed, turned to the people, and said to them:

"This is what happens to misers! Stinginess does not pay!"

Transcribed by Mukhtar Ezra

COMMENTARY TO "THE RICH MISER"

IFA 9400

RACHEL BEN-CNAAN

Our story belongs to the tale type AT 745 ("Hatch-penny," motif N 211.2— "Unavailing Attempt to Get Rid of Slippers" [Thompson 1957, 88]). The story was told by Avraham Barazani, who was born in Baghdad, Iraq, in 1900. In his youth Barazani's friends called him "Dawlish," as, despite his blindness in one eye and a defect in his second eye, he used to hang around Arab villages. Barazani immigrated to Israel in 1950 and lived with his wife in an institution for the blind in Pardes Hanna. He loved to tell folktales, some of which he had heard from wise elderly people in a yeshiva when he was already middle-aged. He used to tell many stories about himself and his own heroic events. He said that, since his youth, he had learned from the Arab villagers how to contact demons, who

helped him return the love of husbands to their wives, or to separate a man from the mistress for whom he'd left home.

Our study aims to examine the present story in light of the rhetorical approach to literature, which explores the speech act and the social context within which it occurs. Rhetoric as a research tool allows the researcher of folk literature to view simultaneously the aesthetic value and the social context of the tale, as well as their complex interactions.

To fully understand the nature of these interactions, we need to trace the rhetorical strategies of our story (Briggs 1988; Abrahams 1967, 146, 11–12). Like any work of art, the folktale has a lasting impact beyond the time spent reading it or listening to it. The persistence of the lasting effect is the result of a sophisticated and controlled winding together of the narrative dimension of the tale with its argumentative layers. It should be pointed out that the aesthetic composition of the narrative organizes the logical arguments through the presentation of serial events of the story in a sequence (Ricoeur 1977, 113). The argument, unlike the narrative, is a series of claims or reasons for actions within the text, and its ultimate goal is to persuade the reader/listener of the just claim by a logical process. The argument must be acceptable both to the storyteller and his recipients (readers/listeners), for the sake of an effective persuasion (Perelman 1982; Worthington 1996, 7). The ongoing relationships between the narrative and the argument exist, as the plot consists of various argumentative expressions (Ricoeur 1977, 113). The narrative is perceived as a discourse activity expressed only in the events recounted. However, since the narrative discourse is inherently dialogic, it may also contain discursive elements such as arguments; therefore the two modes, narrative and argument, coexist side by side, or are woven into one another. Unlike the narrative that presents a sequence of events, the logical argument is a fragment that bears the components of significance and meaning of the text (Andrews 1989, 3). The fusion between the narrative elements of the story and the argumentative components brings the story to its successful completion. Furthermore, these two modes direct the reader to take a positive or negative stance toward the events and the characters of the story.

We will now locate the narrative elements and the argumentative claims in our story. The plot describes a series of amusing episodes that occur one after the other to the rich and stingy merchant named Kassem.

Kassem's repeated attempts to get rid of his old and worn-out shoes are in vain. His shoes keep coming back to him again and again.[1]

The narrative dimension of the plot is logically presented in chronological order—each event follows the previous one: Kassem buys a pair of shoes on the occasion of his son's wedding; the shoes wear out quickly due to his extensive use of them; Kassem visits the bathhouse; he accidentally takes the provincial governor's shoes in the bathhouse. From that moment on the shoes "returned to him" time after time, and each time Kassem paid a fortune for the damages they caused to others.

The storyteller, in parallel to the ongoing narrative, anchors clues consisting of logical and emotional arguments by which he directs his listeners toward a moral idea inherent in both the story itself and the world of reality outside the story. From the narrative sequence alone, one can mistakenly assume that Kassem's shoes conspire against him and that they are his true rivals. The narrator does not describe Kassem's character in a way that enables us to identify with him. On the contrary: He displays a ridiculous caricature of a greedy black-market merchant, and his endless stinginess creates great public nuisances.

These disasters constantly escalate, until a child dies due to Kassem's shoes. Although at the end of each event Kassem is punished heavily, the story does not produce a sense of empathy for him. Quite the opposite: A tone of condemnation is built up by the narrator, reproving Kassem's character traits and at the same time implicitly warning the listeners not to act like him.

The rhetorical pre-opening of the narrative is designed to arouse the attention of the listeners. Both the orator and the folk storyteller draw their moral causes from the broad social context of their words. They use rhetorical devices to convince their audience that the message to which they aspire through their story is morally right and just. One of the basic principles of rhetoric is the presentation of the most important issue of the speech first. The orator, or in our case the storyteller, will present what matters to him repeatedly to make sure that his listeners remember it well. Here's how the storyteller presents our protagonist at the beginning of the story: "There has never been a miser like Kassem El Tandoori, and there will never be such stinginess as his. To this day the people of Iraq, young and old, call extraordinary misers 'Kassem.'" "To this day" connects the textual components of the tale with its contextual components, as it links the fictitious time of the story to the current and realistic time of the storytelling event. The rhetorical link between the fictitious time and the real time allows us to conclude that to this day Kassem El Tandoori is used as a metaphor for Iraqi misers, and to this day negative character traits such as meanness should be denounced.

The end of our tale emphasizes the stinginess and its condemnation, based on symmetrical principles of crime and punishment. The refusal to purchase new shoes, the attempts to eliminate them, and the financial cost of these attempts are presented through reward and punishment measures, as viewed by the society, by way of equivalent retaliation. From the perspective of rhetoric, the storyteller provides the narrative with persuasive argumentation so that his audience can understand the moral nature of his characters. Accordingly the tale activates emotional and moral behavior, which was the narrator's aim in the first place. The narrator relies on the power of his story but also on the moral worldviews of his audience. Thus a balance between the tale's content and the audience beliefs is created, since the norms and values they believe in are reconfirmed by the story.

The conflict in our story occurs not between two opponents but rather between two opposing worldviews. The narrator provides his listeners with logical contrasting systems, leading them to hold an unequivocal position against the protagonist of the story. One is the worldview of "our" hero, who sees no harm in his stinginess and therefore disregards his personal responsibility for his misfortunes. The opposed worldview is that of the reader/listener, who examines Kassem's behavior through the plot, which disguises its didactic intentions in a humorous and comic way, as well as by comparing the worldview of the protagonist to the norms of proper conduct in the real world. To highlight his arguments, the narrator repeatedly focuses on Kassem's greed and his absurd attempts to get rid of his shoes.[2] In the terminology of rhetoric, repetition guides the audience (though not directly) to accept the speaker's ideas (Spiegel, 1994). Our story repeatedly emphasizes and intensifies the use of cheapness and avarice, wealth and poverty, and absurd action against reasonable action, creating an ideological contrasting effect between appropriate standards of behavior and unacceptable ones.

Let us see the rhetorical arguments inherent in the text itself and the arguments outside the text, which are rooted in the moral worldview of the audience. For example, the notion that rich people are always stingy and greedy is common in folk beliefs. It functions in our story as an emotional argument meant to stir the audience's negative feelings toward Kassem, who is unable to make proper use of his wealth because of his extreme stinginess. Even his closest relatives do not feel any sympathy for him and condemn his stinginess, calling him to stop acting so.

Similarly, the stylistic elements of the story create an interpretive framework to the storytelling event. The storyteller's verbal dictionary itself is a rhetorical strategy designed to make the audience understand the story and its lesson. For example, the emphasis on heavy shoes, with their ugly and patched soles, is intended to express through humor and rhetorical exaggeration Kassem's stinginess:

> but soon the soles were torn due to his excessive walking. Kassem asked the shoemaker to fix the soles by adding extra soles to the original ones with the help of some nails. But soon enough he needed to repair his shoes once again, and the shoemaker added more soles on top of the others, and also glued some leather pieces to the heels. Of course, the shoes became very heavy . . .
> . . . A short time later a few fishermen came to the river. They cast their net into the river, and as they lifted it, the net was very heavy. The fishermen thought there was a shark or a whale in the net. To their surprise, they found Kassem's old shoes instead.
> They recognized Kassem's shoes right away . . .

The rhetorical repetitions of Kassem's worn shoes and his refusal to buy himself a new pair of shoes, clarify both the plot line of the story and the logical arguments that are embedded in it. The reason for the hardships that befell our hero is not mentioned explicitly. It is learned from the logical inference resulting from the interactions between the sequence of events (narrative) and the reasons that caused them (argumentation).

Our narrator shows cause and effect only within the superficial relationships existing between Kassem's stinginess and his refusal to buy new shoes. But the repeated description of his big shoes, which look like sharks or whales, together with the detailed repetition of the failure to get rid of them at the end of each episode, function as a logical argument suggesting the real circumstances that led to Kassem's loss of assets. The rhetorical power of the persuasive argument emerges from the correlation between words and events, as if they "really" occurred. This mimetic power gives both the text and the listeners a sense of truth, as if the tale were a true chronology of events that actually took place.

The central leading argument in our story will be logically examined in the following way:

A. Impossible—Kassem walked barefooted because he had no shoes. Obviously this isn't the reason.
B. Possible—The shoes impoverished Kassem. Could be, but not necessarily the main reason presented in our story.
C. Probable—Kassem went barefooted because he wanted to get rid of his shoes. This might be the reason.
D. Certain—Kassem's stinginess made him lose his shoes. This is the conclusive reason.

As soon as we successfully locate the conclusive reason for Kassem's attempts to get rid of his shoes, we avoid the ambiguity in understanding the moral of the story. The logical argument explains the reasons for the hero's action in the text. Hence the set of arguments functions as a trust-building technique for the probability of the story and its logic (Ben-Cnaan, 2004; Frowe, 1989). Not just the narrative but also the logical argument direct the listener to the conclusion that Kassem's extreme meanness led him to disaster.

The logical inference operates beyond the text itself. The reader/listener draws coordinates connecting the fictitious events of the story to the normative system of his or her true life. This is an interpretive process dependent on both the text and the context. It is an intellectual and mental effort of contextualization, which is a technique of interpretation arising from a broad cultural context, much deeper than the narrow and immediate context of the storytelling event (Briggs 1988, 15).

While the narrative flows smoothly, the argumentative information it carries within it is deliberate and manipulative, since it guides the reader to draw conclusions precisely desired by the storyteller—conclusions that go beyond understanding the narrative at its face value. It should be mentioned here that the argument's goal in the plot is identical to its purposes in the real world. The storyteller shows this by presenting a series of logical reasons explaining Kassem's bad luck in the story, but at the same time he compares the story's logic to the pattern of thinking that is part of the accepted norms in the real world.

The storyteller's control over the narrative and at the same time its social context largely depends on his rhetorical skills and his ability to present his ethos as one that suits his listeners' ethos. Like the public speaker, the storyteller achieves control by weaving logical and emotional arguments into the conventional and traditional structure of the folktale. The storyteller ratifies his ethos by using manipulative strategies that have an impact on the listener's reactions to Kassem's conduct. He puts himself in line with the audience, adopting a negative stance toward our hero, focusing on his shoes, which are the symbols of his stinginess. To convince the audience that he is right in his lack of sympathy toward the hero of the story, he adds to the group of critics of Kassem's behavior his closest family: "His family's requests to replace them with a new pair were rejected, despite the words of scorn and derision that came to his ear about the shape of his shoes and his stinginess." Consequently a moral balance is achieved between the narrator's ethos and the listener's ethos.

The folktale, as an artistic act, is designed to entertain the audience. However it is also supposed to affect the audience in some way outside the world of the text. As we have already pointed out, the narrator strives to have his listeners identify with the messages of his story. Thus he makes use of conventional structures and traditional formulas of the folktale, as well as the persuasive techniques of rhetoric. Rhetoric, like folklore, supports society norms and values, to help maintain the continuity of existing social institutions (Graves and Patai 1967; Spiegel 1994; Zoran 2002). Once the listeners identify with the text and believe that the storyteller's ethos is genuine, they tend to grant him their empathy and sympathy, since the existing social conflict in reality comes to life in the fictitious story told to them. In his imaginary creation the narrator gives a name and address to the real problems of his affinity group, and consequently provides the abstract and ideological symbols with traditional forms familiar and understandable.

Kassem's experiences enhance the condemnation directed toward him, since he does not become wiser from the hardships that have befallen him. Accordingly, he does not learn a lesson from the warnings and the repeated punishments: "He turned to the judge and said: 'Your Honor, please save me from my shoes and the trouble they caused me. I am ready to pay any amount that you ask for this favor.'" His stubbornness and stupidity make him think that there is nothing wrong with his behavior. To the end of the story, he believes that the shoes are the source of all his problems. This is how the storyteller concludes his story: "The judge laughed, turned to the people, and said to them: 'This is what happens to misers! Stinginess does not pay!'" The judge's statement functions as a moral lesson, without which the persuasive argument is not fully effective. Laughter is a cathartic release of excessive emotions. Without it, the process of persuasion is not fully materialized. The judge's laughter represents everyone's laughter, gloating at Kassem's misfortunes (Kress 1989, 9–22).

The statement "Stinginess does not pay" unites the narrative with its accompanying logical arguments. It allows the reader/listener to experience a sense of identification with the judge. For the listener/reader, the judge's dignified authority, along with his moral position, is the same as the narrator's, who chooses to end his story with the judge's remarks to emphasize his own moral position and view.

It is obvious that the rhetorical elements of the tale construct the inner logic of the story and its credibility. The lack of sympathy and empathy toward the protagonist of the story, which was formed by the speech act of the narrator, leads and directs the reader/listener to reaffirm the values of his society, values that resonate throughout the story. The argumentative elements of the text clarify the hero's motives, marking and identifying these motives as moral defects worthy of condemnation and severe punishment. As soon as the narrator's negative and hostile attitude toward Kassem becomes clear to the reader/listener, the moral worldview of both the story and the narrator is revealed. This leads to the audience's approval of the arguments inherent in the story and, consequently, to identification with its moral lesson.

Notes

1. See Shenhar and Bar-Itzhak on the story "The Devil Will Separate between Moshe and the Shoe," about the humorous effect resulting from gloating at Moshe's misfortune. As mentioned by Shenhar & Bar-Itzhak (1981, 61–62) his unsuccessful attempts to get rid of his shoe, his anger at the shoe and its exaggerated number of repairs, provide a comic and amusing frame to the story.
2. In our story Kassem's punishment is the result of his greed and stinginess, as well as his inability to enjoy his wealth. In contrast, in the tale referenced in note 1, Shenhar and Bar-Itzhak emphasize the protagonist's tenacious and childish behavior, along with his mechanistic actions, as reasons for his punishment (Shenhar and Bar-Itzhak 1981, 61).

BIBLIOGRAPHY

Aarne, Antti, and Stith Thompson. 1961. *The Types of the Folktale: A Classification and Bibliography*. FF Communications no. 184. Helsinki: Suomalainen Tiedeakatemia.

Abrahams, Roger D. 1967. "Introductory Remarks to a Theory of Folklore." *Journal of American Folklore* 81: 143–58.

Andrews, Richard, ed. 1989. *Narrative and Argument*. Milton Keynes: Open University Press.

Ben-Cnaan, Rachel. 2004. "The Rhetoric of Folktale as a Means to Enhance Children's Reading." PhD diss. Haifa: University of Haifa. [Hebrew]

Briggs, Charles. 1988. *Competence in Performance: The Creativity of Tradition in Mexicano Verbal Art*. Philadelphia: University of Pennsylvania Press.

Frowe, Ian. 1989. "Arguing." In *Narrative and Argument*, ed. Richard Andrews, 55–64. Milton Keynes: Open University Press.

Graves, Robert, and Raphael Patai. 1967. *Hebrew Myths: The Book of Genesis*. Ramat-Gan: Masadah. [Hebrew]

Kress, Gunter. 1989. "Texture and Meaning." In *Narrative and Argument*, ed. Richard Andrews, 9–22. Milton Keynes: Open University Press.

Perelman, Chaim. 1982. *The Realm of Rhetoric*. Notre Dame, IN: University of Notre Dame Press.

Ricoeur, Paul. 1977. "Between Rhetoric and Poetics." In *The Rule of Metaphor: Multidisciplinary Studies of Creation of Meaning in Language*. Toronto: University of Toronto Press.

Shenhar, Aliza, and Haya Bar-Itzhak. 1981. *Folk Narratives from Beit She'an*. Haifa: University of Haifa. [Hebrew]

Spiegel, Nathan. 1994. *The Art of Persuasion: The Speaker and His Audience*. Jerusalem: Magnes Press. [Hebrew]

Thompson, Stith. 1957. *Motif-Index of Folk-Literature*. Vol. 5. Bloomington: Indiana University Press.

Worthington, Ian. 1996. *Persuasion: Greek Rhetoric in Action*. London: Routledge.

Zoran, Gabriel. 2002. *Aristotle/Rhetoric*. Bene Berak: Sifriyat Po'alim. [Hebrew]

SERAH BAT ASHER

IFA 9524

NARRATED BY ELIYAHU MODGORASHWILI (GEORGIA)

The king of the nations, when he wanted to ridicule the Jews, used to issue decrees that would shame them. That day he issued three decrees:

1. That they shall put on funny hats on their heads so that they will be mocked.
2. That they shall wear funny clothes so that they will be laughed at.
3. That they shall wear funny shoes, one red, one black.

He issued these decrees, and the Jews were ashamed to go out.

Once the king went out into the forest, saw a deer, and chased after it, because they (the gentiles) desired game.

The deer was running away, and he chased it, but to no avail. Afterward the deer stopped on one spot. It turned and looked at the king's face, went toward him quickly, and jumped on his head. When it jumped on the king's head, his troops saw it. The king lifted his hands but did not catch it.

The king felt ashamed in front of his troops. He had almost had the deer in his hands. Then the king chased the deer with his horses for a few kilometers, but his troops didn't see the king because he was far away from them.

Afterward the deer ran into a cave that was situated between the rocks, and the king followed it. The cave had a door, and it shut behind him. Inside there was another door. When the deer entered, the door opened, but when the king chased after it, the door didn't open for him, and he was left under lock and key in the dark. Two days passed, and the king was still left in the dark. His soldiers began searching for him. Their search didn't help in anyway, and they didn't find him. After two days the king suddenly saw a beautiful young woman—a female soldier—coming out of the dark with her troops. The darkness lit, and he suddenly saw her and her troops. The female soldier called out to the king to approach her. She said to him: "Do you know me?"

The king said: "No, I don't know you."

She said to him: "I am the deer you were chasing, after I jumped on your head and you didn't catch me." "Now," she said to him: "Why did you impose such a decree on the Jews?"

Afterward the king asked her: "Who are you?"

She answered him: "I am Serah, the daughter of Asher. My uncles went to Egypt, and Joseph, my uncle, introduced himself to his brothers. After a few days, when they got acquainted with each other, they returned home [lit. to the country, i.e. the Land of Canaan]. My uncles called me, and they said to me: 'Play your harp because Joseph the Righteous is alive.' And I took my harp and started to play, and I sang a song: 'My father, my father, Joseph is still alive, and he rules the entire land of Egypt.' Afterward my father [Asher] told me that when I started playing that Joseph was still alive, the *Shekhinah*, the divine presence, rested upon me, and he knew that Joseph was alive. And then he blessed me: 'May you be granted life in the Garden of Eden.' Angels took me, alive, and put me in the Garden of Eden, and I did not taste death."

And afterward the king said to Serah that he would cancel the decrees against the Jews. He promised her that, and she released him from the cave, from the darkness, and he kept his promise and canceled the decrees.

When the king returned home, he invited all the Jews. It was on the Shabbat evening, and he invited all the Jews to him and said to them: "You will keep the Shabbat as you have been accustomed to until now, in joy."

And from among the Jews he picked out one Jew, who was wearing a funny hat, and he took the hat from his head and tore it and replaced it with an ordinary hat, like the king's hat, and put it on his head, and also ordinary shoes and cloths, like every person wears, and he ordered their attendant to do the same for all the Jews.

And he prepared handsome cloths for the Jews, and also shoes. The Jews exchanged their clothes with his servants.

The servants asked: "Why is the king doing this?" And those who hated the Jews were also puzzled, because they didn't know why the king was doing this.

Afterward the king declared to the Jews: "Go in peace, keep the Shabbat with a joyous heart, and with a good heart shall you pray. Make three meals as you are used to doing. On Sunday I'll explain what came over me, what happened to me."

The Shabbat passed. On Sunday the Jews went to the king and gathered there; the king began talking to them about everything that happened to him.

The king asked them: "Do your books mention someone by the name of Serah, the daughter of Asher?"

They answered: "Yes, of course they do. Serah, the daughter of Asher, is the granddaughter of Abraham our father, who blessed Jacob with a life in the Garden of Eden."

This king had one priest, and he invited the priest and said to him: "Remove your hat and the robe that you are wearing. From this day onward you will not be my priest. What you are telling me is a lie; the name of the God of the Jews is truth, and their attendants are truthful."

The priest's days of glory were over. Afterward the king declared that the Jews would suffer no harm, and also that they would pay less money than they used to pay in the stores. Besides that, he built a big synagogue at the same place where he had entered the cave, in commemoration of what happened to him. There the Jews will gather every New Year, every Shabbat, every holiday and festival, and pray in memory of Serah, the daughter of Asher, in the synagogue named after her. And even today this place stands. I don't know exactly, it is written in the Torah that the place stands.

The kindness the king showed to the Jews carried on for three hundred years. He provided horses to people so that those who lived far away could come to pray, and he also planted orchards and trees all around. He even planted seeds so that the cattle would have grazing ground when they arrived on their horses.

A hundred years passed, and the king had already died. A new king rose to power, one who decreed that Jews could not enter with their horses; that they could enter only on foot; and that even if they arrived with their horses they were not to receive water or anything. And then the king's stomach began to hurt, and he shouted that he had a stomach disease. And after the shouts he fell asleep, and he saw in his dream that Serah, the daughter of Asher, was coming to him, and she said: "Why did you prohibit the Jews from traveling with horses and rejoicing together with other Jews on the holidays?"

And afterward he promised her that he would cancel the decree and would give permission to the Jews to rejoice together with their brothers on all the Shabbats and festivals. When day broke, he invited all his servants, and said to them that he gave permission to the Jews to enter with their horses, and they would give them water and grazing and everything, and that's how it was. The Jews used to travel to their brothers with their horses, and they rejoiced on all Shabbats, holidays, and festivals.

Transcribed by Tamar Agmon

COMMENTARY TO "SERAH BAT ASHER"

IFA 9524

DINA STEIN

This miraculous salvation story of a Jewish community—whose time and place are not specified in our tale—is attributed to one woman: Serah, the daughter of Asher. The first documented model of a miraculous rescue of a Jewish community can be found in the biblical tale of the Scroll of Esther,[1] and there too it is a woman who, by physical and spiritual powers, prevents the impending disaster.[2] It seems likely, therefore, that it is no accident that Persia and the Caucasus countries—the areas in which Serah and the salvation story with which she is identified gained much popularity—overlap with the area in which the biblical tale of Esther takes place, and in which the tomb of the Jewish-Persian queen resides. And, just as pilgrimage to Esther's tomb in Hamadan is rooted in the biblical text, so is the

sanctity of Serah's tomb compound, near Isfahan, tied up with stories—stories about her restless figure—beginning in ancient times.[3] The association between the traditions involving Serah and those of Esther finds expression in our tale too, as we shall see later on.

Our story begins by introducing a crisis: A gentile king ("the king of the nations") issues a decree whose main aim is to publicly ridicule the Jews: they are ordered to wear strange clothes and accessories that will humiliate them in front of their neighbors. Indeed, the Jews are ashamed to be seen. The subsequent parts of the narrative will now seek to resolve the various facets of the crisis with which it opened: the inter-religious conflict, the discrimination against the Jews, and their experience of humiliation.

In its second part the story presents the sequence of events leading up to the encounter between the gentile king and Serah. In contrast to the previous section, where the king causes the Jews to be ashamed, here he is characterized as the one who is put to shame: He is embarrassed in front of his army because of the deer's allusive tricks. The underlying principle of the tale's plot is thus intimated; it is "measure-for-measure": Just as the king shames the Jews in public, he himself experiences public shame. However the king is not yet aware of this underlying plot principle, for the simple reason that he does not know that the deer he is trying to capture is not an ordinary animal. For him, external appearance/plot is what counts. And it seems that here we can already discern one of the story's central themes: the question of the recognition and identity of the Jewish congregation. "Do you know [recognize] me?" Serah asks the king, and he of course answers that he does not. The deer, it turns out, is really a beautiful young woman whose name is Serah bat Asher. Yet the king, as a hunter, fails to see her as anything but an animal that he is to hunt down. As a hunted animal the deer serves as a metaphor (or as a metonymy, in the narrative sequence) for the Jews, for their treatment by the king is also governed by external criteria (clothes). However the story overturns the power structure: the hunter becomes a trapped animal whose life and independence are contingent on the willingness of the woman to release him from the cave. The distribution of power between the foreign ruler and the Jewish minority is explicitly played out in the image of the hunter/hunted, and later on of man/woman: as in the Esther story, Serah's beauty and her feminine charms (alluded to indirectly in the cave), no less than the story she tells the king, cause the annulment of the decrees. Moreover, symbolically, not only is Serah the marvelous figure that brings about the salvation of her people, but the actual transformation that her figure embodies—from animal to woman—reflects the transformation the Jews undergo in the unfolding of the narrative's plot.

When the king first turns to the Jews, after hearing Serah's story, he says: "You will keep the Shabbat as you have been accustomed to until now, in joy." Do his words aim at rectifying a decree that was not mentioned (a religious prohibition against keeping the Shabbat), or do they emphasize that now, as opposed to in the past, the Jews are allowed to keep the Shabbat joyfully? It may be that the emphasis the story puts on decrees that address external manifestations (and not internal aspects of cultural-religious life) is rooted in a historical reality (in Persia), in which the Jews were commanded to wear a "badge of shame."[4] Most of the other versions of our story indeed relate the events they depict to the time of Shah Abbas I, in the seventeenth century, when a (failed) attempt was made to impose the "badge of shame" on the Jews.[5] This historical plot is reflected in our story, too, although as it continues, our story clearly departs from any inferred historical setting. The fact that the story repeats the opposition between the external (wearing strange attire in public; a deer) and the internal (keeping the Shabbat; a woman, Serah) may also allude to an extratextual reality in which the Jews were forced to convert while some maintained Jewish practices in secret.[6] Our story may thus allude to a religious conversion, yet its trajectory is of course different: in a reversed fantasy, the king says to the priest that "what you are telling me is a lie; the name of the God of the Jews is the truth, and their attendants are the truth." Unlike another legendary king, the king of Kuzar, this king does not take it upon himself to become a Jew, neither does he turn his kingdom into a Jewish state: it seems that the boundaries of fantasy are confined by some historical measures. The priest, for his part, looses his lofty position. True, our story does not completely follow the well-known model, in which the Jewish minister/advisor prevails over the king's hostile (gentile) advisor—as in the case of Mordechai and Haman. Here, instead of the Jewish advisor there is a woman, and even she appears only briefly, as the messenger connecting the Jewish community to the ruler. Ant yet the echoes of the biblical tale in our story are loud and clear, as is the allusion to the story of Joseph. The last part of our narrative adds that here too (in striking similarity to what happened in Egypt), years pass by and a king rises to power, issuing new decrees against the Jews. Both the story of Esther and the tale of Joseph address themes of exile and redemption, and Serah, the protagonist of our story, is implicated in the heart of these themes. To appreciate this we must return to what she tells the king, after which he utterly transforms his attitude toward the Jews.

Similar versions of the story that Serah tells the king are known from earlier midrashic sources.[7] According to this tradition, Serah is granted eternal life as a reward for having brought to Jacob the good news that his son Joseph was alive.[8] She is mentioned twice in the bible—as one who went down to Egypt with Jacob (Genesis 46:17) and as one who also left Egypt hundreds of years later (Numbers 26:46). The dual appearance of her name in scripture thus served as the basis—or justification—for various traditions of her miraculous figure, who not only lived for centuries but also became immortal.[9] Her longevity (or immortality) signifies continuity and consistency:[10] she is always present; she knows what is hidden from future generations for the simple reason that she, unlike them, was there—when the Israelites went down to Egypt, at the crossing of the Red Sea, in the days of David and Yoav. And it is because of this that Serah is the one who facilitates the redemption from Egyptian bondage: because she holds the signs that were passed down to her by her father, she recognizes—according to those verbal/graphic signs—that Moses and Aaron are God's true messengers, and she is the one who leads Moses to the burial place of Joseph's bones. Since the taking of the bones is a prerequisite for the Exodus, it is Serah, once again, who facilitates the flight from Egypt.[11]

The role Serah plays in the Exodus—which also serves as a model for redemption in the future—provides her with the necessary skills for her redemptive role in our story. Or, in more literary terms, the frequent identification of her figure with the one who played a crucial role in redeeming her people in the past, and as one who gained immortality, explains her appearance in our story. And yet the redemptive model she offers, and the continuity that it implies, is not subsumed in the linear narrative that begins in Egypt and ends in the Land of Israel. According to one tradition, the origin of the Persian community can be traced to before the Babylonian exile (or even prior to the exile of the ten northen tribes).[12] This tradition holds that the Jewish Persian community started with the arrival of Jacob's granddaughter, many years before any exile took place. Serah, according to this legend, was tending her father's flock in the hills of Judea, when one of her sheep wandered off into a cave. In her attempt to retrieve the lost ewe, Serah finds herself in the depths of a cave: the chase is long and tiring, but Serah does not give up. She finally succeeds when the lost ewe exits the cave, close to where the city of Isfahan now stands. (It seems likely that what is referred to in this legend is her tomb compound, and possibly even the "same" cave where the king in our story is trapped.[13]) This is thus a story of a community that does not imagine itself as a product of exiles (Judean or Isrealite)—exiles that interrupted the dream of national redemption, whose roots are in the Exodus from Egypt: An invisible hand brought about the miraculous foundation of the Persian community, parallel to the events that triggered the Egyptian exile and the redemptive model it encapsulates. Therefore it comes as no surprise that, according to the model implied by the tale of the salvation of the community by Serah, the redemption is not reflected in a return to the Land of Israel but rather in improved conditions among the gentiles (mirroring the story of Esther as well as Joseph's rise to power in Egypt). In our story this trajectory, which does not point toward the Promised Land, is implied in its allusion to the story of Esther, when the "badge of shame" is transmitted to the servants, and the priest, just like Haman, is demoted. And moreover: it is now a country that through monuments, such as the synagogue named after Serah, contains immanent holy sites. Yet the end of our narrative, which tells of a king who did not (initially) know Serah-Joseph, also implies that this redemptive model is bound to repeat itself in an endless cycle. Similarly, the foundation story, too, is not devoid of its own ambivalences as a story of a community that imagines its existence as both chthonic and foreign: the community is imagined as a descendant of an ancient mother who emerges out of the Persian land, and yet the origin of that mother resides elsewhere—in the Land of Israel, to which the place itself, near Isfahan, is linked via subterranean routes.[14]

The focus of this discussion has been a version told by Eliyahu Modgorshwili, originally from Kulashi, in Georgia, and written down in Israel in 1973. The wider context obviously informs not only the language of the tale (Serah is describe as a "woman soldier") but also its deep conceptual structure: it is possible that the end point of the biographical plot—that is, the arrival in Israel of the narrator and his life there—explains the addition of the tale's last part, which implies the national redemptive model (the Exodus from Egypt).[15] The narrator's homeland informs some details in the story: the king has a priest—which alludes to a Christian context[16]—and he does not relate the story to any specific time or place. The synagogue named after Serah is mentioned, but the narrator remarks that "even today this place stands. I don't know exactly, it is written in the Torah that the place stands."

Our version combines characteristics of two genres, a legend and a folk tale:[17] It manifestly addresses an inter-religious conflict whose resolution relates to a specific geographical location (typical of legends, and local legends in particular); the heart of the legend lies in the miraculous motif of "Princess Transformed into a Deer,"[18] popular in folk tales. To be sure, the scene where the deer is revealed to the king as a beautiful woman can be read as a hidden longing for matrimony, through which an oppressed minority seeks to be conquered and saved (from the "spell") by the majority. However, this oikotype explicitly does not present Serah as a princess in need of a prince who will undo the spell under which she is put; she herself—or that invisible hand—causes the metamorphosis. After all, she does not marry the king. And yet, although our story is hardly a folk tale, the folk tale element that exists in all the versions of this story provides the legend with a fantasy and a symbolic psychological force that is usually attributed to folktales. Accordingly, this intimates that the construction of individual identity (in the folktale) or the group (in the legend) requires the release of a certain element as a prerequisite for metamorphosis, for change.

The story of Serah, the daughter of Asher, alludes to salvation—not only national salvation (as in the story of Esther or the exodus from Egypt) but personal-individual salvation as well. Put differently, the folktale kernel of the story connects the private and public domains. It turns the story of Serah, told in Israel in 1973, into a national-teleological story (as in the Exodus model); into a story that preserves the memory of life in Persia (or Georgia) as a life that is not contingent on a longing to live in the Land of Israel (as in the Esther Scroll model); and into a story that puts forth the transformative kernel of the individual, without which any communal plot is deemed meaningless.

NOTES

1. This model is also alluded to in the salvation of the city of Abel-beth-maacah by a woman (2 Samuel: 20). See also note 7, below.
2. On this model see, for instance, Yassif 1999 (under the entry "Jewish community: miraculous rescue," in the index, 554). The celebration of a "second Purim" in commemoration of a local miracle (when a threat to the existence of a community was lifted) also embodies this model (Levinski 1955, 297–322).
3. See Soroudi 1979, 263–67; see also Stein 2012, 99–100.
4. See Tobi 1981, 51. Although Itzhak Ben-Zvi's description of the demand that all men in Persia wear western hats (and the Shiites' rebellion against it) refers to a much later period (the 1940s), it might still tell us something about the importance the Jewish story-tellers (from Persia, or as in our case, from neighboring countries) attributed to clothing (Ben-Zvi 1966, 118–19).
5. See, for instance, Soroudi 1979 (note 3 above), 258, regarding the tradition recorded by a seventeenth-century Jewish chronographer, and see also IFA 9695, IFA 13351, and IFA 1389. The prohibition forbidding dhimmis (the protected minorities) from riding a horse is of course known from Muslim contexts. This motif in the last part of our story may also have its roots in the Scroll of Esther, where Haman is condemned to lead Mordechai, who is seated on the former's horse. Be this as it may, in the frame of our tale it clearly constructs a neat symmetry vis-à-vis the king's conduct at the beginning of the narrative, where he is riding his horse while chasing the deer.
6. On the conversion of Jews to Islam in the days of Shah Abbas I and Abas II, see Tobi 1981 (note 4 above); on the Jews of Shiraz and southern Persia, see Loeb 1977, 30–32; 285–87; on the converts of Mashad, see Ben-Zvi 1966 (note 4, above) 127.
7. See *Sefer ha-Yashar*, ch. 14 (Dan 1986, 242–43); on the popular tradition that identifies Serah with the wise woman of Abel, who is also rewarded with entering the Garden of Eden alive, see, for instance, Targum Pseudo-Jonathan to Genesis 46:17. On modern folklore and midrashic origins concerning the figure of Serah, see also Bregman 2005.
8. See also Sabar 1982, 22–23.
9. On the different sources, see Elboim 1965, 124–31; Heineman 1974, 56; Yassif 1985, 104–13.
10. For a detailed discussion, see Stein 2012 (note 3 above), 84–100.
11. On identifying the letters of salvation, see Pirke de-Rabbi Eliezer 48; on identifying Joseph's burial place see, for instance, Sotah 4:6; Mekhilta de-Rabbi Ishmael, beshalah; Mekhilta de-Rabbi Shimon bar Yohai, beshalah; Babylonian Talmud, Sotah, 13a. For a discussion of the sources, see Heineman (note 9 above), 49–56; Kugel 1991, 133–46.

12. On the identification of the Jews of Isfahan with the Jews of the Babylonian exile, see Sorou-di 1979 (note 3 above), 257, and there also the tradition about Serah, who is counted among the first exiles.

13. Loeb 1977 (note 6 above), 274, remarks that this is a well-known Jewish-Persian legend, but he does not provide any specific sources. Although Loeb does not mention her burial spot as the place where she emerged from deep down, and although he does not connect her tomb to the cave of our story, it seems to me likely that these traditions are intertwined.

14. On the motif of the cave connecting the Diaspora and the Land of Israel (in which a goat plays the role of a go-between), see Agnon 1978, 373–75; on Agnon's use of folktales in his tales of Poland, see Bar-Itzhak 2001. In Agnon's tale, as opposed to our tale, the goat leads from the Diaspora to the Land of Israel. (And see Bar-Itzhak [2001], who dis-cusses the ways in which Agnon transforms foundation legends that legitimize life in the Diaspora.)

15. Although this should be qualified: the other versions in IFA (all told in Israel) do not include this additional episode.

16. See Hasan-Rokem 1993, 21.

17. On characteristic features of the folktale and those of the legend, and on folktale motifs in legends, see Hasan-Rokem 2000, 146–52.

18. AT 401: "The Princess Transformed into Deer."

BIBLIOGRAPHY

Aarne, Antti, and Stith Thompson. 1961. *The Types of the Folktale, A Classification and Bibliog-raphy*. FF Communications no. 184. Helsinki: Suomalainen Tiedeakatemia.

Agnon, Shmuel Yosef. 1978. "Fable of the Goat." In *Of Such and of Such*. Jerusalem: Schocken. [Hebrew]

Bar-Itzhak, Haya. 2001. *Jewish Poland: Legends of Origin*. Detroit: Wayne State University Press.

Ben-Zvi, Yitzhak. 1966. *Distant Jews*. Jerusalem: Ben Zvi Institute. [Hebrew]

Bregman, Marc. 2005. "Serah Bat Asher, Biblical Origins, Ancient Aggadah and Contemporary Folklore." in H. Schwartz and B. Razuick (eds.) *New Harvest: Jewish Writings in St. Louis, 1998–2005*. St. Louis: The Brodsky Library Press. 341–353.

Dan, Josef, ed. and intro. 1986. *Sefer ha-Yashar*. Jerusalem: Bialik Institute. [Hebrew]

Elboim, Josef. 1965. "Women Who Entered Paradise Alive." *Mahanayim* 98: 124–31. [Hebrew]

Hasan-Rokem, Galit. 1993. *Adam le-Adam Gesher: The Proverbs of Georgian Jews in Israel*. Jerusalem: Ben-Zvi Institute /Hebrew University of Jerusalem. [Hebrew]

———. 2000. *The Web of Life—Folklore and Midrash in Rabbinic Literature*. Stanford: Stanford University Press.

Heineman, Isaac. 1974. *Legends and Their History*. Jerusalem: Keter. [Hebrew]

Kugel, James. 1991. "Midrashim That Ended Up in the Wrong Place." *Publications of the Israel Academy of Science* 8 (3): 49–61. [Hebrew]

Levinski, Yom Tov. 1955. *Book of Festivals*. Vol. 6. Tel Aviv: Oneg Shabbat. [Hebrew]

Loeb, Laurence D. 1977. *Outcaste: Jewish Life in Southern Iran*. New York: Routledge.

Pirke de Rabbi Eliezer. 1972. A Critical Edition. Codex C. M. Horowitz. Jerusalem: Makor. [Hebrew]

Sabar, Yona. 1982. *The Folk Literature of the Kurdistani Jews: An Anthology*. Translated with introduction and notes. New Haven, CT: Yale University Press.

Soroudi, Sarah. 1979. "The Holy Places of the Persian Jews." *Edot Israel* 2, 257–63. Tel Aviv: Am Oved. [Hebrew]

Stein, Dina. 2005. *Maxims, Magic, Myth: A Folkloristic Perspective of Pirkei deRabbi Eliezer*. Jerusalem: Hebrew University/ Magnes Press. [Hebrew]

Stein, Dina. 2012. Textual Mirrors: Reflexivity, Midrash and the Rabbinic Self. Philadelphia: University of Pennsylvania Press.

Tobi, Yosef. 1981. "The Iranian Jewry." In *The History of the Jews in Islamic Lands*, ed. S. Etinger. Jerusalem: Zalman Shazar Center. [Hebrew]

Yassif, Eli. 1985. *The Ben Sira Tales in the Middle Ages*. Jerusalem: Magnes. [Hebrew]

———. 1999. *The Hebrew Folktale: History, Genre, Meaning*. Bloomington: Indiana University Press.

THE GIRL AND THE DRAGONS

IFA 10106

NARRATED AND TRANSCRIBED FROM MEMORY BY MOSHE ATTIAS (GREECE)

There once lived an old God-fearing woman who followed all of God's commandments. But there was one commandment she had not yet fulfilled and was yearning to carry out all her life: to make the pilgrimage to Mecca and to bow before the Holy Stone before her soul returned to Allah.

The day finally drew near, and the old woman was preparing for the great journey. On the day she was to leave, her clothes packed, her victuals all prepared for the road, and a caravan of pilgrims all set to go, the woman beckoned her granddaughter over and said to her: "My dear, I am about to leave for holy Mecca. I am leaving you the house: Take good care of it while I'm gone. I shall not be long, and with Allah's help I shall soon return home safely." The old woman lovingly hugged and kissed her granddaughter, and left.

Sad and lonely at first, the girl was soon cheered up by her housework. She cleaned, cooked, washed the laundry and the dishes, and so on and so forth, each day with its chores.

One day, as the girl was sewing some clothes, the door opened, and a dragon charged in, calling out: "Stay where you are, pretty girl, and don't move, for I am hungry and will gobble you up to satiate my appetite!"

But the girl, who was clever and brave, did not lose her wits and replied: "I am all set to be eaten by your jaws. But I, too, am hungry. Let me cook a meal for myself before you devour me, and you shall find my flesh even more delicious."

"Fine," said the dragon, for he liked the offer, "but hurry up."

The girl went to the kitchen, took a slice of meat, and began to grind it to make *kobibas*, all the while singing: "Come hither, my neighbor, come and rescue me! A dragon is in my house, and he wishes to devour me!"

The neighbor heard her singing and said to his wife: "I believe the girl is in trouble and seeks help." But the wife soothed his worries, saying: "There is no need to worry, the girl always sings when she does her chores."

But when the two heard the girl sing once again, repeating her plea ever-more forcefully and urgently, there remained no doubt in their mind that the girl was in trouble and in need of help.

The neighbor took his gun, entered the girl's home, saw the dragon, and shot it dead. The girl then put the corpse in a sack, loaded it on the back of the dragon's donkey, which was tied outside waiting for its master, and unfastened the knot. The donkey turned back and returned the corpse to the dragon's family.

When the dragon's mother saw the donkey with the load on its back, she said in her heart: "How wise of my son to send his prey first, before he returns!" She set a large cauldron on the fire, and when the water was boiling, she threw in the dead body. And a herald went around the dragons' camp, inviting all its dwellers for a feast.

All gathered and sat down to eat, when suddenly the mother dragon felt something stuck between her teeth. Taking the piece out of her mouth, she recognized it as her son's ring. Pain and rage engulfed her as she alerted her guests. Silence and sorrow descended on the gathering, and all stopped eating. Then the slain dragon's brother rose and said: "Be brave, Mother! I shall follow my brother's trail and avenge his death!"

The following day, the second dragon mounted his brother's donkey and loosened its reigns, and the donkey led him down his brother's path, straight to the girl's house. The dragon charged in, but could not believe that this young girl was his brother's slayer. Overcome by his appetite, he said: "Stay where you are, pretty girl, and do not move, for I am ready to gobble you up until I fill my stomach with your soft flesh!"

"Gladly," the girl replied. "I will be your prey and satiate your hunger. But why should you eat me while I am hungry? Let me cook a meal for myself and you shall find me even more delicious."

Tempted by her sweet words, the dragon agreed. The girl went to the kitchen and began to grind meat for *kobibas*, and again her singing filled the house. Again the neighbor heard her call and without a moment's hesitation charged in and shot the dragon dead; and, once more, the girl put the corpse in a sack and sent it to the dragon's home, as she had done with his brother before him.

Upon seeing the donkey with its cargo, the mother dragon thought her son had avenged his slain brother and sent her the killer's body. Again she prepared a giant feast to which all her dragon friends were invited. But again, as before, the second son's ring was discovered stuck in her teeth, and the feast turned from joy to mourning.

"What devil has been slaying my sons and sending them back to me?" the dragon mother shrieked. "If ever I lay my hands on him, I will take revenge on him the like of which the world has never seen!"

The third and youngest son rose and said: "My brothers' blood cries out to me from the ground; my brothers' blood cries out for revenge, and I, how shall I remain at peace?"

He said no more, but the following day, at the break of dawn, he set out on his way. To cut a long story short, his fate was no different from that of his brothers. His mother and her guests feasted on his flesh, and when the ring was found in his mother's mouth, a great tumult rose among the dragons. All leaped to and fro in search of the killers, the mother dragon among them. The dragons searched all day, but in the evening they returned to their camp empty-handed.

While the mother dragon was plotting to find her sons' killers and avenge their deaths, the old woman returned from her pilgrimage to Mecca and heard from her granddaughter about everything that had happened in her absence. Knowing full well that the dragons would not rest until they took their revenge, the old woman warned her granddaughter.

And she was right. With the fire of revenge burning in her heart, the mother dragon was considering sundry ruses by which to capture the killer, until at last she settled on one. She dressed as a peddler, packed a flat box with perfumes, fresh-smelling soaps, colorful ribbons, and shiny buttons, hung the box around her neck, and set out wandering around the land.

And so she went from one house to the next, offering her merchandise free of charge in exchange for stories. All jumped at the bargain, and the dragoness's ears were soon filled with an endless abundance of tales, both real and imagined. Our girl, too, heard of the peddler, who one day arrived at her doorstep, offering a piece of merchandise in exchange for a tale; two in exchange for a true story from the girl's own life. The girl mustered her courage, told the peddler of her exploits with the dragons, and, noticing the peddler's keen interest, added some touches of her own.

The peddler lavished praise on the girl's story and gave her seven pieces of merchandise.

"Never have I met a girl braver and cleverer than you," she said. "You shall enjoy much happiness if you agree to wed my son. I guarantee you will like him, for he is very handsome and rich. He will seat you in his palace as his bride, with servants and maids around you awaiting your every command."

The girl's grandmother heard the conversation and warned her granddaughter not to be deceived by the guest's sweet words and promises. But the girl hung on the peddler's every word, as if tangled in bonds of magic, and decided to go with her, ignoring her grandmother's pleas. She followed the peddler to her home, but when they arrived the mother dragon locked her in a cage. "I have captured my sons' murderess!" she cried, "and now you shall come to a swift end. I shall prepare for you a death the like of which the world has never known. First I will feed you, fatten up you with delicacies, until your flesh is soft to the taste, a delight for my dragon friends!"

And so she did. A few months later, when she saw the girl was plump enough, the dragoness set a large cauldron on the fire, then stepped out to invite all her friends to the feast, leaving her half-blind, dimwitted daughter to watch over the prisoner until she returned.

While the dragon mother was away, her daughter saw the girl chewing gum. She came near her and asked for a piece. And the girl said: "Open the cage just a little, so I can reach out and hand it over to you."

And so she did, and the girl gave her a small piece of gum. The dragoness's daughter returned a few moments later and asked for another piece. And again she opened the cage door. The third time, the girl pushed her away and stepped out of the cage, lifted the dragoness's daughter in her arms, threw her into the boiling water, and ran away as fast as she could.

The mother dragon returned with her guests, and when she saw the cage door open, she said in her heart: "How wise of my daughter! As soon as she saw the water was boiling, she threw the girl into the cauldron to have the meal prepared by the time we returned." The merry guests sat down to eat, when suddenly the mother dragon's teeth made a grinding sound. She took a ring out of her mouth, which she immediately recognized as her daughter's. She let out a loud, bitter cry, her heart broke, and she fell dead on the ground.

The girl ran for many hours until she arrived in a big city, the capital of the land. She went to a used clothes store, picked up a boy's outfit that fit her, put it on, and looked just like a boy. The boy (as we shall now call him) wandered the city streets until he arrived at the king's palace and knocked on the kitchen door. The servants opened, but when they saw a boy dressed in lovat garments, they thought he was a common street urchin, pushed him away, and shut him out. When he insisted he be let in, they beat him up. The boy gave a terrifying cry that reached and assaulted the prince's ears, until the latter stepped outside the palace gates to see who was yelling and why. The servants told him about the incident and about the boy's doggedness. The prince took a liking to the boy and ordered that he be recruited into his service at once. When asked for his name, the boy answered: "Lovat!"

Lovat turned out to be a swift and responsible worker, loved by all, and was soon put in charge of the chicken coops and the dovecotes. The days went by, and the boy won the affection of all in the palace.

One day the queen was invited to a lavish wedding at the palace of one of the city's noblemen. Lovat yearned to witness a wedding of this sort. Since he was free to come and go throughout the palace, he snuck into the queen's chambers, picked one of her beautiful gowns, donned it, and went to the wedding.

Before she entered the hall where the wedding was to take place, the young girl approached one of the men she chanced upon and asked: "Would you like to earn two liras?"

"Yes," said the man.

"Then do as I say," she said. "I am about to enter this palace. Wait fifteen minutes, then follow me in, approach me, and say, '*Hanum!* The count is waiting for you and asks that you come at once!' I will then follow you out and pay you."

The girl entered the wedding hall, and immediately everyone was struck by her loveliness and beauty. All huddled around her with much admiration and sought her company. The queen invited her to sit beside her, but before the girl could sit, a man entered and called out: "*Hanum!* The count is waiting for you and asks that you come at once!"

The girl bid everyone a hasty goodbye, and out she went. All looked at each other and asked one another: "Who is this beautiful girl?"—but no one knew a thing about her.

The girl returned to the palace, took off and put away the queen's gown, then returned to her work. At length the queen returned to the palace and met her son, who could see at once the unusual expression on his mother's face. "What is the matter, Mother?" he asked. "Why is your face beset with worry? Did you not enjoy the festivities?"

"What shall I say, my boy?" said the queen. "All was good and merry, until suddenly a stunningly beautiful girl arrived, captivating all who were present. I, too, was taken by her charms;

she is truly fit to be my daughter-in-law. Alas, no one knows her name or where she comes from."

"Why did you not ask her?" the prince wondered.

"I wished to have her seated by my side, but before I could do so, a man entered and said, '*Hanum!* The count is waiting for you! Come quickly!' and she got up and left."

Several more weeks passed, and again the queen was invited to a noble wedding. Once more, the girl wore the most beautiful of the queen's gowns and showed up at the wedding; and once again, a man arrived and announced that the count was waiting for her, whereupon she got up and left. Sad and dejected, the queen returned home; when she had left for the wedding, she told her son, she had but one worry in her heart, but now she had twenty-four, for the marvelous woman reappeared, only to vanish again as swift as lightning. "Again," she reported, "I did not have the chance to speak with her. How happy I could be if only this beautiful girl wed you and dignified my palace with her presence."

"Flies do not kill, but they can certainly embarrass," the saying goes.

And indeed, an opportunity soon presented itself. Several more days passed. The queen was invited to yet another wedding, and the girl, whose ear was hardly deaf to the secrets of the queen's heart, did as she had done before. Little did she know that this time the prince would waylay her as she left the wedding hall, grasp her, and not let go. And when he saw her face, his wits left him. He asked her for her name and the whereabouts of her home, but she did not reply and tried to escape; yet he did not let go, and, realizing that her secret was about to be revealed, she said: "I am yours, and you are mine. Let us exchange rings, and I shall be on my way."

The two exchanged rings, and the girl returned quickly to the palace, took off the queen's gown, and resumed her usual work.

The prince told his mother that he had grasped the girl as she was leaving the wedding and did not let go until she promised to be his bride. Rings, he said, were exchanged. He showed his mother the girl's ring, and the two resolved to visit the girl's home a few days later to collect her. The queen was exultant, the prince even more so, that such a lovely bride was to be his.

Preparations for the trip to the bride's home began. In the kitchen, *kobibas* were made to feed the travelers, and Lovat insisted that he be allowed to make at least one. All laughed and mocked his request, for they believed he had no cooking experience; but at last his wish was granted. He made one *kobiba*, inserting into it the ring he had received from the prince.

In the morning the king and the queen climbed into their carriages and set out on their way, accompanied by the prince and a large entourage. At noon they stopped to eat and were served the *kobibas*. No one wanted Lovat's *kobiba*, no one but the prince, who took a bite and immediately discovered the ring. At once he turned to his mother and said: "Let us return to the palace, my mother the queen, for it is there that my bride resides."

"How so?" the queen wondered.

"Let us return and you will see," he said.

The prince turned back, arrived at the palace early, entered Lovat's room, and said to her: "Why have you fooled me?"

"I have not been fooling you, my prince," she said, "for I love you very much. But how, oh my heart's desire, could I be so bold as to set my sights on the prince?" And she told him all she had done and been through, confessing that she was the one who showed up at the weddings dressed in the queen's gowns, only to rush back to the palace before her absence was noted.

Upon hearing this, the prince took her at once to the queen's chambers, where she chose one of the queen's most beautiful gowns. Delightfully dressed, she then came out of the palace to welcome the king and the queen, who were drawing near. When the queen saw her future daughter-in-law, she stepped down from the royal carriage and lovingly hugged her. The young girl told the queen all she had told her son, the prince, and the queen listened with much interest and with admiration for the girl's wisdom and courage.

The wedding was celebrated a few days later with much splendor and grandeur. The girl remembered her grandmother and sent for her, to let her share in her happiness. The prince and his bride are happy, and so is the queen; all will be good, for them and for us.

COMMENTARY TO
"THE GIRL AND THE DRAGONS"

IFA 10106

DAVID ROTMAN

Not many monster tales are recorded and cataloged in the Israel Folktale Archives (IFA).[1] Eighteen tales in which dragons, ghosts, or monsters are mentioned are documented in the archive, comprising less than one-tenth of a percent of all the folktales included. Of these, our tale is the only one in which the life of a community of monsters is described and its members given a voice of their own, endowing these negative characters with an atypical complexity. Most of the following discussion will focus on the function of these descriptions of the monstrous in our tale.

The tale was narrated and transcribed by Moshe Attias. Born in Thessaloniki, Greece, in 1898, Attias immigrated to Palestine in 1914, becoming the first director of Jerusalem's Municipal Department of Education and Culture after the founding of the State of Israel. Over the years he studied the Sephardic folk songs of Balkan (in particular Greek) Jewry and collected its folktales.

The tale before us is a conglomerate of variations on three common narrative types. Its first section is a variation on novellas belonging to type ATU 956 and its subtypes, in which a girl handles robbers by cleverly calling her neighbors for help (ATU 956B) and having them kill the intruders (ATU 956D). Escaping death, the robbers' leader seeks revenge. He returns to the girl's home dressed as a nobleman, courts her, and lures her to his lair, only to reveal his true identity and threaten her with cruel death. The girl escapes, and the robber is captured and punished. In our version, the realistic intruders (violent men) are replaced with supernatural ones (the male dragons), while the human avenger is replaced with the dragons' mother.

The second component in the conglomerate narrative takes apart and reassembles several variants of the "children-and-monsters" narrative type (ATU 327), in which the child protagonist is captured by a monster and fattened up to serve as the monster's meal (motif K 551.5 in the Thompson index). With resourcefulness and ingenuity, the abducted child causes the monster's progenies, each in turn, to be cooked in the cauldron originally meant for him or her, and to be eaten by the monstrous parent. Finally, the child kills the monster, escapes, and returns home (ATU 328).

The third component in our tale, comprising its final section, is a combination of several subtypes of the Cinderella story (ATU 510).

Conspicuously absent from our version (and present in most others) are the characters of the expelling parents. In other versions, the desirous father and/or the stepmother play a major role in setting off the plot. Here this role is distanced, reduced to the grandmother's temporary desertion of the girl on account of her religious piety, an adjustment possibly meant to sublimate the tensions inherent in the nuclear family and to stress those typical of broader familial circles—a matter to which I will return shortly.

Already on first reading, the adroit manner in which the tale's first two components are integrated to form a unified narrative (henceforth the Dragon Tale) stands at jarring odds with the relatively contrived manner in which these first two components are combined with the third—that is, with the potentially standalone section that begins with the heroine's escape from the dragons' camp (henceforth the Palace Tale). The latter, unlike the first, is completely devoid of supernatural motifs, including those typical of ATU 510 (for example, the supernatural helper, who plays a major role in almost all variations on this type). Also absent from the final section is the violence permeating the first. Replacing these elements are various sexual elements absent from the tale's earlier part: transvestism, seduction, infatuation, and marriage.

Another marked difference between the tale's two sections has to do with the social interactions typical of each. The society in which the Dragon Tale takes place is one with no noticeable governing authority or clear sociospatial boundaries; one marked by evident insecurity, in which members of the dragon community can freely intrude the human space. When her private sphere is left unprotected, the girl must call her neighbor for help. In anthropologist Victor Turner's terms, this section's system of social relations is a "communitas": "an unstructured or rudimentarily structured and relatively undifferentiated comitatus, community or even communion of equal individuals" (Turner 1969, 96). The Palace Tale, by contrast, takes place in an urban space characterized by economic relationships, and in a palace marked by a hierarchy of masters and servants. In Turner's terms, these are the social relationships typical of a "structured community": "a structured, differentiated, and often hierarchical system of politico-legal-economic positions with many types of evaluation, separating men in terms of 'more' or 'less'" (ibid.).

These conspicuous differences call for an examination of the way in which the tale's two primary sections are merged. Solving this problem will contribute to our understanding of the role served by the description of the dragon community in the tale's first section. But to solve this problem, we must first look in more depth at the few elements the tale's two sections do share—most obviously the protagonist, though other characters and motifs recur in both sections as well.

The first of these is the character of the heroine's grandmother. Our tale begins with the grandmother's desertion of the heroine, continues with the heroine's desertion of the grandmother, and ends with a reunion of the two. Conspicuous at each of the tale's crucial junctures—the confrontations with the male dragons, the encounter with the mother dragon, the events at the palace—is the grandmother's utter lack of influence over the heroine's actions. And yet, for the sake of closure, the grandmother reemerges from out of nowhere in the tale's penultimate sentence. The reunion could have occurred at any point after the conclusion of the Dragon Tale; but to achieve this happy result, the protagonist must first complete a certain process that had begun at the story's outset, with the grandmother's initial desertion. The reunion marks the two's coming to terms with that process, the nature of which may be clarified through an examination of the other motifs the tale's two sections share.

Among the most prominent of these motifs are cooking and eating, as well as the discovery of the ring inside the dish in a way that exposes its origin (Motif H 94.2 in the Thompson index). In her work on feminine fairy tales, Dina Stern notes the significance of the baking oven, the baking of bread, and the removal of bread from the oven as symbols of the female subject's self-birth (Stern 2006, 120–21). In our version of the tale, the baking of bread is replaced with the making of the *kobibas*: In the Dragon Tale, the heroine stalls the dragons by making *kobibas*; in the Palace Tale, the *kobibas* she makes for the prince reveal her female identity and make possible her marriage with the prince.

The origins of this latter motif lie in Greece's Sephardic Jewish culture. In her study of Sephardic Jewish versions of tale type ATU 510, Tamar Alexander-Frizer notes the importance accorded in this culture to food and to cooking, an importance reflected in the versions she discusses as well as in ours:

> The motif suits Sephardic culture, in which cooking and food fill an important role in family life. Cooking is the woman's primary function [. . .]. The way to gain acceptance into a new family is to "cook well"; it is also said to be the way to a man's heart. The quality of the cooking is another bone of contention between mother-in-law and bride in their rivalry over the son's affections. The bride tries to present him with dishes like his mother used to make, while the mother-in-law complains that the bride does not cook as well as she does. (Alexander-Frizer 2008, 348–49)

The particular dish in our version—the *kobibas*—may have been the transcribing narrator's choice; it is not the particular dish that is important for our purposes, however, but the recurrence of the same dish throughout the tale.[2] In Turner's terms, the tale's plot can be described as a rite of initiation, with each of the tale's sections paralleling a different stage of the initiation process.

The first stage occurs early in the story, when the girl is left alone. Again in Turner's terms, her desertion by the grandmother symbolizes the "liminal" stage of her initiation, that in which the subject's social status is transformed: "Liminal entities [. . .] are betwixt and between the positions assigned and arrayed by law, custom, convention, and ceremonial" (Turner 1969, 95). At this stage, the deserted girl is characterized primarily by her "feminine" housework, in particular by her cooking. Keeping herself occupied with these chores cheers her up. (As her neighbor later says, she habitually sings while doing them.) But doing these chores is just one of the roles traditional societies assign to their women; the other—the one responsible for turning girls into women—is their sexual role. As the girl is busy sewing, her presexual feminine world is shattered by a male character, the intruding dragon, whose maleness (as well as his brothers') is later underscored by the appearance of the female dragonesses, his mother and sister.

In other versions of the tale, the male intruder is explicitly human; here, the character remains merely symbolic, as does its sexual desire, described here as a "hunger" for the girl's body—a hunger whose sexual character is underscored by the fact that it is precisely at this point, during the dragon's assault, that the heroine's sexuality is noted for the first time (by the male intruder's description of her as "pretty").[3] The girl's escape from the dragon's terror is made possible by her resumption of the traditionally feminine chores to which she is accustomed, in this case the making of the *kobibas*. At this stage, however, she cannot yet handle the intruder independently and relies on her neighbor, armed with his phallic gun, to fend off the assault on her sexuality. The dragons, we learn, are not unlike humans in their vulnerability to shooting—and this, as we shall soon see, is not their only human characteristic.

The description of the making of the *kobibas* at the palace is utterly different. This time the disguised heroine is adamant about making this dish for the prince, doing so of her own initiative and confronting those who, not knowing her gender, mock her for engaging in a feminine activity. Hidden within this culinary symbol of femininity is another such symbol—the ring. Together, these symbols beckon the prince to return to the heroine and help her complete her initiation by consummating her sexuality.

The girl, however, is not the only cook in our story. Paralleling the three episodes in the Dragon Tale in which the girl escapes the male dragons by making the *kobibas* are the three episodes in which the mother dragon cooks and eats her own sons. All three times the feast halts to a grind when the mother discovers her sons' rings in her dish (Motif G 61.2). Rings that find their way into cooked meat are apparently a feature male dragons and human princes share. In the dragons' case, however, the discovery of the rings is associated not with an invitation to sexuality but with the mother's recurrent, chilling discovery that she has eaten her own offspring—a discovery which, at the symbolic level, marks the almost obsessive recurrence of Oedipal relations in the tale. This disastrous (for the mother) result is brought about by the dragons' cannibalistic desire to eat the girl, which, in the second and third assaults at least, can be seen as a direct result of the instinctual, all-too-human violence of the dragons' thirst for revenge and of their wish to defeat the heroine (Stern 2006, 110–11). In this respect, the dragoness's sons are the victims of distinctly human urges—their own, their mother's, and their community's, no less than the girl's.

Yet another reason for the dragoness's recurrent devouring of her sons is intimated by the very different ways in which her cooking and the girl's are described. Whereas the heroine's cooking is described as, "The girl went to the kitchen, took a slice of meat, and began to grind it to make *kobibas*," the dragoness's cooking is described thus: "She set a large cauldron on the fire, and when the water was boiling, she threw in the dead body." The difference is striking. The making of the *kobibas* is an intricate, complex, multistep process, involving the careful selection and preparation of a piece of meat; in other words, it is *cultural*. The dragon's cooking of the victim's flesh is simple, one-dimensional, and violent—in other words, *natural*. The mother dragon does not even pause to take a look at the raw material before she hurls it into the cauldron. And it is this attitude toward the preparation of food—toward her very femininity—that spells her ruin.

The confrontation between the two cooking females culminates with the heroine's capture by the mother dragon, which also marks the apex of the liminal stage of the protagonist's initiation rite—one in which, according to Turner, the liminal entities "are being reduced or ground down to a uniform condition, to be fashioned anew and endowed with additional powers to enable them to cope with their new situation in life" (Turner 1969, 95). What is being "ground down" in our case, is the girl's subjectivity at the apex of her objectification—a process achieved, once again, by way of the focus on food, whereby the girl is turned into an object, fattened up by the mother dragon and waiting to be devoured by her.

On the way to this apex we find another motif that recurs in both sections of the story—the disguise. Because her enemy is disguised as a prospective mother-in-law offering her son as a groom, the girl agrees to leave home, confronts her grandmother (and, at the same time, her own childish past), and walks straight into captivity. This disguise sheds light on certain hints offered at other junctures in the tale. The girl yearns to consummate her sexuality: Longing for a (very rich and handsome!) groom and tempted by the enticing mother-in-law, she "[hangs] on the peddler's every word, as if tangled in bonds of magic." The enticing mother-in-law soon turns out to be a mother dragon; but is the mother dragon not a symbolic realization of the same mother-in-law described in Alexander's above passage, the one who vies with her daughter-in-law for her son's heart, the one who incessantly complains about the bride's deficiencies? By this time, the mother dragon's earlier reactions (such as her repeated exclamations, "How wise of my son!") are cast in a distinctly "motherly-in-law" light. Furthermore, is it not the secret desire of every mother-in-law (and the secret nightmare of every bride in patrilocal societies) to lock out her daughter-in-law, deny her access to her son, and force her to eat her dishes?

If the disguised mother dragon represents the negative, Jungian shadow version of the mother-in-law, the queen represents its Jungian figure of light. As long as the heroine is dressed in clothes primarily designed to conceal her sexuality, the royal mother takes no interest in her. It is when she peels off her disguise, revealing herself as a woman in full flower, that the queen's interest is piqued ("I, too, was taken by her charms; she is truly fit to be my daughter-in-law"). What we have, then, are a masquerading mother-in-law who captures the heart of an innocent girl, and a real mother-in-law whose heart is taken by a masquerading woman.

The mother dragon's role in the heroine's initiation rite is that of a humiliator, similar to that of the Kafwana in the Ndembu coronation ceremonies discussed by Turner (1969, 100–101). The end of the humiliation rite marks also the end of the liminal stage in our heroine's life, whereupon her social environment reverts from a Turnerian communitas to the structured community of the palace. From now on, she is the master of her own fate, carrying herself independently to the last stage of the initiation rite, where her coronation by the royal mother marks the rite's successful conclusion. In the Ndembu rite of passage, the humiliator is also the coronator; in our tale the two complementary roles are separated into two different, if clearly analogous, characters.

This ostensible separation is undercut, however, once we compare the mothers-in-law's views of the bride's proper destiny. The feigned mother-in-law offers her bride the classic role to which patriarchal class societies consign their upper-class women—that of a passive object ("He will seat you in his palace as his bride, with servants and maids around you awaiting your every command"), a variation on the sexualized role demanded of her by the dragoness's sons ("Stay where you are, pretty girl, and don't move!"). It is the royal mother, however—the genuine mother-in-law, the representative of positive post-initiatory family relationships—who turns precisely this "promise" into a reality.

The matriarchal dragon community led by the mother dragon is nothing, then, if not our own human society as it presents itself to the subject of the initiation rite during its liminal stage—that is to say, as an alien threat. During this stage, the male option is represented by the male dragons; the mother-in-law by the mother dragon. The only familial and social relationships available in this sort of community are those of predator and prey. But do these communal elements vanish once the initiation rite is over? Anthropologically speaking, the answer is clearly no, for the rite's purpose is precisely to have the young girl prove her ability to cope with these threatening elements in order to become a mature member of the community. In our folktale, however, the narrative ends thus: "The prince and his bride are happy, and so is the queen; all will be good, for them and for us." This, perhaps, is the tale's advantage over life—the text's over the rite's.

NOTES

1. Marvelous creatures of a different type—demons—make their appearance in five hundred tales documented in the IFA.
2. Moshe Attias wrote some of his tales from memory (Attias 1976). As Tamar Alexander-Frizer notes, his transcriptions tend toward stylization and toward an emphasis on ethnic elements (Alexander-Frizer 2008, 33; 354–55).
3. Much has been written on the analogy between (heterosexual) sex and food, in culture in general and in folktales in particular. Examples pertinent to our discussion can be found in Alexander-Frizer's aforementioned study (2008, 345; 348–49).

BIBLIOGRAPHY

Alexander-Frizer, Tamar. 2008. The *Heart Is a Mirror: The Sephardic Folktale*. Detroit: Wayne State University Press.

Attias, Moshe. 1976. *The Golden Feather: Twenty Folktales Narrated by Greek Jews*. Haifa: Haifa Municipality, Ethnological Museum and Folklore Archives. [Hebrew]

Stern, Dina. 2006. *Violence in an Enchanted World*. Ramat Gan: Bar-Ilan University Press. [Hebrew]

Thompson, Stith. 1955–58. *Motif-Index of Folk-Literature: A Classification of Narrative Elements in Folk Tales, Ballads, Myths, Fables, Mediaeval Romances, Exempla, Fabliaux, Jest-Books, and Local Legends*. Bloomington: Indiana University Press.

Turner, Victor. 1969. *The Ritual Process*. London: Routledge and Kegan Paul.

Uther, Hans-Jörg. 2004. *The Types of International Folktales*. Helsinki: Academia Scientiarum Fennica.

THE KING AND THE OLD WOODCUTTER

IFA 10300

NARRATED BY NISSIM DAMTI (YEMEN)

It is told that long ago lived a very righteous king who was also very wise and understood riddles. One time the king went out to walk in the woods alone. He saw an old man approximately eighty years old, cutting wood. The king felt sorry for the man and went up to him to ask him how he was. The man bowed and answered the king's question seriously, and then continued his work.

The king asked him: "Even?"

The woodcutter answered: "If I had, then I wouldn't have to."

From the woodcutter's answer, the king understood that before him stood a smart and wise man.

Again the king asked: "How are the two?"

The old man answered: "The third one is in between them."

"How are your friends?" the king continued to ask.

And the old man answered: "The package has broken."

"How are your brothers?"

And the answer was: "The far one is close."

The king was astounded by the old man's wisdom and decided in his heart to make his life good, so that he wouldn't have to work anymore and could spend the rest of his days in relaxation, and he wouldn't have to cut wood anymore.

He told him: "I have tried you with riddles, and you have wisdom ten times over. Therefore, listen to me, do not sell cheaply."

The old man smiled and said: "Do not teach the wise."

As soon as the king heard the old man's answer, he left him happily and went on his way.

The king had a vizier. He was a rich man, but he didn't get rich legally. Now the king had found a way to punish him and get rid of him forever.

He said to his vizier: "I am going to ask you four riddles. If you can answer all of them in thirty days' time, I will add to your riches. But if you cannot answer these riddles, I will cut off your head."

In a weak voice and with shaky knees, he answered: "Ask me your riddles; I, your servant hear you."

So the king said: "The first riddle is: 'Even?'" and the answer is: "I had, then I wouldn't have to."

The second one: "How are your two?" and the answer is: "The third one is in between them."

The third one: "How are your friends?" and the answer is: "The package has broken."

The fourth one: "How are your brothers?" and the answer is: "The far one is close."

The vizier left the king with bowed head, thinking about the riddles. He turned to every fortuneteller and magician he could find, but no one could help him with the riddles. The thirty days were up, and there were no answers to the riddles. The vizier was desperate. On the thirtieth day, he went home, said goodbye to his family and friends, drew up his will, and went out to wander the streets, to enjoy the views before his death. On his walk he met the old woodcutter.

The woodcutter greeted him and said: "Why is your face so sad, vizier?"

"Oh woodcutter, leave me alone," said the advisor.

"With the ancient is wisdom; and in length of days understanding" [Job 12:12].

The vizier thought to himself: "I have told my troubles to many people. I will tell this woodcutter; how is he different from anyone else? If indeed there is wisdom in the woodcutter's head." So he turned to him and said: "I will tell you four riddles; let's see if you can solve them."

"Let's hear them," answered the woodcutter.

So the vizier said: "The first one is: 'Even?' and the answer is . . ."

The old man hurried and said: "If I had, then I wouldn't have to."

When the vizier heard the old man's answer, his eyes opened, and his heart widened.

And the advisor continued: "How are the two?"

The old man answered: "The third one is in between them."

"And how are your friends?"

"The package has broken."

"How are your brothers?"

"The far one is close."

The vizier went up to the old man, kissed him on the mouth, and said: "Please tell me, old man, what is the meaning of these riddles?"

"The answer to these riddles will cost you dearly," said the old man.

"I will pay you fifty silver pieces."

"You must be joking; not even hundreds of thousands of silver pieces will be worth the answer to the riddles," answered the old man.

"I'll pay ten thousand silver pieces."

"For the merchandise of it is better than the merchandise of silver" [Proverbs 3:14].

"I'll pay twenty thousand gold coins . . ."

"The gold and the crystal cannot equal it: and the exchange of it shall not be for jewels of fine gold" [Job 28:17].

"All that a man hath will he give for his life" [Job 2:4], thought the vizier to himself, and then he said to the old man: "Wait here for an hour. I'll go home and will be back with something that will please you."

The vizier returned with two porters carrying a trunk filled with precious stones and jewels.

"Take all this and solve the riddles for me quickly," implored the vizier of the old man.

When the old man saw the trunk and what was in it, he changed his mind and told the vizier: One day, on a holiday, the king was walking in the forest and saw me cutting wood. He asked me: "Even?" He meant to say that "even though you are an old man, you are working at such hard labor? And even on a holiday, you do not rest?"

And I answered: "If I had, then I wouldn't have to"—meaning: If had the money, I wouldn't have to be a woodcutter.

The king understood my answer and asked me: "How are the two?"—meaning, "How are your legs?" And I answered him: "The third one is in between them." This means that I am helped by a third leg, a cane.

Then he asked me: "How are your friends?"—meaning, how are your teeth that sit together. And I answered: "The package has broken"—meaning that there are only a few teeth left in my mouth.

The last of the king's questions was: "How are your brothers?"—meaning, my eyes. And I answered: "The far one is close"—meaning, the eyes that used to see far are now only near-sighted. "These are the solutions to the riddles," finished the old man, with a nice feeling of victory.

The vizier hurried back to the king, happy, and with a good heart, and told him the answers to the riddles. The king summoned the old man and said to him: "Old man, old man, didn't I tell you not to sell cheaply?"

"And I answered you: 'Do not teach the wise,' didn't I?" said the old man, and he showed the king the trunk of treasure he received from the vizier.

"A fair price," said the king, who smiled with pleasure at the vizier's great loss of fortune.

Transcribed by Nissim Benjamin Gamlieli

COMMENTARY TO
"THE KING AND THE OLD WOODCUTTER"

IFA 10300

PENINNAH SCHRAM

The informant of this narrative, Nissim Damti, was born in Aden, a city located in southwest Yemen, near the southern entrance to the Red Sea. Damti moved to Israel in 1938. However, apparently due to difficult circumstances, he went back to Aden. Then, some years later, he returned to Israel and lived in Petach Tikva, where he died at the age of sixty-four. Fearing that twenty-one of his remembered folk narratives, as well as his original tales, would be lost, he wrote them in a notebook to preserve them for future generations. In writing these narratives Damti captured the orality of a told tale through dialogue, using short, simple sentences, vernacular language, repetition, metaphoric phrases, and so forth. Damti gave this story, "The King and the Old Woodcutter," to Nissim Benjamin Gamlieli to publish in his book, *The Chambers of Yemen* (1978, 52–54), where it appears in the section titled "Wisdom Stories."

Typologically, this narrative (IFA 10300) belongs to the type AT 921F*[1] ("Geese from Rus"[2]): A tsar speaks in riddles with a peasant who has pleased him. The tsar says; "The geese from Rus [i.e., the nobles] are flying here; be prepared to pluck them." The peasant makes use of this advice with great success.[3] It also features the motif H561.6.1 ("King and Peasant: The Plucked Fowl"): The king gives riddling questions to a peasant, who always interprets them correctly. The king says that he will send the peasant a fowl for him to pluck. The king gives the same questions to his courtiers, who cannot interpret them. They pay the peasant good money for the answers. The peasant tells the king that he has plucked the fowl (Thompson 1956, 426).[4]

Tales involving riddles, a king, his vizier, and a Jew are found in Yemen, which is part of the Arabian Peninsula. Since Muslim Arabs held this region from the seventh to sixteenth centuries, when it fell to the Ottoman Turks in 1538, there is clear evidence that Arabic folktales influenced and shaped the types of folktales Jews related in the Middle Eastern countries—Yemenite tales as well as Sephardic narratives. Not only did Jews transform narratives from other cultures into Jewish variants; they also told Jewish tales, including those from the Talmudic-Midrashic literature. These narratives, in turn, often became international tales, as the fluid folklore process has been active for centuries in every place where Jewish people have traveled and lived. The popular riddling tales were frequently part of this exchange.

Examining the Jewish oral tradition, we find that riddles have always intrigued Jews, as exemplified by the Talmudic *aggadot* and the legends of King Solomon and the Queen of Sheba. Throughout the centuries, Jews also found ways during crises to communicate through cryptic messages and act with cunning and creativity (that is, thinking outside the box). According to Galit Hasan-Rokem and David Shulman, "The riddle form is dialogic, requiring the interaction of self and other. Two levels are joined in the question, only to be disentangled in the answer. The process involved is inherently enigmatic and also transformative. The transition effected leaves reality changed, restructured, its basic categories restated, recognized, affirmed" (Hasan-Rokem and Shulman 1996). Basically, riddle narratives must have two parts: a question and its solution. Within the framework of an often serious "game," riddles take on mysterious and multiple hidden meanings; they require us to analyze those ambiguous meanings to gain a new perspective and to make new connections in our minds. Sometimes listeners get locked into set meanings of words and phrases, but riddles can cause them to understand these words in ways that stretch the mind and entertain them at the same time. Riddles as a literary device can be considered as tiny stories-within-stories.[5]

Since Jews did not always have a protected status or the security to live without pressure to convert during their history in Yemen, there would have been a need to emphasize wish-filled stories narrated by Jews, whereby they demonstrated that they were the cleverest and wisest of people and thus deserving of favor from the ruler of the land. Often in the Middle Eastern and East European narratives, there is a religious confrontation between the Jew and the gentile (a vizier or a priest), with the clever winner (either the Jew or the gentile) sharing the same race or religion as the storyteller and the listeners. Made to match wits, they vie in asking riddling questions and providing answers.[6] An example of this type of tale is IFA 142 (Iraq), "The Tale of a Jew Who Bridled the Wind" (Noy, ed. 1963, 101–4). Frequently these tales of cleverness involve jealousy or envy on the part of the king's evil chief advisor, who undeservedly accuses the Jews of some tragic misdeed (e.g., blood libel) or just wants to get rid of the Jews. However, many Jewish folktales, in both Sephardic and Ashkenazic folklore, frequently focus on the resourcefulness and wisdom of the Jews as well as on riddles and wordplay. Yet in this narrative there is neither a threat to the Jews nor any hostile competition between the Jew and the gentile.

In the frame of this narrative, we find that the king was "very righteous . . . wise and understood riddles," an ideal ruler who no doubt also honored the elders (Jew and non-Jew) in the community. Walking in the woods, he meets an old man chopping wood. In this variant, the old man is not specifically identified as a Jew.[7] This empathetic king asks the woodcutter how he is. What follows is an exchange of brief questions and responses that form four enigmatic riddles. The king, astounded at the poor man's wisdom, decides to help him become wealthy in his old age.

The inner story is about the dishonest vizier, whom the king wants to teach a stern lesson, actually to get rid of him. The king decides to challenge the vizier's ingenuity by telling him he must find out what these riddles mean or else he will be decapitated. The vizier cannot figure out the riddles, nor can he find anyone else to help him, until he encounters the same old man in the woods. Having no one else to aid him, the vizier reluctantly tells the old man about the four riddles. The old man, of course, knows how to complete each riddle in response to the opening words. However, the old man will not settle for any amount of money until the vizier, without any other hope for solving these life-saving riddles, agrees to bring an enormous trunk full of jewels. Only then does the old man explain the riddles to him and thereby fulfill the advice of the king, "Do not sell cheaply." He had indeed "plucked the pigeon" (nobleman) of all his ill-gotten riches. In the end, when the old man recounts what happened, the king is very pleased at this development.

It is interesting to note that this tale differs from many others, where a confrontation between the Jew and gentile ends with the king appointing the clever Jew as his advisor. This does not happen here. In this story, the king uses the riddles to accomplish his two goals, to help the wise old man gain wealth and to justly punish the vizier by depriving him of ill-gotten fortune (in other words, the punishment fits the crime). This tale would thus serve a social function by teaching both the value of wisdom and clever thinking (as exemplified by the old man) as well as the importance of honesty as exemplary behavior, which is preferable to gaining wealth through dishonest means (as exemplified by the vizier).

As a storyteller, I find this type of tale fun to tell because the listeners, along with the vizier, have to try to figure out the enigmatic dialogue between the king and the old man. When I tell this story with older people in the audience, I can see them shaking their heads in recognition of the riddles' solution because they recognize similar troubles with their legs, teeth, and eyes. And when I tell the story to younger people, they nod their heads when they realize that they are not yet clever enough to understand the riddles' meanings, and that they have much yet to learn about life.

Notes

1. In the Aarne and Thompson (1961) classification, it is mentioned as a Russian type: Afanasiev (921B)7.
2. Rus is an old name for Russia.
3. In addition to this variant from Yemen (IFA 10300), this international tale is found in six variants in the IFA. Four of these variants have also been published in other publications, as I indicate here, but none of the seven was published in any IFA publications: IFA 5100, "The Wazir and the Jew" (Morocco); IFA 8443, "The Conversation of the King and the Jew" (Israel, Sephardi; published in Ben Yaakov 1969, tale 9, p. 50); IFA 14012 (Israel, Cherkess; published in Haviv 1990, tale 11, p. 56); IFA 3244, "The Wazir Who Seeks Wisdom and the

Jew Who Helps Him" (Persia; published in Baharav 1968, tale 1, p. 13); IFA 5229, "The Sign Language" (Caucasus; published in Kort 1974, tale 11, p. 51, where it is titled "A Fat Duck to Pluck"; also published in Jason 1976, tale 54, p. 161, as "Wie Rupft Man Eine Ente?"); IFA 6036, "The Tsar and the Wise Old Man" (Poland).

4. There are a number of motifs to be found in this story, in addition to H561.6.1, noted earlier: H501.5 ("Test of Wisdom"); H506 ("Test of Resourcefulness"); H580 ("Enigmatic Statements"—apparently senseless remarks [or acts] interpreted figuratively, prove wise); H585 ("Enigmatic Conversation of King and Peasant"); H599.5 ("Enigmatic Counsel"); H614 ("Explanation of Enigmatic Phenomenon"); H761.1 (Jewish: Neuman "Riddle: Two Are Better Than Three"—two legs better than man with staff in old age); H971 (Jewish: Neuman "Task Performed with Help of Old Person"); H541.1 ("Riddle Propounded on Pain of Death"; Type AT * 922); J1110 ("Clever Persons"); J1250 ("Clever Verbal Retorts"); Q91 ("Reward for Cleverness").

5. For further investigations of the riddling genre, please see the bibliography, especially Hasan-Rokem and Shulman, eds. 1996.

6. Motif H561.6 (Thompson 1956, 426).

7. The ethnographer Yehuda Leib Cahan collected "The Plucked Pigeon" in Eastern Europe. He published the Yiddish tale in his book (Cahan 1931). In Cahan's tale the main characters are a sultan, his vizier, and a Jew washing sheep's wool (not a woodcutter).

BIBLIOGRAPHY

Aarne, Antti, and Stith Thompson. 1961. *The Types of the Folktale: A Classification and Bibliography*. FF Communications no. 184. Helsinki: Suomalainen Tiedeakatemia.

Abrahams, Roger D., and Alan Dundes. 1972. "Riddles." In *Folklore and Folklife: An Introduction*, ed. R. M. Dorson. Chicago: University of Chicago Press.

Ausubel, Nathan. 1957 [1948]. *A Treasury of Jewish Folklore*. New York: Crown. (Includes the folktales of "Riddle Solvers," 87–101; part 5 contains "Proverbs and Riddles," 638–48.)

Baharav, Zalman. 1968. *From Generation to Generation*. Tel Aviv: Mif'aley Tarbut Vechinuch. [Hebrew]

Ben Ya'akov, Avraham. 1969. *The Treasure*. Tel Aviv: Yavne. [Hebrew]

Cahan, Yehuda Leib. 1931. *Yidishe Folksmayses*. Vilna: Yidishe Folklor Bibliothek. [Yiddish]

Camp, Claudia V., 1990. "The Words of the Wise and Their Riddles." In Niditch, Susan (editor): *Text and Tradition: The Hebrew Bible and Folklore*, Atlanta, GA: Scholars Press 1990, 127–51.

Gamlieli, Nissim Benjamin. 1978. *The Chambers of Yemen*. Tel Aviv: Afikim. [Hebrew]

Georges, Robert A., and Alan Dundes. 1963. "Toward a Structural Definition of Riddles." *Journal of American Folklore* 76: 111–18.

Hasan-Rokem, Galit, and David Shulman, eds. 1996. *Untying the Knot: On Riddles and Other Enigmatic Modes*. New York: Oxford University Press.

Haviv, Yfrah. 1990. *The Magic Ring in Golani*. Tel Aviv: Hakibbutz Hameuchad. [Hebrew]

Jason, Heda. 1976. *Märchen aus Israel*. Dusseldorf: Eugen Diederichs Verlag.

Kort, Zebulun. 1974. *The Princess Who Became a Garland*. Tel Aviv: Yehudit. [Hebrew]

Noy, Dov. 1971. "Riddles at a Wedding Banquet." *Mahanayim* 83: 64–71. [Hebrew]

———, ed. 1963. *Folktales of Israel*. Chicago: University of Chicago Press.

Pagis, Dan. 1986. "A Secret Sealed: The History of the Hebrew Riddle in Italy and Holland." Supplement to *Tarbiz IV*. Jerusalem: Magnes Press. [Hebrew]

Pepicello, William J., and Thomas A. Green. 1984. *The Language of Riddles: New Perspectives*. Columbus: Ohio State University Press.

Roberts, John M., and Michael C. Forman. 1971. "Riddles: Expressive Models of Interrogation." *Ethnology* 10: 509–33.

Schwarzbaum, Haim. 1968. *Studies in Jewish and World Folklore*. Berlin: Walter de Gruyter.

Silverman-Weinreich, Beatrice. 2003. "Problemen un Uvdes baym forshn yidishe retenishn." In *YIVO-bleter, naye serye*, 4, 71–88. New York: YIVO Institute for Jewish Research.

Thompson, Stith. 1956. *Motif-Index of Folk-Literature*. Vol. 2. Bloomington: Indiana University Press.

THE WITCH (EL BEDA)

IFA 11575

NARRATED BY YESHUA BEN DAVID (YEMEN)

El Beda is a flesh-and-blood woman who can, just with the use of words, turn a person into an ass or any other animal, or into any form she wishes. To become a *beda* (a witch), the woman has to curse her father and mother for forty consecutive days, commit forty sins, and urinate facing the sun forty times. The one who does all that will for sure become a *beda*, and she will be able to harness magic powers to her service.

One time, El Beda kidnapped a gentile and turned him into an ass. During the day she rode it and used it for her work, and during the nights she transformed him back to his human form as her husband. He became very thin, and his spirit was sad and full of despair. When she saw him so depressed, sad, and bitter, she told him: "I agree to let you return to your wife and sons on condition that one year from now you will come back to me."

The man agreed to the condition and was released from the spell that she had cast on him. But to ensure his return, she asked him to give her a bundle of his head hair. He gave her the hair—not from his head, but from his leather bag, from which he had cunningly cut hair, and gave it to her.

The man returned home to his regular life. And after a year, when he did not come back to El Beda's house as he promised, the witch took the bundle of hair he had given her and invited the hair's owner to come to her. Immediately upon the witch's summoning, the leather bag, which was full of salt and hung on a wall, flew like a feather through the window and disappeared.

Transcribed by Nissim Benjamin Gamlieli

COMMENTARY TO "THE WITCH" (EL BEDA)

IFA 11575

IDIT PINTEL-GINSBERG

The present tale does not belong categorically to one specific genre. It has legend components along with prominent traits of magic folktales that focus on a woman. Laura Stark-Arola has suggested that narratives about women's magic should be considered a genre in itself, carrying a specific social role. This genre indeed overlaps other genres and even coincides with them, but differs from them in its emphasis on sexual attraction toward the feminine body and the couple's sexual and social ties (Stark-Arola 1998, 43–44). These emphases are present in this tale.

It is not possible to allocate the tale to one single tale type, for it is more a conglomerate of various types: AT 334 ("Household of the Witch"); AT 400–459 ("Supernatural or Enchanted Husband"); AT 400 IIIa ("The Hero Wants to Go Home on a Visit"); AT 459d ("An Animal Is Turned into a Handsome Youth").

The tale presents two main characters: a witch and a man. Various motifs connected to each one of them can be discerned. The motifs linked to the witch are G263 (Witch injures, enchants or transforms); D510 (Transformation by breaking taboo); and D567 (Transformation by sunlight). The motifs linked to the man are D132.1 (Transformation: man to ass); D621.1 (Man by day; animal by night).

The tale was recorded by Nissim Benjamin Gamlieli[1] and narrated by Yeshua Ben David, a Yemenite Jew born in 1900 in the village of El'ar, in the Kharaz province. Forty of Ben David's tales are registered at IFA. He heard his folktale repertoire mostly from his father and from an elderly Jew, named Said Eljamdi, who lived in his village (Gamlieli 1978, 465).

The IFA contains 104 tales about sorcerers, fifty-four of which pertain to witches. Twenty-one of the total sorcerers' tales are from Yemen, and nine of these are about witches. Among the Yemenite witch tales, this story is unique in presenting the erotic aspect of the witch, whereas the others focus on her nefarious attributes.

Parts of the tale are considered pseudo-magical. At the beginning, precise instructions about how to become a witch are related, and the end describes a witch practicing what seems to be contagious magic.[2] Despite the tale's style and terminology, there is no connection between the tale and magic praxis.[3]

The beginning of the tale is composed of two basic parts. The first explains the witch's nature: "a flesh-and-blood woman who can, just with the use of words, turn a person into an ass or any other animal, or into any form she wishes." The second part details how any woman can turn into a witch, regardless of her age or religion.

The view that any woman is a potential witch is universal. Many explanations have been offered for this belief (Heinemann 2000). One researcher sees this as stemming from women's biological dissimilarity from men and its projection onto social status; the woman is thus turned into "the other" in the eyes of men (Mauss 1972). Others see it as a projection of men's hidden and unethical desires toward women (Heinemann 2000). Still other scholars see it as originating within power struggles (Sanders 1995), as an efficient way to secure men's hegemony over women's behavior (Larner 1984).

The perception of women as potential witches is echoed in Jewish tradition as well (Bar Ilan 1993), and it grows out of similar roots. The rabbinical literature reflects Jewish men's cultural perceptions (Valler 1999; 2000), and many of its sources express precisely this attitude, as in these examples: "The more wives the more witchcraft" (Mishnah Avot 2:7); "Most women are witches" (Jerusalem Talmud, Sanhedrin 7:13); "The best of women is immersed in witchcraft" (Jerusalem Talmud, Kiddushin 4:11); "Mostly women engage in witchcraft" (Babylonian Talmud, Sanhedrin 67a); "A daughter is a vain treasure to her father . . . if she grows old, lest she engage in witchcraft" (Babylonian Talmud, Sanhedrin 100b).

Women in rabbinical literature were considered as "others" (Baskin 1995) because of their biological difference and its uncontrollable aspects; women were thus identified with nature and impure domains (Rubin 1995). Women were to be banished from religious activity and live on the margins of society, and were viewed by men as a threat to the social order (Bar Ilan 1993; Fishbane 1993; Seidel 1992).[4] The rabbis' judgments of women's nature were guided by men who feared women and suppressed their sexual desire toward them (Hasan-Rokem 1995; Wegner 1991).

According to the opening of our tale, a woman who wishes to become a witch must go through a three-stage process. This process is basically a gradual breaking of laws and conventions connected to three concentric circles of belonging: The internal circle is her parents, which is the human domain closest to her. The middle circle symbolizes society in general. And the outer circle is the public domain and natural world. These three domains cover all the areas of human existence. In the first stage she must curse her parents for forty days, a violation of the biblical commandment "Honor thy father and thy mother" (Exodus 20:12). The connection between this offense and a woman's becoming a witch may be related to the sinners listed in the Mishna as those deserving to be stoned:[5] "These are they who are to be stoned: . . . He who curses his father or mother; he who has criminal connection with a betrothed damsel; the beguiler to idolatry; he who leads a town astray; the sorcerer; and the stubborn and rebellious son" (Mishna Sanhedrin 7:4)

In the second stage, a woman wishing to become a witch must commit forty sins.[6] The tale does not elaborate about the type and nature of these violations, but their implementation is an offense to society as a whole, which is based on respecting the *Nomos*. In this way the woman leaves the civilized human world.

In the third and last stage, the woman must urinate facing the sun. By this act the woman is exposing her intimate parts in daylight for all to see.[7] This is considered the woman's final moral degradation on the path toward total insubordination. As a bodily waste, urine can symbolize a demonstration of power and control through the process of urination, and as such it reflects the woman's transition toward the rejected margins of society.[8] Urinating in the direction of the sun can also be seen as an insult against the sun, and nature's daylight powers in general, in preference for the dark powers of the night.

Thus becoming a witch involves a gradual process of abusing and abandoning human societal norms. It should be emphasized that this process does not include study of or an apprenticeship in witchcraft,[9] although the tale points to a direct affinity between the two: "The one who does all that will for sure become a *beda*, and she will be able to harness magic powers to her service."

The tale focuses on a non-Jewish man kidnapped by a witch. The emphasis on the victim's religion distances the threat from Jewish society but may also tell of and even point to the non-Jewish sources of the tale. The religion of the witch is not mentioned; the reason may be that she has become a being lacking any normative and ethical boundaries, and therefore also lacking any religion.

The relations between the man and the witch are described in a laconic manner, within a few sentences. But the laconic language and the clear imagery actually intensify the hard picture. The active character and initiator is the witch; the man is totally submissive to her authority while he is physically and sexually abused after she turned him into an ass: "During the day she rode it and used it for her work, and during the nights she transformed him back to his human form as her husband."

Man's control symbolizes the cultural domain, while his lack of control is in the natural domain. This relationship, in which the man has no control, is all within the wild and unrestrained natural domain.

The transformation of the man into an ass is not coincidental. This is a common universal and ancient motif (D 132.1).[10] The eleventh-century Persian historiographer Abu Alfaseli Baihaki, in his survey of the various beliefs (which he calls "nonsense") that occur in folktales, presents the example of a tale where an old witch transforms a man into an ass.[11] This motif is present in Jewish sources as well, including Babylonian Talmud, Sahnedrin 67b,[12] Akhimaatz scroll (Yassif 1999, 354). But in our tale this motif constitutes the hidden stratum of the plot and clarifies the relations between the witch and the man.

In Roman classical culture, the ass is considered to possess sexual desire, and is also a phallic object lusted after by women. They are attracted to him, and he satisfies their exaggerated lust (Frankfurter 2001, 491–93). The woman who rebelled and became a witch is also reckless in her unrestrained sexual behavior,[13] and therefore transforms the man into her most desired sexual object, the ass. The man—who during the day is an ass and carries the burden,[14] and at night returns to his human form (but maybe with the sexual characteristics of an ass)—is abused to exhaustion by a woman. It may well be that this treatment projects the most hidden desires of men, but it is obvious that the goal of this tale is to raise objections and create resentment, and to eradicate libidinous actions from intimate ones; to exhort individuals to follow the law and warn both women and men from straying from them.

The next episode in the tale exposes the broken connection between the two characters. This is the turning point where each character changes and returns a bit to the gender attributes society considers proper and desirable for them. The woman is sympathetic to the man's distress: "When she [sees] him so depressed, sad, and bitter," she is ready to return him to his family for a year. For the first time the audience learns of the existence of another family, a wife and sons, from whom he was separated. This detail—the entrapment of a married man—increases the perception of the woman's/witch's recklessness. The most significant change that occurs within the man is his movement from submissive passivity to activity and deviousness. Giving her the hair of his satchel instead of his own hair points toward a few of his changes. He is the initiator in disrupting the bond between him and the witch, for without his hair the witch has no control over him. In this deceit he is revealed as having knowledge of her witchcraft and its usage. He is also revealed as being smarter than the woman. His character is now exposed as that of a man of initiative: knowledgeable, smart, and independent. These are the male traits that are desirable in traditional society.

The woman in this part of the tale is represented as empathetic, stupid (she does not notice the difference between human hair and satchel hair), and naïve (when she believes he will return to her). These are apparently the desirable traits for women in the eyes of the men in the narrating community.

At the end of the tale, the man returns to his family and to his previous life—in other words, to the cultural domain where he rules. At the end of the year, he does not go back to the witch.[15] She tries to return him through witchcraft, using the hair he left for her. Her action reminds one of contagious magic, as she hopes to control him by means of his hair she possesses, but just his satchel full of salt returns to her. Salt is believed to prevent the evil forces' harm (Trachtenberg 1977 [1939]), but it is unclear what its function is in this tale. It may have been hung in the man's house—the cultural domain—to protect the house from evil forces, but it does not prevent the witch's influence over the satchel.

It seems that the function of this tale, similar to that of ancient tales about rebellious women,[16] is twofold. On the one hand it seeks to dissuade men and women from lust and moral and sexual recklessness. On the other hand it wishes to reinforce the fixed norms of traditional patriarchal society (Bar-Itzhak 1982) and the stable gender roles within it.

NOTES

1. This tale was published in Gamlieli's book (Gamlieli 1978, 210).
2. This is a magic praxis based on a continuous contact between the whole and its parts. This term was formulated by James Frazer, who also cites the concept of "contagion." For further reading, see Frazer 1959, 62–70.
3. I would like to thank Dr. Yuval Harari, who very clearly answered my questions in the matter. On magic in folktales, see Shenhar 1982, 72–100.
4. These studies offer surveys of the diverse rabbinical sources in which women are represented as sorcerers.
5. I again thank Dr. Yuval Harari, who pointed out this connotation.
6. The number 40, which appears in this tale, may have no further meaning aside from being a typological number. In Jewish sources there are indeed forty blows given to sinners (see, for example, "Seder Yom Hakippurim," in *Seder Rav Amram Gaon*), but 43 is the number of unintentional sins that require a sacrifice offering (Rambam, Mishnah Torah, Laws of Unintentional Sins 1:4).
7. Laura Stark-Arola, who researched the magic rituals of Finnish women, lists among the rites performed secretly the exposure of the sexual female organ to overcome magical harm (Stark-Arola 1998, 45).
8. For further study, see Douglas 2002, 140–59; Eilberg-Schwartz 1990, 187.
9. Trachtenberg pointed to the historical fact that Jewish women did not have a significant status in the practice of magic (Trachtenberg 1977 [1939], 17).
10. For ancient Greek sources, see Yassif 1999, note 97, p. 530.
11. "An old sorceress turned a man into a donkey, and again another old sorceress anointed his ears with a kind of oil until he was turned into a man again" (Omnidsalar 1984, 205). See also, Bosworth 2004, 17.
12. See discussion on this matter in Yassif 1999, 215.
13. On the perception of the witch as a whore, see Yassif 1999, 354–55.
14. A married man's resemblance to an ass is mentioned in the Midrash Ecclesiastes Rabba 1:1.
15. The refusal to return after a year is reminiscent of the tale "Maase Yerushalmi," where a man is requested to return to a she-demon. But whereas in that tale the man is punished for his refusal by death, in our story the man's refusal is considered positive and acceptable.
16. Baskin defines their functions: "These stories are intended to be didactic: to delineate for men the boundaries of female freedom and to demonstrate to women potential penalties for their attempts to exceed them" (Baskin 1995, 31).

BIBLIOGRAPHY

Aarne, Antti, and Stith Thompson. 1961. *The Types of the Folktale: A Classification and Bibliography*. FF Communications no. 184. Helsinki: Suomalainen Tiedeakatemia.

Alexander, Tamar. 1995. "Design of the Demon Story Genre: Marriages between a Man and a Demon." In *A View into the Lives of Women in Jewish Societies*, ed. Yael Atzmon, 291–307. Jerusalem: Zalman Shazar Center for Jewish History. [Hebrew]

Bar Ilan, Meir, 1993. "Witches in the Bible and in the Talmud." In *Approaches to Ancient Judaism*, new series V, ed. Herbert W. Basser and Simcha Fishbane, 7–32. Atlanta, GA: American Scholars Press.

Bar-Itzhak, Haya. 1982. "Modes of Characterization in the Sacred Legend of Oriental Jews." In *Studies in the Literature of Oriental Jews*, 1–21. Haifa: University of Haifa. [Hebrew]

Baskin, Judith. 1995. "Silent Partners: Women as Wives in Rabbinic Literature." In *Active Voices: Women in Jewish Culture*, ed. Maurie Sacks. Urbana: University of Illinois Press.

———. 1999. "Woman as Other in Rabbinic Literature." In *Judaism in Late Antiquity*, part 3, vol. 2: *Where We Stand: Issues and Debates in Ancient Judaism*, ed. Jacob Neusner and Alan J. Avery-Peck, 65–80. Leiden: E. J. Brill.

Bosworth, Edmund. 2004. "An Oriental Samuel Pepys? Abu'l-Fadl Bayhaqi's Memoirs of Court Life in Eastern Iran and Afghanistan, 1030–1041." *Journal of the Royal Asiatic Society* 14: 13–25.

Douglas, Mary. 2002. *Purity and Danger*. London: Routledge and Paul Kegan.

Dvori, Bilha. 1995. "Why Is a Witch Always a Woman?" *Davar* 30 (4): 12. [Hebrew]

Eilberg-Schwartz, Howard. 1990. *The Savage in Judaism*. Bloomington: Indiana University Press.

Fishbane, Simcha. 1993. "Most Women Engage in Sorcery: An Analysis of Sorceresses in the Babylonian Talmud." *Jewish History* 7 (1): 27–42.

Frankfurter, David. 2001. "The Perils of Love: Magic and Countermagic in Coptic Egypt." *Journal of the History of Sexuality* 10 (3/4): 480–500.

Frazer, James. 1959. *The New Golden Bough*. New York: Mentor.

Gamlieli, Nissim Benjamin. 1978. *The Chambers of Yemen*. Tel Aviv: Afikim. [Hebrew]

Hasan-Rokem, Galit. 1995. "The Voice Is the Voice of My Sister: Feminine Images and Feminine Symbols in Lamentations Rabba." In *A View into the Lives of Women in Jewish Societies*, ed. Y. Atzmon, 95–111. Jerusalem: Zalman Shazar Center for Jewish History. [Hebrew]. French translation: "La voix est la voix de ma soeur. Figures et symbols féminins dans le midrach Lamentations Rabbah." *Cahiers de Littérature Orale* 44 (1998): 13–36.

Heinemann, Evelyn. 2000. *Witches: A Psychoanalytic Exploration of the Killing of Women*. London: Free Association Books.

Larner, Christine. 1984. *Witchcraft and Religion*. Oxford: Basil Blackwell.

Mauss, Marcel. 1972. *A General Theory of Magic*. London: Routledge and Paul Kegan.

Omnidsalar, Mahmoud. 1984. "Storytellers in Classical Persian Texts." *Journal of American Folklore* 97 (384): 204–12.

Pinkola Estés, Clarissa. 1992. *Women Who Run with the Wolves*. New York: Ballantine.

Rubin, Nissan. 1995. *The Beginning of Life: Rites of Birth, Circumcision, and Redemption of the First-Born in the Talmud and Midrash*. Tel Aviv: Hakibbutz Hameuchad. [Hebrew]

Sanders, Andrew. 1995. *A Deed without a Name: The Witch in Society and History*. Oxford: Berg.

Seidel, Jonathan. 1992. "'Release us and we will release you!'—Rabbinic Encounters with Witches and Witchcraft." *Journal of the Association of Graduates in Near Eastern Studies* 3, no. 1 (Spring): 45–61.

Shenhar, Aliza. 1982. *From Folktale to Children's Tale*. Haifa: University of Haifa Press. [Hebrew]

Stark-Arola, Laura. 1998. *Magic, Body, and Social Order: The Construction of Gender Through Women's Private Rituals in Traditional Finland*. Helsinki: Finnish Literature Society.

Thompson, Stith. 1956. *Motif-Index of Folk-Literature*. Vol. 2. Bloomington: Indiana University Press.

Trachtenberg, Joshua. 1977 [1939]. *Jewish Magic and Superstition*. New York: Atheneum.

Valler, Shulamit. 1999. *Women and Womanhood in the Talmud*. Providence, RI: Brown Jewish Studies 321.

———. 2000. *Women in Jewish Society in the Talmudic Period*. Tel Aviv: Hakibbutz Hameuchad. [Hebrew]

Wegner, Judith Romney. 1991. "The Image and Status of Women in Classical Rabbinic Judaism." In *Jewish Women in Historical Perspective*, ed. Judith Baskin. Detroit: Wayne State University Press.

Yassif, Eli. 1999. *The Hebrew Folktale: History, Genre, Meaning*. Bloomington: Indiana University Press.

HOW A BOTTOMLESS BUCKET
SAVED A COMMUNITY

IFA 11739

NARRATED BY SHOSHANA FARIZADA (PERSIA)

[O]nce] there was a town in which a few Jewish families lived. And in this town the Jews lived in peace and quiet. One day there came an order from the sultan to search the Jews to find out what [possessions] they had. And if they didn't have property, he did not care; they should give whatever they had. Every family had to give a million to the sultan, and if not, all families would be put to death.

What does a Jew do when he hears such a thing? They all gather in the synagogue and sit and pray. Suddenly they look up [and behold] someone coming to the synagogue and saying: "What is with you? All of you are crying and mourning. What is [happening] here?" So all of them say: "There is an evil decree against us, and every family has to give a million. And all in all, we are ten or twelve families, and from where will we bring all these millions to give to the sultan?"

Then he said: "That's all?"

They said: "Yes. What do you mean, that's all? It's really bad, how will we manage?"

He said: "Well, someone who grew up among you should take a leaky bucket, a bucket that is open at both ends, and a few meters of rope, and travel to Safed. There he should go, in Safed—he should go to the well in such and such a place, on such and such a street, and throw down the bucket with the rope."

They said: "What are you saying? What will we save with a leaky bucket?"

He said: "What I am telling you, do it."

They get up, they travel with a donkey a few months' journey, and arrive in Safed. They arrive to that place he told them [about]. They search for the well, put the bucket in, throw the bucket down, and pull. [It is] heavy. They pull and pull; they raise it to the top. They see a man lying on a bed. A very luxurious bed. Someone is lying [on it]. When he sees the people who are raising him up, he wakes up. He wakes up, starts: "What do you want? Who are you?"

They, the Jews, say: "Yes! You put this evil decree on us, and our situation is such and such; you must waive the decree or you will not return."

No! Yes! He has no choice! He is in a strange place and far from home, and what will they do? Will they abandon him there? He doesn't know where to go, what or how. Then he says: "So, what do you want me to do?"

They give him a paper and a pen and say: "You must sign that you waive [the evil decree]."

Well, he has no choice; he signs the paper. And they return him.

He returns to his city, the city where he made the decree on the Jews. He says: "Oh, that was a dream I dreamt. What is happening with the Jews? These Jews, they have to bring that money. Impossible, this was just a dream I dreamt. This didn't happen. It is not reality."

Well, the date he gave them at the beginning arrived. He gave them a date, a time to bring the money. The day arrives, the Jews appear. Then he asks: "So, where are you? Did you get it? Did you accomplish the task, or I will finish off all the Jews?"

They bring the paper. They put it in his hand and show it to him. He doesn't believe it. He has no choice; he signed it. His signature is there. He doesn't believe it. What can he do?

Then he cancels his order to finish off the Jews and announces that the Jews must be honored from this day on. Then the Jews believed that God heard their prayer and sent them an angel to guide them, to send them to Safed, and that the decree would be waived.

The Jews knew this was an angel from heaven or Elijah the Prophet. There are some who say: "Do believe this was the hand of God!"

Since then, there is belief, and belief in God and in prayer and in everything; and the main thing is that they believe.

Transcribed by Sarah Loftus

COMMENTARY TO "HOW A BOTTOMLESS BUCKET SAVED A COMMUNITY"

IFA 11739

HEDA JASON

This tale is of the sacred legend genre. This genre has a notable role in Jewish folk literature.[1] Sacred legends comprise more than 20 percent of all stories recorded for the Israel Folktale Archives (IFA) by Jews who immigrated to Israel from Muslim countries. Among the stories recorded by Jews who emigrated from Eastern Europe, the percentage is even higher (Jason 1988, 103; Soroudi 2008, part 2).

The story was told by Shoshana Farizada, who was born in 1937 in the city of Shiraz, in Iran. She immigrated to Israel with her family in 1958, making her home in the city of Beit She'an in the Jordan Valley. In Iran she had heard her stories from her father, who told them mainly in the evenings after work and on the Shabbat, and from her grandmother when the grandchildren gathered around her.

This story was sound recorded in 1978 by Sarah Loftus, who took part in the Beit She'an project.

"Sacred legend" is defined as a folktale presenting a specific problem that a sacred power solves. The solution of the problem takes place within the framework of the community—its value system and rules—and strengthens the existing order. The sacred power works through its agents. These can be humans—a local rabbi or a person known throughout the Jewish world, such as Maimonides—or a preternatural figure, such as the Prophet Elijah. The agent can be also an inanimate article, including manmade objects, such as ritual buildings (synagogues, holy tombs, etc.) and ritual paraphernalia, or natural forces. Sometimes no special agent of the sacred power works in the story, but the very plot is arranged by the sacred power in such a way that the problem is solved in support of the existing social order.

Jewish sacred legends are built on a problem from one of three categories: (1) general human problems (e.g., suffering, illness, fate, death, sin and punishment, etc.); (2) social problems (pitting commoners vs. the elite; conflicts between socioeconomic classes); and (3) Jewish national problems (revolving around Jewish identity in the Diaspora; or arising for a minority community living among a hostile majority). This third group of problems is the subject of about half the sacred legends that are filed in the IFA. Our supposition is that the quantity of stories dealing with a problem reflects the importance of this problem to the Jewish community in the Diaspora (see Jason 1975).

Within the framework of problems of a persecuted minority community, one of the widespread stories tells about a threat to the community's existence from a non-Jewish ruler. The form of the threat is: "If you don't do such and such, the entire community will be put to death or banished." There are two types of persecution: invented threats and real threats. Among the invented threats stand out demands to solve riddles or to accomplish various tasks.[2] Another type of invented oppression is, for example, the demand by the majority non-Jewish community that a Jewish child should be given to them each year for sacrifice on their holiday. An agent of the sacred power rescues the victim and waives the decree. This is the opposite of the blood libels imposed on the Jews. The theme is listed by Gaster as no. 347 in his list of story summaries (Gaster 1924). The story was recorded a few times for IFA—for example, IFA 619, from Jewish immigrants from Yemen;[3] and IFA 842, from Jewish immigrants from Romania.[4] Alongside such stories are IFA stories about actual persecutions, such as imposing a special heavy tax on the Jewish community. This happened many times: Jews were required to pay large sums to the local administrator, and the community leaders were imprisoned. In reality, it was possible to try to circumvent the local administrator—to reach the court of a higher official and obtain a waiver of the decree or the removal of the official, and so forth—with the help of influential Jews or bribery. However this course was not always successful. And here comes the story to comfort the depressed. What actually had a bitter end in the story ends well: The sacred power saves the community from paying excessive, illegal taxes. The rescue is accomplished through an agent of the sacred power (either a human or a sacred being in human form)—a local low-ranking Jew or a mysterious person who appears from outside—and with the help of supernatural forces, as in our story, forces the oppressor to waive the evil decree.

The tale is widespread in the Jewish Diaspora—what could be more Jewish than a story about troubles of Jews if not such an event? Yet this story is also found in early Byzantine Christian writings (fourth century CE). The story describes a group of monks of the early monastic movement who gathered around a charismatic leader. The authorities levied a poll tax on them, as on all other local residents. But the monks have left the active world: They have no income because they do not work but instead pray, and others support them. Thus how will they pay the tax?

The Christian story about the deeds of Father Ammonathas reads as follows:

Once, a clerk came to Pelusium/Pelusion and wanted to demand a poll-tax from the monks as from the laymen. All the brothers gathered around Father Ammonathas to discuss the matter, and decided that a few brothers from the monastery would travel to the Imperator. But Father Ammonathas said to them:—This effort is not needed, it would be better for you to sit quietly in your cells and fast for two weeks, and through the grace of the Messiah, I will accomplish this by myself.

So the monks went to their cells, and the Father also sat quietly in his cell.

After fourteen days, the monks were worried about him, because they had not seen him go anywhere, and said:—The Father has lost our cause.

But on the fifteenth day, the monks gathered again according to the agreement. The Father came to them with a document signed by the Imperator. When the monks saw the document, they were astonished and said to him:—When did you bring this, Father?

The Father said to them:—Believe me, my brothers, that night I traveled to the Imperator, he signed this decree. Then I went to Alexandria and there, I got the clerk's signature. And then I returned to you.

Upon hearing this, they were awestruck and bowed down before him. The matter ended, and the clerk did not bother them again.[5]

Does this sound familiar? It is the same basic story. There is one major difference: the identity of the two communities—one Jewish and the other Christian monks. In the Jewish tale the non-Jewish king is magically transported ("jumping the path," or *kfitsat ha'derekh*) against his will: He is brought to a well in the city of Safed and is returned to his palace. In the Christian story the monk who is living in Pelusion, in a border fortress between Egypt and Sinai (see Pauly-Wissowa 1937, half-volume 37), makes the effort to get to the imperator, who resides in Constantinople, the capital. The monk does this with the help of magic ("jumping the path"). The relationship with the civil authorities differs in the two stories: The monk respects the authorities and its head (the imperator is also the head of the church); the Jew is contemptuous of the non-Jewish authorities and its head, and does not feel obligated to them.

The basic conflict in these two stories is the confrontation between civic authorities and their ideology and minority communities, which profess their own value systems and ideologies. Thus the same narrative can express different viewpoints. Even a folktale that looks "Jewish" can serve a different society; in the present case the two societies share the trait of being an oppressed minority.

NOTES

1. This story was recorded in the framework of the Beit She'an Project (1977–79). The story has been sound-recorded with no editing, and is here translated literally to demonstrate the low-level folk style of live narration by a typical member of the community. A well-trained performer would narrate in a less colloquial style.

2. The story is catalogued in Aarne and Thompson 1961 as no. AT 922.
3. Published in Noy, ed., 1963, no. 154.
4. Published twice: Noy 1960, 114–16; Avitsuk 1965, no. 2.
5. Migne 1864, vol. 65, 135–37. Translated from Greek into Hebrew by Sister Kirsten Pedersen (called Sister Abraham); translated from Hebrew into English by F. Schreiber.

BIBLIOGRAPHY

Aarne, Antti, and Stith Thompson. 1961. *The Types of the Folktale: A Classification and Bibliography*. FF Communications no. 184. Helsinki: Suomalainen Tiedeakatemia.

Avitsuk, Ya'acov. 1965. *The Tree That Absorbed Tears*. Edited and annotated by Dov Noy. IFA Publication Series, no. 7. Haifa: Ethnological Museum and Folklore Archives. [Hebrew]

Gaster, Moses. 1924. *The Exempla of the Rabbis*. London: Asia Publishing Company.

Jason, Heda. 1975. "Conflict and Resolution in the Sacred Legend." In *Studies in Jewish Ethnopoetry*, 63–176. Taipei: Oriental Cultural Service.

———. 1988. *Folktales from the Jews of Iraq: Tale Types and Genres*. Or Yehuda: Babylonian Jewry Heritage Center.

Migne, J. P., ed. 1864. *Patrologiae cursus completus*. Series graeca, vol. LXV. Paris.

Noy, Dov. 1960. "Elijah the Prophet on the Night of the Seder." *Mahanayim* 44: 110–16. [Hebrew]

———, ed. 1963. *Jefet Schwili erzaehlt*. Berlin: De Gruyter.

Pauly-Wissowa. [Pauly, August F. von, ed.] 1893–1978. *Paulys Real-Encyclopaedie der classischen Altertumswissenschaft*. Stuttgart: Meltzer.

Soroudi, Sarah S. 2008. *Folktales of Jews from Iran, Central Asia and Afghanistan: Tale-Types and Genres*. Edited by Heda Jason. Beitraege zur Kulturgeschichte des islamischen Orients, vol. 38. Dortmund: Verlag fuer Orientkunde.

THE MEASURE OF A WOMAN IS TWO, THE MEASURE OF A MAN IS ONE

IFA 11911

NARRATED BY TAMAR LUGASI (MOROCCO)

There was a *hajj*,[*]—he is called *hajj*—he had three daughters. Once, once a year, they go to Mecca. So he told them: "Look, I left you three saplings, flowerpots, to water. The daughter who keeps and she is good, and takes care of herself, she is all right. I shall find for her some . . ."

He told them: "You have everything" they were very rich "you do not lack anything, and take care of yourselves."

Well. The father went with goodbye and blessing.

He has a youngest daughter, very clever. Once she went up to the roof. And she has a flowerpot that she waters. Suddenly a youth came, the prince who was living opposite them, and he told her: "You who water these saplings, for whom do you water? How many leaves do they have?"

She turned to him and said: "You the writer, the wise man, count for me how many stars there are in heaven and how much water there is in the sea and I shall count for you the leaves of this flowerpot."

He said: "She is clever."

She stunned him you know, he had no answer. Two days later, he came to her again. She was drinking some porridge, you know, eating; she dropped some of it and licked her lips with her tongue, and did not notice that he kept an eye on her from the roof, and she went down. Two days later he went up and said: "Licker the daughter of porridge licker from the corners."

She said to him: "Well." She took it to her heart and knew it. And so did he. Two days later he went up with a pomegranate and started to eat from it. One grain fell to the ground; he lifted it and ate it quietly. He came after two days and she told him: "You are a gleaner son of a gleaner."

They kept it so; she did not go there for a week. What did he do? He loved her very much. What should he do, what? He went to an old man and said: "Advise me what to do."

Said he: "Dress up as an old man."

He took some fish, like a fishmonger, and passed by the house: "Fish, fish."

Her sisters went down: "How much?"

He said: "No, I give two kisses and one fish."

So they gave him their cheeks, and he kissed them. They said to the younger sister: "You have no fish, only we shall eat."

[*] *Hajj*—a Muslim who has been to Mecca

And she said: "I cannot do so."

But they forced her, poor thing. They forced her. She went down. She gave her cheek; he kissed her and gave her a fish. She went up, ate, and did not know who he was. How could she recognize the prince, dirty and torn as he was? And she went out. God preserve us. Two days later, she went up again to water the flowerpot. He told her: "We went today among the fish; we were near the house of the lady: we kissed the lady, two kisses and two fish."

And she went. "Oh, what have I done, what have I done"—and she kept it inside her.

She did not go up to the roof anymore. He became ill, very ill. They brought the doctor and the old women. She was also brought. What should she do? She dressed up and called out: "The doctor, the doctor."

Only the nurses did not go out, they said: "Please come in, maybe you will save the prince; he will die and what will happen?"

She entered, and what did she take along? She took excrement of goats and filled a bottle of wine with urine and put it in her basket. And she went in. She told him: "Pardon me," lifted him up, gave him a cup of urine to drink, and fed him with the excrement of the goat; and in the end she lifted his buttocks and put in a radish. Then she lifted her mask and showed him. He cried out. She ran away.

So the father came back from his journey.

"Father," he said, "if you will not ask for me the daughter of the *hajj*, I shall die."

So the sultan went and asked. What could he do? He wanted the daughter of the *hajj*, the young one, her name is Aisha. "We want Aisha."

She said: "Father, I do not want."

There is nothing to do. The king does whatever he wants. He tells her: "My daughter!" Earlier, a daughter could not go against her father's wishes. Or he would kill her . . . "no! No, there is nothing like that." She agreed, what could she do? She told them: "Do you want me to marry the prince?"

She told him: "Well, I want you to prepare for me a tunnel under the house, from one house to another. He will harm me because I told everything to my father."

He [the father] said: "I have money." He was richer than the sultan. He said: "I am ready to do whatever you ask." So he prepared the way to the house. So they started to prepare the wedding. They did the wedding on the honeymoon eve. They sat at the table, she and he, and he said:

"Do you see what you have done to me."

She said: "The measure of woman is two measures; the measure of man is worth nothing."

He told her: "I will throw you into the pit, I will."

She told him: "What do you care, throw me away. Men are worth nothing. Women are those who decide."

He threw her out and told his servant: "Every morning throw her a bottle of water and half a black bread, and black olives." That was her punishment.

Every morning they throw, she goes and eats and laughs. About three months passed, and he told her: "So, what do you say? I want to travel. Say, men are thrice worth; women nothing."

She said: "No, no *siddi*,* no master, I shall not say so." She told him: "Go away. Where are you going?"

He told her: "I am going to Sor." The town of Sor, that is Syria.

She told him: "*Ya siddi*, well be gone, and when do you come back?"

"In two, three days."

She went to her village, to her father: "Prepare."

He began to prepare a tent and a jewel. Red jewels, and a dress, and good servants. She reached the place before him on a horse and started to put up a tent and sat on the bed; she prepared everything for him, and he too went there. Her servant went out alone.

"Why do you run, run?" he said. "Go and tell her that I want to visit her."

So he was courteous to her in order that she let him in. She said: "Well, let him come."

He lay beside her. She said: "On the condition that you give me the sword."

He said: "This?"—and took it off immediately and gave her. And then he drank tea. He got up and went away. Two days later he went back to his town, and she went home.

He said to her: "Ah, you daughter of *hajj*, you don't want to say: The measure of man is two measures . . . I was with a beautiful woman."

She said:—"*Sahtin*† *ya siddi*, to your health, whatever you did. Who is she?" as if she was disturbed by the idea.

Before a year had passed, she had a son. Time passed; every three days he came: "Say: The measure of man is two measures."

So it went on, until a year later he said to her: "I want to travel to Dor." He loves her, wants to take her out of the pit, but he does not want her to be above him, to lift up her head. He was clever, and she was clever. He wants to be more than her, but she does not want so. So he came every three days: "Are you convinced, the daughter of *hajj*, what are you saying?"

She told him: "No, sir. Women are twice, and men nothing, unworthy."

He told her: "Stay there."

In short, every third day he came to say so, until a year had passed. She already has a son, and he tells her: "I want to travel to Dor."

She said: "*Ya siddi*, go in peace and come back. When?"

"In three days."

She went and told her father. The servants did not sleep; they prepared a dress for her, fast, in another color: then red, now green. Everything in green: a green tent, everything. And they made a diamond, and embroidery with diamonds, everything different.

* Siddi—master.
† *Sahtin*—"with health."

She traveled and arrived before him. She prepared her tent; again she changed her servant so that he would not recognize her. And she prepared food, their *kubbe*,[*] prepared tea, and again she waves the fan for her. And she sat.

And the servant went out again. And he said: "Sir, if you see her . . ."

"What? You will not even clean her feet."

He said: "Tell her what I want. If I . . ."

He went and said: "My lord wants to see you."

She said: "Well, let him come."

Now he came and said: "I want to drink something with you."

"Well, on the condition that you give me your crown."

He threw her his crown. Well, they went down.

Then he went back. And went to her and said: "Daughter of *hajj*, are you convinced or not? Do you know that I was with a beautiful woman, I had a wonderful time. So say now: 'The men are twice the women.'"

"No."

And he said: "Stay here."

And then she had a son, and called him Dor. The children grew. And he every three days goes and visits her; the servants give her half a bread. As she throws it away she goes. He finishes his speech, and she goes to her house. Eats, has a good time, is merry. Until a year has passed; then he came and told her: "So, daughter of *hajj*, are you convinced?"

She said: "No, sir. I am not convinced yet."

"What? Say: the men are twice . . ."

She said: "No, women are twice, and the men are nothing."

He said: "You should know that I am travelling to Roma."

She said: "Go in peace and come back. When?"

"In three days."

She said: "Father, prepare everything now in yellow, and diamonds, embroidery, all with diamonds."

He told her: "Everything is ready."

He was such a rich man. The tailors did not sleep; they sat and sewed her dresses, sewed her tent: he brought her a mare, food, not like the former ones. She prepared everything. And she traveled. After two days she did all that she wanted, prepared everything, and again, again she lit a perfume, cinnamon, the leaves of cinnamon. He came and almost fainted. Also the Negro, his servant, fainted. He said: "Go and tell her: I want to visit her." He said: "I want to enter."

She said: "Please." He spoke to her, she said: "On the condition that you give your seal-ring!"

He said: "Take it." He gave her.

---

[*] *Kubbe*—patty of fried meat and semolina

Well. After two days she went back, and he too went home. He told her: "Daughter of *hajj*, I have had a good time, and I have traveled. Say: 'Twice the men.'"

"No sir, never. Twice the women, the men are worth nothing."

He told her: "Do you know that I want to marry in a year!"

"Good luck to you!"

And she completed nine months, and she had a daughter, and called her Roma. Now she had: Sor, Dor, and Roma. And he wanted to marry his cousin. So, the wedding was started.

The children were more than seven years old; they grew each one.

The wedding was prepared. She came to her father and said: "You know, he wants to marry. Prepare clothing for my children."

Well, he prepared clothes of kings for them. She gave each of them something: to the first the sword, to the second the crown, and to the daughter, the ring.

"And now go and tell him as I said." And they went to the house and said: "For God's sake, the house is our father's house, the house is ours, and the dogs throw us out, Sor, Dor, and Roma, our sister. Poor mother, wretched, in the dark, in the pit, and people rejoice. And what does that mean?"

So they said and threw the food. Made it like ash. Throw everything, break the dishes.

The king, the father of the prince, came. He said: "What is this?"

He sees the things, the crown, sees the ring, and children in his image. He said: "What is this, sirs?"

They said: "Yes, sir, Sor, Dor, and Roma, our sister, and our wretched mother in the dark pit. What is this? We are his children, and the wedding is in our house."

"Where?" He took them. They went and took the grandfather to their mother. They saw, looked, and they told him. He went and said: "My son, you made some business behind her back, you did this and that. Now bow before her."

So he did and said: "Thank you." And said to her: "The women are ten times. The men are not worth anything! I have sinned, and I repent."

She told him. They took down Grandfather, he himself gave her the throne, and she became the queen. She herself conducted trials, and she had a good head. And it was joyful. And in that same wedding the grandfather said: "Make a new wedding!"

The same day they made a new wedding; they married and everything was fine.

Transcribed by Galit Hasan-Rokem

COMMENTARY TO
"THE MEASURE OF A WOMAN IS TWO, THE MEASURE OF A MAN IS ONE"

IFA 11911

GALIT HASAN-ROKEM

This story was narrated for me in 1977, in Kiryat Gat, by Tamar Lugasi, born in Morocco in the late 1920s or early 1930s, who immigrated to Israel in the early 1950s with her spouse Avraham Lugasi, a prolific story teller himself. Ms. Lugasi, an attractive, full-bodied woman, narrated sitting on her bed; her legs were pointed straight out on the bed, while her hands intricately played with a light-blue sheer chiffon scarf. The narration was performed in Hebrew, in a melodious Moroccan elocution frequently interlaced with rhymes and proverbs in the Judeo-Arabic language of Moroccan Jews. The pronounced articulation, accompanied by elaborate gesticulation and facial expressions, turned the event into a small theatrical performance—indeed a "room theater," or to be even more exact, a "bed theater." The scarf Logasi soon removed from her head, when she veered from regular speech to narrating, turned into a stage prop: here a tent, there a horse, and then a glamorous dress—all in harmony with the unfolding of the plot.[1]

In addition to my tape recorder and me, present in the tiny room was also Lugasi's youngest daughter, Na'ama; I recollect her being about fifteen at the time. The "theater" performed was thus addressing only women. The truth of the matter is that my purpose that day had been to record Lugasi's husband, Avraham Lugasi (from whom IFA treasures 25 tales that I have recorded, another 14 recorded by Tamar Alexander, and 3 by his son David Lugasi). I was introduced to him about a year earlier by his son, a teacher who studied Hebrew literature at the then-very young University of the Negev (not yet named after David Ben-Gurion). The school was housed in temporary quarters—I taught in a shop at the emergent mall, where people walking by waved at us. I was going to present to Mr. Lugasi the proverb, "The measure of a woman is two, the measure of a man is one"—or in straight language, "women are twice as smart as men"—as part of the fieldwork for my doctoral dissertation. According to the methodology I had developed for my dissertation—reviewing IFA tales with proverbs—I had encountered this proverb in another Moroccan Jewish narrator's tale (IFA 6512, narrated by Maxim Ben Sim'on; Hasan-Rokem 1982, 78–79). I expected Avraham Lugasi to provide another tale, possibly of the same type, to corroborate the structural relationship between the proverb and the narrative, and to expand the cultural context that I could then mine for interpretation. Upon my presenting said proverb to Mr. Lugasi—already then a famous storyteller in various circles—he instantly declined my request for him to tell the story associated with it. The motivation for his refusal was that it would be indecent for a man to tell this story in the presence of women. He thus discreetly exited to narrate the story (which was not recorded) in the adjacent garden in the company of my spouse, and kindly suggested that I listen to his wife's version.

The narrative that I then heard as told by Tamar Lugasi (IFA 11911) is by genre a folktale. The folktale is generally set in a fictional space and time, such as the one *Peter Pan* author J. M. Barrie refers to as "Neverland," and was adopted by folktale scholars as an adequate characterization for the time and space coordinates of folktales as "Never-never-land." This sobriquet suggests the chronotope, a culturally condoned joint constellation of time and space, of the fantastic genre in both its spatial and chronological dimensions (Bakhtin 1981; Todorov 1973). These tales forbid the question "Is this possible?" since the genre allows for everything that may be possible in the conventional framework of each tradition. In this tale the locations sound real enough, but the speed with which the ports all around the Mediterranean Sea—Sor (Hebrew Tsor, known as Tyrus), Dor (Tantura), and Roma (Rome), with supposedly a Moroccan port of departure—are approached, and through a subterranean tunnel to boot in the case of the woman, is certainly fantastic.

In the world of the folktale the king may throw his newlywed wife into a dark pit and not recognize her when she meets him in disguise. Folktales are characterized by formulaic openings, such as "once upon a time, in a distant land," or "beyond mountains and rivers," that constitute a code-switching mechanism oriented toward the audience (Bell 1984) occurring between normal speech and the folktale. In accordance with Axel Olrik's famous Law of the Opening which, together with the Law of Closing, the code-switching completes the framing of the folktale as an aesthetic object within a separate reality (Olrik 1965, 131–32; Lüthi 1987, 49–53; Hasan-Rokem 2000, 270–72).

The study of folktales has made special reference to the relationship of separate realities of the folktale world and the dream world, especially among psychoanalysts. Erich Fromm called it "the forgotten language" (Fromm 1951), whereas Bruno Bettelheim preferred the more general term "enchantment" (Bettelheim 1976). Their general tendency was to emphasize the wish fulfillment function of both genres—folktales and dreams—particularly the fulfillment of forbidden wishes. The folktale—although it may submit its heroes and heroines to horrible, nightmarish adventures—tends to reach á happy end, mostly in the form of a wedding (Propp 1968, 63–64). Accordingly, Tamar Lugasi's tale ends in a wedding, albeit a repeated wedding since the couple was in fact already married. The tendency to always provide a happy ending, interpreted by Bettelheim as a part of the folktale's function in guiding a young person toward a healthy personality, equipped with enough optimism to face the hardships of life—has been condemned by others as an illusionary paradigm misleading its young listeners and steering them into fatalism instead of promoting self-reliance and initiative to action. This accusation has been leveled especially at explicitly fantastic folktales where imaginary beings and fanciful transformations abound. The tale discussed here is more moderate in its scope, and its heroine's achievements are mostly due to her intellectual capacity rather than marvelous or magical helpers or objects. The story thus belongs to the realm of the "realistic folktales" that Stith Thompson termed "novella," after the Italian Renaissance exemplars of the genre (Thompson 1946, 8). Common to both novellas and folktales is their use of a language of symbols (Fromm 1951; in a different vein, see Jason 1971, 184–207). They share the stylistic propensity to bright colors and especially hues of gold and silver, all enveloped in a psychedelic vision. Of all the folk narrative genres, the folktale has the most developed aesthetic features, sensuous proclivities, and a leaning toward art for art's sake (Jason 1971, 166; Lüthi 1987, 14–25). Gifted narrators of folktales excel in stringing together repetitions and triplications, in adorning their discourse with puns, rhymes, proverbs, and riddles.

Possibly the main function of the symbolic language of folktales is to create the overall symbolic atmosphere in the constructed fictional world. From this perspective, the best method is not to explicate each symbol separately, as when solving riddles, but rather to interpret the general symbolic semiotics of the tale. Yet sometimes the symbols weave an enigmatic array that entices the reader to untie their knots. In Tamar Lugasi's tale there are two strings of stark visual symbols that call for specific solutions: (1) the color of the woman's dress and accessories in each of her disguises; and (2) the gifts she procures from the prince in each of their encounters. In the first instance, her dress and accessories are red, then green, and finally yellow. One could almost imagine that the same dress has faded from one meeting to the next. On one symbolic level, and in accordance with the development of the plot, one may interpret that the red of passion is overcome first by the green of fertility and then by the yellow of golden perfection. This could then be seen as a process of maturation which the truly loving woman makes her man undergo—without his awareness—for a better future for their relationship, in contrast to the earlier stage, defined by his dominant and demanding attitude. Alternative symbolic interpretations may produce a very different line of development: red of aggression, green of jealousy, and yellow of betrayal. Notably the three colors match the colors of traffic lights, and since other versions of the same tale type reveal different color schemes, perhaps the influence of urban semiotics can be discerned here.

The gifts, likewise, can be considered in the light of the symbolic values attached to each item. Here too the war of the sexes is projected on concrete objects, and the woman seems to gain all three symbols of royal authority—the sword, the crown, and the ring—topped by the final gain of half the kingdom as well as the prince. But these symbols, like the colors already discussed, and like most symbols, carry double symbolic values. Thus they also become weights and fetters binding the woman to her husband.

There are already quite explicit sexual symbols in the tale in the flirting or courting game between the two before their "first marriage": the porridge she licks with great pleasure; the pomegranates he holds excitedly in his hands; and our imagination steers a quite clear course when the prince announces that he will give the young woman "two kisses and one fish."

The language of symbols of the tale parallels the general scheme of maturation and growth that underlies the plot, characteristically for the folktale genre, in parallel to the structure of puberty rites. Thus usually the hero or heroine begins his or her path in the plot while still happy and inexperienced, in the childhood home. The plot sets them against adversaries and leads them through adventures, and it is usually the assistance of beneficial animals or helpful marvelous beings, together with their own courage and other worthy qualities, that lead them through the various threatening situations that emerge throughout the plot. The prerequisite for the happy ending is a successful passage through the tests and tasks—as in the tale of Tamar Lugasi, where both hero and heroine are tested for their patience and fidelity.

Another possible interpretative perspective of the tale may focus on the liberation process of the woman from her father, who initially braces the bond between them when he demands that she water his plant while he is traveling far from home. Her dependence on him takes the form of the tunnel through which she returns to her father's house to flee the meager and limited existence in which she finds herself as a result of her husband's demands. Thus the virtual "umbilical cord," in the form of the tunnel, on one hand sets her free from her husband but on the other hand prevents a true encounter between husband and wife, since the latter has retreated back to the role of daughter. The marital relationship must now be constructed through a series of disguises before a true and open interaction is established. The husband is initially unable to acknowledge the sharp intellect of his wife and can accept it only after he has been conquered by her sensuous presence as, for him, an anonymous courtesan. As she pampers him with tea, *kubbe*, and cinnamon scent, she allows him to remain the immature being he still is—as his unreasonable demands have proven—without disclosing the fact that in the meantime real children have begun to need and receive her motherly warmth. These children eventually serve in the clever woman's scheme to reunite the family, revealing her situation's curious blend of resourcefulness and powerlessness.

After this curious and tangled course of events, the protagonists are mature enough to enter the real adventure that is waiting for them in what the folktale genre sets as their goal: marriage. But this is where the folktale ends, leaving the scene for other genres to materialize: love songs, lullabies, songs of work and travel, legends, dirges, and in the mixed milieu of tradition and modernity in which the tale was told in the Lugasi home, also the short story, the novel, the TV series, and movies. In today's homes, if at all present, the folktale prepares the younger generation for other genres at the same time as it provides a link to an unbroken chain of tradition.

NOTE

1. The tale, IFA 11911, appears in Hasan-Rokem 1982, 80–84, and is extensively analyzed there, with special reference to the proverb that is repeated by the heroine of the tale, on pp. 84–95.

BIBLIOGRAPHY

Bakhtin, Mikhail Mikhailovitch. 1981. "Forms of Time and of the Chronotope in Novel." In *The Dialogic Imagination*, trans. Carol Emerson and Michael Holquist, 84–258. Austin: University of Texas Press.

Bell, Allan. 1984. "Language Style as Audience Design." *Language in Society* 13 (2): 145–204.

Bettelheim, Bruno. 1976. *The Uses of Enchantment: The Meaning and Importance of Fairy Tales*. New York: Knopf.

Fromm, Erich. 1951. *The Forgotten Language*. New York: Rinehart.

Hasan-Rokem, Galit. 1982. *Proverbs in Israeli Folk Narratives: A Structural Semantic Analysis*. Folklore Fellows Communications 232. Helsinki: Academia Scientiarum Fennica.

———. 2000. "Aurora Borealis: Trans-formations of Classical Nordic Folklore Theories." In *Norden og Europa: Fagtradisjoner i nordisk etnologi og folkloristikk*, ed. B. Rogan and B. G. Alver, 269–85. Oslo: Novus. In Spanish: "Aurora boreal: Transformaciones de las teorías clásicas del folklore nórdico." *Revista de investigaciones folclóricas* 17 (2002): 33–46.

Jason, Heda. 1971. *Genre: An Essay in Oral Literature*. Tel Aviv: Tel Aviv University.

Lüthi, Max. 1987. *The Fairytale as Art Form and Portrait of Man*. Bloomington: Indiana University Press.

Olrik, Axel. 1965. "Epic Laws of Folk Narrative." In *The Study of Folklore*, ed. A. Dundes, 129–41. Englewood Cliffs, NJ: Prentice-Hall.

Propp, Vladimir. 1968. *Morphology of the Folktale*. Austin: University of Texas Press.

Thompson, Stith. 1946. *The Folktale*. New York: Dryden Press.

Todorov, Tzvetan. 1973. *The Fantastic: A Structural Approach to a Literary Genre*. Trans. Richard Howard. Cleveland, OH: Case Western Reserve University Press.

THE REVELATION OF THE
ZADDIK RABBI DAVID U'MOSHE

IFA 12337

NARRATED BY MOSHE DANINO (MOROCCO)

Many legends have been told about the wondrous righteous man Rabbi David U'Moshe, who worked miracles after his death. Most Jews from North Africa are willing to swear that the holy Rabbi David U'Moshe has appeared to them in a dream more than once—some say he appeared to them when they were awake—and granted their requests. In light of this, many Jewish immigrants from North Africa have established synagogues and tombs for this miracle-working righteous man. They have done so in Jaffa and Safed, in Ashkelon and Ofakim, and perhaps in other places as well.

To this day many devotees of this holy man stream to prostrate themselves on his monuments throughout the country, and elsewhere, to pray for the fulfillment of their wishes. Often their wishes are granted.

Moshe Danino, who built a synagogue and monuments in memory of the righteous man next to his house, recounts many of his wonders. Danino will swear to the truth of the following story.

Once his wife, Sarah, fell seriously ill. The doctors told him that she had to undergo a brain operation that might perhaps save her life.

In light of the danger, Danino refused to risk his wife's life and began to moan plaintively in the synagogue he had built in memory of the holy man. He cried out bitterly: "Know, Rabbi David U'Moshe, that if you don't save my wife, I will no longer believe in your greatness."

Suddenly Danino heard a voice speaking to him: "My son, take your wife to the physicians. With God's help no harm will befall her, for I will be with her."

When the woman was wheeled to the operating room, even before the doctors put her to sleep, with her own eyes she suddenly saw the holy man standing alongside her and the doctors.

An operation of the type performed on Sarah, even when it is successful, frequently causes the patient to lose his or her sight, partially or completely. But Sarah came through the surgery successfully and recovered fully from her illness as if she had never been ill.

The doctors believe that she is the first woman ever to undergo this dangerous procedure with such success.

The doctors asked Moshe Danino, Sarah's husband, what his wife had done. He replied: "She is simply a God-fearing woman and has strong faith in the miracles performed by righteous men."

The pious Moshe Danino did not reveal the secret of the righteous man Rabbi David U'Moshe, who had appeared to him and told him what to do.

Transcribed by Nissim Malka

COMMENTARY TO
"THE REVELATION OF THE
ZADDIK RABBI DAVID U'MOSHE"

12337

HAYA BAR-ITZHAK

This story was transcribed in 1979 by Nissim Malka, as it was told to him by Moshe Danino. As we shall see, it is plain from the story itself that it was created in the context of life in Israel as experienced by immigrants from Morocco. From this perspective, it is ethnic folklore. As I have shown elsewhere, ethnic folklore is linked to the traditional folklore that immigrants bring with them from their countries of origin, but it takes shape as a direct result of their encounter

with the Israeli reality. The folklore genres and the system of concepts and symbols brought from their former homes prove to be of great help in the early stages of migration, and make it easier for them to cope with the new world; but they themselves are altered as a result of this encounter. Thus ethnic folklore undergoes modifications, sometimes quite extensive, as compared to the folklore of the country of origin (Bar-Itzhak 2005, 92–96). "The Revelation of the *Zaddik* Rabbi David U'Moshe" affords an instructive illustration of this, and of how the community tries to deal with a new world while not letting go of the cultural values brought from the "old country."

The genre of this story is a *shevach*, to use the ethnic Hebrew term, or a "saint's legend" (*Legende* in German), to use the international scholarly term. At its center are a figure sanctified by the narrating society—in this case, Rabbi David U'Moshe—and a miraculous event that conforms to its traditional notion of holiness.[1] It combines the narrator's original story with the transcriber's comments. The first section—which provides information about the veneration of the saints as practiced in Morocco and revived in various places in Israel, including Jaffa, Safed, Ashkelon, and Ofakim—is supplied by an intracultural transcriber who identifies with the narrator's system of values and norms.[2] It is never really clear whether the story we are hearing is Moshe Danino's or, instead, that told by Nissim Malka, who heard it from Moshe Danino. Although Malka says that Danino is telling the story, it is phrased in the third person.

Various scholars have noted that, starting in the 1970s, Moroccan immigrants in Israel began returning to the ethnocultural pattern of veneration of holy men (Ben-Ari and Bilu 1981, Yassif 1999, 506–29, Bar-Itzhak 2005, 153–66).[3] When they immigrated to Israel, Moroccan Jews had to leave behind the tombs of their holy men, and this naturally reduced the intensity of rituals connected to holy tombs. What is more, in their early years in the country, the immigrants were preoccupied with ensuring their survival and overcoming the culture shock of their encounter with the new country. It was only when they attained a certain degree of economic comfort, especially in the so-called development towns, that veneration of holy men began to revive among Moroccan Jews (Ben-Ari and Bilu 1981).

One of the key aspects of folk medicine among Moroccan Jews was an appeal to holy men or prayers at the tombs of saints to request health and recovery from illness. The present story, which is set in the late 1970s in Israel, affords us an opportunity to study the transformation of Moroccan Jews and how their saints' legends expressed and built a bridge between their new reality and the system of beliefs they brought with them from their country of origin. In this story, the saint stands alongside the physicians and thereby confers legitimacy on Israeli medical care, but without undermining the old traditions.

The story is told as a personal narrative. Recovery from surgery is given the cultural interpretation of a miracle wrought for the narrator and his wife by the merit of the holy man. Many saints' legends are personal accounts of miracles experienced by the narrator, his family, or people he knows; this mode is typical of a genre that is considered to be a true story and enjoys the full credence of the narrating society. It is set in a time of crisis in the lives of the narrator and his wife—a severe illness strikes his wife and could prove fatal. Life in Israel leads them to turn to the conventional medical care that is standard in the country. But the belief in the saint's power remains a key element of their lives. When the narrator learns how critical his wife's condition is, he places his trust in the saint rather than in the physicians; he will not decide on an operation, as they advise, before he receives guidance from Rabbi David U'Moshe.

The mode of addressing the saint, "Know, Rabbi David U'Moshe, that if you don't save my wife, I will no longer believe in your greatness," is rather insolent.[4] It can be understood as reflecting the narrator's emotional state, caused by his wife's health crisis and the cultural crossroads at which he finds himself. The saint's response provides a way to understand the function played by the emergence of saints' legends in Israel for people who live between two such different worlds. The holy man who says, "My son, take your wife to the physicians. With God's help no harm will befall her, for I will be with her," offers comfort to the narrator and his community. The saint confers legitimacy on the norms of the new culture. If he confers this legitimacy and can be found even in this strange place called a hospital, their anxieties are lessened. The saint's revelation to the woman before the operation, with the medical team that is about to put her to sleep, serves as a metaphor for the condition of the narrating society, which lives in two worlds and resolves its existential distress by placing the holy man at the right hand (in both the figurative and literal senses) of both the woman and the physicians.

The success of the operation, and even more so the wife's recovery, are credited to the saint, who stood behind the physicians. The physicians' astonishment at her full convalescence after surgery of this kind enhances the holy man's prestige, and receives the cultural explanation of a miracle wrought by the holy man. The narrator's perspective is the standard view of reward and punishment, typical of saints' legends. Both the fact that the question about the woman's virtues is attributed to the doctors, who are trying to fathom her full recovery, and the answer that she is a "God-fearing woman and has strong faith in the miracles performed by righteous men" are means to reinforce belief in the power of saints.

The conclusion, "the pious Moshe Danino did not reveal the secret of the righteous man Rabbi David U'Moshe, who had appeared to him and told him what to do," reflects the barrier between the two cultures in Israel. The narrating society has managed to find the golden mean between modern medicine and its belief in the power of saints; but it is also aware that the hegemonic culture rejects this belief. As a result, the true story of the holy man remains untold to the world at large and must be incorporated into the internal cultural code known only to members of the community. This also expresses a certain superiority—only we know the secret, the true reason for the doctors' success—that the Moroccan Jews feel vis-à-vis the hegemonic Israeli culture, which generally looks down on them. The story shows, thus, that the first generation of Moroccan immigrants to Israel rejected the radical solution of making a choice between the two worlds and preferred a synthesis that allowed them to survive in the Israeli reality without infringing their sacred beliefs. Nevertheless, the need to turn this world into an internal cultural code is a sign of their alienation from the dominant culture.

NOTES

1. For an extensive discussion of saints' legends, see Bar-Itzhak 1987.
2. On the distinction between intracultural and cross-cultural narration, see Bar-Itzhak 2007.
3. Until the 1980s, the population of approximately 400,000 Moroccan immigrants in Israel constituted the largest single group of *olim* from the Middle East and North Africa. They were visible as a distinct group mainly in the development towns and *moshavim* established around the time they made *aliya*, and less so in the large and heterogeneous urban population centers.
4. This is reminiscent of the unconventional prayers recited by the "innocent" in stories about prayers for rain, as noted by Noy 1959. See also Bar-Itzhak 1978.

BIBLIOGRAPHY

Bar-Itzhak, Haya. 1978. "Gaps Filling Structure in Legends about Bringing Down Rain." *Yeda-Am* 19: 62–68. [Hebrew]
———. 1987. "'Saints' Legend' as Genre in Jewish Folk-Literature (Sample of Oral Stories about Rabbi Israel Ba'al-Shem-Tov, Rabbi Haim Pinto, and Rabbi Shalom Shabazi)." Unpublished Ph.D. diss., Hebrew University. [Hebrew]

———. 2005. *Israeli Folk Narratives—Settlement, Immigration, Ethnicity*. Detroit: Wayne State University Press.

———. 2007. "Cross Cultural Narration in the Nineteenth Century: Jewish Folktales Transcribed by a Polish Author." *Studia Mythologica Slavica* 10: 239–59.

Ben-Ari, Eyal, and Yoram Bilu. 1981. "Saints' Sanctuaries in Israeli Development Towns: On a Mechanism of Urban Transformation." *Urban Anthropology* 16 (2): 243–71.

Noy, Dov. 1959. "The Prayer of an 'Innocent' Brings Rain." *Mahanayim* 51: 34–45. [Hebrew]

Yassif, Eli. 1999. *The Hebrew Folktale: History, Genre, Meaning*. Bloomington: Indiana University Press.

THERE IS NOT A LIVING SOUL

IFA 12434

NARRATED BY ZVI TENENBAUM (GERMANY)

A Jew and a priest met on a train and started talking. During their conversation the priest suddenly closes his eyes and pretends to be asleep, then suddenly wakes up.

The Jew asks him: "Where were you? What did you dream about?"

The priest replies: "I was in the Jewish paradise, where there was a terrible noise and tumult."

The Jew understood immediately what the priest was hinting at, and then it was the Jew's turn to respond to the priest's comments, because the priest's insinuations had angered him.

Then the Jew also "fell asleep" and awoke suddenly.

"What did you dream? Where were you?" asked the priest.

"I was in your paradise. I entered and encountered absolute silence, with not a sound to be heard. I looked around and could not see a single soul."

Transcribed by Avraham Keren

COMMENTARY TO
"THERE IS NOT A LIVING SOUL"

IFA 12434

TAMAR EYAL

One of the most dramatic phenomena in the rich history of the People of Israel is how they were forced to repeatedly defend themselves against every foe and adversary that arose among those nations of the world among whom Israel dwelt. Every generation of the People of Israel had to confront adversaries against whom they were forced to take a stand and argue with enemies, and indeed overcome them in a bitter and prolonged "war of words.'" (Schwartzbaum, 1971, 56)

The reality described in the preceding quotation has been expressed extensively in literature and led to the creation of the polemic genre, which succeeded in gaining a foothold in the world of Jewish folklore.

This story is told by Zvi Tenenbaum, a native of Germany who immigrated to Israel in 1978 and lived in Haifa, where he was in charge of musical education on the city's municipal council. The story raises the issue of polarization between Jews and Christians in contrast to and in defiance of the European Jew's own perception, which held that the Jew must be regarded as inferior to the gentile. This normative perception is replaced in the story of the humoristic dialogue, in which the tables are turned and the priest's sarcastic words of ridicule, expressing malice and hatred toward the Jews, are reversed in the Jew's speech and become words denigrating the Christians.

There is no doubt that the Jew's reaction is harsh and quite unexpected, and when the shoe is put on the other foot, as described here, the humoristic situation is created. When the priest told the Jew that he dreamed a strange and wonderful dream, and in that dream the priest is led into the Jewish paradise, he sought only to slander and ridicule the Jews living among the non-Jews who made their living from commerce and peddling. These Jews are presented as unrefined and materialistic through allusion to the noise and tumult prevailing in their immediate environment. The Jew, in his clever reply, integrates some passages of the priest's story and contradicts them by replacing the object of the story and its setting. Instead of the crowded conditions of the Jews and the terrible commotion prevailing in the Jewish paradise, the Jew, on arrival at the non-Jewish paradise in his dream, finds a deserted and silent place without a living soul. There is just one answer to the questions "Where are the gentiles?" or "Is the non-Jewish paradise really deserted?" and so the priest apparently understood what the Jew meant. The manner in which the story is presented, as a dialogue between the priest and the Jew, illustrates the structural polarization: One voice is that of the mocking, conceited priest, who seeks to insult the Jew and his Jewish faith; the other voice is that of the self-assured Jew, who fights back against the priest and against Christianity in general. True to the stereotype of the priest in Jewish folk literature from the early twentieth century, the priest's words highlight his hatred for the Jews, as he belittles their customs and generally regards them as materialistic and greedy. The title of this story, "There Is Not a Living Soul," appears in the concluding sentence of another version of the same story, "The Jewish Paradise and the Christian Paradise" (see Schwartzbaum 1971, 59–60). In this tale, too, which narrates a confrontation between Jews and Christians, the Jew's courage is apparent as he argues his case in an acrimonious "war of words." He fights back against the priest, arguing tit for tat, without cowering, and speaks without feeling the need to justify himself.[1]

It can be concluded that the direct messages found in the folk story in its various versions[2] result from the protagonists' actions. The Jews are granted an honorable place in the Jewish paradise after death, thanks to their deeds during their lifetimes. In contrast the non-Jews, and even the priests among them, discover that their deeds in this world do not entitle them to life in the gentile paradise after death.

In the story in all its different versions, the Jew makes the gentile—his sworn and hated enemy—into an object of ridicule, as somebody deserving punishment at the End of Days. Here the concept of paradise, which appears in the different versions, is related to the idea of "the world to come" (or "afterlife") mentioned in the *aggadah* of the Talmud and common in the Middle Ages. It should be noted here that, given the belief that the lives of the dead in paradise are absolutely spiritual, the words of the priest referring to "terrible noise and tumult" are perceived in a more serious light. In international folk literature, a parallel story may be found in Thompson's index of motifs as X 438; in the index of types by Aarne and Thompson, it is found at AT 1738 ("The Dream"), which is outlined as: All the priests are in hell. The sick blacksmith sends someone to call for the priest, who initially refuses to come because of the inclement weather. When the priest arrives eventually, the blacksmith tells him about a dream he had in which he went to heaven, and there St. Peter told him that he is not permitted to enter without first visiting a priest. However, there were no priests in paradise, not a single one, because they were all in hell (Aarne and Thompson 1961).

A comparison of this story and the Jewish oikotype of "There Is No Living Soul" leads us to assume that the Jewish narrator opted to use the motif of "no priests in the Christian paradise" and even to extend it to "there is no one at all in the Christian paradise." He thereby expresses his covert wish, shared by the Jews in the Diaspora who were persecuted and threatened by anti-Semitism.

The difference between the two stories is clear: The story of "The Dream" focuses on the conflict against a class background, and features Christian criticism and denigration of the representative of the Christian establishment on earth; the focus of the Jewish folktale is centered on the struggle against a religious background, stressing the Jew's cleverness compared to the Christian's and the fact the Christians are not granted the right to enter paradise. This is an expression of Jewish society's hidden hopes. Using this bitter "war of words," the Jew does at least respond to the priest; he defends his honor and effectively repels his antagonists, driving them down to hell.

We should note here that the opening words of "The Dream"—"All the priests are in hell"— are realized in the conclusion of the Jewish oikotype, owing to the fact that the Christian paradise has no occupants.

It is also noteworthy that in the rich collection of folklore from the Land of Israel compiled by two researchers (Schmidt and Kahle 1930, II, 108), there appears an additional version of this story, with different wording, titled "Where Can One Go for Confession in Heaven?"

> When that dead person arrived at the entrance to the non-Jewish paradise, he met St. Peter,[3] the guard to the Gates of Heaven. St. Peter asked the deceased whether he had already confessed all his transgressions, and the deceased then replied that he had indeed made confession for his sins, except for one sin, which he had preferred to keep to himself and did not confess to. In dealing with this issue, St. Peter ordered him to return to where he had come from, confess to the sin that he had kept hidden, and then return to paradise. This dead person expressed his discontent and asked St. Peter if he would be kind enough to look and find a priest for him in heaven, so that he might confess to him. St. Peter replied that there is not a single priest to be found in heaven, and that the deceased should know better than St. Peter does that if a priest were present there he would not have sent the dead individual back to the mortal world. Then he concluded with the words, "Go off now on your way!"[4]

Like the story of "The Dream," this folk tale also expresses Christian criticism of the priesthood: At the end of the day, the priests are not titled to enter paradise.

Itzik Manger, the poet and writer who was very familiar with Jewish and Christian folkloristic works, chose in "The Story of Paradise" (1982) to refer to these in a paradoxical way. In Manger's writing—in contrast to the Jewish folk work in which the Jewish narrator's covert wish is to see the Christian defeated and humiliated—the narrator wishes to present a world of consensus, tolerance, and mutual understanding between Jews and Christians. The reality molded in the "The Story of Paradise" is perhaps more complex when it comes to the discussion of Jewish-Christian relations. In Manger's work not every Jew is a courageous hero, and not all Christians are anti-Semitic. Where the Jew in Manger's "Story of Paradise" is concerned, we see, instead of daring, the terrible dread of a person in fear for his life; instead of the Jew's act of ridicule, which makes him feel strong and at ease in his argument against the priest, we see the denigration directed toward the Jew, and it is the Christian who mocks him. It seems that while Manger's story owes its origins to the Jewish folk story, it relates to it by way of contrast. Thus Manger's work forms a real world where the non-Jewish paradise is not devoid of Christians but rather populated by anti-Semitic gendarmes as well as noble individuals who are tolerant toward others.

NOTES

1. Haim Schwartzbaum mentions in his book several versions that are similar to this story. These versions appear under the title "Measure for Measure" (Schwartzbaum, 1968, 345–46). It is noteworthy that Schwartzbaum's comprehensive research is based on the Naftali Gross anthology (Gross, 1955), which includes 540 Jewish folktales and fables.
2. See additional versions of the Jewish oikotype (AT*1873 IFA): Schwartzbaum 1968, 345, no. 473 (Hebrew title: "*Midah keneged midah*," or "Measure for Measure"); Sadan 1952, no. 753b, 397; and Mendelsohn 1935, 183 (Hebrew title: "*Gan Eden ha'Yehudi ve'haNozri*," or "The Jewish and Christian Paradise").
3. According to the medieval legend "The Legend of Simon Caiaphas," Peter was in fact a secret Jew who headed the Christian hierarchy but nevertheless still adhered to his Judaism and rejected Christianity.
4. My translation from the German.

BIBLIOGRAPHY

Aarne, Antti, and Stith Thompson. 1961. *The Types of the Folktale: A Classification and Bibliography*. FF Communications no. 184. Helsinki: Suomalainen Tiedeakatemia.

Gross, Naftali. 1955. *Mayselekh un Mesholim*. New York: Aber Press.

Manger, Itzik. 1982. *The Story of Paradise*. Tel-Aviv: Am Oved [Hebrew].

Mendelsohn, Samuel Felix. 1935. *The Jew Laughs: Humorous Stories and Anecdotes*. Chicago: Stein.

Sadan, Dov. 1952. *A Bowl of Raisins*. Tel Aviv: Neuman [Hebrew].

Schmidt, Hans, and Paul Kahle. 1930. *Volkserzählungen aus Palästina*. Band 2. Göttingen: Vandenhoeck und Ruprecht.

Schwartzbaum, Haim. 1968. *Studies in Jewish and World Folklore*. Berlin: Walter De Gruyter.

———. 1971. "Israel and the Nations of the World from the Folkloristic Point of View." *Yeda-Am* 15 (37–38): 56–61. [Hebrew]

RISE EARLY AND HARVEST GOLD

IFA 12443

NARRATED BY YA'ACOV NESHER (ISRAEL, ASHKENAZI)

Mr. Ya'acov Nesher is related to Israel Pollak, founder of Polgat Industries. He told the following story:

Pinhas Sapir, the late Minister [of Commerce and Industry in 1955–65, 1970–72] knew, as we all remember, how to reach out to Jews living abroad and convince them to invest in Israel. In one of his journeys, he went to Chile and there met with Israel Pollak, a millionaire and owner of several textile factories.

Sapir managed to convince him to come to Israel to investigate the possibility of investing money in Israeli industry.

Pollak came to Israel and met with Sapir. He had one condition: He was willing to invest but only in the center area of the country, near Tel Aviv.

During this period [the late 1950s and early 1960s], the area of Kiryat Gat [in the Lachish region, south of the country's center] was being built up, and Sapir wanted to build a [textile] factory in the Kiryat Gat development area.

Sapir scheduled a date to visit the site intended for the new factory [in Kiryat Gat]. As [I] said, the place had to be close to Tel Aviv (and it is known that Kiryat Gat is not close to Tel Aviv). What did Sapir do? He invited Pollak to join him for a trip to Kiryat Gat at five in the morning.

"Why so early?" the millionaire asks.

"I am a very busy man, and this hour is the most suitable for me," Sapir answered.

Pollak agreed. At five in the morning, the two of them left Tel Aviv for Kiryat Gat. At such an early hour, the road was vacant, and Sapir signaled the driver to speed up and shorten the ride. Within less than half an hour, they reached Kiryat Gat. In truth, a half-hour distance from Tel Aviv is no big deal to someone from overseas. Israel Pollak then agreed to build the factory "close" to Tel Aviv. This is how the Polgat Industries and others got started. By now they employ thousands of workers and export their products to numerous countries for tens of millions of dollars.

Transcribed by Avraham Keren

Investors' Encouragement

IFA 21158

Narrated by Ya'acov Shaham (Israel)

Pinhas Sapir was renowned for his ability to attract investors to the distant [southern] Negev area. And how did he succeed in convincing them to invest in the barren Negev, decades ago, after they woke up in their fancy suites in Tel Aviv? It's very simple! Before the esteemed personages entered his car, he would give the following orders to his driver: "Drive at a speed of 135 kilometers [84 miles] per hour."

And to the [prospective] investors coming from Tel Aviv he would say: "My workday starts at five-thirty in the morning. Please come to my car by this time."

The distinguished investors would come, sit in the car; the driver would floor the gas pedal, and they would be in the Negev in a short while.

"You see?" he [Sapir] would then say. "It's only a twenty-minute ride from Tel Aviv."

And the investors would open their wallets. This is how factories like Polgat and many others were built in Kiryat Gat. Only twenty minutes from Tel Aviv! And that was forty years ago, on the roads of those days.

Transcribed by Yifrah Haviv

COMMENTARY TO
"RISE EARLY AND HARVEST GOLD"
AND "INVESTORS' ENCOURAGEMENT"

IFA 12443 and IFA 21158

ILANA ROSEN

IFA contains not only traditional or "classic" stories related to Jewish holy writings, past and present, or to the centuries-long Diaspora, but also stories about the renewed life of the Jewish people in their "old-new land," which came to be called the Zionist (super-) narrative (Shapira 2010; Holtzman 2008; Mintz 1999). The more modern IFA stories include tall tales typical of settlement-and-founding narratives;[1] praise legends with a secular focus; stories that criticize certain traits of the Jewish people; personal narratives reflecting individual, subjective experiences of collective events; testimony; and other novel kinds of folk narratives.

Such is a relatively new story type, recorded in IFA in two rather similar variants, though they were recorded within a few years of one another by entirely different narrators and documenters. This story also appears in one of the memoir volumes of Arye Lova Eliav (head of the Department of Settlement in the Jewish Agency in the early 1950s). The essence of the story is the successful attempt of the minister of commerce and industry, Pinhas Sapir, to convince Israel Pollak, a wealthy Jewish industrialist in Chile (originally from Transylvania, Romania), to invest part of his fortune in a textile factory (later to become Polgat Industries) in the remote southern town of Kiryat Gat. This had to be done while convincing the potential investor that Kiryat Gat, some 65 kilometers (40 miles) south of Tel Aviv, was not really, as Pollak feared, distant from the central area and from potential investors, distributors, infrastructures, banks, and so forth. How does Sapir manage to convince Pollak? He invites him to a tour of the projected factory site at a very early morning hour, when the roads were still empty (relative to that time in the late 1950s and early 1960s), so that the ride lasts less than an hour (and in one variant even less than half an hour). This way, Pollak is convinced of the proximity of Kiryat Gat to Tel Aviv and dares invest in an otherwise barren wasteland location. According to Eliav's memoir, however, Pollak does not really swallow the bait but is impressed by Sapir's determination (or *chutzpah*) and readiness to promote industry in the new State of Israel.

The information about the two variants of this type at IFA and their narrators and document-ers is as follows: IFA 12443 was told by Ya'acov Nesher to Avraham Keren (who added a note about Nesher's being a relative of Pollak). This story is titled "Rise Early and Harvest Gold." Nesher, the narrator, was born in 1912 in the village of Brod (Brid), near Munkács, in the Bereg county of the Austro-Hungarian empire. Nesher immigrated to Palestine in 1928. Because he spoke Arabic, he was asked by Abba Hushi, then the secretary of the Haifa Workers Committee and later the first mayor of Haifa, to work in the Haifa port. Later on he worked in construction, became a member of Kibbutz Givat Haim, and served as *ghaffir* (guard; Hebrew: *notēr*) in the Jewish Settlement Police under the British Mandate during the Arab Uprising (*Ha-mered ha-arvi*, 1936–39). Still later he served in the Haganah pre-state military organization and in Major-General Orde Wingate's Night Battalions. He served as commander of the *yishuv* (pre-state) police and was one of the founders of Kiryat Haim, near Haifa. The other variant, IFA 21158, was told by Ya'acov Shaham to his brother-in-law Yifrah Haviv and is titled "Investors' Encouragement." Shaham was born in 1938 in Tel Aviv and grew up in the Montefiore neighborhood. He first worked as a carpenter and later as an insurance agent. During the Yom Kippur War (1973), he miraculously survived an Egyptian bombardment, an event he recounted repeatedly in later years. The collectors of the two IFA stories—Avraham Keren and Yifrah Haviv—are two of IFA's most prolific documenters. Keren was also a donor to IFA publications and projects. Ya'acov Nesher and Ya'acov Shaham are well-known IFA narrators. Shaham contributed some eight hundred stories and jokes to IFA, and Nesher is a blood relation of Pollak, the secondary protagonist of his story. In addition to the two IFA variants, a very similar story appears in one of Arye Lova Eliav's memoirs (Eliav 1970, 177–79), and it may well be that Eliav recounted it elsewhere in his more than twenty documentary books about his activities in various functions and projects in Israel's first decades, as well as in his public lectures.[2] The fact that the story appears in at least two recorded variants (in addition to Eliav's written version) means that it is of significance both within its environment of creation and in the general context of the Israeli nation-building narrative.[3]

This narrative poses problems for classification in the comparative method used for more tra-ditional folk narratives, as exemplified in the Aarne-Thompson tale-type index. The index has a category of stories about the wise person and the fool, and within it a heading devoted to "Tales of Lying" (AT 1875–1889; Aarne and Thompson 1961, 509–12), containing varied agricultural, mainly European, folk narratives that deal with human relations, at times in the guise of animal fables and figures. The present narrative could be classified there because it is basically a decep-tion narrative, notwithstanding its glamour and (modern) heroism. Yet none of the deceptions detailed under "Tales of Lying" corresponds to this specific plot. In Thompson's motif-index, which features a large category dealing with deceptions (K—Deceptions), there is likewise nothing that conforms to this narrative.[4] The genre of this narrative is partly a personal biographical legend (about Sapir) and partly a personal narrative.[5] Usually such a narrative would be expected to be the account or testimony of someone who was present at the event, but with this story type this is clearly not the case: All three narrators have somehow only heard or learned about the event. It is likely that the three became familiar with the story through hearsay or through their proximity to important personages, as was customary in those decades.[6]

In the public discourse and rumors about eminent personae, ministers, mayors, and others in Israel, Pinhas Sapir was well-known for his so-called Diasporic or Galician cunning and sense of humor, and later for his role as finance minister in an era of financial constraints. In this sense he was compared to Prime Minister Levi Eshkol and Minister Yosef Burg, who were likewise known for their "Jewish" spirit and humor.[7] But in this story, Sapir is still the minister of commerce and industry in the new state. In this time and place it was widely recognized that the young state needed, and was entitled to, the support of world Jewry. The only question for the Israeli leaders was how to implement this understanding. This basic theme is common to all three variants.

A close and comparative analysis of the three variants shows that they vary significantly. In the earlier variant recorded in IFA, told by Ya'acov Nesher, attention is given to the family ties between the narrator and the donor, and it is stated that the initial acquaintance between Sapir and Pollak was created during one of Sapir's fundraising tours in Chile. Sapir does convince Pollak to come to Israel to investigate possible investment in its industry. The visit takes place during the period of the very founding of Kiryat Gat, the capital of the Lachish region in the northern Negev area. Once Pollak is in Israel, "What did Sapir do? He invited Pollak to join him for a trip to Kiryat Gat at five in the morning. 'Why so early?' the millionaire asks. 'I am a very busy man, and this hour is the most suitable for me.' Sapir answered." In this short exchange Sapir exemplifies his initiative and authority: He plans the visit according to his busy schedule, not the rich guest's convenience. The listeners and readers of this story get a clue regarding the choice of the early hour from the contrast between Pollak's statement that "he was willing to invest but only in the center area of the country, near Tel Aviv" and Sapir's wish "to build a factory in the Kiryat Gat development area." This clash of intentions and wishes constitutes the "complication" in dramatic terms; or the "complicity" or "lack" in Vladimir Propp's theory of action in Russian hero tales (Propp 1968, 30, 35); or the "complicating action" according to William Labov's narrative theory (Labov 1972). Upon leaving Tel Aviv, Sapir signals his driver to speed up. This brings them to Kiryat Gat within less than half an hour, which seems a short while to a foreigner used to overseas standards of locations and distances. Following this visit, Pollak agrees to invest in a textile factory in Kiryat Gat, the factory is built, and the story ends on a note of pride and satisfaction: "This is how the Polgat Industries and others got started. By now they employ thousands of workers and export their products to numerous countries for tens of millions of dollars." This summary illustrates the profitability of the investment, even if it was based on a deception, because on the whole the deal was justified financially and ideologically.

In the later variant, told by Ya'acov Shaham, emphasis is put on Sapir's vision and activities related to the distant Negev, an area whose development demanded more energy and resourcefulness than other places in the young state. The identity of the investor is not indicated overtly but can be gleaned from the company's name: Polgat. Sapir's vigor, diligence, and authoritativeness are emphasized even more here than in the earlier variant. Here he announces to the "investors," who are a common, generic entity, "My workday starts at five-thirty in the morning. Please come to my car by this time." In this variant, the early hour and the trick it camouflages are perceived as regular routines in Sapir's relations with "distinguished investors." Accordingly, it is also not specified that he instructs his driver to speed up, apparently because the driver is well versed in his boss's tactics. Eventually, things are summarized succinctly in sentences describing habitual action, such as: "The distinguished investors would come, sit in the car; the driver would floor the gas pedal, and they would be in the Negev in a short while." Moreover, in line with the emphasis on the host and not the guest, we never know what the investor thought of it all and how he acted/responded then or later. Instead, as in the earlier variant, the positive outcome of the trick is emphasized in phrases such as "Polgat and many others."

Arye Lova Eliav's written version positions this narrative in its historical, political, and cultural frameworks. Eliav functioned during this period as director of development for the Lachish area, after having successfully settled many new immigrants during the Mass Immigration period (*aliya gdola*, 1948–53) in many southern villages (*moshavim*). By now there were a few factories in the area of Kiryat Gat: a peanut-processing factory, a cotton gin, and a spinning mill. This was just the right time to establish a "clothing industry" (Eliav 1970, 77), which, like the spinning mill, is viewed as a "Jewish industry" (ibid., 175, 177). Using the same rationale as in the two IFA variants, Eliav ascribes the construction of the spinning mill to himself, or rather to a successful exchange he had with a group of potential investors from the United States. Eliav showed up at a formal meeting dressed like a hard-working pioneer, wearing khaki clothes and "desert shoes" (ibid., 176–77). At first the guests did not believe that he was the manager of the project, but later he convinced them not only that he was the manager but also to invest in a spinning mill. Thus Eliav's initial encounter with the American Jewish investors serves as an introduction to his story about Sapir's meeting with Pollak, the Jewish textile investor from Chile.

Eliav specifies that the minister met Pollak on his South American fundraising tour, and once Pollak came to Israel, Sapir made it his goal to convince him to invest in a factory in Kiryat Gat: "In his first conversation with Pollak [in Chile], Sapir started to praise Israel in general, the Lachish area in particular, and Kiryat Gat even more specifically: the climate is pleasant, there is plenty of water, ample land for development, high-voltage electrical lines nearby, easily available workers, and so on. Thus he continued to outline the advantages of Kiryat Gat" (ibid., 178). Pollak listens but also consults a map and realizes the geographical distance of Kiryat Gat from the center of the country. Yet Sapir persuades him that it is not far away, "a few minutes and you're in Kiryat Gat" (ibid., 178). Sapir's invitation to leave the next day at five in the morning sounds more polite and less authoritative or aggressive than in the two IFA variants. Sapir simply suggests, "Shall we make it five AM?" Pollak is taken aback and exclaims: "At five AM?" but poses no objection beyond that. As for the instruction to the driver to speed up, in this version Sapir gives his driver "a clear signal" to "step down on the gas pedal." It is also indicated that the ride started at a speed of 100 kilometers (60 miles) per hour, but as they left Tel Aviv it went up to 120, and also that they made it to Kiryat Gat in fifty-five minutes. They then visited the hill that was set aside for the factory for only "a few minutes," and "by seven in the morning they were all back in the Tel Aviv hotel" (ibid., 178–79). All this makes the tour seem like a meticulously planned, military-like lightning maneuver, geared toward making the right impression on Pollak but preventing him from thinking over the deal too much. Despite all this, Pollak figures out the trick, yet he admires the motivation behind the machinations and responds to the challenge by founding Polgat Industries. This same company "later enabled the founding of the Oman and Bagir clothing stores, and is still full of potential" (ibid., 179).

To end the discussion of this narrative as told by three very different narrators, two of them orally and one in documentary writing, we must point out that, though it is not a traditional folk narrative, Jewish or otherwise, it still expresses core issues related to the process of the Jewish people's return to their "old-new land." In the main, the narrative looks on this process with humor and with acceptance of the imaginative ploys needed to carry out the Zionist enterprise. Beyond its plot and characterization aspects, then, this narrative addresses general key issues in the modern history and culture of Jews, and subtly pronounces the following realizations:

(1) Alongside the emphasis on the national revival of the Jewish people in its old-new land through physical and preferably agricultural work, there is still an honorable place for more traditional "Jewish" occupations, especially those related to textile, the "Jewish industry" in Eliav's memoir. In the young State of Israel, before it became flooded by cheap Far Eastern merchandise (Hebrew: *konfektsia*), the textile industry flourished and was seen as part of the return-to-the-land ethos through the cultivation of cotton, the raw material for textile products. But it seems that beyond or in addition to the revival of Israeli agriculture, Israeli leaders and functionaries remain connected to Diasporic occupations and commerce, including their manners of persuasion.

(2) Though making *aliya* is vital for the existence of the new State of Israel, it is no less important for the Zionist enterprise that well-off Jews around the world support Israel from wherever they live (and that they better stay there to be able to do so indefinitely). This realization connects to well-known humorous sayings of that period by its renowned "Jewish" figures (like Sapir, Eshkol, Burg, and others): "let's build up the country and go back abroad already"; "no matter how much it costs, as long as it looks modest"; and "how do you make a small fortune in Israel? You go there with a big fortune" (some of these are cited in Nevo-Eshkol 1989, 68–69). The Israeli need for the wealth of Diaspora Jewry is perceived as legitimate, though in later years it was at times criticized in Israeli publicity and public opinion.

(3) The large sums needed for resettling the nation in its land and providing employment for its people must be drawn from world Jewry in roundabout ways, or by outright deception. Wealthy Jews living abroad are not in any rush to part with their money, whether out of fear of losing

too much money too quickly in Israel or because, just like the stereotypical Diasporic rich man, or *gvir*, they cling to their wealth and refuse to part with it even for just causes. Even when an investor has expressed willingness to spend money, it is still incumbent on the locals—even if only for the sake of drama and suspense—to invest special efforts and resourcefulness to show that they deserve the sum. The investor on his part enjoys the dual status of being partially duped and partially too smart to be duped, which enables him to succumb to the trick and even enjoy the whole process, for after all it is for a good cause.

(4) Distance and time are relative entities dependent on the ways things are presented. The same rationale goes for: too much and too little, close and far, closeness and remoteness, duty and right (or privilege), old and new, Jewish and Israeli, agriculture and fashion. Thus this is a legend deployed not only to start the Jewish national existence anew in Israel but also to convince world Jewry of the importance of this project and of their vital part in it. In this way the modern Zionist enterprise is (re-)rooted in the land of ancient Israel, and world Jewry supports it from abroad. Each party merits its practical or symbolic reward in proportion to its investment, and the "lack" or necessity—in folk-literary and in strictly financial terms—is effectively liquidated or (ful-)filled.

NOTES

1. See, for example, the agricultural tall tales about mega-sized vegetables in Siporin 2000.
2. On June 6, 2004, Eliav was a guest speaker at my undergraduate seminar about immigration and settlement in Israel's first years (at Achva College), and it was evident that his oral presentation echoed his written accounts.
3. On the modern Israeli case of nation-building, see Pensler 1998; Cohen-Almagor 1995.
4. Although this category has several very close subcategories or sections; for example, "bluff and trickster tales" in motifs K 1700–1799. See Thompson 1955–58.
5. On ties and borderlines between folk and documentary narratives, see Rosen 2009, 109–12.
6. On Israeli rumor narrative, see Shenhar 1989; Shenhar 1991.
7. On Eshkol's figure and humor, see his daughter Ofra Nevo-Eshkol's book (Nevo-Eshkol 1989).

BIBLIOGRAPHY

Aarne, Antti, and Stith Thompson. 1961. *The Types of the Folktale: A Classification and Bibliography*. FF Communications no. 184. Helsinki: Suomalainen Tiedeakatemia.

Cohen-Almagor, Raphael. 1995. "Cultural Pluralism and the Israeli Nation-Building Ideology." *International Journal of Middle East Studies* 27 (4): 461–84.

Eliav, Arye Lova. 1970. *Leap Forward*. Tel Aviv: Am Oved. [Hebrew]

Holtzman, Avner. 2008. "Gershon Shaked's History of Hebrew Narrative Fiction: A Zionist Enterprise." *Hebrew Studies* 49: 281–89.

Labov, William. 1972. "Transformations of Experience in Narrative Syntax." In *Language in the Inner City—Studies in the Black English Vernacular*, 354–96. Philadelphia: University of Pennsylvania Press.

Mintz, Alan L. 1999. "Fracturing the Zionist Narrative." *Judaism* 48 (4): 407–15.

Nevo-Eshkol, Ofra. 1989. *A Cluster of Humor*. Tel Aviv: Yedioth Ahronot. [Hebrew]

Pensler, Derek Jonathan. 1998. "Narratives of Nation Building: Major Themes in Zionist Historiography." In *The Jewish Past Revisited—Reflections on Modern Jewish Historians*, ed. David B. Ruderman, 104–27. New Haven, CT: Yale University Press.

Propp, Vladimir. 1968. *Morphology of the Folktale*. Austin: University of Texas Press.

Rosen, Ilana. 2009. "Personal Historical Narrative Shaping the Past and Present." *European Journal of Jewish Studies* 3 (1): 103–33.

Shapira, Anita. 2010. "Hebrew Literature and the Creation of the Zionist Narrative." In *Polish and Hebrew Literature and National Identity*, eds. Alina Molisak and Shoshana Ronen, 19–26. Warsaw: Elipsa.

Shenhar, Aliza. 1989. "Legendary Rumors as Social Controls in the Israeli Kibbutz." *Fabula* 30 (1–2): 63–82.

———. 1991. "The Disappearance of the Submarine Dakar: Folklore, Community, and Stress." *Fabula* 32 (1–3): 204–15.

Siporin, Steve. 2000. "Tall Tales and Sales." In *Worldviews and the American West—The Life of the Place Itself*, ed. Polly Stewart, Steve Siporin, C. W. Sullivan III, and Suzi Jones, 87–104. Logan, UT: Utah State University Press.

Thompson, Stith. 1955–58. *Motif-Index of Folk-Literature*. Vol. 2. Bloomington: Indiana University Studies.

THE GIRL WHO EMERGED OUT OF AN EGG

IFA 13876

NARRATED BY ESTHER ELFASSY (MOROCCO)

God was everywhere. Once, there was a wise man who could cure barren women. This man was married to a barren woman, who once asked him: "My wise husband, you can help all the other women, why can't you help me?"

He asked her to remain patient, promised her that her day will come. Since she was not patient at all, she went out, and one day she saw a hen in her backyard. She prayed to God, crying and asking why all the other women had children while she didn't. "Please," she prayed, "let me give birth—even if it be to only one single egg, like the one I just saw." Her wish came true: She became pregnant, and after nine months she gave birth to an egg. She hid the egg in the *kaskas*[*] and kept it a secret, even from her husband.

Nearby, in a hidden place within the city, there was a tall tower. A wicked witch who knew the secret of the woman with the egg lived in the tower. Disguised as a poor woman, she came to the house of the woman who had given birth to the egg and said: "Please lend me your *kaskas* so I can make couscous for my hungry children." The innocent woman agreed and gave it to her. The witch took the *kaskas* with the egg in it and went to her house at the top of the tower. She threw the egg on the floor; the egg broke, and a beautiful girl with long hair emerged out of it. The witch took care of her up until the day she grew up. The girl knew nothing about the world outside the tower. The witch braided a plait from the maiden's hair, with which she could climb up to the tower and go back down. Whenever she came back from her mysterious journeys, she called: "Flower, flower, the daughter of the winds, lower your hair and raise your old woman from depths." And so it happened. One day, a prince went by, hearing and seeing all that happened. He ambushed the witch until she fled, and called the maiden: "Flower, flower, the daughter of the winds, lower your hair and raise your old woman from depths." And so it happened. The girl was surprised to see the prince, because the witch had never told her about the world outside the tower. The prince told her everything about it.

The maiden fell in love with the prince and wished to go with him to the world he had described to her. The prince was afraid of the witch; he warned the maiden and told her about the danger. He suggested that she should ask the witch about the magic spells with which it is possible to overcome her. In due time the maiden lowered the prince down by her hair, and he went to his hiding place. When the witch showed up, she called, as usual: "Flower, flower, the daughter of the winds, lower your hair and raise your old woman from depths." And so it happened. When they

---

[*] *Kaskas* A strainer for draining couscous, a typical North African food.

both went to eat, the girl asked the witch: "Here you are, an old woman, but you have never told me the spells with which one can overcome your power." At first the witch didn't want to reveal her secret, but after the girl asked again and again, she finally answered, as she really loved her. She said: "Here are a pin, a mirror, and a comb. If you throw the pin, everything becomes dark. If you throw the mirror, a river will block the way; and if you throw the comb, thorns will grow everywhere, and I won't be able to step." The witch went to sleep. When dawn came, the witch went away, and the prince showed up. He called the girl, and she lifted him up. She told him the secrets of the witch. They both took all three objects and ran away. When the witch returned and didn't find the girl, she understood that she had run away with the secret objects. She started chasing her until she almost reached her. The girl threw the pin, and it became dark. The witch lighted a magical flashlight. The girl threw the mirror, and a river blocked the witch's way. She crossed it by a boat and almost reached the girl and the prince. The girl threw the comb, and thorns blocked the witch's way. She stopped and couldn't go any farther.

The girl and her beloved prince reached the palace, and after a short time, they got married and lived happily ever after.

The story flowed down with the rivers, and we are left with generous givers.

Transcribed by Ya'akov Elfassy

COMMENTARY TO
"THE GIRL WHO EMERGED OUT OF AN EGG"

IFA 13876

RAVIT RAUFMAN

This tale was recorded in IFA in 1981, by Ya'akov Elfassy, who heard the story from his mother, Esther Elfassy, an immigrant to Israel from Morocco. The tale may be classified as belonging to tale type AT 310 ("Rapunzel"). This tale type includes the following plot stages: (1) The promise of a child—a man promises a witch that he will give her his child; (2) the hair as a ladder—the maiden is imprisoned in a windowless tower; the witch climbs up the tower using the maiden's hair; the prince sees this and does the same; (3) abandonment and blindness—when the witch finds out about the prince, she abandons the maiden in the desert; the prince saves himself by jumping from the tower, and becomes blind; (4) the blindness is cured by the maiden's tears, which fall on his eyes.

The main motifs characterizing the international tale type that exists in the Jewish Moroccan versions are imprisonment in the tower (R41.2), the maiden at the witch's service (G204), and the long hair of the beautiful maiden, which is used as a ladder (S144). The motif of blindness cured by the maiden's tears (F952.1) is missing from the Jewish Moroccan oikotype, and is replaced by the prince and maiden running away and escaping from the witch by throwing three magic objects that block her way. However, the most essential and basic difference between the Jewish Moroccan version and the international tale type lies at the beginning of the story, when a barren woman sees a hen and asks to be able to give birth to an egg.

The unique opening that presents a girl emerging out of an egg is not exclusive to this version but rather can be found in other Jewish Moroccan versions recorded in the IFA, such as IFA 22815, "The Woman Who Gave Birth to an Egg." This tale was recorded more than twenty years before the tale presented here, a fact that raises the possibility that the unique opening that presents a girl emerging out of an egg is not simply an isolated case but rather a common theme among Moroccan Jews.

There are a few possible ways to understand this unique opening. It should be mentioned at the outset that in folklore eggs are commonly connected to creation myths. In the mythologies of many peoples, the world is created by the falling of a cosmic egg (Willis, ed., 1993, 18). Such tales are prevalent in North Africa, where the version discussed here originated. Diverse peoples, scattered far and wide throughout Africa, have described the creation of the world as the shaking of a cosmic egg. From this viewpoint, it might be possible to see the circumstances of the birth of the heroine in the Moroccan versions as an animation of a creation myth that was common in the place where the tale originated. Many mythologies describe the world as being created by, or born out of, destruction, similar to the way in which the heroine emerged out of a broken egg that was powerfully thrown by a supernatural entity—the witch (Willis, ed., 1993, 62, 70, 90). However, I suggest that we understand the act of emerging from an egg as a realization of an idiomatic expression used by Moroccan Jews. This explanation relies on a mental developmental model that suggests viewing idiomatic expressions as bridging the gap between somatic and mental experiences, and between primary and secondary processes.

The idea that wonder tales might reflect mental states, in which both primary and secondary thought processes are involved, can be traced back to the early days of psychoanalysis. In this discussion I will focus on a realization of a metaphor appearing in the present Jewish Moroccan wonder tale in order to exemplify some of the ways in which the wonder-tale genre—with its symbolic, abstract style—conveys its messages in a subtle and sophisticated manner, mixing together primary and secondary thought processes. This is achieved in a variety of ways, such as through the use of idiomatic expressions hidden in the plot. Exposing the meaning of this idiomatic expression allows for a more comprehensive understanding of the plot and helps us touch on the relationships between concrete and symbolic layers of the conscious mind.

In Judeo-Arabic, the language of the Moroccan Jews, the idiomatic expression "emerged out of an egg," means "grew up" (*mitfacts malbeida*).[1] The narrative, indeed, outlines a coming-of-age story about growing up. Usually this idiomatic expression is used in a negative sense. For example, it is common to say about a childish girl that she "hasn't yet emerged out of an egg." A girl who has "emerged out of an egg" is a grown-up maiden, no longer a child. Thus she is ready to get married. I shall now discuss the meaning of this phenomenon: the realization of a metaphor as bridging the gap between concrete and abstract ways of thinking.

In previous works with coauthor Yoav Yigael, I suggested that some idiomatic expressions, in particular those including body organs, have a unique status in human experience as well as a significant role in the way in which the body expresses itself in language (Raufman and Yigael 2010; Raufman and Yigael 2011). Idiomatic expressions were presented in these works as the language's way to describe far-removed and primary experiences whose expressions are part of daily existence, especially in regard to the way they bridge the gap between somatic and mental experiences. In another work (Raufman 2012), I suggested that in many cases identifying the idiomatic expressions hidden behind concrete acts provides us with a way to interpret some of the marvelous elements of the genre.

As mentioned in another discussion appearing in this book (the discussion of the tale "The Six Sisters from the Mountains"), the relationships between concrete and symbolic layers of the conscious mind, and between verbal expressions and somatic symptoms, were studied by Freud during the early stages of the development of psychoanalytic theory. In *Studies on Hysteria*, Josef Breuer and Sigmund Freud described the creation of somatic symptoms as a symbolization of verbal expressions (Breuer and Freud 1955 [1893–95], 20–195). In the same discussion I also presented Yigael's relation to the case description of Cacilie (Yigael 2001, 175–202), in which Freud describes the way the somatic pain had become indicative of a specific kind of psychic suffering. This is how the creation of symbolic conversion is explained: by the simultaneous presence of thoughts accompanied by both physical pain and a given somatic pain. The latter becomes representative of the former by what Freud calls the "associative reverberation of the psychic life" (Yigael 2001, 179–80). In Freud's later works the somatic symptom becomes a representative symbol that implies or stands for an abstract idea or repressed conflict. Conversely, in *Studies on Hysteria*, and in the context of the affiliation between verbal expression and somatic "expression," the symptom is seen as a precise translation of an idiom into a specific sensation (Yigael, 2001, 180). Many other scholars have also related to the connections between idiomatic expressions, or metaphors, and somatic symptoms (Chiozza 1999; Holland 1999; Melnick 1997; Modell 1997; Lakoff and Johnson 1980). The wonder tale, as a tale of magic characterized by the salient of primary processes, gives, in our Jewish Moroccan tale, a concrete expression of feelings and ideas that carry deep meaning. We must remember that, in many cases, the wonder tale's way of describing feelings, emotions, and thoughts is by describing concrete actions. Thus choosing a concrete action to describe the complex process of growing up is quite natural in the realm of the wonder-tale genre.

In this case it is possible to see some of the oikotypification processes—when a plot detail that can be viewed as a realization of an idiomatic expression appears in versions that are told within a society that uses this expression in its language. The case of the Jewish Moroccan version of "Rapunzel"—where the unique opening exists in versions told in Mugrabi—presents a realization of an idiomatic expression that exists in this language. In an article that deals with concrete and symbolic layers in human conscious, Yigael and I demonstrated the way in which idiomatic expressions function to bridge the gap between somatic and mental experiences. We suggested viewing idiomatic expression as the language's way to connect with the primary levels of mental organization (Raufman and Yigael 2011).

It seems that fairy tales in general often describe this phenomenon. Local story versions may frequently reveal the ways in which unique plot details are connected to the language told by the society that preserves these tales. The act of emerging out of an egg appears in versions told by a society that uses the idiomatic expression "emerging out of an egg" in its daily language. This metaphorical expression is not mentioned as such in the Moroccan versions but rather appears in a concrete manner, where a real girl actually emerges out of a real egg.

NOTE

1. I wish to thank the Aberjil family of Zikron Ya'acov, Israel, for assisting me with the interpretation of idiomatic expressions in the Judeo-Arabic of Morrocan Jews.

BIBLIOGRAPHY

Aarne, Antti, and Stith Thompson. 1961. *The Types of the Folktale: A Classification and Bibliography*. FF Communications no. 184. Helsinki: Suomalainen Tiedeakatemia.

Breuer, Josef, and Sigmund Freud. 1955 [1893–95]. *Studies on Hysteria*. S. E. II. London: Hogarth Press.

Chiozza, Luis. 1999. "Body, Affect and Language." *Neuro-Psychoanalysis* 1: 111–23.

Holland, Normand N. 1999. "Cognitive Linguistics." *International Journal of Psychoanalysis* 80: 357–63.

Lakoff, George, and Mark Johnson. 1980. *Metaphors We Live By*. Chicago: University of Chicago Press.

Melnick, Burton A. 1997. "Metaphor and the Theory of Libidinal Development." *International Journal of Psychoanalysis* 78: 997–1015.

Modell, Arnold H. 1997. "Reflection on Metaphor and Affect." *Annual of Psychoanalysis* 25: 219–33.

Raufman, Ravit. 2012. "Idiomatic Expressions in Jewish Wonder-Tales: A New Interpretative Method." *Fabula* 53 (1/2): 20–45.

Raufman, Ravit, and Yoav Yigael. 2010. "'Feeling Good in Your Own Skin,' part 1: Primary Levels of Mental Organization." *American Journal of Psychoanalysis* 70: 361–85.

———. 2011. "'Feeling Good in Your Own Skin,' part 2: Idiomatic Expressions—The Language's Way to Connect with the Primary Levels of Mental Organization." *American Journal of Psychoanalysis* 71: 16–36.

Thompson, Stith. 1955–58. *Motif-Index of Folk Literature*. Bloomington: Indiana University Press.

Willis, Roy, ed. 1993. *World Mythology: The Illustrated Guide*. New York: Henry Holt.

Yigael, Yoav. 2001. "Dual Identification and the 'Weight of Responsibility.'" *Psychoanalysis and Contemporary Thought* 24 (2): 175–202.

THE SALVATION OF THE JEWS OF ARBIL DURING THE RASHĪD 'ALĪ RIOTS, 1941

IFA 13921

NARRATED BY REUVEN ADI (IRAQI KURDISTAN)

There is one belief that our parents related to us and the *goyim* [non-Jews] also told us a day after [the event], and we heard it from them. During the great uprising of Rashīd 'Alī in 1941, when they killed 960 Jews in Baghdad,[*] the rioters reached us. I remember that well.

I was about eighteen years old.[†] We went up to the roofs; we used to sleep on the roofs in the summer. In the summer we did not sleep in the rooms. Everyone went up to the roofs and slept there. The roofs were surrounded by a fence of sorts, a sort of railing.

Suddenly we heard the yells of *goyim* who came bearing swords, to kill us. What did we do? All the Jews began to recite Psalms. That is the belief in God's mercy. They locked the gates that were made of wood, and went upstairs to cry. All cried. And to where did the *goyim* reach? They reached that *tchak*.[‡] That exactly was the borderline. The first Jewish house was next to it. After that were a few coffeehouses.

Next day we were told by the *goyim*, those who participated in this demonstration, and I cannot verify whether this is true or not. But next day the *goyim* already related that they saw three old men wearing white clothes who said to them, to the *goyim*: "You're stupid. You're going to kill the Jews? Now the governor will phone the military base (that was very near the city, almost inside the city); he will inform the army. The army will come and arrest all of you. Go first and kill the governor, and then attack the Jews."

And indeed they went back, in reverse, to kill the governor. Meanwhile the governor had fled to the military base. Meanwhile they set on fire his car, which was parked near the *kishle*.[§] The governor saw the rioting and gave an order to the army, which arrested them all. Next day they said that the Jews have a great God, very great. Why? Because they saw this and that. And that is the very truth.

Transcribed by Haya Gavish

---

[*] Actually, the number of those killed in Baghdad was 150 to 180.

[†] In his curriculum vitae Reuven Adi noted that he was born in 1928; thus he was only thirteen years old at the time

[‡] A tomb sacred to both Jews and Muslims, located in the center of the Jewish ghetto, near the Jews' stores.

[§] A word used by Ottoman Turks to denote barracks for soldiers. The *kishle* often served as headquarters for officials.

Commentary to
"The Salvation of the Jews of Arbil during the Rashīd 'Alī Riots, 1941"

IFA 13921

Haya Gavish

euven Adi, an active member of the Zionist underground in Arbil, related his story in the framework of a research project titled "Arbil as Reflected in the Eyes of Its Former Residents."[1] The story most prevalent among members of that community related to their wondrous salvation during the riots of 1941. I heard six versions of this episode,[2] indicating how important it was even many years after the event. Reuven Adi's story is a classic example of a memory narrative[3] of the Jewish narrative type: supernatural intervention to rescue a community threatened by a mob.[4] I choose to discuss his version of the event, while relating it to the additional versions, all in a folkloric-historical context.

Reuven Adi was born in 1928 in Arbil, in Iraqi Kurdistan. At the age of eighteen, he joined and became an active member of the Zionist underground in Arbil; he was the leader of youth groups. He immigrated to Israel in 1950. On the journey from Arbil, which lasted several weeks, he became ill. In Israel he lived first in Kibbutz Yagur, but after his family immigrated, he moved to Jerusalem. He now lives in Tel Aviv, where he serves as a cantor and a copyist of religious texts in the synagogue named after Nahum the Elkoshite, in Tel Aviv.

Adi's story opens with the riots conducted against the Jews of Baghdad on June 1–2, 1941, after the fall of the pro-Nazi regime of Prime Minister Rashīd 'Alī al-Jīlānī and before the British forces entered the city. In these riots, known as the "Farhud"[5] (Cohen 2010, 159–72), 150 to 180 people were killed, about 700 were wounded, and some 1,500 Jewish stores and homes were looted; altogether there were about 2,500 people physically victimized or suffering damage to their property (Yehuda 1992, 9–26; Meir-Glitzenstein 2004, 13–15).

Adi then described the development of the episode in Arbil, an important provincial capital strategically located between Mosul and Kirkuk. Although Arbil is in the Kurdish sector of Iraq, most of its inhabitants were Turkomans (Brawer 1935, 246–47; Brawer 1944–46, 204–13).[6]

The Jews of Arbil earned their livelihood primarily from shoemaking, dyeing, and trading in fabrics. A few owned stores, and some engaged in barter with the Kurds.[7] The community was traditionalist-religious, and even maintained a small yeshivah for the study of Jewish religious law. Despite differences in oral testimonies regarding relations between Jews and Muslims in Arbil, it appears that, aside from occasional violent incidents, relations were proper, though there was friction of an economic and nationalist nature between the two communities.[8] This continued until the attempted pogrom in the Jewish ghetto of Arbil in June 1941.

In contrast to written documentation relating to events in Baghdad, there is very little concerning what happened at that time in Kurdistan. We know that the Jews of Zakho were ordered to collect a large quantity of gold, a decree that was suspended only when the regime fell (Gavish 2010, 240–45). It is also a fact that ten Jews were murdered in Sondur, and that the residents in the Jewish quarter in Kirkuk remained within it for several weeks for fear of rioters (Habbas 1943, 102–4).

Reuven Adi's memory narrative combines facts with supernatural, imaginary elements. The objective of the facts is to lend credibility to the event and how it unfolded, and particularly to transmit a message that will strengthen belief in the power of Divine Providence. The personal experience of the narrator, identical to the experience undergone by the community, lends greater authority to this tendency.[9]

The narrator describes the sense of immediate danger and the panic that were the lot of the community. That is why his narrative has a dramatic element evinced in hearing voices ("Suddenly we heard the yells of *goyim* who came bearing swords") and emotional outbursts ("all cried"). The sense of danger is enhanced when Adi introduces realistic facts into his story: "We went up to the roofs [. . .] In the summer we did not sleep in the rooms [. . .] All the Jews began to recite Psalms [. . .] They locked the gates that were made of wood, and went upstairs to cry."[10]

In an introductory interview to his narrative, Reuven Adi spoke about the *tchak*, a tomb sacred to both Jews and Muslims in the Jewish quarter:

Tchak, yes, there was such a place, but there was not much belief in it. People believed that it was [the tomb of] a prophet, but it was a single tomb in the middle of a square in the center of the ghetto of the Jews, near their stores.[11] It was a tomb with a small fence about 25–30 cm [high] around the tomb, and it was said that this was a *tchak*. That is how this tomb was called. We don't know what a *tchak* is, a sort of prophet in Kurdish.[12]

It could be that mention of the *tchak*[13] was meant to make it clear that there was but a short step between the Jews and their deaths, because the mob had advanced very close to them. The panic and fear were very clearly enunciated in the narrative even many years later, and were accompanied by motions of the hands and intonations conforming to the description. The episode ended with acts of punishment, deescalation, and reconciliation. The sense of calm is also present in the closing part of Hayyim Pinhasi's testimony: "We rested after a few days, we rested."[14]

Adi concluded his narrative with a moral that strengthened belief in Divine Providence: "The governor saw the rioting and gave an order to the army, which arrested them all. Next day they said that the Jews have a great God, very great. Why? Because they saw this and that. And that is the very truth."

The deeply emotional experience of sudden and wondrous salvation was expressed in "the belief" related to Adi and other members of the community by their parents and the *goyim*— that it was three elderly men who, by a clever stratagem, turned the mob away from the Jews to attack the governor of Arbil. These three anonymous figures—whom no Jew saw with his own eyes—gave rise to amazement and motivated members of the community to try to learn more about them.

Like Adi, Shelomo Rabi also stressed the atmosphere of reconciliation between the Jews and their non-Jewish neighbors after the attempted pogrom. He supplied a description of the three old men as related by one of the leaders of the rioters: "Mahmud Tchicho, who led the mob and afterward became my friend, told me that the old men had glowing eyes and were of more than middle height. They held staves in their hands. [. . .] If there are people who emerged from their graves to defend you, then you are a people of Heaven."[15]

Belief in wondrous salvation by three old men was the basis for a legend[16] created and told in Israel by the children of individuals who were in Arbil,[17] and Reuven Adi's memory narrative exemplifies how the legend began to evolve.

Adi's narrative is, as noted, one of six diverse, somewhat poetic, interpretations by members of the Arbil community of an event that apparently took place in 1941; it left an indelible mark on the Jews of the city but lacks any written documentation. However we can learn something about that period, the atmosphere, and the episode and its causes from oral documentation by informants from Arbil. In his testimony Salih Yosef Nuriel, the last head of the Arbil Jewish community, who was also active in the Zionist movement (Gavish 2010, 161–62; 308), related primarily to the atmosphere and actions that preceded the attempted pogrom. "There was a Zionist club in the synagogue," he said. This club had a library of Zionist books that Nuriel lent out to young people in the community. His testimony continues: "We burned it [the library] during the time of Rashīd ʿAlī. There were many Zionist books, more than 400 to 450; this was a terrible time. During the Rashīd ʿAlī riots [. . .] they were also in our place [. . .] like in Baghdad. But there was no robbery. There was no murder. Only talk."

In the continuation of his testimony, Nuriel referred to attempts by members of the community to prevent the massacre: "It would have been foolhardy [to collect arms]; when facing every Jew there are a thousand Nazis, what will arms help?" He added: "[The pogrom] did not take place, but there was fear. A few times [members of the community] came to me [and said]: 'Let's congregate in the synagogues.' We had four large synagogues. I told [them]: 'By that you are opening the door. If the *goyim* know that we are hiding, that we are afraid, they might attack us. [. . .] Don't be afraid.'" He added that "in the time of Rashīd ʾAlī [the governor] was Salih Zaki. [The rioters] attacked him, they set his car on fire."[18]

In a personal memory narrative, Ya'acov Uriel (formerly Nuriel), the son of Salih Yosef, presented his own interpretation of the event in a much more realistic manner. Earlier, in an interview, he absolutely denied the possibility of miracles: "I don't believe in miracles. Every miracle can be explained as a human act."[19] In his personal memory narrative, he said:

When in 1941 they got ready on "the black night" to annihilate the Jews, the governor of the city and the commander of the city battalion surrounded the city and the rioters, who were advancing on the Jewish neighborhoods. There was fierce opposition between the police and the city residents who wanted to harm the Jews. The rioters set afire the car of the governor of the city. The army surrounded the city and didn't allow the rioters to draw near. I remember that next day at five in the morning I went to the governor's house to see his car that had been burnt. [. . .] In my opinion, the Jews were saved then because the governor was a man of prestige and because he decided not to let the mob attack the Jews. That is why he called the army into the city to defend the Jews.[20]

Following the pogrom in Baghdad, Iraqi Jews no longer felt secure or able to survive in that country.[21] The Jewish community of Baghdad underwent far-reaching changes, even if not immediately, and the Jews of Arbil apparently felt the same, even if the pogrom against them had been prevented. Among them were some who decided to fulfill the age-old longing for the Land of Israel and even took some practical steps in that direction. This is attested in the testimony of Ya'acov Uriel, who explained why he fled Arbil in 1945 with four other young fellows. They reached Palestine only in 1947, after undergoing difficulties and imprisonment on their journey:

Iraq and Arbil, in any case, were no "paradise" for Jews. This was especially made clear during the revolt of Rashīd 'Alī. [. . .] All those years of quiet were before the revolt. Because of the revolt you could sense that this peace and quiet was also somewhat colored by hatred. The Jew's success, the money he accumulated through his trading—all these influenced the locals. Though not every minute or at all times, but when they had the opportunity they would certainly do things against the Jews. [. . .] We did not leave [for Palestine in 1945] because of persecutions. But when you go to the synagogue you hear about Jerusalem in the prayers. Then you yearn for something that was but is no longer, and want that thing again. The Books of Ezra and Nehemiah motivated people to go up [to the Land of Israel] and build. Add to this the agitation among the young people after the Rashīd 'Alī revolt and the attack by the Muslims that came so suddenly [in order] to exploit the situation against the Jews. These things motivated the young people to move to a new place.[22]

In his testimony, Uriel even attempted to portray intensified feelings in the Jewish community of Arbil that a new situation, one of change, was at hand:

After the Rashīd 'Alī revolt and the pogroms, the Zionist movement acquired greater significance and influence than previously. The youth were enthusiastic about it. It may be that some of the grownups were more restrained in this matter, but Zionism was very popular. All the young people were mobilized and were organized in groups such as *hakhsharot*[23] and for studying the [Hebrew] language, etc.

Further on in his testimony, Uriel maintained that "the Zionist movement began in Arbil in 1941."[24] He was mistaken when he made an immediate connection between the rioting and the beginnings of the Zionist underground in his city. The Zionist branch in Arbil, like the other ones in northern Iraq, was established only five years later, in 1946. The Arbil branch, called "Alonim" (oak trees), was the most active one in Kurdistan, according to the sources at our disposal, and the young people flocked to it with the encouragement of the older members of the community (Meir-Glitzenstein 2004, 108–9).

It may very well be that intensive underground Zionist activity in Arbil during these years stemmed from the trauma and the sense of helplessness felt by the community a few years earlier and from the desire of the youngsters to find a solution for and change the situation.

NOTES

1. Haya Gavish, Arbil file, IFA.
2. See four additional versions in the IFA: Hayyim Pinhasi (no. 13928); Shelomo Rabi (no. 12062); Menashe Sho'an (no. 13938); and Weizman Hayyim (no. 13918). A fifth version, that of Ya'akov Uriel, is in the Arbil file, supplement, 286–87.
3. For the term "memory narrative," see Gavish 2010, 4–5. For the difference between a classic memory narrative, related in the first person and expressing beliefs and supernatural elements, and the personal narrative, which also includes secular and personal values, see Langellier 1989, 253.
4. On the basis of the IFA's expansion of the Aarne-Thompson international classification of folktales, we can classify Reuven Adi's narrative of supernatural intervention to rescue the community from a mob as AT *730. For this type of narrative and its unique structural characteristics—such as the reason for the attack, where and when it occurred, the rescue, and the manner in which this was done and its results—see Marcus 1977, 98–109.
5. According to Nessim Kazzaz, "Farhud" was the underground name of Yūnis al-Sab'āwī, a Jew-hater and one of the leaders of the uprising, who appointed himself governor of Baghdad on May29, after Rashīd 'Alī and his henchmen fled the city. Al-Sab'āwī's followers were actively involved in the murderous events of the two days of the Farhud in Baghdad (Kazzaz 1991, 206–7).
6. Salih Yosef Nuriel, the head of the Arbil Jewish community, made an interesting comment about this: "The residents in the city did not feel that they were Kurds, but rather Turks and Arabs. They were ashamed to say that we are Kurds." Salih Yosef Nuriel, Arbil file 21 (11), Oral History Division, Institute of Contemporary Jewry, Hebrew University of Jerusalem, 33.
7. Information supplied by Reuven Adi, Nabi Faraj, and Mordechai Yohanan: IFA, Arbil file, supplement, 135–37, 159–65. Abraham Ben-Ya'acob quotes the memorandum prepared by

Ben-Zion Yisraeli, a member of Kevutzat Kinneret, who visited Arbil in 1934. He noted that the Jews were losing their hold on the traditional crafts, which were being taken over by Muslims (Ben-Ya'acob 1980, 94).

8. For Jewish–Muslim relations, see IFA, Arbil file, supplement, 85 (testimony of Menashe Sho'an); 291 (testimony of Ya'akov Uriel); 163, 172, 177 (testimony of Reuven Adi); and 159–60 (testimony of Nabi Faraj).

9. A memory narrative in which a personal experience is combined with some true basis tends to increase the belief of the audience in the supernatural elements in the story; see Yassif 1999, 421–22.

10. See also the version of Hayyim Pinhasi (IFA 13928) about this aspect. The description of the Jews on the roofs as the mob tries to reach them is reminiscent of the biblical narrative about the wondrous rescue of the residents of Jerusalem from the besieging forces of Sennacherib during the days of King Hezekiah; Isaiah 37, esp. v. 36.

11. Adi also described the Jewish neighborhoods: "The entire Jewish quarter was flat. There were a few Jewish neighborhoods. Three Jewish neighborhoods [. . .] this was a Jewish ghetto in which lived no more than four Arab families. [. . .] It wasn't a ghetto like in Eastern Europe, but still a ghetto [. . .] Jewish neighborhoods together." Reuven Adi, IFA Arbil file, supplement, 134–35; see also Menashe Sho'an, ibid., 82.

12. Reuven Adi, IFA Arbil file, supplement, 145; Menashe Sho'an, ibid., 89.

13. It is also noted in the narrative of Hayyim Pinhasi (IFA 13928).

14. Hayyim Pinhasi, IFA Arbil file, supplement, 250.

15. Shelomo Rabi, IFA Arbil file, supplement, 64.

16. For this genre, see Dégh 1995, 226–35.

17. For example, Weizman Hayyim, an anthropologist, whose parents were born in Arbil; IFA Arbil file, supplement, 5, 49–66.

18. Salih Yosef Nuriel, Arbil file 21 (11), Oral History Division, Institute of Contemporary Jewry, Hebrew University of Jerusalem, 25, 33–34, 49, 60.

19. Ya'akov Uriel, IFA Arbil file, supplement, 315.

20. Ibid., 286–87.

21. For the way in which the pogrom influenced Jewish life in Baghdad, see Atlas 1971, 17–27; Meir-Glitzenstein 2004, 14–15.

22. Ya'akov Uriel, IFA Arbil file, supplement, 285, 295.

23. Lit. "training groups"—generally for Zionist agricultural settlement.

24. Ya'akov Uriel, IFA Arbil file, supplement, 287.

BIBLIOGRAPHY

Aarne, Antti, and Stith Thompson. 1961. *The Types of the Folktale: A Classification and Bibliography*. FF Communications no. 184. Helsinki: Suomalainen Tiedeakatemia.

Atlas, Yehuda. 1971. *Up to the Scaffold: The Deeds of the Underground in Iraq*. Tel Aviv: Ma'arachot. [Hebrew]

Ben-Ya'acob, Abraham. 1980. *The Jewish Communities of Kurdistan*. Jerusalem: Kiryath Sefer. [Hebrew]

Brawer, Abraham J. 1935. "From the Episode of My Travels in Syria, Babylon, and Assyria." In *A Tribute to David: Jubilee Book in Honor of David Yellin*, ed. Simha Assaf, Ben-Zion Dinaburg, and Shmuel Klein, 246–47. Jerusalem: Reuven Mass. [Hebrew]

Brawer, Abraham J. 1944–46. *Road Dust*. Tel Aviv: Am Oved. [Hebrew]

Cohen, Hayyim. 2010. "The Anti-Jewish Farhud in Baghdad, 1941." In *Al-Farhud: The 1941 Pogrom in Iraq*, ed. Shmuel Moreh and Zvi Yehuda, 2–17. Jerusalem: Magnes Press.

Dégh, Linda. 1995. "The Process of Legend Formation." In *Narratives in Society: A Performer-Centered Study of Narration*, 226–35. FF Communications No. 255. Helsinki: Suomalainen Tiedeakatemia, Academia Scientiarum Fennica.

Gavish, Haya. 2010. *Unwitting Zionists: The Jewish Community of Zakho in Iraqi Kurdistan*. Detroit: Wayne State University Press.

Habbas, Bracha. 1943. *Close Yet Distant Brothers*. Tel Aviv: Am Oved. [Hebrew]

Kazzaz, Nessim. 1991. *The Jews in Iraq in the Twentieth Century*. Jerusalem: Ben-Zvi Institute. [Hebrew]

Langellier, Kristin M. 1989. "Personal Narratives: Perspectives on Theory and Research." *Text and Performance Quarterly* 9 (1989): 243–76.

Marcus, Eliezer. 1977. "The Confrontation Between Jews and Non-Jews in the Folktales of Jews of the Islamic Countries." PhD diss., Hebrew University of Jerusalem. [Hebrew]

Meir-Glitzenstein, Esther. 2004. *Zionism in an Arab Country: Jews in Iraq in the 1940s*. London: Routledge.

Yassif, Eli. 1999. *The Hebrew Folktale: History, Genre, Meaning*. Bloomington: Indiana University Press.

Yehuda, Zvi. 1992. "The Pogrom (Farhud) of 1941 in Light of New Sources." In *Al-Farhud: The 1941 Pogrom in Iraq*, ed. Shmuel Moreh and Zvi Yehuda, 9–26. Jerusalem: Magnes Press.

THE "CATTISH" FIRE IN CHELM

IFA 14232

NARRATED BY MORDECHAI HILLEL KROSHNITZ (POLAND)

In Chelm they suffered from a severe mouse epidemic—something terrible. Thousands of thousands of them. They didn't know what to do. No solution! There weren't any cats.

One bright day some Chelmer visited another town; suddenly he sees in a certain house there is a cat.

"What kind of animal is it?" he inquires with the house owner.

He said: "Oy, this is a very good animal."

"What does it do?"

"It catches mice, destroys them."

"What?! Listen, sell me this animal! We . . . I'll pay you as much as you want! In our place, in Chelm, one just can't live because of the mice."

He paid him money for the cat, brings the cat home, and announces: "From today onward, I have such an animal that destroys mice. And whoever pays me, I'll give him, I'll lend him the cat."

Fine, the Chelmers come one after the other, each one pays him money, and he gives him the cat to take home. But such a cat, such an expensive animal that does such an important job, of course, you don't treat it by chasing it away and such . . . So the cat would enter a house, would immediately begin causing damage: jumped on tables, threw plates, broke, dropped glasses. Milk, drank the milk; cream, ate the cream; took meat from the pots . . . The point is, that at the end they decided that this is a pest cat, which causes such harm that they have to get rid of it.

How do you get rid of it? They took the cat out of town and left it there. The cat went right back! So how do you succeed in doing it? So comes one and says: "We need to take the cat up, to the tallest building, which is the synagogue, lift it to the roof and throw it down."

They took the cat, put it on the roof of the synagogue, and threw it down.

The cat immediately jumped on its feet, escaped, and again began to walk about and cause damage!

What do you do? They decided that once again they will raise the cat to the rooftop, yes, and the synagogue beadle [shamash] will hold it in his hands, and they will throw the beadle along with the cat, and this way it will surely be killed. And so they did: They took the beadle, the beadle held the cat, and they threw them down. So the beadle got killed, and the cat escaped! No choice, no solution. They cannot get rid of the cat. So comes one wise man and says: "Gentleman, I have a solution."

"What is it?"

"We will take the cat, put it in a house, shut it all around so that it can't escape, and burn it. We will burn the house, and so the cat will burn up as well."

Well, they did as that guy advised them. They shut the cat in a house, sealed it all around, the doors were locked—not only locked but they also shut them with nails, so that they couldn't be opened—and they kindled the house. The cat was burned, the house was burned, but along with the cat the whole town was burned, because the houses were made of wood. So the whole town was burned down.

This was the first fire caused not just by fire but by the fault of a cat; and since then it was written in the history of Chelm as "The Cattish Fire."

And this teaches us that against a destructive person or thing you don't have to use even more destructive means. You need to find a solution to the problem and not solve it in the easiest manner, which is the most dangerous.

Transcribed by Ayelet Oettinger

COMMENTARY TO
"THE 'CATTISH' FIRE IN CHELM"

IFA 14232

AYELET OETTINGER

The story "The Cattish Fire in Chelm" (IFA 14232) is a conglomerate assembled from the two narrative types AT 1281 and AT 1310. These tales are international and have parallels in many languages.[1] In AT type 1281 ("Burning the Barn to Destroy an Unknown Animal"), a cat is brought to a land in which there are no cats in order to fight a plague of mice (F708.1, "Country without Cats"). Before long the damage the animal causes exceeds the benefit gained from it; thus the decision is made to get rid of it by capturing it in a building that is set on fire. In our tale this attempt to kill the cat is preceded by two other attempts, based on AT 1310 ("Drowning the Crayfish as Punishment"). The tale of the crayfish belongs to the story type in which people, out of ignorance, attempt to kill an animal in ways that, due to the animal's unique characteristics, enable it to escape. The three futile methods the people of Chelm use to try to get rid of the cat show their foolishness and increase the humor of the story.

The humor inherent in the first attempt to kill the cat—by tossing it off the roof of the synagogue—does not emerge only from the incongruity between this strange solution and the more effective way to dispose of a cat. Truly, people who are not familiar with cats don't necessarily know about their ability to jump from high places and remain unscathed. Instead the gist of the humor comes from the lack of proportion between the goal (to prevent the damage the cat causes in houses), which is logical and suits the events, and the choice to act in an unsuitable and illogical way (killing the cat) to achieve it. The lack of logic in the solution undertaken by the people of Chelm derives from the fact that it is exaggerated. The cat is a useful animal that helps the Chelmers defeat the mouse plague; the only problem is that it does damage to their homes because the people of Chelm treat the cat as if it were a sacred animal. Once their radical behavior becomes problematic, they adopt the other extreme: They decide to kill the cat, without ever thinking of other, intermediate options that might allow them to enjoy the cat's help while restricting its movements to prevent further harm.

The second solution the people of Chelm arrive at is even more amusing. To the humor derived from the gap between the simple problem and the extreme solution are added the qualities of automatism—of rigidity and not learning from experience. After the first trial failed, the people of Chelm should have figured out that cats falling from high places land on their feet. Yet instead they repeat the same act—only this time they entrust the cat to the beadle to prevent its escape. The humor lies in the fact that the people of Chelm did not properly interpret the sequence of events they witnessed: The cat first escaped death, and only then ran away; but the Chelmers ascribe the failure of the first attempt to the cat's flight rather than to its ability to survive the fall. More-over, although the people of Chelm apparently know that falling off a roof can cause death, they compartmentalize this knowledge: They apply it only to their target—the cat—not thinking that the beadle might also die in the process. The beadle's death demonstrates and enlarges the gap between the trivial damage the cat caused and the ill-advised and radical manner with which the people of Chelm deal with it. They are thus portrayed as grotesque in their mechanical rigidity and misapprehension of events.[2]

Only after the second attempt to kill the cat by throwing it from the roof fails do the people of Chelm internalize that this is not the way to get rid of it. They decide therefore to lock the cat in a house and set it on fire. This method is as incongruous as the first two in that it is even more extreme in its consequences, endangering not only the beadle but the whole town.

The story type AT 1281 has two parallels in the IFA. One of them was told in Yiddish by an informer from Linsk who related the tale as an incident that took place in his town (IFA 7124). The other was told by an informer from Turkey, who attributed the foolish actions to monks (IFA 17, published in Alexander and Noy 1989, 165–66; Jason 1975, 223–24). In this story type and its IFA parallels, the cat-owners panic because they are afraid the animal, with which they are not familiar, will not be satisfied with a diet of mice and will eventually devour them as well. Their decision to burn the cat derives from their fear of the unknown. Their anxiety over being killed gives a psychological rationale for both the radicalism of the deed and its lack of rationality.

It should be noted in this context that the mere idea of cat-burning is not without precedent in many European countries, for in medieval times it occurred as part of the traditional bonfires held on the eves of Saint John's Day and Easter. In all these cases the cats were burned out of fear, since folklore ascribed to them magical and demonic powers, such as the casting of the "evil eye," creating natural disasters, poisoning people with their breath, and drinking the blood of sucklings. Furthermore cats were perceived as the embodiment of witches and as bearing the image of the devil itself (Rogers 1998, 45–72). Fear of the cat as a harmful animal is mentioned in the Talmud as well, which states: "It is permissible to kill a cat, and it is in fact a sin to keep it" (Babylonian Talmud, Tractate Baba Kamma 80b).[3] In the Jewish context the manner by which the cat is killed bears an additional meaning, for pushing the condemned to their death from a height is the manner by which stoning (*sekila*) is implemented. Stoning is the first of four types of capital punishment executed by the rabbinic court (*mitot beit din*, Mishnah Sanhedrin, 6:4), while burning (*serefah*) is the second (ibid., 7:1). To the Jewish listener familiar with the rabbinic sources, it seems as if the people of Chelm judged the cat according to the order of capital punishment types mentioned in the Mishnah. Further humor lies in the fact that the people of Chelm do not even consider the next two types of capital punishment—decapitation (*hereg*) and strangulation (*chenek*)—which are more suitable than stoning and burning for the extermination of unwanted animals.

The parallel stories emphasize the foolishness of the Chelmers' behavior in the tale under discussion. The people of Chelm are not afraid of the cat and do not avoid touching it, as is obvious from the fact that they catch it several times to destroy it. Their extreme and reckless action is the result of a minor discomfort that lacks the psychological legitimacy of the parallel stories. They act out of sheer foolishness that exceeds normal behavior. A sane person, foolish as one could be, will not attempt to kill an animal by jumping with it from a tall building or by locking it in a house set on fire (Jason 1975, 205–8). Hence Jason perceives the people of Chelm and other societies of numbskulls as "kind of in-between beings identified through their quality of distorted thinking. They stand between humans and dead souls" (ibid., 222–23).

The story of the "'Cattish' Fire" takes place in Chelm, a commercial city near Poland's eastern border, southeast of Lublin. Jews may have lived in Chelm from as early as the twelfth century, and they continued to do so until the Holocaust period, when the entire Jewish town was exterminated. Still, in Jewish folklore and humor, the city of Chelm will live forever as a legendary-fictive Jewish town whose inhabitants acquired the reputation as good, well-meaning, happy, hardworking, and gentle, but mainly gullible, fools who are detached from reality; they have no wise men, wise fools, or even tricksters among them. The stupidity of the Chelmers motivates their ridiculous behavior. They display absurd misunderstandings, absurd ignorance, and absurd disregard for facts. They have poor judgment and engage in foolish imitation. They are shortsighted: They do not notice or comprehend the consequences of an action and fail to see the natural, logical connection between cause and effect. Hence they act automatically, invent absurd scientific theories, and do everything in the reverse of what ordinary people do. The environment of Chelm is molded like the real, mundane world of the narrating community, but it differs in that, for example, common things (such as cats) are unknown in it. This isolated territory exists outside the realms of ordinary human society (represented in the story by the person who lives in "another town" and sells the cat to the Chelmer). According to Jason, the world of numbskulls—Chelmers and others—is located "between the two worlds, this world and the afterworld" (ibid., 209–10).

Noodlehead towns like Chelm exist in the folk humor of other countries, cultures, and societies, including Abdera and Boeotia (the land of fools) in ancient Greece; Emesa in Persia; Kampen in the Netherlands; Altstatten in Switzerland; a large number of cities in Germany;[4] and more than forty-five towns in fifteenth-century England (Luomala 1966). Cognate stories of fool-towns are told in Syria, India, China, Russia, Japan, Pakistan, Sri Lanka, and other countries (Jason 1975, 197).[5] In Jewish folklore and literature throughout the ages, other places earned reputations as noodlehead towns as well: The Babylonian Talmud mentioned the city of Papunia in Iraq (Tractate Pesachim 42a). In the Middle Ages we learn that collective foolishness was attributed to dwellers of the East in general and to the inhabitants of Acre and Assyria in particular.[6] Among the Jews of Salonica and the Judeo-Spanish–speaking Jews in the Middle East, the town of numbskulls is Maceda (Attias 1976, 23); and in Eastern European folklore of the nineteenth century, foolishness was ascribed in Poland to the people of Poznan, as well as to those of Chelm (Friedman 1981, 562). In Israel the colony of Mescha received this reputation among the collective agricultural labor settlements. In addition the IFA contains three stories, narrated by informers from Morocco, about "the Wise Men of Chelm from the Atlas Mountains," pertaining to the villagers living there (IFA 9570–9572).[7] Yet despite this variety it can be said that "Chelm" is the name most rooted in Jewish folklore as the village of foolish simpletons, of whatever provenance; this may be due to the similarity in sounds between its name and the Hebrew word *holem* ("a dreamer"), since gullible fools, detached from reality, can be perceived as daydreamers.

Tales of the people of Chelm have been told ever since the end of the sixteenth century, probably under the direct influence of tales about the Schildburg fools. These tales were translated from German into Yiddish in 1597 (under the title *Schildburg, A Short History*), and achieved extreme popularity among the Jews of Middle and Eastern Europe (Ausubel 1948, 320; Friedman 1981, 562). Chelm stories were first compiled in 1867.[8] During the twentieth century the literature of Chelmer stories grew immensely, mainly in Hebrew and Yiddish. Stories were compiled into Chelm tale collections and anthologies of Jewish humor. Many Chelm tales were edited as children's literature.

The Israel Folktale Archives contains thirty-two Chelm tales, fourteen of which were told by the narrator of this story, Mordechai Hillel Kroshnitz, who was my grandfather.[9] The other tales were related by informers from Poland (14 stories), Romania (2 stories), and Moldova (2 stories). The Chelm stories in the IFA are not jokes but rather humoristic stories having a short, condensed plot, and which achieve a comical climax through hints, agreed-upon codes, anti-codes, and surprises.[10] Humor is interlaced into the Jewish milieu, as Chelm is portrayed as the typical Jewish settlement (*shtetl*) that prevailed throughout Eastern Europe until the twentieth century, all of whose inhabitants were Jewish. Indeed even the sophisticated way in which the people of Chelm draw conclusions may be a satire of the *pilpul* exercises of Talmudic scholars.[11]

The Jewish milieu is also evident in the story in the choice of character (the beadle) and place (the synagogue). The synagogue and the fire link the fictional setting with the realistic and geographical city of Chelm, which was well known both for its magnificent synagogue—one of the earliest synagogues in Poland (Brick 1981, 78–79)—and for the fire that broke out in the Jewish quarter and left half of the city's Jewish population's homes roofless.[12]

Yet despite the Jewish characteristics, it is difficult to conceive the stories of Chelm as expressing "Jewish humor," which is typically defined as being told by Jews about Jews, and mocking their defects.[13] Oring has determined Jewish humor as having derived from the conceptualization of Jewish history as one of suffering, rejection, and despair (Oring 1992, 112–21). "Laughter through tears" is conceived as a "philosophic" and "exalted" way of dealing with everyday life and facilitating it. In addition, Jewish humor is explained as a "defensive" humor, supplying a weapon that enables the Jew to feel superior to his surrounding society, as if saying, "We are better than you even in laughing at ourselves." Yet in the case of the Chelm tales, the shortcoming sneered at—foolishness—is the exact opposite of the stereotypical characteristic of the Jewish people.[14] There is also a "pathological" concept of Jewish humor, according to which such humor is seen as irrational self-criticism that the narrators direct toward themselves. Yet one cannot argue that in Chelm tales the listening audience identifies with the characters described. On the contrary, they do not define themselves as belonging to the same social or collective identity.[15] The fact is that the social milieu of the joke as populated with Jewish people does not bear any ethnic or religious significance. The Chelm tales are not concerned with the Chelmers' Judaism. Rather, the stories revolve around the Chelmers' foolishness—a human weakness that is universally mocked throughout the ages.[16]

According to psychoanalytic/relief theory, gloating at and ridiculing fools have psychological motives: They enable the storyteller and his audience to discharge anger and aggression (Freud 1953–74, 8: 9–238; Bergson 1911). In addition laughter arises from the "sudden glory" felt when listeners recognize their superiority over the groups depicted as foolish in the story. The sense of superiority also creates the liberating laughter, which can be perceived as the main aim of the joke.

An additional way of interpreting laughter caused by the fool is according to Oring's theory of "appropriate incongruity," which claims that humor is a response to grasping appropriate interrelations of elements from distinct, incongruous fields (Oring 1992, 1–15; Palmer 1994, 93–110). The tales of the people of Chelm supply a classic example of this theory, since in all of them humor derives from the cognitive contradiction between the Chelmers' inner logic—apparently appropriate for the problems they face—and reality, proving all their solutions incongruent and wrong.

Yet it is exactly this appropriateness (even if incongruous) that enables the tale-teller to refer to the people of Chelm as "wise": In many stories they are referred to as "the wise men of Chelm" (not as "fools"), and this is not meant only ironically. In fact, the Chelmers' folly does not derive from witlessness but rather from a lopsided logic that focuses on a specific problem but does not widen to see the whole picture. Thus their solutions are wrong, detached from reality, and unpractical.

Another characteristic enabling us to see the people of Chelm as wise is the "street smarts" enfolded in their stories. As a storyteller, Mordechai Kroshnitz conveyed these "street smarts" by adding a few sentences of his own insights to the ends of his Chelm stories, after the narrative yet still in the realm of the storytelling context. In all fourteen IFA Chelm stories narrated by Kroshnitz, he added interpretations of the Chelmers' behavior to impart lessons and values, underscore general principles, and clarify the tales' virtuous morals or satirize negative but realistic human behavior. In most cases these additional interpretations include examples taken from different sectors of life (work, society, politics, etc.), reflecting Kroshnitz's opinion and knowledge gained from experience with leaders and officials, conventions and parties, political matters, and, mainly, general human behavior. With the creative act of adding the supplements to the stories, the narrator ensures that they cease to be humoristic tales; instead they are placed in the realm of morality and wisdom literature. The tales thus become exempla: illustrative "teaching stories" or parables used to impart lessons and values. The additions to the stories' conclusions constitute their morals. Indeed, Kroshnitz regarded his tales to be "fables" or "parables" (both referred to by the same word in Hebrew: *mashal*). He connected the supplements to the stories using sentences such as, "This is the parable. What is its moral?" or "This sounds like a children's tale, right? But it is not a children's story; it is a parable: a folk tale with an intention." The change in genre is not at the expense of the humor conveyed in the stories, for the moral arrives only after the liberating laughter and not in place of it. The sudden awareness of the truth presented in the tales illuminates them in a totally different light; and as in satire, this forces the listeners who have just laughed at the folly of others to digest everything anew, in view of the relevant truth imparted—and to search for the folly in them.[17]

In medieval times, truth and satiric criticism were often put in the mouth of the fool.[18] His special position as a simpleton (or an actor impersonating one) gave him freedom of speech and guarded him from the punishment that would otherwise be the consequence for those who know right from wrong and are responsible for their words. In the case of Kroshnitz's interpretation of the tales of Chelm, the moral stands apart from the humoristic fiction and is superficially applied onto the story by the storyteller. As far as I know, there is no other case of using Chelm tales as parables with an explicit moral. The stories transcribed in the IFA were conveyed by Mordechai Kroshnitz to us, his grandchildren, during family gatherings that took place mainly on weekends and holidays, usually around the table, between meals. Frequently he told these and many other Chelm tales when the moral suited particular circumstances. Over the years Kroshnitz presented a lecture to various audiences titled "Chelm: Fable and Moral," during which he used to interpret the tales of Chelm in the same manner.

Oring claims that a storyteller's repertoire can bear a deep personal meaning. Hence one can ascertain the nature of the tale-teller by the way he tells the tale, even if originally they were composed by others (Oring 1992, 94–111). The fact that Kroshnitz told and retold the stories of Chelm for years suggests that he considered them meaningful and also reveals his character. For example, in the tale discussed here, Kroshnitz taught that "against a destructive person or thing, you don't have to use even more destructive means." He concludes, "You need to find a solution to the problem and not to solve it in the easiest manner, which is the most dangerous." Pacifism, wisdom, and right behavior characterized him, and he tried to teach these to his grandchildren not only by his own example but also through stories. Only now, as I look back, do I see that, apart from entertainment, the joyous family gatherings involved also a didactic goal: to teach the younger generation knowledge, moral virtues, and ways of behavior—a goal worthy of a grandfather telling stories to his grandchildren.

NOTES

1. There are known versions in Finnish, Swedish, English, German, Dutch, Hungarian, Russian, Turkish, Chinese, and other languages.
2. This motif is found in another IFA story (of which only an extract exists), titled "A Rooster's Burial" (IFA 1494), also told by a narrator from Poland. The story relates how the people of

Chelm punished a rooster that broke a mirror by burying it while it was held on the beadle's lap. In this case, too, the rooster escaped, and the beadle died.

3. This was noted in the context of a cat that has bitten off the hand of a child. It is interesting to note that, later in the discussion, permission is given to breed cats, as they help to keep the house clean. Yet this applies only to black cats, while white cats are perceived as dangerous.

4. Including Buxtehude, Iglau, Mutschingen, Pirna, Schildburg (Schild), Schwarzenborn, Hafenstadt, and Teterow.

5. It should be mentioned that in some of the villages the people are not truly dumb but rather wise people pretending to be fools as a subterfuge. The people of Schildburg, for example, were so famous for their wisdom that rulers of their district forced them to serve in their palaces as advisors. Feigning stupidity helped the people of Schildburg avoid being taken from their homes. Similarly, the villagers of Gotham did so to prevent King John from passing onto their land and expropriating it, basing their behavior on the medieval belief that folly is contagious.

6. See Alharizi, *The Book of Tahkemoni*, assembly 46. Alharizi attributes collective foolishness to Eastern Jews in general, and to inhabitants of Assyria in particular, due to their poor speech, illiteracy, and stinginess. The people of Acre are regarded by him as fools, probably due to the author's dispute over the writings of Maimonides with some sages of France who dwelled there. Attributing collective foolishness as an invective resulting from a personal dispute can be found also in the Babylonian Talmud, such as in the epithets "foolish Babylonians" (Pesachim 34b; Yoma 57a; Beitzah 16a; and others) and "foolish Galilean" (Eiruvin 53b).

7. IFA contains more stories about groups of fools similar to the "fools of Chelm," yet they are not defined spatially as "cities" of fools (see Jason 1975).

8. In the chapter "*Di khokhmes fun eyner gevisen shtot*," included in a small booklet titled *Blitsende Vitsen Oder Lakhfiln* (*Lightening Jokes and Laughter*), published by an anonymous author in Vilna (Vilna: Avrohm Ytshak Dvorzshetsky). See Friedman 1981, 562.

9. Mordechai Hillel Kroshnitz (born in Baranowice, Belarus, 1915; died in Nahariya, Israel, 1998) received a traditional Jewish education. From a young age he was active in the Zionist socialist youth movement *Frayheyt* (Freedom). By the age of seventeen, he served as the official of the district council, organized the Vilna branch, and joined the Shachariya Kibbutz in Vilna, where he met Mina-Tamar, whom he married in 1936.

   During World War II, Kroshnitz escaped from the Nazis, first to Lubcha, and then into the interior of the USSR, until he reached Samarkand, Uzbekistan. He fought in the Red Army and was wounded at the Siege of Leningrad. At the end of the war, he returned to Poland and was sent by the Zionist party to organize activities in the Upper Silesia district. Kroshnitz was the kibbutz manager of Bytom, in which Jewish survivors (*she'erit ha-pletah*) were gathered. He became one of the leaders of the survivors in Germany, a delegate to and a lecturer at the survivor congresses, and a representative of Poland Jewry at the World Jewish Congress in Switzerland (1948). During the Israeli War of Independence, he was active in organizing illegal immigration to Palestine and in raising funds. In 1949 he made *aliyah* to Israel with his wife and two children. He worked as secretary of the clerical union in Haifa until he retired. Afterward, until the age of eighty, he volunteered as a labor law advisor to the Israeli workers' union.

10. For the definition of a "humoristic story" and the distinctions between it and a "joke," see Oring 1992, 82–93.

11. According to Ausubel, the Jewish nature of the stories is expressed in the Jewish settings; in the behavior of the characters according to Jewish customs, manners, and traditions; and also in many aspects of Jewish irony and wit (Ausubel 1948, 321).

12. Although responsibility for setting this fire is ascribed to the authorities, who hoped thereby to turn the Polish city into a Russian county town, rather than to incinerate a cat (see Vasermann 1981, 430).

13. See, for example, the anthology of jokes and humorous stories, Spalding 1969. For an attempt at understanding the development of Jewish humor, see Bermant 1986. For a collection of essays about the subject of Jewish humor, see Oring 1992, 112, and the reference mentioned there.

14. Such as greed, which was attributed to Jews at different periods (see Oring 1992, 126).

15. This is determined on the basis of a conclusion drawn by Ben-Amos (1973), that the pretensions of "self-criticism" or a "masochistic character" of a "Jewish joke" are based on relations of social identification between the narrator and the object of the joke (such as a matchmaker's mockery of matchmakers).

16. See, for example, Swain 1932; Palmer 1994, 24–53. The idea that Jewish humor regarding fools parallels that of international humor fits with Oring's claim that presenting Jews as a "laughing" people reflects the wish to portray Jewish culture as humanistic in nineteenth-century Europe (Oring 1992, 117). According to this theory, humor is one of the signs of civilized humanity.

17. Satire is an artistic protest, which in its essence stands for the wish to convey a conceptual element aimed at improving the future by rejecting the existing reality, and in confronting it with an idealistic, desirable past. Aside from the idealistic element motivating the satirist to criticize reality, satire also involves pleasure—wit and humor—both as an aim in itself and as a way of luring the readers to read, and thus expose them to the criticism conveyed in it, as a sweet coating to a bitter pill. Both ends exist in satire in different dosages, until it is defined as the art of telling the truth through laughter, and as a critical and entertaining distortion of the familiar (Snodgrass 1996, 405).

18. This, for example, was the main function of the court jester, and it characterized the Mother Folly figure in the plays of "The Joyous Societies," as well as the players in the "sotties" and the "feasts of fools"; see Swain 1932, 4; 62–64; 98; 109–12.

BIBLIOGRAPHY

Aarne, Antti, and Stith Thompson. 1961. *The Types of the Folktale*: *A Classification and Bibliography*. FF Communications no. 184. Helsinki: Suomalainen Tiedeakatemia.

Alexander, Tamar, and Dov Noy. 1989. *The Treasure of Our Fathers: Judeo-Spanish Tales*. Jerusalem: Missgav Yerushalaim. [Hebrew]

Alharizi, Yehuda ben Shelomo. 2001. *The Book of Tahkemoni: Jewish Tales from Medieval Spain*. London: The Littman Library of Jewish Civilization.

Attias, Moshe. 1976. *The Golden Feather: Twenty Folktales Narrated by Greek Jews*. Haifa: Haifa Municipality, Ethnological Museum and Folklore Archives. [Hebrew]

Ausubel, Nathan. 1948. *A Treasury of Jewish Folklore*. New York: Crown.

Ben-Amos, Dan. 1973. "The Myth of Jewish Humor." *Western Folklore* 32: 112–31.

Bergson, Henri. 1911. *Laughter: An Essay on the Meaning of the Comic*. London: Macmillan.

Bermant, Chaim. 1986. *What's the Joke?—A Study of Jewish Humour Through the Ages*. London: Weidenfeld and Nicolson.

Brick, Avraham. 1981. "In the Footsteps of Chelm's Jewish Community's Hidden Light." In *Chelm Congregation's Memorial Book*, ed. Shimon Kantz, 57–90. Tel Aviv: Irgun Yotzei Chelm. [Hebrew]

Freud, Sigmund. 1953–74. *The Standard Edition of the Complete Psychological Works of Sigmund Freud*. 24 vols. Trans. under the general editorship of James Strachey, in collaboration with Anna Freud. London: Hogarth Press and the Institute of Psycho-Analysis.

Friedman, Philip. 1981. "Chelm's Tales." In *Chelm Congregation's Memorial Book*, ed. Shimon Kantz, 561–62. Tel Aviv: Irgun Yotzei Chelm. [Hebrew]

Hodgart, Matthew. 1969. *Satire*. London: Weidenfeld and Nicolson.

Jason, Heda. 1975. "Numskull Tales: An Attempt at Interpretation." In *Studies in Jewish Ethnopoetry: Narrating, Art, Content, Message, Genre*, 197–234. Taipei: Chinese Association for Folklore.

Luomala, Katharine. 1966. "Numskull Clans and Tales: Their Structure and Function in Asymmetrical Joking Relationships." *Journal of American Folklore* (The Anthropologist Looks at Myth) 79, no. 311 (January–March): 157–94.

Oring, Elliott. 1992. *Jokes and Their Relations*. Lexington: University Press of Kentucky.

Palmer, Jerry. 1994. *Taking Humour Seriously*. London: Routledge.

Rogers, Katharine M. 1998. *The Cat and the Human Imagination: Feline Images from Bast to Garfield*. Ann Arbor: University of Michigan Press.

Singer, Isaac Bashevis. 1973. *The Fools of Chelm and Their History*. Trans. Isaac Bashevis Singer and Elizabeth Shub. New York: Farrar, Straus and Giroux.

Snodgrass, Mary Ellen. 1996. *Encyclopedia of Satirical Literature*. Santa Barbara, CA: ABC-CLIO.

Spalding, Henry D., comp. and ed. 1969. *Encyclopedia of Jewish Humor: From Biblical Times to the Modern Age*. New York: Jonathan David Publishers.

Swain, Barbara. 1932. *Fools and Folly during the Middle Ages and the Renaissance*. New York: Columbia University Press.

Vasermann, Shneor. 1981. "Paths of Life." In *Chelm Congregation's Memorial Book*, ed. Shimon Kantz, 423–36. Tel Aviv: Irgun Yotzei Chelm. [Hebrew]

Wisdom of a Man and Slyness of a Woman

IFA 15825

Narrated and transcribed from memory
by Yiftah Avrahami (Persia)

The head of the merchants' guild hung a sign in his store on which was written: "Slyness of a Woman, Wisdom of a Man." A sly woman passed by, read the sign, and became very upset. It annoyed her so that she promised herself to show the head of the merchants' guild her sly power, so that he will know that the two—slyness and wisdom—belong to a woman, and that man is just a vessel made by the woman's hands.

One day she put on her makeup, and adorned and perfumed herself so beautifully that no man could withstand her charms. She entered the store and started praising the merchant with all her qualities, asking him about his family status; she learned that he was single. She told him: "A merchant of your status deserves a beautiful girl from the highest rank, maybe even the daughter of one of the well-known and famous *hajjis*."

The merchant asked her: "Do you know of such a person?"

She replied: "Sure, of course. Among all the wealthy people, I know one *hajj* who has a beautiful daughter; no one is like her in the whole world. But for some reason, whoever asks for her hand, the *hajj* refuses to marry her off, claiming that his daughter is ugly, blind, and limps. It is not appropriate to marry her off, and it is not worth talking about her. And up until now he rejected all the suitors, and no one knows the reason. Nevertheless, she has no defect or flaw. Maybe a man like yourself, wise as it is written on your sign, may overcome the problem, and marry the only daughter of the *hajj* and enjoy your life."

The merchant became very enthusiastic as a result of the woman's lies and started to check out the nature of this *hajj* and his greatness. He found out that he really was a wealthy man and that he had an only daughter who had reached puberty, but he refused to marry her off.

Well, he sent messengers to talk to the *hajj*'s heart and to ask for his daughter's hand. But His Honor the *hajj*, as usual, told the messengers that, unfortunately, his daughter has many defects, and it is inappropriate to marry her off. But the messengers did not give up easily, and in the name of the merchant they promised that he would accept the *hajj*'s daughter with all her defects and flaws. His intention was to attach himself and marry into a worthy family such as that of His Honor the *hajj*, and not to one of a common man from the market. He does not fall for the charms of a woman; the important thing is that she belongs to wealthy people like the *hajj*.

Well, the *hajj* agreed and asked the merchant for a written commitment so that he would never divorce his daughter due to her defects. And the merchant, who was captivated by the woman's words, signed the commitment and handed it over to the *hajj*.

They made a magnificent wedding. The marriage procession started, and the time came to receive the bride into the groom's house. The woman ran to the merchant's house and told him: "Are you going to bring your bride like a common man? You have to prepare a fancy palanquin, and bring her with great honor to your house."

The merchant agreed, and they brought the bride with great honor to his house. The merchant went to greet the bride, but she was blind, armless, and limping, deformed and ugly, and could barely move. The merchant knew that he had fallen into a trap.

The woman came to wish him good luck (*mazel tov*), and the merchant burst into tears and complained about his bitter fate. However the woman comforted him. She could solve the problem on condition that he removed the sign in his store and sent her a suitable fee for her efforts. The merchant did not object and agreed to her terms. Then she told him: "For now on you should keep quiet and say nothing, and in three days tell the *hajj* that your relatives wish to come to the *hajj*'s house and visit him to wish him good luck" (*mazel tov*).

After three days he gathered all the town's poor and all the beggars and put them on donkeys. They took noisy musical instruments and started drumming and singing on their way to the *hajj*'s house. The *hajj*, who had decorated his palace for the reception of the wealthy, the rich, and the great merchants, was waiting for the arrival of the honorable guests. He heard the sound of the musical instruments and came out to see who was singing. He saw all the miserable and disadvantaged people of the town coming to his house, and wanted to chase them away in case the guests would arrive and see these common people, thereby damaging his honor. Suddenly, he felt the presence of his son-in-law, who stood at the head of this crowd. He was the one who had invited all these miserable people, and he wanted to chase them away, but his son-in-law said: "These are my relatives, and no one is allowed to tell me who will be my relatives."

The *hajj*, who saw that he was dealing with the paltry, plain people, begged his son-in-law to return his daughter to his house, and he would compensate him for the harm he caused him as a result of the wedding.

In return he just had to drive these people out of his house, so they wouldn't damage his honor and his status. And so it was done. The *hajj* compensated the groom, and the groom compensated the bride.

And the woman proved that women have slyness and deception but are also wise, and men are nothing compared to them.

COMMENTARY TO "WISDOM OF A MAN AND SLYNESS OF A WOMAN"

IFA 15825

LIMOR WISMAN-RAVID

A devious woman is walking down the street, and suddenly she sees a sign hanging above a shop: "Slyness of a Woman, Wisdom of a Man." She doesn't like what she reads. Why? We learn the reason immediately when she starts to act. She wants to prove that a woman is not just devious but wise as well, and that her wisdom is greater than men's. It was already said that "God blessed the woman with more wisdom than he gave to the man" (Babylonian Talmud, Nida 45b). And what else shall we discover about that woman when we continue to read the story? That she is devious and not necessarily wise; that she is hot-tempered; that she is a greedy, manipulative liar who takes advantage of her beauty. This character who moves the story has many qualities, not all of them necessarily moral. Is she married? Does she have children? The storyteller doesn't say anything about it. He, like all popular storytellers, says only what is important for the story, and in the current case it is important that we shouldn't know the family status of this woman who walks freely down the street, arranging fates, coupling couples, and destroying them with her own hands.

Now, let's look at another character in the story: the *hajj*'s daughter. Who is this anonymous young woman?[1] She is a handicapped "woman," unworthy of being married to a man: Ugly, blind, and lame, she hardly moves; she is worthless, to the extent that her father, the *hajj*,[2] doesn't want her to get married at all, except to the "prince," who more than anyone else insists on marrying her and promises that he will never get rid of her. The *hajj* knows what men want—a spouse, a mother, and a housewife—and his daughter will not be able to fulfill any of these duties. She is not beautiful and not even attractive; she doesn't move, and she has a lot of handicaps, so how can she be the queen of her home? It's no exaggeration to say that it would be ill advised for her to be a mother. Most would agree with that statement, and at any rate it's quite likely she would not be able to bear children. If this is the case, she is not a woman at all, according to the tale. So what is she? She is an object, and all the characters in this story—the devious woman, the merchant, and the *hajji*—would agree with that assessment. The expressions "women's slyness" and "women's wisdom" are not relevant in referring to this character, for she is simply not a woman.

In the following pages I would like to discuss the story by confronting characters who belong to different social groups: men and women, healthy people and handicapped individuals. The central confrontation in the story is that between a woman and men, as it can be deduced from the title of the story, and the goal of this confrontation is to achieve control, gain power, and change the socioeconomic status of the woman. This confrontation reveals one of the weakest segments of society, one usually illustrated in folk literature in an unpleasant light: those who are handicapped. The "crippled" woman (a word that is rooted in the Hebrew root meaning "beaten, defeated") in this story has no form, literally and figuratively, and also no content, just like the other crippled people described in the stories gathered at IFA.

The storyteller, Yiftah Avrahami, was born in 1926, in the city of Honsar, in Tlat, a province of Iran. Avrahami studied at *heder* for ten years and at a Persian elementary school for six. At the age of eighteen, he joined his father's trade business. In 1951 he immigrated to Israel and settled in Maslul, a rural settlement in the south. He wrote down more than seventy stories from memory. He had heard these stories in various situations, from Jewish merchants who visited the family store in Iran; during long winter nights when people gathered to drink tea and coffee together and tell stories; and also on the road during his business trips.

AN UNUSUAL NOVELLA

What we have here is a novella—that is to say, a realistic story—that is focused on a woman, and its central characters are regular people (not kings and princes). The story deals with wisdom and "love," both concepts that usually move the plot in novellas and contribute to resolving them.[3] Although romantic love and the relationship between man and woman are major characteristics of novellas, and are usually counted among the achievements of the novella's characters,[4] in our novella these concepts are being ridiculed and subjected to mockery, abandoned for other loves— love of honor, love of money, love of being in control of others—and result in the collapse of the family unit rather than its establishment.

As far as the narrative tale type, this novella belongs to the Jewish oikotype "The Revenge of the Wise Woman" (AT 1406*A), but it has also components of the narrative tale type AT 1441 ("Old Woman Substitute") and the oikotype "The Scholarly Rabbi's Daughter Who Looks like a Beast" (AT 873*A). It is important also to cite the motif C195 ("The Advice of a Wicked Woman"). A swindle plot is at the center of the novella, and thus it may also be seen as a swindle novella as defined by Jason (Jason 1971, 37). It is set in the Islamic world and lacks Jewish characteristics.

Let us turn first to the oikotype, "The Revenge of the Wise Woman." There are several versions belonging to this oikotype at the IFA.[5] In these versions, which originate from the Middle East, a wise woman wants to prove to a man that she has better qualities than he does, and she advises him to ask for an important person's daughter's hand in marriage. When the man marries the daughter, following the wise woman's advice, he discovers that his young wife is ugly/crippled/a woman-beast. The wise woman helps him get rid of his wife, and then marries him herself. The ending in these stories is a happy one, but not everything is so rosy. Although the heroine proves she was right and marries the man, the secondary character of the handicapped woman is forced even further to the side. She is taken out of sight so she won't disturb the festivities, and she sinks into the dungeon of forgetfulness.

There are various differences among the versions: In IFA 1710 the wise woman marries a wealthy shoemaker, and she suspects that he is not faithful to her. She tests him by appearing to him in disguise. He falls in love with her, and she sends him to her "father," the dervish, to ask for her hand. Of course she sends him to a dervish whose daughter suffers from all kinds of diseases. The shoemaker marries the sickly daughter, finds out about her illnesses, gets rid of her, and returns to his wise wife after he learns his lesson and is flooded with love.

In another version in IFA, the wise woman makes a rich man/merchant prince fall in love with her. (In IFA 5647 the wise woman is elderly and makes him fall in love with her granddaughter.). She then sends him to her "father" to ask for her hand. Here again he is not the woman's actual father but rather a dervish, imam, rich man, and even a butcher. In each of the versions, the wise woman tries to prove something: that she is wiser, a more adept swindler, more furious, and so forth. In all the versions except for the present one, the story ends with a marriage,[6] as it does in any novella.

In all the versions the handicapped woman—or as she is called in IFA 3441, "the monster"—is silent throughout the story and disappears at its end. If she is not silent, she "is stuttering, so [the man] can't understand at all what she is saying" (IFA 2880), or she answers by "screaming like an animal" (IFA 1710). That is to say, she can't converse with anyone, and she is as unaware as an animal. Getting married to such a woman would cause any man to lose his happiness. For instance, in IFA 3441, the fabric merchant, "who was usually a joyful person and satisfied with his life, lost his desire to live. He lost weight because he spent his days thinking about how to get out of his troubles—thinking and thinking but not finding a clue."

In each version the handicapped woman is rejected for a different reason: In one of them she is paralyzed; in the second one she is stricken with scabies and lice; in the third one she is ugly, stinking, and stuttering; and in the fourth she is ugly to the extent that her upper body is like that of a donkey. In IFA 5647 she is more tolerated by those around her, despite her paralysis, and this is thanks to her beauty and cleverness. As her father says: "God has punished me, because he took from her the ability to walk." When her handicap is revealed to the public on her wedding day, the prince, who is "benevolent and merciful," makes her disappear during the ceremony and disperses the guests; the following day he sends her back to her father's home, with compensation. At the end of the story, the good prince marries the maiden who delivered him into the arms of the paralyzed daughter. Of that maiden the storyteller remarks, "besides beauty, God blessed her with a perceptive heart and a thinking brain," and he concludes the tale with these words: "and [the prince] governed with benevolence and mercy over his citizens, because he always listened to his wife, who also excelled in beauty and wisdom." The (legitimate, in the eyes of the story-telling society) exclusion of the paralyzed woman from any public domain and from any proper social processes, and the fictitious morality of the prince and his wife, are to blame for the very annoying silence of the story.

A Woman

We will now discuss two questions: Did the devious woman prove her argument, and what else did she prove?

To answer the first question, we will examine the meaning of the words "wisdom" and "sly-ness." "Slyness" is defined in the Ben Yehuda dictionary as "a skill of wisdom and sharpness in cheating and trickery." In the *Present-day Dictionary* (*Milon ha-hove*) it is defined as "brilliance, sophistication, inventiveness, or trickery used to deceive, to defraud, and to manipulate in order to obtain something untruthfully."

And how is the word "wisdom" explained? In the Ben Yehuda dictionary, it is "the deep under-standing, the intelligence, the wide knowledge in anything." In the *Present-day Dictionary*, it is "knowledge and experience for the benefit of man and society." In the Hebrew online dictionary *Rav Milim*, it is "intelligence, understanding, good judgmental ability, good thinking; the highest ideal of life, as suggested by various philosophies."

The lexical interpretations of these two words demonstrate that the word "wisdom" is positive, demonstrating morality, fairness, and righteousness, while the word "slyness" is negative, exhibit-ing selfishness, deception, and lack of consideration for others. Wisdom benefits the wise person and those around him; slyness benefits only the devious person himself, who thinks nothing of resorting to cheating and trickery to achieve his goal.

The devious woman did prove part of her argument: She demonstrated that a man in her hands is like raw material in the hands of the creator. But in her actions she showed primarily devious-ness. She didn't demonstrate intelligence, sensitivity, learnedness, or idealism. What else did the devious woman prove? That her deviousness is one characteristic among the traits of an unreli-able women: She gets angry easily when she sees the sign; she envies men's status; she looks for respect and admiration; she uses her beauty to trick the merchant; she acts hypocritically when she gives him compliments; she betrays his trust and cheats him and the *hajj*; she is selfish and pro-motes primarily her own goals; she ignores the needs of others; she causes suffering to others and doesn't nurture female solidarity with the handicapped woman; she is cruel and domineering, and covets power and money; she is a blackmailer who is ready to get the merchant out of his entanglement for monetary compensation.

The actions of the devious woman demonstrate not only the qualities she possesses but also those she lacks—especially love and compassion, qualities considered to be typically fem-inine. The devious woman plays the masculine game based on gaining control and supremacy, and she uses it to maneuver her way in the world. Unlike the case in the other tales—where the devious/wise woman marries the hero—in this story the woman despises the institution of marriage, and she dismantles the family unit, as if to say, "A wise woman did not build her home."[7]

As mentioned earlier, the woman does not belong to anyone, and she strives for maximum independence even as she objectifies the feminine body—both her own and the handicapped woman's. She objectifies her own body to convince the merchant to listen to her advice, and she objectifies the body of the *hajj*'s daughter to highlight her social inappropriateness and ineligibility to function as a feeling and thinking human. Thus the devious woman uses the handicapped woman for her own needs, and by doing so she creates a division between her and "that" woman. This boundary also separates healthy women and handicapped women in real life, and feminist researchers who study handicaps talk about it broadly.[8] They have found that the social status of handicapped women is much lower than that of women in general. Handicapped women are considered "others" by healthy women, by society in general, and by the larger handicapped community, which reflects the same gendered power relationships as in society as a whole.

To complete this part of the discussion, I propose that the behavior of the devious woman can also be interpreted in a different way: as the behavior of an independent being who has feelings, needs, and desires, and who wishes to transform the regular status of women in a patriarchal society. But the painful price paid by the other characters due to the nature of and actions committed by the devious woman strengthens the negative stereotypes of women in general. Evidence for this interpretation can be found in the words of Yiftah Avrahami, the storyteller who recounted this tale from memory. Referring to the women depicted in his tales and to the circumstances under which these tales are told, Avrahami said:

> Sometimes students ask me [if they can] copy part of these stories, and they pose this question: "Why is it that in so many stories there are disloyal women?" And my answer is that I don't write the stories out of my own head, but I hear them from others, and I write what I heard from the tellers. [. . .] And I just now remember a story I heard during my first business trip, when I was still a young man. [. . .] The intention of a story is to shorten the journey and pass time. Well, how one can pass time and shorten the journey? Like this [. . .] and that is how they pass their time; we used to gossip about women, until the journey was over.

HALF A WOMAN

The *hajj*'s daughter, the handicapped woman in the story, is definitely seen as an object. She is passed from hand to hand, and she is defined by others according to her faults and her visible defects. This woman is submissive and invisible. She can't see and she doesn't make noise; she never looks at others, not even at the hands that transfer her from one place to another. Thus she will never be a "subject," as defined by Sartre,[9] and certainly not Buber's desired and unfound "you" (Buber 1959).[10] She will forever be an "object," subjected to the observations of others and not observing them herself. She will always be passive, submissive, and accepting of the judgment of the other—not present in life, not involved in a human dialogue, not having any bond with others, not a person, not-a-woman.

Because she is blind, in both meanings, and she doesn't say a word, we don't know how she feels when she is given and taken away; we can only guess and feel sorrow over it. Because the other characters do see and talk, we know what they think and how they objectify the other, and we should feel regret over that as well. The voice of the "normal" characters reveals the attitude of the telling society toward its weak and handicapped members. This society turns the handicapped human being into a nonhuman, and by doing so it enables handicapped beings' exclusion from human society and pushes them to a neglected corner. Thus handicapped people in such a society cannot have a normal way of life; their handicap is not only physical but also social, as is emphasized in studies of disabilities.[11]

The *hajj*'s daughter, who is known only as the *hajj*'s daughter, is completely captivated by the other. When she is brought back to her hidden residence, order is returned. Once again she doesn't disturb—aesthetically or spiritually—all the healthy and beautiful people who live next to her.

The expressions used to describe handicapped people in the folkloric literature sometimes reflect the attitudes the society telling these stories has toward such people. So it is also in this novella about a swindle, which is not committed to morality or to values, and therefore describes the handicapped woman using a single quality—her bodily and spiritual impairment—and as an object for abuse that must be excluded from the public. There isn't in this novella, or in the novella genre in general, any attempt to educate, to teach manners, or to denounce negative qualities,[12] and thus there is no condemnation of the attitude toward the *hajj*'s daughter. This contributes to and even ensures the preservation of the stereotypes of handicapped men and women, because the story's plot deals—as is typical of a novella—with an extreme situation. Stories like this one destine handicapped people to worthless and unfulfilled lives, and justify their continued social exclusion, discriminatory treatment, and vulnerability in the face of strong social groups.

And Two Men

It appears that the two men in this story are made of similar raw material: Both are deceived by the woman, whether directly or indirectly, and both behave and act similarly, which puts them in a negative light in the eyes of the twenty-first-century reader.

The merchant is described as a naïve person, simple and hasty, who, like many men, is captivated by the false charms and nonsense of beauty; tends to see women as objects intended to fulfill his economic, sexual, and paternal needs; cheats when he needs to; and prefers money over love. The lesson he learns in this story is simple: It is better not to be involved with women—not for their honey and not from their sting; one should not listen to their advice and never marry them.

Similar things—and even more—can be said about the *hajj*: Despite his name, which implies holiness and virtue, he is not a holy and moral man, and he doesn't fulfill his duties as a parent. Throughout the story he cares for himself more than he cares for his only daughter, and he even prefers to take care of the needs of strange men than to take care of his daughter's. This can be deduced from his refusing—out of masculine fraternity—to marry his daughter to the men who ask for her hand in marriage. This can be deduced also from the haste with which he dismantles his daughter's marriage, after she finally found a groom, just so no harm is done to his own honor and status. The class attribution is even more important to him than masculine fraternity, the filial love of daughter and father, the continuation of the dynasty (she is his only daughter), and the preservation of his holiness. If he cannot marry his daughter to a rich man, it is better that she not marry at all. Clearly he does not care for her; she most likely will not produce grandchildren; and he already earned his points in heaven when he visited Mecca.

CONCLUSION: A PERSONAL NOTE

Throughout time women have used various strategies to "manage" their way in the masculine world. They have done it by, among other things, adopting a masculine world-view and fighting against it. The devious woman in this story fights against men's opinions of women, and she succeeds somewhat in overcoming them. If I were to try to defend her, I would say that she was active all along the way; she never gave up, and she never failed.

However, the behavior of the two women in the story leaves me, as a woman, somewhat frustrated. I would like to address each of them separately. I would be glad to tell the devious woman that if she wants to be wise, she had better make peace with her femininity, respect the other, and identify herself with a woman who is weaker than she is and who is discriminated against because of her physical disabilities. I would be happy to get closer to the *hajj*'s daughter as well, to take her hand in mine and teach her what her father never taught her: to not hide herself from the public and to be active; to not remain silent; to express in full voice her experiences; and to require consideration for her special needs, just as women with special needs have begun to do today. Fortunately, our world today is more accessible and tolerant than before toward women in general as well as toward handicapped women and other, less privileged social groups in particular.

NOTES

1. The other characters in this plot do not have names either, as is typical of folktales.
2. He holds the title "hajj" because he fulfilled the sacred commandment of going to Mecca.
3. Regarding these attributes of novella, see Yassif 1999, 371; Jason 1971.
4. See more on this topic in the type index by Aarne and Thompson (1961): AT 850–AT 869.
5. IFA 1710 (Turkey), IFA 2880 (Egypt), IFA 3441 (Persia), IFA 5647 (Yemen).
6. In IFA 1710—in the reinforcement of the marriage.
7. According to Proverbs 14:1: "A wise woman builds her house; a foolish woman tears it down with her own hands."
8. The reference to handicapped women as "different" is discussed by several female researchers: Asch and Fine, eds., 1988; Corker and French, eds., 1999; Morris 1991; Price and Shildrick 1999; Russell 1998; Wendell 1996.
9. According to Sartre (1966, 252–302), man situates himself as a subject by looking at others whom he turns into objects. Sartre emphasizes the centrality of objects and subjects as constituting self and "other."

10. The possibility of becoming "you" is not achievable for the handicapped woman: She cannot hold a conversation; she is not equal, not present, and not active. This "you," Buber (1959, 10) wrote: "is not anymore a thing among things and is not made of things. It is not a he or a she, that another he or she are limiting and diminishing them, they are not a point in time and in space [. . .] not a loose collection of qualities that have name and attribute. But: you has no neighbor and no combination. Not him and none but him, but: everything else exists in its own light." And also: "the relationship to a you with no separation, between the me and the you there is no conceptual separation, no prejudice and no imagination [. . .] between the me and the you there is no barrier of purpose, desire or shortcut" (ibid., 7).

11. The research on handicaps distinguishes among disability, limitation, and handicap. These three categories enable researchers to focus on the oppressing environment and on the social structure (Abberley, 1987; Oliver 1990), which turn the person who has disabilities into a handicapped, "beaten person." According to Wood (1980, 27–20), impairment "[in] the context of health experience . . . is any loss or abnormality of psychological . . . physiological, or anatomical structure or function. . . . [A] disability is any restriction or lack (resulting from an impairment) of ability to perform an activity in the manner or within the range considered normal for a . . . human being. . . . [A] handicap is a disadvantage for a given individual, resulting from an impairment or a disability, that limits or prevents the fulfillment of a role that is normal (depending on age, sex, social and cultural factors) for that individual."

12. The swindler novella has nothing to do with morals or ethics. These are the qualities of actors in sacred legends. The actor in the novella represents purely mental attributes and is evaluated within the story according to the good or bad use he makes of these faculties. "The swindler's immoral acts and even his crimes are not condemned according to the society's norms but admired as successful exploits" (Jason, 1971, 37). As Jason notes, the sacred legend is different from the novella. As a didactic genre, the sacred legend expresses a positive attitude toward people with impairments. But in the sacred legend as well, the impairment is the key quality that represents these characters, and the attitude toward them is patronizing. Here too they are seen as anomalous and needy, and their appearance is used to glorify the personality of the saint who is at the center of the story. This saint tries, at times, to cure them, or he reveals another quality that characterizes them and is destined to compensate for their impairment. (See, for example, the Hasidic story "The Flute," in its different versions, where the righteous person reads the deep secrets of mute souls.)

BIBLIOGRAPHY

Aarne, Antti, and Stith Thompson. 1961. *The Types of the Folktale: A Classification and Bibliography*. FF Communications no. 184. Helsinki: Suomalainen Tiedeakatemia.
Abberley, Paul. 1987. "The Concept of Oppression and the Development of a Social Theory of Disability." *Disability, Handicap and Society* 2: 5–12.
Asch, Adrienne, and Michelle Fine, eds. 1988. *Women with Disabilities*. Philadelphia: Temple University Press.
Buber, Martin. 1959. *The Hidden Dialogue*. Jerusalem: Mossad Bialik. [Hebrew]
Corker, Mairian, and Sally French, eds. 1999. *Disability Discourse*. Buckingham: Open University Press.
Jason, Heda. 1971. *Genre: An Essay in Oral Literature*. Tel Aviv: Tel Aviv University.

Morris, Jenny. 1991. *Pride Against Prejudice: Transforming Attitudes to Disability*. London: Women's Press.

———, ed. 1996. *Encounters with Strangers: Feminism and Disability*. London: Women's Press.

Oliver, Michael. 1990. *The Politics of Disablement*. Houndmills, Basingstoke: Macmillan.

Price, Janet, and Margrit Shildrick. 1999. *Feminist Theory and the Body*. Edinburgh: Edinburgh University Press.

Russell, Marta. 1998. *Beyond Ramps: Disability at the End of the Social Contract*. Monroe, ME: Common Courage Press.

Sartre, Jean-Paul. 1966. *The Look, Being and Nothingness: A Phenomenological Essay on Ontology*. New York: Citadel Press.

Thomas, Carol. 1999. *Female Forms: Experiencing and Understanding Disability*. Philadelphia: Open University Press.

Wendell, Susan. 1996. *The Rejected Body: Feminist Philosophical Reflections on Disability*. New York: Routledge.

Wood, P. N. H. 1980. *World Health Organisation International Classification of Impairments, Disabilities, and Handicaps*. Geneva: Office of Publications, WHO.

Yassif, Eli. 1999. *The Hebrew Folktale: History, Genre, Meaning*. Bloomington: Indiana University Press.

MOTHER'S GIFT IS BETTER THAN FATHER'S GIFT

IFA 16131

NARRATED BY HAYA (HADJADJ) MAZOUZ (TUNISIA)

So, there it is: The present from the mother is better.

Once there was a king; he had a daughter whom he loved very much. His wife died, and he remained without a wife. Years passed, and people came and said: "Sir, take a wife, how can you stay alone?"

He said to them: "No, I don't want my daughter to suffer. She'll have a stepmother who will mistreat her, make her work, give her this . . . I want my daughter to be pampered and spoiled. I don't want her to suffer."

People said: "Nonsense. You will care for your daughter even if you have a wife. You may find a good woman who will continue to spoil her the same way you do."

In short, they continued to nag. He finally asked a woman to marry him. He told her: "Listen, woman, don't do anything for me. Whatever you feel like doing for me, do to my daughter. I want her to feel as if her own mother is at home."

She said: "Fine. I will do whatever you want."

The daughter is always well dressed and coiffed, bedecked, and does nothing, very spoiled. When the king goes to work, she said to her: "What are you doing sitting like that? Your father spoils you; would you rather grow up to be just a chunk of meat? Now get up, quick. Quick! Dust the furniture, wash the floor, work!"

She started working. [She] was scared, shaking. When she knew the father was about to come home, she tells her: "Quickly, wash yourself and get dressed; go sit up on the bed!"

And that's how they did it. When they sit to eat, she said to the daughter: "If you tell your father anything, I will double your workload."

When she finishes eating, she brings her things to embroider. She teaches her how, gives her bedsheets to embroider. She tells her: "Do this and do that."

At first it was difficult for the daughter, but then she got used to the work. She learned to embroider, got a sewing machine, and learned to sew. And her father doesn't want her to sew or embroider, or do anything, he wants her like a picture.

[Esther Schely-Newman: Displayed.]

Just be careful, do not touch her.

And when the father comes home, they quickly put away the machine, hide the embroidery and all; they clean the house and leave no sign. The daughter just sits there, well dressed.

Days came and days went; people came to ask for the daughter's hand. She got married. What did the father give her? What did he not give her? Carts with blankets and clothing, gold and silver and all, everything very nice. He gave her everything. She moved to another town. Her luck arrived. Let's say, he lives in Jerusalem and she lives in Eilat. He had no choice, her fate was in Eilat.

Every three, four months, the daughter comes to visit her parents, and her father gives her more and more, and she lived very well.

Days came and days went, her husband, the poor one, was fired from his work. And the children, she had six or seven children. Whatever she brings [from her father] is not enough. The situation got worse; how much can she ask from her father?

She took out the machine and started sewing. People came to her and she made dresses, clothing for children, for adults, and [she] makes money on a daily basis. Every day she had clients, and she could buy food and whatever is needed for the children.

So one day she had some free time, and she wrote him a letter:

"Father: I, thank God, I have all I need and do not need anything; the children are well. But tell your wife [I (Haya Mazouz) have told you 'mother,' but she (in the letter) said to him, tell my father's wife]: Her present is the biggest. Her present does not end, and yours is already gone."

When the father got the letter, his daughter is well and the kids are well, but "your present is finished, everything you gave me is gone. And what the other one gave still remains." He went to his wife. He knew that his wife did not give anything. When she left, she did not give her a thing, while he filled up as much as possible. [He] asked her, "Tell me what you gave my daughter? I gave and gave and gave, and she said that mine is gone and yours still remains?"

She told him: "*Yufa mal el jeddin, utak'ad san'at el yeddin*" [Arabic: "Ancestor's fortune will end, hands' profession remain"].

So he asked: "What do you mean?"

She told him: "You spoiled her and left her doing nothing. And you kept telling me, watch and watch, don't let her do nothing. Meaning, don't let her do housework. But I did not follow your instructions or leave her the way you said. I taught her housework, sewing, and embroidery. Now that her situation has changed, she embroiders and sews and is able to support her children."

"Ho, my poor daughter will reach this situation?"

Immediately he went and collected more gold and silver and things to send her. But how much can he send? Her hands sustain her. He told her: "There was never a woman like you." Meaning "You raised her better than I did. As much as I spoiled and cared for her, you did much better."

Transcribed by Esther Schely-Newman

THE SHOE

IFA 16132

NARRATED BY HAYA (HADJADJ) MAZOUZ (TUNISIA)

I will tell you about a king who did not have children. He was quite miserable when he sat for dinner with his wife; he notices, he feels that they have no children, and can hardly eat.

One day, sometime after, let's say one night, while he's sleeping, a *naib*, a *naib*, naib came—meaning someone who cares for them. The *naib* told him: "If you want a son, he will die on the eve of his wedding. If you want a daughter, all your fortune will disappear."

For him it is a difficult choice. He went to his wife and told her: "Please move my bed to the other side," and she did.

Again the *naib* came to him asking: "What did you decide, a boy or a girl?"

Again he woke up and told his wife: "Move my bed."

She said: "What is wrong with you? What happened?"

So he said to her: "I'll tell you the truth, I'll tell you. A *naib* came to me and said, a son will die on his wedding night, and a daughter will make me poor."

She said: "Ask for a girl. What can we do, a boy will die. What good will that bring us? But a daughter, you are king; you have so much, even if you lose it, something will still be left."

He listened to her. When the *naib* came the third time: "So, what did you decide?"—he told him: "Okay, let it be a girl. Okay."

Next morning he went to his work as usual.

A month or two later, the wife became pregnant. From the moment she was pregnant, the man started to go backward. Whatever he does, instead of gaining, he loses. Instead of winning, he is losing.

His wife indeed had a girl, and she grew up; when she was five or six, the king took it to heart. He had nothing left, a king who has nothing. The king began to worry and wonder, became depressed, and died.

The king died, and the daughter was left with her mother. The girl is now about ten, eleven. She sells items from the house, like we do now when you have some antiques; you take it out to sell. She sells the king's antique items, and she eats, and her daughter eats. She had a servant who works elsewhere, but he comes to visit because he worked for them for many years.

Three, four more years went by, the girl is fifteen or sixteen, and there was nothing left, nothing. One day when the servant came, she told him: "Do me a favor and sell the door." The door must have been of good quality. "We'll sell the door and get a simpler one."

He sold the door, had enough to eat for two, three weeks, and that's it, finished. Finally she said: "Let's sell the house and rent a room somewhere."

They sold the house, had enough for one or two years, they used the money from the house, and that's it. They had nothing, they were poor.

One day the mother was worried, the daughter worried. She said: "Mother, you know what we should do? Sell me as servant in the market."

"I will sell you as servant?"

She told her: "There is nothing else to do. You are hungry, I am hungry, we have nothing to wear, nothing to eat, and we'll both die, we can't pay rent. Sell me and live off my money, end of story."

The mother did not agree; for some time she refused. At the end there was no choice. Went with her to the market, went to sell her. She is standing in the market selling her, and there goes . . . who can go to the market to buy a girl? Only rich people. Servants are only for the rich who need servants. *Ali Mjala* [Arabic: "By her luck"] that day a king from another town was passing by and saw that beauty. She did not colored her black or else. A beautiful young woman is standing. He told her: "What do you want for her?"

"Let's say, a million."

"Here, lady, take two million and give her to me."

The mother asked for a million and got double. She was pleased, but on the other hand, she started crying. He told her: "Why are you crying? Do you want more? I'll add."

So she told him: "No, I don't want more money. It's only that she is my daughter. And if you love her and love me, and you really want a servant in the house, I will do it."

He said: "Please come."

He took both women and went home. Arranged his house, or it was already fixed, and married the daughter. And the other woman remained as servant, her daughter in the house. She got along very well with her mother because they were together all the time, and continued with their lives. And he is king, ruling over his people, and all is well.

One day he was expecting, let's say . . . like he is in Israel and he is expecting seven boats from America, one boat probably with weapons, one with food, another with some merchandise . . . seven boats, each with some different fare. He dressed up in regular clothing, not as a king, and went near the port, where the boats arrive. He went there, and as luck has it, the boats were late. There is a kiosk or a café there. He sat, took a chair and sat. He is sitting, and there were also other rich people. They too were waiting for their merchandise—not a king or something—waiting for one, two, or seven boats. He was sitting on the side, did not interfere with their conversation. And they were telling all kinds of stories. One is saying: "There is no trust in women. Women can never be trusted."

And the other says: "As for me, I cannot believe my wife. I leave the house, and who knows what she can do."

Other men said similar things. This one speaks one way, and the men got deep into the conversation. And he sits and listens; it got him very angry. So he told them: "This is not true, you should not be talking like that. My wife doesn't even know what the street is like. She doesn't even get out of the door. Not true, not all women are the same. There are different kinds."

They started arguing, him too. They said: "Let's make a bet."

"What should we bet on?"

He said: "If you want to make a bet, I have seven boats that should be arriving soon. If you bring me something from my wife, a proof that you were with her, if any one of you will go to her and bring a proof from her, I will give you the seven boats. And if you don't bring a thing, you give me seven boats with the same value."

They said fine. Shook hands and said: "We will give you."

Which one of them will do that? One man said: "I will go." And he went; the rest stayed waiting for their boats.

He went to do his thing, and the king told him: "You have three days in your hands. If you bring no proof, you lose."

That man took money from his friends, got dressed, and went to the address he received. He got there. No open window, no door opens, no one gets in, no noise, nothing. From the morning to the evening, he circles the building and nothing. If he goes back without proof, his friends will kill him. What will he do now? On the next morning, it is the same story. All day he walks here and there. Suddenly an old woman came by. She told him: "What are you doing here? Since yesterday all you do is circle around; what do you want?"

He told her: "I have a problem. If you help me, I will give you whatever you want."

"Tell me what it is all about."

He told her what . . . why he came. She said: "Don't worry. I will help you. I will set her up. Go to the carpenter, make a box. Not a box, a chest for a person"—meaning a long one for him to fit in, even sitting up—"and I will say: 'this is my daughter's trousseau, put it inside the house, I have nowhere to leave it.' And you will be inside the chest, and in the middle of the night get out and look, bring something, look at her, this or that."

He told her: "That's a good idea."

He went to a carpenter, told him: "Prepare the chest quickly, within two three hours."

The carpenter stopped all his work and made the chest. He gave him a large sum of money and gave the same amount to the old woman. They quickly waited for him outside. The carpenter hurried up to make the chest, and gave it to him. The old woman put him in and took it to the house. And they don't open the house, did not see anything. He got into the chest, and she closed it well, locked from the inside so that he can open it.

Now she knocks on the door. The mother comes out: "Who is it?"

She said to her: "Where is your daughter?"

She told her: "My daughter is inside."

"Tell her I want to talk to her."

Well, a woman came, an old woman, not . . . she said to her:—"*Ya bint achti*" [Arabic: "Daughter of my sister"]—to the mother, not the daughter—"*Ya bint achti, tach aliya el lel*" [Arabic: "Daughter of my sister, the night has fallen on me"], "it is night and I have no place to put this chest. Put it inside, just for one evening; in the house, and tomorrow early I will take it. I could find no cart or someone to carry it for me."

So she said: "Mother, do you have a niece?"

She said: "I have no one."

"So where did you get this daughter of your sister, this aunt?"

She said: "No, I don't have an aunt." She said: "I have no aunt."

She started to nag, and she replied: "I do not want to bring the chest in."

The old woman continued to nag and nag, let's say from twelve noon to eight at night. And she cries at the door: "Daughter of my sister, oh daughter of my sister," knocking on the door and disturbing them. Finally, the daughter got such a headache and said: "Come on, Mother, open the door, and let her bring in the chest. We will leave it in the yard; we will not bring it into the rooms, in the courtyard. And in the morning we will give it back to her, early in the morning, and that's it. My head is splitting open!"

She told her, and they opened the door, brought the chest in, did it together, I don't know how they dragged it in. Her daughter's trousseau, brought it into the courtyard. What is the courtyard? It is walled in, and in the middle, there is no roof, it is open, you can see the sky. And inside you close the door behind it. You have rooms and everything. Like the houses over there [in Tunisia]. They . . . she, when they brought in the chest, the woman became nervous. She went to her mother and said: "Mother, I am terrified of this chest. Let's go into our rooms and close the door. Let's sleep or talk inside the room. I don't want to see the yard or the chest of this woman."

From haste and fear, she dropped one of her shoes in the courtyard, and it laid there. And the shoe sparkles, *matruz bel adsh* [Arabic: "it is embroidered with sequins"], and it has her initials and her husband's. She went in, what do I know, one of her shoes fell off. She might have thrown the other in the room and did not pay attention to it. She got into bed, started to chat, the mother and daughter, until they fell asleep. In the morning . . . well, leave them for now. They are asleep.

And the guy found that it was quiet, no talking or nothing. He opened the chest and got out. He got out, looking around, the wall is green.—If I tell him: "I was in your house, and your wall is green," he will say: "No, you could have climbed on the roof and saw the color." I'll tell him: "Your wife has big eyes and black hair, and she is pretty"—"you climbed on the roof and saw her." I'll tell him: "She is tall, she is short"—"you climbed on the roof and saw her from above."

What should he do? He failed in everything. He wandered around, wandered around. He will tell him the shape of the house, a door on the left, a door on the right, and this . . . "but you climbed on the roof and brought all these details, it is all visible from the top." What will he do? Just when he was about to give up, and going back into the chest, he passed near it. Suddenly he saw something shining. What is that shining thing? It is her shoe. Oh, a house shoe, a slipper, this will save him. He took the slipper with him into the chest, closed it, and waited for the morning.

In the morning the old lady, what can I tell you, you can't even distinguish between a black and a white thread, and she knocks on the door: "*Ya bint achti*" ["My sister's daughter . . ."]

She said: "Give it to her, give her that chest quickly." "*Kib sha'da heya wal zeaz natcha*" [Arabic: "Damn her and damn her trousseau"].

She gave her the chest, and she left. And the other one got up, made the house, and then:

"Mother, my shoe, I cannot find the pair."

She looked for the second shoe and did not find it. She said: "You know, this chest, there was something in it, I am sure."

Well, she did not find the shoe, what can she do? Fly to the sky? She did not find it! But she felt since the morning that the shoe was lost and all. Now it is noon, and her husband should be home for lunch. She prepared everything and waited for him.

And that man came in the next morning and told him: "You see? There is no trust in women. I was with her three days, had a good time with her, finally I told her, 'Please let me have some memento.' She loved so much she said, 'Here take it, one for you and one for me, I will have one left and you have one.' She said, 'Here my initials are embroidered on it.'"

When he saw this, he died on the spot. What did he do? The boats just arrived, just arrived and were docked; he left it all and went. Just went.

She was looking out the window toward the direction where the husband usually comes and saw him, she said: "Look here, Mother, he is arriving."

In the evening she saw him passing by the house, but he did not enter or come home. She said: "That's interesting, I saw him arriving, but he did not come in."

When the mother heard, "Here he comes," she went into her room. Each one has a room, and the daughter set the dinner on the table, and waited and waited and waited; finally she covered the food and went to bed.

He came late, exactly at midnight, when both women were asleep. He came in with a pack of razors, a pound of salt, a pound of hot pepper. And he started cutting her and putting salt and pepper; she begins to wake up but faints for all the blood that's flowing. Finally he reached her face. He said: "This face is so pretty, I don't want to ruin it, I will not touch the face." He made cuts all over her body, put her into a burlap sack, and threw her near the water. There was a beach there; the sea is not too far, threw her.

She was in that sack, when the man threw her, the tide brought her back to the beach, and she remained there, not in the water, at the edge. Now he did what he wished and went back to sleep. Early in the morning . . . he was not in his court for three days, was absent three days, so he went to work early.

The mother woke up in the morning, prepared eggs with sugar, made jam, made coffee, made . . . they will get up and eat.

And now, [back to] the young woman. Early in the morning a physician, riding his horse, was passing by the beach. Horses, when they smell people, they stop. He tries to make the horse move, but the horse refuses to go. Finally he got off and said to himself, let's see what is that. He found the sack, opened it, and saw a beautiful woman, just the face. He took her quickly to his house on the horse. He doesn't even know if she is alive or dead, just took her to check. He heated some water, started to wash her, removed all the salt and pepper, gave her an injection against pain, saw she was still alive, her pulse and all. Gave her injection against pain, patched her up, cared for her, and gave her medicine, until she woke up.

She said: "Where am I? Where am I at?"

He told her: "I found you on the beach, and you were like this and like that, and now I am taking care of you, as it happened I am a doctor."

All right. He asked: "When you'll get better, will you marry me?"

She replied: "Why not, I will marry you. You saved my life, why not?" And he was caring for her.

The other one, the mother, was waiting for her daughter and son-in-law to get up. It is already eight, nine, and they are not up yet. Desperate, she opened the door to the street. She asked a woman who passed by: "I don't know, my son-in-law came in last night, and they are not up yet. I don't know if I should knock on their door or not, I don't know what to do."

The woman told her: "What are you talking about; the king is in his court since six in the morning."

"What, then my daughter is in the room." She opened the door and did not find her daughter. Where is her daughter? She started beating herself and crying. People came to the king and said: "*Ya shdna el saltan*" [Arabic: "Your majesty"], "what can we tell you, your wife is not home and your mother-in-law is crying."

He came home, pretending he knows nothing. He came weeping and crying. He probably is weeping for those seven lost boats. He cries and screams: "What happened, what happened?"

And she said: "I got up as usual and was waiting for you to get up and for her to get up."

He said: "I left her sleeping in bed, how could that be?"

She said: "She knew that [something was wrong with the] chest yesterday, she was terrified, and could not find her shoe. She was fearful, knew something wrong was there."

He asked her: "What, what, what chest, what shoe?"

She told him: "These three days: an old woman came two days ago screaming, 'My daughter's trousseau, bring it in,' and nagged us all day. Finally I let her in. We went inside our room quickly and closed the door and in the morning she could not find her shoe, it fell out at night."

"You did not see who came?"

"No, I did not see."

When he heard that, he understood what happened. He said to himself what stupidity, how stupid could he be. Why did he not come and ask his wife, where is her shoe, and she would have told him. He would have shown this man. What would he do now with the boats? If he goes to him now and said you lied, how can he prove it? Where is the wife? You killed a person! The moment he heard the mother, he ran to the beach, found nothing. And now, he just received two strokes at once, not only his property but his wife as well, and he was cheated.

Well, now the doctor is treating the woman. She is well. No signs on her body, perhaps just a little, but almost no scars. She was healthy and all is good. Now the doctor wants to marry her. She said: "We can't marry until I go to the *hammam* [bath house]. We'll bring a rabbi to do what needs to be done. Why, are we animals to marry just like that?"

—"All right, what do you want to do?"

[Esther Schely-Newman: She did not tell him she is married? Haya Mazouz: No, she did not say a thing. What can she tell him? Nothing.]

He took her to the *hammam*. After a few days he took her to the *hammam*. He is waiting outside, and she went in. The owner of the place saw her, so pretty; *nadrav piya* [Arabic: "He was struck"]. He told her: "Would you like to marry me?"

She said: "Why not? Why not marry you? Would I ever find someone better? I will marry you."

She told him: "But just one condition, I want to have a private room."

He showed her several rooms. She looked where the window is facing in each one and chose one with a window facing the street. She said: "Fine"—and went into the bath, said: "I do not want to be disturbed. I want to stay a whole hour in the water."

He said fine. She went into the water and thought: "This one is waiting at the door outside, this one is waiting at the door inside, what should I do?" What did she do? She did not bathe or anything but tried to open the window. She broke it and escaped through the window, and ran away. The man saw that an hour passed by; she asked not to be disturbed for a whole hour. He sent a woman to check. They knocked on the door, no answer. Opened the door and found no one, just a broken window. She broke the window and left. He was astonished, lost the woman and also a window. When he got out, the doctor asked him where the woman that came in is. He told him: "What was she wearing?"

He said: "A pink dress."

He told him: "That woman with the pink dress broke a window and got out."

"She left?"

They said: "Yes, she left."

"Oh, how much money I have lost, all the medicine, the injections. She left?"

They said: "Yes, she left."

The doctor went home, *myet* [Arabic: dying]. He went back home desperate; he not only lost money, she also tricked him. And the bath owner was angry but said nothing.

She was running, all evening she was running. She arrived somewhere and met a black man. A black man saw her and said: "Where are you going?"

She said: "I am looking for"—let's say—"how to get to Jerusalem."

[ESN: She wanted to get back to her town? HM: Yes, her town.]

He said: "Come, I will take you to Jerusalem, but will you marry me in return?"

She said: "Why shouldn't I marry you?"

And he, the black man, worked at some king's house. He went to the king and brought the girl with him. He went into the king's house and said: "Look what I found. I brought a woman from the street, and I will marry her tomorrow."

And the king said: "No way, how come you marry her! Go away, black man, you nigger, you dirty. Why! I will marry her! You will take such a beauty? This woman is for me, not you. Go away!"

And what can a servant say to the king? He cannot say anything. Then the king told her: "Let's get married tonight."

She said: "You know what, we can't marry from one moment to the next. Sleep alone tonight, and I will sleep in another room. And tomorrow morning you bring a rabbi"—sure, she already went to the [ritual] bath—"we'll get ready and marry. Why not, would I ever find someone better than a king?"

He believed her because she spoke so nicely. He said okay, he gave her a room and a key: "Lock the door so you will not be afraid."

All is fine. She rested for an hour or two on the bed, thinking: The black man is waiting, the king wants her. What would she do, marry him? No way. What did she do? Opened the door in the middle of the night, found all the house quiet, and *bdat harbat* [Arabic: "ran away"]. She ran as fast as she could, to escape as far as possible.

She is walking and walking. She is walking, and just at daybreak, at daybreak, she finds an old man with a donkey, old, seventy or eighty years old, white beard, white hair, with a donkey, and he has a *jellaba*, wearing a *jellaba*. He said: "Hey, where are you going?"

She said: "I am going where my legs take me."

"Would you like to marry me?"

She said: "Why not marry you? That's a good idea. Let's get married. But here is an idea. I'll tell you what we'll do." She said: "Look, you are old and I am young, whoever sees me will say, 'What? You are marrying this one?' They will take me away from you. Give me your *jellaba*, I will wear it, and you put on my dress, until we get to your house and no one will notice."

He said: "You are right." He gave her his *jellaba*, and she went behind a tree and gave him her dress. He put on her dress, but until he got off his horse it takes time, got off the donkey. She said: "Wait, I will get on the donkey, and you ride behind me"—okay, behind the girl, why not? She got on the donkey, and he, struggling with the dress, putting on her dress, she took the stick and hit the donkey: "Go"—and escaped.

He said: "Come back, give me my donkey. I don't want you, just my dress, I don't want you."

She said: "You dirty old man, you want to marry your daughter? Stay where you are!"

She left that poor man with her dress, stumbling and falling, running and falling, and she rode the donkey and went away. It started to get dark, night. She is now on the donkey going from one place to the next, from town to town, doesn't know where she is going, any road she takes she doesn't know where she is, knows nothing.

At that time the king of another town died. They say, whoever gets to the city gate, a person or a horse, will be king. They opened the gate, whoever comes first will be king. And who comes when the gates opened? The old man with the *jellaba* and the donkey, you understand? They said: "Great, this man with the *jellaba* is old, but seems young, a young-old man." With a wide *jellaba* you don't see breasts or woman's body. And she arranged her clothing like a man, but old men's garb. They said: "This is a young man dressed like an old person." They brought him in and told him: "You will be king; our king died, and whoever gets first into the city should be king."

Now, her father was king, her husband was king, she can also be king. They took her. Now dressed up in these clothing, no one say, "Hey woman, marry me," nothing. They took her, and she became king. Now king's outfits are sewn large, and no one can notice what she is, she fixes herself.

Days passed, and time went by, and the word got out about a new good king. Whoever goes to him succeeds in his quest and comes out with a good solution, meaning, no one is disappointed. The doctor heard about him and said, "I should go and tell him my story—that I treated a woman and spent a lot of money. Maybe he will help me." The doctor started his journey, going from town to town, until he arrived. She immediately recognized him. There were many people waiting for her, but she started with him. She left the line of people waiting and called him: "What do you have?"

He said: "I have a long story."

"What's the story?"

[He told her how] one day he got up and found a body on the beach, it was a woman's body, all cut up. He took care of her, spent a lot of money. She went into the bath house and ran away. "And I wasted lots of money. Perhaps you can help me find her or repay me the expenses."

She said: "Why not?"

She had lots of servants there: "How much did you spend?"

"Two million."

"Give him four!"

He took the four million and returned home very pleased. He said [to himself], the woman went away, she is gone. The important thing is that he got his money back. She felt sorry for him, he spent all that money on her to no avail; at least he'll have money, money so he will be pleased.

The doctor went to the *hammam* owner and told him: "You know what, I went to that king and got some money back."

The *hammam* owner said: "I will go, too, maybe he will give me back at least the price of the window."

Now the word is out that there is a king, *Sultan el Ḥaq* [Arabic: "sultan of justice"]. The black man heard: "I will go and tell him about the king that snatched the woman." You understand?

The old man said: "I will go and tell him about the woman who took my donkey and *jellaba*."

The mother was unhappy and crying and all. She told her son-in-law: "Let's go to Sultan el Ḥaq and tell him how my daughter disappeared. Let us tell him and see what he can do for us."

He knew that he threw her into the sea and she is gone, but just to calm the woman, he told her: "Let's go."

One day she woke up, the sultan got up in the morning and finds her mother, her husband, the old man in the dress, the *hammam* owner, they all arrived the same day. She sees the old man in the dress and wants to laugh, but hides it. He walks in the dress and trips, still in the same dress—until they had money to buy—still in the same garment. She saw him in the dress. And her mother, she saw her and felt sorry for her, sitting on the side. She saw her husband, she said:

"This is going to be a difficult day." So she went out and said: "People, I will see this person, and that person, all the rest wait for tomorrow." She cannot take care of all of them together. "Those will be for tomorrow."

Well, first she took the *hammam* owner. "What do you have?"

"I have a *hammam*. A pretty woman came; no . . . A woman came into my *hammam* and broke a window."

So she said: "Tell me, you did not say anything to her?"

He told her: "No."

She said: "Listen, if you come to me, you must tell the truth."

"No, she was just pretty, and I told her, 'Would you like to marry me?' and she agreed."

She told him: "Tell me, good-looking people and ugly people come to you. What do you mean you marry her if she is pretty? What, do you have any sense? How do you behave? However, believe me; you deserve to lose your head. But well, how much does the window cost? One pound? Take two and go away, you dare come and complain? Be off quickly!"— and he left.

The black man came in. She went by order.

[ESN: Going from easy to difficult? HM: No, by the order, how she met them.]

So she says to the black man: "Yes, what about you?"

He said: "I was on the road one night, I saw a beautiful woman running. I wanted to help her and asked her to marry me; she agreed, and I went with her to the king . . ."

She told him: "You find a woman, you are black, and you are going to marry a pretty white woman? Where do you think you are? You deserve to lose your head. But no, we won't do that. You deserve nothing. What are you complaining about?"

"The king took her from me."

"Go tell the king . . . no, we will send . . ."—she sent a warrant to bring the king in haste. The king did not come to complain. She is waiting now for the king. She has all day set aside just for them, for their trial. The king came.

"Tell me where is the girl that . . ."

He told her: "The black man brought her and I took her."

She told him: "How could you, as king? A woman can't find her family, she is left out in the street. Instead of you watching for her and searching for her family, you tell her to marry you? You call yourself a king? Quickly chop his head off, this is not a king, he is a fraud. Cut his head off."

Finished, she is done with him. Now whose turn is it? The old man. The old man came in weeping: "I had a donkey and a *jellaba*, and a woman came and took them away from me."

"And what did you tell her?"

"That I will marry her."

"How do you, an old man, marry a young woman?"

"What can I do, I told her, and she agreed."

"All right, all right, you are an old man, or else you would be worse. Give him two donkeys, two *jellabas*, and two walking sticks. Let him go." The old man left happy with two donkeys. Now it was the turn of her husband and mother.

"Yes, what do you have?"

He says to her: "Listen [using female form], I will tell you the truth"—[I (Haya Mazouz, narrator) am speaking in female form, but he is a male]—"I will tell you the truth, I want to tell you all I have on my heart, however, not in front of the mother. I want to tell it to you alone."

The mother wants to tell her story, so she said, "Okay, I will receive the mother first, and then I will listen to you." She brought in the mother.

"Listen, my son-in-law went out for three days to receive some merchandise, to take some merchandise, to bring and get merchandise, and he did not come home for three days. He was supposed to come for lunch and did not; he should have come home for dinner and did not. My daughter and I are in the house. One woman comes to us and talks about a chest. She brought in the chest. And the shoe was lost. In the evening she waited for her husband to come, for my son-in-law. She went to sleep in her room, and she [I] went to sleep in my room. In the morning I did not find my daughter." Since that day she cries day and night, and doesn't know where her daughter has gone.

She told her: "Don't cry, and don't worry, I will take care of it and bring your daughter."

"You can bring me my daughter?"

She told her: "Yes."

"Do you know her?"

She said: "I have things to attend to, I will fix it. We'll see what we can do."

"Do you promise?"

She said: "I promise."

She went to her husband and said: "Listen, this mother will stay as my guest today." And she brought her into the house. She told her: "Come and rest." She went to her servants and said: "Give her lunch and let her rest."

She went to her husband and said: "Now, what do you want to tell me?"

He said: "Listen, I will tell you the truth, everything. But do not tell my mother-in-law the truth. I will tell you the truth, but do not tell her the truth."

She said: "All right." She knew there was something in here. "What did happen?"

He told her: "Look, I went to bring some merchandise, the seven boats from the port." Now she knows that he really went indeed to bring those things. "And there were men sitting; one says my wife is like this, and the other says my wife is like that, and one says, 'There is no trust in men' [*sic*: should be 'in women']. And me, it made me angry. I said, 'Not true, there is no one like my wife. My wife doesn't get out of the house, doesn't open a window, doesn't see anyone, no one sees her.' And one man said to me, 'Do you want me to bring something from her? I will bring you a proof that all women are the same.' So we made a bet, if he brings a proof from her, he will get those seven boats, and if he brings nothing, they will give me seven. So after three days, I indeed gave him. He brought me her shoe with her name and mine, and said, 'Here, I was with her three days and she gave me.'"

So she said: "And how come you did not ask your wife how it was? How she gave the shoe? And how were the three days? You should check first. And then, what happened?"

He said: "I will tell you the truth, I was angry. I brought razors and cut her, threw her to the sea. You are a king, if you want to kill me, kill me. You want to slaughter me, slaughter me. Do whatever you want."

[ESN: Did the king tell him that later he knew it was not true, when the mother told him? HM: He told him that the mother told him so and so, and why didn't you check first; that the mother told him about the chest.]

"And you do with me whatever you want. I am broken. The mother cries all the time about her daughter; I have lost my wife and lost my stuff as well."

The next day, she has soldiers, sent a hundred soldiers: "Quickly bring those men, what are their names?" He gave her their names, and they went to bring them. They came. She asked him: "You tell me who the man who brought you the shoe is."

"Tell me, how did you get to the woman?"

"I was with her three days and was inside the house."

She told him: "Liar! You did not. An old woman brought you inside a chest. And you remained outside in the corridor, in the courtyard. And the courtyard is closed; you found the shoe outside by chance. By chance the woman forgot her shoe outside. Now you will give him back the fourteen boats with all the merchandise. Return it all, or you lose your head."

And he, when she told him everything, it was finished, nothing else to say. They went with policemen and brought the fourteen boats. He said: "Now the fourteen boats, I am glad that I got them, but my wife is better than all that."

She said: "We'll see about your wife; wait and see if we find her. We don't know. We'll see if you threw her into the sea."

He took his fourteen boats, and those seven crooked guys, they killed them, they hung them.

Now she told him: "It is evening now, night. A break. You go back to your home"—to her husband—"with your boats, and as for your mother-in-law, I really feel for her, let her rest here. Tomorrow we will bring her back to you. Let her stay with my mother and sister in the house."

So he said to his mother-in-law: "Listen, I am going home, the king wants you to stay some more to investigate about your daughter tomorrow."

She said: "All right." She told him: "One more thing, you are invited for lunch tomorrow in my house."

He said: "Okay." After all he too is a king, and they want to have some business together.

In the evening she went into the house. The mother said: "You really have contact with my daughter, did you see her?"

She said: "Yes, I have. We'll arrange something. She was looking for you for a long time. We'll see how we'll get in touch with her. We will bring someone to have her over here. Eat something first."

She said: "I can't eat until you tell me, tell me how."

So she told her: "Do you have a sign, a mark on her back, something?"

She said: "Yes, she has a red mark on her back, a birthmark."

She said: "Wait here, let's see what we can do."

What did he do? The king got his clothes off, put on women's garb, and combed her hair to the familiar way, and went out. "Do you know me?"

"Where did you come from? Where have you been?"

"Do you want to see the birthmark?" She showed her the mark.

"You are my daughter."

She started to hug her, kiss her, and cry: "How did this happen?"

She told her: "Mother, all you saw today, you saw all these people out there? All these were my experiences [lit., passed on my head]." So she told her everything that happened. And the mother was very, very happy. "This is indeed the just king, this is the just king." She stayed up all night, she and she telling each other what happened, and what with the shoe. This one is happy, the other crying, talking all night long. In the morning she told her: "Don't say a thing to my husband."

And he came, arranged all his business. At noon they set the table, all nicely arranged. And now he is as the king. They sat together and talked, stories about this and that and merchandise, and all. Then he said: "Tell me, if I bring you your wife, what you would do?"

"My wife? You'll bring me back my wife?"

He could not say near the woman that he threw her into the sea.

"Where will you bring her from?"

He said: "She is alive, she is somewhere, I can bring her over."

The mother sits there, pretending not to know anything. She went quickly and changed her clothes. The mother told him: "Here is the daughter. You see, here she comes."

"And where is the king?"

"The king disappeared." So they hugged and all, and she told him the entire truth, that she herself is the king. So he told her, now look, he will have to rule the two places, combine them. All his riches and her riches that he is now the king. And she remained living in wealth, and he lived in wealth, and she took it all and succeeded. And this, since she was so poor and with no luck, finally she had double luck and had all that wealth.

Transcribed by Esther Schely-Newman

COMMENTARY TO "MOTHER'S GIFT IS BETTER THAN FATHER'S GIFT" AND "THE SHOE"

IFA 16131IFA 16132

ESTHER SCHELY-NEWMAN

Like many other women's folktales, "The Shoe" and "Mother's Gift" refer to women's role and place. In patriarchal-traditional societies—such as the Tunisian Jewish community in the middle of the twentieth century—women are expected to be modest, helpful, and devoted wives and mothers. Gendered roles are learned by girls at their mothers' knees, through observation, participation in domestic life, and listening to their elders. Folktales are an important pedagogical tool in the process of acculturation: Through entertainment they teach the right and wrong ways of the group, and they validate social order and apply social pressure (Bascom 1954). As demonstrated by Hejaiej (1996), women's issues and desires are metaphorically discussed within the domestic-female domain, behind closed doors. Narrative events are opportunities for exploring other possible paths of life, dreams, and wishes; explicit and implicit subversive meanings are nested in the tales (Zipes 1983).

These two tales were narrated by Haya Mazouz in 1984–85 as part of a large collection of tales, the result of fieldwork conducted for my master's thesis in folklore (Schely-Newman 1986).[1] For the occasion of the IFA jubilee book, I again visited the informant in July 2005, and found that her passion for narrating had not diminished in the twenty years that passed. She loves to tell stories to her grandchildren, and to complain, as before, about the lack of patience of the younger generation. What changed during these passing years is my own point of view, now being more attuned to gender perspective. The new reading of the tales allows me to focus on explicit and implicit subversive meanings.

I begin with presenting the narrator and her repertoire, then proceed to a second, feminist, reading. The narrator was born in 1943 in Gabès, a small town in southern Tunisia. Her family immigrated to Israel in 1950, but returned to Tunisia two years later because of the difficult conditions in Israel. In 1956 they left Tunisia once more to settle in Israel. At twenty-one she married Yehuda Mazouz, also from Tunisia, and they reside in Lod, a small town in central Israel. Yehuda comes from a family of storytellers, and several stories narrated by his parents are found in IFA. I first met Haya Mazouz when I arrived to interview Yehuda about his parents' repertoire. To my delight I found in her a copious source of tales, and she thus became the focus of my research. The fieldwork lasted for several months, during which I recorded thirty-eight different complete folktales and personal-experience stories, as well as abstracts of other tales.[2] For example, when telling stories about *jinni*, she mentioned that these supernatural beings frequently appear in other tales. Mazouz admitted she loves stories, always seeking to hear and read new ones, retelling them even when alone, to herself, so that she would not forget them. She was therefore pleased with the opportunity to narrate for an interested audience, to a visitor who came especially for that purpose and who listened, recorded, and asked for more. She used to make lists of the stories she knew, and was pleased to receive a printed copy of her repertoire. When, in 2005, I called on her again, she was eager to retell the stories I requested. Despite the passage of time since the first time I heard the stories, there were very small differences between the versions of the tales.

This remarkable collection of stories focuses on women. Only fourteen of the thirty-eight have a male main character. Furthermore, most of the stories related different periods of the female characters, not just specific episodes, thus establishing a "biography" and allowing us to analyze the emerging female image. The stories follow women's lives: beginning with a birth as the less-than-desired offspring—boys are preferred—then evolving into a maiden who requires protection; finding a husband; having children and experiencing motherhood; and finally moving into old age. Good and docile women are rewarded by finding their mates and having children, and those who stray are punished. The happy ending restores the proper social order. However, while at first the tales seem to conform to patriarchal order, a subsequent reading permits a different interpretation.

Feminist criticism of female characters in folktales focuses on stories originating from Europe, in particular as they became popularized through children's books and animated movies, mainly by Disney corporation (Rowe 1986; Stone 1975). In the popular Western tales, the passivity of heroines is emphasized; active heroines rarely show up at Disney's studios. Marcia Lieberman, who studied stories appearing in popular collections, found that they reflect a segregated and limited image: The positive heroine is always pretty, quiet, good-natured, and submissive. She is rewarded by marrying a man of a higher status. Those who prefer to travel less traditional paths—the daring, the curious, those refusing to marry—are punished by trials and tribulations, suffering, and wandering until they reach their proper destination: marriage or reunification with the lost husband. Rescue, in these tales, frequently arrives from a male source, not the heroine's own initiative (Lieberman, 1986). Married life rarely appears in the tale, just the courting period. The schematic conclusion, "and they lived happily ever after," says nothing about the day after. This one-dimensional image deprives girls and boys of the chance to identify or experience other options. Instead popular folktales reaffirm the unequal patriarchal power structure.

In non-Western tales other models may be found. Paradoxically, in patriarchal societies where men and women lived in parallel-separate worlds, we can find female initiative and activity. Alongside female jealousy and bickering crones, witches, and stepsisters attempting to harm the innocent heroine, there are also stories of help extended by women and feelings of sisterhood. This may be so because, in the Judeo-Muslim cultural sphere, women are the significant others in female life; they protect and afford security for each other. In tales from these cultural spheres, marriage is not the happy ending, just another episode. Only when women have children does their status become secure (Alexander 1993; Bar-Itzhak 1993; Schely-Newman 1990). The stories I chose from Haya Mazouz's repertoire exemplify these characteristics.

"Mother's Gift Is Better Than Father's Gift," is a female version of tale type AT 949, of which many variants are recorded in IFA.[3] Similar to the masculine version, the story proves the importance of work for survival regardless of status or origin. AT 949 tells about a prince who learns to weave rugs at the demand of a maiden he wants to marry—a trade that saves his life when he is kidnapped and enslaved.[4] The tale in this collection refutes another common motif in folktales: that of the wicked stepmother. A widowed king, who initially refuses to wed so that his beloved daughter will not have a stepmother, makes his new wife swear to treat the daughter as her own. He fears that a stepmother will mistreat her, while he wants her "to be pampered and spoiled." The father wants his daughter to be "well dressed and coiffed, bedecked, and [to do] nothing. [. . .] [H]e wants her like a picture." The stepmother, however, has other plans: Taking advantage of the father's absence, she forces the daughter to do house chores, warning her to keep it a secret. Unlike Cinderella or Snow White, who marry princes after proving their docility and domesticity, the heroine of this tale marries according to her social status. Her domestic skills are used when the financial situation changes. The supposedly wicked stepmother is proven to be responsible and caring. A woman should not stay idle: "Your father spoils you; would you rather grow up to be just a chunk of meat?" Indeed, the stepmother treats her as a real daughter and teaches her necessary survival skills. When the impoverished daughter girds her loins and uses the skills she learned from the stepmother, she also finds time to teach her father a lesson. It is the stepmother who solves the riddle for the father, quoting a proverb saying that, while family fortunes may disappear, manual skills remain forever.

All variants of AT 949 celebrate women's resourcefulness: it is the woman who realizes the importance of skills and who insists on obtaining skills. The bride-to-be (or stepmother in our story) will marry only a person who has a profession, even if the groom-to-be is a prince. Real life proves that social status may be of no value in times of emergency. A trade not only supports the person but may save one from hunger (in our story) and even from death (in other variants). Between the lines, a subversive message against the social order, where fathers are in charge, is voiced: Women's illogical demands or disobedience ensure survival, not traditional norms. A different view of women's role in society is exposed: For men the woman is a decorative element to be displayed at balls (Cinderella), in a glass coffin (Snow White), or in a golden cage (Gilbert 1986). The female gaze penetrates the decorative façade and reveals women's responsibility for their own fate.

Recognition for women's resourcefulness and the tension between decorative element and active agent are even more obvious in the second story. "The Shoe" is a conglomerate of several types of AT 880 ("Proofs of Fidelity and Innocence").[5] In this long, almost picaresque, tale we follow a woman through childhood, marriage, betrayal, persecution, rise to glory, and final reunification with her husband.

Her fate was foretold: She will bring misfortune to her parents, a king and queen. The father dies of heartbreak, and the mother is not able to support her beautiful maturing daughter. The situation goes from bad to worse, until the daughter suggests that her mother sell her as a slave so they may both survive. Luckily, she is bought by a king, who takes her for a wife and allows the mother to join their household. However this is just the beginning of more complications. Her husband, proud of her beauty and chastity, succumbs to a wager with another man, who procures a false proof of the wife's infidelity. The enraged king assaults his wife and throws her near-dead body into the sea; but the body is found by a doctor who heals her, and she continues to be "thrown" from one man to another, until she manages to resolve the situation and is reunited with her husband.

Yet we may ask—did she contribute to her fate? Is Lieberman's suggestion, that curious and active heroines are those who suffer, universal or is it valid only in the Western Christian world? In this story the impoverished widow and her daughter try to survive by slowly selling everything they own, including the door of the house. This may be a turning point, as the door is the barrier between inside and outside, between the private-female and the public-male spheres.[6] When nothing is left to be sold, and with nothing else to protect them from the male gaze, the daughter is put on display, to be sold as a slave. The centrality of the barrier between the private and public spheres is evident from the text itself: "door" and "window" are used frequently, appearing twenty-five and fourteen times, respectively.[7] Selling the door and displaying the young woman in the marketplace leads to more exposures, and the young woman finds herself all alone, where only men roam. In many other stories, the fates of heroes are predestined, but the actions of their spouses help to save them from their curse (e.g., "Beauty and the Beast"). In this story, however, the woman is the one who is left alone—her own husband falls for the treachery of the man who provided a fake proof of her infidelity. She is also deprived of female company (her mother) and must rely on her own initiative. She uses her body, first being sold in the marketplace, and then promising herself as a reward to her suitors, but she escapes them all, finally finding refuge by hiding in men's clothes. Her body hidden behind male garb, she can use her wisdom, and she rules with great success: People come from near and far to the court of *Sultan el Ḥaq*, the "just king." The denouement brings together all the people who took part in her life—and she rewards and punishes them justly. The regretful husband gets the best reward: He is rejoined with his smart wife and receives another kingdom.

The tale seems to express patriarchal power relations: As a woman the heroine could escape only by using different ruses; as a man she has the power to punish and reward others. And when she reveals herself to her husband, "[H]e will have to rule the two places, combine them. All his riches and her riches that he is now the king." Her achievements are summarized in the closing sentence: "And this, since she was so poor and with no luck, finally she had double luck and had all that wealth." The curse she was born with—to bring poverty—has been removed. All's well that ends well: The story ends with the woman being happily reunited with her husband.

In the tale, the men use items that are feminine in nature—the man trying to prove the wife's treachery hides in a chest (womb), and finds a shoe in the yard, which is produced as a proof of infidelity.[8] The shoe, a feminine symbol, shifts in meaning from a marker of union between a man and a woman (as in Cinderella) to one designating betrayal. Here too the story is about one of a pair of shoes, but unlike the case in Cinderella, where the prince looks for the foot matching the shoe, the missing shoe has been appropriated: The owners' names—husband's and wife's—are embroidered in sequins. The shoe, left outside by mistake, perhaps indicates the woman's carelessness, as the closed gates prove insufficient protection. The shoe, a symbol of woman's sexuality, is not supposed to be outside, accessible to the gaze and touch of a stranger. Indeed, like the shoe, the woman is exposed as the story evolves.

However this tale, like the previous one, has subversive undercurrents that allow for a different perspective on male-female relations. The male figures are not inspiring; they cannot cope with significant changes in their lives: The king-father is unable to face a turn of fate and dies, leaving his wife and daughter with no protection. The king-husband is unable to see his "traitorous" wife; he cuts her and then stuffs her in a burlap sack, and throws her into the sea. All men are guided by stereotypes about women: Women are competitive, they cannot face defeat. And all men are lechers, regardless of age or social status: They want to lay their hands on any beautiful woman who crosses their path.

The story includes two older women who represent the good fairy (the mother who helps her daughter but has limited resources) and the wicked old woman, who is willing to sell the woman's chastity for sufficient money and advises the man how to get the needed "proof." The young woman is the only character worthy of admiration: She is the power that moves the plot, and she is the one who goes through different adventures until reaching the happy ending. Despite the lack of a supportive environment, she is able to cope with the difficulties. She does not hesitate to use her looks to trick the men she encounters in her wanderings.

Visual representations are crucial in this story as well. Men see the woman as an object to be protected behind walls or to be exposed as a trophy: It is the husband's bragging about his wife's chastity that brings about the wager. The slippers, a private item that symbolizes the couple's unity, are decorated too lavishly: They are visible, calling for attention, just like the conjugal harmony and chastity the king is eager to proclaim. Perhaps the shoe, too, like the wife and her domestic behavior, should not be exposed. All the men can perceive about a woman within the public sphere is an object of desire to be addressed in sexual terms: "Will you marry me?" In this context all a woman can do is to hide behind walls or men's garb, until she reaches safety—in marriage.

Stories function to entertain and acculturate; audiences or readers find in them role models and messages that help internalize social norms. However, although folktales transmit traditions from generation to generation and thus maintain and reproduce social patterns, the dynamics of narration, the tension between tradition and change, and the flexibility of the genre—for example, references to the context of narration—allow narrators to transmit implicit messages that may resist the same tradition they supposedly glorify (Bascom 1954). These two tales and other personal narratives show that even in the traditional Jewish-Tunisian society we find narrators who challenge, if not overtly reject, traditional gender relations. Men are capable of giving material goods: money, gold, status—visible items with questionable value. Women give their daughters explicit and implicit survival skills, hidden messages that encourage self-reliance and trust of other women. The mothers' present is the narration itself—intangible, invisible, but more reliable than what fathers may give.[9]

NOTES

1. Department of Hebrew Literature, under the supervision of Dr. Galit Hasan-Rokem.
2. Most narration was in Hebrew, interspersed with Judeo-Tunisian phrases or words. At my request, she also narrated one of the stories in Arabic.
3. Originally narrated on July 17, 1985. At that time Haya Mazouz referred to the story by a different name, *San'at el yeddin* (lit. "Hands' Profession").
4. Weaving connotes a variety of meanings that are frequently gendered, as in the Greek myth of Ariadne, turned into a spider and weaving/writing literally from her guts. In other cultural spheres weaving was a male occupation.
5. Originally narrated on July 24, 1984.
6. In the 1984 version the initiative for selling the door is not clear: "Three, four more years passed, the daughter is now fifteen or sixteen, there was nothing left. Nothing. One day the servant came, and she told him, 'Do me a favor and sell the door for me.'" In 2005 I specifically inquired as to who asked to sell the door. The narrator said it was the mother.
7. Counted in the original Hebrew text. A different type of barrier also appears: The gates to the town are mentioned three times.
8. In 1984 Haya Mazouz gave the story the title *"Firdet el prill"* ("Dainty Half a Pair"), while in 2005 she called it *"Firdet el tarliq"* ("House Slipper"). In both stories it is one shoe of a unique pair designed for interior (bedroom?) use.
9. These characteristics can be found not only in traditional tales but in other genres as well, such as personal narratives that are frequently told in Israel (Schely-Newman 2002).

BIBLIOGRAPHY

Aarne, Antti, and Stith Thompson. 1961. *The Types of the Folktale: A Classification and Bibliography*. FF Communications no. 184. Helsinki: Suomalainen Tiedeakatemia.

Alexander, Tamar. 1993. "Haninat Allah: A Jewish-Yemenite Version of the Cinderella Story." *Pe'amim* 53: 124–48. [Hebrew].

Bar-Itzhak, Haya. 1993. "Smeda Rmeda Who Destroys Her Luck with Her Own Hands: A Jewish Moroccan Cinderella Tale in an Israeli Context." *Journal of Folklore Research* 30 (2/3): 93–125.

Bascom, William. 1954. "Four Functions of Folklore." *Journal of American Folklore* 67: 333–49.

Gilbert, Sandra. 1986. "The Queen's Looking Glass." In *Don't Bet on the Prince*, ed. Jack Zipes, 201–8. New York: Methuen.

Hejaiej, Monia. 1996. *Behind Closed Doors: Women's Oral Narration in Tunis*. New Brunswick, NJ: Rutgers University Press.

Lieberman, Marcia. 1986. "'Some Day My Prince Will Come': Female Acculturation through the Fairy Tale." In *Don't Bet on the Prince*, ed. Jack Zipes, 185–200. New York: Methuen.

Rowe, Karen. 1986. "Feminism and Fairy Tales." In *Don't Bet on the Prince*, ed. Jack Zipes, 209–26. New York: Methuen.

Schely-Newman, Esther. 1986. "Women's Life in Tunisian Folktales: Reality and Symbolic Reflection in one Woman's Repertoire." Master's thesis, Hebrew University of Jerusalem. [Hebrew].

———. 1990. "Zin el Gamra: A North African Snow-White." *Jerusalem Studies in Jewish Folklore* 11–12: 76–101. [Hebrew].

———. 2002. *Our Lives Are but Stories: Narratives of Tunisian Israeli Women*. Detroit: Wayne State University Press.

Stone, Kay F. 1975. "Things Walt Disney Never Told Us." *Journal of American Folklore* 88 (347): 42–50.

Zipes, Jack. 1983. *Fairy Tales and the Art of Subversion*. New York: Methuen.

Between the Sun and the Moon

IFA 17414

Narrated by Ibrahim Kweider Sbechat (Israel, Bedouin)

There was an Arab *emir* [Arab king], and one son was born to him. How proud he was of him, and he is an Arab *emir*. He brought him a private school teacher. He [the teacher] began teaching him.

One day the teacher told him: "Oh, Muhammad, Allah will bless the Prophet Muhammad. If you see a dream, and you are glad with it, do not tell it to anyone, not to your mother and not to your father and not to me!"

He said: "Why, sir?"

He said: "Just as you see it in a dream, you will see it in your lifetime, if you not tell it. If you tell it, it will disappear. You will not see it anymore."

One night of the nights, he saw a dream: [He saw himself] asleep between the sun and the moon. He was very glad about it. When his mother woke him, he was angry with his mother because the dream disappeared when he got up and opened his eyes. When the boy got up angry, she tried to [convince] him to wash himself. He did not want to wash. She tried to [convince him to] drink tea, coffee, he did not want. He picked up his book and went to school angry. She went and told his father in the *diwan* (guestroom). His father sent for him. They brought him. He said to him: "Why are you angry? Why did you not bathe? Why did you not drink tea and you did not drink coffee?"

He did not answer. The father swore: "If you do not tell me what is going on, I'll sell you away to [someone]! As slaves."

They used to sell slaves. Bargain and sell. The child continued to insist, he did not want to tell him. He swore about him, and he sold him. He gave him to his slave, and he said to him: "Put him behind you on the horse and go, let us say, to Jenin,* and sell him. But sell him and bring him back. Do not sell him to Abu Khalil and let him stay sold. It is because of the oath I swore in divorcing his mother. Sell him to Abu Khalil and bring him back!"

The slave did not respond to these things. Abu Khalil took him and returned to his home; he went to a far-away country. Abu Khalil is satisfied with the child. The child is like an apple, and he is a polite boy. Came the wife of Abu Khalil and said to him: "Son, you, don't you have any father and any mother?"

He said: "I have a mother and father, [otherwise] from where I was created?"

---

* It is a typical custom of folk-storytellers to use landmarks from the immediate surroundings with which he and his audience are familiar.

She said: "How did they sell you?"

He said to her: "I saw a dream, and I did not want to tell them about it, and because I would not tell them about it, they sold me. My father swore of me in divorcing my mother [that is to say, if I do not speak, he would divorce my mother], and I did not want to tell him, and of course they sold me."

She began to flatter him so that he would tell her. He said to her: "Are you better than my mother and my father? My mother and father, I did not tell them, then why should I tell you?"

She was angry with him and complained about him, and when her husband came [home], she said to him: "This child, either drive him away or sell him!"

He said: "Why, so and so [the teller does not give her name]?"

She said: "*Foko ve-takhto!*"* She put [the idea] in his mind.

However, Abu Khalil, he had a friend, an Arab *emir*, as they say, a head of a state. He [Abu Khalil] had of course friends in other places. When coming to the market to sell him, without comment, and here is the son of his friend, traveling to his country. He bought the child. When he bought him, they went. They were satisfied with him.

As it happened to him here, it happened to him there. The woman tried to [convince him] to tell her, and he did not want to tell her. She said to her husband: "Sell him. We do not want him; his behavior is not good!"

He came, punished him, tortured him, and put him in jail. He brought him to jail one day, two days, ten, twenty, Allah knows. They forgot him.

Some [time] passed, and the child was dying of hunger and thirst. He started screaming and crying and calling to Allah, be he praised and exalted, to release him from his grief. He went out of the jail. But the house is big, wide, a palace. And in the palace, there is a king's daughter, the daughter of the head of the state. He began to run, he came into the kitchen, came to the food, which was steaming. He ate and drank and returned to his place [in jail].

The *emir*'s daughter, the king's daughter, looked at the food. No one took it [but yet], someone ate of it. She told her mother. Her mother said to her: "The handmaiden is hungry. Add food and pay attention to the handmaiden."

She began to notice that every day some food is missing. Someone ate it. She began to spy on the person who eats the food, is it the handmaiden or someone else? She encountered this slave after he ate, and he wanted to go back to the place where he was. Anyhow, later she caught him. She said to him: "You're a man, or a demon?"†

He said to her: "I am human."

She said to him: "What happened to you?"

---

* Unclear expression—literally, "His upper and his under"; the meaning may be: he is mad or crazy—everything is upside down with him.

† In Arabic: "*Inte ins wala dgin?*"

He told her, he told her his story. She let him stay at her place. She tried to [convince] him to tell her. He said to her: "I will not tell you!"

Well, never mind.—She said to him: "In any case, I'll let you stay here with me. There is no one with me but Allah."

He remained with her of course. The food that her mother began to bring her was enough for two people.

One day Abu Khalil brought to the daughter's father a pair of horses, one dobbin and one a noble horse. But both were of the same sort and same color and same length. None of them is different from the other, not in height or in size.

He said to him: "I want you to recognize the noble horse and the dobbin. If you can identify them, you'll gain both of them, and I'll give you such and such financial reward. If you don't identify them, you'll give them back and pay such and such tax . . ."

He [Abu Khalil] came to the *emir* who kept with him the child. He put riders on them. They went to the racing field; both horses rode head to head. They could not tell the dobbin from the noble horse: same headway, same color, and same size.

He was angry, and he went to his daughter in the palace.

She said to him: "What happened to you, Daddy? I see that you are not satisfied."

He said to her: "Hush, my child. A certain king brought me a pair of horses, of the same color and same height, and so and so, in order that we will identify who is the dobbin and who is the noble horse, and we cannot tell them apart; the experts do not recognize them and the riders cannot identify them. In the race field, [they have] the same speed; one does not succeed more than the other does!"

In any case, she went to the boy. She said to him: "The problem is such and such."

He said to her: "I'll solve it."

She went to her father, she said to him: "Leave me alone for twenty-four hours. I will give you an answer!"

He left her.

He [the boy] said to her: "Let every horse stay overnight in [a separate] place, and let them starve. The dobbin, far from you, the listeners,* will start to eat his own excrement. The noble horse will keep standing. It will not eat its own excrement, it will not smell it, and on one leg, it will continue to stand, the noble one. The other [the dobbin] will start to walk and to eat its own excrement."

Indeed, when they tied them, it was true: the dobbin, from its hunger, eats its own excrement, and the noble one, stands on one leg, slim.

---

* When the storyteller mentions something loathsome or disgraceful, he addresses his listeners with "Far from you, the listeners."

He identified it. He gave him signs [that show the difference between the horses] and won [the bet]. He also brought him a pair of gems. He said to him: "If your money is as heavy as these gems, I'll give you my daughter, Sun, as a bride!"

His daughter's name was Sun, and the daughter of the *emir* who bought the child, her name was Moon. "I'll give you my daughter, and I will pay you a monetary tax all my life, that is to say, I'll be under your protection. And if you don't solve it, you'll give me [your daughter] Moon, and you'll be in my custody all the time, that is, under my protection; you'll pay my godson, you'll pay a monetary tax."

He said: "[I wish] his house will fall down, far from me.* How stupid is he! This gem, all my money, and the government's money will not be equal to it? Bring us a handful of gold."

They put it on the scales. The gems stayed at the bottom of the scale, and the gold rose up. Anyone who has money or his family has money, they brought pure gold, no coin, only gold. Finally, he was confused; nothing remained in his family, not [even] the women's gold. Whatever they put on the other side was useless.

He was like a blind man. He went and told his daughter. She said to him: "Leave me alone for twenty-four hours."

She went to the boy. The boy is hidden in her closet. When her father comes, she hides him. She said: "Come on, the problem is such and such."

He said to her: "The condition [is that] I want the sun and the moon."

She said: "How can he agree with our words?"

He said to her: "Tell your father: You have a prisoner that you blamed unjustly and imprisoned on such and such date. Open the prison and visit him. If he lives, he will solve it; and if he is dead, it means that you remain constantly under the protection of that king! And I, when I meet him, we will sign a contract. If he agrees, he will give me the sun and moon, and I'll solve it. If I don't [solve] it, he will behead me!"

She said to him: "It is reasonable."

He said to her: "Bring me, make me barley and boil it, so I can take a bath [of barley water] so that my body would be yellow, that is, looks like I'm ill."

The end of this story is good, very good!†

When her father came, she said to him: "I saw a dream in which there is a boy in the prison, and he is the one who can solve it if he is still alive."

He [the *emir*] had forgotten him. He clapped his hands and started to go. He called the guard and said to him: "The boy whom you imprisoned, where did you put him?"

He said to him: "I put it in a certain place."

He said to him: "You feed him and give him to drink?"

He said to him: "By God, I forgot him. What do you want, it was long time ago!"

---

* A sort of curse.
† The storyteller addresses his audience and calms them: Don't worry.

He went, he found him in a state of dying. He washed himself with barley water and made himself dead. They brought doctors and began feeding him and the like. After a few days, he recovered, because, of course, he had no illness.

Finally, they made the contract, the *emir* and the boy. He said to him: "Give me a written contract. Sign it, so I will solve it."

He said to him: "What do you want? I'm ready to give it to you."

He said to him: "I want the sun and moon. I want nothing more from you, and I am the son of such and such man of such and such place."

He signed and gave it to him.

"Give me the jewels and give me the balance and give me some gold pieces."

They said: "Oh, what's that?"

The viziers said: "What is this? This guy wants to solve it?"

When they brought the scales and the gold, they put the gems on one side and some pieces of gold on the [second], and brought some soil, some earth. They put it on the gem. And the scales balanced.

He said to him: "[The gems are like] the eyes of a person; one can compare these stones to the human eyes, and the eye of a man is never satisfied but when it is covered with earth! [When man dies]."

He stood up; he joined Sun and Moon. He married them and returned to his father.

Transcribed by Yoel Perez

Commentary to
"Between the Sun and the Moon"

IFA 17414

Yoel Perez

In 1982 I conducted fieldwork among Bedouin tribes in the Galilee region (Northern Israel). I recorded more than one hundred stories from Bedouin informants of various tribes. The stories were recorded mostly in Arabic, written down in spoken Arabic and in Arabic in Hebrew transliteration, and translated into Hebrew by Bruria Horowitz. All the stories are listed in the Israel Folktale Archives Named in Honor of Dov Noy (IFA). Some of them (about 10 percent of all the collected material) are published in English, accompanied by comments, in Raphael Patai's book (Patai 1998).

The story "Between the Sun and the Moon" was recorded from the narration of Ibrahim Kweider Sbechat, a Bedouin janitor from the tribe Rumaneh-Sbechat, who works in the regional council Basmat-Tiv'on. (Basmat-Tiv'on is a Bedouin settlement near Kiryat Tiv'on.) This is the only story I recorded from him. The text presented here is a literal English translation.

In the folklore of many cultures, dreams are considered to bear messages from the future and the fulfillment of hidden wishes. The story I chose to present here belongs to type AT 725 ("A Dream about Future Greatness").[1] It is an adolescence story that reflects maturation processes and generational power struggles.

The story takes place over a long period. It describes the hero's biography from birth to adulthood. Already at the beginning of the story, the storyteller places a foreshadowing hint in the mouth of the hero's teacher: "Just as you see it in a dream, you will see it in your lifetime." And indeed the central axis of the story is a dream the hero dreams in his youth and fulfills as a grown man.

At the beginning of the story, we hear about the good relationship between the father and his son: "How proud he was of him." The father cares for his son's education and brings a private teacher to teach him. However, the same teacher is indirectly the cause of the change in the father's attitude toward his son. The teacher warns his pupil that his dream will come true only if he keeps it to himself and does not tell it to anyone: "If you see a dream, and you are glad with it, do not tell it to anyone, not to your mother and not to your father and not to me!" But this advice causes a conflict between the boy and his parents. We are told that the parents do not accept the boy's attempt to resist, hold his own opinion, and rebel against their authority. The conflict begins between him and his mother, but the latter perpetuates the conflict rather than ignoring it. She rushes to tell the father about the son's behavior.

The father behaves recklessly. He vows that if the boy does not obey his request to reveal his secret, he will divorce his wife. The father, like the mother, does not try to solve the conflict peacefully. He escalates it, and in trying to suppress the boy's rebellion, he puts himself in the position of having to choose between the boy or his mother—between selling the boy or divorcing his wife. When the boy remains recalcitrant, the father must keep his word and actually choses the woman over his son.

It seems that the crisis reflects an Oedipal struggle between the father and his son. The son is perceived as a threat, as one who competes with the father for the mother's love, and the father tries to keep him out of the house. But once it actually happens, the father regrets his rashness and tries to rectify the situation by giving an order to the slave to sell the boy and then redeem him immediately.

The slave does not carry out the father's directives, or as the narrator says it, "The slave did not respond to these things." He sells the boy and does not redeem him. Does he fulfill the innermost desire of the father to get rid of his son, or is he perhaps jealous of the preferred status of his master's son and wants to take revenge? The narrator does not give us a definite answer. From an artistic point of view, it stimulates our curiosity, leaves the situation unclear, and enables us as listeners some "leeway." This part of the story thus creates the crisis between the two generations and the infrastructure for further development of the plot.

But this is not the only generational crisis in the story. The future bride of the hero manages a complex relationship with her parents, one that in a way is in opposition to what is happening in the family of the hero. The princess's mother harasses the hero, defames him in her talk with the *emir*, and in fact causes the *emir* to throw him into jail. The narrator tells us that what happened to the hero with the wife of Abu Khalil, the first buyer, happened to him also with the other buyer's wife, the wife of the *emir*. He tells us that the first woman "began to flatter him so that he would tell her," meaning she tried to seduce him in a sexual manner; and when he refuses the seductions, she turns to her husband and blames the hero of misconduct. It seems to be an accusation of sexual assault, but the expression the narrator uses—*foko ve-takhto!* ("his upper and his under")—is unclear and could be interpreted in many ways. However, what strengthens the impression of the sexual assault complaint is the description of the hero's beauty in an earlier paragraph: "The child is like an apple, and he is a polite boy." The story is also repeated with the other woman. Therefore we find here a hint, in parallel to the Oedipal complex vis-à-vis the boy, of an Electra complex as the girl and her mother compete for the affections of the same man.

The first woman, by the way, wonders about the circumstances that led to the hero's expulsion from his parents' house and brought him into slavery. The woman actually tries to understand how such a pretty and nice boy—"polite" as the narrator describes him—could be sold into slavery by his parents. The boy's answer is also interesting, "My father swore of me [i.e., swore about an issue that concerns me] in divorcing my mother, and I did not want to tell him, and of course they sold me." The boy takes for granted his father's decision and does not blame him. I will refer to his acceptance of this verdict when I discuss the connection between our story and the Islamic version of the Joseph story in the Qur'an.

But let us return to the relationship of the princess and her parents. Here we find a reverse symmetry. The girl encounters a problem: Someone is eating her food. She turns to her mother for help. The experienced mother suspects her handmaiden, advises her daughter to increase food rations, and to keep an eye on the actions of the handmaiden. (The puzzling actions of the suspected handmaiden in a way parallel the puzzling behavior of the slave at the beginning of the story.) The mother does not tell the father what happened. She prefers to end the matter peacefully.

The daughter soon discovers the hero of the story in her room. Like her mother, she is impressed by his beauty and his nice manners. She falls in love with him and hides him. This is a rebellion against the customary rules of morality. Like the boy, she has an independent position of her own. The princess also has a secret that she must not reveal to her parents—neither to her mother nor to her father. Later she must resolve the conflict and find a way to inform her parents of the boy's presence without being condemned for inappropriate behavior.

Unlike the boy, the girl finds a middle ground; she *invents* a dream that allows her to reveal her secret to her parents and still achieve her goal of marrying the hero. The symmetry, then, is completed through a fictional dream that corresponds to the boy's real dream, one that would also come true and enable the girl to solve her critical crisis.

Another symmetrical plot point is the recklessness of the two fathers: The recklessness of the *emir*, who falls into the trap of his opponent and is tempted to take on solving the riddles, is equivalent to the recklessness of the father at the beginning of the story, which led to the selling of the boy into slavery.

Thus the circle is completed, and both heroes—Mohammed and the princess—overcome the youthful crises and accomplish their goals. In this respect we can say that the story has a comedic character in the classic sense: The story begins with an initial problematic social crisis between the authority of "tribal elders" (the parents) and the younger generation, who rebels against authority and demands change and renewal. The crisis is diminished, as it does in comedy, and the parental figures are not condemned but rather neutralized as they lose their power.

The struggle between the generations is a central axis of the whole story. The two young people fight for their right to keep their own place and get the legitimation of their adulthood from the previous generation. It should be noted that the struggle goes beyond the family boundary. The boy must resist the seduction of the older women who covet him for his beauty and character, and later he must overcome the mistrust and contempt shown by the viziers when he comes to solve the riddle ("They said: 'Oh, what's that?' The viziers said: 'What is this? This guy wants to solve it?'")

Up to this point I have looked mainly at the content of the story and its literary structure; I showed how both dreams—the "real" one and the fictional one—from a literary perspective, have a major role in the story: The whole story revolves around the dreams. Now we can ask: What is the role of the dreams in the *heroes' lives*?

It seems to me that the dream in this case is a form of communication. The hero's communication with himself and the basic spiritual experience within him form a sort of nucleus around which he develops his emerging personality. Freud argues that at the foundation of each dream there is a hidden wish. The dream of the hero is a dream of future greatness, one that expresses his desire to find himself elevated to the heavenly bodies. However, the fulfillment of the dream does not happen by itself. The hero carries out his dream actively, by turning it into his destination and a touchstone of his life. The important thing is not the specific content of the dream but rather the importance he attaches to it. The hero directs his life according to the principle he received from his teacher: keeping the secret. Each of the secondary heroes—the mother, the father, the two women, and the princess—is examined and judged by his or her attitude toward this secret. Only the princess, who is ready to accept the hero as he is, without trying to learn his secret—that is to say, his crystallized independence—passes the test and therefore becomes the realization of his dream.[2]

What is the role of the fictional dream in the princess's life? If we keep with the idea of inverse symmetry that was proposed earlier, we could say that in her case there is a reverse movement. She has to reconcile two opposites. She is torn between loyalty to her parents and accepted tradition on the one hand and the need to follow her heart's desire on the other. If the hero has *fulfilled a dream*, then it can be said that she was *fulfilling reality* through a fictional dream.

But in a closer look, the symmetry is not inverse but equivalent: Each of the characters uses the dream to overcome obstacles and achieve a goal. Each of them tries to control his or her life and fate. He does it by clinging to the principle, while she does it by sophisticated manipulation of her father through a dream that never happened.

Her dream seems manipulative, and it is perceived—being false—as inferior in relation to the "real" dream of the hero. But we must look at it in a broader perspective: The princess is facing a crisis, and it is not only her personal crisis. The fates of her father and the entire kingdom are at stake. Imagine what the "script" of the story would be if the riddle was not solved: The princess's father would become a slave to Abu Khalil, she herself would marry him against her will, and the hero would die of starvation.

The idea of a fictional dream was the initiative of the princess. The hero only offered her the outline: He wants to sign an agreement with the *emir* that would ensure his release and his marriage to his beloved, Moon, and to the other girl, Sun; so he offers to tell the king about the prisoner who was forgotten in prison. He can solve the riddle, and he is willing to guarantee it at the risk of losing his head. He also offers to pretend he is dying by using the trick of the barley water.

But beyond this, he does not tell her how to put the plan into action. The princess is the one who has to execute the plan, explaining that she knew of the prisoner's existence and his fate—forgotten and starving—without raising the suspicion that she knew him, and persuading her father that this forgotten prisoner has the necessary knowledge to solve the riddle.

The girl found the perfect solution: She takes advantage of the Bedouin outlook regarding the significance of dreams. She thus intelligently adapts her actions to the social customs of the tribe without giving up her ambitions. Her society has absolutely no tolerance for the girl's having sex with a stranger (or even a friendly relationship, since the narrator hides from our eyes what happened while the hero stayed in her room, leaving it to our imagination). Since Arab society attributes supernatural power to dreams, she describes a dream that removes any suspicion, and assures that her father is convinced about the young boy's ability to solve the riddle the experienced viziers failed to resolve. (And the narrator, whom I consider an unusual storytelling master, indeed bothers to tell us later that the viziers disdained the boy's ability to solve the riddle, so indeed there was a real necessity to establish the status of the boy through a dream.) Moreover, when the girl describes her dream to her father, she omits the boy's suggestion that he guarantee the solution with his life: "If I don't [solve] it, he will behead me!" Instead she says to her father: "I saw a dream in which there is a boy in the prison, and he is the one who can solve it if he is still alive."

This is the point where our wonderful storyteller, with his natural eye for drama, felt the most suspenseful moment in the story had arrived, and between the description of the boy's plan and the description of its actual implementation by the girl, he inserted the soothing words, "The end of this story is good, very good!"

Thus one can say that the young girl's fictional dream is not just a manipulation but a wonderful way to describe her proactive initiative in adapting herself to tribal tradition, fulfilling the desire of her heart and saving her father and the entire kingdom. Moreover, it seems that the way the heroine chose to face her problems is much more resourceful and imaginative than that of the hero, who persistently only keeps his secret at all costs.

Here I've given the princess the status of a central hero, equivalent to the status of the hero, and I have good reason to do so: Our narrator sings an ode to the youth, and to the ways by which young people confront the world around them. He presents both the masculine way and the feminine way, and it seem to me he much more prefers the feminine way.

Another subject that is worthwhile discussing is the content of the riddles. The first riddle relates to the question of how to distinguish between a noble horse and a workhorse that seem identical in their external appearances and skills. This riddle is rooted deeply in the Bedouin world, where breeding noble horses has always had great importance. But beyond that is the hidden symbolism connected to the plot of the whole story: Distinguishing between the horses is a metaphor for distinguishing between people. A person's true face is revealed in a state of crisis, when he is stressed and pressured. The noble horse that is not "tempted" and does not debase itself by eating its droppings is a symbol of the hero who keeps his dignity and values—even at times of crisis. The hero manages to solve the riddle by relying on his life experience.

Noble origin is also an important issue in Bedouin society, which treats slaves and orphans contemptuously. By her questions the first woman tries to find out whether the boy is an orphan, and he replies firmly: "I have a mother and father, [otherwise] from where I was created?" Toward the end of the story, the hero tells the *emir*: "and I am the son of such and such man of such and such place." That is to say, he emphasizes that he comes from a high-level family and he is therefore worthy of marrying *emirs'* daughters.

The second riddle is also a clearly symbolic one. It concerns the human greed that knows no bounds, and here we can also say that the hero solves it by relying on his experience with greedy women.

Dreams and the solving of riddles often evoke associations with the biblical story of Joseph. Indeed, if we compare our story to the Joseph story, we will find that the similarity is not coincidental.

The similarity is reflected in motifs as well as in the overall format of the story. The story of Joseph in the Bible is built as a long novella that describes the life of the hero from his birth until his death. Joseph was the eldest son of his previously barren mother, Rachel, and he became the pampered and favorite son of his father. In his dream he sees the heavenly bodies—the sun, the moon, and stars—which symbolize his adolescent struggles and his future greatness. Thereafter his father's attitude toward him changes, and he scolds his son for his dreams of greatness. Our story also covers an entire life story from the birth of the hero to his adulthood and the moment when his dream comes true.

Since our story is told in an Islamic society, we must compare it not to the biblical tale of Joseph but to its later version in the Qur'an, to which many elements were added from midrashic and Islamic legends. An entire chapter in the Qur'an (chapter XII) is devoted to Joseph's story. In later Islamic writings, there are additional expansions to the story. For example, in the Qur'an the reaction of Jacob to the sun, moon, and stars dream (the dream of the grain sheaves is not mentioned in the Qur'an) is, "My (dear) little son! Relate not thy vision to thy brothers, lest they concoct a plot against thee: For Satan is to man an avowed enemy! Thus will thy Lord choose thee and teach thee the interpretation of stories." Jacob to a certain extent plays the teacher's role in our story, instructing Joseph to tell his dream to no one.

Joseph's brothers are jealous of his superior status and eventually sell him into slavery. In our story, the hero has no jealous brothers; the jealous figure is the slave who does not fulfill the instructions of his master.

The act of selling the hero also finds its analogy in the Joseph story. Reuben does not intend to abandon his brother, but events evolve in such a way that, after Joseph is thrown into the pit, he is sold into slavery and taken from his homeland. In our story, as well, the hero's father intended to sell him for only a limited time, but the father's intention was thwarted by the slave. In Midrash Bereshit (Genesis) Rabbah (chapter 86), Rabbi Levi says about Joseph: "A slave buys and a son of a maid servant sells and a freeborn is a slave to both of them."

In the Bible Joseph's voice is not heard at the time of the sale. He is completely passive. But later, when his brothers go to Egypt, we hear an echo of what happened many years earlier in their conversation: "And they said one to another: 'We are verily guilty concerning our brother, in that we saw the distress of his soul, when he besought us, and we would not hear; therefore is this distress come upon us'" (Genesis 42:21). In the Islamic narrative tradition, however, it was said of Joseph, "He bore his suffering in silence, and there was one saying in his mouth: everything is from Allah, and man should not doubt His deeds." There is also an echo of this acceptance in the hero of our story's words: "I did not want to tell him, and *of course* they sold me."

One of the most prominent elements in the Quranic tradition is the description of Joseph's beauty, which was also based on later Jewish traditions. According to the Qur'an, the wife of the governor presents Joseph before her friends while they peel apples with sharp knives; impressed by his beauty, they cut their fingers. This story has become a central theme in Islam, and the scene is depicted on many art objects—carpets, pictures, and miniatures—throughout the Muslim world. In our story, we find an echo in the narrator's remarks, "Abu Khalil is satisfied with the child. The child is like *an apple*, and he is a polite boy."

Later, the temptation motif appears once again, and the hero is thrown into jail after an accusation of sexual harassment. Like Joseph, our hero is also forgotten and left to rot in jail, and his rescue, like Joseph's, is due to his ability to decipher obscure meanings. Joseph solves the officers' dreams and the dreams of Pharaoh. Our hero solves the riddles that were proposed to the *emir*.

There is a strong connection between riddles and dreams. Joseph is a dream interpreter, but he also solves problems, using a cup for divination: "And Joseph said, What is this thing which you have done? Had you no thought that such a man as I *would have power to see what is secret?*" (Genesis 44:15).

Joseph marries Asenath, the daughter of Potiphera, the priest of On—that is to say, a woman of high status. Our hero marries two *emirs'* daughters. Midrash Bereshit (Genesis) Rabbah identifies Potiphera with Potiphar, and suggests that Joseph married the daughter of the woman who tried to seduce him (Midrash Bereshit Rabbah 86:3). Our story, as we have seen, follows the same script.

Another interesting analogy to the biblical Joseph stories is the use of the number 2 instead of 3, the usual typological number in folktales. In Joseph stories, all the dreams appear in pairs: Joseph's two dreams, the ministers' two dreams, and Pharaph's two dreams. In our story, we find the number 2 repeatedly: The hero finds himself in a dream between two celestial bodies—the sun and the moon. The hero refuses twice to reveal his secret, to his mother and to his father. The hero was sold twice. Two women try to force him to tell his secret. There are two riddles, and in each of them, two objects—two horses and two gems—and the hero gains two wives. The two gems symbolize two eyes. The motif of a man's eyes being insatiable eyes until they are covered with earth also appears in the Babylonian Talmud, in the story of Alexander's visit to heaven (Babylonian Talmud, Tamid 32b).

One can assume a possible influence of the story of Sendebar (Syntipass) on our tale. In the frame story of Sendebar, the hero, the king's son, is also ordered by his teacher to keep a secret (actually not to talk for a certain time even to his father). The king's concubine tries to entice the hero to kill his father and marry her, and when he does not agree, she accuses him publicly of attempting to rape her. Here also the king is described as a reckless man who is ready to kill his son without inquiry (Epstein 1967).

I have examined here a Bedouin folktale that revolves around the dream theme. The analysis of the story clearly exposes a variety of beliefs related to the perception of dreams in the folktale: the dream as precursor of a wish fulfillment, as a driving force in the hero's life, as an axis and guiding principle of his life, as a source of authority, and as an instrument by which the weak one can triumph over the strong one. The dream is perceived both from the perspective of the dreamers and from the perspective of the listeners as a sign from heaven, a real message from God. In the popular thinking, there is a strong connection between dreams and riddles: The dreamer, like Joseph, is revealed as a solver of riddles.

Folktales pass from one generation to another generation, from father to son and from mother to daughter, thus it is not surprising to find that the subject of relations between generations plays a central role in such stories. Our story reflects the struggle between the two generations: The young people attempt to have their parents treat them like adults who have the right to act on their desires. The story also emphasizes the extent to which parents' actions affect the fates of their children: The hero is sold into slavery because of the recklessness of his father, and the *emir*'s daughter could share the same fate due to the recklessness of her father.

Finally, I would say that the whole folktale expresses something of the spirit of a dream. As human beings, we live in a world with ambiguity and uncertainty, where things are more hidden than known. The folktale, like the dream, expresses a hidden wish at the heart of all of us: The desire to control our destiny instead of being a pawn in the hands of unknown forces. In the story, as in a dream, we have the possibility of weaving another reality that strengthens our confidence in the world order, the triumph of justice over evil, and the fulfillment our desires.

But the good storyteller, as I showed here and throughout my analysis, nevertheless succeeds in maintaining a certain ambiguity. Just as in dream, there are unmistakably fundamental, enigmatic elements, and the heroes must interpret their dreams; thus in a good story things are not so cut and dried. The plot of the story has a convoluted course, and not everything is known to us, the listeners. We must fill in the gaps using our imagination. This is true in stories as much as it is true in real life—where we also must decode the signals and interpret them throughout the course of our lives. This is a source of pain and sadness, but also a source of beauty and excitement in both the dream story and reality.

Notes

1. In the Israel Folktale Archives there are eleven parallel stories: Morocco (6106, 9160, 9481), Egypt (7007), Turkey (1025), Yemen (6399), Iraq (1590), Kurdistan (6762, 8820), Iran (11571), and a Samaritan version (1481). Worthy of note is the version that Galit Hasan-Rokem recorded from the Moroccan storyteller Abraham Lugasi (9481). In Bushnaq 1986, there is an interesting Iraqi version.

2. We know nothing about the other girl he marries, Abu-Khalil's daughter. The names "Sun" and "Moon" (*Shams* and *Gumar* in Arabic) are not conventional. They appear in other Bedouin stories as the names of literary heroes. Sun, Abu-Khalil's daughter, is not examined and judged by her attitude to his secret, but one can assume that the hero knew her when he stayed in Abu-Khalil's house, and perhaps he had some expectations of marrying her.

Bibliography

Ashkenazi, Toviyah. 2000 [1956]. *The Bedouins in Eretz Israel*. Jerusalem: Ariel. [Hebrew]

Brosh, Naama, and Rachel Milstein. 1991. *Bible Stories in Islamic Painting*. Jerusalem: Israel Museum.

Bushnaq, Inea. 1986. *Arab Folktales*. New York: Pantheon.

Epstein, Morris. 1967. *Tales of Sendebar*. Philadelphia: Jewish Publication Society of America.

Freud, Sigmund. 1950. *The Interpretation of Dreams*. New York: Modern Library.

Hasan-Rokem, Galit. 2000. *Web of Life: Folklore and Midrash in Rabbinic Literature*. Stanford, CA: Stanford University Press.

Meyohas, Josef. 1928. *Children of Arabia: Bible Legends, Prophets, Legends*. Tel Aviv: Dvir. [Hebrew]

Noy, Dov. 1970. *Form and Content in Folktale*. Jerusalem: Academon. [Hebrew]

Patai, Raphael. 1998. *Arab Folktales from Palestine and Israel*. Detroit: Wayne State University Press.

Rivlin, Josef Yoel, trans. 1963. *Al Qur'an*. Tel Aviv: Dvir.

THE WIDOW AND HER DAUGHTER

IFA 17478

NARRATED BY RIVKA DANIEL (INDIA)

A rich widow once arrived from the Land of Israel with her daughter and another eight hundred people; they settled in an ancient port city named Caranagor.

In those days, they believed that widows brought bad luck, and she was forbidden to walk in the streets. Therefore the woman, who was brave, married a seven-year-old boy, so that she would no longer be a widow, and lived quietly in the neighborhood.

One day the ruler's son rode his horse through the neighborhood and, by chance, saw the widow's daughter. He fell in love with her and wanted to marry her. His father, the raja, came to ask for the girl's hand in marriage, but the mother (Kadamvatach was her name) unequivocally refused to wed her daughter to a non-Jew. The poor prince fell ill from love, and the raja became very angry and ordered all the Jews to leave the city that very night; otherwise, everyone would be put to death.

The Jews fled in fear, but Kadamvatach and her daughter ground their jewelry into dust and threw it into the pond. They themselves swallowed diamonds and died. Until today, the name of the pond is "the Jewish Pond," and the hill above it, "the Jewish Hill."

They say that at the bottom of the pond one can still find small pieces of gold.

Transcribed by Efrat Shalev

COMMENTARY TO
"THE WIDOW AND HER DAUGHTER"

IFA 17478

HAYA MILO

This tale was recorded by Efrat Shalev, of Yesod HaMa'ala, and narrated by Rivka Daniel, who was born in the city of Cochin, on the Malabar coast, in 1912. Daniel studied at the local Jewish school until sixth grade. Afterward her mother had difficulties financing her schooling, and she moved her to the Saint Tereza Convent School, an all-girls' school, where she pursued her studies in history. Daniel was an excellent student, and she completed twelfth grade, but she didn't manage to finish all of her exams because her father fell ill. Thereafter Daniel worked in her father's place as a ticket-taker at the ferry office. For a while she worked in a government office. During World War II she joined the British navy; she made *aliya* to Israel with her younger sister in 1951 and went to live on Kibbutz Neot Mordechai, where she first worked in the kitchen

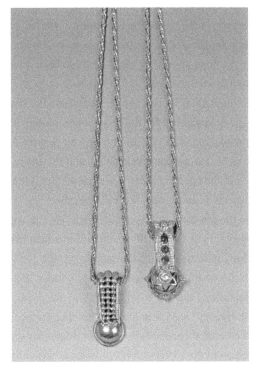

cooking kosher food for the local Cochin group. Later she worked in the clothing warehouse. Daniel's stories were passed down to her from her maternal grandmother. Because of her interest in history, she became especially intrigued by tales about places and origin tales. She was accustomed to telling her stories to family members.

"The Widow and Her Daughter" belongs to the historical legend genre, a Jewish oikotype (AT *730). The story begins as a legend of origin that tells the listener about the original settling of the Jews in the ancient port city of Carnagor, and ends as a destruction legend (Bar-Itzhak 2001) that explains why the Jews were driven out of the city and how "the Jewish Pond" and "the Jewish Hill" got their names.[1] These motifs are not fully developed in the tale and serve only as a sort of framework for the main plot line, which focuses on the character of a rich Jewish widow who refuses to marry her daughter to the raja's son. In response to this refusal, the furious raja drives all the Jews out of his city. The widow and her daughter do not flee, as the other Jews do, but rather commit suicide by swallowing their diamonds.

This plot line follows the well-known narrative of "tales about women during the dark days," historical stories that usually relate to a specific time and place, and which occur during the days when the Jewish community was in great danger. The salvation of the community in these tales comes in the form of a heroine. Although these tales have been common among Jews throughout the generations, they are unique in that they allow women, who are traditionally identified with weakness and moral inferiority (Atzmon, ed., 1995, 15), to become unconditional "heroines"— both of the tales as well as in regard to the protesting of norms through expressions of heroism and bravery, which save the community from its persecutors. In all the tales of this type, the heroine is confronted with a masculine figure who is "other," the non-Jew.[2]

In these stories we can find three basic models of confrontation between the heroine and the non-Jew (Bar-Itzhak 2001, 192–94).

In the first model, constructed along the lines of the biblical story of Esther, the heroine gives up her innocence for the good of her people. In this case, although the behavior is not normative, the woman wins the admiration and respect of the people. The breaking of the taboo is seen as a noble act, which saves the lives of the entire Jewish community threatened with destruction.[3]

In the second model, constructed along the lines of the biblical story of Yael and Sisera,[4] the woman kills the non-Jew but pays the price with the loss of her innocence. The most prominent in the group of archetypal heroines who belong to this group is Judith, to whom Jewish tradition attributes the saving of the city of Jerusalem from the hands of Holofernes, general of the Assyrian army of King Nebuchadnezzar.[5]

In the third model, the heroine chooses death so as not to come into contact with a non-Jew. In most of the cases, on the way to her death, she deceives the non-Jew who desires her. These stories lend legitimacy to the heroine's suicide, where the non-Jew threatens her purity. Although the heroine chooses the most forbidden act according to the Jewish religion, she wins the admiration of the society; the people speak of her as someone who has died a martyr's death (*Kiddush Hashem*, the sanctification of God's name through martyrdom), and her death serves only to intensify her image and memory in the eyes of the society that is telling the story.[6]

It would seem that the present story belongs to the last model. A reading of the story according to the accepted narrative appears as a hegemony that views women as a source of danger and threat not only to the "stability of public life" but to life itself. The daughter's beauty (which is not explicitly mentioned but is hinted at when the raja's son falls in love with her at first sight), exposed to the public, puts the Jewish community at risk of destruction, and the sexuality of the woman becomes her tragedy and downfall, along with that of the entire community.

However the text does not fulfill all the conditions of a conventional narrative; its deviations allow for a reading that places at its center a female character—and one who criticizes the social norms of her time. "A subversive act in the text," writes Orly Lubin, carries with it . . . a double meaning: On the one hand, the text conveys a line of accepted norms in regard to medium, genre, style, themes, and ideologies, while on the other hand, it also allows for the absorption of another—often opposite—message, which enables the extrication of a system of norms and judgments that doesn't answer the needs of the hegemonic center but rather presents an alternative from the margins. (Lubin 2003, 76)

How is a subversive reading carried out? A subversive reading of hegemonic texts reveals a crack, instabilities in the text, which make possible alternative normative thoughts of independent thematic organization by the reader who excluded, so that its subject is positioned as an autonomous center, in contrast to the normative system that organizes the story. Choosing this type of action indicates a leaning on textual elements as well as the breaches that appear and disturb it, in order to suggest its alternative reading, regardless of whether it's possible to claim that the author's purpose was to encourage this type of reading or not. (Lubin 2003, 78)

BREACHES AND CRACKS

What are the breaches and cracks that allow for an alternative reading of the tale "The Widow and Her Daughter"?

The first breach is in the second paragraph, in the words: "In those days, they believed that widows brought bad luck, and she was forbidden to walk in the streets. Therefore the woman, who was brave, married a seven-year-old boy, so that she would no longer be a widow." This paragraph deviates from the story's main thematic line, which focuses on the question of the relations between the local inhabitants and the Jews (according to the teller herself), and turns the listeners' attention to a different theme—the question of the public status of widows.[7] The paragraph stops the story's narrative flow and does not contribute to the main plot. Likewise, it does not relate to the previous paragraph except in that it makes reference to the mother's widow status. The second breach derives from the first. It is clear that the widow, rather than her daughter, stands at the tale's center. Even though it is the daughter's innocence that is threatened, it is her mother, the "rich and brave" widow, who is at the heart of the tale. The daughter is hardly mentioned in the story; Kadamvatach—the widow (the only character in the story who has a name)—is clearly the heroine. Another crack is the absence of a rational explanation for the most meaningful act in the text: the suicide of the widow and her daughter. Why didn't the widow and her daughter escape along with the other Jews? The text provides no convincing explanation for this act, and the act of suicide isn't explained in the text but rather in its response to external genre-related norms. Similarly, we are also left with the unique manner in which the widow and her daughter commit suicide. The F1041.1 motif—"Unusual Death"—is well known in folktales, but it is necessary to examine each unusual death within the framework of the specific text in which it appears.

The breaches and cracks allow for the suggestion of an alternative reading of the story, one that relies on its "deep structure."

THE DEEP STRUCTURE

According to the understanding of Claude Lévi-Strauss, reliance on the deep structure calls for the breaking down and rearranging of the text, together with the motif or plot units, which have a shared meaning. The "cutting and joining" (breaking down and putting together) of the text reveals a system of thematic contrasts at its base (Lévi-Strauss 1969). The importance of a system of contrasts at the foundation of the text is based on understanding the basic covert notional question that exists under the surface, underneath its overt expression and wording.

The question is presented without a solution and requires a decision, as regards the fields of relation outside the related story. In the question, which represents the deep pattern, we can identify the unifying foundation of the story. The question does not split the text in two directions but rather positions them according to their contrasting affinities (Barzel 1993).

Two plot units confront one another in this story, and at the center both are the subject of marriage: the marriage of the widow to a seven-year-old boy opposite the marriage of her daughter to the son of the raja. Both of these marital models are undesirable. The first is accepted by Jewish society, while the second remains a taboo that cannot be broken. In the first example—the widow's choice to marry a seven-year-old boy—the heroine takes control of her destiny by deviating from the social norms and ridiculing them.[8] She refuses to accept her diminished status as a widow and so eliminates it by ridiculing the institution of marriage—the only institution that provides women with the right to a public existence. The text's subversive nature is expressed by the fact that it is precisely in this paragraph that the teller directly characterizes her heroine as "brave." The widow's bravery lies in her courage to change her own destiny, to act within the normative framework, while emptying it of content. Apparently the Jews do not confront the heroine, and the Jewish community accepts this act, despite its subversiveness.

The second model—marriage between the daughter and the raja's son—is not realized. In this case, the heroine takes upon herself the cultural taboo and does not deviate from it. Her courage, in this case, is revealed in her choice to commit suicide along with her daughter rather than flee in fear with the rest of the Jews. In response to these norms, it seems the story determines the limits of personal "rebellion." As long as the heroine rebelled only against the norms of society, the society itself accepted this rebellion, but the moment the norms restricted and confined the cultural identity at the very basis of Jewish existence, the limitations became too difficult and inflexible, and the heroine herself was no longer interested in breaking them. When one taboo stands opposite another taboo, one chooses the less worse of the two.

The contrasting attitudes of both units allow for the examination of the accepted rules of social organization in regard to women, the limited ability of women to maneuver within these rules, and the heavy personal price one must pay for breaking them.

The question of why the widow and her daughter didn't flee together with the other Jews may find an answer in the social area, in the axes of contrast that illustrate the relations that exist in the story:

Axis A	Axis B
singular (the widow)	plural (800 Jews)
adult (the widow)	child (the 7-year-old boy)
woman (the widow, the daughter)	man (the raja, the son)
Jewess (widow)	non-Jew (the raja)
named (the Widow Kadamvatach)	nameless (all the other characters)
married (the widow)	unmarried (the daughter)
bravery (the widow)	fear (the Jews)
stay (the widow, the daughter)	leave (the Jews)
death (the widow, the daughter)	life (the Jews)

We see that Axis A is entirely depicted by the story's heroine, while Axis B reflects the rest of the story's characters. The deep structure reveals a system of binary contrasts, in which the widow is positioned in contrast with the local Jewish surrounding environment as a whole. Axis B shows that the contrast that exists in regard to the story's surface structure—between the Jews, that is, whom the widow represents, and the locals—is not the only contrasting axis, and may possibly not even be the main contrasting axis. The contrast in the story's deep structure is also apparent in the intensity of the relations between the widow and the Jews themselves. The relationships that are revealed in the story are not only those between the Jewish community and the local community but those existing within the Jewish society itself.

It would seem that the contrast presented by the teller between the Jews who chose to flee "in fear" and the "brave" widow may also suggest a deeper relationship—between the woman who dared to "stretch the limits" and the society that accepted this act but remained silent. The widow is exceptional. When she takes a stand opposite the raja, she stands alone. The Jewish community does not support her but rather leaves her to her fate. Perhaps this is her punishment for being different and for daring to ridicule her community's norms. From this point of view, the text authorizes the belief of the people, already mentioned at the beginning of the story, that "widows brought bad luck." The ousting of the community from Carangaor is the bad luck they receive because of the widow and her daughter.

The level of the relationships in the text may also provide an answer to the question of why the widow and her daughter specifically commit suicide by swallowing diamonds. A woman's jewelry, apart from its significance as a social symbol and a sign of a certain economic situation, is also a sign and symbol of her femininity, since its role is to externalize and emphasize her beauty and feminine sexuality. Accordingly, jewelry also depicts a source of social power, as well as a source of the heroine's weakness as a woman. On the surface the acts of swallowing the diamonds and grinding the jewels into powder can be interpreted as the heroine's deceiving of the non-Jew, as it were, according to the norms of the narrative model. These acts prevent him from taking her money, in terms of her suicide and that of her daughter, who would otherwise inherit her wealth. In terms of the deep structure, the heroine "pays," in a double sense, for daring to undermine the norms of the public order and trying, by marrying a seven-year-old boy, to deviate from her proper place in society. Her money cannot protect her, and she can't use it to escape and build a new life for herself in another place within the framework of the community. Therefore all that remains for her to do is to take her wealth with her to the grave. At the same time, on the surface level the heroine chooses to die for *Kiddush HaShem* in order to remain a part of society. On the deep level this choice is made because there is, in fact, no other choice; it is only through this act that she can find her way back into the bosom of Jewish society.

The question of why the story places at its center the widow rather than the daughter as its heroine is answered on the narrative's deep level. The text provides a "voice" for she who has no voice; it depicts the heroine's attempts to give herself a strong personal identity and to control her own destiny within the framework of the normative system that diminishes her power. The story presents the individualistic voice of a woman who doesn't have the traditional, stereotypical attributes of most women, such as sensitivity, compassion, or empathy. Instead this woman has financial and personal power. However this strength turns out to be a double-edged sword. The text's subversion is limited because the heroine's ability to rule her own destiny is also limited. The end of the story brings the heroine back into the heart of Jewish society but doesn't allow her to be saved from the "bad luck" intended for her from the beginning of the story.

The hidden patterns in the story examine the possibility of the existence of a feminine power figure within the framework of a social and cultural space that perceives women as negligible and mute. The main questions formulated from these contrasts are: Is it possible for women to wield power over their own destiny or not? And what is the price of this power?

Notes

1. For details on the characteristics of "origin legends" and "destruction legends," see Bar-Itzhak 2001.
2. See Bar-Itzhak's discussion of the story "The Girl and the Cossack" in this book.
3. For this model, see: Bar-Itzhak 2001, chapter 4.
4. Yael killed Sisera with cunning, after presenting herself as an ally: "Then Yael, Heber's wife, took a nail of the tent and took a hammer in her hand and went softly unto him, and smote the nail into his temples, and fastened it to the ground: for he was fast asleep and weary. So he died" (Judges 4:21).
5. The Book of Judith is one of the Apocrypha books, part of the Greek canon of Septuagint ("LXX"). Originally the book was written in Hebrew, but the original was lost, and the version known today is taken from the translated version of Septuagint. Joshua Grintz translated Septuagint into Hebrew in 1956. The book is named after the narrative's heroine, Judith, who saved the Children of Israel from the soldiers of Assyria. The Assyrians laid siege to the city of Bethuliah (a fortified city on the way to Jerusalem) and cut off its source of water. After a month's time, the water was finished, and the city dwellers of Bethuliah decided to surrender to the enemy. However, the city's rulers opposed the surrender. Judith, a rich and beautiful widow, respected by all, decided to save the people. She went to the enemy camp, where her beauty soon vanquished the heart of the military general, Holofernes. After drinking wine, he became drunk, and Judith cut off his head with his sword. After the death of

Holofernes, the Assyrian army began to flee. The Israelites chased after them and defeated them. At the end of the story, Judith returns to her city and lives there, still much adored, until she is very old.

6. The best-known model from Jewish folklore of this type is "Solika the Just," which may be found in various variations of IFA Tales: 10357, 10359, 11257, 13949, 14964, 17574, and 20943–20948.

7. Traditionally, the status of widowhood was perceived as a state of lack and absence; the absence of the husband from the woman's life was emphasized rather than the terms of her existence (the widow as a woman in her own right). This negative traditional conception of the widow is common in Jewish culture—even to the extent of expecting widows to throw themselves on the funeral pyres of their husbands (*sati*). Widows who declined this practice and chose to live instead were banished from all social celebrations out of the belief that their situation would bring bad luck to the celebrants. The etymology of the word "widow" in various languages—Hebrew, through Latin, and from there to modern-day English—testifies to associations with the qualities of muteness and silence (the Hebrew root for the word "widow" is "mute"), a lack or emptiness (*chera* in Greek). In Indian languages, there are many expressions for "widow": *rand, raki, randi*—all of which mean "prostitute" (Casler 1999).

8. In this context it is important to mention the subjects of *yibbum* and *haliza*, which may allow marriage between an older widow and a young boy, as it is written in Deuteronomy 25:5: "If brothers live together, and one of them dies, and has no child, the wife of the dead man shall not marry outside to a stranger; her husband's brother shall go in to her, and take her to him for a wife, and perform the duty of a husband's brother to her." The law of *yibbum* says that, if a married man dies and is without children, one of his brothers should marry his widow and inherit his wealth; if a son is born to this union, he will continue the line of the brother who died without a son. However there are many cases where, for the good of both the widow and the brother, no marriage should take place, as when there is a large age difference. In such cases the woman is released by means of *haliza*, and she may marry another man, except for a *cohen*. Since the storyteller doesn't give us any details about the young groom (the boy) or his origins, we cannot know for certain whether the marriage between the widow and the boy resulted from the necessity of *yibbum* and the refusal of *haliza* (perhaps because of the widow's wealth) or from the choice of the widow herself. Whatever the reason, there remains the storyteller's comment that the widow is "brave" in regard to this act.

BIBLIOGRAPHY

Atzmon, Yael, ed. 1995. *A Glimpse into the Lives of Women in Jewish Society*. Jerusalem: Zalman Shazar Center for Jewish History. [Hebrew]

Bar-Itzhak, Haya. 2001. *Jewish Poland: Legends of Origin*. Detroit: Wayne State University Press.

Barzel, Hillel. 1993. "The Question of Deep Structure—Bible and Literature Readings According to the Hypotheses of Lévi-Strauss." *Journal 77* 44–45: 30–39. [Hebrew].

Casler, Jeanine. M. 1999. "Aging and Opportunity: Growing Older in Clara Reeve's School for Widows." *Journal of Aging and Identity* 4 (2): 111–26.

Lévi-Strauss, Claude. 1969. *The Raw and the Cooked*. London: J. Cape.

Lubin, Orly. 2003. *Woman Reading Woman*. Haifa: Zmora Bitan. [Hebrew]

THE BOY WHO WAS KIDNAPPED AND BROUGHT TO RUSSIA

IFA 18140

NARRATED BY HINDA SHEINFERBER (POLAND)

Once upon a time, those who captured children came and took only one boy. He was like thirteen years of age (after his bar mitzvah). He came out of the synagogue with his *tefillin* [phylacteries]. And they captured him, gagged his mouth so he cannot shout, put him on a wagon, and transferred him far, far away to Russia.

They gave the boy to a childless family. They started to take care of him. The boy cried a lot; he missed his parents and wanted to go home. He did not want to eat their food, which was not Jewish. He did not eat and became thin and looked ill. The man brought home a doctor who told him: "If you want to have a child of your own, give him what he wants. Buy new utensils for him—new pot and a dish, fork and spoon—and give him so he can prepare his own food and he will start eating."

The boy said that if he will see how they are milking the milk, he would drink it. Then they began to make potatoes with milk, butter also is permitted to eat because when making butter it does not catch anything that is gentile. So there is butter, potato, and he drinks the milk straight from the cow, and was already in a better mood and started to study. The man brought him a teacher who will teach him Russian because he knew only Yiddish.

And the boy had grown. In Russia people joined the army at the age of twenty-five. He was maybe seventeen or eighteen and already went.

But before, when he was still young, when he had his *tefillin*, what will he do with it? He found a tin box, closed it, dug a hole not far away, made himself a marker, buried the *tefillin*, and went to the army.

He was already old. Not old but had a long beard, and all the army clothes also were too big for him, and big boots. He looked old. One night before he was through with the army, he came to the gentile's house, dug up the *tefillin*, took them, and ran away. He wanted to find his parents, to be among Jews; he did not forget this, his whole life.

He went from one town to another and of course had dust and dirt and mud on his boots and clothes; he slept in the woods and went from town to town and did not find his parents.

One time he came to one town, and it was snowing and cold, and he was hungry. Somewhere he saw a light; he knocked on the door and entered. There was an old couple who were very frightened: Who can knock on the door, maybe thieves? But he had knocked and knocked, so they said: Among Jews, if you want to make a *mitzvah* "it is ordered for life,"* a human being for life; let it be a thief, a murderer, we will open the door.

They opened the door and saw a gentile. The woman and the man were talking with their lips: to let him in or not? And then they were saying again: "It is ordered for life," we have to save him. So they let him in, made tea, gave him food, brought him to the small room they had where they had a bed. He closed the door and slept, but the old couple could not sleep the whole night from fear that he might kill them. There was silence. In the morning he did not open the door. They put their ears against the door and do not hear a thing. Then she opened the door quietly and looked. She sees him standing like a statue, he does not move. She cannot see his face, he is just standing. She calls on her husband, so he can see him too. Then he, without speaking, only with his hands, calls her to enter a bit. She goes inside, and he does not move; she goes a little more until she almost reaches the table, where he stands, and she sees on it a bag with *tefillin*. Then she almost fainted.—What is it?—She turned her head, her eyes, and read. This was embroidered with Hebrew letters. She could not get over it anymore, when she came closer and saw her son's name on the *tefillin* bag. She turned her face to his and saw him wearing the *tefillin*, and she understood why he was standing like this and not moving: He was saying the *Shmone Esrei* prayer when you have to stand straight. She fainted, and he saved her.

He had found his parents.

Transcribed by Hadarah Sela

---

* Meaning that Jewish laws and deeds (*mitzvot*) are intended to secure lives and not endanger them.

COMMENTARY TO
"THE BOY WHO WAS KIDNAPPED AND BROUGHT TO RUSSIA"

IFA 18140

HAGIT MATRAS

The phenomena of Kidnapping of children, has been known through history. Sometimes it occurs out of jealousy or revenge, or in order to profit from a ransom. In recent years we face the increasing of cases where children had been kidnapped from their home and brought for adoption to another country, privately or by a profitable organization. This also appears within the family in a process of separation, when a parent has abducted a child from home in order to gain custody.

Such incidents prompted international authorities to legislate a special law known as the Hague Convention on the Civil Aspects of International Child Abduction (Bergman and Witztum 1994).

In "The Boy Who Was Kidnapped and Brought to Russia," the child is kidnapped as he leaves the synagogue and is transferred "far away to Russia." He is given to "a childless family" for adoption. The description of the capture itself, the efforts of the child and his adoptive parents to adjust to one another, and the behavior of the boy while growing up—his deeds and appearance—are well situated in the temporal and spatial frame of the story. The final meeting with the old couple—their fears and curiosity up to the discovery and identification of their lost son—are described in great detail, as are their expressions and emotions. The end of the story—featuring the bag of *tefillin*, the son's stillness while praying the *Shmone Esrei*—is dramatically linked to the opening of the story: the boy's exit from synagogue carrying the *tefillin* and his concern over its safety during his army service. There is some vagueness surrounding the purpose of the kidnapping itself: Was it for adoption? For conscription? Why did the adoptive parents agree to let him go?

We may gain some insight by looking at another story, "The Rabbi and the Kidnapped Children" (IFA 18161), which was told by the same narrator, Hinda Sheinferber (Poland):

A long time ago there was in Russia such a custom where they sent killers and strong robbers to Poland to capture children six or eight years of age—does not matter what age—and bring them to far away Russia, where they wanted to bring them up.

. . . And in one town they captured eighteen children all at once and held them in a prison. And the town's rabbi heard about it but could not get to them, to remind them not to forget the fact that they are Jews. What did he do? The rabbi dressed as a poor man, sat outside all night, slept outdoors. The guards woke him up and asked him: "Who are you?"

He replied: "I am a thief."

"Thief? You ought to be in prison."

So they put him in together with the children. He started to tell them not to forget that they are Jewish, but they are still young, so they have to remember *Shema Yisrael*, which is the symbol of the Jewish religion, and if they will remember it, God will help them to stay alive.

Sheinferber was born in Mogielnica, Poland, in 1904. She grew up in a very Orthodox family and learned reading, writing, and prayers. She was married in 1926, and one week later came to Israel with her husband, David Aharon Sheinferber. They lived in Jerusalem, where their two sons were born. Life there was a struggle, and after six years they moved to Haifa, where they had a daughter. After their second-born son was killed during the War of Independence (1948), their lives revolved around the loss and their memories. Hinda was the center of the extended family. Her house was always open to guests, and even to strangers. Her husband passed away in 1968, and afterward she lost her oldest grandson in a car accident.

Sheinferber spent most of her adult years studying the Bible and reading Yiddish literature. These formed the basis for the story repertoire she knew and loved to narrate. She also memorized the folktales her mother told her and tales from the area where she grew up. She was able to find the right story for each situation, and this became a way for her to express her own point of view.

There is no doubt that these two stories spring from a common environment and complete one another. Although they do not specify the kidnapping of Jewish children, the trajectory of the stories and the salvation through the intercession of a rabbi or religious objects clearly point in this direction.

Both stories suggest a "personal narrative" or a "rumor story," which prepares the audience for what is to come: a cruel reality softened by some hope and comfort, a moral ending highlighting the sacred values of Judaism.

The first story's structure follows this rough outline: kidnapping, adoption, observation of Jewish laws in a hostile environment, the search for parents and home after years of absence, hospitality, the identification of the son by a certain sign, and, finally, recompense. In the second story we have details of the kidnappers and their purpose, imprisonment, the rabbi's wisdom, and, finally, hope.

The IFA collection contains only a few stories in which the kidnappers are human beings and the final resolution occurs through heavenly intercession. God's messenger on earth, commandments, the use of sacred elements, a dream, and miraculous saving are all motifs of sacred legend that are found in such stories.

"The Jew as Priest" is one example (IFA 9806):[1] A boy is kidnapped while still a baby and is raised as a gentile. He is returned to his faith as a result of a dream that shows him his true faith. "The Girl Who Was Kidnapped by Gypsies" (IFA 8563; Hechal 1970, 77–78, tale no.4),[2] resembles our original story: A personal sign on the baby's garment helps to identify her even after she grows up. We see this motif in yet another story: "Elhanan the Pope" (Sade 1983, 201–2).[3]

The kidnappers in all these stories are agents of the state in charge, among them are thieves and murderers, nomads and outcasts, or others who are on the margins of society. The kidnapping itself is carried out by an order or as personal retribution. In all these stories there is a happy ending: The boy returns to his own religion, to his homeland, to his family.

Folk behavior have gathered all kinds of means to protect children and prevent such harms as kidnappings. Creatures believed to pose real dangers of this kind are in general called witches and child-eaters.[4]

These were widely known throughout Europe during the Middle Ages and can be found in the writings of the Ashkenazi Hasidim. Yosef Dan recalls the use of the term *shatria* for a witch who eats children (Dan 1968, 189). Moshe Gideman explains that the belief in a *shatria* (a woman who came from the forest) or *brosha* (a witch), like other folk beliefs described in detail in books of Jewish customs, charm books, and in the writings of Ashkenazi Hasidim, originated in the Brothers Grimm's books and in non-Jewish superstitions (Gideman 1972, 161, 159–69). I also would note here the story of the *brosha* who played the role of midwife but in fact strangled newborn babies, turned some babies into animals, and transformed people into animals (Grunwald 1982).[5]

Customs used to protect babies also include the reciting of psalms and prayers, the use of charms and amulets, and the execution of certain ceremonies.[6] If these prove insufficient, mediators of special spiritual potency are summoned to influence those "forces." *Toldot Adam* presents a story based on such event. The story describes how a baby was saved as a result of an incantation ceremony performed by a Rabbi, on "more than one hundred thousand . . . men and women wizards and witches. . . . Flames of fire emanate from their mouths . . . while they play with the newborn baby." At the same time, the mother held a replica of her child made out of straw.[7] The book *Toldot Adam was first published in* the beginning of the eighteenth century in Lemberg (Lviv) area (now Ukraine), and contains—among other charms and medical formulas dealing with birth and children—the writings of two famous Rabbis who were also known as 'Ba'aley Shem' (the 'name' owners) and had lived in the area one hundred years earlier. This particular story is related to R' Eliahu of Chelm who lived in the area one generation before them and had found a tradition of using certain magic formulas for such occasions.

The story begins like a folk tale: "Once there was . . ."; however it might be a rumor story or a sacred legend: this tale that was transmitted by oral tradition, was well known in the area. It is written to a threatened audience in great details as a reminder and a useful tool.

The act of switching children (German: *kinder verwechseln*; Yiddish: *benemin*) is related to women witches as well as to ghosts: *Toldot Adam* brings "an amulet for a woman in confinement who is susceptible to the switching of her sons at birth, by Lilith or Machalat or women-witches that have such power."[8] Yet it seems that witches carry out tricks and transformations on the child, whereas demons tend to exchange the child with one of their own. The inception of the literary genre about these two sorts of "switching" would be an interesting topic for further study.

The concept of "switching children" close to their birth, still exist in folk narratives in modern times. See for example: "The Lost Princes" (IFA 5751; Noy 1970),[9] "Two Golden Kids" (Grunwald 1982), "The Girl and Her Seven Brothers" (Koen-Sarano 1994)[10]. Textual analysis that follow such stories show their strong connections to the genre of the folk-tale: the transformation of a child into an animal and his travails leading up to the happy and just ending, carry the reader/listener by waves of imagination.

In the translated and annotated edition of the Grimm legends by Donald Ward, we find many switching/kidnapping stories where babies are taken by a wild woman from the mountains, by a mountain ghost, by elves or demons, or by the devil himself (Ward 1981, tale nos. 50, 82, 83, 88, 90, 91, 153). In these legends we encounter the "other world" that tries to enter and live in the human world by transforming children. The exchanged child carries special signs, and the anxious parents usually know how to take care of them and how to get rid of them. Child kidnapping (also referred to under the categories "changeling," "stealing," "abduction," *Kinder-roub*, *Wechselbalg*) is committed while the parents are away and the baby is unsupervised; the parents are usually working in the field or at such tasks as shoeing or forging. Ward's comparative analysis refers to other variants in different cultures. The creatures responsible for the capture belong to the unearthly world. The baby is usually saved through prayer, pilgrimage to a sacred place, or a ceremony that involves a holy person or an act of a holy nature. The overall formula of the stories thus belongs to the sacred legend genre.

Stories about switching children by evil forces are known in many societies and are still told today. I will now turn to some examples, excluding the "Lilith" variations (as a kidnapper/eater/killer of babies who sucks their blood), which are subjects that must be studied separately.

Among the IFA stories from Yemen—which deal with our subject and were told to Heda Jason by the Shwili family but not published—I have found one story about a boy who was changed into a wooden doll as punishment for a curse (IFA 1449: "Demons Took a Child and Brought Him Back"; transcribed by H. Jason from Yeshayahu Shwili). The boy did not go to sleep, and the mother burst out at him, saying: "The demon take you!" The boy was returned only after a rabbi conducted a transformation ceremony and "threatened the demon."

Andre Elbaz (1982) relates a story told to him by his mother, titled "The Baby who was Kidnapped by a Jnun."[11] The story apparently described an actual incident and was transmitted within the family tradition: "A baby disappeared from the room where she was sleeping alone, and was returned after a ceremony of prayers, incense, and candle-lighting was performed. The room had one window that faced the grave of a holy Muslim figure." Similar stories are told to this day by people who come from North Africa; some are "faith stories" and others "personal narratives" or "rumor story."

Stories that involve kidnapping by demons or fairies were common and well collected among immigrants from the British Isles to Eastern Canada. In a collection of about one hundred traditional stories from Scotland (Bruford and MacDonald, eds., 1994), mostly legends or sacred legends, eighteen are connected to "sea men and fairies." In their annotations to the texts of these legends, the editors discuss the strongly held belief that "fairies cannot cross water"—whether salted seawater or flowing rivers—to bring back a kidnapped child.

Substitution of a child by a supernatural being is usually carried out while the child is left alone, without his parents' supervision.[12] In another collection from Nova Scotia from the 1930s, annotated according to the folklore theory of that time (Fraser 1931), we are introduced to stories describing the switching of human children with those of devils and fairies. Here too the exchanges occur while the human child is left unprotected: during the agricultural season, while his parents are working in the fields, during the passage of seasons, on Christmas day, and so forth. This usually occurs when no customary precautions are taken, such as carrying a piece of iron to ward off the malign forces. The return of the child is usually carried out by consulting experts who compensate the fairies, perform rituals, and use the fairies' children—who had been left in place of the human ones—as bargaining chips. There can also be an entering into the "fairy world" to confirm where the real child is being kept, and perhaps the chance to find a certain object to bring back as a proof of the existence of "the other world." The texts are written in Gaelic, the language in which they were told, which reflects their origins in the folk culture passed down in the society through oral tradition.

In a seminar I taught at the Hebrew University Folklore Department in 1998, I asked students to collect folk narratives dealing with the subject of kidnapped children. They collected versions with gypsies, nuns, and Lilith as child kidnappers; these were narrated by people from Syria, Egypt, and Morocco. Other stories collected during the seminar were connected to the kidnapping of children who had emigrated from Yemen to Israel during the first years of the state's establishment, a topic that received wide attention through the media that year (Caspi 1997). These stories were mostly of the personal narrative or rumor genre. Analyzing them brought up many details that resembled the kidnapping stories I have discussed above.

Stories about kidnapping, changelings, and stolen children have common features. The child's disappearance is usually related to the breaking or violation of proper social order: leaving children unattended, deserting them outdoors, saying prohibited words aloud. These typically occur during periods when parents perform agricultural labor in the fields, as during harvest seasons; during rites of passage; at the change of seasons; or when emigrating from the country of origin. The catalyst might be immigrating to a new land, moving to a new house, looking for medical aid, changing jobs, and so forth. The kidnapper might be an outsider to a place or culture: an avenger or manipulator with enigmatic demands who holds a position of power. The new reality can produce "culture shock," which raises people's level of anxiety and is sometimes expressed in personal narratives, rumor and other storytelling genres. These narratives were transmitted orally until they received literary expression within a well-known literate framework (Bar-Itzhak 1993). Fear of unknown dangers, which is a central theme in these stories, relies on an existing reality—(children's kidnapping or deliberate switching occur to this day, as do babies' deaths due to unknown causes) but is transferred to a new place and situation.

Many of the stories were told as true accounts and held an essential element of belief. They relied on personal and cultural factors without doubting their real-world credibility. Classification of the stories as "legend" or as "belief legend" is due to their wide distribution in modern society. Their social role is based on the power of the unconscious—both of the tellers and of the audience—and on the reality of their contents (Dégh 1971).[13]

These stories have both visible and symbolic messages and play a didactic role. The cruelty described in them can be transformed into a happy ending through salvation, a miracle, or simply a good deed, as in "The Boy Who Was Kidnapped and Brought to Russia."

Notes

1. "The Jew as Priest" (IFA 9806) was transcribed by Malka Cohen, as told to her by Tova Retler (Romania). See Cohen 1974, 79–80, story no. 56, and the notes on p. 190.
2. The story "The Girl Who Was Kidnapped by Gypsies" (IFA 8563) was transcribed by Ronit Bernstein-Dotan, as narrated by Avraham Urmosa (Syria).
3. For additional versions, see Sade 1983, notes on p. 190.
4. See *Toldot Adam* paragraph 124 (Matras 1980).
5. See Grunwald 1982, story 59, "Tricks of Brosha the Witch," and accompanying notes for its versions in IFA.
6. See *Toldot Adam* paragraphs 12, 19, 80, 86, 104, 105, 113, 119, 16; *Zchira*; and other charms and medicine books (Matras 1980, 83–87, 144–46; Matras 1997).
7. See *Toldot Adam* paragraph 86.
8. See *Toldot Adam* paragraph 80.
9. Noy 1970, 133–36, tale 45, and the notes on pp. 214–15. See also the discussion of IFA 8902 in the present volume (48–50).
10. Narrated by Rivka Cohen-Arieli.
11. Tale no. 49, narrated in French by July Elbaz.
12. Bruford and MacDonald eds., 1994, tales 69a and 69b; notes p. 475. Story 69b is "A Fairy Changeling," narrated by Nan MacKinnon of Vatersay (350).
13. For discussion of memorats, see Shenhar 1994, 105–35. See also the discussion in "Memorat Stories in Sifrei Sgulot u'Refuot" (Matras 1997, 107–8, 156–57; 224, nn. 132–33).

*B*IBLIOGRAPHY

Bar-Itzhak, Haya. 1993. "Israeli Reality in the Traditional Narratives of Yemenite Jews." *Tema* 3: 130–43. [Hebrew]

Bergman, Zeev, and Eliezer Witztum. 1994. "Kidnapping of a Child by a Parent and the Syndrome of Ignoring a Parent." *Sichot* 9.1 (November): 115–29. [Hebrew]

Bruford, Alan, and Donald A. MacDonald, eds. 1994. *Scottish Traditional Tales*. Edinburgh: Polygon.

Caspi, Arie. 1997. "Where Is the Child? There Was No Kidnapping or Conspiracy: The Story of Immigration in the Early Years of the State Has Turned into an Infernal Thing Owing to Ignorance, Paranoia, and Discrimination." *Ha'aretz* supplement, September 5. [Hebrew]

Cohen, Malka. 1974. *Mi-pi ha-am*. Annotated by Haim Schwarzbaum. Tel Aviv: Yeda Am. [Hebrew]

Dan, Yosef. 1968. *The Esoteric Theology of Ashkenazi Hasidism*. Jerusalem: Bialik Institute. [Hebrew]

Dégh, Linda. 1971. "The Belief-Legend in Modern Society: Form, Function and Relationship to Other Genres." In *American Folk Legend*, ed. W. Hand, 55–68. Berkeley: University of California Press.

Elbaz, Andre E. 1982. *Folktales of the Canadian Sephardim*. Toronto: Fitzhenry and Whiteside.

Fraser, Mary L. 1931 [1975]. *Folklore of Nova Scotia*. Toronto: Catholic Truth Society of Canada.

Grunwald, Mayer.1982. "Spaniolic Folktales (*Consejas*)." In *Folklore Research Center Studies* 6, 197–213. Jerusalem: Magnes Press/Hebrew University. [Hebrew]

Gideman, Moshe. 1972 [1897]. *A Book on Doctrine and Life in Western Countries in the Middle Ages*. Jerusalem: Makor. [Hebrew]

Hechal, Edna, ed. 1970. *A Tale for Each Month, 1968–1969*. Haifa: Haifa Municipality, Ethnological Museum and Folktale Archives. [Hebrew]

Koen-Sarano, Matilda. 1994. *Consejas i Consezikas: Stories and Folk Tales from the Jewish-Sephardic World*. Jerusalem: Kana. [Hebrew and Ladino]

Matras, Hagit. 1980. "*Sifrei Sgulot*: Customs and Belief in Folk Medicine, According to the Book 'Toldot Adam.'" Master's thesis, Hebrew University, Jerusalem. [Hebrew]

———.1997. "*Sifrei Sgulot u'refuot* in Hebrew: Contents and Origins (Based on the Books Printed in Europe during the 18th century)." PhD thesis, Hebrew University, Jerusalem. [Hebrew]

Noy, Dov. 1970. *Jewish Folktales from Tunis*. Jerusalem: Jewish Agency, Haifa Municipality, and Israel Folktale Archives. [Hebrew]

Sade, Pinchas. 1983. *Sefer Hadimyonot shel Ha-Yehudim.—Jewish Folktales*. Jerusalem: Schocken. [Hebrew]

Shenhar, Aliza. 1994. *The Story, the Storyteller, and the Audience*. Tel Aviv: Hakibutz Ha'meuchad. [Hebrew]

Ward, Donald, ed. and trans. 1981. *The German Legends of the Brothers Grimm*. 2 vols. Philadelphia: Institute for the Study of Human Issues.

THE IMPOVERISHED AND WANDERING JEWISH TENANT

IFA 18800

NARRATED BY DAVID ITSICOVITC (ROMANIA)

A poor, elderly Jew came, wishing to meet the rabbi to talk to him and ask for his advice. When his turn came, he met the rabbi, and in tears told him that he had no way to support himself and did not want to be a burden on anyone.

The rabbi listened to the poor man's life story, thought a great deal, and then said: "Listen to me: You should wander from place to place, and in every Jewish community you reach and are hosted in, you should tell tales. Any tale you know, you should tell."

The unfortunate soul wandered from place to place, from community to community, and he slept everywhere, either at a Jew's home who invited him to stay over or in synagogues where in the winter it was warm from the oven made ready for the worshipers, or in a room designated for the wanderers.

When he arrived at Jewish homes, especially the rich ones, on Shabbat, he told a tale for every one of the Shabbat meals,* three tales on Shabbat.

Once he arrived on a Friday night and entered a synagogue and waited for someone to invite him as a guest for Shabbat. In this town apparently not too many were hosting. He sat in a corner, prayed the Shabbat prayer with everyone else, and hoped for the best.

On this Shabbat eve, one of the local wealthy Jews arrived late for prayer; for him the Shabbat evening prayer was delayed, and they finished late.

When the synagogue was almost empty, the rich man saw the poor one sitting in a corner, staring at the departing worshipers, expecting someone to invite him.

The rich man approached and asked him if he wanted to accompany him, to be his guest for this Shabbat. The poor fellow rejoiced and went with him.

The rich man used to invite the poor to his house and asked them to tell everybody stories they knew. This poor man said he would tell a story as well. Everyone waited to hear a story from his mouth, but he did not make a sound. The poor guest opened his mouth, but nothing came out of it. He was silent; silent and ashamed.

In the morning they went to the synagogue, and when they came back, they sat, ate, and sang the Shabbat songs, and waited to hear any story from the stranger. But he said that his head was

---

* According to Jewish law, during Shabbat one is required to eat three meals: the first one on Shabbat eve (Friday night), the second one after the Saturday morning prayer, and the third on Saturday evening.

really empty; he did not remember a thing—nothing. The rich man, his household, and the poor shook their heads and thought that the poor fellow was a little bit mentally disturbed. They thought it, but did not speak a word, for it is forbidden to shame a person.

On Shabbat afternoon they prayed *Mincha*[*] and sat to eat the third meal. And then the night fell after the *Maariv* prayer.[†] When they sat around the table, after the *Havdalah* service,[‡] the poor man told his host: "Sir, I am ashamed to say that I forgot all the stories I can tell. But if you allow me, I will tell a completely different story. I do not know what happened to me."

And this is the story: A Jew was a tax collector for a gentile landlord in Poland. The gentile landlord gave him this job and the right to collect taxes due to him every year from the farmers in the villages that were the gentile landlord's property. The tenant farmers worked all year, with all their strength, to be able to feed their children and their families, and also to pay the taxes the gentile landlord imposed on them. There was a drought in the region for the third year, and they barely had what to eat. Obviously they could not give the Jew any amount of money for taxes. The gentile farmers saw the Jew as the landlord's messenger and hated him because he took money and crops from them. They considered him the main culprit.

The gentile landlord himself used to visit his estate a few times a year. Most of the time he enjoyed life in the big city with the counts and the rich men, in their luxurious palaces with their beautiful ladies. The first year the Jew arrived empty-handed and told the gentile landlord about the drought, he forgave him and told him to try collecting the taxes from the villagers. The second year he scolded the Jew and informed him that he would punish him if he didn't bring him the money he is owed.

The Jew left broken-hearted. He saw the sorrow of the villagers who worked from sunrise till sunset, without rain. They even started slaughtering their cows to have something to eat and not to feed. They reached their last piece of bread. And what will they give to the Jew who came and claimed money? They saw him as the main culprit. The Jew himself did not have food. From time to time he walked or traveled to his old rabbi in the nearby town and got from him spiritual support and also a few coins from the community's charity fund.

When the gentile landlord arrived during the third year and heard that the Jew did not have money for him, he beat him with a whip. He called his servants and ordered them to throw the Jew into a pit, along with his wife and four children. The gentile landlord did not even listen to the Jew plead that he is not to blame. It is so simple: The villagers don't have food, so what will he take from them?

The servants obeyed the gentile landlord's orders and threw all the Jew's family into a pit, which was once a well, and left so they would not hear the cries of the children and their mother.

---

[*] *Mincha* is the afternoon prayer.

[†] *Maariv* is the evening prayer.

[‡] *Havdalah* (literally: differentiation) is the ritual performed on Saturday evening to mark the end of the Shabbat

And the Jew stayed silent and prayed. What will happen to him and his wife, who was pregnant in addition to his four children?

His lips whispered: "God be my help, and in you I will put my trust, there is no savior but you."

Two nights they were there, and nobody came to the pit to see what happened to them. On the third night the father heard approaching footsteps. He listened and heard the voice of the doyen of the court servants whisper: "Listen, I am lowering to you something to eat and a pitcher of water. Nobody should know I was here."

Done and gone. He did this every few nights.

After a month the woman gave birth to a girl, and there was nothing with which to treat her. The father took his upper garment and wrapped her with shreds he cut from it. When the old servant heard about the baby's birth, he offered to have his wife raise her. Her parents feared that she would grow up in a Christian home and refused to give her up. They asked him to bring whatever he could for her.

Two other villagers who heard what was done to the Jew came to him at night and offered to take his first-born son and drive him away from the village, and God have mercy on him.

The parents consulted each other; they talked to their eldest son, who was eleven years old, and decided to accept the offer of the good gentiles. They knew that the Jew was good and not guilty of anything. On one of the nights, they lowered a ladder, and their eldest son separated from them. He climbed, entered a carriage, they covered him with straw, and they drove him to town. There he got off, separated from them, and remained alone.

After a few months the gentile landlord remembered the Jew, and when he heard that he and his family were still alive, he ordered them to be taken out and expelled from his estate. In the cart given to him by a kind farmer, they left the place and arrived at the rabbi's town and settled there.

More than twenty years passed, and there was no trace of their son. In all the Jewish communities they asked, inquired, and sought in vain.

Here the poor guest turned silent, sighed, lowered his weary head, and covered his face with his hands.

The *Melave Malka* dinner* was forgotten by all and silence filled the place.

Then the host asked: "Do you know if this story is true? If it is, are the parents of this child still alive? Where are they and their children?"

The poor storyteller guest said: "I am his father. But my wife is long dead from grief and aggravation. His brothers are fine."

"I am this boy!" the rich man cried, and embraced his father with excitement and tears.

"Blessed be the Almighty who did not leave me," they both whispered, and their tears met.

Recorded by Ya'acov Avitsuk

---

* *Melave Malka*, literally "the Queen's Escort," is the name of the third meal of Shabbat; Shabbat is referred to as a "queen," and this meal is eaten at the end of the Shabbat.

Commentary to "The Impoverished and Wandering Jewish Tenant"

18800

Rachel Zoran

The text is a conglomerate in which one story is framed within the other: The hero of the framing story is a storyteller, an impoverished Jew who, following his rabbi's advice, made his living wandering among Jewish communities and telling stories of all kinds.[1] The turning point occurs when he meets a rich man who from time to time invites poor people to his home and asks them to tell stories. When his turn comes he opens his mouth but is unable to utter a word. Later he remembers one single story, an "entirely different" tale, and tells it to the rich man and his guests. This (framed) story proves to be about the narrator and the listener, the poor man and the rich man. It transpires that they are father and son, forced to separate and now reunited through the story.

The story told by the poor father to the rich son can be regarded as a "redeeming tale," since it concerns both the narrator and the listener; when they become aware of that fact and recognize each other, they are redeemed through their reunion. The main subject of the entire text is thus redemption through the act of narrating. The connection between the framing and the framed story exemplifies how the act of narration can make *Tikkun* (repair, restoration) in the worlds of both narrator and listener.

The possibility of such *Tikkun* is systematized and analyzed in the field of bibliotherapy. Bibliotherapy is an art therapeutic method that suggests including in the therapeutic discourse a "third voice": that of the literary text, through which the entire therapeutic process takes place. The *Tikkun* process in the present story follows the narration of a text that turns out to be the life story shared by the narrator and the listener: What is presented in the narrative interaction first as a "third voice" (the framed story) emerges as a first-person story common to the two participants in the narrative act.

At the beginning of the plot, the poor man is presented as having told all the stories he knows, but having forgotten them, so that only a single story remains.[2] The various stories told by the poor man for his living and heard by the rich man seemingly for his pleasure become transformed into a single story, the "different" one: a special and hence a redeeming tale. This transformation is the focus of the plot, and it bears its secret and hidden meaning, which is the ability to make *Tikkun* in the world through storytelling.

The mutual recognition occurs at the end of the text, apparently as a surprise but in fact having taken shape gradually. This indicates that to transform a tale into the "single story," the one that redeems, mere chance cannot suffice: A certain guiding hand is needed.[3] Let us trace the stages through which the secret of the story is built and revealed.

At the beginning the *Tikkun* is set forth in its tangible aspect: the poor man's ability to make a living out of storytelling, following the rabbi's advice. This advice, which seems material, actually has a spiritual aspect as well, since it somehow suits the poor man's personality as depicted in the prologue: He is an elderly man, no longer fit for hard work but capable of storytelling. Moreover, his life experience can probably ensure that he possesses an abundance of stories. Thus the first *Tikkun* brought about by the stories is material wellbeing, but this is conditioned on a life of wandering, which means no home or family.

But the hidden plot, the real aim of the journey as revealed at the end, is at this stage still hidden within the story's folds. This expected course of events is reversed when the "natural" order of "a story for a bed and a meal" is disrupted: This time the Jew wanders to a town where there are few hosts, and he stays on Shabbat eve without being invited for a meal. The poor Jew remains the last person in the synagogue; he sits in the corner, prays, and hopes for the best. At this point the plot is interrupted; the reader/listener, along with the poor Jew, expects a turn in the situation.

Sure enough, by chance, one of the rich men of the town is late, and the Shabbat evening prayer had been delayed especially for him. He sees the poor man in the corner and invites him to his home. This is no ordinary encounter. Despite the coincidence, the situation created here seems controlled and intentional: the rich man came late to the service, and the poor man remained alone after it without any host. The rich man is known to invite poor people to his home and ask them to tell stories, and this precisely is the poor man's profession. There is thus a full symmetry: staying after prayers together with latecoming; storytelling together with story consuming. This harmony hints at some guiding hand.

Yet even after this temporary solution, the plot does not flow smoothly but rather is blocked once again: When the moment comes to "pay" for the meal, the poor man forgets all his stories and is unable to utter a word. As it was earlier at the synagogue, when the absence of a host among the congregants left room for the one host who came late, so is it here also: All the stories known to the storyteller are forgotten. When his memory returns, on Saturday night, after Shabbat ends, he recalls only one story, which will give rise to mutual recognition. That is, to effectuate a *Tikkun* the story must somehow change from one story among many to one story, a single and special tale, which may deeply touch narrator and listener alike. This dialectical tension between presence and absence, one and many, silence and narration, remembering and forgetting, is thus the force that drives the plot.[4]

The story was told by David Itsicovitc, who was born in the village of Negresht, near the town of Vaslui, in Romania (year unknown). In 1909 Itsicovitc married Rachel Gutman Iliovitc, and they had nine children. One of them, Ya'acov Avitsuk, transcribed this story. During World War I Itsicovitc was conscripted. He served at the front and later in the interior of Russia. He would hear wandering rabbis and preachers who came to Vaslui, and then retell the stories he heard from them. He told stories every Shabbat eve, and the children would listen intently. He also told stories at the synagogue on festivals but especially at the "third meal," on Saturday night, after Shabbat ended, and relatives would come and listen to him. His talent was revealed especially on Passover eve. For each festival he had his special stories, which he told slowly, accompanied by hand gestures and facial expressions and variations in his voice. When he told of shooting or noise in general, he used the cutlery and crockery. Sometimes he rose in the middle of the telling and walked around to enact the hero's actions. Eighteen stories told by him are recorded in IFA.

Our story brings to mind two other tales that are clearly interconnected: "The Ba'al Shem's Servant" from *Praises of the Ba'al ShemTov* (*Shivhey ha-Besht*) and "The Forgotten Story," S. Y. Agnon's literary adaptation of the Hasidic tale. In certain points the tales are alike, or even the same, and in others they differ no less significantly. Limits of space prevent a detailed comparison of the tales here, but I would like to deal briefly with the central turning point in all three. This concerns the tales' "secret": forgetfulness of all the stories except the single, redeeming tale. Beyond this likeness, the contrasts among the three stories in regard to this feature may also indicate their differences in context and literary character.

"THE IMPOVERISHED AND WANDERING JEWISH TENANT"

After the rich man invited the poor man to his home and gave him a meal, as was his wont with all the poor people whom he asked to tell stories, the host and all the guests waited to hear the poor man's tale, but he did not say a word. He opened his mouth without uttering a sound. He was silent and shamefaced.

It was the same the next morning. The poor man said that his head was empty; he did not remember anything. The rich man and his guests thought that something was wrong with him, but did not say a word lest they offend him. Only at the third meal, after *Havdalah*, did the poor man say to his host, "Sir, I am ashamed to say that I forgot all the stories I can tell. But if you allow me, I will tell a completely different story. I do not know what happened to me." At this point the poor man begins the tale, which proves to be the redeeming one.

"The Ba'al Shem's Servant": A Tale from Adat Zadikim

The Ba'al Shem's servant is a compulsive storyteller who wanders among the Jewish communities and tells the Ba'al Shem's tales. He arrives at the house of a rich man known to pay a lot for new tales about the Ba'al Shem. He is made warmly welcome, and is asked at once to tell something of the "wonders and fearful things which he has seen with the Ba'al Shem" (Rodkinzon, Adat Zadikim 1897, 24). He wants to relate something, "and lo, he has forgotten all the tales as if he had never laid eyes on the Ba'al Shem" (24). This frightens him, but he passes it off as owing to the travails of the journey. But even after a night's sleep, the servant remembers nothing, "since he has forgotten the Ba'al Shem entirely, as if he had never known him" (24). The situation recurs the next morning, "and the rich man had great sorrow and the servant twice as great" (24). All that day the servant was "like a shocked man and did not remember a single act" (24). After the *Mincha* prayer the rich man went home happy and lighthearted. He invited to his meal distinguished guests, and showed respect and honor to the servant as he would to one of the great rabbis.

And the servant felt as if his stomach was pierced by a sword, since he knew that he had no refuge, as he had no single story to tell, because he forgot everything, as a child being born forgets all the Torah he has known in the higher world.

The guests implored him, but—

He was sitting dumb and shocked, like a ship that has lost its oars in the midst of the sea. [—] All of a sudden he was healed and remembered one single tale, wonder of wonders, and then in his mind he praised and thanked God for that story of reminiscence.

"The Forgotten Tale" by S. Y. Agnon

The Ba'al Shem's servant, Reb Jacob, who after the Ba'al Shem's death wanders among the Jewish communities and tells of his late master's wonders, arrives after seven months at a rich man's house, having heard that he is ready to pay much money for tales about the Ba'al Shem. The rich man settles him in the attic and asks him to wait until Shabbat eve—the time for tales. After dinner Jacob is suddenly unable to remember anything: "since he forgot all that had ever happened to him [—] as if he were born that same day" (Agnon 1987, 160–64).

The townspeople who have come to hear the tales mock and scorn him, but the rich man is patient and suggests they wait till the next day—perhaps he will remember something. But at breakfast, too, Jacob is unable to remember anything, and he tells the rich man that he feels that "it is not a mere coincidence, since such a thing had never happened to him" (Agnon 1987, 161).

The rich man then suggests they wait for the third meal, but then, too, Jacob cannot remember anything, and he becomes very sad. The people of the town keep taunting him, and "the righteous man, Reb Jacob, accepted everything with love and prayed to God" (Agnon 1987, 161).

When on Saturday night, after Shabbat has ended, he remembers nothing, he tells himself that it may be a sign from heaven, not a coincidence, and decides to return home. Hearing this, the rich man asks him still to wait three more days. Since the servant is unable to remember even then, he takes his leave of the rich man, who gives him a generous donation and lets him go.

As he climbs onto the wagon, Reb Jacob suddenly remembers a "fearful story" (Agnon 1987, 162) about the Ba'al Shem, and he returns to the rich man's house and asks his servant to inform him that he has remembered a precious tale. The rich man invites him to his room and says to him, "Please, do tell," and he tells.

The structure in all three versions is obviously the same, but several points may reveal a different concept in each. Let us examine these differences through several components of that scene:

1. the time span between forgetting and remembering;
2. the reaction to the forgetfulness of the narrator (the poor man) and of the listener (the rich man);
3. the way the narrator remembers the story after his silence, and the story's special quality.

In the tale "The Impoverished and Wandering Jewish Tenant," the time span is the shortest: from Friday night, when the rich man meets the poor man in the synagogue, to Saturday night, after *Havdalah*. The poor man becomes ashamed because of his forgetfulness, and the rich man and his guests think that he has lost his wits but say nothing so as not to offend him. The poor man feels that "his head [was] really empty," but he does not know why. Only when he remembers the "other story" on Saturday night does he express his feelings about the forgetfulness: "I do not know what happened to me." With these words he refers not only to the act of forgetting but more especially to the fact that, when he does remember, it is only one tale; this he defines as a completely different story, which it later transpires is about himself and his son, as we saw earlier.

The expression "a completely different story" attests that the narrator distinguishes this story from the other stories he told in his wanderings. This is a specifying predicate, used before the tale was actually told. Only after telling it is its real "otherness" revealed, since it unites the narrator/father with his lost son. Moreover, until the end of the story, we do not know what these forgotten stories are; they are probably tales heard, or perhaps actually experienced, by the poor man, since according to his rabbi's command he had to tell "any tale you know."

The meaning of forgetfulness in this case is nothing but the need to empty the poor man's mind of all the stories he knows in order to lead him to the other story, the only one about himself and his son—the rich man listening to him—without either knowing the other's identity. What the poor man certainly does know is that he is telling the rich man the story of his own life, and that is enough to define the story as "other," unique among all the stories, even before the rich man's identity is revealed. Moreover, the fact that the events in the story actually happened is critical, since this alone allows the narrator and the listener to identify each other, and hence be redeemed.

The short time span between forgetfulness and recalling may be regarded as serving the centrality of the inner story, and it sheds light on the function of forgetfulness as clearing and making room. This interval permits the narrator's mind to be "cleansed" of all the stories he knows, which will induce him to recall his life story, pivotal in which is his parting from his son. The "guiding hand" in this case is what mysteriously makes him forget, and later remember—but narrator and listener alike seem innocent and ignorant of its real purpose. Only in retrospect does it become clear that what seemed to be coincidental was an intentional chain of events.

In "The Ba'al Shem's Servant," the wandering seems longer. Throughout that time the servant never loses hope of becoming rich from the mission imposed on him by his master before dying, with the promise that he will make his living out of it. The kind of tales he has to tell is known from the outset: the wonderful stories about the Ba'al Shem. Until this point the narrated time is far longer than the time of narration, and it is clear that on the many passing days the servant "remembers" the Ba'al Shem's stories and tells them. Only after the preacher tells him that there is a wealthy man who may make him rich for his stories is there a kind of "shortcut," and he immediately sets off for the rich man's home, where he asks permission to tell his stories.

Now, when everything seems to happen at a rapid pace, the process is blocked by the servant's forgetting the stories. His immediate reaction is fear: For him this means forgetting the Ba'al Shem himself. He feels as if "he had never known [the Ba'al Shem]." His fright is a natural response to the feeling that he has lost his teacher and master.

At first the servant ascribes his forgetfulness to fatigue from the hardship of the journey, and the wealthy man, his eagerness notwithstanding, lets him rest and even go to the bath house. But even later he cannot remember anything "since he has forgotten the Ba'al Shem entirely, as if he had never known him." The experience is very hard: A major part of the servant's biography is erased from his mind, and he is shocked. Then the servant seems to grasp that this is not mere forgetfulness, and he sinks into pondering the situation. But the wealthy man keeps on pleading with him; the absence of a response causes him great sorrow, "and the servant twice as great." Clearly, the rich man and the servant now have a common interest: The servant's sorrow is indeed the greater, since it is accompanied by a sense of loss of identity, but the rich man's sorrow is great too. At this point, however, his sorrow can be understood only through his unrequited passion for tales about the Ba'al Shem.

As time passes from Friday to Saturday night, both parties' distress worsens; that of the servant reaches its climax on Saturday night, when the rich man invites him to a meal as if he were one of his most distinguished guests, but he experiences a complete emptying of his mind. At the height of this crisis—"wonder of wonders"—he recalls a story, only a single one.

As in the previous text, here too recollection brings relief, and when the narrator finishes his tale, both he and the listener are redeemed: The rich man had to hear the servant's story to attain his full atonement; this story took him from darkness to light, and having heard it, he bestowed on the servant half his fortune, as he had vowed. But the poor man is redeemed not only from his poverty but also from the feeling that he has lost his identity and never knew the Ba'al Shem. That is, he experiences at one and the same time material and spiritual redemption. The rich man, on the other hand, whose full redemption depends on his hearing the single story about himself, attains it after the recollection.

The redemption process, which is completed at the ending of the text, may be regarded as having started already in the time span between forgetting and recalling. Unlike in the "Tenant" tale, here not only does forgetfulness clear the way for the "single story" but, by means of the delay it creates, it allows either participant to enter into a dialogue on the meaning of forgetfulness and its connection to the story that is eventually recollected, a tale of atonement that is followed by atonement in the real world.

In Agnon's version this time span, with the possibilities it opens for self-examination, is even longer, and the time that passes from Jacob's arrival at the rich man's house to the moment of recollection is almost a week.[5] Upon arrival he is accommodated in the attic and asked to stay until Shabbat eve, the time when people assemble to hear the Ba'al Shem legends. Until that day he is not aware that he has forgotten all the stories. From the moment of forgetfulness, a drama seems to take place in both participants' minds. The drama in Jacob's mind is overt, while the rich man's drama is revealed only in retrospect, when it becomes clear that he has known all along that it is Jacob who is about to tell him the story that will bring about his atonement.

Jacob's suffering is immense, but he feels no loss of identity, as he believes that what has happened is not mere coincidence: The forgetfulness has a certain reason, even if it is hidden from him. The time span is prolonged even more as the rich man asks him to stay three more days after the Shabbat, and, as we learn in retrospect, that period is dedicated to prayer and self-examination on the rich man's part. The remembering is different here as well: Jacob is already on his way back, having given up hope of recalling anything, and only on the wagon does he remember the story. Unlike in the Hasidic tale, here the possibility of remembering is entirely renounced, and that complete renunciation alone facilitates recollection. While the poor man in the first story feels shame and confusion, and the servant in the second story feels fright because of the loss of his master, in Agnon's version Jacob recognizes the role of Providence in his forgetfulness and directs his prayer to God. Moreover, by leaving the place and forgoing the chance of easy enrichment, he makes room for the story. Only in doing so does he recall, when he is about to leave, the "fearful story," the "precious story" (Agnon 1987, 162). This time, however, it is not a tale for which he will be paid but a special story that will change his own life and his hearer's.

Forgetfulness, as the story's main theme, and as representing its secret, is explicitly expressed at the ending of the Hasidic version where, according to the generic convention, the narrator addresses the readers:

So far the tale. And the one who has been granted understanding by the Holy One Blessed Be He may understand how many wonders are in the story, and the greatest of all wonders is that the servant has forgotten all that he remembered except this tale alone. And it means that had he remembered all the tales, he might have told him other tales and not this one, and therefore he forgot everything about the Ba'al Shem and had only this one, so that he was forced to tell precisely it, in order to make the rich man know that his atonement is complete. ("The Ba'al Shem's Servant" from Adat Zadikim, 24)

The Hasidic narrator says explicitly what in the other version is implied in the actions, but the conclusion is common to all three: For the tale to render complete *Tikkun*, it must be isolated from all other tales, acquire a space of its own, and become indispensable and unique—the one story.[6]

If one considers these points of resemblance, the Hasidic version at face value seems structurally more perfected and condensed. But the focus of the drama in the tenant's tale is actually elsewhere: It is a family drama, in contrast to the religious drama in the Hasidic version. This may become clearer when we examine the internal stories.

In the Hasidic tale and in Agnon's adaptation, the internal story is identical: It is the tale of the atonement of the rich man, and the condition of full atonement compels him to listen to his own story. In our text the internal story is wholly different. The setting is indeed similar, and it concerns the conflict between the gentile and Jewish worlds, but the distress in the tenant's story is personal, and it has to do with loyalty to family and community. Accordingly, the narrative solution, the redemption, is also different: Our story is not about atonement; the redemption is entirely personal—the reunion of father and son, who were forced to part when the son was eleven years old. Moreover, in the Hasidic versions the narrator is an innocent witness, a kind of emissary relating the story without understanding its meaning. But in the tenant's story the narrator is certainly aware that he is telling the story of his own life with its particular trauma, and even if at that stage he still does not know that the listener is his son, the very act of narration is a kind of confession, which has a comfort of its own—the comfort felt by one who gains the opportunity to tell the tale of his life.

The uniqueness of the tenant's story as a family tale is echoed also in its narrative situation. In all the stories there is an internal narrative situation related as part of the story. But in the tenant's story, the resemblance between the fictional narrative situation and the external, real one is striking. The internal story is told by a father to his son. The external narrative situation is that of a father, the Romanian Jew David Itsicovitc, who tells the story to his son, Ya'acov Avitsuk, the informer. Usually the documentation of the informer and the narrator is an extra-textual element, but in this case one is tempted to include them in the fictional structure, seeming clearly to form a mirror image.

Without knowing anything about the narrator and the informer except the details recorded in IFA and presented with the story, we may see that the family has experienced immigration (from Romania to Israel), and we know that such an experience affects the adult and the younger generation differently. While the adult generation finds it hard to become accustomed to the new place and preserves something of its foreign character, the younger generation adjusts more easily and adopts some of the characteristics of the new place. Here we see that the father kept his original family name, Itsicovitc, and the son adopted a new, Hebraized name, Avitsuk. Yet despite the Hebraizing, this name still preserves some of the original sounds; moreover, its meaning has to do with fatherhood and strength: *Avi-tsuk* means "father of a cliff." Perhaps through this name change the son tries to create a different life story for himself and his father, or perhaps for his own son, too. In any event, the new name signifies him as a local person, while the father's original name signifies him as an immigrant. Here the kind of relationship between the poor wandering father and the rich son is identifiable.

The son records stories for IFA, and for this purpose he needs immigrants, including his own father, as narrators, just as the rich man needs the wandering storytellers. In this tale the father may offer his son something "different": perhaps no longer folkloric tales, as is the norm with IFA, but his own personal story. Or perhaps no longer the powerful Zionist narrative, as implied in the name "Avitsuk," but a story about wandering and hard-pressed people. Be that as it may, he tells a story that makes it possible for the immigrant father and integrated son to recognize each other again.

My intention has been to point out the possibilities suggested by the narrative activity. It can only be hoped that every one of us find his or her own "unique" story, which may make a Tikkun of the worlds of narrators and listeners alike.

Notes

1. On the Jewish storyteller, see Bar-Itzhak 1994.
2. See the motif of forgetting a story in "A Story Short" in the TV series *The Storyteller* (1988) by Jim Henson.
3. In this story and in the following ones, the guiding hand is that of Providence; hence these are religious legends. Bibliotherapy concerns a process by which the therapist mediates between the patient and the text, thus he or she can be regarded as the "guiding hand": He or she fosters the transformation of the literary text in the dialogue from an "alien" text, which has no interest in the reader, to a special "first-person" text. Moreover, even the text itself, being ambiguous—that is, having a potential of addressing various kinds of readers—may also address each reader individually.
4. This force exists not only in the general course of the text but also in the internal story told by the poor man, which concerns a conflict between Jews and gentiles over money. The landlord claims his share in the harvest through the tenant/narrator, and when the crop fails, he punishes the tenant for not paying and thrusts him and his family into a pit. Precisely in these circumstances the gentiles prove to be of various qualities; one of them helps the tenant and his family, and eventually saves them and brings about the adoption of the elder son (the rich man). In an analogue to the general course of the story, the redemption of the tenant's son also takes place through the contact with the single gentile who saved him. And here too the redemption occurs through the disconnection of the elder son's story from that of the rest of the family. This is of course not full redemption, as long as the rest of the family still suffers at the hands of the landlord. Complete redemption takes place only years later, after the reunion of father and son.
5. In Agnon's story the storyteller is named, but the rich man remains anonymous. This feature is significant, as it indicates that no less than the rich man—perhaps even more—the storyteller is the hero of the tale.
6. In bibliotherapy a similar thing happens. From the general assembly of stories and literary texts, those that can be included in the bibliotherapeutic dialogue become unique and special

time and again, according to the circumstances, character, and special needs of the patient. The single story, which is isolated from the text, is in many cases also the story that links the patient to the therapist.

BIBLIOGRAPHY

Agnon, S. Y. 1987. *The Tales of the Ba'al Shem Tov.* Jerusalem: Schocken. [Hebrew]

Bar-Itzhak, Haya. 1994. "Narration and the Components of Communication in the Jewish Folk Legend." *Fabula* 35: 261–81.

Bettelheim, Bruno. 1976. *The Uses of Enchantment: The Meaning and Importance of Fairy Tales.* New York: Knopf.

Rodkinzon, Michael Levi. 1897. *Adat Zadikim.* Lemberg: J.D. Suess. [Hebrew]

Zoran, Rachel. 2000. *The Third Voice: The Therapeutic Qualities of Literature and Their Application in Bibliotherapy.* Jerusalem: Carmel. [Hebrew]

THE QUEEN AND THE FISH

IFA 20959

NARRATED BY MINA ABU-ROKAN (ISRAEL, DRUZE)

There once lived a king in one of the lands. And there also lived a fisherman. The fisherman went fishing one day, when suddenly he caught a large, colorful fish. He did not sell it; instead, he gave it to the king.

The king liked the fish and let it swim in his pool, where he used to sit every day with his family and ministers.

And every day, as they were all sitting by the pool, the fish would spit tar at the queen. The queen was angry and said to the king: "Order the fisherman to come and explain why this fish keeps spitting tar at me!"

And the king ordered the fisherman to come forth, and he asked him: "Why does this fish spit tar at the queen?" And the fisherman told him he did not know.

In his anger, the king told the fisherman he had three days to tell him why the fish was spitting tar at the queen, or else he would lose his head. The fisherman returned home and told his daughter what had happened. The daughter went to the sheikh, told him the entire story, and asked him what to do.

And the sheikh said to her: "Go to the king and tell him: 'If the fish talks, the queen will be sorry.'" And he told her a story about one man who had caught a large, beautiful beast and kept it alive, for it was very beautiful indeed. One day, as the man sat down to eat with the beast by his side, water began to drip from the rock overhead into his empty cup. When the cup was full, the man wished to drink from it, but the beast pushed the cup away, and all the water spilled on the ground; the man picked up the cup and filled it up again in order to drink from it; but once again the beast pushed it away, and all the water spilled on the ground, until finally, in his wrath, the man beheaded the beast. But no sooner had he done so than he looked up and saw that the rock was dripping not water but blood; and he said: "I wish I had not beheaded the beast." And the sheikh said to the fisherman's daughter, "Go to the king and tell him: 'Better go to sleep angry than sorry; and if the fish talks, the queen will be sorry.'"

So the fisherman's daughter went to the king and told him the story exactly as the sheikh had told it to her. But the king answered that he wanted to know why the fish was spitting tar at the queen; and he said to her that she has two days left, or else he will behead both her and her father.

The following day the daughter returned to the sheikh, explaining that if she did not return to the king within two days and explain why the fish was spitting tar at the queen, the king would behead both her and her father.

So the sheikh told her another story: There once was a lumberjack who used to chop wood every day and sell it. One day he gave his horse some food to eat; but when he woke up the next morning, he saw gold where the horse's food had been. And he said in his heart that he wants to know where the horse found his gold, so that he could bring more and make himself rich enough to stop chopping wood. At night the man hid behind the trees and watched the horse, when suddenly the horse transformed into a young woman. The lumberjack said, "I can see you!"—but as soon as the woman heard him, she vanished, and with her vanished the gold. And the lumberjack was sorry he had spoken out and said, "I wish I had never spoken." And if the fish talks, the queen will be sorry.

And the sheikh told the fisherman's daughter, "Go to the king and tell him this story." So the fisherman's daughter went to the king and told him the story. But the king said to her, "I [still] don't know [the answer]. You have only one day left. If you do not tell me why this fish keeps spitting tar at the queen, I will behead both you and your father."

So the fisherman's daughter returned once again to the sheikh and repeated what the king had said. And the sheikh said to her, "Go back to the king and ask him to order the queen and her maid and all the other women in the palace to go to the pool, enter the water, and swim with the fish; then [he] will know why the fish has been spitting tar at the queen."

The king followed the sheikh's advice, and all the women in the palace obeyed—all except the queen, who refused to enter the pool with her maid. But at last she complied; and when she entered the pool and her maid disrobed, it turned out that the maid was not a woman but a man, and that the queen was cheating on the king with his servant. So the king divorced the queen, beheaded the servant, and gave many gifts to the fisherman and his daughter.

Transcribed by Lina Abu-Rokan and Galia Shenberg

COMMENTARY TO
"THE QUEEN AND THE FISH"

IFA 20959

TSAFI SEBBA-ELRAN

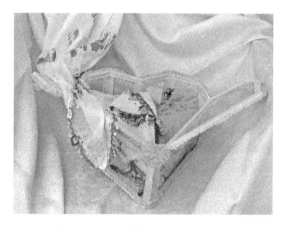

genuine culture of seafaring and seamanship was largely absent from Jewish life until the founding of the Israeli Merchant Fleet by the fledgling State of Israel. Even then resource allocation and social recognition remained far from obvious with regard to seamanship. In the absence of an indigenous history of seamanship, Hebrew seamen had to import traditions, behavior patterns, and idioms from British sea culture, often Judaizing and Hebraizing them to serve their particular needs (Sebba 2002, 17–22).

This disengagement from seafaring is evident also in the modern folktales documented by the Israel Folktale Archives (IFA), where sea tales—depicting the marine world and the seafarer's way of life—are relatively rare.[1] Fish, however, figure more prominently in the Israeli folktale, where they appear not only in the form of a Shabbat dish but also as messengers of God sent to reward the righteous, return the lost, rescue those stranded by storm, fulfill wishes, and lead sailors through shortcuts at sea. As symbols of blessedness and fertility, fish (gematric value: *dalet* + *gimmel* = 7) figure not only in folktales but also on Jewish amulets and in Jewish ceremonies and rituals, helping to make the "otherness" of the sublime sea more familiar and comprehensible even in the context of Jewish culture.[2]

I have chosen to discuss "The Queen and the Fish" (IFA 20959; AT *895) because it is featured prominently in the IFA, appearing in no fewer than twelve versions.[3] In addition, the tale is instructive with respect to the cultural symbolism of water in general and the marine realm in particular. The version presented here was transcribed in the Druze town of Isfiya, by Lina Abu-Rokan and Galia Shenberg. The narrator, Mina Abu-Rokan, was born in Isfiya in 1940 and is the daughter of Sheikh Lebib Abu-Rokan, a government official and religious leader well known among Israel's Druze population. Married since 1958 and a mother of seven, Mina Abu-Rokan has always taken an interest in folktales. As a child she listened avidly to stories told by her grandmother, her parents, and Druze elders—stories she now passes on to her own grandchildren and to anyone who may take an interest in the subject. It is worth noting that the version presented here is very similar, both thematically and poetically, to Jewish versions of the tale.

In what follows I shall focus on two themes I consider central to the tale; compare our version with parallel versions cataloged in the IFA; and reflect on familiar literary motifs featured in the tale.

The Scourging Water

At the story's two poles, as its title suggests, stand the fish and the queen. The fish gives the adulterous queen (in other versions, the promiscuous princess) away by spitting tar at her (in other versions, by laughing or spitting), and as a result the queen is punished.[4] In doing so, the fish represents and helps enforce an accepted social norm of female fidelity and chastity within the family.

The world to which the fish belongs is a distinctly male one. Brought to the palace by the fisherman (in other versions by the king's vizier or, in one variant, by the fisherman's daughter), the fish helps the king uncover the adulterous queen and regain control of life in the palace. That a fish should serve as a symbol of the male world is hardly surprising. In psychoanalysis fish have long been seen as a phallic symbol, and in Jewish culture, among others in the ancient Middle East, fish figured in contexts of fertility and sexuality. From antiquity the sea and the adjacent seashore and seaport were considered weak links in the communal chain, places where women and girls were frequently exposed to the threat of sexual violence, as the story type "The Man Who Never Took an Oath" (AT 938), as well as seven of the twelve seamen tales in the IFA, attest.[5]

The queen (or the princess), who in four versions refuses to see or stay with the fish, is motivated by warranted fear, then, for the fish is alien to the female environment on which she relies for social support. The solution to the riddle of the fish's behavior is delivered, however, by the fisherman's daughter (in other versions by her proxies), not by a male character. She consults with the sheikh—the representative of religion and wisdom—who offers her the solution to the mystery in the form of short fables she is to deliver to the king. Meant as hints to the king, the fables also serve to warn him that solving the riddle may bring calamity on his family. Different versions of the fables are included (if at all) in different variations of the tale. The first tells of a beast that repeatedly spills the water collected with great effort by its master; the latter kills the animal in retaliation, only to find that the water had been contaminated with blood (in other versions, with some drug or venom), and that the trusty animal had in fact saved him.[6] The fable hints, first, that we, as well as the fisherman's daughter, should trust the fish even if we do not yet understand its actions; and, second, that the water of the queen's pool may in some sense be contaminated.

The second fable tells of a horse that produces gold for its master, a lumberjack. Eager to uncover the horse's secret, the lumberjack follows the beast, only to find it has transformed into a young woman. He reveals himself to her, but she is startled and runs off with the gold.[7] Again we learn that we should trust animals and content ourselves with their hints without trying to decipher them in full. In two versions of the tale (IFA 7353 and 14934), a child (substituting for the fisherman's daughter) sees a royal vizier kicking a mare and warns him he might blind the foal in her womb. In a fable featured in four other versions (IFA 292, 2674, 4135, and 7353),[8] a loyal parrot brings the king a magical weed from which a fruit of youth sprouts. The king's envious vizier poisons the fruit, putting the blame on the parrot; the king has the parrot killed, only to find the truth about the fruit's wondrous qualities. In another fable (included in just one version, IFA 14934),[9] a loyal dog protects an infant from a snake while the child's parents are away; finding blood on the canine's mouth, the alarmed parents kill the dog, only to come belatedly to the truth. In all these stories, loyal animals help their masters, only to be killed or harmed due to the latter's incomprehension, ingratitude, and haste—faults replaced by deep remorse once the truth comes out.

The stories in our version all offer clues to solving the riddle of the fish's behavior. First, there is the fish's positive characterization as the king's loyal helper and benefactor, the equivalent of the other fables' trustworthy animals. Second, the threat posed by the first fable's poisoned water anticipates the queen's eventual trial-by-water. Finally, the second fable's horse-cum-woman hints at the servant's female disguise. What the sheikh's clues are meant to suggest to the king (and perhaps also to the fisherman's daughter) is that the solution to the fish's riddle has to do both with water and with the maid's true identity.

The sheikh's third and final suggestion returns us to the main plot's denouement. The fisherman's daughter, the sheikh now suggests, should tell the king to invite all the women of the palace for a swim in the pool; once the women disrobe, all present (in nearly all versions a large crowd of men) would be able to see that the queen's maid was in fact her male lover. In all versions except two, the king (or his delegate) has the queen (or the princess) and her lover (or lovers) killed, not without cruelty. In both versions that tell of "relations" with adulterous women, water functions not only as a "social enema" but also as a purifier, cleansing the adulteress of her impurity and sin, like ritual immersion in the *mikveh*.

That the story's denouement should take place around a pool is hardly an accident. In the Bible water serves as the backdrop for mythical lovers' encounters; in Greek mythology and its various folk derivatives, water represents sexual temptation in the form of nymphs and sirens. Poolside scenes offer their characters ample opportunity for undressing; and, as a female character in one version of our tale (IFA 16328) reminds us, our encounters with water often carry erotic meaning. It is therefore hardly surprising that the queen's lover and sex life should be exposed at the pool, or that water should play a role in exposing them. It is near water that the truth comes out; it is there that the adulterous female characters are either cleansed or, in most versions of our tale, punished and executed.

In Judaism, moreover, water is associated with laws concerning female adultery. According to Numbers 5:12–31 ("This is the law of jealousy when a woman goes astray and defiles herself while married to her husband," 5:29), a wife suspected of infidelity is to be subjected to a trial by water, whereby she must drink holy water from the Tabernacle mixed with dust from the Tabernacle floor. If the water harms her, she is pronounced guilty and punished; if she emerges unharmed, she is acquitted. A similar trial by water is described in Exodus 32:20 where, to be forgiven for their worship of the Golden Calf, the Israelites must drink water mixed with dust from the calf's graven image. The link these biblical associations form among water, sexuality, and purity/impurity hints further at the queen's adultery and anticipate her eventual punishment.

Interestingly, the fisherman in our version sends his daughter to the sheikh instead of going himself. In other versions, the messenger who solves the fish's riddle and exposes the adulterous queen is a wondrous boy or dwarf, the unnatural offspring of the fisherman's daughter or wife.[10] In medieval versions, the king's delegate (eunuch, deputy, etc.) travels far and wide in search of a person capable of solving the fish's riddle, until a young girl is found who is up to the task. In all versions, then, the character responsible for uncovering the truth, in person or by proxy, is a young woman; and it is precisely this young woman whom the tale seems to address all along.[11]

Our tale describes a young girl who undergoes an initiation of sorts by mediating between the sheikh and the king. The girl, we learn early in the story, is chaste (for example, she wears a veil) and a virgin. All along the sheikh's fables warn her to stay away from the water. The sheikh does not wish to solve the riddle for her; but neither does he want her to ask the fish. What we, through the girl, seem to learn from the water (the fish, the pool) is the traditional conservative lesson that women's proper place is at home. The female characters in the tale's various versions—the princess shut in her room like Solomon's daughter in her tower; the queen confined to the palace and to female company alone—are constrained in their movement, isolated from male or even human company, required to remain sexually pure, and punished cruelly for breaking these rules. Their only choice is between chastity, fidelity, and the social seclusion they entail—and death. In this respect, our tale continues a long tradition of maritime gynophobia according to which women bring bad luck at sea, fracture the male fraternity of seamen, and tempt men by exploiting their weaknesses only to ensnare them in the end.[12]

Our tale underscores, then, the links between bodies of water (and water in general) and sexuality or eroticism. Moreover, it stresses the *scourging* role of water: The same water that casts women in a negative light also helps consecrate female fidelity, chastity, and domesticity via the distinctly male ritual of the adulterous woman's purification and penalization.

THE SILENCE OF THE FISH

Those who keep silent are sometimes said to be "quiet as a fish," perhaps because fish, unlike other animals, make no sounds, and the sea with which they are associated is often identified with silence. The association of marine animals, especially fish, with sounds or aural stimuli has developed from this widespread assumption. The sirens, with their lethal singing, tempted seamen to moor their ships and then killed them. To have the sea-goddess Amphitrite, Poseidon first sent a singing dolphin to woo her (Fink 1998, 196, 59). Seductive singing also characterizes Andersen's little mermaid, who in order to become human must give up her beautiful voice and let her tongue be severed. As these examples and many others indicate, the voices and sounds of the sea have retained their mysterious, magical allure in cultural consciousness across the ages.

Against this background, it is not insignificant that it is by laughing, singing, speaking, or secreting various substances from its mouth that the fish in the tale's various versions delivers its covert message. First, it is against the conventional association of fish with silence that our fish's ability to produce sounds is seen as a marvel, proving the validity and reliability of its message. (The fish in our tale is similar in this respect to the gold fish or whale that teaches the language of animals to a boy in AT 670.) Second, as noted earlier, the sounds produced by the fish are culturally associated with sexuality (and are in this respect a contemporary folk variant of the sirens' seductive voice).[13] Representing as it does fertility and sexuality, the fish's voice, certainly its laughter, discloses the sexual meaning of its actions. The tension between silence and speech is thus a guiding element in the tale. The fisherman's daughter—the sheikh insists all along—should persuade the king to keep quiet. Not once, nor twice, but three times the fisherman's daughter repeats her warning, "If the fish talks, the queen will be sorry" (a phrase the story's transcriber took care to write down on a separate line). Similarly, the two fables embedded in the tale instruct us to respect the animals' silence and accept their actions without further questioning. By asking her to warn the king not to reveal the queen's secret, the sheikh aims to teach the fisherman's daughter that silence is sometimes better than attempts to expose the truth. Unconvinced, the king insists that the fisherman's daughter interpret the fish's laughter. Finally, when the queen's secret is revealed and the adulteress is punished, all seems to return to order.

The sheikh's efforts to forestall the king's attempts to interpret the fish's hints suggest, however, that the tale may also have an alternative, pro-female message, at odds with its harsh message concerning the fate of wayward women. According to this alternative interpretation, the sheikh, wishing to protect the queen, asks the fisherman's daughter to appease the king with fables to dissuade him from looking further into the fish's actions. The sheikh's lesson to the fisherman's daughter, in this interpretation of the tale, is not the harsh one about chastity and sexuality but rather about the importance of silence. Though the story cannot but end in full knowledge and with a thorough interpretation of the fish's clues, for a while it seems as though the sheikh aims to protect the queen, using his fables to show the young girl another, less conventional, method of coping with the king's demands, a method of subterfuge and silence. She should accept things as they are and keep the truth under cover, to leave the wayward woman unpunished and the violated social norms unrectified. As she finished telling the story, the narrator told the transcriber, "And this is the story I've told you, Lina, and hid under your hand." The meaning of the comment is not entirely clear to me; it seems, however, that the narrator was hiding something in her hand and alerted the transcriber to this fact. Perhaps she meant to stress that hiding is an option, using her gesture to reinforce the sheikh's message that covering, hiding, and keeping quiet are important social skills—no less important than honesty, fidelity, or chastity.

The fisherman's daughter may thus be interpreted as representing a social alternative to women's conventional status. The expectation that she will solve the riddle; her intelligence and resourcefulness, which some of the versions emphasize; her freedom of movement, which enables her to serve as a messenger among the king, the sheikh, and her father—all these are antithetical to the conservative restrictions imposed on the tale's central female figure, the queen. That this alternative is present in our tale (alongside the more conventional view of women's status and fate) is a fact well worth noting.

The tension between silence and speech is typical of numerous seafaring tales, especially those of an erotic nature commonly associated with seaman (Sebba 2002, 65–67). Seafaring tales about the value of family, especially those told on shore, often feature manipulative ploys whose purpose is on the one hand to tell, on the other to conceal or obscure the violation of social norms. In this respect, as in others already discussed, no character is more apt than the fish to deliver the enigmatic message of the queen's infidelity. The message's erotic nature; its conservative focus on the value of virginity or fidelity; and the speech used to deliver it, which contains within it the possibility of silence—all these place the fish in our tale in a unique position from which we can learn much about the sea as a cultural symbol and as a space of lived experience.

NOTES

1. Tales of the sea are included in the IFA under the categories "seafarers," "sailors," "seamen," "fish," "the Red Sea," "the Dead Sea," "the Mediterranean," and "lakes."
2. The fish often substitute for other animals in Jewish tales as, for example, in the "animal languages" folktales (AT 670). See Noy 1971, 171–208; Shenhar 1970, 58–59.
3. The versions of the tale known to me are IFA 292, 2036, 2674, 2996, 4135, 4741, 6367, 7353, 7572, 14934, 16328, and 20959. IFA 4135 is the only version without a fish; instead, the king dreams of forty crows pecking his head. This latter version was published in Noy 1967, tale no. 48, pp. 95–98. One of the inner tales in the story (about a dove spilling a poisoned cup on its master) was published in Noy 1976, tale no. 34, pp. 92–93. Our story appears also in several medieval collections as Ibn Zabara's *Sefer Hasha'ashuim* (*Book of Delights*) along with an Indian version of the story. The laughing fish is replaced in Zabara's version with a jumping monkey, probably under the influence of other familiar versions from the Middle Ages. See Ibn Zabara 1925, 35–43.
4. In our version (IFA 20959), the fish spits tar. In another version (IFA 4741), the fish pelts the queen with three pieces of coal. In yet other versions the fish laughs or spits.
5. For an extended discussion of this tale, see Yassif 1984–85, 32–37. See also Corbin 1995, 14.
6. In other versions the animal is an eagle, a bird, a fowl, or a parrot; in the international type AT 916 II C, it is a falcon.
7. This fable resembles Aesop's "The Hen That Laid Golden Eggs," where the titular hen is slaughtered because its owner hopes to get rich quickly by finding a lump of gold in its entrails.
8. See also AT 916 II D.
9. See also AT 178A.
10. In these versions, the fisherman (or lumberjack) finds a skull and grinds it to dust after it threatens to kill forty men. The fisherman's daughter accidentally swallows the dust and is impregnated by it; she gives birth to a boy, usually through her nose or by spitting, so that her virginity remains intact. This version of the tale is discussed in the context of immaculate conception in Zlotnik 1945–46, 49–58.

11. The only exception is IFA 16328, in which the message about female infidelity is delivered by a fish peddler who alerts the man of the house to his wife's suspicious aversion to fish.
12. Sebba 2002, 37, note 1; Ariel 1999, 7–42.
13. See IFA 2727.

BIBLIOGRAPHY

Ariel, Avraham. 1999. "Joseph Conrad's Final Victim." In *Seamen*, 7–42. Israel: Ladori: [Hebrew]
Corbin, Alain. 1995. *The Lure of the Sea*. Middlesex: Penguin.
Fink, Gerhard. 1998. *Who's Who in Greek Mythology*. Jerusalem: Hed Artzi. [Hebrew]
Ibn Zabara, Joseph Ben Meir. 1925. *Book of Delights*. Ed. Israel Davidson. Berlin: Eshkol. [Hebrew]
Noy, Dov. 1967. *Jewish Folktales from Morocco*. Jerusalem: Jewish Agency, Haifa Municipality, and Israel Folktale Archives. [Hebrew]
———. 1971. "The Jewish Versions of the 'Animal Languages' Folktale (AT 670): A Typological-Structural Study." In *Scripta Hierosolymitana*, 171–208. Jerusalem: Magnes.
———. 1976. *The Jewish Animal Tale of Oral Tradition*. Haifa: Haifa Municipality, Ethnological Museum and Folklore Archives, Israel Folktale Archives. [Hebrew]
Sebba, Tsafi. 2002. "Like a Tree Planted on Sea Waves: The Personal Narrative as a Door to the Seaman's World." Master's thesis, Tel Aviv University. [Hebrew]
Shenhar, Aliza. 1970. "Folktales of the Sea." Master's thesis, Hebrew University. [Hebrew]
Yassif, Eli. 1984–85. "The Story about the Man Who Never Took an Oath: From a Jewish to an Israeli Oikotype." *Jerusalem Studies in Jewish Folklore* 8: 32–37. [Hebrew]
Zlotnik, Y. L. 1945–46. "Those Conceived Unnaturally." *Sinai* 18: 49–58. [Hebrew]

THE PHARMACIST'S BURIAL

IFA 21021

NARRATED BY ZALMAN (KASTROL) BEN-AMOS (BELARUS)

1Moray ve-rabosay
azoy vi ikh bin a magid,
un gey fun shtot tsu shtot
ikh bin gekumen in der shtetl Samakhlavitsh.
5 Oy, moray ve-rabosay, ikh bin gekumen in der shtetle Samakhlavitsh,
meg ikh aykh dertseyln vos iz dortn geshen.
Es iz geshtorbn dortn der apteyker, yimakh shmoy vezikhroy.
Er hot gegesen trayfene zakhn un er hot mekhalel geven dem shabes.
Un ez er iz geshtorbn, hot di familye im gevolt bagrobn.
10 Oy, vos hobn zey im geton?
Me hot im begrobn in der erd.
Oy, moray ve-rabosay, oyf morgn, az di familye iz gekumen oyfen keyver,
vos habn zey gezen?
Di erd hot im aroysgevorfn.
15 Moray ve-rabosay,
Di familye hot nit gehat vu ahintsuton zikh mit im.
Hot zi im genumen, dem mes, dem peyger, un araingevorfn in taykh.
Ober oyf morgn, az zey zenen gekumen tsum breg taykh,
vos hobn zey gezen, moray ve-rabosay?
20 Der mes ligt vayter baym breg fun taykh.
Oy, moray ve-rabosay, di familye hot nit gehat vu ahintsuton zikh mit im.
Hobn zey bashlosn, zey hobn im genumen un geleygt a fayer.
Un hobn genumen un im aroyfgeleygt oyfn fayer.
Oy, ober der roshe iz geven aza groyser, aza treyfnyak,
25 Az der fayer hot im nit gebrent.
Un, moray ve-rabosay, der muser-haskel fun dem vos iz?
Az me darf zayn frum,
me darf nit zayn kayn treyfnyak,
me darf hitn gots toyre.
30 Oy, moray ve-rabosay, az ir vet geyn in gots veg, un ir vet hitn di toyre,
vet aykh der fayer brenen,
der vaser vet aykh trenken,
un di erd vet aykh nemen.
Bimheyro beyomeynu, omeyn.

"The Pharmacist's Burial" Translation

1 My masters and teachers,

Because I am a *maggid*,*

And go preaching from town to town,

I once came to the town of Samakhlalovitch

5 Oy, my masters and teachers,

I came to town of Samakhlalovitch

I have to tell you what happened there.

The pharmacist—may his name and memory be blotted out—died there.

He used to eat *treif*† food and desecrated the Sabbath.

10 And when he died, the family wanted to bury him.

Oy, what did they do to him?

They buried him in the ground.

Oy, my masters and teachers, in the morning, when the family came to the grave,

What did they see?

The earth had cast him out.

15 My masters and teachers,

The family did not know where to put him.

They took him, the deceased, the corpse, and tossed him into the river.

The next morning, when they came to the riverbank,

What did they see, my masters and teachers?

20 There was the deceased again, lying on the riverbank.

Oy, my masters and teachers, the family didn't know where to put him.

They decided, they took him and built a fire,

And went and laid him in the fire.

Oy, but he was so wicked, such a sinner,

25 That the fire didn't burn him.

And what, my masters and teachers, is the moral of this?

You should be pious,

You should not be sinners,

You should observe God's Torah.

30 Oy, my masters and teachers, follow God's way and observe the Torah.

So that the fire will burn you,

The water will swallow you,

And the ground will take you.

Speedily in our days, amen.

---

* A preacher
† Nonkosher

Commentary to
"The Pharmacist's Burial"

21021

Dan Ben-Amos

My late father wondered from time to time about what I was actually doing. "Professor-shmofessor, but what do you do?" he would ask. For sure, he had long resigned himself to the fact that I would not be among the pioneers like he was. After all, the roads were paved, and it was no longer necessary to put over the land, as he did, "a dress of concrete and cement."[1] He also realized that the newcomers to Israel had their own houses, many of them better than his own, and it was not necessary to build new developments as he had. In his heart he had secretly hoped that I would at least be an army officer, as he was in the Haganah,[2] or an engineer, as he wished to be but could not, because World War I disrupted his plans. My preoccupation with folktales seemed somewhat odd to him, but he tolerated it. I could not say that he did not love books, poetry, and theater, and could not appreciate the importance of folktales, but for him all these were considered hobbies, not real work. Once, when he read a Hebrew manuscript of an article of mine that he found on the table in our "living room"—as we pretentiously called that room in our shack—he said to me: "You know, my son, you are pretty smart." I was surprised because this was the first time he had given me such a compliment, qualified as it was. I thought that he had read my article and followed the logical development of my ideas, or my arguments against my critics. But in answering my question he said: "If you can make a *parnuseh*[3] from *bobeh mayses*,[4] you are pretty smart."

When my parents visited with me at my home in Philadelphia, my father queried me more about the actual nature of my work. Two years earlier, I had returned from Benin, Nigeria (Bradbury 1957; idem 1973; Ryder 1969; Roth 1968; Spahr 2006), and I explained to him what I had done there. "In that case," he said, "let me tell you some stories, and you will record them." After I had set up the tape recorder, he stood up and assumed a posture, the significance of which was not clear to me at the time, and told the tale "The Pharmacist's Burial."

Upon completion, I asked my father, but he was not able to tell me from whom he had heard this parodic sermon, nor whether there was any specific preacher at whom it was directed. By

1968, forty-four years after he had left his hometown of Minsk, Belarus, the story blended into the pool of his cultural memory on which he drew for this performance.

Parodies of sermons were hardly a new phenomenon, and they are certainly not unique to Jewish society. The complaint of the prophet Jeremiah, "I have become a constant laughing-stock, everyone jeers at me" (Jeremiah 20:7), evidences the social attitude toward a variety of preachers that has prevailed since biblical times. The editors of the midrashic literature included sermons in their collections but not parodies on sermons. When a particular exegetical interpretation was amenable to a humoristic interpretation, the editors made the audience, rather than the preacher, the target of the satire. For example, while it is possible to consider the comment of Rabbi (second century) in his sermon—"One woman in Egypt brought forth six hundred thousand at a birth" (Song of Songs Rabbah, 87 [1:15,3])—to be a parody of the sermon, the editors presented it as a rhetorical strategy to wake up the dozing audience rather than as a ridicule of the preacher.

Parodies are available in Jewish literature from the end of the twelfth and the beginning of the thirteenth century (Davidson 1907, 3–29), but these ridicule neither sermons nor their preachers. Yet in the Christian church there were already, at that time, parodic sermons. Sander Gilman, who studied them, has distinguished between Latin parodies, which are extant in famous preachers' collections, and which were performed in churches and monasteries, and popular vernacular parodies, which were delivered in rural churches, markets, city squares, and along the highways but which are now extinct (Gilman 1974, 11). The earliest evidence for parodic sermons is available from 1260, when they were condemned in a regional church proclamation by the council of the Province of Cognac (Gilman 1974, 18; Hoffmann-Krayser 1903). The parodic sermons were delivered in the medieval Christian church during the *Festum innocentium* (Feast of the Holy Innocents), celebrated on the twenty-eighth of December, in commemoration of the children whom Herod murdered after the apparition of the star to the Wise Men (Matthew 2:16–18). In these festivities, children were permitted to elect a child-bishop, and the occasion served as the core ritual from which the celebration known as *Festum stultorum* (Feast of Fools) was developed (Gilman 1974, 16–28). It was celebrated on or about the feast of circumcision, which took place on the first of January, and it was at this feast that parodic sermons were performed (Gilman 1974, 16–28). In Jewish society, the Purim holiday served as the context for the ritualistic formation of parody (Davidson 1907, 209–63),[5] but over the years parodies extended beyond the boundaries of the Purim holiday and were applied to different social aspects. Parodic sermons are available in the nineteenth and twentieth centuries (Saperstein 1989, 91, n. 4).

During the nineteenth century preaching became an integral part of community life in the Pale of Settlement. There were two types of preachers: community-appointed and itinerant preachers. While the community-appointed preachers were salaried public servants, the livelihood of the itinerant preachers depended on public generosity in the communities they visited. They were poor and lonely people, dedicated to their mission, and their only gratification was their audience's admiration. Some of them were learned men who knew the Bible backward and forward, and were familiar with the ethical literature. They preached in the Lithuanian cities and *shtetlekh* to an audience that knew and respected their religious value. Every sermon lasted long hours, during which the preacher moralized, appealed to God to improve the lot of His people, urged his listeners to follow their religion and tradition, consoled the miserable, and threatened the sinners and the secular Jews with severe punishments, describing horrific scenes in hell. The audience, which filled the synagogue to capacity, responded in affirmation and sobbing (Assaf 2002, 135, 428 n. 67; Caplan 2002, 43–58, 127–31; Gliksberg 1940; Greenbaum 1995, 110–15; Luz 1988, 16, 107–8, 217–20).[6]

The present text is an oral parody of such sermons. The repeated usage of the addressing formula "my masters and teachers" (lines 1, 5, 12, 15, 19, 21, 26, 30), which serves as a rhetoric shift in unfolding the narrative, the immediate repetition (lines 2 and 3; 9 and 11; 19, 21, 22, 23), and the accumulative repetition (lines 11–31) are distinctive features of oral performance (Jousse 1990), and the exaggerated use of some of them is a parodic device. It is possible to assume that, in the split and divided Jewish society of the second half of the nineteenth century, the *Maskilim*, who "stood for the spread of the Enlightenment among the Jews but rejected full integration in Russian society" (Luz 1988, 29),[7] the Zionists, and the socialists ridiculed the preachers. But does this parody ridicule preaching in general, the sermon as a genre, or an individual preacher whose style, themes, and manners it imitates? When my late father performed this sermon for me, for him the image of the preacher it targeted had already been blurred. But there is evidence that this parodic sermon targeted a specific preacher who was popular in the cities and *shtetlekh* of Lithuania and Belarus, singling out his preaching style and themes. This evidence is to be found in the short story of Eleazar Schulmann (1837–1904), "*Ikesh u-ftaltol*" ("Stubborn and Perversed"), which appeared in *Ha-Shahar* in 1873:[8]

The preacher of Zelem! Who among us has not heard of him? Is not he the man for whom the earth trembled when he spoke, and who uprooted mountains with the words of his mouth? Is not he the man of whom all the jokers make fun, and whose speeches they imitate! Has not he already voiced his morals in Palzah,[9] for several days and miraculously also in Palzah "he took up his theme"[10] and amazed all his listeners.

And so that you, dear reader, will be amazed as well, we shall quote for you a few of the words he spoke in Palzah, saying: "My masters, the earth was filled with lawlessness" (Genesis 6:11, 13; Ezekiel 8:17), and none cares. Crime piles upon crime, and none cries like a crane. . . .[11] My masters, would not a hen raise its voice when it lays an egg, and you give birth to evil spirits and demons with your evil acts, and still you do not make a peep. The leopard has its spots and would not hide them—and you hide spots and your evil acts. . . . The grocer let you buy on credit, and you go around,[12] but he let you buy on credit balm and medicine, and you go around your hair and beard with scissors. Let it be that this will be your last round and the ground will swallow you! "For evil men will be cut off" (Psalms 37:9) whoever wears short clothes, his days will be shortened, and whoever wears long trousers, the days of his leprosy on his belly muscles will lengthen for your top hats worms will eat you up, for your gloves heaven will strike you dead. This too has to be said: "My masters! When an evil man dies, all the evil men of the land quack together, if he is buried in the ground would not the ground throw him away saying: 'you do not have any share and inheritance[13] in me'; if he is thrown into the fire, he will not burn, and if he is placed in front of worms, they will turn away from him. Therefore my masters, do not sin, 'do what is just and right,'[14] then the land will swallow you, you will burn together in fire, and the worms will eat you up."[15]

In the first paragraph of his story, Schulmann attested that already in his lifetime this preacher suffered the ridicule of jokesters, and was subject to parodic imitations of his sermons. Moreover he singled out the present parodic sermon, with a minimal variation—worms instead of a river—as an example of the arsenal of ridicule with which his critics assailed him. In his account Schulmann assumed a satiric attitude toward the preacher, changing his town's name from Kelme to "Zelem": an "idol" in Hebrew (2 Kings 11:18) and a "crucifix" in Yiddish. To his readers it was clear that he referred to the *Maggid* of Kelme, a well-known figure in the second half of the nineteenth century in the cities of Lithuania and Belarus:

From 1859–1860 and onward, a short, skinny, bearded man, with dark complexion and dark untidy hair, about forty years old, traveled through the cities of Lithuania and Zamut.[16] He probably was from the city of Kelme in the Kaunas [Yiddish: Kovno] district, and so he was known. He preached and moralized in houses of study, captivating the masses, and in particular the pious women. His sources were not the Talmud and the midrashic literature, and he hardly drew from them. But his forceful rhetoric and sharp tongue were amazing. He preached in a powerful voice for three to four hours without a break, standing on the podium and a bucket of water at his feet, from which he drank from time to time until it was almost empty. His sermons included not so many moral lessons and clever fables; rather they were distinguished by his verbosity. He cursed those who did not observe the Shabbat, dressed in non-Jewish garbs, and so forth. Such were his metaphors: "The rooster has a comb on his head, but it would not comb his head on the Shabbat, while the tailor does not have a comb, and he combs his head on the Shabbat. Whoever puts on white vest on his heart, his heart would be shredded to pieces." In most of his sermons he described what happened in hell, and the suffering of the *Apikoroses*[17] there, as if he were an eyewitness. His following syllogism is well known: "The *Apikoroses*, may their name be blotted out, say that there is no hell, but the proof is that Mapu[18] and his friends were certainly in hell, and this is the proof that there is hell." The rabbis did not like his sermons, but they did not protest them because the people followed him, and every time he preached, the house of study was full to capacity. (Syrkin 1918, 197–98)

This description, which is based on memory, is corroborated by the recollection of others who were not necessarily eyewitnesses but who drew their information from oral tradition or from written or oral testimonies of the contemporaries of the *Maggid* of Kelme, as the preacher Moshe-Yitzhak ben Noah (1828–99 or 1900) was known. He was likely born in the *shtetl* of Jeziernica, near the city of Slonim, in Belarus. He was first appointed as a preacher at the age of twenty-two in the town of Kelme—hence his nickname—but after three years the community expelled him for defaming one of its wealthy men (see Friedmann 1926, 8). He then served as a community-appointed preacher in several towns and at the same time became an itinerant preacher, traveling as distance permitted.[19] In his sermons he preached the ideas of the Musar movement, but he was not an actual disciple of Rabbi Israel Salanter (1810–83), the founder of this movement, and only spread its ideas.[20]

He moralized against sins affecting the relationship of man to God and against sins affecting the relationship of man to his fellow man. He talked mainly about integrity, honesty, fairness in negotiation, and about strict observance of weights and measures in trade—on the usage of precise and well-balanced scales—on avoidance of any lies and deceptions, on sincere intention in prayers, and on studying the Torah for its own sake, and so forth, and so forth. His principle moralizing strategy was to threaten with the punishments awaiting the sinners. He skillfully, vividly, and imaginatively described the Seven Departments of Hell, the lashes of fire and sulphur, the terrifying, gaping inferno that was ready to swallow up the wicked men—a real Jewish incarnation of Dante. His enflaming sermons centered on the themes of the rewards and punishments for good and evil. His performances, in a traditional, melancholic melody, shocked his listeners and caused—not only in the women's section—scenes of mass hysteria, punctuated by the sound of sobbing, sighs, and groans. Fear and terror struck the audience, bringing them to a mass confession and repentance for sins they committed and did not commit, as they were scared by the scenes of hell and captivated by his powerful locution (Lichtenstein 1961–79, 66–68).

Indeed, the available descriptions of him sermonizing attest to a sweeping audience enthusiasm.

> While he preached the house of study transformed into a "valley of vision" (Isaiah 22:1, 5). The men's section and the women's section were full to capacity, and many sat on the window sills and the tables, and all were holding their breath, listening to the sermon. The powerful and pleasant preacher's voice was rolling over the dense sea of heads, and an electric current seemed to pass through the listeners, who were carried away, in spite of themselves, by his pleasant voice from the lower to a mystical and a spiritual world. (Gliksberg 1940, 453)

In contrast to his listeners, the *Maskilim*—whom he critically targeted—ridiculed him, and the present parody, which is based on a logical paradox, is one of those that are extant. It entered into the canon of Jewish humor and is included in several joke anthologies (Ausubel 1977, 382;

Druyanow 1935–38, 1:184, no. 475; Mendelsohn 1951, 59; Miller 1937, 195, vh. "maggidim," no.22; Olsvanger 1965, 167–69, no. 263; Olsvanger 1949, 46–47, no. 51).[21]

But in the process of the parody's canonization, its wit somehow dulled. It transformed from a performed to a reported joke. Quite likely, the dramatic imitation was the mode of ridicule employed in mockery of the *Maggid* of Kelme, as Schulmann seems to describe. My father reconstructed such a performance as he learned it in Minsk, his hometown in Belarus, where he came in direct contact with the society and culture of the audience and the critics of the *Maggid* of Kelme, though he was born in 1898, shortly before the *maggid*'s death. Such a direct cultural contact is absent from most of the published versions, and even the narrators of the two other IFA versions, who told the parody orally, were distant from its primary culture, and hence did not tell but reported the joke.[22]

NOTES

In preparing the English version of this article, I was assisted by David Assaf, Dvora Gilula, Joshua Levinson, and David Roskies, and I would like to thank all of them.

1. The metaphor occurs in a popular song known variously as "*Shir Boker*" ("Morning Song") or "*Shir la-Moledet*" ("A Song for the Motherland"), written by the Israeli poet Nathan Alterman (1910–70) and included in a volume of his collected songs, *Pizmonim ve-Shirei Zemer*, 2:302–3. The poem is sung to a melody by Daniel Sambursky [Samburski] (1909–77), which he first composed for a play by Shaul (Sally) Levin, *Die einzige Loesung* ("The Only Solution"; 1931), produced in Berlin and then performed in the film *L'Chayim Hadashim* (*The Land of Promise*; 1935) with the words of Alterman's song (Samburski 1969). For the song and melody, see Bronzaft and Samburski, eds., 1947–51. The song is available on several recordings, one of which is *Alterman* (Tel Aviv: Mediadirect, 2004), 1, no. 15. It was among the Zionist songs that shaped the *Yishuv* culture of the 1930s and 1940s (Ben-Yehuda 1990, 96).
2. The underground military organization in the *Yishuv* period in *Eretz Yisrael* from 1920 to 1948. For studies of its history, see Allon 1970, 133–35; Bauer 1970; Dinur, ed., 1954–72; Syrkin 1947; Yona 2001.
3. "Make a living" in Yiddish; a Hebrew word of unknown origin that is first seen in the Talmudic-midrashic literature (e.g. Babylonian Talmud, *Berakhot* 50b). Its pronunciation in modern Hebrew is /parnasáh/, but my father, who spoke Hebrew fluently, gave it a deliberate Yiddish twist.
4. Yiddish for "folktales"; literally, "grandmother's tales."
5. Steinschneider 1902–4: 46 (1902): 176, 187, 275, 280, 372, 376, 473, 478, 567–82; 47 (1903): 84–89, 169–80, 279–86, 360–70, 468–74; 48 (1904): 242–47, 504–9.
6. Direct reference to the *Maggid* of Kelme (Caplan 2002, 127).
7. For a recent historical study about them and their movement, see Feiner 2004.
8. *Ha-Shahar* 4 (1873): 281–93. *Ha-Shahar* was the leading literary Hebrew monthly of the period, published in Vienna (1868–84).
9. A fictional name.
10. Schulmann's satirical description of the preacher is studded with biblical phrases that intertextually add a satirical dimension. The phrase "he took up his theme" is associated in the Bible with the figure of Balaam, son of Beor in Pethor, whom Balak hired to curse the

Israelites as they crossed the desert and approached their destination. See Numbers 23:7, 18; 24:3, 15, 20, 21, 23.

11. In idiomatic Hebrew, "to shout at the top of one's voice."

12. Schulmann quotes a pun the preacher made. To sell on credit and to go around something are two verbs that pun in Hebrew.

13. A biblical idiom that recurs in Genesis 31:14; Deuteronomy 10:9, 12:12, 14:27, 14:29, and 18:1.

14. A biblical idiom that recurs in prophetic discourse, for example, Jeremiah 22:3, 15; 23:5; 33:15; Ezekiel 18:5, 21; 33:14, 19.

15. Quoted from Davidson, ed., 1972, 2:264–65. Motifs E411.0.6, "Earth rejects buried body," and *E411.0.6.1, "Water rejects corpse," occur already in midrashic literature in references to the corpses of the Egyptians: "Another Interpretation: *Thou Stretchedst Out Thy Right Hand*. This tells that the sea would cast them [the dead Egyptians] out to the land and the land would throw them back into the sea." *Mekhilta de-Rabbi Ishmael*, 2:67–68 (Tractate Shirata 9 [Exodus 15:12–16]).

16. Samogitia, the region of western Lithuania, known in Hebrew and Yiddish as Zamet or Zamut; in Lithuanian: Žemaitisa; in Polish: Žmudž; in Russian: Zhmud.

17. In rabbinical literature, and henceforth in Jewish traditions and languages, the term refers to heretics, and to Jews who deny the basic tenets of Judaism (BT *Sanhedrin* 99b–100a). The term derives from the name of the Greek philosopher Epicurus (341–270 BCE), who sought to build his philosophy on the basis of experience. For discussions of his life and teachings, see Bailey 1928; Diogenes Laertius 1995, "Epicurus," in *Lives of Eminent Philosophers* 2:528–677 (bk. 10.).

18. Abraham Mapu (1808–67) was one of the major exponents of the Haskalah movement and the author of *Ahavat Ẕiyyon* ("The Love of Zion," Vilna, 1853), a biblical novel that represents a turning point in modern Hebrew literature. He was born in Slobodka, a suburb of Kaunas (Kovno), the same district from which the *Maggid* of Kelme came. For his biography, see Patterson 1964.

19. According to information his son offered to Kalman Lichtenstein, he served as a preacher in the following cities: Kelme (1840–52), Slonim (1847–50), Zagare [Yiddish: Zhager] (1853–57), Oshmyany (1858–59), Minsk (1860–62), Slonim (1863–80), Mlawa (1881–85), Grodno (1886–97). In 1898 he moved to Lida, where he died. See Lichtenstein 1961–79, "The History of the Slonim Jewish Community," 275, note 314. Lichtenstein points out that this chronology is not consistent with information available from other sources.

20. Descriptive, evaluative, and historical writings about the *Maggid* of Kelme are available. A selection is: Gliksberg 1940, 453–56; Katz 1954, vol. 2: 395–402; Lichtenstein 1961–79, 66–68; Luz 1988, 16; Mark 1958, 222–36; Etkes 1982, 198–99; Syrkin 1918, 197–98.

21. The *Maggid* of Kelme became the butt of jokes and anecdotes; see Lipson 1968, 1:18, 73, 163–67, 231, nos. 45, 184, 409–15, 632; 2:42–43,105–7, 208, nos. 964, 965, 1163–67, 1538; 3:41, 146, 164, 245–48, nos. 1871, 2179, 2225, 2489–92.

22. There are two other versions of this tale in the IFA. The first is IFA 7745, "The Sinner's Punishment," which was told by Itsik Fishman (Poland) and recorded by Shelomoh Shtifman:

> One of the *maggids* stood on the synagogue podium and preached in a pleasant melody:
>   There was a sinner who died. Naturally, they buried him, but the ground did not want to accept him. They threw him into the water, but the river ejected him. They

threw him into the fire, but the fire did not consume him. The *maggid* took a short break and said: "If you are righteous, I promise you that the ground will accept you, the river will not eject you, and also the fire will consume you."

The second tale, IFA 9755, "So Said the Maggid," was told by Moshe Zhabotinsky (Kiev, Ukraine) and recorded by Malka Cohen; it was published in Cohen 1974, 116, no. 92:

A *maggid* preached in a house of study: "Embarrassed are the eyes that see that: Women are going out to the market with uncovered hair. How great is the sin, and how severe is the punishment!"

The *maggid* illustrated his statement with a story about a woman who died. The next day they found her grave open, and the corpse lying face down. A Hasid happened to come to the cemetery, and seeing the corpse, he said: "This impudent woman well deserves not being accepted by the ground, because she walked around the market without a head covering."

And also I, as a *maggid*, say: "This will be the end of all the impudent women. Therefore, Jewish women, watch out to have your head covered, so when your day comes, the ground will accept you."

About the distinction between performed and reported speech, see Bauman 1977; Bauman 1986; and Hymes 1975.

BIBLIOGRAPHY

Allon, Yigal. 1970. *Shield of David: The Story of Israel's Armed Forces*. London: Weidenfeld and Nicolson.

Alterman, Nathan. 1979. *Pizmonim ve-Shirei Zemer*. 2 vols. Tel Aviv: Hakibbutz Ha'meuchad. [Hebrew]

Assaf, David, ed. 2002. *Journey to a Nineteenth-Century Shtetl: The Memoirs of Yekhezkel Kotik*. Raphael Patai Series in Jewish Folklore and Anthropology. Detroit: Wayne State University Press.

Ausubel, Nathan. 1977 [1948]. *A Treasury of Jewish Folklore*. New York: Crown.

Bailey, Cyril. 1928. *The Greek Atomists and Epicurus*. Oxford: Clarendon Press, 1928.

Bauer, Yehudah. 1970. *From Diplomacy to Resistance: A History of Jewish Palestine 1939–1945*. Philadelphia: Jewish Publication Society of America.

Bauman, Richard. 1977. *Verbal Art as Performance*. Rowley, MA: Newbury House Publishers.

———. 1986. *Story, Performance and Event: Contextual Studies in Oral Narrative*. Cambridge Studies in Oral and Literate Culture 10. Cambridge: Cambridge University Press.

Ben-Yehuda, Netiva. 1990. *Autobiography in Israeli Folksongs*. Jerusalem: Keter. [Hebrew]

Bradbury, R. E. 1957. *The Benin Kingdom and the Edo-Speaking Peoples of South-Western Nigeria. Ethnographic Survey of Africa*. Western Africa, pt. 13. London: International African Institute.

———. 1973. *Benin Studies*. Ed. Peter Morton-Williams. London: Oxford University Press for the International African Institute.

Bronzaft, Moshe, and Daniel Samburski, eds. 1947–51. *A Book of Songs and Melodies for the Schools and for the Folk*. 3 vols. Jerusalem: Kiryat-Sefer. [Hebrew]

Caplan, Kimmy. 2002. *Orthodoxy in the New World: Immigrant Rabbis and Preaching in America (1881–1924)*. Jerusalem: Zalman Shazar Center for Jewish History. [Hebrew]

Cohen, Malka. 1974. *Mi-Pi ha-Am*. Annotated by Haim Schwarzbaum. Tel Aviv: Yeda Am. [Hebrew]

Davidson, Efraim, ed. 1972. *Our Mouth's Laughter: Anthology of Humor and Satire in Ancient and Modern Hebrew Literature*. 2 vols. 2d ed. Hulon: Biblos. [Hebrew]

Davidson, Israel. 1907. *Parody in Jewish Literature*. New York: AMS Press.

Dinur, Ben-Tsiyon, ed. 1954–72. *The History of the Haganah Book*. 3 vols. Jerusalem: Ha-Sifriyah ha-Tsiyonit. [Hebrew]

Diogenes Laertius. 1995. *Lives of Eminent Philosophers*. The Loeb Classical Library. Cambridge, MA: Harvard University Press.

Druyanow, Alter. 1935–38. *The Book of Jokes and Wit*. 3 vols. Tel Aviv: Dvir. [Hebrew]

Etkes, Emanuel. 1982. *Rabbi Israel Salanter and the Beginning of the "Musar" Movement*. Jerusalem: Magnes Press. [Hebrew]

Feiner, Shmuel. 2004. *The Jewish Enlightenment*. Philadelphia: University of Pennsylvania Press.

Friedmann, Eliezer Elijah. 1926. *Book of Memoires* [1858–1926]. Tel Aviv: Author's publication. [Hebrew]

Gilman, Sander L. 1974. *The Parodic Sermon in European Perspectives I*. Wiesbaden: Steiner.

Ginzburg, Pesah, ed. 1947. *Poetry of Labor: An Anthology*. Tel Aviv: Neuman. [Hebrew]

Gliksberg, Shim'on Ya'akov. 1940. *The Sermon in Jewish Society*. Tel Aviv: Mosad ha-Rav Kuk. [Hebrew]

Greenbaum, Masha. 1995. *The Jews of Lithuania: A History of a Remarkable Community, 1316–1945*. Jerusalem: Gefen. [Hebrew]

Hoffmann-Krayser, E. 1903. "Neujahrsfeier im alten Basel und Verwandtes." *Schweizerisches Archiv für Volkkunde* 7: 202–3.

Hymes, Dell. 1975. "Breakthrough into Performance." In *Folklore: Performance and Communication*, ed. Dan Ben-Amos and Kenneth Goldstein, 11–74. Approaches to Semiotics 40. The Hague: Mouton.

Jones, Howard. 1989. *The Epicurean Tradition*. Routledge: London.

Jousse, Marcel. 1990. *The Oral Style*. Trans. Edgard Sienaert and Richard Whitaker. The Albert Lord Studies in Oral Tradition 6. New York: Garland Publishing.

Katz, Dov. 1954. *The Musar Movement: Its History, Personalities, and Methods*. 4 vols. 2d ed. Tel Aviv: Avraham Tsiyoni. [Hebrew]

Lauterbach, Jacob Z., ed. 1933. *Mekilta de-Rabbi Ishmael*. 2 vols. Philadelphia: Jewish Publication Society of America.

Lichtenstein, Kalman. 1961–79. "The History of the Slonim Jewish Community." In *Pinkas Slonim: Record and Face of a Town—Ruin of the Community, In Memoriam.*, ed. Kalman Lichtenstein. 4 vols. 1:3–280. Tel Aviv: Irgun 'ole Slonim be-Yisra'el. [Hebrew]

Lipson, Mordekhai. 1968 [1929–38]. *From Generations of Old: Folktales and Conversations, Sayings and Jokes, Inventions and Riddles, Conduct and Manners, That Are Common Among the Folk about Jewish Personalities, for Generations*. 4 vols. Tel Aviv: Achiasaf. Reprint of Tel Aviv: Dorot, 1929–38. [Hebrew]

Luz, Ehud. 1988. *Parallels Meet: Religion and Nationalism in the Early Zionist Movement (1882–1904)*. Trans. Lenn J. Schramm. Philadelphia: Jewish Publication Society.

Mark, Jacob. 1958. *In the Company of the Generation's Great Personalities*. Jerusalem: Gevil. [Hebrew]

Mendelsohn, Samuel Felix. 1951. *The Merry Heart: Wit and Wisdom from Jewish Folklore*. New York: Bookman Associates.

Miller, Salem. 1937. *Fun'm Yidishn Kval: The Gist of Jewish Jest*. Winnipeg: Dos Idishe Vort.

Olsvanger, Immanuel. *L'Chayim*. 1949. New York: Schocken.

———, ed. 1965 [1931]. *Rosinkess mit Mandelen: Aus der Volksliteratur der Ostjuden—Schwänke, Erzählungen, Sprichwörter, Rätsel*. 2d ed. Zürich: Verlag der Arche. Reprint of Basel: Schweizerische Gesellschaft für Volkskunde.

Patterson, David. 1964. *Abraham Mapu, the Creator of the Modern Hebrew Novel*. London: East and West Library.

Roth, H. Ling. 1968 [1903]. *Great Benin: Its Customs, Art and Horrors*. New York: Barnes and Noble. Reprint of Halifax: F. King and Sons.

Ryder, Alan. 1969. *Benin and the Europeans, 1485–1897*. Ibadan History Series. New York: Humanities Press.

Samburski, D. 1969. "Autobiography." *Tatzlil* 9: 180–82. [Hebrew]

Saperstein, M. 1989. *Jewish Preaching, 1200–1800: An Anthology*. Yale Judaica Series 26. New Haven, CT: Yale University Press.

Spahr, Thorsten. 2006. *Benin-Bibliographie: Mehrfach systematisierte, bilingual kommentierte Bibliographie zur Geschichte der Edo-Kultur im Königreich von Benin (Süd-Nigeria)*. (Benin-Bibliography: Multiply Systematised and Bilingually Annotated Bibliography on the History of the Edo-culture in the Kingdom of Benin [Southern Nigeria].) Mammendorf: Pro LiteraturVerlag.

Steinschneider, M. 1902–4. "Purim und Parodie." *Monatsschrift für Geschichte und Wissenschaft des Judentums* 46–48.

Syrkin, Joshua Ben Ya'akov. 1918. "Portraits." *Reshumot* 1 (1918): 195–98. [Hebrew]

Syrkin, Marie. 1947. *Blessed Is the Match: The Story of the Jewish Resistance*. Philadelphia: Jewish Publication Society of America.

Yona, Amnon. 2001. *Missions with No Traces: Sixty Years of Israeli Underground National Security*. Jerusalem: Devora Publishing.

THE WISE WOMAN

IFA 21307

NARRATED AND TRANSCRIBED FROM MEMORY BY BERTA LIEBER
(WHO HEARD THE STORY FROM AN ETHIOPIAN WOMAN)

A woman sensed that she was losing her husband's love. She went to the village's magic sorcerer, who advised her about ways of winning back her husband's love.

The magician told her: "If you bring me three whiskers from a lion's mustache, I will give you advice."

The woman left, in despair. How could she carry out such a complicated and dangerous task?

Her strong desire to restore her husband's love overcame all the obstacles. She went off and slaughtered a lamb and sliced it into pieces. She put the pieces in a sack, put the sack on her back, and went off to the forest. She climbed to the top of a high tree and waited. A lion came and rested at the bottom of the tree. She threw the meat onto the ground; the lion ate the meat and was curious about where this mysterious gift came from. The lion looked up, saw a black face, and went up toward it.

The next day, the lion returned to the same place. The woman climbed partly down the tree and threw another piece of meat. The lion looked up, and went off. The next day, he came back to the same spot. The woman climbed farther down the tree and threw another cube of meat. The lion ate, looked up, and went off again.

The same thing happened again and again, until the seventh day. This time the lion ate its meat straight out of the woman's hand. Then it quietly fell asleep. The woman pulled three whiskers from the lion's mustache, and ran to the sorcerer happily. "I brought what you wanted, and so now you must give me advice," she cried. The magician replied: "If you were so wise and knew how to capture a lion's heart, you don't need my advice. You will figure out on your own how to restore your husband's love for you."

COMMENTARY TO "THE WISE WOMAN"

IFA 21307

ALIZA SHENHAR

F eminist researchers have long rea-
soned that male hegemonic strategies laden within the foundations of
cultural thinking created different types
of discrimination and oppression against
women. These patriarchal perceptions,
which serve as frames for male cognition,
are built on a binary patriarchal division
between activism and passivity, culture and
nature, head and heart, rationalism and
emotionalism, logic and pathos, father
and mother. The first terms appear to

describe the man (activism, culture, head, rationalism, logic, father) and the second terms the
woman (passivity, nature, heart, emotionalism, pathos, mother).

In her ground-breaking book, *The Second Sex*, Simone de Beauvoir emphasizes that women
were humiliated by men throughout history, to the point of being treated as objects. In male
society, the woman is viewed as the male's "other," and owing to the jaded comparison between
woman and man, patriarchal society denied a woman's status as an independent subject. By turning women into objects, such society deprived a woman of the opportunity to take responsibility
for her life; power and authority remained in male hands.

An analysis of this tale shows that it does not perpetuate these patriarchal viewpoints and is,
to a large extent, devoid of hegemonic gender standards.

The tale was recorded and narrated by Berta Lieber, who does not recall the identity of the
Ethiopian woman from whom she heard it. Lieber was born in Bukovina (where Austrian rule
gave way to Romanian sovereignty) in 1920. She immigrated to prestate Israel in 1939. For her
first four years in the country, she was a member of Kibbutz Shamir and worked as a nurse, partly
in Afula's hospital. Later she married and moved to Haifa, where she continued to work in the
medical field. In 1948 she established the health fund's medical branch in Haifa's downtown area
(today known as the health fund's Gliker branch). After she retired, Lieber did volunteer work
with new immigrants; subsequently, she recorded stories in Braille for blind people, and from
1990 until her death in 2007, she volunteered at the Israel Folktale Archives.

There is no clear record of the circumstances of the tale's narration, but it can be surmised that the story, which was told by a woman, perhaps in a company of women, was told not only to entertain but also to encourage an alternative, corrective approach, and to deconstruct conventional approaches from a feminist perspective.

The heroine of our story, who wants to restore her husband's love for her, personifies the female stereotype: woman = emotions and heart. She does not find an answer for her distress; at a critical juncture in her life, prior to her recognition of the potential inherent in her female personality, she follows the customary pattern in patriarchal society and turns to an all-knowing male, here represented by the magician, since authority and power belong to males and she lacks independent status.

The condition stipulated by the magician creates a major change in the female image; as a result of his advice, she turns into a self-aware subject and the possessor of autonomous borders. She mobilizes her feminine resources and goes off to the forest (nature = feminine qualities) while demonstrating activism (a male trait) and rational prudence (also a male trait).

In her volume on psychoanalysis, *Women Who Run with Wolves*, Clarissa Pinkola Estes examines an archetype of the "wild woman," along with processes in a woman's education. Where is such a wild woman to be found? Estes says that she walks in the deserts, the forests, and the oceans. In fact, the heroine of this tale, a version of a wild woman, walks in the forest; and thanks to her ingenuity, courage, and wisdom, she manages to bring the lion close to her and to take three whiskers from its mustache, just as the sorcerer demanded. The woman emerges here as someone who represents the masculine pole—strength, courage, and also patience, rather than emotion, weakness, and dependency. Despite her inferior status as a woman, she is not liberated by a man but rather pursues an independent, successful path, discovering in the end that a woman has tremendous hidden, unrealized potential, and that this capacity can be tapped to bring about substantive change in her life.

The lion, which is basically trained by the woman through the feeding ritual, is in many cultural and folk traditions identified as the "king of the beasts," and is perceived as a symbol of power and heroism.

It bears mentioning that, in Ethiopian tradition, lions have great symbolic import. The Ethiopians' belief in Hebrew origins, as descendants of royalty and priests, remains deeply ingrained in their consciousness. "The eternal lion of the tribe of Judah" was inscribed on the Ethiopian royal seal. Incidentally, the lion cub of Judah served as the symbol of the new Hebrew city of Jerusalem; and the lion was the symbol of the tribe of Judah, particularly the royal house of David.

The heroine of our story thus notches a symbolic victory over the male beast; and in keeping with an ancient folk-mythology tradition, such a triumph is particularly sweet. Her lack of awareness of this triumph creates dissonance between what was expected to happen and what happens in fact, and this gap yields the tale's humorous dimension.

As the representative of the male establishment, the magician certifies the woman's heroic triumph. A person who managed to conquer a lion's heart by using wisdom certainly has the power to reconquer her husband's heart.

The tale's main character is a heroine. It also features a magician, whereas the third figure, the woman's husband, is mentioned but does not take an active part in the narrative. In contrast to the religious legend holding that heroes are always masculine characters, the heroes of literary novellas, as in the case of this tale, are mainly women. The popular novella has a romantic character, and as a result of its expressive character, there is a tendency toward hyperbole, wherein the exaggeration emphasizes the storyteller's message.

According to IFA oikotype classification, this tale correlates to AT 293*J (IFA: "Debate of Tongue and Other Body Parts").

BIBLIOGRAPHY

Beauvoir, Simone de. 1949. *Le deuxieme Sexe*. Paris: Gallimard.
Estes, Clarissa Pinkola. 1992. *Women Who Run with Wolves: Myths and Stories of the Wild Woman Archetype*. New York: Ballantine.

WATER FOR THE GUEST

IFA 21882

NARRATED BY FAIZA BISHARA (ISRAEL, CHRISTIAN ARAB)

An unknown poet was passing through the village [of Tarshiha]. He was very thirsty, so he knocked on the door of one of the houses. A beautiful young maiden opened the door, and he asked her for a drink of water. The young maiden went back into the house and brought him a jug filled with sweet, cool water, which she gave to him. The poet looked into the jug and saw some straw in the water. The poet slowly began to drink the water, so as not to drink the straw as well.

When he had drunk his fill, he returned the cup to the maiden and said: "How wonderful this water would be, were it not for the straw at the bottom."

The maiden replied: "I dropped the straw in on purpose, because I saw that you were thirsty and tired, and I was afraid that you would drink it all in one gulp and be ill."

The poet was amazed by her wisdom and beauty and said: "*Wa rashahatni il, fatah bemaeha tarshiha*. The maiden gave me water, drop by drop."

And that's how the village got its name.

Transcribed by Rita Daoud Bishara

THE MAIDEN AND THE GUEST

IFA 21883

NARRATED BY IBRAHIM DJAIEM (ISRAEL, MUSLIM)

One day, a poet was passing by the spring next to the village, and there he met a maiden drawing water from the spring. Desperate with thirst, he asked her for a sip of water. [After drinking], he looked upon her and began to recite poetry. One line of verse was as follows: *Wa rashahtni il, fatah bemaeha tarshiha*. Gently, she gave me water, drop by drop.

Transcribed by Rita Daoud Bishara

THE GRAVE OF SHEIKH JAMAL IL-DIN

IFA 21884

NARRATED BY AHMAD DARBE (ISRAEL, MUSLIM)

During the time of the Crusades, in this place (Tarshiha), a warrior of the holy war was buried, named Shiha Jamal il-Din. His grave is on the hilltop, which is called il-Mujhed. Shiha fought against the Crusaders, fell in battle, and was buried in this place.

They said: "*Tar Shiha*"—Shiha flew, Shiha's head flew. Over time, the "t" became a "th" and the name became Tarshiha.

Transcribed by Rita Daoud Bishara

TAR–SHIHA

IFA 21885

Narrated by Basma Darbe (Israel, Muslim)

In the army of Salah il-Din Yusuf ibn Ayyub, there was a commander by the name of Shiha Jamal il-Din, who was killed on Mt. il-Shiha Mujhed. When he was killed, his head flew from the mountaintop down to the village (Tarshiha).

The people said: "*Tar-Shiha*"—Shiha flew, Shiha's head flew. And ever since, this has been the name of the village.

Transcribed by Rita Daoud Bishara

Commentary to "Water for the Guest," "The Maiden and the Guest," "The Grave of Sheikh Jamal il-Din," and "Tar-Shiha"

IFA 21882, IFA 21883, IFA 21884, IFA 21885

Amer Dahamshe

These stories offer the reader various explanations behind the name of the village of Tarshiha.[1] The etiological inquiry into the meaning of the name—how it came to be and its origin, according to the people—appears repeatedly throughout all the stories, in spite of their varying content and the way in which they are constructed. Therefore, in this analysis, we perceive the stories as one entity with similar lines of thought rather than as completely separate units.

The stories were recorded by Rita Daoud Bishara, and told by four different storytellers who live in Tarshiha, so we will provide some background information about each.

Faiza Bishara was born in the village of Tarshiha in 1912 and died in 2002. When she was two years old, her parents died, and she was raised by her aunt. She married at the age of nineteen and was a widow by the age of thirty-two. Alone, she raised five children, and made a living by doing various difficult jobs: housecleaning, cooking in the house of an elderly man, and weaving clothes. Her efforts were rewarded, and she was blessed in the raising of her children, who grew up and were educated at institutions of higher learning. One of the comforts of her hard life was to listen to the stories of the women in the village, at their houses or while she worked. So, over the years, she became a veritable "walking encyclopedia" of folk legends and traditions, folksongs and proverbs.

Ibrahim Djaiem was born in the village of Tarshiha in 1944, the son of one of the village's first Muslim families to settle there. Djaiem grew up in the lap of Arab tradition. Because of the family's difficult economic situation, he had to leave school after the eighth grade. He then learned his father's trade, stone masonry. He is still a stone mason to this day, and the profession has been passed down to his own son as well. The villagers were accustomed to gathering together at night, after an exhausting day of work, and telling stories. This is how Djaiem came to know so many stories.

Ahmad Darbe was born in the village of Tarshiha in 1936. His family was among the first in the village. During the Israeli War of Independence in 1948, his family fled to Syria and Lebanon, where they wandered from village to village. During this period family members often collected and told stories. After several months of wandering, they returned to the village, where difficult living conditions prevailed; there was no indoor plumbing or running water to be had. Ahmad Darbe studied at school until the twelfth grade in Kfar Yasif. After completing his studies, he helped his father with agricultural work, after which he began working as a truck driver, his profession until today. In the village he and his brother were educated in the ways of the Arab tradition; they worked during the day and gathered together at night to listen to the stories of others and tell some of their own.

Basma Darbe was born in the village of Tarshiha in 1943. During the Israeli War of Independence in 1948, her family fled to Lebanon, where they wandered from camp to camp, until her father found work as a hotel manager in Beirut, where Basama Darbe studied and completed her high school education. She then married a cousin, Ahmad Darbe, who lived in Tarshiha, and so, in 1972, she returned to her village. Her grandmother used to tell her stories about Tarshiha, about its people and the ways of life in the village. She came back to the village with a double heritage: a Palestinian village heritage and a Lebanese heritage.

RESEARCH BACKGROUND

The motifs that appear under the letter "A" in Thompson's motif-index are mythical-etiological motifs; they deal with the mythical origins of natural phenomena and creation stories, and explain the questions of "why" and "how" (Thompson 1955–58). The criteria concerning the source of things or objects are reflected in the stories that explain how the village of Tarshiha first came into being and received its name; however, these stories also relate the way in which the village got its name during historical time, and not at the beginning of Creation.

Stories that explain place names belong to the subtype of "place legends" or "place stories," and are often defined by origin stories—etiological stories that explain the source of place names, natural phenomena, or exceptional places in the natural environment, such as a river with a strange shape, an unusual stone, a plot of land that is unusually barren or exceptionally fertile, as well as manmade objects (Alexander-Frizer 2000, 116; Yassif 2005, 6; Shenhar 2000, 165). In this context, it is important to look at Haya Bar-Itzhak's discussion dealing with legends that relate to Jewish Polish place names. Her discussion deals with name-*midrashim* (homiletical explanations). The name-*midrash* is incorporated into a literary work and creates a legend of origin. (Bar-Itzhak 2001).

The research branch that deals with place names—the way in which places receive their names—is known as *toponymy*, the theory of geographical locations. This concept derives from two Greek words: *topos*, or place; and *onoma*, or name (Kadmon 2000, 3). Etiological stories about place names are stories that ask for explanations about why a place is called what it is and the meaning behind the name. The study of toponymy and place names encompasses broad sources, including language-oriented, geographical, topographical, and historical research. Over the past years attention has also been given to political aspects connected to place names. Nevertheless, the study of nomenclature in folk etiology and literary work (see Bar-Itzhak 2001; Dahamshe 2002)—the subject of our discussion—is scarce.

The study of toponymy in general and Arabic toponymy in particular, as it has been conducted until today, is based on permanent grammar and phonetic rules, and mainly focuses on the lexical form. In addition it largely relies on travel books, dictionaries, and lexicons, often ignoring local folk stories as well as internal cultural interpretations.

This is the picture that comes to light from the contributions of the geographers and Arab travelers and explorers of the Middle Ages, who recorded many names based on literary and phonetic rules. However, these names weren't always in keeping with the customary pronunciation of the local residents, which were closer to the original form (Il-Helew 1999, 43). Western explorers and scholars who arrived in Israel at the end of the nineteenth century perceived the lexical Arabic form of the name as an epistemological tool for identifying biblical sites and their names (see Robinson 1970; Smith 1927). Study of the lexical form of the Arabic name is also a prominent subject of both Jewish (Kliot 1989; Vilnay 1985) and Arab modern-day researchers (Sharab 2000). These recent studies, as well as those of Western scholars, for the most part show subjective inflections, and the study of their place names are frequently subjugated to ideological needs.

However, more important, the geographic names used by the Arabic-Palestinian society living in Israel and the Occupied Territories when it was still an agrarian and partially nomadic society are, for the most part, enveloped in the twilight of the past. These names were passed on by word of mouth and, in most cases, were never actually written on any map and never documented or studied. In Israel the Israel Folktales Archives (IFA), established by Dov Noy, has been active since 1955. One of the major driving forces behind the establishment of the archives was the desire "to preserve the folktales that were passed down through oral tradition over the generations among the *various ethnic groups that made aliya to Israel or lived in Israel*, by collecting, preserving and documenting them" (emphasis mine). The strength of this statement does not hold true for Arabic folktales: In 2001, when I started writing my Master's thesis on the place names of Arab settlements (Dahamshe 2002), the number of tales in the IFA was 22,000, of which only 1,268 (5.76 percent) were Arabic tales. Of the overall number of tales in the archive, only 12 tales (0.054%) were about Arab place names.[2]

The place names of this Arabic-Palestinian society live on in its memory; they suffer from the type of forgetting that goes hand in hand with Palestinian internal-cultural processes, and even more so from the evasion and concealment of the Israeli ruling institutions. As a result these names are disappearing from academic and research dialogues and discussions. The absence of research in regard to place names anchored in the local and oral Palestinian tradition is a necessary, multilayered evasion of the mapping of the state, and a source of serious contention, when it comes to research that investigates the outcome of the historical mapping of this land.[3] At the same time it is also an evasion of another type in regard to the distribution of knowledge, which originates in the social history and ways of life of the local society.

To further support these statements, I will present several of the studies that recognize the essential nature of the spatial definitions of the local people. Riva Berleant-Shiller, who studied geographical names on the island of Bermuda in the Lesser Antilles, mentions that field studies and interviews with locals are a source of important ethnographic information, and can illustrate and enrich theories and hypotheses in the field of toponymy. In her opinion we should observe the uses of land and, in this way, come to better understand the daily lives of the locals, becoming more familiar with their heritage, spoken language, and the place names that are not written on maps (Berleant-Shiller 1991, 92–93, 100). Linguistic anthropologists perceive place names as a form of cultural documentation that produces essential information not only about morphology and the contents of the physical environment but also regarding the way in which people experience their environment and perceive and conceptualize their surroundings (Basso 1988).

Along these same lines, folklorists, anthropologists, and geographers have acknowledged the contribution of storytellers and local traditions to our thinking about place-names, place identity and experiences of place. (Canaan 1929; Baily 1984; Nicolaisen 1979). In the following discussion about place-name stories documented among the local people—the Palestinian-Arab society—I hope to make up for some of the lack of toponymy research in this field.

THE STORIES: DISCUSSION

The following discussion begins with the stories I have chosen to examine; however, attention will also be given to the textual foundations that relate to the creation of a name: its structure, pronunciation, notional-conceptional foundations, and the structural aspects connected to the ideas that arise from the name.

According to the first and second etiology (IFA 21882 and 21883), which will be discussed together because of their similar thematic aspect, the origin of the name *Tarshiha* is based on a love story between a poet and a maiden who meet as a result of the poet's thirst. The meaning of the name is the drinking of water, given drop by drop—*Tarshiha*—into the mouth of the poet, by the hand of the maiden. However, this meaning doesn't result from either the place's characteristics or the water itself. The etiological explanation relates to the human reality and is simply a conceptualization of the love relations of traditional Arab society.

As was said in regard to the content involved in the creation of a village's name, its meaning is taken from classical Arab love stories of a young man (usually a shepherd or field worker) and a woman who meet as a result of the young man's thirst.

As the plot develops, the subject of the name takes on a poetic meaning proclaimed from the mouth of the Arab poet, in response to an idea that began with the maiden's heart's desire. The chance meeting, initiated by the hand of fate, is used by the poet and the maiden as an opportunity to seek out the possibility of love through the expression of their various skills and legends. The maiden is endowed with several unique qualities: She behaves according to custom with respect to offering hospitality to guests, and she quenches the poet's thirst. She is young, pretty, and clever. Although first presented as someone who acts in innocence, she knowingly places a bit of straw (or chaff) in the jug, out of concern for the poet.

However, in my opinion, with this act the maiden engages in a strategy whereby she tests the poet, examining the possibility of a love connection between the two.[4] The maiden's clever act may also be interpreted from within the folk medicine framework: She prevents the poet, who is suffering from extreme thirst, from drinking all the water down in one gulp and makes sure the guest drinks the water in small sips. Thus the feminine character tries to arouse the man's feelings of love without leaving behind any traces that might lead to trouble in a conservative patriarchal society, which forbids relations between men and women outside the marital framework.

In addition, the poet's words—"*Wa rashahtni il, fatah bemaeha tarshiha*": "The maiden gave me water, drop by drop"—don't simply relate to the fact that he received water and swallowed it drop by drop. He addresses the maiden using the general pronoun *fatah* (maiden) and words of poetry, words of praise—a sign that his soul has bonded with hers. At the same time, these words are a demonstration of the poetic ability and pleasant style of the wandering poet.

The leitmotif centers on the element of *water*: thirst drives the poet to the village; the maiden draws water and offers it to the wandering poet. As a result the poet praises both the manner in which the water is served as well as the maiden who slakes his thirst. The drinking water serves as a mediating link between the poet and the young woman, and the benefits of this natural resource are used to weave the beginnings of a romantic relationship. From this triangular context the name *Tarshiha* is created, but the characters' influence—the human factor—is of the highest importance in regard to the coming into being of the name's linguistic form. The characters in this legend do not have names. It is possible that this anonymity is anchored in the patriarchal values that enforce a taboo on a meeting between the two sexes, not to mention when lovers' names are spoken about in public.

The poet's wooing of the young woman, as well as her wooing of him, are hinted at, and are also reflected through the spatial objects and their location. The space itself carries hidden messages and acts as a metaphor for social beliefs and relations (Lévi-Strauss 1975). The meeting place of the young woman and the poet is the nearby spring; according to an additional version, they meet on the threshold (of the young woman's house). According to cultural tradition, a spring is an ideal place for a meeting between a man and a woman, as is clearly reflected in these examples: Moses meeting with Jethro's daughters at the well (Exodus 2:16); Isaac's meeting with Rebecca (Genesis 14:16–18); Jacob's meeting with Rachel (Genesis 29:9–10; see also Patai 1936, 10–11).

The meeting between the sexes at the spring receives legitimization in the Arab tradition, while this meeting is explicitly forbidden in other places, such as on the path, on a road, or out in nature. The origin of this unspoken legitimacy is anchored in the reality of traditional village life, where it was customary for men to water their herds and for women to draw water for drinking, cooking, and household needs at the spring or well. This realistic necessity transformed the spring into a romantic "umbrella" under which deeds and actions relating to love and marriage naturally occurred. The words "next to the village" in relation to the spring hint at the borderline nature of its location, and this is also reflected in regard to the threshold of the house. A borderline space, be it a spring or threshold, is a symbolic meeting place, a transformation from the absence of connection between the sexes to its realization. Even more important is the notion of water which, according to the people's beliefs, is a symbol of fertility, sexuality, and eroticism (Cirlot 1978, 364). In regard to the spatial details and characters' movements within this space, we can identify a clear interaction between the internal and the external, area and depth—the poet: the maiden, open space (the threshold): closed space (the inside the house), external: internal (the poet leaves his village; the maiden goes into her house), fatigue: calmness. This reflects the characters' movements against the spatial background and emphasizes the characters' feeling of eroticism and fertility.

Therefore, etiological stories that create local place names after a first meeting between a young man and a young woman serve as a reminder of Arab social norms that relate to love relations in days past.[5] It is also possible that stories requiring the etiological foundation challenge the patriarchal concept, which does not recognize either the wisdom of women or their longings for the opposite sex. Thus the repressed feminine voice is a part of the etiological legend and resides within it. In fact, the origin of the name, explained by the local meeting, is taken from the social reality that relates to the way in which men and women meet in Arab culture in general. Hence this expression is not limited to specific events in the village of Tarshiha, whose name is explained in the stories under discussion.

I will now examine the third and fourth stories, IFA 21884 and 21885, which will be discussed together because they share a similar thematic aspect. These stories explain the name of the village by relating to the religious-military acts of leadership (of the military commander, Shiha). They are set in the distant past, which is very significant in the eyes of Muslims living in Israel. The origin of the name is explained by two minor pictorial stories: the arrival of the commander named *Shiha*, who fought for the village in the army of Salah il-Din, and his battle against the Crusaders, who kill him and throw his head from the mountaintop. This dramatic scene is stamped on the memory of the local inhabitants who, in their amazement, said: "*Tar Shiha*" ("Shiha's head flew"). The interpretation of the name incorporates two Arabic words (which have two meanings) into one word, "Tarshiha," creating a linguistic sign that identifies the village. Over time, the word undergoes linguistic changes, and the "t" becomes a "th."

The name of the commander is central to the associations that developed and explains the original name. The commander-warrior is defined by the verb-adjective unit *mujahed* (holy war warrior) and the space, which illustrates his willingness to become a martyr. Through this characterization, the symbolic aspect of the figure is expressed.[6] In other words, ascribing the name of the village to a Muslim hero and commander of a historical event clearly conveys an interreligious interaction, whose foundation is the disharmonious relations between the Muslims and the Crusaders.

Folklore often reflects a somewhat extreme process of polarity: the reinforcement of group values and internal unification through legends that glorify figures who are admired and respected by group members on the one hand, and aggression toward the outside, external world on the other (Alexander-Frizer 2000, 46). The interpretation of the village's name serves to establish the nature of the relations between Muslims and Crusaders, which mirrors a self-awareness of the "ethnic self." The figure of the warrior, acting out of religious passion and in the service of Salah il-Din, is exalted through comparison to the collective figure of the Crusader. In the awareness of religious Muslims, Crusaders are perceived as heretics and enemies who strive for the destruction of Islam; hence Muslims are obliged to engage in ongoing *jihad* (holy war) against them (Prawer 1963, 526–30). This ideology serves to commemorate Shiha; therefore, his actions win the admiration of the group members, who keep his memory alive in perpetuity by giving the village his name. Thus we can conclude that the name of the village is symbolic and is accompanied by both a religious meaning and an extensive group identity.

From the analysis presented here, and in light of the fact that the origin of the name of the village of Tarshiha is explained by etiologies with different themes, we see that the sense of the place—that is, the nature of the affinities existing between human beings and space (Shamai 1991), of the local Palestinian-Arab people and the surrounding space—according to the various traditions of this society, is quite complex and nonhomogenous. The place's past and identity are not completely clear. It is rather like a woven tapestry of identities and meanings: a gender-oriented, local identity (the woman comes from within—she is one of us; the man is from outside, a stranger) and a historical Islamic identity, which relates to historical-epic dimensions. The placement of the name's interpretation along a synchronous-paradigmatic continuum reveals that the named village, as a space, is at one and the same time comprised of a rich tapestry of places, constructed in various ways and containing diverse elements. These elements include social identity, where one of the expressions is the gender-oriented identity of meetings between a man and a woman in traditional Arab society, and the Islamic-battle identity, which connects the spatial aspect with the religious aspect.

Thus every place within the village lends it a different spatial identity. It may be that these different identities, expressed in the etiological stories, are also reflected in the ethnic identity of the storytellers themselves. As mentioned, the stories about Tarshiha were recorded by a Christian student, Rita Daoud Bishara, who documented them at a certain stage during her studies. From the stories we discover the ethnic identity of the storytellers: the Muslim, Ahmad Darbe, attributes the origin of the village's name to the military commander in the army of Salah il-Din; as opposed to the Christian, Faiza Bishara, who explains the origin of the village's name through a social story about gender relations within the local culture.

Here pleasure and entertainment are not the only reasons for the telling of stories; it is the message the story wishes to impart to its listeners that is of greater importance. Each of the versions is connected to a separate spatial identity that attempts to reinforce the reflection and presence of the group telling the story. The version that explains the name through the legend of the maiden and the poet is a legend type that illustrates compromise and balance between the social forces of different religious ethnic groups that share the same social traditions and customs.

Space is not just a physical place; it is also a cultural construction (Tuan 1980, 14; Wagner 1986). Place names create the physical space as a text of cultural identity (Azaryahu 2000, 83). In other words, the way in which the space is constructed in legends shows the values of the "collective self." In the legend that interprets the village's name through the meeting between the maiden and the poet, a beneficent space is described in which the physical and emotional needs of the poet are satisfied. The provision of water slakes both his thirst and his fatigue, and improves his emotional state, while the absence of water, especially in the desert, hints at danger and threat. In the village setting people know one another, and here the door opens for satisfying the emotional urges. In addition the space, and all of its related components—water and maiden—provide the poet with a stage on which to express his poetic prowess. The poetic and oratory vehicles in this story lend a certain beauty and cheerfulness to the space. In contrast, the story that interprets the place name through the head of the warrior theme spreads a feeling of terror onto the space. Nevertheless, the death of a warrior in a holy war in a local place and the description of the village as an arena of battle both serve to intensify its humble geographical aspect to historical-epic proportions, and lend spiritual meaning to the space. Either way, in spite of the contrast in spatial constructions, it seems that the space described in the stories contains emotional qualities that differentiate it from its surroundings.

And what about the real space described in the legends? According to the analytic interpretation, the legends all take place in a real environment or space. The Arab village is the setting, and within its spatial borders it exists as a real, geographical natural/artificial entity in which the action takes place. In regard to the topology of the space's range, we can use Heda Jason's stories' model, according to which the storyteller and his community of listeners are positioned at the center, and around which exist ever-widening circles of other spaces (Jason 1971, 153–63). The legends in our study express the concepts of "our village," "our state," and "our world beyond the Land of Israel." The objects that organize "our village," the specific village, are connected to the village's externalities: the spring, water, the house, the hill and mountain; the village's space is designed as the center of attention. The "state" and "the world beyond Israel" lack a geographical definition and are not identified by name. It may be that this lack of identification directs the plot toward the absence of a "named" space.

The naming of the village, according to the Arab people's way of thinking, relates to Arabs who came from another country/state or their relation to and participation with the locals, where immigration and movement of the population have an influence on etymological developments. Tracing the creation of the name shows a four-cycle progression. The first cycle involves the appearance of a figure from outside the village; the second, his visit in the village; the third, his enjoyment of the village or events that relate to his destiny; and the last, the naming of the figure, and his actions carried over and inscribed as the name of the place, or the way in which he glorifies the village and its residents, thus establishing the name. In the last cycle the locals also take part, mainly in adopting the name and bequeathing its history—the name is given, as it were, by consensus, and on the plot level it serves as a metaphor for cultural unity.

Clearly, legends that explain the origin of Arab place names don't present facts but instead convey attitudes and feelings directly connected to the social experience shared by Muslims and Christians alike, and to the Muslim historical legacy, rather than to the place itself. Therefore, the local identity presented in the story that explains the name Tarshiha is external, not local, and not Galilean at all.

It would appear that the main relationship between the names and the etymologies are twofold: (1) a morpheme-sound relationship—the etymology dictates the sounds of the name through linguistic-content–based foundations, sometimes with a slight change; and (2) a semantic relationship—the literary episodes, which come one after another in a cause and effect format, lead to the interpretation of the origin of the name and bring its contextual meaning to light.

Moreover, the etiological legends—despite the difference in the explanations regarding the name's origin—create a text which, on an aggregate level, is similar, according to which the Arab name is born in a "natural manner," rather than by a formal, official order or decision. The Arab name was not determined through discussion around a table or by any type of predetermined decision or plan (see also Benvenisti 1997, 12). The Arab form of the name came into being through an unpredictable evolutionary process, and in response to historical and personal circumstances.

NOTES

1. Tarshiha: An Arab settlement in northern Israel.
2. See www.ifa.haifa.ac.il; accessed August 10, 2010.
3. On the essentialness of Arabic names for identifying biblical, Greek, and Roman names, see Elitzur 2009, 1; Benvenisti 1997, 25–26.
4. The notion of a test and task for the lover and future husband, and their various revelations, appears in the Thompson Motif Index (1955–58), H310–H499, especially in the motifs H310 and H335. See also IFA 20694 ("Jamil and Hend"; Meron, Shehadi, and Masarwi 1997, 243–41).
5. Folk legends tend to wander from a cultural environment to other spaces and, during their transfer, to adapt themselves to the absorbing culture (Honko 1981). Here the legend, whose purpose is to explain the name of a place (Tarshiha), is told not as an etiological story in the book: 1 Kings 17:8–16. The legend relates to Sidon, not far from Tarshiha, but is also the place where the biblical story of Elijah, who comes to ask for water and bread from a poor widow, takes place. An identical story to the biblical version is told by Arabs from the upper Galilee, about the abundance of water in the village of Peki'in, next to Tarshiha. But this story focuses on the prophet who comes to ask an elderly local woman for some water. The last story appears in Falah and Shenhar 1978, 24. This story was also mentioned in Shenhar 2000.
6. In regard to the representative and typical character, see Even 1992, 52–53.

BIBLIOGRAPHY

Alexander-Frizer, Tamar. 2000. *The Beloved Friend and a Half: Studies in Sephardic Folk Literature*. Jerusalem: Magnes/Ben-Gurion University of the Negev Press. [Hebrew]

Azaryahu, Maoz. 2000. "Hebrew and Hebraization: Aspects of Creating Cultural Identity." *Jewish Studies* 40: 77–88. [Hebrew]

Baily, C. 1984. "Bedouin Place-names in Sinai." *Palestinian Exploration Quarterly* 116: 42–57.

Bar-Itzhak, Haya. 2001. *Jewish Poland: Legends of Origin*. Detroit: Wayne State University Press.

Basso K. H. 1988. "'Speaking with Names': Language and the Landscape among the Western Apache." *Cultural Anthropology* 3 (2): 99–130.

Benvenisti, Meron. 1997. "The Hebrew Map." *Theory and Criticism* 11: 7–30. [Hebrew]

Berleant-Shiller, Riva. 1991. "Hidden Places and Creole Forms: Naming the Barbudan Landscape." *Professional Geographers* 43 (1): 92–104.

Canaan, Taufik. 1929. "Studies in Topography and Folklore of Petra." *Journal of the Palestine Oriental Society* 9: 136–218.

Cirlot, Juan Eduardo. 1978. *A Dictionary of Symbols*. London: Routledge.

Conder, Claude Reignier, and Horatio Herbert Kitchner. 1881. *The Survey of Western Palestine: Arabic and English Name Lists*. Trans. E. H. Palmer. London: Committee of the Palestine Exploration Fund.

Dahamshe, Amer. 2002. *The Names of Arab Settlements in the Galilee in the Folk Narrative*. Master's thesis, Hebrew University. [Hebrew]

Elitzur, Yoel. 2009. *Ancient Place Names in the Holy Land: Preservation and History*. Jerusalem: Academy of the Hebrew Language. [Hebrew]

Even, Yosef. 1992. *Dictionary of Literary Terms*. Jerusalem: Akademon. [Hebrew]

Falah, Salman, and Aliza Shenhar. 1978. *Druze Folktales*. Jerusalem: Hebrew University. [Hebrew]

Honko, Lauri. 1981. "Four Forms of Adaptation of Tradition." *Studia Fennica* 26: 19–33.

Il-Helew, Abdallah. 1999. *Tahkikat tarichia lughaweia fe il-asmaa il-jughrafia*. Beirut: Besan. [Arabic]

Jason, Heda. 1971. *Genre: An Essay on Oral Literature*. Tel Aviv: Tel Aviv University.

Kadmon, Naftali. 1994. *Toponomasticon*. Jerusalem: Carta. [Hebrew]

———. 2000. *Toponymy: The Lore, Laws and Language of Geographical Names*. New York: Vantage Press, 2000.

Kliot, Nurit. 1989. "Arab Settlement Names in the Land of Israel Compared to Hebrew Settlements Names." *Horizons in Geography* 30: 71–79. [Hebrew]

Lévi-Strauss, Claude. 1967. "The Story of Asdiwal." In *The Structural Study of Myth and Totemism*, ed. E. R. Leach, 1–48. London: Tavistock.

Meron, Yoram, Carmela Shehadi, and Nimer Ahmad Masarwi. 1997. *Seed of Pomegranate: The Woman in Arab Folktales*. Givat Haviva: Jewish-Arab Center for Peace. [Hebrew]

Nicolaisen, Wilhelm Fritz Hermann. 1979. "Field Collecting in Onomastics." *Names* 27: 162–78.

Patai, Rafael. 1936. *The Water*. Tel Aviv: Dvir. [Hebrew]

Prawer, Joshua. 1963. *The History of the Crusaders Kingdom in the Land of Israel*, vol. 1. Jerusalem: Mosad Bialik. [Hebrew]

Robinson, Edward. 1970. *Biblical Researches in Palestine and the Adjacent Regions*. Jerusalem: Universitas Booksellers.

Shamai, Shmuel. 1991. "Sense of Place: Towards an Empirical Measurement." *Geoforum* 22 (3): 347–58.

Sharab, Muhamed. 2000. *Mu'ajam asmaa il-modon wa-alkora al'arabia wa-il-felestinia*. Aman: No publisher noted. [Arabic]

Shenhar, Aliza. 2000. "Local Legends about the Land of Israel in Druze Folktales." *Ariel* 22 (144–43): 173–65. [Hebrew]

Smith, George Adam. 1927. *The Historical Geography of the Holy Land*. London: Hodder and Stoughton.

Stewart, George. 1975. *Names on the Globe*. New York: Oxford University Press.

Thompson, Stith. 1955–58. *Motif Index of Folk Literature*. Bloomington: Indiana University Press.

Tuan, Yi-Fu. 1980. "Rootedness versus Sense of Place." *Landscape* 24: 3–8.

Vilnay, Ze'ev. 1985. "The Names of the Arab Settlements." *Encyclopedia Ariel*, vol. 9 (addenda), 65–675. Tel Aviv: Hasade Library. [Hebrew]

Wagner, Roy. 1986. *Symbols That Stand for Themselves*. Chicago: University of Chicago Press.

Yassif, Eli. 2005. "On Space and Memory: Local Legends in Arabic Israeli Culture." In *Village Tales: Anthology of Arab Folk Tales*, 5–12. Givat Haviva: Jewish-Arab Center for Peace. [Hebrew]

Do Not Bequeath, for You Will Be Poor

IFA 22649

Narrated by Yossi Bar Sheshet (Morocco)

Once, in a small town, there was a wealthy, happily married man who had seven beautiful and remarkable sons. The sons grew up, got married, and respected their parents. Each time another son hosted his parents for the holidays, they all came home. So life continued until one day, may it not happen to us, the mother of the family got sick with a grave illness; doctors and drugs did not help, and she passed away. The sons sat *shiva* at their father's home, and when they arose from the mourning period, his firstborn son told him: "Dad, do not worry, you will not be alone. We will continue to host you as before; we will come to you for the holidays, and you will be fine as in the good old days. Do you, my brothers, agree?"

"May it be so!" replied the brothers.

The sons returned home, each one to his wife, the older ones to their children and their duties, and the father remained alone in his house. Not long after, his loneliness was difficult to bear; every corner reminded him of happier days. He looked at the fine vessels, the beautiful furniture, the banking securities in his drawers, and the possessions he accumulated, and he thought to himself: "What good is it that I have all these things?" But his thoughts quickly passed by . . .

Days and weeks passed, and the sons kept their promise. The firstborn son started, and the youngest one completed: every Shabbat evening one of the sons invited him to his house, and so his solitude was dissipated. But during his visits he saw that some of his sons lacked furniture, some of his grandchildren did not have warm clothes for the winter, and he heard sighs about their harsh livelihoods. Then he decided: "I will bequeath all I have while I am still alive, so the situation of my sons and grandsons will improve. What profit is there for me; I am old and lonesome? I can be satisfied with little, and they will feel good." So he said, and so he did. He called out his seven sons and told them: "My dear sons, I considered and decided that you should not wait for my death to inherit from me! I will share my possessions while I am still alive, and will enjoy your joy. My firstborn, according to the inheritance law, will get twice as much as the rest of his brothers, and each of the six others will get an equal part. And so I will divide my possessions into eight parts: two to the oldest, and one of six to each one of his brothers."

When he finished talking, he handed each of them a list of objects, possessions, money, banking securities, and everything he owned, and then blessed them: "May you abound and prosper, and in your bliss I will rejoice."

The sons rejoiced. Each one of them took his share and returned to his home with light hearts and heavy possessions, for their father was a wealthy man, and even one-sixth for the six was significant.

A week came to pass, two weeks passed, and on the third week, the firstborn son came to his father: "Father, come to us for Shabbat night."

The father, without any belongings, was in despair; even his stature was low, and when he sat down at the table, while eating soup, his hand trembled, and some of the liquid spilled on the white tablecloth. His daughter-in-law frowned but did not say a word. When the son walked his father back to his house, the father told him: "I saw the face of my daughter-in-law, your wife, may she live, and it was not like every other day . . ."

"Why do you think so, Father?"

"When the soup spilled and the white tablecloth got soiled, she frowned."

"It doesn't matter, Father . . . Never mind . . . We will continue to invite you in turn . . . Next week my second brother will host you, and after him the third one, as it used to be before our mother's death, may her soul rest in peace."

After a week, the father was hosted by the second brother. His hands shook while he drank his tea, and the expensive porcelain teacup fell on the floor and shattered into pieces. His daughter-in-law frowned but did not say a word. And so it happened with the third son, the fourth, the fifth, the sixth, and the seventh. And all their wives told their husbands: "Enough! We won't tolerate our father-in-law anymore in our houses! Today a plate, tomorrow a kettle, and the day after tomorrow he may harm the baby in the cradle!"

On the eighth week of the turn, the oldest brother did not invite him. A week later no one came. And so on, during all the coming weeks. The father sat, lonesome and bored, and thought: "Why did I bequeath all I had, while I am still alive? Now they don't want me. How will I bring them back to me? How will I bring them back to me? How will they respect and love me again?"

He thought and thought, until a smile arose on his face. On the very same evening, he went to his youngest son and told him: "Come to me secretly tonight, and tell no one that I called you."

"What is the matter, Father?"

"Hush, son, I have to talk to you; you won't be sorry."

In the evening, the son told his wife: "A fabric merchant is coming to town, and I have to meet him, to check merchandise for our store. I will come home late. Don't worry." He said goodbye to her and his two young children, and walked slowly, around and around, so no one would recognize him, to his father's home. When he arrived he saw his father offering him a chair. He took a chair and sat very close to him. The father whispered: "My dear youngest son."

"Yes, Father?"

"I have a secret to tell you. But I have to make you swear to me to keep it secret. It should not be disclosed, not to your wife or to your children, not to your brothers, and not to your sisters-in-law, not to anyone at all!!! Do you promise me?"

"My word of honor."

"So listen: Here, down in our wine cellar, I have hidden a treasure! After my death, it will be all yours."

"But why me, my dear father?"

"Because I love you as Jacob loved Joseph, and you should have the honor. Now go home, and remember, as it is written: Put a bridle on your mouth."

"Yes father, as it is written in Psalms: I will keep my mouth with a bridle [Psalms 39:2]. Farewell, Father."

"Farewell, my son."

The youngest son left happy and upbeat, and returned to his home. His wife stared at him and said: "Your face is glowing, and your eyes rejoice! Was the fabric deal successful?"

"Way beyond my imagination and dreams!" he told her.

"Sit and eat."

"No, I am too excited. I will go to bed. Goodnight."

The next day the father called the sixth son and told him the exact same thing he told the youngest son. And so, during the seven days of the week, he called his sons. From that day on, all seven of them, and not to mention their wives, started to look after the father. This one was cleaning his house. This one was cooking. This one was ironing. Every single day he was invited by another son, and he did not have a dull moment. He was now loved and respected twice as much as when their mother was alive, may her soul rest in peace.

Years passed by, the old father got ill, and his sons did not leave his bedside. One was coming, and when he left, the other one came, until he closed his eyes forever and passed away, and was buried near his wife.

His seven sons came to his house and sat *shiva*. All the town's honorable people came and left, for the deceased was a well-respected and important man. They honored the sons, consoled them, and spoke in favor of their father. And so the seven days passed, and the week of mourning ended. Slowly, the consolers left, and the sons and their wives remained. The sons sent their wives home to the children, and they stayed by themselves, sitting on the carpet; no one left his place. An hour passed, two hours, three hours, no one said anything; none of them spoke.

Then the oldest brother got up and said: "My brothers, I am sure that our father told each one of us the secret of the treasure in the wine cellar, and this is the reason why no one is leaving. We can no longer sit here in shame. Let's all stand up, go down to the cellar, and see what our father left us. We will try to divide it equally so we won't quarrel. And this time, I will give up my double share. We will divide it into seven parts, all equal. Do you agree?"

"Yes."

"Good, let's go to the cellar."

They started to go down, each one restraining himself from running in front of the other. The firstborn opened the door to the cellar and looked around.

"Here is the crate!" he called.

They surrounded the large crate on the cellar's floor.

"And here is the key to the lock," said the youngest.

"Well, open it!" said the firstborn.

The youngest son opened the crate, his hands shaking. His brothers, next to him, helped him lift the cover, and they looked inside.

"What's in there?" asked the firstborn son.

"A sealed envelope."

"Give it to me."

They gave him the envelope. The firstborn son opened the envelope and took out a folded piece of paper. He spread out the page, stared at it, and did not say a word.

"What? What is written there? Tell us! Tell!" called all the six with excitement.

"Well, I will read it to you! Here is written: 'Damned is the one who bequeaths while he is still alive!!!'"

Transcribed by Yifrah Haviv

COMMENTARY TO "DO NOT BEQUEATH, FOR YOU WILL BE POOR"

IFA 22649

DOV NOY

This tale belongs to the international folktale type AT 982 ("Supposed Chest of Gold Induces Children to Care for Aged Father") This is a widespread folktale type.[1] At IFA there are forty-six different versions, including the present one, from East and West:[2] Afghanistan (2), Bulgaria (2), Caucasus (1), Egypt (2), Iraq (2), Israel (1), Israel Mizrahi (1), Israel Arab (1), Israel Druze (1), Israel Muslim (1), Kurdistan, Iraq (1), Libya (1), Morocco (11), Poland (3), Romania (6), Russia (4), Tunisia (1), Turkey (1), Yemen (3).

In this tale, some motifs can be discerned:

P236.1	Folly of father giving all property to children before his death
S20	Cruel children and grandchildren
J152.*7	Wisdom from old man
Q281.1	Ungrateful children punished
K476.2	False articles used to produce credit

Folktales dealing with aging are numerous. In the Aarne-Thompson Index of folktale types (1961), there are a few types related to this tale topic:

AT 980	Ungrateful Son Reproved by Naïve Actions of Own Son
AT 980A	The Half-Carpet
AT 980B	Wooden Drinking Cup for Old Man
AT 980C	Dragging Old Man Only to Threshold
AT 981	Wisdom of Hidden Old Man Saves Kingdom

The message in the tale types is close to the one in our tale: to reflect the improper, harsh treatment of an elderly person until it is suitably resolved.

Our tale was recorded by Yifrah Haviv in 2004, from the teller Yossi Bar Sheshet, who was born in Morocco in 1949. Bar Sheshet immigrated to Israel in 1955, to Moshav Hazorim. Since 1976 he has worked as an Egged cooperative bus driver in the Lower Galilee Municipality, and drives pupils to the Kadoori School and back. This is how he met his tale recorder, Yifrah Haviv, who worked at this school. Bar Sheshet is a storyteller full of enthusiasm and humor, with exciting and brilliant narrative abilities.

Since IFA's first years, various versions of this tale have been recorded: the first was IFA 274, from Romania; later the tales IFA 1482, told by an Israeli Arab, and IFA 1711, from Turkey, were recorded. These three tales were registered at IFA in 1958. Thus this tale has been told for more than fifty years, at least, and is still told today. The reason may be the relevance of the plot, which is universal and timeless: the reversed affinity between an aging father and his sons, whom he cared for in his younger days and their youth, to the point when he is unbearably dependent on his ungrateful children in old age.

On the revealed level, the tale intends to implant the desirable commandment, according to the Torah, "Honor thy father and thy mother" (Exodus 20:12; Deuteronomy 5, 16) and "Honor the face of the old man" (Leviticus 19:32)

On the hidden level, this tale reveals the reality to us, the audience. It deals simultaneously with the cohort of the "father" and in doing so, appeals to elderly people who identify with the father's suffering, and it appeals as well to the "sons," the grown sons for whom caring for their parents is a burden, and who seek ways to evade this responsibility. This tale simultaneously evokes recognition of the sons' negative feelings toward their father and their guilt over having these thoughts. Over both of the two groups hovers the understanding that every human being will eventually reach this situation in his life, when the ones who now are giving care will with time become the ones who will need care. And from this point on, the desired resolution is a single one: to implement the normative behavior in order to ensure proper relations between the generations.

The tale opens with a very condensed sentence that describes concisely a long period of time during which a wealthy and happy family is well-provided for and the children are raised until they marry. This ideal existence, characterized by the proper, caring relations between the parents and their seven sons, continues until the death of the mother. As the sons sit during the week of mourning for her, they promise that they will continue to treat their father well. Indeed, they keep their promise, up until the point when their father decides to bequeath them his belongings while he is still alive. From that point on, the sons' attitude toward their father gradually changes. The audience understands in retrospect that the idyllic existence was simply for the sake of appearance. The sons did not act honestly, out of respect for their father, but instead from hypocrisy, so that they would be rewarded. And indeed, once they get their rewards, the ideal turns into a nightmare.

The old, penniless, and helpless father is left completely at the mercy of his sons and daughters-in-law. At the end, he is totally abandoned by them and remains lonely.

This lowest moment is the tale's turning point. The father regains his composure and comes up with an idea.[3] The old man undergoes a transformation, from being controlled and weak to being the leader and the initiator, when he tells each one of the sons separately that he has hidden a treasure for him only. Following this deceit, which does not encounter any objection—not in the tale and not from the audience (in fact it might be quite the opposite)—the sons' attitude toward their father improves. At this stage the change occurs in the father only, and not in the sons. They continue to be portrayed as greedy as they seek the hidden part of the inheritance. Its existence is their motivation to once again devote themselves to caring for their father.

The sons' real inner change occurs only after the father dies, in a scene that parallels the one described at the tale's opening, as they sit *shiva* together to mourn a parent's death. On this occasion, the sons begin to understand their father's ruse. The firstborn son is the first to comprehend that the promise seemingly given to just one of the sons was in fact delivered to all of them. Harmony is about to return to the brothers' relationship, as the firstborn suggests that they divide the new inheritance into seven equal parts. After opening the chest, they discover that the father bequeathed them a message of common sense, based on his bitter experience: "Damned is the one who bequeaths while he is still alive!!!"

It seems that the father's voice rose from the grave, sorrowfully but humorously summarizing the truth of the human condition that cannot be changed.

NOTES

1. See, for example, Ratzabi 1965, 455–58; Gross 1955, 276; Schmidt and Kahle 1918–30, 123; Schwarzbaum 1968a, 236; Schwarzbaum 1968b, 36; Bolte and Polivka 1913–32, v. 14, 172; Krzyzanowski 1952–53, no. 946, n. 4; Barash 1958, 109–12.

2. Some of them were published: IFA 3089, "The Will," Afghanistan (Kort 1974, 91–92, tale 20); IFA 7231, "Dividing the Will," Afghanistan (Ben-Zion 1969, 58–60, tale 10; Noy 1967a, 51–53, tale 5); IFA 1921, "Respecting the Father Because of a Chest," Tunisia (Noy 1970, 162–63, tale 61); IFA 5044, "The Inheritance," Libya (Noy 1967b, 138–39, tale 60); IFA 6544, "Respecting Father and Mother," Persia (Baharav 1968, 173–74, tale 62); IFA 274, "The Sons Who Did Not Respect Their Father," Romania (Yeshiva 1963, 15, tale 4); IFA 6599, "The Father Ruse," Bulgaria (Shtal 1976, 79–80, tale 27). For a textual analysis of AT 982's several versions, see Yeshiva 1963, 26–28.

3. In the majority of the versions, the father is not the one who has the idea but instead hears it from his friend. See IFA 7231, "Dividing the Heritage," Afghanistan (Noy 1967a, 51–53, tale 5; 104–5 n.).

BIBLIOGRAPHY

Aarne, Antti, and Stith Thompson. 1961. *The Types of the Folktale: A Classification and Bibliography*. FF Communications no. 184. Helsinki: Suomalainen Tiedeakatemia.

Baharav, Zalman. 1968. *One Generation to Another*. Tel Aviv: Tarbut Ve'chinuch. [Hebrew]

Barash, Asher. 1958. *From the Conversations of the Arabs*. Tel Aviv: Massadah. [Hebrew]

Ben-Zion, Yehoshua. 1969. *Folktales from Afghanistan*. Haifa: Haifa Municipality, Ethnological Museum and Israel Folktale Archives (IFA). [Hebrew]

Bolte, Johannes, and Georg Polivka. 1913–32. *Anmerkungen zu den Kinder und Hausmärchen der Brüder Grimm*. 5 vols. Leipzig: T. Weicher.

Gross, Naftali. 1955. *Mayselekh un Mesholim*. New York: Aber Press.

Kort, Zevulun. 1974. *The Princess Who Turned into a Bouquet*. Tel Aviv: Yehudit. [Hebrew]

Krzyzanowski, Julian. 1952–53. *Mądrej gowie dość dwie słowie*. 2 vols. Warsaw: PIW.

Noy, Dov. 1967a. *A Tale for Each Month 1966*. Haifa: Haifa Municipality, Ethnological Museum and Israel Folktale Archives (IFA). [Hebrew]

———. 1967b. *Jewish Folktales from Libya*. Jerusalem: Jewish Agency, Haifa Municipality, and Israel Folktale Archives. [Hebrew]

———. 1970. *Jewish Folktales from Tunis*. Jerusalem: Jewish Agency, Haifa Municipality, and Israel Folktale Archives. [Hebrew]

Ratzabi, Yehuda, ed. 1965. *The Book of Ethics by Zacharia Al-Dahri*. Jerusalem: Ben-Zvi Institute. [Hebrew]

Schmidt, Hans, and Paul Kahle. 1918–30. *Volkserzählungen aus Palästina*. Band 2. Göttingen: Vandenhoeck and Ruprecht.

Schwarzbaum, Haim. 1968a. *Studies in Jewish and World Folklore*. Berlin: Walter De Gruyter.

———. 1968b. "International Folklore Motifs in Petrus Alphonsi's Disciplina Clericalis." *Sefarad* 21 (1961): 267–99, 22 (1962): 17–59 and 321–44; 23 (1963): 54–73.

Shtal, Abraham. 1976. *Stories of Faith and Morals*. Haifa: Haifa Municipality, Ethnological Museum and Israel Folktale Archives. [Hebrew]

Thompson, Stith. 1955–58. *Motif Index of Folk Literature*. Bloomington: Indiana University Press.

Yeshiva, Miriam. 1963. *Seven Folktales*. Haifa: Haifa Municipality, Ethnological Museum and Israel Folktale Archives. [Hebrew]

THE BROKEN OATH

IFA 22832

NARRATED BY LEVANA SASSON (ISRAEL, SEPHARDI)

There was a girl whose parents sent her to study far away from their home, and she went to learn there. When she finished her studies, she wanted to return to her parents' home to visit them. She decided to go to them. As she went along, she suddenly lost her way and came to a field in a very distant place. She looked right and left and realized this was not her way, not the road to her parents' home. She walked and walked and did not see any inhabited place. She began to become tired and became very thirsty, since it was very hot. Suddenly, she opened her eyes and saw a well with a rope descending into it. She lowered herself into the cistern with the help of the rope; she drank, but she could not manage to climb up again. She began to cry and scream, but there was no one to come to her aid. Suddenly, a fellow passed by; he heard the voice coming up from the well and became very frightened. He peeked into the well and saw a woman inside it. He was sorely frightened; he did not understand how there could be a person in this isolated place.

He asked the young woman: "Do you belong to the humans or the demons?"

She answered him: "I am human." She cried and pleaded for him to take her out of the well.

The fellow said to her: "If I take you out, you will give me everything I ask for."

She was so petrified that she said: "Whatever you ask, I shall do."

He said to her: "Make an oath on it for me."

So she swore an oath. He worked hard until he managed to take her out of the well. She told him how she had come to be in it.

And he said to her: "Now you must fulfill your promise. I want to sleep with you."

She tried to rebuff him and asked: "What city do you come from?"

He replied: "I am from hither and yon, and I am a *cohen*."

And she began to tell him where she was from, from which family and which city, and she queried him: "If you are from a holy family, how is it that you want to act like a beast, without *ketubah* [marriage contract] and *kiddushin* [proper marriage ceremony]? Come to my father and to my mother, speak with them, and I will marry you respectably."

He agreed, and they swore a pledge to each other.

The fellow said: "Who will be a witness for us?"

And they decided that the heavens, the weasel that passed by, and the well would be their witnesses, and they determined to meet after a certain amount of time passed.

"Good-bye, good-bye," and each went on their own way.

The girl kept her promise, and she refused anyone who asked to marry her. One time, a young man came from a different city; he was very rich, wise, and learned, from a distinguished family. He heard about this young woman. He sent people to her father to speak with him about giving his daughter to him in marriage. When the father heard that this was a good match, he was very pleased.

So he said: "I shall ask my daughter, and I shall give you an answer."

He went to his daughter and said to her: "Until now I did not pressure you to marry anyone of those who came to you, but now I know that this man who has come to inquire of you is handsome, wise, and rich, and you will find no one better than he in the entire world. You absolutely must not toss this pearl out of your hand and banish luck. Whether you want to or not, I am forcing you to marry him."

Her mother, too, came and appealed to her emotions that she should marry him. She saw that both her father and her mother were pressuring her; she had no choice, and she decided to feign insanity. She began screaming, tore her clothes, and threw rocks at whoever followed her.

And that man forgot his oath, married another woman, and had a son. The child grew and was already three years old; and they loved him and were very happy with him. One day, the child was walking about the yard, and a weasel came and strangled him. They cried sorely about the strange death [*mita meshuna*] of their son. The woman decided to have another child. This child fell into a well and died on the spot. His mother sat day and night, crying over her son; she could not be consoled. She sat and thought: "Why did two such misfortunes befall me, one after the other? We must certainly have done something wrong."

She called her husband to the room and said to him: "Apparently we have committed some sin for which we are being punished, and our children are dying strange deaths, not once but twice. We must look and think, What did we do? I have sat and reflected continuously, and I have not found anything for which I think I must be punished through such difficult retribution. From the time I was a small child through today, I have always only done good deeds, and I have not done anything bad to anyone. I want you to search and remember, what did you do when you were young? Perhaps we can do something so that we will not continue to be punished."

He sat weeping, trying to remind himself. He thought and thought, and suddenly he remembered the oath that he had made to that young woman, that they would not marry anyone else. He told his wife the whole story, and she understood why all these troubles had befallen her. She immediately asked her husband for a *get* [a divorce] and the fulfillment of her *ketubah*. He was miserable; he loved his wife very much, but he had no choice. And she said to her husband: "Go right now to that young woman that God has given you and fulfill your oath, before we have other victims." They went to the rabbi; she received her divorce document and went home. And he went to the city where she had told him her parents lived, and he asked about her. Everyone told him that she had gone crazy long ago and that there was no reason to go to her.

He replied to them: "In any event, I want you to show me her father's house."

He went to the man and said to him: "I know you have a daughter. I want you to give her to me for a wife."

Her father answered him: "Yes, I had a daughter like a jewel. Don't remind me of her, lest I become too sad. She can no longer marry anyone."

He responded: "No matter, I want her. Do me a favor and take me to her."

Her father let him into [her room], and she began to throw all kinds of things at him, to yell, and to drive him out.

He said to her: "You don't recognize me; we have met only once, when I encountered you in the field [when you were] inside the well." Then he told her the entire story. When she heard him, she could not believe it and asked that he tell it again; so he told her the story again.

And she immediately told him: "Because of you and because of the oath, I have suffered for a number of years, but I kept my oath."

He told her everything that had happened to him.

Without delay they called for her mother and her father and told them the whole story; and they were very happy.

And they said: "If that is the situation, now we understand what happened. You didn't tell us anything."

They immediately prepared everything for the *huppah* [lit. wedding canopy, meaning the wedding ceremony] and held a large wedding; they had many sons and daughters, and enjoyed grandchildren, wealth, and dignity.

Transcribed by Tamar Alexander

COMMENTARY TO "THE BROKEN OATH"

IFA 22832

TAMAR ALEXANDER

This story, which is titled "The Tale of the Weasel and the Well" in the Hebrew sources, is one of the most widespread tales in Jewish culture, so it can be seen as an infrastructure story. It appears in written as well as oral literature, in Hebrew and in the three main Jewish languages: Yiddish, Judeo-Spanish (Ladino), and Judeo-Arabic. This is a vital story that first appears in the Babylonian

Talmud (*Ta'anit* 8a) and has continued down to our times in various genres, including stories, legends, novellas, poems, and plays.

In Talmudic times the story was so well known that Rabbi Ammi mentions it as the example that proves the verse, "Truth springs up from the earth, and justice looks down from heaven" (Psalms 85:12). Rabbi Ammi lived in the third century CE, and Rabbi Hanina, in whose name the legend was transmitted in *Sefer ha-Ma'asiyyot* in the Gaster edition (Gaster 1968 [1924], 74, par. 89), lived about one hundred years earlier. We thus learn that this was, apparently, a legend disseminated orally before the Talmudic era. The story of the legend itself is not cited in the Talmudic text but rather in Rashi's commentary to that passage. On the same page (*Ta'anit* 8a), a different version appears in the commentary of the Tosafists.

Also during Rashi's time, the story appears in an entirely different version in the dictionary *He-Arukh*, by the eleventh-century rabbi Natan ben Yehiel (Ben Yehiel 1926 [1531]). The text of *He-Arukh*, replicated and formulated, appears in Geonic responsa, but it seems that Rashi was not familiar with it. Perhaps the stories were written at the same time, according to different oral traditions, though it is also conceivable that each writer adapted the story in line with his own manner and style.

Both versions of the story are included in the two main anthologies of legends in Hebrew, *Mimekor Yisrael* (Bin Gorion 1966, par. 295) and *Sefer ha-Agadah* (Bialik and Rawnitzki 1967 [1908], 484, par. 50). A later medieval version is included in *Sefer ha-Ma'asiyyot*, and it is almost identical to that in *He-Arukh*. At the beginning of the nineteenth century, the story was included in the collection of stories *Oseh Pele*, edited by Yosef Shabetay Farhi (Farhi 1959 [1846], 53–55). *Oseh Pele*, which is a basic collection among Sephardic and Eastern Jewry, was written in Hebrew and translated into Ladino. "The Tale of the Weasel and the Well" has many different adaptations across genres. In the Enlightenment period, it even became known as a play (Lasky 1860; Werbel 1852; Goldfaden 1972, 133–94). In modern Hebrew literature the story served as a solid foundation for various works, such as *Ba-Emek* (*In the Valley*) and *Kalonymos and Naomi*, by Berdyczewski (Berdyczewski 1965, 197–205), and *Shevu'at Emunim* (*Betrothed*) by S. Y. Agnon (Agnon 1966, 216–98).

The story's subject is an oath that has been breached, and its main motif is that of "the double match": a real match that fails owing to the disruption of the ideal match.[1] The story appears in *Midrash Me'am Lo'ez*, which is the most important literary work written in Ladino. Jacob Culi, the author of *Me'am Lo'ez for Genesis* (Culi 1730),[2] who probably was familiar with all the previous versions, chose as the basis for his version that of the Tosafists, which is an intermediate text between Rashi's short, tragic text and the detailed, more positive, more popular text by the author of *He-Arukh*.[3]

The narrative context of *Me'am Lo'ez* is the interpretation of the Genesis verse 31:51–52, in which Laban makes Jacob pledge not to mistreat his daughters and to protect them.

In the international tale type index (Aarne and Thompson 1961), this story is included in the group of tales of fate, AT 930. Yet there is an essential difference between fate stories like "King Solomon's Daughter in the Tower," in which the father prevents the marriage of his daughter to her potential spouse because of differences in wealth and status, and "The Tale of the Weasel and the Well." In our story the parents are not involved, and the conceptual axis of the tale is the pledge made by the couple themselves. There is no economic obstacle or class gap between them. This is an internal Jewish story, classified as oikotype AT 930*F, which casts doubt on the belief that divine providence determines events from the outset and stresses instead humankind's freedom of choice. From the minute the pledge was formulated, there was no escape from the chain of events. But were it not for the oath, perhaps the tale would have ended with the rescue of the girl who had fallen into the well. Yet the girl could have given up and relinquished the pledge, as in a parallel story with King Solomon as the judge, in which the youthful oath of a couple is annulled and each one of them marries a different spouse (Gaster 1968 [1924], story 111–12). Instead we are presented with a tragic story in which the protagonists set out on a road from which there is no return.

The Sephardic oral story tradition in Ladino did not choose the version from *Me'am Lo'ez*, preferring instead the version in *Oseh Pele*, which is based on the text of *He-Arukh*, perhaps due to its happier ending.

In the narrative tradition of Ladino-speaking Jews of Spanish origin, there is no doubt about the importance of the midrash *Me'am Lo'ez* as a bridge between Hebrew literature and the Ladino-reading public, and as a bridge between written and oral stories. Customarily, *Me'am Lo'ez* was read aloud on Sabbaths, within the family circle. It is only natural that this story would then be relayed in other contexts, such as through the rabbi preaching in the synagogue, a mother telling the tale to her children, or a woman conveying it to her female friend.

Of no less importance among Sephardic and Eastern Jews was the collection *Oseh Pele*, which exemplifies the juncture between a written and an oral story. For the version of "Tale of the Weasel and the Well," Farhi, the book's author, relied mainly on the version in *He-Arukh*.

The version under discussion here was told to me in Hebrew by Levana Sasson, a native of Jerusalem, as she heard it from her mother, Merkada, who was born in a small village near Istanbul. The story's plot is very close to that in *Oseh Pele*. The fact that this book was found among Levana Sasson's deceased mother's effects bolsters the assumption that she had read the stories in the anthology and afterward related them orally, at every opportunity when she had an audience of listeners. According to her daughter, Merkada did not need any special context for storytelling. She simply wanted to tell a story. She would say to her daughter, "Come listen to a nice story."

Similarly, Levana Sasson told the story in Ladino to Matilda Koen-Sarano (Koen-Sarano 1999, 250–55). The story in Hebrew is much more detailed and replete with dialogue; the style of speech is in the middle linguistic register. The exposition was updated to the modern day and does not fit well within traditional social norms: for example, the daughter leaves the family to study. The importance of education is also prominent when the candidate for marriage is described as "wise, and learned." The first time Levana Sasson told me the story, she said a snake, rather than a weasel, killed the elder son, and she characterized the girl in the well as a sprite rather than a demon. After Sasson read my comparative analysis to the other versions of the story, she "corrected" herself; in the current version, she includes the weasel, and the girl is described as a demon, as is customary in most versions of the story. As Levana understands it, this is a true story, and she displays a sympathetic attitude toward the two female figures in the story. The girl is not an arrogant, wealthy, and conceited person who tempts fate by wearing a great deal of jewelry and walking in a field by herself, as in the *Oseh Pele* version, but rather a student returning home, losing her way, and crying out of fear.

The second woman, the wife, observes the commandments, as does Sasson herself, and she believes that maintaining a religious way of living merits a better life and protects her from misfortune.

The sympathy of the storyteller also goes out to the young man, who is forced to leave his beloved wife because of the pledge he made in his youth. "He loved his wife very much, but he had no choice."

Sasson, herself the mother of three children, also does not forget the suffering of the girl's parents, who are not mentioned at all in parallel stories. Only at the end do they understand what happened to their daughter, and they rejoice greatly.

In all versions, whether written or oral, the expression Rashi used to describe the death of the children—that is, they died a "strange death" (*mita meshuna*)—is preserved. Even when the story is related in Ladino, this phrase is maintained in Hebrew, as it is also in Sasson's version.

Many storytellers express a preference for the written stories, claiming, "I read this in a book." Levana Sasson took the trouble to place on the table both *Oseh Pele* as well as *Me'am Lo'ez* as proof of the correctness or importance of the story. The oral tradition is perceived as insufficient for the representative of an academic education.

I documented another version of this tale as told by Rosa Alboher, who was born in Jerusalem to a family originating from Salonika. In regard to this version, Alboher points out that she read the story in *Midrash Me'am Lo'ez*, even though her version differs greatly from the one there; upon concluding the story she noted, "This story is a true story and happened here in the Land of Israel at the time of King Solomon." The link to the figure of Solomon has some support in the narrative tradition. The Gaster collection (Gaster 1968 [1924], 74, par. 89) contains a story about King Solomon as a judge; the internal story relates the tale of a boy and a girl who swore allegiance to each other. But the girl changed her mind and wanted to marry someone else. She went to the young man to seek release from her pledge, and she indeed obtained her goal. The motif of a pledge of fealty, certainly, is similar to that in "The Tale of the Weasel and the Well"; here, however, there is no tragedy but rather forgiveness and release from an oath.

In his article regarding "The Tale of the Weasel and the Well," Dov Sadan (Sadan 1957, 367–81, 467–76) cites the Eastern European version of the story, which was written down in 1915 and published by Samuel Lehmann in a collection of stories in Yiddish. The story's protagonist swore an oath to the young woman, and the witnesses to it were the heavens, the earth, and a tree. The young man forgot his pledge, but the young woman did not release him. When the Russians captured the village, they hanged the fellow on the tree, and from then on the tree was fossilized: It was impossible to break its branches. Sadan correctly concludes that a folktale that continues to live in oral tradition must frequently change and adapt itself to the new context.

Within the framework of the personal story—which is a narrative of personal experience told in the first person or a story about someone known from the nearby environment—I recorded many tales told by Sephardic women in Jerusalem that were connected to the breaking of promises made when young. Some of these end tragically, as, for example, in suicide or death from deep sorrow, rather in acquiescence to the situation and deriving consolation from one's children. Yet in none of these stories was there an oath made in the presence of witnesses; neither was there the harming of children. These life stories are typical of a society in which marriages are determined according to considerations (for example, economic class or family pedigrees) that in many cases run counter to those of the couple. Stories like "The Tale of the Weasel and the Well" or "The Broken Oath" provide a different case, having a unique tripartite structure of sin-punishment-correction (except for the Rashi version, which offers no correction). In the personal stories there is no punishment and no resolution, but rather a tragic conclusion in which the woman refuses to accept the situation and commits suicide or takes to her bed and dies; or she may accommodate to the situation, with each person marrying someone else, whether they want to or not.

"The Tale of the Weasel and the Well" is in the genre of a novella that may be classified somewhere between a legend—which is considered an event that did occur—and a fictional tale. In the novella taking place in the real world, there are no wondrous turnabouts or supernatural elements. Elements that go beyond reality may be explained by events that occur by chance: the meeting next to the well, the weasel that came by, and the death of the children.

The novella places at the center the figure of the woman and the relations between her and the man. In "The Tale of the Weasel and the Well," the man is an anti-hero situated in a dual system of relations. The two women are domineering and active; they direct the life of the man and find the solution. The story's power, and perhaps with that its vitality, is in the conclusion, which coalesces from the story's structure as an insoluble situation in which both women are right.

The resolution of the plot in the return to the first couple does not have sufficient force to resolve the harm done to the two women. The corrective marriage will not restore the children who were killed, or compensate for the marriage that was destroyed or for the years in which the young woman grew older and lived disguised as an insane person, barely remembering for whom she was waiting. More than a love story, this is a conceptual story about the power of an oath, and the plot solution is thin and superficial. The networks of relations among the figures does not lead us to the declared final formulation of *Oseh Pele*, "They lived in happiness and wealth; they enjoyed sons and assets." Thus we return to the initial version of the story in Rashi, who leaves his protagonists with no way out. This seems to be so also for the endings of the contemporary personal stories, which are based on actual biographical events.

The various versions of "The Tale of the Weasel and the Well," and the varied links among them, together create a unit of multifaceted stories that form a fundamental element of Jewish culture in general and of Sephardic Jewish culture in particular.

Notes

1. For a discussion of this motif, see Feingold 1984, 22–49.
2. See Culi 1730. On the stories of *Me'am Lo'ez for Genesis*, see Landau 1980.
3. For a detailed analysis of the story in *Me'am Lo'ez*, see my book, Alexander-Frizer 2008, 45–70.

Bibliography

Aarne, Antti, and Stith Thompson. 1961. *The Types of the Folktale: A Classification and Bibliography*. FF Communications no. 184. Helsinki: Suomalainen Tiedeakatemia.

Agnon, Shmuel Yosef. 1966. *Two Tales: Betrothed, Edo and Enam*. Translated by W. Lever. London: V. Gollancz.

Alexander-Frizer, Tamar. 2008. *The Heart Is a Mirror: The Sephardic Folktale*. Detroit: Wayne State University Press.

Ben Yehiel, Natan. 1926 [1531]. *Sefer Arukh Ha-shalem*. Vienna: Menorah. [Hebrew]

Berdichevsky [Berdyczewski], Micha Yosef. 1965. "Kolonimos and Na'omi." In *Kol Kitvei Berdichevsky*, vol. 1: 197–205. Tel Aviv: Dvir. [Hebrew]

Bialik, Haim Nachman, and Yehoshua Hone Rawnitzki. 1967 [1908]. *The Book of Legends*. Tel Aviv: Dvir. [Hebrew]

Bin Gorion, M. J. 1966. *Mimekor Yisrael: Classical Jewish Folktales*. Translated by I. M. Lask. Bloomington: Indiana University Press.

Culi, Ya'acov. 1730. *Me'am Lo'ez: Bereshit*. Constantinople.

Farhi, Yosef Shabetay. 1959 [1846]. *Sefer Oseh Pele*. 3 vols. Jerusalem: Bakal. Reprint of Livorno, 1846. [Hebrew]

Feingold, Ben Ami. 1984. "The Pre-Ordained 'Double Match' Theme." *Jerusalem Studies in Jewish Folklore* 7: 22–49. [Hebrew]

Gaster, Moshe. 1968 [1924]. *The Exempla of the Rabbis*. New York: Ktav.

Goldfaden, Avraham. 1972. *Shulamite*. Jerusalem: Bialik Institute. [Hebrew]

Jechielis, N. 1926. *Aruch Completum Sive Lexicon: Targumicis. Talmudicis et Midraschicis*. Vienna: Hebrauscher Verlag. [Hebrew]

Kagan, Zippora. 1983. *From Aggadah to Modern Fiction in the Work of Berdichevsky*. Tel Aviv: Ha'kibbutz Ha'meuchad. [Hebrew]

Koen-Sarano, Matilda. 1999. *Legendas: I Kuentos morales de la tradision djudeo-espanyola*. Jerusalem: Nur.

Landau, Luis. 1980. "Content and Form in *Me'am Lo'ez* of Rabbi Jacob Culi." PhD diss., Hebrew University. [Hebrew]

Lasky, Moshe. 1860. *Ne'emnei Erez (The Weasel and the Well)*. Lvov: M. I. Landa. [Hebrew]

Sadan, Dov. 1957. "On the Legend of *The Weasel and the Well*." *Molad* 15: 367–81, 467–76. [Hebrew]

Werbel, Eliahu. 1852. *Trustful Witnesses or The Weasel and the Well*. Vilna: Yosef Reuven Ram. [Hebrew]

THE GATE TO THE GARDEN OF EDEN IS BENEATH A WOMAN'S FEET

IFA 22833

NARRATED BY ELIEZER PAPO (YUGOSLAVIA, SEPHARDI)

Poor Joha was married to a difficult, rigid, overbearing, and temperamental woman. Whatever he did was not good enough for her. If he came back from the market with meat, she would berate him. "What did you think, that you are a prince, that we can permit ourselves to eat meat on a weekday?" If he would bring vegetables, she would yell at him: "What, do I look like a cow to you? Go bring this to your mother, that she may eat grass, that befits her."

Poor Joha, what could he do? He secluded himself in his immediate surroundings, taking his lumps and suffering. But one day, when she asked him to stand on all fours so he could serve as the base for the *payla* [washbasin] since her base had broken, even the patience of Joha ran out. He stood straight up and calculatedly and contemplatively left the house. He walked on and on, without paying attention to where, and suddenly he found himself in the desert.

Oh, *Dio santo* [blessed Lord]! How could he go back now? He looked right and left, and suddenly he saw two passersby. He asked them: "Would it be possible to accompany you until we reach some town?"

They said to him: "Your servants have nothing more than a single prayer that we recite every day, and the heavens open, and all the delicacies of the world descend prepared. But we are sworn not to hand it over to anyone, and we are also forbidden from letting anyone who does not know the prayer to enjoy it."

He said to them: "Surely I am familiar with it. Otherwise, how would I be able to exist here in this desert with nothing in hand?" They believed him. At noontime one of the men said to Joha: "The time has come to eat, would you kindly pray?"

He replied to him: "No, you are two, while I am one. One of you pray." Okay—and that fellow began to pray, and Joha watched his mouth to perhaps be able to discern the text of the prayer. While the man was still praying, behold the heavens were opening up, and a table full of all the delicacies of the world descended to the ground. They took [it], recited a blessing, broke bread, and ate their fill. The next day, the second fellow said to Joha: "Today, it's your turn."

"No," responded Joha, "you are two, while I am one; you pray, and tomorrow I will pray."

He said and he did [*Lo dicho, lo ficho*]. That fellow prayed, and Joha again tried to read the text of the prayer from his lips, but again this was in vain. The man finished his prayer with one *Shema*, the heavens opened, and the scene from the first day was repeated. The following day at noontime, Joha already understood that there was no prudence and no counsel; he had to perform the act and pray. What did he do? He lifted his eyes upward to the heavens and said to the Master of the universe:

> You are Master of the universe,
> All comes from you and returns to you,
> So what do you care,
> About whatever formula of prayer?
> What these two have prayed,
> I know not, and my forefathers, too, did not know,
> But to you, O Lord, is righteousness,
> And to us is disgrace,
> Take this miserable prayer of mine,
> As if it were theirs,
> And may my intention before you be acceptable,
> For you are too great
> To be strict with me.
> And why should this day be different,
> My life is always held in your hands,
> And were it not for your great mercy,
> We would have died heretofore.

At that moment the gates of heaven opened, and three tables descended. One held meat and choice dishes, the second fruits and sweets, and the third coffee with a *nargila* [hookah] and a backgammon board. The two were filled with great wonder, and Joha as well, who had no fear in his heart, for the hand of the Lord is not limited; he too was astonished by the last miracle being greater than the first. They felt tremendous awe, but people do not exist from awe. In the end, they took and blessed, drank and ate, washed and blessed, drank and smoke, and began talking. Joha said to them: "Now, since you realize that I too have the prayer, tell me the version that you usually recite."

They said to him: "What we say is very simple":

> Master of the universe,
> By virtue of Joha's suffering,
> At the hand of his wife the snake,
> Give us today our daily bread,
> And fulfill all our needs.

At that moment, Joha understood that creatures exist in this world by virtue of him. He said to himself: "What, I should lose such a large treasure of rights?" He returned to his wife and from the doorway said to her: "Where is the washbasin, and where should I stand on all fours?"

This is what people say: "La puerta de Gan Eden esta basho los pies de la mujer" ["The gate to the Garden of Eden is beneath a woman's feet"].

Eyos tengan bien I mozotros tambien [That they should merit all good: they, and we as well].

Komo fue verda asi mos venga la geula [Just as this was the truth—so the Redemption shall come].

I si era de mentira ke mos venga el Mashiah [And if this was false—then the Messiah shall come].

Transcribed by Tamar Alexander

COMMENTARY TO
"THE GATE TO THE GARDEN OF EDEN
IS BENEATH A WOMAN'S FEET"

IFA 22833

TAMAR ALEXANDER

Joha is a well-known figure in the Eastern folktale in general and in Sephardic stories in particular.[1] Joha stories are common among all centers of Sephardic dispersion.[2]

The origin of the name Joha is uncertain. The oldest literary record for this name can be found in collections of anonymous Arab stories dating to the ninth century (Rejwan 1984, 7–8).[3] In Turkish stories from the late Middle Ages there appears a figure whose name is Nasser a-Din Hudja, which resembles that of Joha. According to Turkish narrative tradition, there was indeed a man named Nasser a-Din Hudja, and his tombstone is located in the Turkish city of Konya.

In Turkey the Jewish figure and the Turkish figure merged, creating a new name composed of the two earlier names: Nasser a-Din Hudja effendi Joha. In the seventeenth century, after the Turks captured part of the Maghreb countries, the stories about Nasser a-Din Hudja reached North Africa as well and merged with stories of the same type that were common in local tradition. On the eastern coast of Africa and in Iraq, parallel stories were attributed to Abu Nuwas.

The non-Muslim world also bears evidence of stories that parallel those about Joha. In Sicily the folk fool has the name Giufa (Corrao 1991), which sounds very similar to the name Joha.

In every culture, including the various Jewish groups, there is the figure of the fool around whom jokes are woven, such as Hershel of Ostropol, Mottke Chabad, and Shaike Feiffer among the Jews of Eastern Europe (Schwarzbaum 1962).[4] In the Ethiopian tradition he is known as Abba Gevar Hanna (Alexander and Eynat 1996, 119–91). The unique personification of the figure depends on the context and the conditions under which the character operates.

In his attitude toward his environs and the attitudes of those around him, the figure of Joha is two-faced, like Janus: a prankster and a trickster, yet still a fool. Joha is a simpleton and a rogue, a finagler and a mark, a clever person who "fixes" others and a fool and a victim who falls into any trap.

Joha the simpleton is full of good will and carries out missions with purely good intentions but without flexibly adapting to conditions, so he fails in carrying out the tasks assigned to him. Joha understands things literally, and in his innocence, he performs whatever has been asked of him to the letter. The way he executes his task misses the mark and causes laughter. Joha sees certain situations as problematic, even though an ordinary person would perceive it as posing no difficulty at all. When he finds himself in these situations, he comes to conclusions he considers logical but which the ordinary person would consider absurd. He thus is liable to draw conclusions based on a basic lack of knowledge of the laws of nature and of reality. At the polar opposite to his innocence, which stimulates laughter and a sense of superiority in the listener, stands the fool. Roles reverse, and it turns out that the person considered inferior, such as Joha, has been graced with true superiority and wins the esteem of the Lord.

In contrast to Joha the innocent victim, who believes everything and arouses sympathy and pity in the listener's heart, this Joha has the opposite appearance. This Joha is a trickster who uses ruses to obtain his goals, even at the expense of others. Jokes of this type are called practical jokes. The hero is boastful when he describes how he managed to trick someone for his own benefit or to prove his cleverness. According to this narrative tradition, Joha earns his living from his tricks. In many stories he is the court jester.

By intentionally playing the social role of buffoon and fool, he is permitted to mock sacred topics, including those regarding God, death, honoring one's father, and desecration of the body. He can express what others do not even dare.

Humoristic stories such as Joha tales, which deal with relations between man and woman, with exploitation of man's greed, or his yearning to be victorious over death, are universally human, and found in every culture. Yet there are Joha stories that are unique to Jewish culture and are based on "inside" cultural knowledge.

Many phrases put in Joha's mouth in the intrastory dialogue, or phrases expressing the narrator's attitude toward Joha, became generalizing phrases that describe the all-too-human condition. They became disengaged from the story and gained the status of proverb or saying. These proverbs were created from the narrative situation, and at times it is impossible to understand them without being familiar with the story's plot. The link to Joha is obvious, to the point that sometimes the name Joha does not even appear in them. That is, the proverb summarizes the story and derives from it, but there is no longer any need to tell the entire story to the group members—it is enough to state the proverb. There is also a contrary, more common phenomenon: the attribution of general proverbs to Joha. In this case, the proverb is loaded with the cluster of meanings that the image of Joha carries with it.

These phenomena attest to the wide distribution of Joha stories among members of the group, to the extent that there is no need to tell the whole story but only to summarize its moral in the form of a proverb. Moreover, the meaning of proverbs of this type are likely to be clear only to the group members who know the story. After the phrase has been separated from the story and turned into a proverb, it is then possible to adapt it to other stories. These proverbs are concrete, and not metaphorical; they describe a situation possible in reality.

Another phenomenon that attests to the role of the figure among members of the group is the fact that Joha has gone beyond the literary contexts and functions also in contexts of daily behavior to mark a characteristic or deed through an expression or idiom, such as "the luck of Joha," or "with the taste of Joha." Moreover, the name Joha turned into a lexeme. Thus there is no need for a story, or even an idiom or expression. It is sufficient to say the name, such as "What a Joha," or "She has a Joha husband," and this suffices to indicate characteristics or modes of behavior.

I chose to discuss the story "The Gate to the Garden of Eden Is beneath a Woman's Feet" because of its singularity, in that most of the characteristics of the Joha stories I've described are concentrated in this story, whereas usually in each story only one or two characteristics appear. In this story Joha appears as an innocent and a victim as well as a trickster, but also as a righteous person in whose honor the world is nourished. This is a story unique to Jewish culture in general and Sephardic culture in particular, and it is summarized through the figure of the narrator in the concluding proverb.

This story was told by Dr. Eliezer Papo, who was born in Sarajevo, Yugoslavia, in April 1969, and immigrated to Israel in 1991. Dr. Papo is a lecturer in Sephardic literature at Ben-Gurion University of the Negev. He currently serves as the deputy director of the Moshe David Gaon Center for Ladino Culture at Ben-Gurion University. The story presented here was related by Papo from his memory of a tale he heard in Sarajevo from Ben-Zion Campos. In many stories the figure of the wife of Joha appears. In all the stories she is depicted as a woman who causes him great injustice. She is a swindler who is ugly and always angry, and she visits neighbors' homes in contradiction of Sephardic norms, according to which a woman must stay in her own home. She is mercilessly domineering of Joha and abusive toward him; finally, she leaves home with Joha's best friend. These stories are usually related by men, and they are intended to warn against the nature of women. Yet one must keep in mind that Joha is a lowly figure, and thus these jokes provide ambiguous certainty to the listener that such things could not happen to him, for he is not such a fool as Joha.

In the story at hand, Joha's wife is described as a "rigid, overbearing, and temperamental woman." As much as Joha tries to placate her, he cannot succeed. She has complaints and retorts for everything he does. Joha, who is described here as his wife's victim, takes everything quietly, until she asks him to stand on all fours and serve as the base of the washbasin. Not only is this demand particularly humiliating, both regarding the physical position as well as the woman's attitude toward him as an object, but one may even see in it an erotic allusion to an exchange of the role in which the husband demands that the wife stand on all fours in a sexual position. This is where the first turning point in the story occurs. The submissive Joha rebels and leaves home. While trudging in the desert, he meets two men who know a secret prayer with magic power, by the virtue of which, every time it is recited, delicacies descend from the heavens. Revealed at another turning point is the trickster facet of Joha, who confidently claims to these men that he, too, knows the prayer. Twice he manages to manipulate them and make them continue to pray, with the false claim that he does indeed know the prayer. On the third day (a formulaic number), he can no longer evade the issue and is forced to pray himself. Now our story comes to a third turning point, and Joha turns into a completely righteous person who does not know how to pray, but his prayer is accepted by virtue of his pure heart.

This motif belongs to the tale type AT 827("A Shepherd Knows Nothing of God"). The Jewish oikotype is called "The Simpleton's Prayer," and its number is AT 827*A (Aarne and Thompson 1961).[5] These stories deal with a naïve person who does not know how to pray properly, but his simple, defective prayer is accepted by virtue of his pure intention, since God loves the heart ("God wants what's in the heart"). Joha in our story does not know how to pray. He speaks with his maker in an egalitarian form and in simple, spoken language: "What do you care," he asks the Lord, "about whatever formula of prayer?" He consciously seeks a response to his prayer in honor of his pure intention: "May my intention before you be acceptable." In contrast to the prayer of the simpleton who does not boast of his pure intention, and usually does not ask anything for himself, here Joha prays for a material goal to his benefit: to receive food and drink. Perhaps in the background of this prayer stands a well-known song for *Havdalah*, which is sung in Ladino at the end of every Shabbat and in which the worshiper asks from the Lord, among other things, "bread to eat and wine to drink" (Romero 1991). After the hoped-for miracle occurs, the men reveal to Joha the text of their prayer, and then it turns out their prayer is also not a typical one; the great surprise is that Joha himself is the hero of their prayer, as if he were a great *zaddik* (righteous person). God showers them with delicacies by virtue of Joha's suffering at the hands of his wife: "At that moment, Joha understood that creatures exist in this world by virtue of him." The final turning point in this story of many switches is that Joha quickly returns to his home and asks his wife "Where is the *payla* [washbasin], and where should I stand on all fours?" And what looks like humiliating submission to his wife is now perceived as the measure of supreme righteousness of someone who is willing to suffer in order to nourish the world.

The storyteller concludes the story with a proverb summarizing its moral. I term this a "narrative proverb." The proverb is not dependent on a story, since the story is already embedded within it. "The summarizing storyteller"[6] relates the chain of events objectively and from afar, as it were. He is situated outside the plot and looks at it from a bird's eye view, whether he is involved in the event or not. The phrase, which the narrator in this position chooses to utter, is the result of a choice among many phrases. The proverb can function separately from the story. And, indeed, Eliezer Papo attests that this proverb is very common among members of the Sephardic community in Sarajevo, while the story is much less known.

Papo heard the story among a group of men on Shabbat eve in the community building of Sarajevo, shortly before entering the synagogue. On that occasion, the synagogue's beadle described how he had become a widower and subsequently remarried, encountering difficulties and problems between him and his wife. To that Ben-Zion Campos, one of those present, responded: "Oh, there is a story about that," and he related the story we are discussing. According to Papo, the story was understood as a one of consolation for men who have difficulties with their wives. One may expand on this and say that the story is intended to affirm the group norms of maintaining the value of family and marriage, even at the price of troubles and having to bear insults. Direct attention to this topic is found in the book *Pele Yo'ets* by Rabbi Eliezer Papo of Sarajevo. This is a *musar* book (an ethical work) that was written in Hebrew and translated into Ladino, and it is widespread among the community members. Rabbi Papo addresses both men and women and preaches for the preservation of domestic harmony at all costs, since for the suffering in this world there will be recompense in the world to come:

> And a woman who has had the misfortune of having a mate who is a bad person, a good-for-nothing beater and curser, who stomps on her and is a fornicator, should accept the judgment of the heavens and suffer and not flee to save herself, for the full benefit of her reward will be in the world to come. . . . To be sure, a man whose lot it has been to fall in the clutches of a difficult woman, like a bone stuck in his throat, must be careful. He is being put to a severe test and needs the wherewithal to behave calmly and amicably toward her for the honor of the Divine spirit, whoever has a bad wife will not see Gehenna [hell]. . . . It was worthwhile seeking an evil wife if he could withstand the experience, since whoever passes the test will not inherit the dual situation of Gehenna [suffering now and later], but accept [the situation] with love and receive his reward for his effort. (Papo 1824, section alef)[7]

This means that Rabbi Papo not only promises a reward in the world to come for suffering in married life in this world, but even goes to the extreme and declares that, for a man who is confident in his ability to suffer, it is worth marrying a bad women to meet the test and receive his reward in the next world.[8] Rabbi Papo does not place all the responsibility on the woman and demands only patience from her, as accepted in traditional society, but also considers the role of the man.

In the deep underpinnings of the Joha story, which is intended to amuse, stands a most serious ethical social norm that does not ignore the daily reality in which married life frequently is difficult and problem-laden.

The innocent, childish figure of Joha enables the audience of listeners to see things from the childish point of view as a game position of play. The amusing situations in which he finds himself allow the adult listener to respond like a child playing a game. Joha understands instructions and advice in their literal meanings but is unable to transfer instructions from one situation to another and from one context to another. He does not have basic knowledge about the laws of nature and reality, and he thereby enables us to laugh from our sense of superiority. The listener can identify with Joha the trickster, however, from a different position, since Joha expresses forbidden desires and does things the listener would perhaps like to do but does not dare to think about within the norms of society. Thus, for example, it is possible to express a feeling that is unacceptable according to social norms but which definitely exists: joy at someone else's downfall. Many of the situations in which Joha finds himself are embarrassing: He fails, is beaten, falls, but rather than sympathize with him, we laugh, the same way we laugh about his victims. Joha permits the listener to overcome feelings of pity and frustration and to allow the listener to extract himself from difficult situations. Joha's flippant attitude toward sacred issues or those that strike terror in people's hearts, such as death and God, help the listener overcome deep fears and attenuate tension. Laughter is a social phenomenon (Hertzler 1970). It occurs in society, and it has social significance. Laughter is a social implement intended to punish an inflexible person, one who is not fit for society owing to his rigidity. Laughter is a corrective for this extreme rigidity. It enables the expression of solidarity among the society's members or hostility toward those who stand apart from it.

Laughter is double-edged as a social instrument: On the one hand it helps preserve the norms within the group; on the other it reinforces the fact of individualism as opposed to acquiescence to society. Thus laughter serves as a tool for withstanding pressure. It is no wonder, then, that Joha appears in both guises: as the trickster who rebels against social conventions and acts for his own benefit against society, its rules, and its values, and as the fool, whose lack of ability to adjust to the rules of society and its reality make him the object of mockery.

The uniqueness of the story under discussion is in the perceptual turnabout between its beginning and its end. Joha the antihero, the ludicrous victim whose wife humiliates him, is revealed precisely because of this position as a righteous person by whose virtue miracles take place. The humiliating opening position becomes a characteristic of piety. Yet this is a funny story—in the way it is told, by its very attribution to Joha, by the triviality of the miracle, and by its many plot-linked surprises and twists and turns.

The story is anchored in Jewish culture and in Sephardic group culture, both in its plot and in its context of utterance. The diners do not forget to ritually wash their hands and recite the blessing before eating. The story was related right at the onset of Shabbat, before entering the synagogue in the Jewish community building in Sarajevo. It is spiced with expressions in Ladino, and it closes with the ending formulas common in Ladino and which are apt for the ambiguity of the story: If these things are true, the Redemption will come; and if they are false, the Messiah will come. Either way, the same hope is being expressed. Whether this is a humorous story or a somewhat sad, bitter tale about married life, the wheel stops at the same point: the importance of marriage and the value of domestic harmony, despite its high price.

NOTES

1. On the figure of Djuha in the Sephardic story, see Alexander-Frizer 2008, 354–69. On proverbs concerning Joha, see Alexander-Frizer 2004, 125–65.
2. For a comprehensive collection of stories on Joha in Sephardic culture, see Koen-Serano 1991.
3. Rejwan (1984) presents more than 230 stories on Joha from the Arabic tradition and considers the source of the name in the Jahwan tribe, affiliated with the Prophet Muhammad.
4. For a broad discussion of the topic, see Krasney 1993.
5. On the Jewish oikotype, see Noy 1961, 34–45; on this tale type among Sephardic group members, see Alexander-Frizer 2008, 259–71.
6. On this term, see Alexander and Govrin 1990, 1–34.
7. I wish to thank Dr. Eliezer Papo for the reference to this source.
8. This concept, which sees suffering in this world as a test meant for the benefit of man, so that he may increase his reward in the world to come, is salient in the ethical teachings of the *Hasidei Ashkenaz* in the thirteenth century. See, for example, Alexander-Frizer 1991.

BIBLIOGRAPHY

Aarne, Antti, and Stith Thompson. 1961. *The Types of the Folktale: A Classification and Bibliography*. FF Communications no. 184. Helsinki: Suomalainen Tiedeakatemia.

Alexander, Tamar, and Amela Eynat, eds. 1996. *Tarat Tarat: Jewish Folktales from Ethiopia*. Tel Aviv: Miskal, Yediot Aharonot. [Hebrew]

Alexander, Tamar, and Michal Govrin. 1990. "Story Telling as a Performing Art." *Assaph: Studies in the Theatre* 5: 1–34. [Hebrew]

Alexander-Frizer, Tamar. 1991. *The Pious Sinner: Ethics and Aesthetics in the Medieval Hasidic Narrative*. Tübingen: J. C. B. Mohr.

———. 2004. *Words Are Better Than Bread: The Judeo-Spanish Proverb*. Jerusalem: Yad Ben-Zvi Institute/Ben-Gurion University Press. [Hebrew]

———. 2008. *The Heart Is a Mirror: The Sephardic Folktale*. Detroit: Wayne State University Press.

Corrao, Francesca Maria. 1991. *Giufa*. Milan: Oscar Mondadori.

Hertzler, Joyce Oramel. 1970. *Laughter: A Socio-Scientific Analysis*. New York: Exposition Press.

Koen-Serano, Matilda. 1991. *Djoha Ke Dize? Kuentos Populares Djudeo-Espanyoles*. Jerusalem: Kana.

Krasney, Ariela. 1993. *The Badḥan*. Ramat Gan: Bar Ilan University. [Hebrew]

Noy, Dov. 1961. "The Prayer of an 'Innocent' Brings Rain." *Mahanayim* 51: 34–45. [Hebrew]

Papo, Eliezer. 1824. *Pele Yo'ets*. Istanbul (Constantinople): Ha-Levy Printing House.

Rejwan, Rahamim. 1984. *Juḥah*. Tel Aviv: Zmora, Bitan. [Hebrew]

Romero, Elena. 1991. *Noche de Alhad, Coplas sefardíes*. Córdoba: Ediciones el Almendro.

Schwarzbaum, Haim. 1962. "Famous Folk Jesters in Israel." *Mahanayim* 67: 57–63. [Hebrew]

Killing the Snake

IFA 22849

Narrated by Yosef Goldman (Poland)

When we arrived, the place was utterly desolate. I sent my wife and daughter to my sister in Haifa and stayed here alone. Every afternoon I used to go out and try to plant a garden. One day I come back and cross the threshold. I saw there was a stick on the threshold, but I didn't pay any attention to it and stepped over it. No sooner had I entered the room than I see that the stick is following me—it wasn't a stick but a snake, which began to dance in front, while blocking my path back to the door.

What could I do? There was no place to run to, and in Poland I had never had anything to do with snakes. I look around, and next to me I see the bucket we had received from the Jewish Agency. In those days, when we came from Poland, I was healthy—I must have weighed around a hundred kilos. I grab the bucket, put it over the snake's head, and sit on it, and, what do you expect, my weight severed its head. I was petrified! I took the snake by the tail and ran to my upstairs neighbors, who were oldtimers from Afula. They heard the story and began to roar with laughter, because the snake wasn't poisonous.

Transcribed by Haya Bar-Itzhak

COMMENTARY TO "KILLING THE SNAKE"

IFA 22849

HAYA BAR-ITZHAK

I recorded this story, which was told by my father, Yosef Goldman, as part of a project to collect the immigration and absorption stories of Polish Jews in Israel.[1] I had already heard him tell the story on many occasions. When I was young I used to call the story "The Polish Jew Fighting the Israeli Monster"—the title I gave the first article I published about the absorption stories of Polish Jews in Israel (Bar-Itzhak 1998).

My late father was born in 1918 in Poland. He was a graduate of the *Tarbut* school, where he acquired his perfect if somewhat old-fashioned Hebrew. His parents, Rachel (née Kozioł) and Rabbi Simcha Goldman, immigrated to Palestine before World War II, and passed away before my father's arrival in Israel. My father was a Zionist and ardent secularist, and he joined the Ha'khshara (a training program for pioneers who intended to make *aliya*) of the He'halutz movement in Poland. His plans to come to Israel didn't materialize because of World War II. His first wife, Esther, perished in the Holocaust, along with their only son. He himself was conscripted and served in the Polish army and then in the Red Army. After the war he married my mother, Menucha (Manya) Pundik. When it became possible to make *aliya* from Poland, after Wladyslaw Gomułka came to power in 1956,[2] we did so.

My father was a gifted storyteller. I still remember many of his tales. This one, like other immigration and absorption stories I have studied, exemplifies the creation of folklore by immigrants drawing on the experience of their *aliya*. The narratives make use of familiar cultural patterns that the immigrants brought with them from the "old countries," but their new creations are a direct result of their migration and everything associated with it, and can therefore come into being only after they have made the move and in a fashion that is determined by all the factors involved in their change of country.

This story, like other absorption stories told by Polish Jews who arrived in Israel in the late 1950s, grew out of the new situation and the anxieties it generated, including their fear of certain animals viewed as primeval beings—snakes, scorpions, lizards, and chameleons—which the narrator and his city-dwelling listeners knew only from books. The story exposes the anxieties of the narrating society, but the mere act of telling it serves as a kind of catharsis. These stories provide a way to vent the anxieties through the mere act of expressing them. The story is a metaphor for the situation of the immigrants from Poland, who feel they have moved to a primordial wasteland. In this respect, it expresses the binary opposition between nature and culture, to use the terminology of Claude Lévi-Strauss (Lévi-Strauss 1963, 206–323). The hero is characterized as someone who has moved from a civilized habitat to a place where nature (which he tries to civilize by planting a garden) lies bare, overrun with primeval creatures.

Settlement in an unfamiliar place, according to Mircea Eliade, resembles an act of creation. The alien region is associated with chaos and precreation. The act of settlement turns chaos to cosmos by means of a ritual that realizes it (Eliade 1991, 9–10). The story of the transition is an expression of, as well as a part of, the ritual itself. The transition, represented in the story by the crossing of the threshold, traps the hero in a state of no exit. His back is to the wall, while the monstrous snake "dances" in front of him, blocking the way out. This is how these immigrants conceived of their situation. They were aware that there was no way to return to the former situation which, although it did not lack difficulties, was known and familiar. Hence the only way out (in both the concrete and figurative senses) was to confront the Israeli monster and, if possible, to overcome it.

The hero of the story has no means appropriate for dealing with his new situation. "In Poland I had never had anything to do with snakes," he insists. Nor is the gear he has received from the Jewish Agency of much use in this encounter. Here we have implicit criticism of the absorption process itself. Nevertheless, the hero is a doer. Instead of throwing in the towel, he grabs the bucket he has received from the Jewish Agency—although it is certainly not the tool he needs for his mission—because it is all he has to hand. But in addition to the Jewish Agency bucket, he also makes use of an asset he retains from his past: experience of life, the ability to improvise, a capacity to withstand perilous situations and survive. Thus, even though the bucket is the wrong tool, his inventiveness and willingness to meet the challenge lead him to victory.

Interwoven through the story is a vein of humor that the narrator directs at himself. The fact that an experienced adult has allowed himself to be trapped creates the self-directed irony typical of Eastern European Jewish humor (Noy 1962, 118–21; Oring 1992). His battle against the snake-monster—using an aluminum bucket, he decapitates the creature by sitting on it—is a genuinely comic scene. The humorous climax of story, in which his Israeli neighbors inform him that the snake isn't poisonous, turns the entire plot into a tempest in a teapot, reflecting the narrator's attitude toward himself and his listeners, and his ability to see the humorous side of their anxieties.

All the same, even if it turns out at story's end that he was not locked in combat with a fearsome serpent but only a harmless garden snake, neither the narrator nor his listeners see it as much ado about nothing. The incident is important precisely because it exemplifies the immigrant's trapped situation and forces him to take a stand and act. It reflects the optimism of the Polish immigrants who came to Israel in the late 1950s, after having survived World War II and the Holocaust: You have to deal with a difficult situation, no matter what. What is more, the story illustrates that even though the Israeli host society did not provide the immigrants with the tools they needed for their absorption, they could use what they had received if they remembered that they possessed other resources drawn from their past lives—perseverance, resolve, ingenuity, and the ability to manage in situations of hardship and pressure. From this perspective, the story affirms the positive self-image of the narrating society, alongside its characteristic self-irony.

This story, like other absorption narratives I have studied (Bar-Itzhak 2005), points to the importance of folklore for the migration process. The creation of folklore is a means of dealing with the culture shock,[3] a manifestation of the chaos immigrants experience in the process of immigration and settlement in a new place; but it is also means to turn the chaos into a cosmos (as Eliade puts it), by using cultural tools from the past and adapting them to the new reality. In this way, folklore serves as a means to digest the changed situations, to cope with them, and to construct a bridge over them while using resources drawn from both cultures, the old and the new.

NOTES

1. For an extensive discussion of these stories, transcribed in Upper Nazareth, including the one discussed here, see Bar-Itzhak 1998, 191–206.
2. Historians have labeled the wave of Polish *aliya* from 1956 to 1960 the "Gomułka *aliya*," after the Polish Communist leader who permitted the Jews to leave the country. A total of 42,289 Polish Jews arrived in Israel, most of them in 1957 (29,529). For more on the topic, see Bar-Itzhak 2005, 57–68.
3. On culture shock and the creation of folklore, see Kirshenblatt-Gimblett 1978; Bar-Itzhak 2005, 57–90.

BIBLIOGRAPHY

Bar-Itzhak, Haya. 1998. "Les Juifs polonais face au 'monstre' israélien: Récits d'aliya en Israël des Juifs polonais." *Cahiers de littérature orale* 44: 191–206.
———. 2005. *Israeli Folk Narratives: Settlement, Immigration, Ethnicity*. Detroit: Wayne State University Press.
Eliade, Mircea. 1991. *The Myth of the Eternal Return or Cosmos and History*. Bollingen Series XLVI. Princeton, NJ: Princeton University Press.
Kirshenblatt-Gimblett, Barbara. 1978. "Culture Shock and Narrative Creativity." In *Folklore in the Modern World*, ed. Richard M. Dorson, 109–21. The Hague: Mouton.
Lévi-Strauss, Claude. 1963. "The Structural Study of Myth." In *Structural Anthropology*. New York: Basic Books.
Noy, Dov. 1962. "Is There a Jewish Folk Joke?" *Mahanayim* 67: 49–56. [Hebrew]
Oring, Elliott. 1992. *Jokes and Their Relations*. Lexington: University Press of Kentucky.

THE FLYING CAMEL OF THE LEVANT FAIR

IFA 22876

NARRATED BY ZIPORA ZABARI (ISRAEL)

In the twenties, twenty and so, a very important man came from America who wanted to help Israel. So he and Dizengoff* wandered around on horses from place to place. Dizengoff showed him the different neighborhoods: "Little Tel Aviv," which was covered with sand dunes, "Mugraby" where everything was just sand dunes, "Allenby"—sands too; only "Nachalat Binyamin" had a little eh . . . was covered with some asphalt, and from here to "Allenby" down there was only sand, and so forth. Then he tells him: "Here! You see!"

Later on he took him a little farther, to "Balfour" above; there it was even worse, a desert! Then the man says: "Here you want to have a second America?" he says to Dizengoff.

So he says: "Yes, yes, here will be a second America, it will be a Little America."

So he tells him: "You know what?" He says to Dizengoff, "When a camel will have wings and fly, when the camel will fly, then you will have here a Little America."

So he says to him: "Fine. I hope that with the help of God, the camel will fly for us."

So this is the reason Dizengoff chose the flying camel as a symbol of the Levant Fair Exhibition. People said: "What is this, a flying camel? Camels have wings?"

Later on they knew what it was.

Transcribed by Nili Aryeh-Sapir

---

* Meir Dizengoff (1861–1936) was the first mayor of Tel Aviv from 1911 until his death.

COMMENTARY TO
"THE FLYING CAMEL OF THE LEVANT FAIR"

IFA 22876

NILI ARYEH-SAPIR

O ral and written stories that deal with Tel Aviv's reality of the 1920s and 1930s communicate in different ways the powerful yearnings of Tel Aviv's founders and shapers to actualize their dream in reality and to transform the city into a metropolis.

This story was told by Zipora Zabari, who was born in Neve Tzedek in 1908 to a family that emigrated from Yemen in 1888. In her youth Zabari was a dairy maid in Tel Aviv's neighborhoods. In 1928 she took part in the *Malkat Esther* (Queen Esther) competition that preceded the city's Purim celebrations. These competitions were hosted in Tel Aviv by the dancer Baruch Agadati as part of the city's Purim's balls. Zabari was crowned *Malkat Esther* by the mayor, Meir Dizengoff. Later on she traveled to Europe and became an actress and acrobat. She returned to *Eretz Yisrael* on the eve of World War II. On her return she settled in Kerem Hateimanim, in Tel Aviv.

From this tale, which has oral and written versions, we can extract a clear message, shaped with focused tools, that seeks to prove that yearnings may transform into reality. Meir Dizengoff, the first mayor of Tel Aviv, had repeatedly proven his intent to develop the city and make it an urban and economic center of the Middle East.[1] In the anecdote before us, the dialogue between the American guest and the mayor reflects their respective world views, which are clearly in opposition. The American perceives Tel Aviv's reality (and possibly *Eretz Yisrael*'s reality) as static and hopeless: a reality in which camels shall always pace the desert's sands. In his view, any attempt to change and transform the desert's nothingness into the reality Dizengoff hopes for is not only doomed to failure but should be understood as totally impossible. With his words he attaches wings to the camel—the symbol of the country's desertlike and desolate reality—and this winged image comes to symbolize a supernatural and improbable motif that characterizes the fairy tale.[2] The winged camel is used here as a complex symbol that demonstrates and fortifies the guest's unequivocal opinion that there is no chance such changes can take place either in Tel Aviv or in *Eretz Yisrael* as a whole. Thus the symbol receives a metonymic character.

In contrast, in Meir Dizengoff's eyes a flying camel symbolizes a challenge; for him it represents his opposing world view. Symbols that appear to represent impossibility are meant, in Dizengoff's view, to be actualized. Such seemingly incongruous symbols were frequent in the realities confronting the Jewish people whose task it was to renew *Eretz Yisrael*. They were experiencing the transformation of an unproductive state into a productive and independent state, a process that appeared to external foreign viewers as an impossible mission. Those who experienced this transformation created the symbols in the very early stages to represent the reality for which they yearned. They did so to accelerate the self-actualization process of the Jewish people in their country. Indeed, the special powers of these symbols facilitated this goal. The initiators and innovators of this process thus sought to eliminate the polarity between reality and dream, and make the dream into reality.

The international Yerid Hamizrach (Levant Fairs) Exhibitions of the 1930s were among the central economic events of the period. These exhibitions displayed the cultural, industrial, and trade achievements of many countries and the *Yishuv*. These exhibitions thus conveyed several messages: (1) They emphasized the central role of Tel Aviv in the country and the world as the host city for such an important economic event; and (2) they were a metonymy of the entire *Yishuv*, which had succeeded in making the camel fly. Thus the tale discussed here receives its meaning only in relation to the special historical and social context of this period. Its messages are entirely dependent on the context. Told during this period, it transmitted encouragement and fortitude at a time of building and actualizing, when there was a great need to reshape the Jewish entity in Israel as a productive group that stood by itself, in direct opposition to its character in the Diaspora. The image of the flying camel thus became a visual icon for many people of the *Yishuv* during this period.[3]

This story about the past was told retrospectively, in the present day. It was transmitted as a way to set the past as an example for the present. In this version of the anecdote, relayed in my interview with Zabari, she repeatedly compared the past reality of Israel in general and Tel Aviv in particular—characterized by idealism and by people's limitless loyalty to the sacred cause of actualizing the nation—with the shallow values of the present, which she viewed as sliding irrevocably downward. In Zabari's view, the Yerid Hamizrach Exhibitions and Tel Aviv's Mayor Dizengoff, the entrepreneur with the vision behind this enterprise, were worthy examples for the message she wished to convey to me, as they embodied the unique qualities of the past that effectively built the nation.

Notes

1. On the declared intent of Meir Dizengoff to make the city a state center, see, for example, a letter from 1929 from the chairman of the city council of Tel Aviv, Meir Dizengoff, requesting various institutions' contributions to support the Purim events in order to attract large crowds to the city (Tel Aviv-Yafo Municipal Archives, section 4, file 2 5/R).
2. The motif of the winged camel appears in Thompson's *Motif Index of Folk Literature* (1955–58) as B 47.
3. The flying camel's statue stood permanently atop a pole at the entrance square to Yerid Hamizrach. It is used to this day as the symbol of the Israel Trade Fairs and Convention Center (Shtukman 1966).

Bibliography

Aryeh-Sapir, Nili. 2006. "The Foundation of Urban Culture and Education: Stories of and About Ceremonies and Celebrations in Tel Aviv in Its First Years." *Dor Ledor* 26: 36–46. [Hebrew]

Shtukman, Dita, ed. 1966. *From Levant Fairs to Tel Aviv Fairs*. Tel Aviv: Yerid Ha'mizrach, Chevra Le'ta'aruchot. [Hebrew]

Thompson, Stith. 1955–58. *Motif Index of Folk Literature*. Bloomington: Indiana University Press.

Honor Your Guest,
Though He May Be a Beggar

IFA 22913

Narrated by Hamza As'ad Abu Zidan (Israel, Druze)

There is a story I heard from my father. There was a family here, Taher, who were among the notables of the village (Mghar). At the entrance to Sheikh Abu Sa'id's house in the neighborhood, there was a small market, and near the house was a tree. One day a man came and sat under the tree; he was one of those who came to beg for alms.

Now when Abu Sa'id saw him, he called for his servant and told him: "Call this man, he seems to need help."

Now when he entered his house and looked at him, he said: "This man may have been forced to beg for alms. Bring a sheep and slaughter it, and invite the man to eat. Also invite the *mukhtars* [village heads] and the sheikhs of the village."

They brought him, slaughtered a sheep, fed the man, and dined alongside him. Now when the sheikhs came, they said to Abu Sa'id: "Who are your guests, O Abu Sa'id?"

He said: "This man you see here."

They said: "What . . . have you slaughtered a sheep for a beggar?"

And he said: "Yes I have. I saw him. Allah knows he belongs to a respectable family, and this man is not a beggar."

The days came and went, and one day Abu-Sa'id had to go to pay taxes in the Gaza area. When they reached Gaza, they saw a man there who seemed trustworthy, a man of respectable family.

At the moment this man saw them, he ran up to them in the road and said: "Abu Sa'id, you and your companions are my guests today."

He said: "How? Where did you learn my name?"

He said: "I will tell you later where."

He took them into a house. And the door of this house could be entered by a man on horseback, so tall and wide was it. The man slaughtered a sheep for each one of them—five sheep for the five men. And then he said to them: "What is your desire?"

They said: "We came to pay the money and taxes."

The man sent one of his servants to the *wali*, who collects the money and taxes, and told him: "Bring the receipt for the money and taxes owed by Mghar, and I will give you the money. And you, honor us and dine with us at midday."

Now while he was serving them, the *wali* came. And the host who had invited them told Abu Sai'd: "Abu Sa'id, invite him!"

Said the *wali*: "Are you Abu Sa'id?"

And even before, on their arrival, Abu Sa'id had said to him: "I want to know why? Where do you know me from?"

So he said: "I am the beggar you noticed. Once I came to your door, and you slaughtered a sheep for me."

Now he said to the group of men who were gathered there: "I want to know who is more honorable, Abu Sa'id or I?"

His companions who were there said to him: "You slaughtered five sheep, and he slaughtered one!"

And he said: "No. He slaughtered the sheep for a beggar, and thus he is more honorable than me. I knew who Abu Sa'id was, and knew who the people with him were, and that is why I slaughtered a sheep for each one. He is more honorable than me."

This is my story, and it is now finished.

Transcribed by Yoram Meron

Al-Jazzar and Muhammad al-Qablan

IFA 22924

Narrated by Muhammad 'Arsan Majid Abu Zeid (Israel, Bedouin)

One night Muhammad al-Qablan was visited by three beggars dressed in rags, and beggars . . . came to Muhammad al-Qablan: "Peace be upon you, O sheikh."

"And upon you be peace. You are welcome."

They entered and sat in his house. He gave orders to his workers, slaughtered for them, cooked for them, and hosted them. Three days of hospitality, as is customary. His paternal cousins came and said to him: "O Sheikh, what is the matter with you? These are beggars, not equals."

He said to them: "Uncles, for me all men are equals, I do not distinguish between beggars and guests. Each deserves to be honored."

They were his guests for three days, and he offered them full hospitality, a full welcome. And after three days he took them to the coastal plain, and they returned to their home. The affair was forgotten, one could say; about a month and a half or two months passed.

And all of a sudden al-Jazzar called for Muhammad al-Qablan. This Muhammad al-Qablan was told by his relatives: "He who is called to al-Jazzar does not return. May God lighten your burden."

They said their goodbyes, consoled him, and held a party for him that night. He clothed himself, made his ablutions, and set on his way. He went down to Acre, to al-Jazzar's palace, where he saw the guards posted along the way: "Hello, hello."

He said: "I was called for by al-Jazzar."

They said: "Who are you?"

He said: "I am Muhammad al-Qablan, of the Tababshe, of the tribe of Tababshe and the Arabs of al-'Aramshe."

They said to al-Jazzar: "Muhammad al-Qablan is here at the gate, and he asks to see al-Jazzar. Did you call for him?"

He said: "Let him in."

He came in shivering, of al-Jazzar! He was shaking with fear. As to the slaughter he went, to the inside of the palace: "Peace be upon you."

"Upon you be peace."

Al-Jazzar was sitting, preparing himself. He said: "Are you Muhammad Qablan?"

He said: "I am Muhammad al-Qablan."

He said: "Is it true that a month or two [ago], three beggars came to you?"

He said: "With your permission, I am your vassal, O Jazzar, O Sheikh, they came to me, and I hosted them and honored them, and gave them all they required."

He said: "If you see them, will you recognize those three beggars?"

He said: "Of course, they were with me for three days."

He called for his two viziers, his assistants. They were dressed exactly the same.

He said: "True, O Sheikh, these are the two. I hosted them, Uncle, did I host you or did I not? I hosted you, slaughtered for you, and everything."

They said: "True. And who is the third?"

He said: "The third . . . ?"

A smile appeared on al-Jazzar's face . . . he said: "With your permission, not you . . . ?"

He said: "Me, truly, it was me."

He said to him: "With your permission, Sire, forgive me, I should have hosted you more properly."

He said: "This you did for beggars; what would you have done had you known that I am al-Jazzar?"

He said: "Had I known that you are al-Jazzar, I would have slaughtered three hundred heads of sheep and goats . . . Three hundred would I have slaughtered, all those in the pasture, in the village, I would slaughter for you."

Al-Jazzar honored and hosted him, and he stayed with him for two days, and was appointed sheikh of seven clans, of seven tribes. That is, all the tribes in this area, he was appointed sheikh over them, and presented with much money and honor, and given all the tribe of Aramshe for his command, and he went home.

And the children of Aramshe were glad, and celebrated for a month, and danced, and sang, and Sheikh Muhammad al-Qablan was made sheikh of seven tribes.

That is the story.

Transcribed by Yoram Meron

Commentary to "Honor Your Guest, Though He May Be a Beggar" and "Al-Jazzar and Muhammad al-Qablan"

IFA 22913 and IFA 22924

Roni Kochavi-Nehab and Yoram Meron

On an April day in 2004, we drove up to the village of Arab al-Aramshe on the Lebanese border (incidentally, the only Arab village in Israel surrounded by a security fence) to hear and record the stories of the inhabitants. Our visit was part of an extensive project intended to present Jewish and Arab readers with a collection of local stories, including one from every Arab locality in Israel.

Our host was Muhammad 'Arsan Majid Abu Zeid, a professional bus driver and amateur storyteller known throughout his village and the area. The story about the tribe of Aramshe and the sheikh of the tribe, which we heard from the sheikh, seemed to us to fit our purpose from the first hearing, so we recorded it as he recounted. At his suggestion, the story was named after its protagonists: "Al-Jazzar and Muhammad al-Qablan."

The same day, we continued to the village of Mghar, where our host was Hamza As'ad Abu Zidan, who received us in his attractive *mdhafe*, or drawing room. After coffee was served and the formalities were over, Hamza told us a story that had occurred in his village and which he had heard from his father. We were truly amazed to hear him tell the very same story we had heard a few hours earlier. The heroes and locations were different, but the story was almost identical. Hamza's story is titled "Honor Your Guest, Though He May Be a Beggar."

The two stories were told in response to the question: "What story [in the narrator's opinion] best represents the village?" Both stories were told the same day by chance, but their similarity underscores the importance of hospitality in the hierarchy of values in Arab society.

HONOR AND HOSPITALITY PRACTICES

Both stories revolve around the precept of hospitality. The protagonist is tested to see whether he observes the precept even in the case of beggars, the most inferior class of this society. In both stories the hero performs his duty in contradiction to the advice of his relatives and friends and local notables, who disdain the beggar guest and deem him unworthy of investment of effort and money, and therefore see no reason or need to host him.

These stories echo the account of the angels who came to Abraham (Genesis 18:1–8) and the practices of hospitality described in it, which are identical to those of the heroes. Like Abraham, the hosts in our story hasten to invite the strangers to stay in their tent or house, receiving them with great honor without asking their identity and the reason for their visit. Like Abraham, the hosts here slaughter sheep or camels for the guests and prepare a feast in their honor.

On this point the two stories presented here differ most: Muhammad al-Qablan, in Muhammad 'Arsan's story, receives the three beggars who have come to him, hosts them, and slaughters sheep for them without suspecting who they are. But Abu Sa'id, the hero of Hamza As'ad's story, recognizes the beggar as an honorable man, saying: "Allah knows he belongs to a respectable family, and this man is not a beggar."

Nevertheless, by observing the precept of hospitality, our heroes pass the test and are rewarded. Muhammad al-Qablan is appointed sheikh of all seven tribes of al-Aramshe and wins riches and honor, and Sheikh Abu Sa'id is received royally in Gaza, his taxes are paid, and he is honored with a visit of the *wali*, or provincial governor, in the home of his host.

The precept of hospitality is one of the most important and respected virtues in Arab society, from the Jahiliyya period through the appearance of Islam and to this very day. This commandment originates in the difficult conditions of life of the nomadic tribal society in the Arabian desert. The Bedouin cannot survive in the desert without this assistance, which protects him and guarantees his existence. This is the origin of the custom demanding that guests be hosted, without asking the reason for their visit, for three and a third days. During this time the guest's every need must be attended to, and he must be protected and sent safely on his way. To this day the Arabs are known for their hospitality and proud of this virtue.

The two stories we have find five parallels in IFA. In all these the protagonist or the protagonist and his wife pass a test of decency and respect for the other. In most cases the tester is not God but a majestic ruler, and the reason for the test is not part of the story.[1]

THE RULER DISGUISED AS A BEGGAR

In both stories important people appear at the host's home disguised as beggars. In Muhammad 'Arsan's story, the guest is al-Jazzar himself, accompanied by two of his counselors, and in Hamza As'ad's story, the disguised beggar is the *wali*—the Ottoman governor of Gaza.

This act of the disguised ruler, together with his assistants and counselors, mingling with the people is known to us from as early as the stories of Haroun al-Rashid, the famous Abbasid caliph (ruled in Baghdad from 786 to 809 AD) whose caliphate was marked by economic and cultural prosperity. In these stories Haroun al-Rashid is described as a justice-seeking ruler, governing with wisdom and honesty and winning great admiration. He often appears disguised as a beggar, meets with common people, tests their virtues, and rewards them.[2] Similarly, in the two stories under discussion, we meet a ruler whose subjects fear his punishment but respect and admire his character. The ruler is very human, treating his subjects with respect and a measure of affection, assisting them and promoting them after testing them secretly.

AL-JAZZAR

Al-Jazzar is the nickname of Ahmed Basha (1720–1804), governor of Syria, Lebanon, and Palestine under Turkish rule. He was infamous for his great cruelty, beheading more than seventy thousand rebellious Bedouins in Egypt—thus his name "al-Jazzar," or "the butcher." Al-Jazzar's seat was in Acre, which he fortified in anticipation of Napoleon's invasion. It is told that he imbricated the skulls of the executed in the walls and fortifications of Acre. It is also told that he would starve insurgent prisoners of war to death, roast their flesh, and feed it to his hungry prisoners. Al-Jazzar was buried in Acre, in the lavish mosque named for him (Cohen 1960, 313, 319; Shamir 1965, 203–4). Thus it is understandable that the people of al-Aramshe, in 'Arsan's story, bid Muhammad al-Qablan farewell when he was called to al-Jazzar's palace, saying, "He who is called to al-Jazzar does not return." But in the story we meet a different, even kind, al-Jazzar. Again, the protagonist who has passed al-Jazzar's test is thereafter appointed sheikh of the seven tribes of al-Aramshe, and his people "celebrated for a month, and danced, and sang." The multifaceted figure of al-Jazzar appears again and again in the many stories we have collected in the villages of the Galilee. In the stories of IFA, on the other hand, it is the only one so far.

While the story told by Hamza As'ad Abu Zidan treats the precept of hospitality and compares two acts of generosity, Muhammad 'Arsan Majid Abu Zeid's story underlines the status of Muhammad al-Qablan, who, due to the quality of his leadership, was appointed "sheikh of seven tribes." This story, chosen by its narrator to represent his village, is intended to praise the tribe led by al-Qablan, which was promoted by al-Jazzar to rule over the entire area.

THE HONOR OF THE HOST

In Hamza As'ad's story we find an additional test, when the ruler tests his followers and asks them "who is more honorable"—he himself, who slaughtered five sheep for his guests, or the host who slaughtered one sheep? The ruler rejects his followers' flattering response and states that the host who slaughtered a sheep for a beggar—without knowing his identity and without discriminating between rich and poor—is more generous than the ruler who slaughtered five sheep for his guests as a reward for their actions. This serves to praise the virtues of generosity and respect for guests—any guests, including beggars.

At the end of Muhammad 'Arsan's story, the host tells the ruler: "Had I known that you are al-Jazzar, I would have slaughtered three hundred heads of sheep and goats." This expresses the custom of receiving lords with gifts as numerous and precious as possible, as a kind of insurance policy for the future.

In this context we may mention the expression common among Arabs, "*akram min Hatem,*" "more generous than Hatem." This refer to the actions of the boy Hatem, who slaughtered a camel for each of his guests and went so far as dividing the rest of his father's camels among them. As Hatem explained to his father: "With this act I have brought you immortal fame!" And indeed, his act is considered a paradigm of generosity to this day.

Likewise in the story under consideration, the Gazan host slaughters a sheep for each of his guests, and this exaggerated generosity serves to bring honor to his name. The more the host does for his guests, the more his fame as a generous and hospitable man will spread, enhancing his status in his village and among his tribe, and even in the entire region.

To this day, custom dictates that a sheep be slaughtered in honor of highly regarded guests and on special occasions.

As mentioned earlier, the two stories find five parallels in IFA. Three of these are told by Muslim narrators, and two by Jews.[3] The plot in four of the five parallels is identical: Unlike in our cases, the host is a poor man who shares his remaining food with the beggar he finds at his doorstep, even when he has nothing left to eat. Later—and here the parallelism appears—it turns out that the beggar is a ruler, a superior minister, or, in the Jewish versions, a magician or hidden saint. In all versions the generous poor man is rewarded materially for his hospitality and generosity.

An exception is the Druze story (IFA 22089), which is parallel in plot details and historical framework to the version told by Hamza As'ad Abu Zidan. In this story, the background for the test of hospitality is the exaction of taxes from the inhabitants of the country by an absentee ruler. The story's purpose is to praise the residents of Usfiyeh, which fought each other for the honor of hosting the guests and fulfilling the obligation of hospitality without knowing the reason for the tax collectors' visit to the village. Their generosity wins them the respect of the ruler, who waives their tax obligations and brings a stream of new residents to the village.

In the other versions, the host is poor. In the story told by 'Ali 'Ayesh (IFA 7243, Israel, Muslim) and Abu Mahmoud (IFA 13152, Israel, Bedouin), the poor man's reward is brought about by a miracle, when a treasure is discovered under the peg of his tent. These two stories are identical in most details, but only one mentions the name of Haroun al-Rashid. In both, as in all parallels, the poor man is invited to the ruler's palace after passing the test of hospitality. But unlike in the other parallels, here the two do not meet, and the king does not identify himself as the beggar who appeared at his home. The poor man who comes to the ruler's abode finds him praying and decides that if the ruler has turned to God for help, so should he. When he returns to his tent, he changes its location ("a change of place, a change of luck," as the Hebrew saying goes, or as the story says: "Move the stake and peg, and God will redeem his slave"). While posting the stakes at his new location, he finds a treasure and becomes rich. The poor man is not rewarded during his visit to the ruler's palace, but rather receives his reward mysteriously, through divine intervention. Thus the moral importance of the commandment of hospitality is brought home.

The Jewish versions differ from the others in involving supernatural events, while all the Muslim versions are historical legends related to specific times, places, and personalities. This is also true of the two stories recounted here.

In Kalman Gurevitch's Lithuanian Jewish version (IFA 5747), as well as in the Persian Jewish equivalent told by Shmuel Qadusi (IFA 750B), the poor man's reward comes from the hands of a supernatural entity. In the first it is a hidden saint, and in the second, a magician who presents the poor man with a golden sculpture that brings riches. The other versions, like our own, feature a flesh-and-blood ruler. The Jewish parallels are also missing the sociohistorical context, focusing on the test that occurs when a beggar or vagrant reaches the house of the poor man, who hosts him with generosity beyond his means, giving up what little he has.

In some versions, the behavior or response of others is detailed as a contrast to the host's generosity. In Qadusi's story, the wife's response to her husband's deeds ("Why did you give him everything, leaving nothing for us?") contrasts with the host's generosity and enables the narrator to present the promise of a reward in the magician's answer to the wife. The story begins and ends with the relationship between the generous poor man and his envious rich neighbor. In the opening the rich man's cruelty to his poor neighbors is related, and in the final episode the rich man, covetous of their newfound wealth, is of course punished.

In both stories published here, the supporting characters in the story represent a position opposed to that of the generous man. The ruler negates it when he praises the greatness of the generous host. And so, in Hamza's story, when the generous host invites the *mukhtars* and sheikhs of the village to the feast he is holding for the beggar:

> . . . they said to Abu Sa'id: "Who are your guests, O Abu Sa'id?"
> He said: "This man you see here."
> They said: "What . . . have you slaughtered a sheep for a beggar?"
> And he said: "Yes I have. I saw him. Allah knows he belongs to a respectable family, and this man is not a beggar."

And similarly, in Muhammad 'Arsan's story:

> His paternal cousins came and said to him: "O sheikh, what is the matter with you? These are beggars, not equals."
> He said to them: "Uncles, for me all men are equals. . . . Each deserves to be honored."

The theme of the local leader tested for his hospitality by a ruler disguised as a beggar is common in Arabic folktales; less so in Jewish ones. Its purpose is to strengthen existing customs, to testify to other virtues of the local leader, and to vouch for the character of the village as a locality to which it is an honor to belong. Motifs of generosity toward beggars that is rewarded materially, however, are common in all folk traditions—Jewish and Arab alike.

NOTES

1. Other versions of this tale from the Israel Folktale Archives (IFA) include: IFA 5082, "The Golden Statue" (recorded from father, Zemah Qadusi: Jewish, Persian Kurdistan); IFA 7243, "The Poor Man, the Dervish, and the Treasure" (told by 'Ali 'Ayesh: Jaffa, Israel, Arab), IFA 5747, "One of the 36 Righteous Men" (told by Kalman Gurevitch: Jewish, Lithuania); IFA 13152, "Haroun al-Rashid Upholds Simplicity" (told by Abu Mahmoud: Israel, Bedouin), IFA 22089, "'Aquila Agha Al-Hafi" (Majid Abu Rukan: Usfiyeh, Israel, Druze).
2. See another version of this tale: IFA 13152.
3. These versions are related to the following tale types: AT *776 ("Miscellaneous Divine Rewards"); AT *776 IC3 ("A Person Provides Hospitality"); AT *776 IIC 3 ("The Person Is Rewarded by a King"); AT 750B ("Hospitality Rewarded").

BIBLIOGRAPHY

Aarne, Antti, and Stith Thompson. 1961. *The Types of the Folktale: A Classification and Bibliography*. FF Communications no. 184. Helsinki: Suomalainen Tiedeakatemia.

Cohen, Aharon. 1960. *The Arab East*. Merhavia: Sifriat Poalim. [Hebrew]

Shamir, Shimon. 1965. *The History of the Arabs in the Middle East in Modern Times*. Tel Aviv: Reshafim. [Hebrew]

THE YOUNG MEN WHO DRANK ARAK AT AL-KHADER

IFA 23000

NARRATED BY ZAHRA ABDI KHAMRA (ISRAEL, MUSLIM)

This story was told to me by my mother. It is about these young men who drank arak.* They brought it in cans. My mother told me: "They came from the villages. I don't know which ones. They came and brought sheep with them." My mother swore that the arak was in cans, this is how they got the arak out. . . .† And you know how it was then. They would drink. They got drunk and went swimming. There was not even a two-day old chick there.‡ You know Abu Khaled, who was in charge of the place, cannot see [blind]. All the people that were there were elderly, veterans. Everyone walked with a cane. They all came to the door, shouting: "Hey, Sidna Al-Khader,"§ and kissed the place. My mother began to cry: "They kissed Al-Khader, the door." Yes, they lay down [bowed] on the floor, asking for help: "*Tanibin 'alek*" [in Arabic]— Extract them alive. "Hey, Mar Elias,"¶ they called . . .

My mother said: "Within seconds, someone came in a boat. One man took so many people out [of the water] and threw them [onto the shore]. And then no one ever saw him again, he disappeared."

[Roseland Da'eem: What happened to the young men?]

They lived. Every one of them. She said, "No one was injured."

[RD: Did they get out of the water?]

They got out. He pulled them out, one by one. He took them out and threw them on the beach. He took them out with an oar. He had oars with him. This is how he took them out [of the water]. He would pull one [out of the water] and throw him out, pull one [out of the water] and throw him out. Maybe close to fifty people, and no one ever saw him again; he disappeared. What is the meaning of this?

[RD: How was he dressed, do you remember?]

My mother said: "He was dressed up, he was dark and wearing a black suit." My mother said that she saw him dark and fat.

[RD: Was your mother there?]

* A kind of liquor.
† Accompanied by hand gestures.
‡ Arabic saying, meaning "there was absolutely no one there."
§ The holy site of Elijah's Cave in Haifa is called "Al-Khader" by Palestinians.
¶ Mar Elias, the Arab Christian name for Elijah.

My mother was living there, she saw him, saw him when he came in the boat. After all, the women came in droves, and sat down on the beach. It wasn't like today, with cars and people and crowds. These events happened over sixty years ago, maybe sixty-three years ago. It wasn't like today, no cops, like . . . And nobody paid attention to anyone then.

[RD: What did you say that they said: "Hey Al-Khader, hey Mar Elias"?]

"Hey Khader, hey Mar Elias, we beg you, we swear by your life (*bihyatak*). Hey Khader, hey Mar Elias, '*Ya Abu Al-'Abbas,*' save the young men." Yes, and then he began to pull them out of the water and toss them onto land, pull them out of the water and toss them onto land, pull them out of the water and toss them onto land.

This is the story my mother told, she would tell this story every time.

[RD: Now you have told me that Al-Khader is the Prophet Elijah's cousin?]

Yes, his first cousin [related through their mothers].

[RD: And here they said "Hey Khader . . ."].

"*Ya Khader, Ya Abu Al-'Abbas, Ya Saint [Mar],*" yes, "*Ya Mar Elias.*"

[RD: They turned him into one figure here].

Yes, they say: "Al-Khader Abu 'Abbas." They said: "Al-Khader. Mar Elias, Khader, hey Abu Al-'Abbas, hey Mar Elias." I heard my mother say that all the time.

[RD: That they are cousins?]

Yes, cousins. My mother would say that they are cousins. I heard my mother say that. And it's true, they are related to one another. There is a mountain between them. One above the other.*

Transcribed by Roseland Da'eem

---

* Indicating the distance between the Cave of Elijah, below Mount Carmel, and the Carmelite Monastery, on Mount Carmel.

COMMENTARY TO "THE YOUNG MEN WHO DRANK ARAK AT AL-KHADER"

IFA 23000

ROSELAND DA'EEM

I recorded the story "The Young Men Who Drank Arak at Al-Khader" in Arabic, in Haifa (April 1999), as it was told to me by Zahra Abdi Khamra, a Muslim Palestinian woman who was born in Haifa in 1936.[1] The narrator related several stories about Al-Khader, the Arab cultural figure who corresponds to the Prophet Elijah (*Mar Elias*). She heard some of the stories from firsthand sources, and others are based on her own experiences. The story discussed here had been told to her by her mother, who witnessed the events herself. Her story is characterized by her dramatization, which the narrator relates fluently, accompanying her words with gestures and body movements.

According to the Aarne-Thompson tale type index (1961), the story belongs to the category of religious tales. Subjects that recur in religious tales include (1) "God Repays and Punishes" (750–79 AT), and (2) "Truth Comes to Light" (AT 780–89). The story "The Young Men Who Drank Arak at Al-Khader" belongs to the first category. The prominent theme here is the reward received by the faithful for their obedience to the values and norms that entitle them to justice, in this case, their visit to the holy place and their plea to the saint for help.

The story is similar to the Jewish oikotype AT *776 ("Miscellaneous Divine Rewards").[2] As the Jewish oikotype, the story is divided into three parts: (1) A person upholds religious commandments;[3] (2) he is rewarded by the Prophet Elijah; and (3) he is saved from death.

The story has one parallel in the Israel Folktale Archives (IFA), "The Prophet Elijah (Mar Elias) and the Fire" (IFA 10341), narrated by a Christian Palestinian, but it is missing the first part of the oikotype.

The researcher Hasan El-Shamy (2004) wrote an index to literary tale types in Arab culture. He classified type 776, in parallel to the Jewish oikotype (AT *776), as "Contest between Saint and Druid (Magician): The Saint and His Faith Win" (El-Shamy 776), which contains the theme

"The Saint Disguised as Help." It is interesting that this story is actually more similar to the Jewish oikotype than to the Arab cultural types.

The story discussed here underwent different literary and artistic adaptations. Haifa artist Abed Abdi, the narrator's brother, made a series of illustrations that were inspired by the story he had heard from their mother. The written version of the story was published in the book by Salman Natour, *Wama Nasayna* (*Unforgettable Memories* [Natour 1998]). In that version Al-Khader made the rescue mission five or six times, thus saving several men at once, in contrast to the version of the story told here, which describes fifty to sixty rescue missions. It is interesting to note that Natour heard the story from the father of the same narrator.

The saint figure in the story is a combination of the Prophet Elijah (Mar Elias) and Al-Khader. Mar Elias, who is the biblical Prophet Elijah, is also central to the Jewish tradition as a legendary folk figure who appears in various forms, becoming supernatural in folk belief. Elijah's role is to reward kindness, heal the sick, enrich and save from death, but also to punish (Noy 1966). In the New Testament in Arabic, he is known as "*Eliyya Annabi*" (the pronunciation resembles that of the Hebrew term for "Elijah the Prophet"). Christians sanctify him primarily as a prophet of Israel and for his war against the fanatical prophets of Ba'al, the equivalent of Christianity's struggle against idolatry. Accordingly many churches bear the name "Mar Elias" within Israel-Palestine, Lebanon, and Syria ('Arraf 1993).

The biblical Prophet Elijah, who lived on Mount Carmel, is known by the Arabic names "Elias" or "Mar Elias," and identified with Al-Khader within the Arabic tradition. Al-Khader, the legendary figure associated with the "faithful God-fearing" figure in the Koran (The Cave Chapter [Surat Al-Kahf]: 60–82), is sometimes likened to, identified with, or confused with the Prophet Elijah (Mar Elias). At times the sacred places of Elijah are also attributed to Al-Khader (Augustinovic 1972).[4]

The motif "Taboo: Asking Questions" (C 410), which is also noted as the tale type "God's Justice Vindicated" (759 AT), appears in the Koranic story of Al-Khader. This motif is common to the literature of different nations of the ancient Near East and also appears in rabbinic legends (as in the tale of Rabbi Yehoshua Ben Levi's journey with Elijah, who does strange deeds.) According to folk belief Al-Khader is a saint or prophet; those who call his name three times will be saved from theft, fire, drowning, despotism, the devil, a snake, or a scorpion. The sky, land, and sea obey him. He is the representative of God on sea and land. He appears and disappears at will and flies in the sky. He lives in Jerusalem. He prays on Fridays in the mosques of Mecca and Medina (Saudi Arabia) and on the Mount of Olives (Jerusalem). He eats truffle mushrooms and celery. He meets Elijah and goes on pilgrimage with him to Mecca every year. He drinks from the waters of the Zamzam (Zumzum) well[5] and can find water under the earth (Wensinck 1933, 8: 374–56).

As mentioned already, there are both similarities between and confusion over the Prophet Elijah and Al-Khader. These are intensified in a place like Haifa, where two holy places exist close to each other: one identified with the Prophet Elijah and the other with Al-Khader. The local Palestinian population also does not clearly distinguish between them (Augustinovic 1972).

In our story, the Prophet Elijah/Al-Khader performs a miracle. He rescues a group of men who visited the Cave of Elijah the Prophet—which residents call Al-Khader—ate mutton, drank "arak . . . in cans," went to swim in the sea nearby, and nearly drowned. Those who witnessed the incident panicked and prayed fervently. They knelt down, kissed the walls of the cave, cried, and called for help. Suddenly, a man appeared in a boat, rescued the men, and disappeared. According to the narrator's belief, it was Al-Khader. When calling for help, the believers used the Arabic phrase "*Tanibin 'alek*," which means turning to or asking for help, particularly the assistance of saints. Its literal meaning is "I seek help," but the phrase is more powerful than that simple statement. It contains a plea for the kind of help that saves people from catastrophe, as when a person in distress pleads for the miracles of the saints and the divine world (Badawi and Hinds 1986; Canaan 1980 [1927]). In this story, the people seeking help kissed the walls of the holy site, ran toward the beach, raised their hands up to heaven, called the various names for the Prophet Elijah (Mar Elias and Al-Khader), and bowed to the ground. Their supplication is accompanied by body movements expressing humility and meekness. The saint responded to the cries of the believers and their calling his name. That is how the Prophet Elijah rewards people who believe in him.

According to the holistic approach (as distinguished from the literary-aesthetic approach), which sees the story as composed of different elements, a tale's genre is determined by the relation of its various components to one another and to the story as a whole.[6] The story is thus considered a "saint's legend": a tale whose central figure is a saint revered by the society that tells the story. Haya Bar-Itzhak (1987) dealt with the poetics of Jewish saints' legends. In my Master's thesis on saints' legends in Arabic culture (Da'eem 2005), I found that the poetic elements determined by Bar-Itzhak match those of the Arabic-language genre. This story is also given in the supernatural, numinous, miraculous mode, where a person is confronted with supernatural forces. In our story, the men are in mortal danger, nearly drowning, and are faced with forces of nature as exerted by the supernatural world. The supernatural character of the Prophet Elijah/Al-Khader appears in the human world to save the men from death, as a reward to the believers who sought his help and prayed. Thus the men who visited a holy place before swimming in the sea were rewarded.

The supernatural character of the Prophet Elijah/Al-Khader appears in the story in the guise of a human in the middle of the sea, and makes use of objects from the realistic world. The cultural interpretation is that a holy figure has suddenly appeared to come to the rescue.

The story is a saint's legend centered on a sanctified character, but it is also a local legend that takes place in part in Elijah's Cave in Haifa. The Cave of Elijah the Prophet (Al-Khader) is located at the foot of Mount Carmel, on the Mediterranean Sea. The sea fulfills a plot function. In those days (the period in which the story is set), nothing separated the cave and the sea—no cars or traffic—unlike today, when the main road between Haifa and Tel Aviv bisects them. The narrator thus describes the place as it was in the past. She provides a very concise description: The Prophet Elijah is above, on the mountain (referring to the Carmelite convent), while Al-Khader is at the foot of the mountain (referring to the Cave of Elijah). One is above the other. The cave is not described in detail. The cave and the sea are described in a way that serves the plot. The explanation provided by the narrator's mother, who claims to be witness, is that indeed all the women went down to the sea, and she explains how they got there. The explanation is necessary today, because anyone who hears the story knows that there is a highway and buildings that obstruct the free movement between the sacred place and the sea. But then, when the events occurred, and young people nearly drowned, the place was completely empty.[7]

The story is a folk literary work that draws its existence from the society where it was told and the culture and customs of that society; it reflects the spiritual and material culture and various social attitudes. The story describes a visit to a holy place undertaken with the twin goals of healing and leisure. The narrator's mother, who was ill, lived for two years in the Cave of Elijah.[8] She swore that the information she conveyed was true, and that what she saw really happened. Throughout the story the narrator kept repeating the words: "My mother says," "my mother would say," and "my mother swore." Hence we learn about the importance of "the word" and the significance of firsthand evidence in this genre. Despite the narrator's society's belief in miraculous supernatural powers, it is necessary to verify repeatedly the dramatic picture of the bowing masses and the appearance of the man in the boat with oars, which is described by the narrator under oath, while validating the word of an eyewitness.

The story illustrates a striking phenomenon among mixed societies: the use of words from the different languages prevalent in that society. In ethnically mixed Haifa, for example, the narrator used the word "automobile." This word came into Arabic under the influence of the British; the younger generation of today does not use this term anymore, and some even cannot understand it. On the other hand, the narrator used the saying "there was not even a two-day old chick" (*"fish sous ibin yomen"*), which means there was no one there. Of course, someone who does not speak the Arabic language will have trouble understanding this phrase without explanation.

The sheep the men brought with them is a symbol of the redemption of the son of Abraham (Ishmael or Isaac). It is served as a sacrifice at the Muslim Festival of Sacrifice ('ed Al-Adha) and slaughtered during fulfilment of vows. Bringing sheep to a holy place, slaughtering them, and sacrificing them is an observance of a folk religious cult. Both Christians and Muslims slaughter or sacrifice sheep and lambs in fulfilment of vows or as entertainment. Certain conditions are required for the selection of the lamb intended for slaughter in fulfilment of vow ceremonies. Eating lamb meat can indicate economic status, and the fact that the story specifies that the men ate lamb, the most expensive meat, indicates their distinguished economic status (Canaan 1980 [1927]).

It is not clear in the story if the sheep are a kind of offering or intended for fulfilment of a vow, or if the men planned a hike and took sheep with them to roast on an open fire. This latter interpretation is reinforced by the fact that they came equipped with cans of arak for feasting and entertainment. It should be noted that, according to Islam, alcohol use is prohibited. Since the narrator is Muslim, she might be implying that there was a divine punishment for drinking arak in a holy place, but this cannot be determined with certainty. In Haifa, a mixed society, Muslims and Christians live together, and many Muslims drink alcohol, despite the religious prohibition.

The fact that the men brought arak in cans reflects the well-known practice of distilling arak at home and storing it in cans.

The narrator says: "And you know how it was then. They would drink." The narrator could be seen as apologizing for past alcohol consumption by implying that less alcohol is consumed by Muslims today due to the influence of the Islamic movements.

The social relations between residents of Haifa and those from the countryside are also reflected in the story. The tale takes place in the Cave of Elijah, on the seashore. The men who came from villages, according to the narrator, drank arak, went swimming, and began to drown. The men are not from the city of Haifa. Mentioning the village origins of the men may reflect the attitude of Haifa urban-dwellers toward the rural guests who came to visit the city's holy places, since most of the communities at that time were rural.

In summary, this story is both a saint's legend and local legend about the Prophet Elijah in Haifa. The story structure is compatible with the elements and characteristics of these genres, and expresses the spiritual and material culture of the Arabs of Haifa. The story reflects the Arab people of Haifa's belief in the Prophet Elijah (Mar Elias)/al-Khader and the supernatural qualities attributed to him in this dramatic tale. The tale's description of believers bowing to the ground and a sailing saint battling the forces of nature at sea comprises what Olrik, according to epic laws, calls a "tableaux scene" that gives expression to the idea of the tale.

NOTES

1. In my master's thesis (Da'eem 2005), the story was transcribed using the Latin alphabet. For this chapter I rewrote the tale in the original Arabic and translated it into English in a way that preserves the original language to the extent possible.
2. According to the Israel Folktale Archives classification of Jewish oikotypes.
3. In the stories in the Israel Folktale Archives, the hero is a rabbi or a poor man.
4. Al-Khader is also sometimes associated with Saint George.
5. A holy well close to Al-Ka'ba in Mecca.
6. Heda Jason defined the components by which the genre is defined according to modus, character, time, space, and objects (Jason 1971).
7. In recent years a footbridge was built from the cave to the sea, but for many years the road was inaccessible to pedestrians.
8. This information was gathered in a conversation prior to the telling of the story and not through the story itself.

BIBLIOGRAPHY

Aarne, Antti, and Stith Thompson. 1961. *The Types of the Folktale: A Classification and Bibliography*. FF Communications no. 184. Helsinki: Suomalainen Tiedeakatemia.

'Arraf, Shoukri. 1993. *Tabaqat Al-'Anbia' wa Al'Awlia' Alsalihin fi Al'Ard Al-Muqaddasa—Tabaqat Al-'Anbia' wa Al'Awlia,* j2. Mi'ilya: Ila Al'omq. [Arabic]

Augustinovic, A. 1972. *El-Khader and the Prophet Elijah.* Jerusalem: Franciscan Printing Press.

Badawi, Al-Sayid, and M. Hinds. 1986. *A Dictionary of Egyptian Cairo*. Cairo: American University in Cairo Press.

Bar-Itzhak, Haya. 1987. "'Saints' Legend' as Genre in Jewish Folk-Literature." PhD diss., Jerusalem: Hebrew University. [Hebrew]

Canaan, Taufik. 1980 [1927]. *Muhammedan Saints and Sanctuaries in Palestine*. Jerusalem: Ariel Publishing House.

Da'eem, Roseland. 2005. "Local 'Saints' Legends' Told by Christian and Muslim Tellers in the Context of the Elijah Cave and Carmelite Monastery." Master's thesis, University of Haifa. [Hebrew]

El-Shamy, Hasan M. 2004. *Types of Folktales in the Arab World: A Demographically Oriented Tale-Type Index*. Bloomington: Indiana University Press.

Jason, Heda. 1971. *Genre: An Essay in Oral Literature*. Tel Aviv: Tel Aviv University.

Natour, Salman. 1998. *Wama Nasayna*. Ram-Alla: Mu'assat Tamer. [Arabic]

Noy, Dov. 1966. *Introduction to Rabbinic Literature*. Jerusalem: Hebrew University. [Hebrew]

Propp, Vladimir. 1968. *Morphology of the Folktale*. Austin: University of Texas Press.

Thompson, Stith. 1955–58. *Motif Index of Folk Literature*. Bloomington: Indiana University Press.

Wensinck, Arnet Jan. 1933. "Khader." In *The Encyclopedia of Islam*, vol. 8, 347–56. Trans. Yuonis Abd Al-Hamid. Cairo: D.N.

THE ROAD ON THE HOLIDAY OF SHAVUOT

IFA 23011

Narrated by Aharon David Rabinovitch (Belarus)

A heavy winter gripped the land that year, and the snowstorms had not stopped their raging for a whole month. The roads lay forgotten underneath a cloak of whiteness, and all contact between the towns and the neighboring villages had ceased completely. A wealthy merchant needed to transfer a load of glass to the fair that was meant to take place in the next town, across the river, which at present was frozen.

The merchant went to the wagon-owners of his town and asked if they were inclined, in exchange for generous payment, to transfer the glass to its destination in time for the opening of the fair. Now, on the best of days, the road to this town was a bad one and much in need of repairs. On a snowy winter's day, it was treacherous, indeed. One Jewish wagon-owner, a man with many children, agreed to do the job. The merchant clearly stipulated that the glass was to be delivered whole and in one piece to its destination. In the event of any damage, the wagon-owner would be held responsible and need to pay compensation.

Early the next morning, as the snowstorm continued to rage with cold and blinding intensity, the wagon-owner set out on his way with horse and wagon, now packed with the glass. After a long and exhausting day of travel, as evening fell and they approached the river, the horse stumbled and fell. The sledge slid off the path, struck a rock, and the entire load of glass was smashed all to pieces.

The wagon-owner returned to the town with his lame horse and a wagon full of glass shreds.

When the merchant heard about the misfortune, he immediately went to the wagon-owner's home and demanded compensation for the damage.

"I am the one who should be paid!" cried the wagon-owner. "My horse, the source of my livelihood, has broken his leg, and will not be able to walk for many days!"

"You made a promise to me!" shouted the merchant. "We had an agreement. You are breaking your promise, which is explicitly forbidden in the Torah."

"Where in the Torah is this written?"

"It is written," the merchant insisted. "It is written in the Book of Judges."

"But when were we given the Torah?" asked the wagon-owner.

"We received the Torah on Shavuot."

"On Shavuot?" echoed the wagon-owner hotly. "On the holiday of Shavuot, the road was like a violin,* it was like day,† and there was no problem getting to the market!"

Transcribed by Itzhak Ganuz

---

* From the Yiddish: "*Vi a fidl*" (literally: "The road was as straight as a violin string").
† From the Yiddish: "*Zi iz geven vi a tog*" (literally: "The road was visible, as in the full light of day").

Commentary to
"The Road on the Holiday of Shavuot"

IFA 23011

Itzhak Ganuz

This story was told by Aharon David Rabinovitch, who was born in Belarus in 1890. In the town of his birth, Rabinovitch was a butcher who came into daily contact with Jews from neighboring towns and villages, and he listened to their stories. He loved to tell stories as well, and often seasoned his tales with popular jokes from the people with whom he did business throughout the day. He came to Israel in 1947, after surviving the Holocaust. He settled in Tel Aviv and died in 1963.[1]

Our story is unique, as it does not belong to any particular tale type, but its ending is similar to the general AT 929 tale type ("The Clever Defense"). In the IFA, there are 140 stories that include wagon-owners or coachmen. Most of this collection was recorded by Ashkenazi Jews. Ninety-four of the stories originate in Eastern Europe. Twelve additional stories were told by Ashkenazi Jews from Israel.[2]

The function of the coachman or wagon-driver in the economic fabric of the town and Jewish village in Eastern Europe was of the greatest importance. The transfer of goods and people from place to place—along bad roads and paths that weren't paths, through cold days and colder nights, snow, wind, floods, and mud, and at the mercy of robbers who would lie in wait to attack and rob travelers—gave their profession a place of special importance.

The story begins with an exposition of the physical disconnection among the towns and villages in the area. This disconnection is caused by the bad state of the roads, as a result of a severely harsh winter; in the words of the story: "all contact between the towns and the neighboring villages had ceased completely." A wealthy merchant who ignores the physical conditions insists on delivering fragile goods to the fair taking place "across the river, which at present was frozen over." Emphasis on the merchant's wealth and his unwillingness to forego a promising business opportunity creates, in the listener, a negative attitude toward this character, and happiness at the predictable and inevitable misfortune in the meeting of the fragile glass and the slippery ice.

The teller again stresses the fact that the roads are very bad when he mentions that, on the best of days, the road was bad, while on a snowy winter's day, it was treacherous. At this stage, the merchant is the character who drives the plot. He approaches the collective character of the "wagon-owners." No details are given about their reactions or responses, but as the plot continues, we understand that they all refuse the job. The only one willing to take on this impossible task is a man who seems to be in a state of financial distress or trouble, described as a Jew "with many children," who apparently acts out of need, having no other choice.

Thus the conflict between the wealthy merchant and the poor man reaches its first stage. The audience of listeners knows there is no way out. It naturally identifies with the character of the wagon-owner, expects that he will take the job on himself, and that he will fail. The tension mounts once the merchant lays down the conditions involving compensation for any ensuing damage caused to the goods along the way. This is an impossible stipulation, because of the physical conditions and also because of the wagon-owner's financial situation, even though his poverty is never explicitly stated.

It is clear that the storyteller sides with the wagon-owner. Perhaps this is why he never actually says that the wagon-owner agrees to the merchant's conditions. The wagon-owner's righteousness is emphasized in the following paragraph. For one whole day the wagon-owner, his horse, the wagon, and the load of glass struggle against the harsh snowstorm. As night falls the horse collapses and falls, causing the sledge and wagon to slip, upon which the glass shatters. The guilt falls on the wagon-owner, and his dedication, perseverance, devotion to his goal, and desire to fulfill the conditions of the business deal are stressed.

The injustice of the wealthy merchant toward the wagon-owner is expressed as the story continues: The merchant, when he hears about the misfortune, demands compensation according to the agreed-upon conditions.

Here the conflict reaches its peak. The wagon-owner, who up until this point has been attentive, compromising, and servile to the wealthy merchant, suddenly surprises us with his response as he demands compensation for himself because his livelihood has been harmed. Victory is won when the wagon-owner solves the problem by using scholarly wisdom from the Torah to back him up. Here for the first time we also see that the wealthy merchant is also a Jew, and the conflict turns to focus on the internal, social, and socioeconomic contexts. The tension rises still further as a result of the threat to the accepted norms of Jewish society relating to mutual responsibility (moral responsibility among Jews).

Reference to the "giving of the Torah," as an emphasis for the validity of the conditions, has several meanings: not just a dry look at the finer points of the Torah, but an attempt to address the essence of the Torah—that same sensitivity to social justice, and mutual responsibility, that supposedly characterizes Jewish society.

The wagon-owner's clever answer is generally reminiscent of tale type AT 929 ("The Clever Defence"). Yet it is difficult to understand his witticism. Is it really true, as the wagon-owner claims, to say that the Torah is valid only during the season in which it was given? Indeed, this seems inconceivable. It is clear that here the wagon-owner is revealed to be far cleverer than the wealthy merchant.

The listening audience, which completely identifies with the wagon-owner, participates in the happiness of his victory. The injustice and tension accompanying the economic gap in Jewish society are immediately rectified.

Although in our story the character of the wagon-owner is portrayed in a positive light and arouses both empathy and sympathy from the listening audience, this character is not always thusly portrayed. Wagon-drivers and coachmen—simple people, further from the Book and the written word than those who deal with scholarly or holy matters or than even craftsmen—for the most part are portrayed in a negative light in most Yiddish stories and proverbs, as in these examples:

The wagon-driver rides long miles, his face toward the horses, until he, himself, becomes a horse. ("*A baal agala fort azoi lang mitn ponim tzum ferd biz er vert alein a ferd.*")

O God, liberate us from exile and from wagon-drivers!
("*Loz undz ois got fun galut un baal agalot.*" [Stutchkoff 1950, 117])
Wagon-drivers drink alone (a glass of vodka). ("*A baal agala trinkt alein.*")[3]

This idea is also expressed in the prayers of the Days of Awe:

And he was as clay in the hands of the Creator, like Man in the hands of the wagon-owner.
("*Vi der parshoin beim baal agala in der hant.*")

This negative way of relating to wagon-drivers is also reflected in IFA tale 4077 ("Why There Were Two Messiahs"), recorded by Nachmat Tzion and told by Reizl Wolff, of Poland.[4] The wagon-driver in this story is annoying. Through the questions he asks the rabbi he tries to present himself as a clever scholar, but his questions are insipid and bothersome.

In IFA tale 2844 ("The Clever Wagon Driver Tests His Three Sons"), told by Jacob Rawer, of Poland, the wagon-driver is characterized as a wise man who knows how to give advice, and who needs to predict the mishap that will befall him during his journey. Therefore, in answer to his youngest son, he sees the continuity of the profession as it passes from father to son, like many other professions and businesses in those days.

The wagon-driver's helper was referred to as a "*schmeisser*" (a beater or whipper). On long journeys, when the wagon-driver would lie down and rest, it was the *schmeisser*'s responsibility to keep the horses moving and make sure they didn't stray off the road. One of the stories tells about a wagon-driver who was looking for a *schmeisser* to work with him. One boy turned up. The wagon-driver decided to put him to the test and asked him:

"Tell me, what would you do? It is night, there's a rainstorm raging all around. You are in the middle of the journey; there are no houses or people around for miles. A wheel breaks, and it's black as pitch in every direction . . ."

The young man didn't know what to say and stood there, silent, depressed, and dumb-founded by the wagon-driver's shockingly dismal description.

"Know this," shouted the wagon-driver, "it is bad! Very bad! It is bitter as gall!" ("*Siz biter vi gal.*")[5]

In the case of a tragedy or misfortune, the wagon-driver also knows how to make clever excuses to explain away the cause of the problem and shrug off all responsibility and guilt; often the same arguments are taken from the Jewish holy books and literary sources. Together with this, he bends the truth to his own benefit, of course. Such is the case described in our story, IFA Tale 23011 ("The Road on the Holiday of Shavuot").

Memoirs and memorial (*yizkor*) books copiously relate how difficult and exhausting it was for wagon-drivers to make a living. Perhaps this is why wagon-drivers were famous for being overly critical of and rude to their passengers. In his memoirs, Yekhezkel Kotik describes a man who was referred to him as a student in this way: "I looked upon the young man and straightaway, I didn't like his looks. Too tall, big-boned, large, thick hands—he looked just like a wagon-driver" (Kotik 2005, 58).

Many stories about wagon-drivers are prefaced by brief introductions, such as: "There once lived a Jewish wagon driver, whip in hand. It was as if he and his whip were one—inseparable. In this way, he lived his life, together with his loyal horse, far from enlightenment and the higher dealings of Jewish life, sunk in a daily life of coarseness and the material world" (Chaham 2005).

Mordechai Ben Yehezkel's story "Ritual Slaughterer—Wagon-Driver" is taken from the book *The Faith of the Righteous* (Warsaw, 1955) and also, according to rumor, from the character of the man who is the subject of the story: ". . . and this wagon-driver was not ignorant and uncultivated, as were most wagon-drivers, because as a youth he had learned in the study house, and he had the spark of Torah in him, and it was only the changes of time that brought him to this profession" (Ben Yehezkel 1957, 275).

According to different interviewees in the books of Naftali Gross, wagon-drivers were perceived as simple, non-educated people, at times naïve: "the wagon-driver who didn't know it was forbidden to beat one's wife" ("*Der baal agala yung vos hot nit gevust az men tor nit shlogn a veif*" [Gross 1955, 171]).

Wagon-drivers and coachmen are depicted as very sensitive about their honor, and crave the respect and appreciation of others. The wagon-driver's passengers in these tales often include personages of high status: rabbis, merchants, and Jews dedicated to holy works—and he, a simple wagon-driver, tries to overcome his feelings of inferiority. This is expressed in IFA tale 6649 ("The Coachman and the Rabbi Who Changed Places"), recorded by Motel Adar from West Galicia:

A baal agala fun a rav hot ein mol gezogt cum rav: ir hot azoifil kavod. Lomir zich baitn mit di erter vel ich oich hobn a bisl kavod. Der rav hot zich gebitn mit di erter un azoi zajnen zej ongekumen in a shtetl un cugeforn zum beit amidrash. Fun beit amidrash zejnen arois oifnemen dem rav. Im opgebn kavod un derbei im gefregt er zol zej farentfern a kashie fun der gemore vos zej farshteien nit.

Dem rav (baal agala) hobn zich di fis ongehoibn shoklen. Er hot zich ober bald gechapt un gezogt: Oich mer a kashie! D-os ken doch afile mein baal agala farentfern!

Translation:

One day, the rabbi's coachman said to him: "You receive so much respect; let's change places, so that I, too, can get some respect."

The rabbi and the coachman changed places, arrived at the town, and went to the study house. The people flocked out of the study house to welcome the rabbi and pay their respects, and then asked him to solve a question from the Talmud which they didn't understand. The rabbi's [coachman's] legs began to tremble, but he quickly regained his composure and said:

"Ah, but this is no riddle at all! Even my coachman can solve it!"

In the memoirs of refugees from the Holocaust and those who managed to emigrate from Europe prior to the grasp of destruction and extermination, wagon-drivers were remembered fondly. It is worth mentioning the observations of Zelda Sapperstein, born in Kaminitz, near Brest in Lithuania, whose memories reflect the period before World War I and up until the 1930s.[6] This is how she describes wagon-drivers:

There were wagon-drivers in our town. Good Jews, they were fair and honest. They would take travelers to Brest. The journey, I remember, took all night. The poor horse would struggle to pull the wagon with his last ounce of strength. More than once, it was necessary to get down from atop the wagon and push, helping the horse to get the wheels moving once again. . . . There was a beadle who worked in the study house, a cantor, a *mohel*, a ritual slaughterer, and someone who called the Jews to prayer at the synagogue. The main thing was that Jews lived—from the wind, from the air. They lived with confidence, sure that the Master of the Universe would help them . . . and thank God, He helped . . . daughters were married . . . they took bridegrooms and received "full maintenance" [*oif kest*]: the young couple received full support from the bride's father for the first few years . . . they were content, they tasted Life, and when it was over, their souls were returned with love to the Master of the Universe . . . because it is the end of every man to die. . . . Man is but ashes and such is his end. . . . Blessed be the True Judge.[7]

In the book *Sefer Ha-Prenumeranten* (Yiddish: *Book of Subscriptions* [Cohen 1975, 255, entry 7221]), we see among other things a list of the people who signed and purchased holy books in the town of Kaminitz Litovsk. The list includes twenty titles, among them, *The Path of the Righteous* by Menachem Tzvi Maksin (Warsaw, 1893), who sold the town eighty-eight copies—a relatively large circulation for a book in those days in such a small settlement.

Hasids appreciated the wagon-drivers' labor, their knowledge of the roads, and their ability to overcome the strange and various difficulties with which they were often faced. There is a story about the father of Reb Avraham Matityahu from Shtefanesht, who once set out from the town on a carriage journey with his young son. In the middle of the journey, he told his son to sit up on the box in place of the coachman and drive the horses. The youth, who in time would be the next *rebbe*, did so. His father was said to have remarked: "My son already holds the reigns of the world in his hands" ("*Majn kind ken shoin firn di velt*").

Something personal. It was the 1930s, and I, a boy, studied in the *Tarbut* Hebrew school in the city of Lida (today in Belarus, formerly Poland). It was the last day of school; school reports had been handed out to the pupils, and the summer vacation was just beginning. I was walking home from school, my school report, which I had just received, clutched in my hand. I passed by the marketplace, where the wagon-drivers stood with their horses and wagons. One of them got up and called out: "So, kid, let's see your school report, what kind of grades did you get?" In all innocence, and with no hesitation, I showed him my school report. He looked it over carefully, scratched his big head, white from a sack of flour, and pronounced: "*Nu*, this is a good road, for both a wagon and a sledge!" ("*Nu, siz a gute veg sai mitn vogn un sai mitn shlitn!*")

NOTES

1. Three of his five children were murdered in the Holocaust. One of his sons and his daughter, Sarah Schiff, had been active in the Zionist movement abroad. Sarah had been imprisoned by the Soviets prior to World War II. During the German occupation, she joined the partisans.
2. The distribution of the stories from Eastern Europe includes: Poland (54); Russia (22); Eastern Europe, no specification (7); Lithuania (5); Latvia (3); Belarus (2); Ukraine (1). One version that is very similar to our story is IFA 1987 ("The Wagon-Driver and the Giving of the Torah Festival"), recorded by Schwartzboim in 1960. The story's essence is as follows: The rabbinical court decreed, according to the laws of the Torah, that a wagon-driver who fails to reach his destination according to the agreed-upon time loses his wage. The wagon-driver claims that, since the Torah was given on Shavuot—that is, in the summer—it cannot discuss things that occur during the winter and times of heavy rainfall.
3. I recorded this saying from a Polish émigré in the 1950s.
4. The storyteller gives the rabbi the name "the Sharp Rabbi of Salant." We assume this refers to Rabbi Salanter (Lipkin) Yisroel (1810–83), the founder of the Morality Movement. When the rabbi was twelve years old, he went to study in a yeshiva in Salant, Lithuania, and his nickname is taken from this town. It is the way of folktales that their tellers relate to their characters as if they were well-known figures of that generation, popular figures of their times, and in this way they lend force to the related events. Still, it is impossible to be sure of the exact identity of this character or any other, although we have an idea of the time and place. Moreover, the

nickname "the Sharp" was known to be attributed to Rebbe Eisel Sharp, rather than Rebbe Yisroel of Salant.

5. I recorded this tale during the 1950s, as narrated by R. Aharon David, of Blessed Memory, born in Lida, western Belarus.

6. Zelda Sapperstein's handwritten Yiddish memoir was sent to the journal *Yeda Am* by Esther Hanani, of Haifa, on March 2, 1982, and it is archived at Yeda Am archives.

7. For more information on Kamieniec Litewski, see *Pinkas Ha-Kihillot, Poland*, 1969–2006, index p. 328.

BIBLIOGRAPHY

Ben Yehezkel, Mordechai. 1957. *A Book of Fairytales* 1. Tel Aviv: Dvir Publications. [Hebrew]

Chaham, A. 2005. "From the Book of the Righteous, the Mysterious Messenger." *Amodia*, supplement, January 3, 2011. [Hebrew]

Cohen [Kagan], Berl. 1975. *Sefer Ha'prenumeranten*. New York: Bibliotek Fon Yiddish Teologishen Seminar. [Yiddish]

Gross, Naftali. 1955. *Mayselekh un Mesholim*. New York: Aber Press. [Yiddish]

Kotik, Yekhezkel. 2005. *Journey to a Nineteenth-Century Shtetl: The Memoirs of Yekhezkel Kotik*. Detroit: Wayne State University Press, in cooperation with the Diaspora Research Institute, Tel Aviv University.

Pinkas Ha-Kehillot, Poland (*Notebook of the [Jewish] Communities*), *Volhyn, Polesia*. 1969–2006. 5th edition. Jerusalem: Yad Vashem. [Hebrew]

Stutchkoff, Nahum. 1950. *Thesaurus of the Yiddish Language*. New York: YIVO.

APPENDIX 1. IFA TALES: ETHNIC DISTRIBUTION, 2013

Ethnic Group	Tales	Ethnic Group	Tales	Ethnic Group	Tales
Afghanistan	529	Iraq	1451	Latvia	49
Africa	45	Israel, Armenian	9	Miscellaneous	27
Algeria	23	Israel, Ashkenazi	977	Moldova	54
Argentina	47	Israel, Baha'i	1	Morocco	2132
Austria	5	Israel, Bedouin	302	Persia	817
Belarus	130	Israel, Circassian	76	Poland	2878
Brazil	2	Israel, Christian	249	Rhodes	5
Bukhara, Uzbekistan	213	Israel, Druze	493	Romania	621
Bulgaria	87	Israel, General	3424	Russia	400
Canada	32	Israel, Karaite	7	South Africa	13
Caucasus	98	Israel, Muslim	672	Spain	20
Chile	2	Israel, Oriental	299	Syria	270
Czechoslovakia	109	Israel, Samaritan	56	Tunis, Arabic	1
Eastern Europe	120	Israel, Sephardic	841	Tunisia	814
Egypt	280	Italy	51	Turkmenistan	1
England	5	Kazakhstan	2	Turkey	383
Ethiopia	184	Kurdistan	5	Uganda	1
France	16	Kurdistan, Iraq	719	Ukraine	826
Georgia	93	Kurdistan, Persia	246	Uruguay	1
Germany	95	Kurdistan, Turkey	43	USA	43
Greece	83	Lebanon	57	Yemen	1587
Holland	3	Lebanon, Christian	2	Yugoslavia, Ashkenazi	67
Hungary	570	Libya	286		
India	117	Lithuania	183	Yugoslavia, Sephardic	51

APPENDIX 2.
IFA PUBLICATIONS SERIES

Noy, Dov. 1962. *A Tale for Each Month, 1961*. Haifa: Haifa Municipality, Ethnological Museum and Folktale Archives. (In Hebrew) [12 tales]

Ben-Zion, Yehoshua. 1962. *The Father's Will*. Haifa: Haifa Municipality, Ethnological Museum and Folktale Archives. (In Hebrew) [13 tales]

Yeshiva, Miriam. 1963. *Seven Folktales*. Haifa: Haifa Municipality, Ethnological Museum and Folktale Archives. (In Hebrew) [7 tales]

Noy, Dov. 1963. *A Tale for Each Month, 1962*. Haifa: Haifa Municipality, Ethnological Museum and Folktale Archives. (In Hebrew) [12 tales]

Weinstein, Esther. 1964. *Grandma Esther Relates*. Haifa: Haifa Municipality, Ethnological Museum and Folktale Archives. (In Hebrew) [18 tales]

Baharav, Zalman. 1964. *Sixty Folktales*. Haifa: Haifa Municipality, Ethnological Museum and Folktale Archives. (In Hebrew) [60 tales]

Kagan, Ziporah. 1964. *A Tale for Each Month, 1963*. Haifa: Haifa Municipality, Ethnological Museum and Folktale Archives. (In Hebrew) [12 tales]

Avitsuk, Ya'acov. 1965. *The Tree That Absorbed Tears*. Haifa: Haifa Municipality, Ethnological Museum and Folktale Archives. (In Hebrew) [36 tales]

Tsedaqa, Ratson. 1965. *Samaritan Legends*. Haifa: Haifa Municipality, Ethnological Museum and Folktale Archives. (In Hebrew) [12 tales]

Kagan, Ziporah. 1965. *A Tale for Each Month, 1964*. Haifa: Haifa Municipality, Ethnological Museum and Folktale Archives. (In Hebrew) [12 tales]

Bribram, Gershon. 1965. *Jewish Folk-stories from Hungary*. Haifa: Haifa Municipality, Ethnological Museum and Folktale Archives. (In Hebrew) [14 tales]

Noy, Dov. 1966. *A Tale for Each Month, 1965*. Haifa: Haifa Municipality, Ethnological Museum and Folktale Archives. (In Hebrew) [12 tales]

Marcus, Eliezer. 1966. *From the Fountainhead*. Haifa: Haifa Municipality, Ethnological Museum and Folktale Archives. (In Hebrew) [40 tales]

Haviv, Yifrah. 1966. *Never Despair*. Haifa: Haifa Municipality, Ethnological Museum and Folktale Archives. (In Hebrew) [7 tales]

Nehmad, Moshe. 1966. *The New Garment*. Haifa: Haifa Municipality, Ethnological Museum and Folktale Archives. (In Hebrew) [5 tales]

Pipe, Samuel Zanvel. 1967. *Twelve Folktales from Sanok*. Haifa: Haifa Municipality, Ethnological Museum and Folktale Archives. (In Hebrew) [12 tales]

Mizrahi, Hanina. 1967. *With Elders Is Wisdom*. Haifa: Haifa Municipality, Ethnological Museum and Folktale Archives. (In Hebrew) [40 tales]

Noy, Dov. 1967. *A Tale for Each Month, 1966.* Haifa: Haifa Municipality, Ethnological Museum and Folktale Archives. (In Hebrew) [12 tales]

Sider, Fishel. 1968. *Seven Folktales from Boryslaw.* Haifa: Haifa Municipality, Ethnological Museum and Folktale Archives. (In Hebrew) [7 tales]

Noy, Meir. 1968. *East European Jewish Cante Fables.* Haifa: Haifa Municipality, Ethnological Museum and Folktale Archives. (In Hebrew) [6 tales]

Seri, Rachel. 1968. *The Holy Amulet.* Haifa: Haifa Municipality, Ethnological Museum and Folktale Archives. (In Hebrew) [12 tales]

Hechal, Edna. 1968. *A Tale for Each Month, 1967.* Haifa: Haifa Municipality, Ethnological Museum and Folktale Archives. (In Hebrew) [12 tales]

Guter, Malka. 1969. *Honour Your Mother.* Haifa: Haifa Municipality, Ethnological Museum and Folktale Archives. (In Hebrew) [12 tales]

Fus, Dvora. 1969. *Seven Bags of Gold.* Haifa: Haifa Municipality, Ethnological Museum and Folktale Archives. (In Hebrew) [7 tales]

Hechal, Edna. 1970. *A Tale for Each Month, 1968–1969.* Haifa: Haifa Municipality Ethnological Museum and Folktale Archives. (In Hebrew) [24 tales]

Noy, Dov. 1971. *A Tale for Each Month, 1970.* Haifa: Haifa Municipality, Ethnological Museum and Folktale Archives. (In Hebrew) [12 tales]

Noy, Dov. 1972. *A Tale for Each Month, 1971.* Haifa: Haifa Municipality, Ethnological Museum and Folktale Archives. (In Hebrew) [12 tales]

Hechal, Edna. 1973. *A Tale for Each Month, 1972.* Haifa: Haifa Municipality, Ethnological Museum and Folktale Archives. (In Hebrew) [12 tales]

Aminoff, Irit. 1974. *The Emir and the Widow.* Haifa: Haifa Municipality, Ethnological Museum and Folktale Archives. (In Hebrew) [12 tales]

Shenhar, Aliza. 1974. *A Tale for Each Month,* 1973. Haifa: Haifa Municipality, Ethnological Museum and Folktale Archives. (In Hebrew) [12 tales]

Rabach, Berl. 1975. *The Kept Promise.* Haifa: Haifa Municipality, Ethnological Museum and Folktale Archives. (In Hebrew) [6 tales]

Haimovits, Zvi Moshe. 1976. *Faithful Guardians.* Haifa: Haifa Municipality, Ethnological Museum and Folktale Archives, (In Hebrew) [18 tales]

Noy, Dov. 1976. *The Jewish Animal Tale of Oral Tradition.* Haifa: Haifa Municipality, Ethnological Museum and Folktale Archives, Israel Folktale Archives. (In Hebrew) [60 tales]

Attias, Moshe. 1976. *The Golden Feather.* Haifa: Haifa Municipality, Ethnological Museum and Folktale Archives. (In Hebrew) [20 tales]

Stahl, Abraham. 1976. *Stories of Faith and Morals.* Haifa: Haifa Municipality, Ethnological Museum and Folktale Archives. (In Hebrew) [36 tales]

Noy, Dov. 1978. *A Tale for Each Month, 1974–1975.* Jerusalem: Hebrew University and Israel Folktale Archives (IFA). (In Hebrew) [24 tales]

Falah, Salman, and Aliza Shenhar. 1978. *Druze Folktales.* Jerusalem: Hebrew University and Israel Folktale Archives (IFA). (In Hebrew) [30 tales]

Pinhasi, Jacob. 1978. *Folktales from Bukhara.* Jerusalem: Hebrew University and Israel Folktale Archives (IFA). (In Hebrew) [10 tales]

Noy, Dov. 1979. *A Tale for Each Month, 1976–1977*. Jerusalem: Hebrew University and Israel Folktale Archives (IFA). (In Hebrew) [24 tales]

Noy, Dov. 1979. *A Tale for Each Month 1978*. Jerusalem: Hebrew University and Israel Folktale Archives (IFA). (In Hebrew) [12 tales]

Babay, Refael. 1980. *A Favor for a Favor*. Jerusalem: Hebrew University and Israel Folktale Archives (IFA). (In Hebrew) [10 tales]

Keren, Abraham. 1981. *Advice from the Rothschilds*. Jerusalem: Magnes, Hebrew University. (In Hebrew) [28 tales]

APPENDIX 3.
IFA–INITIATED PUBLICATIONS

Alexander, Tamar, and Dov Noy. 1989. *The Treasure of Our Fathers*. Jerusalem: Misgav Yerusha-layim. [Hebrew]

Bar-Itzhak, Haya, and Idit Pintel-Ginsberg. 2008. *The Power of a Tale: The Jubilee Book of IFA*. Haifa: University of Haifa. [Hebrew; 53 tales.]

Bar-Itzhak, Haya, and Aliza Shenhar. 1993. *Jewish Moroccan Folk Narratives from Israel*. Detroit: Wayne State University Press. [21 tales.]

Noy, Dov. 1963. *Folktales of Israel*. Chicago: University of Chicago Press. [71 tales.] Spanish trans.: *Contos da Diaspora*. São Paulo: Editôra Perspectiva, 1966.

———. 1964. *Jewish Folktales from Morocco*. Jerusalem: Jewish Agency, Haifa Municipality and Israel Folktale Archives (IFA). [Hebrew; 71 tales.] English trans.: *Moroccan Jewish Folktales*. Jerusalem: Jewish Agency, 1966. [71 tales.] French trans.: *Contes Populaires Racontés par des Juifs du Maroc*. Jerusalem: Organisation Sioniste Mondiale, 1965. Spanish trans.: *Cuentos Populares Narrados por Judios Marroquies*. Jerusalem: Organización Sionista Mundial, 1965.

———. 1965. *Jewish-Iraqi Folktales*. Tel Aviv: Am Oved. [Hebrew; 120 tales.]

———. 1966. *Jewish Folktales from Tunis*. Jerusalem: Jewish Agency, Haifa Municipality and Israel Folktale Archives (IFA). [Hebrew; 71 tales.] French trans. *Contes Populaires Racontés par des Juifs de Tunisie*. Jerusalem: Organisation Sioniste Mondiale, 1968.

———. 1967. *Jewish Folktales from Libya*. Jerusalem: Jewish Agency, Haifa Municipality and Israel Folktale Archives (IFA). [Hebrew; 71 tales.]

Shenhar, Aliza, and Haya Bar-Itzhak. 1981. *Folktales from Beit-She'an*. Haifa: University of Haifa. [Hebrew; 30 tales.]

———. 1982. *Folktales from Shlomi*. Haifa: University of Haifa. [Hebrew; 7 tales]

Appendix 4.
Additional Annotated Publications
of IFA Tales

Avitsuk, Ya'acov. 1985. *The Fate of a Child*. Edited and annotated by Esther Schely-Newman. Tel Aviv: Amir. [Hebrew; 28 tales.]

Baharav, Zalman. 1968. *One Generation to Another*. Annotated by Dov Noy. Tel Aviv: Tarbut Vechinuch. [Hebrew; 71 tales.]

Ben-Amos, Dan. 2006. *Folktales of the Jews*, vol. 1. *Tales from the Sephardic Dispersion*. Philadelphia: Jewish Publication Society. [71 tales.]

———. 2007. *Folktales of the Jews*, vol. 2. *Tales from Eastern Europe*. Philadelphia: Jewish Publication Society. [71 tales.]

———. 2011. *Folktales of the Jews*, vol. 3. *Tales from Arab Lands*. Philadelphia: Jewish Publication Society. [60 tales.]

Cohen, Malka. 1974–79. *Mi-Pi ha-Am*. 3 vols. Annotated by Haim Schwarzbaum. Tel Aviv: Yeda Am. [Hebrew; vol. 1: 113 tales; vol. 2: 206 tales; vol. 3: 306 tales.]

Jason, Heda. *Märchen aus Israel*. 1976. Dusserldorf: Eugen Diederichs Verlag. [80 tales.]

Jefet Schwili Erzählt. 1963. *Hundertneunundsechzig jemenitische Volkserzaehlungen aufgezeichnet in Israel 1957–1960*. Herausgegeben von Dov Noy. Berlin: Walter De Gruyter. [169 tales.]

Kort, Zebulun. 1983. *Jewish Folktales from Afghanistan*. Edited and annotated by Haim Schwarzbaum. Jerusalem: Dvir. [Hebrew; 75 tales.]

Rand, Baruch. 1967–68. *Together, the Tribes of Israel*. Jerusalem: Ministry of Education. [Hebrew] This series in simplified Hebrew includes Jewish folktales from Iraq (7 tales), Kurdistan (8 tales), Morocco (8 tales), Persia (9 tales), Poland (6 tales), Romania (6 tales), and Yemen (6 tales).

Narrators

Zahra Abdi Khamra
The Young Men Who Drank Arak at Al-Khader (IFA 23000)

Mina Abu-Rokan
The Queen and the Fish (IFA 20959)

Hamza As'ad Abu Zidan
Honor Your Guest, Though He May Be a Beggar (IFA 22913)

Reuven Adi
The Salvation of the Jews of Arbil during the Rashīd 'Alī Riots, 1941 (IFA 13921)

Muhammad 'Arsan Majid Abu Zeid
Al-Jazzar and Muhammad al-Qablan (IFA 22924)

Moshe Attias
The Girl and the Dragons (IFA 10106)

Yiftah Avrahami
Wisdom of a Man and Slyness of a Woman (IFA 15825)

Abner Azoulay
Rabbi Ephrayim Elnekave and the Lion (IFA 6432)

Yossi Bar Sheshet
Do Not Bequeath, for You Will Be Poor (IFA 22649)

Avraham Barazani
The Rich Miser (IFA 9400)

Yeshua Ben David
The Witch (El Beda) (IFA 11575)

Faiza Bishara
Water for the Guest (IFA 21882)

Simcha Bracha
Death as a Godfather (IFA 1937)

David Cohen
The Girl and the Cossack (IFA 1935)

Yaffa Cohen
The Six Sisters from the Mountains (IFA 7370)

Heftsiba Dadon
The Cat Demon (IFA 8902)

Nissim Damti
The King and the Old Woodcutter (IFA 10300)

Rivka Daniel
The Widow and Her Daughter (17478)

Moshe Danino
The Revelation of the *Zaddik* Rabbi David U'Moshe (IFA 12337)

Ahmad Darbe
The Grave of Sheikh Jamal il-Din (IFA 21884)

Basma Darbe
Tar-Shiha (IFA 21885)

Ibrahim Djaiem
The Maiden and the Guest (21883)

Esther Elfassy
The Girl Who Emerged Out of an Egg (IFA 13876)

Esther Elizra
The Princess in the Wooden Body (IFA 6859)

Shoshana Farizada
How a Bottomless Bucket Saved a Community (IFA 11739)

Leah Gad
The Wise Sheikh and the Menorah (IFA 8271)

Sima Goldenberg
The King Who Trusted His Kingdom to His Daughters (IFA 7202)

Yosef Goldman
Killing the Snake (IFA 22849)

David Itsicovitc
The Impoverished and Wandering Jewish Tenant (IFA 18800)

Dr. S. Z. Kahana
The Hanukkah Miracle: Hannah and Her Seven Sons (IFA 1724)

Zalman (Kastrol) Ben-Amos
The Pharmacist's Burial (IFA 21021)

Zevulun Kort
The Miserly *Mohel* and the Demons (IFA 5151)

Mordechai Hillel Kroshnitz
The "Cattish" Fire in Chelm (IFA 14232)

Ibrahim Kweider Sbechat
Between the Sun and the Moon (IFA 17414)

Berta Lieber
The Wise Woman (IFA 21307)

Tamar Lugasi
The Measure of a Woman Is Two, the Measure of a Man Is One (IFA 11911)
Long-Time Jerusalem Resident
Stone in the Temple Originated from Sinai (IFA 553)

Haya (Hadjadj) Mazouz
Mother's Gift Is Better Than Father's Gift (IFA 16131)
The Shoe (IFA 16132)

Eliyahu Modgorashwili
Serah bat Asher (IFA 9524)

Haya Nahumzon
The Bride and the Demon (IFA 335)

Ya'acov Nesher
Rise Early and Harvest Gold (IFA 12443)

Aharon Nini
Stone Restrains Redemption (IFA 489)

Dov Noy
The Old Synagogue in Prague (IFA 502)

Eliezer Papo
The Gate to the Garden of Eden Is beneath a Woman's Feet (IFA 22833)

Aharon David Rabinovitch
The Road on the Holiday of Shavuot (IFA 23011)

Levana Sasson
The Broken Oath (IFA 22832)

Ya'acov Shaham
Investors' Encouragement (IFA 21158)

Hinda Sheinferber
The Boy Who Was Kidnapped and Brought to Russia (IFA 18140)

Israel Ber Schneersohn
The Dance of the Ari (Rabbi Isaac Luria) (IFA 3590)

Zvi Tenenbaum
There Is Not a Living Soul (IFA 12434)

Shimon Toder
The Story about Dobush (IFA 5167)

Zipora Zabari
The Flying Camel of the Levant Fair (IFA 22876)

TRANSCRIBERS

Lina Abu-Rokan
The Queen and the Fish (IFA 20959)

Tamar Agmon
Serah bat Asher (IFA 9524)

Tamar Alexander
The Broken Oath (IFA 22832)
The Gate to the Garden of Eden Is beneath a Woman's Feet (IFA 22833)

Haim Dov Armon
The Hanukkah Miracle: Hannah and Her Seven Sons (IFA 1724)

Nili Aryeh-Sapir
The Flying Camel of the Levant Fair (IFA 22876)

Yeshayahu Ashani
The Dance of the Ari (Rabbi Isaac Luria) (IFA 3590)

Moshe Attias
The Girl and the Dragons (IFA 10106)

Ya'acov Avitsuk
The Six Sisters from the Mountains (IFA 7370)
The Impoverished and Wandering Jewish Tenant (IFA 18800)

Yiftah Avrahami
Wisdom of a Man and Slyness of a Woman (IFA 15825)

Zalman Baharav
The King Who Trusted His Kingdom to His Daughters (IFA 7202)

Haya Bar-Itzhak
Killing the Snake (IFA 22849)

Dan Ben-Amos
The Pharmacist's Burial (IFA 21021)

David Cohen
The Girl and the Cossack (IFA 1935)

Deborah Dadon-Wilk
The Cat Demon (IFA 8902)

Roseland Da'eem
The Guys Who Drank Arak at Al-Khader (IFA 23000)

Rita Daoud Bishara
Water for the Guest (IFA 21882)
The Maiden and the Guest (21883)
The Grave of Sheikh Jamal il-Din (IFA 21884)
Tar-Shiha (IFA 21885)

Ya'akov Elfassy
The Girl Who Emerged Out of an Egg (IFA 13876)

Mukhtar Ezra
The Rich Miser (IFA 9400)

Nissim Benjamin Gamlieli
The King and the Old Woodcutter (IFA 10300)
The Witch (El Beda) (IFA 11575)

Itzhak Ganuz
The Road on the Holiday of Shavuot (IFA 23011)

Haya Gavish
The Salvation of the Jews of Arbil during the Rashīd 'Alī Riots, 1941 (IFA 13921)

Galit Hasan-Rokem
The Measure of a Woman Is Two, the Measure of a Man Is One (IFA 11911)

Yifrah Haviv
Investors' Encouragement (IFA 21158)
Do Not Bequeath, for You Will Be Poor (IFA 22649)

Rachel Heller
Death as a Godfather (IFA 1937)

Avraham Keren
There Is Not a Living Soul (IFA 12434)
Rise Early and Harvest Gold (IFA 12443)

Billy Kimhi
The Princess in the Wooden Body (IFA 6859)

Zevulun Kort
The Miserly *Mohel* and the Demons (IFA 5151)
The Wise Sheikh and the Menorah (IFA 8271)

Berta Lieber
The Wise Woman (IFA 21307)

Sarah Loftus
How a Bottomless Bucket Saved a Community (IFA 11739)

Nissim Malka
The Revelation of the *Zaddik* Rabbi David U'Moshe (IFA 12337)

Yoram Meron
Honor Your Guest, Though He May Be a Beggar (IFA 22913)
Al-Jazzar and Muhammad al-Qablan (IFA 22924)

Dov Noy
Stone Restrains Redemption (IFA 489)
The Old Synagogue in Prague (IFA 502)
Stone in the Temple Originated from Sinai (IFA 553)

Ayelet Oettinger
The "Cattish" Fire in Chelm (IFA 14232)

Yoel Perez
Between the Sun and the Moon (IFA 17414)

Moshe Rabi
Rabbi Ephrayim Elnekave and the Lion (IFA 6432)

Esther Schely-Newman
Mother's Gift Is Better Than Father's Gift (IFA 16131)
The Shoe (IFA 16132)

Hadarah Sela
The Boy Who Was Kidnapped and Brought to Russia (IFA 18140)

Efrat Shalev
The Widow and Her Daughter (17478)

Galia Shenberg
The Queen and the Fish (IFA 20959)

Shimon Toder
The Story about Dobush (IFA 5167)

Moshe Vigiser
The Bride and the Demon (IFA 335)

Scholars

Prof. Tamar Alexander, Ben-Gurion University of the Negev
The Broken Oath (IFA 22832)
The Gate to the Garden of Eden Is Beneath a Woman's Feet (IFA 22833)

Dr. Nili Aryeh-Sapir, Hebrew University and Tel Aviv University
The Flying Camel of the Levant Fair (IFA 22876)

Prof. Haya Bar-Itzhak, University of Haifa
The Girl and the Cossack (IFA 1935)
The Revelation of the *Zaddik* Rabbi David U'Moshe (IFA 12337)
Killing the Snake (IFA 22849)

Prof. Dan Ben-Amos, University of Pennsylvania
The Pharmacist's Burial (IFA 21021)

Dr. Rachel Ben-Cnaan, University of Haifa
The Rich Miser (IFA 9400)

Dr. Roseland Da'eem, University of Haifa
The Guys Who Drank Arak at Al-Khader (IFA 23000)

Dr. Amer Dahamshe, Hebrew University
Water for the Guest (IFA 21882)
The Maiden and the Guest (21883)
The Grave of Sheikh Jamal il-Din (IFA 21884)
Tar-Shiha (IFA 21885)

Dr. Tamar Eyal, University of Haifa
There Is Not a Living Soul (IFA 12434)

Prof. Larisa Fialkova, University of Haifa
The Story about Dobush (IFA 5167)

Mr. Itzhak Ganuz, *Yeda Am*
The Road on the Holiday of Shavuot (IFA 23011)

Dr. Haya Gavish, Hebrew Union College
The Salvation of the Jews of Arbil during the Rashīd 'Alī Riots, 1941 (IFA 13921)

Prof. Galit Hasan-Rokem, Hebrew University
The Measure of a Woman Is Two, the Measure of a Man Is One (IFA 11911)

Ms. Edna Hechal, University of Haifa
The Miserly *Mohel* and the Demons (IFA 5151)
The Cat Demon (IFA 8902)

Dr. Heda Jason, Jerusalem
How a Bottomless Bucket Saved a Community (IFA 11739)

Dr. Esther Juhasz, Hebrew University and University of Haifa
The Wise Sheikh and the Menorah (IFA 8271)

Dr. Roni Kochavi-Nehab, Hazorea
Honor Your Guest, Though He May Be a Beggar (IFA 22913)
Al-Jazzar and Muhammad al-Qablan (IFA 22924)

Prof. Rella Kushelevsky, Bar-Ilan University
The Hanukkah Miracle: Hannah and Her Seven Sons (IFA 1724)

Prof. Avidov Lipsker, Bar-Ilan University
Rabbi Ephrayim Elnekave and the Lion (IFA 6432)

Dr. Hagit Matras, Hebrew University
The Boy Who Was Kidnapped and Brought to Russia (IFA 18140)

Mr. Yoram Meron, Givat Haviva
Honor Your Guest, Though He May Be a Beggar (IFA 22913)
Al-Jazzar and Muhammad al-Qablan (IFA 22924)

Dr. Haya Milo, University of Haifa
The Princess in the Wooden Body (IFA 6859)
The Widow and Her Daughter (17478)

Prof. Dov Noy, Hebrew University
Do Not Bequeath, for You Will Be Poor (IFA 22649)

Dr. Ayelet Oettinger, University of Haifa
The "Cattish" Fire in Chelm (IFA 14232)

Dr. Yoel Perez, Achva College
Between the Sun and the Moon (IFA 17414)

Dr. Idit Pintel-Ginsberg, University of Haifa
The Bride and the Demon (IFA 335)
Stone Restrains Redemption (IFA 489)

The Old Synagogue in Prague (IFA 502)
Stone in the Temple Originated from Sinai (IFA 553)
The Witch (El Beda) (IFA 11575)

Dr. Ravit Raufman, University of Haifa
The Six Sisters from the Mountains (IFA 7370)
The Girl Who Emerged Out of an Egg (IFA 13876)

Prof. Ilana Rosen, Ben-Gurion University of the Negev
Rise Early and Harvest Gold (IFA 12443)
Investors' Encouragement (IFA 21158)

Dr. David Rotman, Tel Aviv University
The Girl and the Dragons (IFA 10106)

Prof. Esther Schely-Newman, Hebrew University
Mother's Gift Is Better Than Father's Gift (IFA 16131)
The Shoe (IFA 16132)

Prof. Peninnah Schram, Yeshiva University
The King and the Old Woodcutter (IFA 10300)

Prof. Howard Schwartz, University of Missouri
Death as a Godfather (IFA 1937)

Dr. Tsafi Sebba-Elran, University of Haifa
The Queen and the Fish (IFA 20959)

Prof. Aliza Shenhar, Max Stern Yezreel Valley College
The Wise Woman (IFA 21307)

Prof. Dina Stein, University of Haifa
Serah bat Asher (IFA 9524)

Ms. Limor Wisman-Ravid, Tel Aviv
Wisdom of a Man and Slyness of a Woman (IFA 15825)

Prof. Eli Yassif, Tel Aviv University
The Dance of the Ari (Rabbi Isaac Luria) (IFA 3590)

Dr. Yael Zilberman, Ben-Gurion University of the Negev
The King Who Trusted His Kingdom to His Daughters (IFA 7202)

Dr. Rachel Zoran, University of Haifa
The Impoverished and Wandering Jewish Tenant (IFA 18800)

Narratives According to Ethnic Groups

Afghanistan
The Miserly *Mohel* and the Demons (IFA 5151)
The Wise Sheikh and the Menorah (IFA 8271)

Belarus
The Pharmacist's Burial (IFA 21021)
The Road on the Holiday of Shavuot (IFA 23011)

Bulgaria
Death as a Godfather (IFA 1937)

Ethiopia
The Wise Woman (IFA 21307)

Georgia
Serah bat Asher (IFA 9524)

Germany
There Is Not a Living Soul (IFA 12434)

Greece
The Girl and the Dragons (IFA 10106)

India
The Widow and Her Daughter (17478)

Iraq
Stone Restrains Redemption (IFA 489)
The Six Sisters from the Mountains (IFA 7370)
The Rich Miser (IFA 9400)

Iraqi Kurdistan
The Salvation of the Jews of Arbil during the Rashīd ʿAlī Riots, 1941 (IFA 13921)

Israel
Investors' Encouragement (IFA 21158)
The Flying Camel of the Levant Fair (IFA 22876)

Israel, Ashkenazi
The Hanukkah Miracle: Hannah and Her Seven Sons (IFA 1724)
The Dance of the Ari (Rabbi Isaac Luria) (IFA 3590)
Rise Early and Harvest Gold (IFA 12443)

Israel, Bedouin
Between the Sun and the Moon (IFA 17414)
Al-Jazzar and Muhammad al-Qablan (IFA 22924)

Israel, Christian Arab
Water for the Guest (IFA 21882)

Israel, Druze
The Queen and the Fish (IFA 20959)
Honor Your Guest, Though He May Be a Beggar (IFA 22913)

Israel, Muslim
The Maiden and the Guest (21883)
The Grave of Sheikh Jamal il-Din (IFA 21884)
Tar-Shiha (IFA 21885)
The Guys Who Drank Arak at Al-Khader (IFA 23000)

Israel, Sephardi
Stone in the Temple Originated from Sinai (IFA 553)
The Broken Oath (IFA 22832)

Lithuania

The Bride and the Demon (IFA 335)

Morocco
Rabbi Ephrayim Elnekave and the Lion (IFA 6432)
The Princess in the Wooden Body (IFA 6859)
The Cat Demon (IFA 8902)
The Measure of a Woman Is Two, the Measure of a Man Is One (IFA 11911)
The Revelation of the *Zaddik* Rabbi David U'Moshe (IFA 12337)
The Girl Who Emerged Out of an Egg (IFA 13876)
Do Not Bequeath, for You Will Be Poor (IFA 22649)

Persia
How a Bottomless Bucket Saved a Community (IFA 11739)
Wisdom of a Man and Slyness of a Woman (IFA 15825)

Poland
The Old Synagogue in Prague (IFA 502)
The Girl and the Cossack (IFA 1935)
The Story about Dobush (IFA 5167)
The "Cattish" Fire in Chelm (IFA 14232)
The Boy Who Was Kidnapped and Brought to Russia (IFA 18140)
Killing the Snake (IFA 22849)

Romania
The King Who Trusted His Kingdom to His Daughters (IFA 7202)
The Impoverished and Wandering Jewish Tenant (IFA 18800)

Tunisia
Mother's Gift Is Better Than Father's Gift (IFA 16131)
The Shoe (IFA 16132)

Yemen
The King and the Old Woodcutter (IFA 10300)
The Witch (El Beda) (IFA 11575)

Yugoslavia, Sephardi
The Gate to the Garden of Eden Is beneath a Woman's Feet (IFA 22833)

TALE TYPES

AT 178A, ATU 178A	IFA 20950
AT 293*J (IFA)	IFA 21307
AT 310, ATU 310	IFA 13876
AT 311, ATU 311	IFA 7370
AT 327, ATU 327	IFA 10106
AT 328, ATU 328	IFA 10106
AT 332, ATU 332	IFA 1937
AT 332 I	IFA 1937
AT 334, ATU 334	IFA 11575
AT 400–424, ATU 400–424	IFA 11575
AT 400 IIIa, ATU 400 (1)	IFA 11575
AT 401, [no ATU]	IFA 9524
AT 425, ATU 425	IFA 7370
AT 459 d, ATU 459	IFA 11575
AT 461A, [no ATU]	IFA 1937
AT 476*, ATU 476*	IFA 5151 and 8902
AT 476*-*A (IFA)	IFA 5151 and 8902
AT 510, ATU 510	IFA 6859, IFA 10106
AT 510 Ib, ATU 510	IFA 335
AT 510B, ATU 510B	IFA 6859
AT 670, ATU 670	IFA 20959
AT 725, ATU 725	IFA 17141
AT *730 (IFA)	IFA 914, IFA 13921, IFA 17478
AT 745, ATU 745	IFA 9400
AT 750–779, ATU 750–779	IFA 23000
AT 750B, ATU 750B	IFA 22913 and 22324
AT 751A*, [no ATU]	IFA 1937
AT 759, ATU 759	IFA 23000
AT *776 (IFA)	IFA 22913 and 22324, IFA 23000
AT *776 IC (IFA)	IFA 22913 and 22324
AT *776 IIC3 (IFA)	IFA 22913 and 22324
AT *776 IIIA (IFA)	IFA 22913 and 22324
AT *776C-B (IFA)	IFA 6432

AT 780–789, ATU 780–789	IFA 23000
AT 817*, ATU 817*	IFA 335
AT 827, ATU 827	IFA 22833
AT 827*A (IFA)	IFA 22833
AT 873*A (IFA)	IFA 15825
AT 881, ATU 881	IFA 16131 and 16132
AT 882, ATU 882	IFA 16131 and 16132
AT *895 (IFA)	IFA 20959
AT 916 II c, ATU 916 (3)	IFA 20959
AT 916 II d, ATU 916 (4)	IFA 20959
AT 921F*, ATU 921F*	IFA 10300
AT 922, ATU 922	IFA 11739
AT 923, ATU 923	IFA 7202
AT 923A, ATU 923A	IFA 7202
AT 923B, ATU 923B	IFA 7202
AT 929, ATU 929	IFA 23011
AT 930, ATU 930	IFA 22832
AT 930*F (IFA)	IFA 22832
AT 934E, ATU 934	IFA 1937
AT 938, ATU 938	IFA 20959
AT 949 [no ATU]	IFA 16131 and 16132
AT 956B, ATU 956B	IFA 10106
AT 956D, ATU 956D	IFA 10106
ATU 956	IFA 10106
AT 980, ATU 980	IFA 22649
AT 980A, ATU 980	IFA 22649
AT 980B, ATU 980B	IFA 22649
AT 980C, ATU 980C	IFA 22649
AT 981, ATU 981	IFA 22649
AT 982, ATU 982	IFA 22649
AT 1164D, ATU 1164	IFA 1937
AT 1187, ATU 1187	IFA 1937
AT 1281, ATU 1281	IFA 14232
AT 1310, ATU 1310	IFA 14232
AT 1406*A (IFA)	IFA 15825
IFA 1441, ATU 480A	IFA 15825
AT 1738, ATU 1738	IFA 12434
AT 1862B, ATU 1164	IFA 1937
AT *1873 (IFA)	IFA 12434
AT 1875–1889, ATU 1875–1999	IFA 12443 and 21158

Index

Page numbers in *italics* refer to figures.

CPSIA information can be obtained
at www.ICGtesting.com
Printed in the USA
BVHW091128190919

558844BV00005B/10/P

9 780814 342084